Major Voices:
19th Century American Women's Poetry

Major Voices
19TH CENTURY AMERICAN WOMEN'S POETRY

SELECTED POEMS
WITH INTRODUCTIONS BY
Shira Wolosky

The Toby Press

The Toby Press

First Edition 2003

The Toby Press LLC
POB 8531, New Milford, CT. 06676-8531, USA
& POB 2455, London WIA 5WY, England
www.tobypress.com

ISBN 1 59264 040 0, *paperback*
ISBN 1 59264 041 9, *hardcover*

A CIP catalogue record for this title
is available from the British Library

Typeset in Garamond by Jerusalem Typesetting

Printed and bound in the United States by
Thomson-Shore Inc., Michigan

For my husband Ariel Weiss
and my sister Rickey Wolosky Palkovitz

Preface

Anthologies tend to include a large number of poets with a handful of texts for each. Here, instead, I have concentrated on fewer poets whom I consider especially expressive of nineteenth-century American women's poetry, and have included a relatively large number of their texts. A small number of poems cannot give real entry into the world and work of a poet, cannot allow a reader any genuine encounter with the writer, her sense of things and sensibility of words. In this collection, I have chosen a substantive number of texts from each writer, reflecting their wide and varied range of poetic topics, styles, and interests. This can give a much better sense of who they are, and of the world in which and of which they wrote. I have, however, limited myself to poems that are short rather than long (Sigourney was paid by the word), and have generally included more texts from poets whose work has not been collected than from those whose has been. The poems I have grouped without regard to the chronology of their composition, following instead an order placing them according to kind or type, so as to establish a sequence of reading that will give a sense of each poetic mode and also of how each opens into and connects to the others. The poets themselves have been ordered loosely rather than strictly according to birth, placing poets with more or less contemporary birthdates according to the chronology of subjects or concerns their poems mainly address; that is, according to the way their poems are situated within the course of the nineteenth century itself.

As to the introductory essays that follow, in these I have given biographical accounts of each poet, but have been more concerned to provide a guide to the poems themselves. Each introduction is meant to make available categories of reading, interpretive frames for seeing the particular modes of each poet, as an aid to entering their texts. There has also been an eye to the links between the poets, the way each one approaches or develops concerns visible in the others. This I believe enriches each one, as well as gathering to a larger image of who women were and what and how they wrote in the nineteenth century. The "Bibliographical Comments" list the primary texts on which this selection has been based. In this volume, I have tried to represent the very wide range of women's expressions and interests, their historical experience and religious sensibility, their critique of society and sense of their own changing roles, in ways that make their writing available not only to readers of poetry and literature, but also to historians, to historians of religion, to cultural critics, and to all who are interested in women's studies.

Contents

ix

Introduction:

Women's Voices

From the time of their writing; of their going out of print almost immediately upon the death of their authors; and through their gradual reintroduction into literary history, women's poetry of the nineteenth century has been characterized essentially as domestic, albeit with varying judgments. In the nineteenth century, viewing the poems as domestic made them acceptable, popular, diminutive and safe. As with so many other women's activities, women's writing could be consigned to the comforting and appropriate domain of the woman's sphere. Yet even in this guise, the poems signaled women's entry into new areas before closed to them. Barriers had been gradated, guarding not only against publication as unmeet to women's modesty, but against attaining the literacy necessary to take one's place in literature: first to read at all, and then to read enough of the cultural property so as to be able to contribute to it. Such opportunity only arose to large extent with the American Revolution, and its opening to women—first in Philadelphia in 1787—of secondary education in the form of female seminaries. This already entailed a political and civic dimension. If women were not yet permitted to vote and hold office, they nonetheless married and mothered male citizens who could do so. Education became part of their republican participation. In the immediate case, it gave to them the tools for literary endeavor, which is why the nineteenth is the first century in which one can speak of women's poetry to any large extent.

What ensued was a veritable riot of circulation. And domesticity, at least as a perceived category, opened to women the avenue down which they could make their poetic way—not least to being acceptable to publishers. As Rufus Griswold, the poetmaker (or, as in Poe's case, unmaker) of the period's literary respectability, warns in introducing his groundbreaking 1848 *Female Poets of America*: "We are in danger of mistaking for the efflorescent energy of creative intelligence, that which is only the exuberance of personal 'feelings unemployed.'" In such manner was the poetry promoted and dismissed.

This notion of women's poetry as domestic has persisted in many ways even into more recent attempts to recover it. Women's poetry becomes a poetry of confinement, which defines not only its settings but becomes its central topic as frustration and conflict over its own limitations. Or, most recently, the disdain with which domesticity was regarded is being reversed into a positive mode of female self-expression. Literary and cultural criticism has come to focus on domesticity in its aspect as sentimental writing, recasting it and rescuing it from the dismissive condescension it has suffered in established literary opinion. This rereading of domesticity has been important work, largely treating novels but also poetry. Nevertheless, establishing sentimentality as the major mode of women's poetry risks reducing its variety and multifocal energies, which go beyond, although they include, the sentimental.

Nineteenth-century women's poetry instead can be shown to offer a wide range of topics, and even types or subgenres, of poems. One central and organizing energy, however, is the question of voice. The poetry is about having a voice and having it heard; about making the invisible visible, the silent audible, and the tensions between these impulses and ordinances, between realms newly opening, and those still normative or coming to critical awareness. Voice itself emerges as a foundational figure or image in the poetry: in the guise of naming, addressing, conversing, of the poetic venture itself.

With regard to types or kinds of poems, a number can be specified. These recur from poet to poet and mutually illuminate both texts and contexts.

There are *'lady'* or *'woman'* poems. These propose, explore, question, and juxtapose just what being a lady or woman might entail. There are many different womanly figures: young wives, old women, teachers, artists, elegant women, housewives, sisters, mothers, girls, working women, fallen women, prostitutes. Poems repeatedly consider marrying and not marrying and their social roles, the belonging and exclusions of the married and unmarried. The many texts centered in these figures and roles often inscribe confusion, as the notion of woman itself was becoming confused and contested under the nineteenth century's rapidly changing circumstances. Poems of this sort range from meditations on womanhood and wifehood to parodies and ironies, especially in Phoebe Cary, on single women and marriage markets; and to Gilman's ideological parables such as "Females," "More Females," and "Unsexed."

There are poems of *'missed-dialogues'*, in which women and men talk past each other, as if each were speaking a different language, living in a different world. These can take explicit dialogue form; or they can be the unspoken thoughts of the woman or man; or a third person account that may nonetheless be cast through these gendered viewpoints, in explicit or implicit misunderstanding with each other. Larcom's "Getting Along," Jackson's "Two Truths," and Wilcox's "A Holiday" are outstanding examples.

There are poems of the *'double-standard'*, a very live topic during the period, as increased urbanization and immigration, with its dislocations, meant increased isolation from traditional sexual and social contexts as well as a growing industry in prostitution. But of course the double standard is an ancient and enduring distribution of morality. The sexual double standard, which condemned without reprieve a girl who 'fell into sin,' whether by seduction or out of economic duress, while the men who seduced or who paid for sexual services retained their social and even moral status undisturbed—this is a recurrent subject and also structure for woman poet after poet. (Indeed, the moral reform or purity movement, attempting to criminalize not only prostitutes but their male clients so as to impose on men the same sexual standard as applied to women, was one of the first and most durable—and unsuccessful—reform movements undertaken by women in the nineteenth century). These include Harper's "The Double Standard," "The Contrast," and "The Revel;" Phoebe Cary's "The Outcast;" Howe's "Outside the Party;" and Gilman's poems on prostitution, "One Girl of Many" and "Unmentionable."

The double standard takes on, however, ever broader implication as these poets invoke it not only in a narrow sexual sense, but in a social and cultural one. The nineteenth century witnessed the transformation of America from an agricultural and mercantile society into an industrial urban one, where economic values increasingly pushed aside earlier virtues of republican commitment and religious community. It was women who took up these marginalized values; women who inherited republican virtue, the service to the common good, (often through church societies), despite their own lack of citizenship rights such as voting and holding office, and the rising tide of ideology of the separate spheres.

The *'separate spheres'* themselves make up a topic and topos of women's poetry: that is, the separate spheres as an ideology in complex tension and even counter-fact against the course of events taking place. The spheres are hortatory rather than strictly descriptive. The separation of work from home that marks the rise of industry is a residential fact. That women were relegated to the latter while men went off to the former is an ideological premise. In practice, many women participated in many activities situated not in the home but in the community. Some of these seemed and were extensions of what women did at home: schooling, care for the sick, the needy, the aged, the orphan—all of which are treated in women's poetry of the period. Yet other commitments and involvements can be described as 'domestic' extensions only by way of distortion: abolition, Indian rights, women's rights, urban activism, the politics of republicanism, war—all are firmly in the public sphere and all are fully present in women's poetic writing. The notion that women's poetry is domestic and not public is itself a product of ideology, rather than its basis in evidence. The division itself pivots around an ideological slurring

4

of categories, especially that of economics. The gendered division proves to be much more economic/not economic than public/private. But what makes economy public, except its geography outside the home? This is a question women poets themselves ask, in poems of *'social-economic critique.'* Their social analysis turns on the bifurcation of American values into economic self-interest as against community service. This division is not merely spatial. Community service also takes place in the home, in the family life women largely build. The distinction, rather, is axiological. Gender becomes a map not only of roles and restrictions but of broad social values and commitments: to the economic self or to larger senses of selfhood as invested and embedded in community life and the common good. In this sense, poems of the separate sphere are not only domestic but also political. *'Political poetry'* is a fundamental and overarching category of the women writers.

Poems of politics and gender take their place in the larger category of *'poems of history.'* These poems may be called documentary. They present—which is to say recognize, attend, and enter into record—women's viewpoints and experiences which general history has tended to omit. Included here are poems on the landing in America, as in Sigourney's "Pilgrim Fathers" and "The Fathers of New England;" and poems of the Westward movement, as Sigourney's "Western Emigrant," Larcom's "Call to Kansas" and "Elsie in Illinois," Harper's "Going East," Alice Cary's "Growing Rich" and "West Country." War looms through the verse as seen, judged, and imagined from home (especially in Larcom and Howe), and with recurrent treatments of the Lincoln assassination (Larcom's "Tolling," Alice Cary's "Abraham Lincoln," and Phoebe's "Own Good President," Howe's "Requital"). Political commentary as protest, analysis of the polity, republican reflections, as well as particular *'causes'* such as abolition and Reconstruction (especially in Harper), Indian rights (especially in Sigourney), and, not least, women's rights all are persistently addressed in women's poetry (of special interest here is Phoebe Cary's poem "To Miss Susan Anthony.")

'Religion' remained, at least until the later part of the century, an overarching and penetrating realm for women, one might say in

every venture. The recent critical categories of race, class, and gender treat religion as if it were somehow absorbed into these prior rubrics. This is not the case, in the nineteenth century certainly, nor again in ours. Religion takes many poetic forms. There are poems of the *Bible*—early exercises, intentionally or not, in feminist biblical interpretation. Women poets are reading and interpreting the Bible from a new angle, i.e. their own. This means looking at different texts than was traditionally the case; or looking at traditional texts differently. Poems feature biblical women, even women outcast or deviant in the tradition such as Hagar (in Harper's "Dedication Poem"), Delilah (in Wilcox), Rizpah (in Harper), and especially Vashti. The scorned queen of the *Book of Esther* becomes heroine in Harper, Jackson, Wilcox. Or, poets reread standard texts, as Sigourney does in her "Ark and Dove" as a feminized version of Noah and the Flood; or in renderings of Abraham as near Matriarch in Sigourney's "Abraham at Macpelah" and Harper's "Burial of Sarah." Dickinson has critical readings of, as well as appeals (in this selection) to Moses, David, and various New Testament promises. The *hymnal* form is the primary base in Dickinson in very complicated ways, but is also a central form in Larcom, the Cary sisters, and an important background in Sigourney and Howe. Through all poems of the Bible, and inescapable even for those who are religiously conservative, is the very fact of women reading Scripture and writing biblical interpretation. The authority to interpret, and also to preach, had always been male (except among the Quakers). Men had controlled all instruments of language in religious tradition. Women's poetry shows this monopoly to be breaking—a monopoly declared most forthrightly by Elizabeth Cady Stanton at the first women's right convention in 1848 in Seneca Falls, against men's having "usurped the prerogative of Jehovah himself, claiming it as his right to assign for her a sphere of action, when that belongs to her conscience and her God."

Yet not all women who pursued this path were radical. Lydia Sigourney was very devout and, as far as she knew, perfectly conservative. Through her advice books, she was herself an important force in constructing and defining a separate sphere for women—advice, however, she did not quite follow herself in her very public and profitable career as professional writer (including giving this advice). Larcom, Harper, the Cary Sisters, even Julia Ward Howe were likewise devout, and very active in their churches. These tended, it is true, to be liberal churches with emphasis on the inner spiritual encounter with God in sanctification of every soul. In terms of the women poets, their faith strengthened them to pursue what they often thought to be their calling. Daring to speak, to write, was invested in them rather than theirs to claim through personal assertion. This was not mere strategy. It is not a question of women 'using' religion in order to emerge into public light and voice. Their emergence was rather justified as mission, without which these women would not have so ventured. At issue are, first, social norms—the silence of women not least in church, as set down by St. Paul in his ministry: "Let the woman learn in silence with all subjection. But I suffer not a woman to teach, nor to usurp authority over the man, but to be in silence" (1 Timothy 2: 11–12). There is as well a genuine value of modesty not as repression (which it very often indeed is) but as a certain structure of the self: a structure which sees the self as not only self-defined but in intimate, ultimate definition in terms of others. This derives in older religious visions of the self, but also in women's senses of themselves as embedded within their social lives as a positive identity, and as committed to a political, republican vision of participation in the commonwealth.

In poetic terms, this religious-political drive took shape as prophetic vocation, in *prophetic poems*. Here Julia Ward Howe's "Battle-Hymn of the Republic" is outstanding, not least in its cultural success. The vision is religious, but as an American *civil religion* which sees the nation itself as fulfilling a providential and moral destiny—again a recurring topic throughout women's poetry. And it is a woman who delivers this message, in a repeatedly dramatized self-reflective declaration of this very act of vision: mine eyes have seen, I have seen, I have read. A woman thus becomes public prophet, a prophetic voice that recurs in Sigourney's "Imitation of Parts of the Prophet Amos," Harper's "Bury Me in a Free Land," Larcom's "The Weeping Prophet," Lazarus's "New Ezekial," and even in Dickinson in a poem like "My Triumph Lasted Till the Drums." The hymnal

7

echoes through such ventures, as a public communal address structured around participation by the congregation in its rhythms and phrasings. In them, the poet's voice is not focused on the self. Rather, it draws its energy and strength from the authority of its claims and the urgency of its delivery.

For later writers in the century, religion has become less a cause than an effect. Poets may continue to use religious language, but they do so in order to put forward their own visions rather than having their visions defined by religious frameworks. This is the case in Ella Wheeler Wilcox, who pretty much invents her own spirituality, as in her experiments with theosophy. Charlotte Gilman uses religion largely as a figure for positions she does—and does not—approve. Both poets still engage biblical and religious discourses. Both re-write the creation story of Adam and Eve, for example, but with very altered gender alignments (in both, these poems are addressed "To Man" or "To Men.)" In "The Real Religion," Gilman proleptically casts issues that will emerge in feminist theologies. The two as well strongly appeal to American civil religion as grounding both self and community.

At issue is a kind of redefining of religious allegiances or of the balance among religious terms, giving rise to a poetic mode or topic among the women writers which can be called *metaphysical revision.* Dickinson's work presents a rigorous and even systematic metaphysical critique. But throughout the women's verse are dialogues between soul and body—an ancient form recast through the transformations of nineteenth-century culture; poems attempting new conceptions of perfection as this-worldly rather than focused in the next world; and poems of the body itself. What emerges is a new pull towards the body—its legitimate claims, its validity as a genuine and positive sphere of experience. There are even poems—Howe's "Amanda's Inventory," Wilcox's "The Women," and Gilman's "This is a Lady's Hat" and "The Cripple"—which approach the body as a political topic, presenting women's dress and comportment as a mode of discipline and control over them. Such poems often stand in tension against the older hierarchy elevating soul and its metaphysical corrolaries, creating in the texts ambivalent, somewhat unstable structures and preferences. Yet something new is being recorded: a critique of perfection, a dissatisfaction with older metaphysics, also registered in a widespread Emersonianism and tributes to Emerson, a new embrace of time over eternity.

Here as elsewhere in nineteenth-century women's historiography, conservative and progressive or even radical impulses are not simply oppositional. The poetry reveals just how volatile these categories can be. This remains an argument in feminist discourses: do the concessions made in the context of advances work to limit and indeed betray their possibilities? Was women's continued acceptance of the social norms of family and modesty, defining themselves through traditional roles as mother, wife, daughter, only a check on their further progress? Many of the social-public activities women engaged in were, as we have seen, justified as extensions of their domestic roles, even when in fact not really like them. In my view, an opposite argument reflects more the case: that conservative motives and concessions ultimately unleashed progressive outcomes, contrary to their intention, in a transformative process that could not be controlled. Domesticity opened a door out of the house. Modesty became a mode of self-presentation, in fact a topos in women's writing through which the woman emerges into a public—i.e. published—identity. Traditional feminine preoccupations and energies became a politics of community responsibility—which could, again, take conservative turns, as in Wilcox's and Gilman's nativism, as well a progressive ones, as in Wilcox's poetic and Gilman's political feminism. As to religion, in America in general and certainly for the women presented here, this was as much a liberal force as a conservative one. The Protestant structure of individual encounter with God and personal conversion experience, albeit in the context of a church community; in conjunction with the specific social history of America, including multiple groups, none of which was able to establish a hegemony over the others; with open spaces always available for those who wished to pursue their own forms of worship: all of this made possible a liberal religious experience in America. The greatest exception was in the South. As Frances Harper strongly denounces in "Bible Defence of Slavery," in the South an authoritarian and hierarchical church was enlisted to justify and strengthen slave society. In the North and

West, a sense of each self as sacred and inviolable was often rooted in religious sensibility in complex relation with political liberalism.

Such mutual transformation or penetration of categories especially marks women's poetry considered as '*sentimental*,' a topic lately under much discussion. Sentimental writing has come to be explicated and defended as a political appeal through personal emotion; and as constituting in effect a social attitude of women according to the values they held and wished to uphold, of attachment, connection, and responsibility. In poetry, this can take shape as laments and consolations for dead babies and dead children—or, as in Dickinson, a focus on dead people generally; although Dickinson on the whole is more stark and even grotesque than sentimental. There are other sentimental poems with strong political force, as in Harper's slave auction and slave mother poems or Sigourney's Indian poems. Sentimental poems of religion offer transcendent event or consolation, although they also often present and perform a mode of American civil religion, in missions for social causes.

There is a tendency, however, even in defenses of it, to see the sentimental as transforming political into private emotion; when instead often in the poems private sensibility is directed outward toward public action. And sentimentality remains only one mode of women's poetic writing, which can itself take a variety of forms and functions. This includes a strong trend of deflationary or poetic '*counter-forms*': counter-sentimental, counter-melancholic, counter-romantic, counter-ballads, and especially in Phoebe Cary and Gilman, various modes of parody. The women writers can be very wry about their own domestic setting, training, and sensibility.

Women writers themselves are surprisingly varied in background, status, religion, and ethnicity. The image of women poets as genteel, domestic, and as coming from an established well-to-do class, is simply untrue. Indeed, the men poets of the century are much more uniform in this regard than are the women. Most men were comfortably-off—including a goodly number of Harvard alumni and professors—with well-established and defined social and gender roles according to their regions. The exceptions are Poe as failed Southern gentleman, Whitman as man-of-all-trades, and Stephen Crane as ne'er-do-well journalist. And even they, like the other male poets, were white and Protestant, which remained the case until the turn of the century with Paul Laurence Dunbar. Among women, in contrast, only Howe and Emily Dickinson were born into a typical elite class. Lazarus was wealthy, but Jewish. Frances Harper was a free black. Her first work was in domestic service, although she eventually became self-supporting through her writing—as did Lucy Larcom, who worked in the Lowell Mills; Lydia Sigourney, who was the daughter of a gardener-handyman; the Cary sisters and Ella Wheeler Wilcox, all poor farm girls from out West (although Wilcox married well). Helen Hunt Jackson and Charlotte Gilman likewise came from financially modest if more intellectual backgrounds, becoming self-supporting through professional writing and lecturing.

Moreover, these women had far more struggle with gender definitions than did the male poets, again excepting Poe, Whitman, and Crane; and especially in relation to their vocation of writing. There is evident throughout the century a severe tension between marriage and writing. These tend to be in inverse relation to each other. Of the women treated here, Larcom, Alice and Phoebe Cary, Dickinson, and Lazarus did not marry. Harper and Jackson wrote before or after marriage; Sigourney and Howe in ongoing conflict with their husbands; Gilman after divorce and recreating marriage in a new image. To be professional and self-supporting launched a whole new construction of the female self. It must also be emphasized, however, that for these women not all inherited social norms and roles were negative and restrictive. They could also be sources of strength, values, and a strong sense of identity, especially in terms of female relationships with each other. This is the case with mother/daughter and teacher/student relations in Sigourney; and with sister relations, explicitly in the Cary sisters, implicitly in Dickinson. Dickinson lived with her sister Lavinia. Her relations to her sister-in-law Susan Gilbert Dickinson were intimate and sharing in literary senses as well, as was also her relations with her Norcross cousins and Helen Hunt Jackson through Dickinson's circulation of her poems in letters. The Cary sisters, Howe, and Gilman were actively associated with women's groups of various kinds. There is, that is, a female world of community which provided for these women writers a context for creative effort and sustenance.

When dealing with women's poetry, the question of aesthetic value is inevitably raised. In some ways it is a peculiar question. Contemporary male poets, even those as unpopular as Poe, Whitman, and Crane, never went out of circulation as the women poets did. However popular the women had been in their lifetimes, the minute they died and were buried so were their works (the exception, as usual, is Emily Dickinson, who evaded this indignity by not publishing at all). Longfellow, Whittier, Oliver Wendell Holmes Sr., James Russell Lowell, even Timrod and Lanier have editions of their work available throughout the nineteenth and twentieth centuries. Most were included in literary histories, curricula (which the Harvard Professors compiled), and in anthologies. These male writers on the whole are not more accomplished or interesting than their women compeers. From this angle, to ask the question of value is to ask the question of gender. From another perspective, it is to pose a general question of literary history. Literature has its distinctive modes, setting it off from other forms of language. Within these criteria—which are not resolutely stable—certain works are art of highest accomplishment. Others, as gauged through different approaches, are variously accomplished, interesting, engaging, curious, stimulating, provoking, moving, or valueless. The women's poetry collected here fit into all these categories except the last. As such, they are extremely valuable from a range of interests. They are sources of historical material for women's experiences and viewpoints, just beginning to become part of the written record in the nineteenth century, with the advent of women's higher education except for the very privileged few. They provide social and political analysis of tremendous interest to current discussions, especially of republican traditions in America. They are records of religious experience and transformation, in complex relation to other cultural trends. The poems are, that is, of interest to historians, political theorists, historians of religion, critics of culture and society, and of course to feminists (as well as to women and men in general). Poetry emerges as a central avenue of women's self-expression and participation in public discourse in the nineteenth century, addressing diverse interests and engagements.

But beyond these numerous and significant uses, the poems also stand as poetry. They are rhetorical and formal organizations of language in controlled, at times self-reflective construction, negotiating complex relations between poet, subject, figure and audience. And besides their value as discrete texts, they together form that literary history, indeed that body of literature itself, without which no text, even great ones, can be grasped, appreciated, or even written. The notion of art as cut off from society, from history, from anything but language (as if language is itself not social and historical!) is very specific to a certain period—our own—and in this sense is itself, in a strangely self-denying way, highly historical. Literary art hears, takes up, represents and transforms the voices circulating around it, analyzing or distributing or synthesizing, echoing and answering the words in the mouths of the myriad speakers and actors amidst which it flourishes. It is a peculiarity of women's literary as of other forms of women's history that it has been highly discontinuous. Because of the failure to reprint or report women's texts or actions, each generation of women has had to begin anew, to discover for herself avenues that had in fact been, inaccessibly to her, marked out before her by other, earlier pioneers. Yet the accumulation of efforts and the surprising continuities or cross-junctions between texts suggests interesting commonality in women's experience and expression.

Emily Dickinson can serve as limit case. Even she, for all her abstractness and remoteness, writes words from the world around her: of marriage and worship, of war and success. Women writers contemporary to her display the gender constructions, social forces and tensions, political issues and events that are, in Dickinson, often disguised; but which come to notice exactly through the contexts of other women's writing. To miss this is to miss a great deal. But these other women are worthy of attention in their own right. They are saucy and insightful, protesting and affirming, sentimental and political, all within forms of literary representation that are, depending on the writer, elaborate or straightforward, and eminently worthy of analysis.

What marks this women's writing, perhaps surprisingly, is a complex multiplicity of identities. The women define themselves along a number of planes: through gender; through their vocation as poet; through their national identity as American; and through their religious background. Each of these categories is undergoing enormous change, in themselves and in relation to each other. For women they are disjunctive to start with, if not outright conflictual. To be a woman at the beginning of the century, for example, meant to be lacking in legal, economic, and citizenship rights, with few opportunities for higher education, no leadership roles in church, and a wide range of social strictures regarding personal conduct. Through the century's course, genuine (although still limited) change began to occur: new property rights, new seminaries and then colleges for women, new emergence as speakers and preachers, new professional opportunities, new voluntarist social activities, first through church societies and then into a wider range of causes and organizations, including that of women's rights. The definition of womanhood and its relation to other activities necessarily also registered such changes, in professional, religious, and political directions. Moreover, American society itself was changing: in its populations, its economy, in transportation and communication; in its move from slavery through the cataclysm of war and into efforts at Reconstruction; through new religious forms and practices; new political organization and rules of participation. What the women poets register is a sense in these developments of increasing splits not only in terms of gender but within American society. The pursuit of wealth seemed to leave every other desire behind, economic self-interest to empty public, shared spaces, personal gain to increasingly squeeze civic life.

Just how each of these women's identities will—or will not—stand in relation to the others is a fundamental structural concern in these poets, most sharply and defiantly drawn in Emily Dickinson, who again here directs interpretive strategies to other women poets, even as she benefits by the conjunction with them. Textually, these complex identities come to focus in the figure of the poet herself, in poems on *poetry and the poet*. The poet is a figure the women had to construct essentially from scratch, in tension with their other identities. Woman had existed in poetry before only as Muse. With the woman as poet, the Muse figure becomes awkward. Some—for example Howe and Dickinson—conjure "Masters" to or for whom they wrote, as in Howe's "My Master" and Dickinson's "My Life Had Stood A Loaded Gun." But this occurs at the risk of reduction of one's own agency and authority. Or, poets may imagine feminized Muses—the figure of America, for example, in Lazarus's "New Colossus," not to mention her homoerotic poem "Assurance." Dickinson's relation to Susan Gilbert Dickinson comes to mind, whether erotically or as part of a community of women as audience and support, such as certainly occurred between the Cary sisters and with Sigourney and her students. Religious identity also entered in new alignments with that of woman and poet. As religious calling, women could speak and write, in preaching and in poetry. As American poet, women could critique, envision, protest, and promote values that they had long conducted and continued to represent and embrace.

The strains and responses to them induced through these changing and interacting identities can be seen in still another poetic form characteristic of women: that of '*apology*' and renunciation on the one hand (Dickinson and Jackson both wrote poems called "Renunciation;" compare Howe's "An Apology" and Lazarus's "Acceptance"); or, as its mirror image, poems addressed to *opportunity* (in Jackson), aspiration (in Lazarus), fame (in Alice Cary), or attainment (in Wilcox). Almost all the women poets collected here wrote both sorts, with texts often oscillating between them. In such cases, to apologize is also to defend, to disclaim also to claim. This double-faced mode recalls Anne Bradstreet, the first American woman and indeed poet to publish. Her "Prologue" to her *The Tenth Muse* (published in 1650, reissued in 1867) can stand as prologue to the women's poetry that followed her. There she declares she "will not sing of wars, of captains, and of kings / of cities founded, commonwealths begun"—public matters reserved for (male) epic poets; (although in fact she proceeds to write sweeping histories). Her "Prologue" continues in what will become a paradigmatic mode of concession that also makes an argument:

Men have precedency and still excel,

> It is but vain unjustly to wage war;
> Men can do best, and women know it well.
> Preeminence in all and each is yours;
> Yet grant some small acknowledgment of ours.

Conceding to men precedence—although the remark about unjust wars may retract what she has just offered as praise—she nonetheless defines a place for herself. Within this apologia, she puts forward her own cause. For if she grants to men "Preeminence in all," she likewise asks that they in turn "grant some small acknowledgment of ours." When Bradstreet concludes the "Prologue" with the request of no "bay" leaf crown, but a kitcheny "Thyme or parsley wreath," she in effect is laying claim to her own writer's domain, defined by herself with enormous wit and some reproach as to more pompous ambitions.

Bradstreet was able in this way to blaze her path to poetry. In some sense, much is here conceded: the uncertainty of women's right to speak or stand forward, her discomfort in doing so, her willingness to cede to men the first place. Yet by these means she, and other women, have found strength to speak not only against, but through their sense of appropriate positioning. In this way they were able to imagine themselves as poets, not in betrayal or abandonment of their nineteenth-century senses of self, but in mobilization of it. The authority they claimed would be not for their own sakes but in the name of vision and commitment. Here to be a poet and to be a visionary prophet or a republican come together. Like Whitman's political vision of the poet as not apart from, but among those he addresses, leadership would not be imposition. Women's poetic voice discovers and launches itself as representative—not imperious, but as a mode of public participation, service and address.

Bibliographical Comments

I n the case of women poets of the nineteenth century, their work immediately went out of circulation on their deaths regardless of how popular they may have been, or how many editions of their poetry may have been published during their lifetimes. This was in distinction from male nineteenth poets who may have enjoyed a similar popularity and followed many of the formal norms as the women did, but who remained always available in editions of collected poems, in curricula, in anthologies, and in literary histories, many of which they themselves compiled. The exception, as usual, is Emily Dickinson, whose career followed an inverse course, of non-publication in her lifetime and various editions slowly eked out from her manuscript collections until her complete poems appeared in the Thomas Johnson edition in 1955. The work of nineteenth-century women poets was therefore mainly ignored or unknown by writers of the twentieth.

Only in the years since women's history and feminist literary studies have been initiated has the work of these poets begun to be recovered. Now more and more of their material is available. Here I include, in alphabetical order by poet, new collected editions of poetry; original volumes and internet sources from which I have selected texts; memoirs and autobiographical material, biographies and other documentary material I have drawn on in preparing the introductions.

Alice and Phoebe Cary

There is no collected poems of the Cary sisters. Poems here were selected from: *The Poems of Alice and Phoebe Cary*, New York: Hurst and Co. Pub., 1850; and from materials available in the *Making of America* internet archive at the University of Michigan: *The Poems of Alice and Phoebe Cary*, Philadelphia: Moss and Brother, 1850; *Early and Late Poems of Alice and Phoebe Cary*, Boston: Houghton Mifflin, 1887; *Poems*, by Alice Cary, Boston: Ticknor and Fields, 1855; *The Poetical Works of Alice and Phoebe Cary with a memorial of their lives by Mary Clemmer*, New York: Hurd and Houghton, 1876; *Poems and Parodies by Phoebe Cary*, Boston: Ticknor and Fields, 1854; *The Poems of Phoebe Cary*, New York: Hurst, 187?.

There is no biography of the Cary sisters, nor did they write autobiographical memoirs. Phoebe wrote about Alice in "Alice Cary," *Ladies Repository*, July 1871. A fuller account was written by Mary Clemmer in "A Memorial of their Lives," included as introduction to *The Poetical Works of Alice and Phoebe Cary*, 1876. This was based upon interviews with relatives and friends, Phoebe's account of Alice, and Clemmer's own memoir. There is a "Legacy Profile" of Alice Cary by Judith Fetterley and Marjorie Pryse, *Legacy* 1, no. 1, 1984.

Emily Dickinson

There are two complete editions of Emily Dickinson's work: Thomas Johnson's *Poems of Emily Dickinson*, 3 vols. Cambridge, Mass. Harvard University Press, 1951; Bruce Franklin, *The Poems of Emily Dickinson*, 3 vols. Cambridge, Mass.: The Belknap Press of Harvard University Press, 1998. Facsimile reproductions of Dickinson's 'fascicle' manuscript pages are available in Bruce Franklin, *The Manuscript Books of Emily Dickinson*, 2 vols. Cambridge, Mass.: The Belknap Press of Harvard University Press, 1981.

Dickinson's letters are collected in *Letters of Emily Dickinson,* ed. Thomas Johnson. Cambridge, Mass.: The Belknap Press of Harvard University Press, 1958. Documentary material surrounding her is contained in Jay Leyda, *The Years and Hours of Emily Dickinson*, 2 vols. New Haven: Yale University Press, 1960. Richard Sewall's *The Life of Emily Dickinson* 2 vols. New York: Farrar, Straus and Giroux, 1974 has been the standard biography. Since then, many many accounts of Dickinson have been published.

Charlotte Perkins Gilman

There is no complete works of Charlotte Gilman, either in verse or prose; nor is her poetry available at this date on the internet. The best source for her writing is her own journal, *The Forerunner*. There are two volumes of poetry in print: *In This Our World*, New York: Arno Press, 1974; and *The Later Poetry of Charlotte Gilman,* ed. Denise D. Knight. Delaware: University of Delaware Press, 1996.

Gilman's own memoir she called *The Living of Charlotte Perkins Gilman*, Madison: University of Wisconsin Press, 1953/1990. Other documentary material includes: *The Diaries of Charlotte Perkins Gilman*, ed. Denise D. Knight, Charlottesville: University of Virginia, 1994. The 'standard' biography is by Ann J. Lane, *To Herland and Beyond*, New York: Pantheon Books, 1990.

Frances Watkins Harper

There is a *Complete Poems of Frances E.W. Harper,* ed. Maryemma Graham, New York: Oxford University Press, 1988. Biographical and other material on her are available in *A Brighter Coming Day: A Frances Harper Reader,* ed. Frances Smith Foster, New York: Feminist Press at the City University of New York, 1990. There is also *Discarded*

Legacy: Politics and Poetics in the Life of Frances Ellen Watkins Harper, by Melba Joyce Boyd, Detroit: Wayne State University Press, 1994. A contemporary account of Harper is provided by William Still, *The Underground Railroad,* Philadelphia: Porter and Coates, 1872/ New York: Arno Press, 1968. There is a "Legacy Profile" on Harper by Elizabeth Ammons, *Legacy* 2, 1985, 61–6.

For general background on the spiritual world in which Harper lived, compare: *Sisters of Spirit: Three Black Women's Autobiographies of the Nineteenth Century*, ed. William L. Andrews, Bloomington: Indiana University Press, 1986.

Julia Ward Howe

There is no complete works of Julia Ward Howe, nor is her poetry available at this date on the internet. There are two main collections of her poetry: *Passion Flowers,* Boston: Ticknor, Reed, and Fields, 1853; *Later Lyrics,* Boston: J.E. Tilson and Company, 1866. Howe's memoir, "Reminiscences," appeared in the *Atlantic Monthly* Vol. 83 March 1899. There is as well a memoir by her daughters, Laura E. Richards and Maud Howe Elliott, *Julia Ward Howe: 1819–1910*, Boston: Houghton, Mifflin, 1916. Both are available on the internet.

Biographies of Howe include: Deborah Pickman Clifford, *Mine Eyes Have Seen,* Boston: Little, Brown and Co., 1978; Louise Tharp, *Three Saints and a Sinner*, Boston: Little, 1956. There is a great deal of biographical material on the internet. Another source is *Julia Ward Howe and the Woman Suffrage Movement: Selections from Speeches and Essays* ed. Florence Howe Hall, Boston: Dana Estes and Co., 1913.

Helen Fiske Hunt Jackson

There is a complete *Poems by Helen Hunt Jackson*, Boston: Roberts Brothers, 1873/ New York: Arno Press, 1972. Biographies of Jackson are: Ruth Odell, *Helen Hunt Jackson*, New York: Appleton Century,

1939; Evelyn Banning, *Helen Hunt Jackson*, New York: Vanguard Press, 1973 and Rosemary Whitaker, *Helen Hunt Jackson*, Boise: Boise State University Press, 1987. There is also a "Legacy Profile" by Rosemary Whitaker, "Helen Hunt Jackson" *Legacy* 3 No. 1 Spring 1986, 56–60.

Lucy Larcom

Selections from Larcom have been taken from: *The Poetical Works of Lucy Larcom,* Boston: Houghon Mifflin, 1868; and from materials available on the *Making of American* internet archive at the University of Michigan website: *The Poems of Lucy Larcom,* Boston: Fields and Osgood, 1869; and *An Idyll of Work,* Boston: J.R. Osgood and Co., 1875; Biographical material on Larcom is available through her own memoir, *A New England Girlhood,* Boston: Houghton Mifflin, 1889. There is a biography by Daniel Dulany Addison, *Lucy Larcom: Life, Letters, and Diary,* Boston: Houghton Mifflin, 1894, and by Shirley Marchalonis, *The Worlds of Lucy Larcom*, Athens, Georgia: University of Georgia Press, 1989. Shirley Marchalonis also wrote a "Legacy Profile" on Larcom, *Legacy* 5, no. 1, Spring 1988, 45–51.

Emma Lazarus

A new collection, although not complete, of Emma Lazarus has become available: *Selected Poems and Other Writings*, ed. Gregory Eiselein, Toronto: Broadview Literary Texts, 2002. A fuller collection is available in Josephine Lazarus, "Emma Lazarus," *The Poems of Emma Lazarus, 2 Vols.* Boston and New York: Houghton, Mifflin, 1889.

    Letters of Emma Lazarus were edited by Ralph L. Rusk, Columbia University Press, 1939. Lazarus wrote a large amount of prose, which remains uncollected. Biographies on Lazarus include: Heinrich Jacob, *The World of Emma Lazarus*, New York, 1949; Eve Merriam, *Emma Lazarus: Woman with a Torch*, New York: Citadel, 1986; and Dan Vogel, *Emma Lazarus*, Boston: Twayne, 1980.

Lydia Huntley Sigourney

There is no collected poems of Lydia Sigourney. Poems here are selected from: *Poems*, New York: Leavitt and Allen, 1860; *Illustrated Poems*, Philadelphia: Carey and Hart, 1849; *Poems*, Philadelphia: Key and Biddle, 1834; and materials available through the *Making of America* internet archive at the University of Michigan: *The Weeping Willow* Hartford: H.S. Parsons, 1847; *Poems* New York: Leavitt and Allen Bros., 1841; *Pocahontas and Other Poems,* New York: Harper and Bros., 1841; *The Man of Uz and Other Poems*, Hartford: Williams, Wiley and Waterman, 1862. Sigourney wrote a memoir, published posthumously: *Letters of Life*, New York: Appleton and Company, 1866/ Arno Press, 1980.

The 'standard,' condescending biography of Sigourney is: Haight, Gordon S. *Mrs. Sigourney, The Sweet Singer of Hartford*, New Haven: Yale University Press, 1930. There is also a *Legacy Profile* by Mary De Jong, *Legacy* Volume v, no. 1, Spring 1988, 35–43.

Ella Wheeler Wilcox

There is no edition of collected poems by Ella Wheeler Wilcox. Poems here are selected from: *Poems of Optimism*, London: Gary and Hancock Ltd., 1915; *Poems of Pleasure*, Chicago: Morrill Higgins and Co., 1892; *Poems of Progress*, Chicago: W.B. Conkey Co., 1909; *Poems of Passion*, W.B. Conkey Co., 1883; *Poems of Power*, Chicago: W.B. Conkey Co., 1901; *Poems of Problems,* W.B. Conkey Co., 1914. A great deal of material is available at the *Ella Wheeler Wilcox Society* website and at the *Making of America* internet archive at the University of Michigan website: *Custer and other Poems*, W.B. Conkey, Chicago: 1896; *How Salvator Won and Other Recitations*, New York: E.S. Werner, 1891; *Shells*, Milwaukee: Hansen and Story, 1873; *Poems of Pleasure*, London: Gay and Bird, 1900; *Poems of Affection*, London: Gay and Hancock, 1920; *Poems of Reflection*, Chicago: M.A. Donoghue and Co., 1905; *Poems of Power*, W.B. Conkey, 1902; *Poetical Works of Ella*

Wheeler Wilcox, Edinburgh: Nimmo, Hay and Mitchell, 1917; *Hello Boys*, London: Gay and Hancock, 1919; *Poems of Experience*, London: Gay and Hancock, 1910. "The Captive" is from *Yesterdays*, London: Gay and Hancock, 1916.

Wilcox wrote two autobiographies: *The Story of a Literary Career*, 1905; and *The Worlds and I*, 1918. There is a biography by Jenny Ballou, *Period Piece: Ella Wheeler Wilcox and Her Times,* Boston: Houghton, 1940; mostly noteworthy for calling Wilcox "not a minor poet but a bad major poet."

Lydia Huntley Sigourney: 1791–1865

Introduction

Lydia Sigourney is, in literary history, the cliché of nineteenth-century American women's poetry. In the event, what her work does offer is an initiation into many of the features and terms for the poetry to follow her. The first American woman to make poetry her professional career, she was scorned by the (male) literary establishment. Dismissed as a domestic and sentimental "sweet singer," Sigourney is the model of Mark Twain's parodic poet Emmeline, who "could write about anything you choose to give her to write about just so it was sadful" and who died because an undertaker got to a funeral first. She was called a "gemmy" poet by her biographer, and by Poe an imitator in the "sweet images, the cares, the sorrows, the gentle affection of the domestic hearth." Yet Sigourney is an incisive writer, variously witty and ironic, resolutely political in her interests and address, and highly attentive and determined regarding women's roles, viewpoints, and experiences. Her work probingly investigates and even invents questions of history from the vantage point of women; of women's religious understanding and involvement; of women's lives in sustained critical comment against surrounding social values. Her topic of dead babies and children is one among others, and serves as a figure for a range of pressing issues in the ways American women were coming to define themselves in the century following the Revolution. Finally, her self-representation in her work offers a complex sense of the woman poet as this role accords—and fails to do so—with other womanly roles and senses of selfhood.

Sigourney's biography reads like the instruction books she so successfully produced—itself a testimony to how large was this need in a period of rapid social change. Born the daughter of the gardener-handyman on the Lathrop estate in Norwich, Connecticut, Lydia was patronized/matronized first by Mrs. Lathrop and, on her death, by wealthy Lathrop family connections and especially Daniel Wadsworth. Through them she received a fine education—including instruction in Hebrew and Latin; and help in launching a teaching career at girls' seminaries: first in Norwich in 1811, where she unusually included poor and African-American girls among her students; and then in Hartford in 1814, where her curriculum substituted academic study and moral development for embroidery and domestic crafts. She also began to publish her poems. These professional achievements were threatened by the third social advantage sponsored by Wadsworth, her marriage to the well-off merchant Charles Sigourney in 1819. His opposition to his wife's employment and publication led to the end of her teaching career and resistance to her publishing—as he put it, she had thrown off "that mantle of modesty with which the female character should ever be shrouded." However, financial setbacks came to her rescue. Her writing—in her own name rather than anonymously after 1833—emerged as an important source of income for her family and the support of her parents. She was an astute businesswoman and prolific writer, neither of which entirely accord with the advice she offers in her guide-books for young ladies. Her husband's death in 1854 released her to a satisfactory widowhood as a professional writer in the midst of a community of her students and readers.

Sigourney offers a vivid instance of the complexity of relation between conservative and progressive impulses in the context of women's history. Far from being plainly oppositional, nor only a case where conservative commitments contain and undermine radical ones, the two can augment each other in surprising ways. Conservative intentions in fact often fail to constrain radical consequences. In Sigourney's case, an intense piety—what Poe called her "lofty aspirations of a redeeming Christianity"—provides the framework for all her other undertakings and her understanding of the world. Yet her religion worked to give her a sense of her own authority and voice. It confirmed her in commitment to women's viewpoints and moral activism; and it is the basis of a strongly critical stance against many trends in the society around her, including, perhaps unintentionally, gender, economics, and politics.

"To a Shred of Linen" can serve as a compendium poem, introducing Sigourney's poetic voice and self-representation, as well as the main arenas of her work. Its scene is housekeeping; its subject, the speaker's failure to excel in this role. It is a very tongue-in-cheek poem. Its opening gesture is one of conscious history. Norms have changed, and an older generation of goodwives would not approve of her activities, which is to say her diversion of attention from homemaking to reading and writing books. Actually, she is perfectly happy not to receive this voice of judgment past; nor does she court the approval of "some spruce beau" who, with canny sardonic humor, she knows to rely on women's labor for his own spoiled luxury. Social history in turn extends into material history: the production of the linen, mainly by women supervised by men; the life linen leads in the homes of women, rapidly changing from farmhouses to bourgeois interiors; and finally its fate of being made into paper. But this last image has been a figure for poetry throughout, as the poet very intentionally offers this linen as a "thread of discourse" she herself is weaving. Poetry, as is the case often in women's writing and in Sigourney's own poem "Statue of the Spinning Girl," is associated with and represented by the woman's art of clothmaking. This homely image is at once feminine and modest, even self-deprecating—a modesty so characteristic of female writing as to be a topos. Nineteenth-century women tend to present themselves uncertainly. Their sense of voice, of right to speak and to command an audience, emerges in tension against their sense of place in relation to others. Pure self-assertion is not their norm. This is registered in Sigourney's gesture at the poem's end to a "worthier bard" than herself. Yet she does speak, here and in her poetry; does present herself, for all her humble restraint. And her strength to do so is also hinted in this poem, in the image of Moses' rod—a figure for her own pen. For Sigourney, the authority to speak and write comes from her sense of sanction by moral cause and religious warrant.

Just how strong this sense of moral cause can be as a motive for writing is seen in the poem "Indian Names." Sigourney was a passionate, rare, and of course unsuccessful supporter of Native American rights. In "Indian Names" she attempts to make visible and hence undo the erasure of the Native American, giving voice to their silencing. The poem attests the fundamental relation between language and polity. The importance of naming, and poetry's power to do so, becomes a mode of national shaping, even as America is presented here as a linguistic event. Here, as in her other poems on Native Americans ("The Funeral of Mazeen," "Our Aborigines," "The Indian Girl's Burial") she accuses her own culture of betraying its principles—rebuking the "pale brow'd brother's guilt" in "The Funeral of Mazeen," even while she acknowledges the humanity and value of other cultures. This moral stance, however, contains a certain fissure. While affirming respect for other cultures, her own Christianity remains the measure. In "The Suttee," and more strongly in "The African Mother at her Daughter's Grave," Sigourney views the Indian and African as worshipping "idol-gods" and "invoking gods that could not save." Yet these poems also show the awakening effect of Sigourney's Christian moralism. It strengthens her sense of injustice, specifically of injustice against women, and her critical judgment of established, male norms.

"The Suttee" is in many ways a sentimental poem; but in this it also illustrates some of the structure and strength of sentiment. A growing number of feminist critics have reexamined and reinterpreted sentiment as political and public appeal, rather than private indulgence. This is often the case in Sigourney. "The Suttee" dramatizes the anguish of mother and child, to defy and accuse the social-religious system which destroys her. Perhaps the embarrassment of emotional attachment is just what the text intends to expose, acknowledge and mobilize. It is Sigourney's means of forcing recognition of the humanity of women and, if still in her specifically Christian terms, of other groups as well. "The Indian Girl's Burial" extends the dignity of attachment and mourning to Native Americans, opening to her mostly female readers an avenue of recognition of each in the other. "The African Mother" explores and describes foreign customs with dignity, and if it finally frames them as pagan vs. Christian, it also opposes human African against an inhumane "race of pale-browed" slave traders.

Reading through Sigourney's work, the gendered orientation is remarkable. This pronounced sense of women as organizing category, as perspective, as mode of experience, situates her sentimental poetry. Poems of gender cluster around mothers and daughters and babies, marriage and school, and death. But death is a varied and complex figure. One of its senses of course is mortality: not that more babies died in the nineteenth century than before it (only two of Sigourney's five children survived to adulthood); but that family ideology had changed into the nurturing attachment of the separate sphere of the home. Sigourney's work marks—indeed was part of—the construction of the separate spheres as gender ideology. Yet she also signals how, at the very moment of the separating of the spheres, contrary currents were likewise emerging. Woman-at-home as ideology and also geography came into being exactly as women were leaving the home in post-Revolutionary culture: to school, on missions, in voluntary societies, in moral reform, temperance and other campaigns, into the work force, and eventually, for women's rights.

Sigourney's sentimental, Emmelinish verse on dead children, for example, records both these contrary and simultaneous social directions. Mourning at once affirms attachment in and to the home, but also its rupture—and not only in death. "Death of an Infant" strangely changes the dying infant into furniture: an odd reflection on housekeeping, and recording grief as strongly (at least) as it does consolation. Marriage is just as great a disruption in Sigourney as death is, with the one often a figure of the other. In poems like "To an Absent Daughter," "Forgotten Flowers to a Bride," and "The Bride," it is hard to tell whether the departed daughter has died or wed. In either case she is lost to her mother. Marriage, like death, breaks into female relationship. School also takes on a fatal figuring: not only as separation, but as conflict about woman's proper place and role. Sigourney was part of the pioneering move into higher education for girls launched by the Revolution, dedicated to participatory citizenship—if not for females themselves, then at least as companions to husbands and instructors to sons. Yet to go to school entailed leaving the home, not to mention new life possibilities. Sigourney's "Sister" hence dies—of ambivalence as it were—while "Absent at School." The "School of Young Ladies," even as it registers the excitement of new opportunities, almost immediately cringes under a dark fear of their inevitable disappointment and concludes in death imagery.

Through all her commitments, Sigourney's vision remains founded in religion. Yet this points in a number of different and not always consistent directions. Tensions are evident in the poem "A Name." Opening, as do many of her poems, with a biblical reference—here to Babel—the poem enacts a major dilemma of women's writing, the difficulty of even claiming a name, of having a voice. Sigourney at once yearns for, and also hesitates and worries about the grounds of her naming and writing. There is a hesitation of self-assertion: except in the name of some larger vision, some greater commitment which justifies, directs, and fuels her efforts. Such appeal to a greater cause informs all of Sigourney's poems on religious topics, as well as her historical vision, itself framed in terms of sacred history; and ultimately poetry itself. What is striking is how Sigourney focuses, in religion and history, on women's experience in quite revolutionary ways. "The Ark and Dove," for example, is a re-writing of the Bible from a woman's viewpoint, focusing on female figures such as contemporary feminists have set out to do in biblical interpretation. Sigourney re-names the story, making Noah and the Flood into the Ark—as image of the domicile—and the Dove, as female heroine (perhaps based in her studies in Hebrew, where the Dove is a feminine grammatical form). As heroine, the Dove ventures forth in the name of rescuing others to find safe landing. Framed as a scene of mother instructing daughter, the poem ends with the hope that the young girl will grow to be "like that exploring dove."

Sigourney not only feminizes the Bible, but claims its authority. Her poem in "Imitation of Parts of the Prophet Amos" (a title at once venturesome and diffident: imitation, parts, male—yet still, in the model of the prophet-figure) depicts the prophet being called from his humble beginnings and his essentially domestic role as shepherd to "forsake thy flock and be the Seer of God." The ensuing account of God's sustenance in prophecy dramatizes Sigourney's own poetic calling, her conflict over leaving her "tender lambs" yet sense that God, who has summoned "the rough-clad man to leave his simple flock / with strength will gird him." This is the basis for her daring to be a poet at all, and her view of its role of mediating leadership. The poem ends with an homage to the splendor of creation that strongly recalls Edward Taylor's writing, whom of course she could not have read. "Abraham at Macpelah" approaches another male figure, yet again in very feminized terms. This patriarch emerges in effect as matriarch, not only defined through his love for Sarah (compare Frances Harper's "Burial of Sarah") but taking on her qualities of hospitality, grace, humility, and the "labouring breast" of sorrow.

Sigourney's historical poems are continuous with her religious ones. "Pilgrim Fathers" and "The New England Fathers" (anthologized by Griswold) despite their titles highlight the arrival of women on the New World shores, women's confrontation with the wilderness as it assaulted their family life. It is "matron and maid and fragile child" who made the pilgrimage; they who had courage; they who suffered the "babe bereft" and "heart-sickness" for lost homes, the "sever'd" link to "habitable earth." Just so, "The Mother of Washington" celebrates a feminine national geneology, re-inserting women into history and acknowledging their public life. "The Western Emigrant" depicts the movement westward through the sense of displacement, as well as opportunity, felt by children and wives. It is, again, biblical narrative and religious devotion that launches and interprets the venture—America as "Haran's wild"—to which Sigourney is strongly committed in republican terms. "On the Admission of Michigan into the Union" offers an elaborate and witty conceit of an American polity established by Founding Mothers, governed by an etiquette of civility. The American possibility of expansion as inclusion, for the first time in history instituted not as colonization but federalization, is central to this vision of republican opportunity and feminized equality.

Yet Sigourney is also anxious about the betrayal of these principles. "On the Admission" goes out of its way to insist on the Indians who are not admitted, who have been excluded from this American picture. Just how far the poem may be ironic as to the actual lack of participation of women in government is difficult to gauge. In "The Volunteer," Sigourney does not hesitate to register woman's devastation at men's wars. And "The New England Fathers" uses the memory of the founding as warning against its abandonment. Sigourney's is a republican warning against the "Mammon" whose "bloated luxury" increasingly "eats the core from manly virtue." Civic virtue, devotion to the public good, was giving way to increasing economic self-interest and social organization in a way she denounces.

It was women in fact who in the nineteenth century were largely inheriting these revolutionary republican values as men were not. It is women who engaged in works of public service, while men increasingly engaged in works of labor and profit. It is a strange twist that dubbed as "separate sphere" what in practice involved community life: care of children, of the ill, of the elderly, of urban development, health, social relationships. What the separate spheres do indicate is the increasing separation of values—not into domestic as against public, but communal as against economic. "Benevolence" blasts this division. The work of woman's voluntarism, benevolence is opposed against private "treasure-chambers." "A Cottage Scene" is the very image of home as haven in a heartless world, but as such it is a critique of "weary commerce." "Statue of a Spinning Girl" aligns womanly values of "patient industry and household good" against male "lordly halls"—and with art. As sculpture and as craft, the "Spinning Girl" represents women's poetry, in both its modesty and its ambition. Sigourney in her memoir calls hers a "kitchen muse" and herself "a woman of all work and an aproned writer;" or, as she writes in "The Muse," "I've written poetry, sooth to say, in the oddest places." She nonetheless presents "Poetry" as a "holy thing" (Poe's favorite Sigourney line) and, in "The Sacred Poet," as the "mouth for an immortal mind"—by which she means "an honour from the hand of God." "In deep humility," she continues; and in opposition against the increasingly crushing value of "prosperity," the poet still goes forward, dedicated to high values, to immortality. With deeply feminized imagery, viewpoint, and values, she opposes in her texts and her enterprise the needle and the pen against the sword.

Poems

To a Shred of Linen

Would they swept cleaner!—
                              Here's a littering shred
Of linen left behind—a vile reproach
To all good housewifery. Right glad am I,
That no neat lady, train'd in ancient times
Of pudding-making, and of sampler-work,
And speckless sanctity of household care,
Hath happened here, to spy thee. She, no doubt,
Keen looking through her spectacles, would say,
"*This comes of reading books*:"—or some spruce beau,
Essenc'd and lily-handed, had he chanc'd
To scan thy slight superfices, 'twould be
"*This comes of writing poetry*."—Well—well—
Come forth—offender!—hast thou aught to say?
Canst thou by merry thought, or quaint conceit,
Repay this risk, that I have run for thee?
—Begin at alpha, and resolve thyself
Into thine elements. I see the stalk
And bright, blue flower of flax, which erst o'erspread
That fertile land, where mighty Moses stretch'd
His rod miraculous. I see thy bloom
Tinging, too scantly, these New England vales.
But, lo! the sturdy farmer lifts his flail,
To crush thy bones unpitying, and his wife
With 'kerchief'd head, and eyes brimful of dust,
Thy fibrous nerves, with hatchel-tooth divides.

—I hear a voice of music—and behold!
The ruddy damsel singeth at her wheel,
While by her side the rustic lover sits.
Perchance, his shrewd eye secretly doth count
The mass of skeins, which, hanging on the wall,
Increaseth day by day. Perchance his thought,
(For men have deeper minds than women—sure!)
Is calculating what a thrifty wife
The maid will make; and how his dairy shelves
Shall groan beneath the weight of golden cheese,
Made by her dexterous hand, while many a keg
And pot of butter, to the market borne,
May, transmigrated, on his back appear,
In new thanksgiving coats.
                              Fain would I ask,
Mine own New England, for thy once loved wheel,
By sofa and piano quite displac'd.
Why dost thou banish from thy parlor-hearth
That old Hygeian harp, whose magic rul'd
Dyspepsia, as the minstrel-shepherd's skill
Exorcis'd Saul's ennui? There was no need,
In those good times, of trim callisthenics,
And there was less of gadding, and far more
Of home-born, heart-felt comfort, rooted strong
In industry, and bearing such rare fruit,
As wealth might never purchase.
                              But come back,
Thou shred of linen. I did let thee drop,
In my harangue, as wiser ones have lost
The thread of their discourse. What was thy lot
When the rough battery of the loom had stretch'd
And knit thy sinews, and the chemist sun
Thy brown complexion bleach'd?
                              Methinks I scan
Some idiosyncrasy, that marks thee out
A defunct pillow-case.—Did the trim guest,

To the best chamber usher'd, e'er admire
The snowy whiteness of thy freshen'd youth
Feeding thy vanity? or some sweet babe
Pour its pure dream of innocence on thee?
Say, hast thou listen'd to the sick one's moan,
When there was none to comfort?—or shrunk back
From the dire tossings of the proud man's brow?
Or gather'd from young beauty's restless sigh
A tale of untold love?
                    Still, close and mute!—
Wilt tell no secrets, ha?—Well then, go down,
With all thy churl-kept hoard of curious lore,
In majesty and mystery, go down
Into the paper-mill, and from its jaws,
Stainless and smooth, emerge.—happy shall be
The renovation, if on thy fair page
Wisdom and truth, their hallow'd lineaments
Trace for posterity. So shall thine end
Be better than thy birth, and worthier bard
Thine apotheosis immortalise.

Indian Names

Ye say, they all have passed away,
That noble race and brave,
That their light canoes have vanished
From off the crested wave;
That 'mid the forests where they roamed
There rings no hunter's shout;
But their name is on your waters,
Ye may not wash it out.

'Tis where Ontario's billow
Like Ocean's surge is curl'd,
Where strong Niagara's thunders wake

The echo of the world,
Where red Missouri bringeth
Rich tributes from the west,
And Rappahannock sweetly sleeps
On green Virginia's breast.

Ye say, their cone-like cabins,
That clustered o'er the vale,
Have fled away like withered leaves
Before the autumn gale:
But their memory liveth on your hills,
Their baptism on your shore,
Your everlasting rivers speak
Their dialect of yore.

Old Massachusetts wears it
Within her lordly crown,
And broad Ohio bears it
Amid her young renown;
Connecticut hath wreathed it
Where her quiet foliage waves,
And bold Kentucky breathes it hoarse
Through all her ancient caves

Wachuset hides its lingering voice
Within his rocky heart,
And Alleghany graves its tone
Throughout his lofty chart;
Monadnock on his forehead hoar
Doth seal the sacred trust,
Your mountains build their monument,
Though ye destroy their dust.

A Name

"Let us make us a name, lest we be scattered abroad."
GENESIS, XI, 4.

Make to thyself a name,
Not with a breath of clay,
Which, like the broken, hollow reed,
Doth sigh itself away;
Not with the fame that vaunts
The tyrant on his throne,
And hurls its stigma on the soul
That God vouchsafes to own.
Make to thyself a name,
Nor such as wealth can weave,
Whose warp is but a thread of gold,
That dazzles to deceive;
Not with the tints of Love
From out its letters fair,
That scroll within thy hand shall fade
Like him who placed it there.
Make to thyself a name,
Not in the sculptured aisle,
The marble oft betrays its trust,
Like Egypt's lofty pile;
But ask of Him who quell'd
Of death, the victor, strife,
To write it on the blood-bought page
Of everlasting life.

The Suttee

She sat upon the pile by her dead lord,
And in her full, dark eye, and shining hair
Youth revell'd.—The glad murmur of the crowd
Applauding her consent to the dread doom,

And the hoarse chanting of infuriate priests
She heeded not, for her quick ear had caught
An infant's wail—feeble and low that moan,
Yet it was answer'd in her heaving heart,
For the Mimosa in its shrinking fold
From the rude pressure, is not half so true,
So tremulous, as is a mother's soul
Unto her wailing babe.—There was such woe
In her imploring aspect,—in her tones
Such thrilling agony, that even the hearts
Of the flame-kindlers soften'd, and they laid
The famish'd infant on her yearning breast.
There with his tear-wet cheek he lay and drew
Plentiful nourishment from that full fount
Of infant happiness,—and long he prest
With eager lip the chalice of his joy.
And then his little hands he stretch'd to grasp
His mother's flower-wove tresses, and with smile
And gay caress embraced his bloated sire.
As if kind Nature taught that innocent one
With fond delay to cheat the hour which seal'd
His hopeless orphanage.—But those were near
Who mock'd such dalliance, as that Spirit malign
Who twined his serpent length mid Eden's bowers
Frown'd on our parents' bliss.—The victim mark'd
Their harsh intent, and clasp'd the unconscious babe
With such convulsive force, that when they tore
His writhing form away, the very nerves
Whose deep-sown fibres rack the inmost soul
Uprooted seem'd.—With voice of high command
Tossing her arms, she bade them bring her son
And then in maniac rashness sought to leap
Among the astonish'd throng.—But the rough cord
Compress'd her slender limbs, and bound her fast
Down to her loathsome partner.—Quick the fire
In showers was hurl'd upon the reeking pile;—

But yet amid the wild, demoniac shout
Of priest and people, mid the thundering yell
Of the infernal gong,—was heard to rise
Thrice a dire death-shriek.—And the men who stood
Near the red pile and heard that fearful cry,
Call'd on their idol-gods, and stopp'd their ears,
And oft amid their nightly dream would start
As Frighted Fancy echoed in her cell
That burning mother's scream.

On the Admission of Michigan into the Union

Come in, little sister, so healthful and fair,
Come take in our father's best parlor a share,
You've been kept long enough at the nurse's, I trow,
Where the angry lakes roar and the northern winds blow;
Come in, we've a pretty large household, 'tis true,
But the twenty-five children can make room for you.

A present, I see, for our sire you have brought,
His dessert to embellish, how kind was the thought;
A treat of ripe berries, both crimson and blue,
And wild flowers to stick in his button-hole too,
The rose from your prairie, the nuts from your tree,
What a good little sister—come hither to me.

You've a dowry besides very cunningly stor'd,
To fill a nice cupboard, or spread a broad board,
Detroit, Ypsilanti—Ann Arbour and more—
For the youngest, methinks, quite a plentiful store,
You're a prog, I perceive—it is true to the letter,
And your sharp Yankee sisters will like you the better.

But where are your Indians—so feeble and few?
So fall'n from the heights where their forefathers grew!
From the forests they fade, o'er the waters that bore
The names of their baptism, they venture no more –
O soothe their sad hearts ere they vanish afar,
Nor quench the faint beams of their westering star.

Those ladies who sit on the sofa so high,
Are the stateliest dames of our family,
Your thirteen old sisters, don't treat them with scorn,
They were notable spinsters before you were born,
Many stories they know, most instructive to hear,
Go, make them a curtsy, 'twill please them, my dear.

They can teach you the names of those great ones to spell,
Who stood at the helm, when the war tempest fell,
They will show you the writing that gleam'd to the sky
In the year seventy-six, on the fourth of July;
When the flash of the Bunker-Hill flame was red,
And the blood gush'd forth from the breast of the dead.

There are some who may call them both proud and old,
And say they usurp what they cannot hold;
Perhaps, their bright locks have a sprinkle of gray,
But then, little Michy, don't hint it, I pray;
For they'll give you a frown, or a box on the ear,
Or send you to stand in the corner, I fear.

They, indeed, bore the burden and heat of the day,
But you've as good right to your penny as they;
Though the price of our freedom, they better have known,
Since they paid for it, out of their purses alone,
Yet a portion belongs to the youngest, I ween,
So, hold up your head with the "Old Thirteen!"

The Ark and Dove

"Tell me a story—please," my little girl
Lisped from her cradle. So I bent me down
And told her how it rained, and rained, and rained,
Till all the flowers were covered, and the trees
Hid their tall heads, and where the houses stood,
And people dwelt, a fearful deluge rolled;
Because the world was wicked, and refused
To heed the words of God. But one good man,
Who long had warned the wicked to repent
Obey and live, taught by the voice of Heaven,
Had built an Ark; and thither, with his wife,
And children, turned for safety. Two and two,
Of beasts and birds, and creeping things he took,
With food for all; and when the tempest roared,
And the great fountains of the sky poured out
A ceaseless flood, till all beside were drowned,
They in their quiet vessel dwelt secure.
And so the mighty waters bare them up,
And o'er the bosom of the deep they sailed
For many days. But then a gentle dove
'scaped from the casement of the ark, and spread
Her lonely pinion o'er that boundless wave.
All, all was desolation. Chirping nest,
Nor face of man, nor living thing she saw,
For all the people of the earth were drowned,
Because of disobedience. Nought she spied
Save wide, dark waters, and a frowning sky,
Nor found her weary foot a place of rest.
So, with a leaf of olive in her mouth,
Sole fruit of her drear voyage, which, perchance,
Upon some wrecking billow floated by,
With drooping wing the peaceful Ark she sought.
The righteous man that wandering dove received,
And to her mate restored, who, with sad moans,

Had wondered at her absence.
> Then I looked
Upon the child, to see if her young thought
Wearied with following mine. But her blue eye
Was a glad listener, and the eager breath
Of pleased attention curled her parted lip.
And so I told her how the waters dried,
And the green branches waved, and the sweet buds
Came up in loveliness, and that meek dove
Went forth to build her nest, while thousand birds
Awoke their songs of praise, and the tired ark
Upon the breezy breast of Ararat
Reposed, and Noah, with glad spirit, reared
An altar to his God.
> Since, many a time,
When to her rest, ere evening's earliest star,
That little one is laid, with earnest tone,
And pure cheek prest to mine, she fondly asks
"The Ark and Dove."
> Mothers can tell how oft,
In the heart's eloquence, the prayer goes up
From a sealed lip: and tenderly hath blent
With the warm teaching of the sacred tale
A voiceless wish, that when that timid soul,
New in the rosy mesh of infancy,
Fast bound, shall dare the billows of the world,
Like that exploring dove, and find no rest,
A pierced, a pitying, a redeeming hand
May gently guide it to the ark of peace.

Imitation of Parts of the Prophet Amos

I from no princely stock, or lineage came,
Nor bore my sire, a prophet's honour'd name,
But 'mid the Tekoan shepherds' manners rude,

My speech was fashion'd, and my toil pursued.
O'er hills and dales I led, o'er streams and rocks,
The wandering footsteps of my herds, and flocks,
I fed them where the fruitful valleys fling
Their first, fresh verdure, on the lap of spring;
Or where the quiet fountains slowly glide
Their fringed eyes, among the flowers to hide;
And when the noontide sun, with fervid heat
Upon the tender lambs, too fiercely beat,
I guided, where the mountain's sheltering head,
A sable shade, across the landscape spread.
There, while they sank in slumber, soft and meek,
I wandered forth, my simple meal to seek,
The juicy wild fig, and the crystal tide
My strength renew'd, and nature's wants supplied.
When sober twilight drew her curtaining shade,
And on the dewy lawn my flocks were laid,
In my rough mantle, by their side reclined
I gave to holy thoughts my wakeful mind;
The stars, that in their mystic circles move,
The sparkling blue, of the high arch above,
The pomp of eve, the storm's majestic power,
The solemn silence of the midnight hour,
The silver softness of the unveil'd moon,
Spake to my soul of Him, the Everlasting One.
Once as I woke, from visions, high and sweet,
And found my flocks reposing at my feet,
Saw morning's earliest ray, the hills invest,
Stream o'er the forest, touch the mountain breast,
Glance o'er the glittering streams and dart its way,
Thro' the damp vales, where slumbering vapours lay,
Methought, within my heart, a light there shone
More clear, and glorious than the rising sun,
And while my every nerve with rapture thrilled
A Power Supreme, my soul in silence held.
Quick to the earth, my bending knee I bowed,

My raised eyes fixing on a crimson cloud,
Which from its cleaving arch, the mandate bore,
"Go shepherd, lead thy much-lov'd flock once more!"
My trembling lips now press'd the soil I trod,
"Shepherd, forsake thy flock, and be the seer of God."

Uprising at the heavenly call, I laid
My crook and scrip beneath the spreading shade,
"I go, I go, my God!" my answering spirit said.
Thro' the rude stream I dash'd, whose foaming tide,
Came whitening o'er the mountain's hoary side;
But pressing on my path, I heard with pain,
The approaching footsteps of my cherished train,
And wept, as gazing on their fleecy pride,
I thought, who now their wandering steps should guide.
Yet still, within, the hallow'd impulse burn'd,
And soon, its answering thoughts my heart return' d;'
"My tender lambs, my unfed flock, adieu,
My God, a shepherd will provide for you,
One kind as I have been, whose care shall guide
You, where fresh pastures smile, and fountain glide;
Hand unseen, a voice and purpose true,
Divide you from my charge, and me from you."
What tho' my rustic speech and shepherd's dress
But ill a prophet's dignity express,
What tho' the doom I bear, be dark with fear,
And grate repulsive on the guilty ear,
What tho' my heart beneath fierce tortures break,
And I, a martyr's fiery death partake,
Yet He, who summoned from yon distant rock,
The rough-clad man to leave his simple flock,
With strength will gird him, for his wants provide,
And quell the clamours of the sons of pride.
With fearless brow, I sought his haughty foes,
Where proud Samaria's regal ramparts rose.
But lo! the wasted suburbs, parch'd and dry

Spread a brown heath, to meet the wondering eye,
The smitten verdure, and the sterile plain,
Disclosed the march of a devouring train,
Before whose face, the fruitful earth was fair
Behind, a prey to famine, bleak and bare.
The wasted herds, a poor, neglected train,
Sought their accustom'd food, but sought in vain
Some, mad with hunger, spurn'd the flinty clay
And some in pangs of death, despairing lay.
Then, low to earth I bent my drooping head,
As one who mourns his dearest idol dead,
"My God!" I cried, "my God, arise and see,
Thy chosen people's fearful misery!
The sick land mourns its harden'd children's sin,
Thy wrath devours without and guilt within:
Ah! who shall drooping Israel's strength repair,
If thou dost cast him from thy succouring care?"
An answering voice was heard, it spake to me,
God spake from heaven—"This judgment shall not be."
Soon, nature's languid form, reviving fair,
Sang praises to the God who answers prayer;—
Vanish'd the reptile host, the withering stem
Spread forth anew, the bud reveal'd its gem,
Deep mourning earth, her robe of joy resum'd,
And spicy gums, the summer gales perfum'd.
A flame!—a flame!—its awful ravage spread
With quenchless wrath and indignation dread,
Fed on the domes of pride, with angry sweep
And hiss'd defiance at the watery deep.
Ah!—who shall stay its rage, or curb its power.
Our God! protect us, in this dreadful hour.
You first the plague and wants of war shall vex,
The captive's yoke shall cling around your necks,
And you shall groan, in servitude and scorn,
Like the slave sorrowing o'er his dead first-born.
Ah sinful nation!—of thy God accurst,

Thy glory stain'd, thy crown defil'd with dust,
Go,—hide thee ill Mount Carmel,—dive the deep,
Plunge in the slimy cells where serpents cleep,
Make through the earth's dark dens, thy secret path,
Yet canst thou shun the purpose of His wrath.
"Hence, to your woods," they cried, "your herds and flocks,—
Go, drive your few sheep o'er the rugged rocks,
Who bade you dare to quit the lowing throng?
Who made you judge of violence and wrong?"
He, who beheld me, at my humble toil,
Content and cheerful, ill my native soil,—
He, who beholds you, from the frowning skies,
And all your wrath and arrogance defies;
He call'd me from my flocks and pastures fair,
He gave the message, which I boldly bear,
And which I bear till death:—so breathe your ire,
And wreak such vengeance, as your souls desire
Say,—whose strong arm compos'd this wondrous frame?
Who stay'd the fury of the rushing flame?
Who made the mighty sun to know his place?
And fill'd with countless orbs yon concave space?
Who from his cistern bade the waters flow
And on the spent cloud hung his dazzling bow?
Who drives thro' realms immense his thundering car
To far Orion and the morning star?
Who light to darkness turns?—and night to death?
Gives the frail life and gathers back the breath?
Who gave this ponderous globe, with nicest care
To balance lightly on the fluid air?
Who raised yon mountains to their lofty height?
Who speeds the whirlwind in its trackless flight?
Who darts thro' deep disguise, his piercing ken
To read the secret thoughts and ways of men?
Who gave the morning and the midnight birth?
Whose muffled step affrights the quaking earth?

Who curb'd the sea? and touch'd the rocks with flame?
Jehovah, God of Hosts, is his tremendous name.

Abraham at Macpelah

Deep wrapp'd in shades
Olive and terebinth, its vaulted door
Fleck'd with the untrain'd vine and matted grass,
Behold Macpelah's cave. Hark! hear we not
A voice of weeping? Lo, yon aged man
Bendeth beside his dead. Wave after wave
Of memory rises, till his lonely heart
Sees all its treasures floating on the flood,
Like rootless weeds. The earliest dawn of love
Is present with him, and a form of grace,
Whose beauty held him ever in its thrall:
And then, the morn of marriage, gorgeous robes,
And dulcet music, and the rites that bless
The Eastern bride. Full many a glowing scene,
Made happy by her tenderness, returns
To mock his solitude, as the sharp lance
Severs the quivering nerve. His quiet home
Gleams through the oaks of Mamre. There he sat,
Rendering due rites of hospitality
To guests who bore the folded wing of Heaven
Beneath their vestments. And her smile was there,
Among the angels. When her clustering curls
Wore Time's chill hoar frost, with what glad surprise,
What holy triumph of exulting faith,
He saw fresh blooming in her wither'd arms
A fair young babe, the heir of all his wealth.
Forever blending with that speechless joy
Which thrill'd his soul, when first a father's name
Fell on his ear, is that pale, placid brow
O'er which he weeps. Yet had he seen it wear

Another semblance, tinged with hues of thought,
Perchance unlovely, in that trial-hour,
When to sad Hagar's mute, reproachful eye
He answer'd naught, but on her shoulder laid
The water bottle and the loaf, and sent
Her and her son, unfriended wanderers, forth
Into the wilderness. Say, who can mourn
Over the smitten idol, by long years
Cemented with his being, yet perceive
No dark remembrance that he fain would blot,
Troubling the tear. If there were no kind deed
Omitted, no sweet healing word of love
Expected, yet unspoken; no light tone
That struck discordant on the shivering nerve,
For which the weeper fain would rend the tomb
To cry forgive! oh, let him kneel and praise
God amid all his grief. We may not say
If aught of penitence was in the pang
That wrung the labouring breast, while o'er the dust
Of Sarah, at Macpelah's waiting tomb,
The proud and princely Abraham bow'd him down,
A mourning stranger, mid the sons of Heth.

Pilgrim Fathers

What led the pilgrims through the wild
On, to this stranger land,
Matron and maid, and fragile child,
An uncomplaining band?

Deep streams their venturous course oppos'd,
Dark wastes appall'd their eye;
What fill'd them on that trackless way,
With courage bold and high?

What cheer'd them, when dire winter's wrath
A frosty challenge threw,
And higher than their trembling roofs
The mocking snow-drift grew?

When in its wasted mother's arms,
To famine's ills, a prey,
The babe bereft of rosy charms
Pin'd like a flower away?

And when the strong heart-sickness came,
And memory's troubled stream,
Still imag'd forth fair England's homes,
That lull'd their cradle-dream,

When no lone vessel ploughed the watch
News from her clime to bear,
What nobly bore the stricken soul,
Above that deep despair?

What gave them strength, 'mid all their toil
In every hour of need
To plant within this sterile soil
A glorious nation's seed?

The same that nerv'd them when they sank
To rest, beneath the sod,
That rais'd o'er death, the triumph song
Prayer, and the faith of God.

The Fathers of New England

How slow you lonely vessel ploughs the main!
Amid the heavy billows now she seems
A toiling atom; then, from wave to wave

Leaps madly, by the tempest lash'd, or reels
Half wreck'd through gulfs profound.
                                    Moons wax and wane,
But still that patient traveller treads the deep.
—I see an ice-bound coast toward which she steers
With such a tardy movement, that it seems
Stern Winter's hand hath turn'd her keel to stone,
And seal'd his victory on her slippery shrouds.
—They land! they land! not like the Genoese
With glittering sword, and gaudy train, and eye
Kindling with golden fancies. Forth they come
From their long prison, hardy forms that brave
The world's unkindness, men of hoary hair,
Maidens of fearless heart, and matrons grave,
Who hush the wailing infant with a glance.
Bleak Nature's desolation wraps them round,
Eternal forests, and unyielding earth,
And savage men, who through the thickets peer
With vengeful arrow. What could lure their steps
To this drear desert? Ask of him who left
His father's home to roam through Haran's wild,
Distrusting not the guide who call'd him forth,
Nor doubting, though a stranger, that his seed
Should be as ocean's sands.
                                    But yon lone bark
Hath spread her parting sail. They crowd the strand,
Those few, lone pilgrims. Can ye scan the woe
That wrings their bosoms, as the last, frail link,
Binding to man, and habitable earth,
Is sever'd? Can ye tell what pangs were there,
With keen regrets, what sickness of the heart,
What yearnings o'er their forfeit land of birth,
Their distant, dear ones?
                                    Long, with straining eye,
They watch the lessening speck. Heard ye no shriek
Of anguish, when that bitter loneliness

Sank down into their bosoms? No! they turn
Back to their dreary, famish'd huts, and pray!
Pray, and the ills that haunt this transient life
Fade into air. Up in each girded breast
There sprang a rooted and mysterious strength,
A loftiness, to face a world in arms,
To strip the pomp from sceptres, and to lay,
On duty's sacred altar, the warm blood
Of slain affections, should they rise between
The soul and God.
                        Oh ye, who proudly boast,
In your free veins, the blood of sires like these,
Look to their lineaments. Dread lest ye lose
Their likeness in your sons.
                        Should Mammon cling
Too close around your heart, or wealth beget
That bloated luxury which eats the core
From manly virtue, or the tempting world
Make faint the Christian purpose in your soul,
Turn ye to Plymouth-rock, and where they knelt
Kneel, and renew the vow they breath'd to God.

The Western Emigrant

An axe rang sharply 'mid those forest shades
Which from creation toward the skies had tower'd
In unshorn beauty—There, with vigorous arm
Wrought a bold Emigrant, and by his side
His little son, with question and response,
Beguil'd the toil.
                        "Boy, thou hast never seen
Such glorious trees. Hark, when their giant trunks
Fall, how the firm earth groans. Rememberest thou
The mighty river, on whose breast we sail'd,
So many days, on toward the setting sun?

55

Our own Connecticut, compar'd to that,
Was but a creeping stream."
                              "Father, the brook
That by our door went singing, where I launch'd
My tiny boat, with my young playmates round
When school was o'er, is dearer far to me,
Than all these bold, broad waters. To my eye
They are as strangers. And those little trees
My mother nurtur'd in the garden bound,
Of our first home, from whence the fragrant peach
Hung in its ripening gold, were fairer, sure,
Than this dark forest, shutting out the day."
—"What, ho!—my little girl," and with light step
A fairy creature basted toward her sire,
And, setting down the basket that contain'd
His noon's repast, look'd upward to his face
With sweet confiding smile.
                            "See, dearest, see,
That bright-wing'd paroquet, and hear the song
Of yon gay red-bird, echoing through the trees
Making rich music. Didst thou ever hear,
In far New England, such a mellow tone?"
—"I had a robin that did take the crumbs
Each night and morning, and his chirping voice
Did make me joyful, as I went to tend
My snow-drops. I was always laughing then
In that first home. I should be happier now
Methinks, if I could find among these dells
The same fresh violets."
                         Slow night drew on,
And round the rude hut of the Emigrant
The wrathful spirit of the rising storm
Spake bitter things. His weary children slept,
And he, with head declin'd, sat listening long
To the swol'n waters of the Illinois,

Dashing against their shores.
                              Starting he spake—
"Wife! did I see thee brush away a tear?
'Twas even so. Thy heart was with the halls
Of thy nativity. Their sparkling lights,
Carpets, and sofas, and admiring guests,
Befit thee better than these rugged walls
Of shapeless logs, and this lone, hermit home."
"No—no. All was so still around, methought
Upon mine ear that echoed hymn did steal,
Which 'mid the church, where erst we paid our vows,
So tuneful peal'd. But tenderly thy voice
Dissolv'd the illusion!"
                              And the gentle smile
Lighting her brow, the fond caress that sooth'd
Her waking infant, reassur'd his soul
That, wheresoe'er our best affections dwell,
And strike a healthful root, is happiness.
Content, and placid, to his rest he sank;
But dreams, those wild magicians, that do play
Such pranks when reason slumbers, tireless wrought
Their will with him.
                              Up rose the thronging mart
Of his own native city—roof and spire,
All glittering bright, in fancy's frost-work ray.
The steed his boyhood nurtur'd, proudly neigh'd,
The favorite dog came frisking round his feet,
With shrill and joyous bark—familiar doors
Flew open—greeting hands with his were link'd
In friendship's grasp—he heard the keen debate
From congregated haunts, where mind with mind
Doth blend and brighten—and till morning rov'd
'Mid the lov'd scenery of his native land.

The Volunteer

Thou'lt go! Thou'lt go!
               In vain, thy stricken wife,
A poor, unconscious infant in her arms,
And thy young children, clinging to thy hand
Implore thy stay. Thine aged parents bend
In prayer, and sorrow. Hath the battle-field
Such charms for thee, that thou wilt tread on all
That love and nature give, and rush to reap
Its iron harvest?
            Lo! the roughen'd men,
Thy boon companions, 'neath the neighboring hedge
Do wait for thee. The vow hath past thy lips
And thou must go.
            So, hence away, and share
Such pleasures, as thy chosen course may yield;
The stirring drum, the pomp of measur'd march,
The pride of uniform, the gazer's shout
Of admiration, the alternate rest
Of idleness in camps, and toil that wastes
The nerveless limb, and starts the sleepless eye.
Take too, the stormy joy of deadly strife,
Spill blood, and trample on the mangled form
And like a demon, drink the groans of pain.

Yet sometimes, when the midnight bowl is drained
And thou art tossing in thy broken dream,
Bethink thee, soldier, of a cottage home
All desolate, its drooping vines untrained,
Its wintry hearth unfed, and she, with cheek
As pale as penury and woe can make,
(Why dost thou start?) and her once blooming ones
Some at hard service, where their bitter bread
Is scantily doled out, and some who ask
Her shuddering heart, for what she cannot give.

—Still doth the vision open?
                    There are graves!
The white-hair'd father hath his rest in one,
And she, who died lamenting for the son
Who snatch'd the morsel from her feeble hand,
Nor sought her blessing when he went to war,
Sleeps in the other.
                    Dreamer! wake not yet.
Mar not the sequel. Toward the peaceful shades
Of his own village, comes a poor, lone man
Whom misery and vice have made their own.
His head is bandaged, and his swollen limbs
Drag heavily. He hath no threshold stone,
No friend to welcome.
                    Is this he who scorn'd
His heaven sworn duties, and his humble home,
And chose his pittance from the cannon's mouth?

The Mother of Washington
On the laying of the corner-stone of her monument

Long hast thou slept unnoted. Nature stole
In her soft ministry around thy bed,
Spreading her vernal tissue, violet-gemmed,
And pearled with dews.
                    She bade bright Summer bring
Gifts of frankincense, with sweet song of birds,
And Autumn cast his reaper's coronet
Down at thy feet, and stormy Winter speak
Sternly of man's neglect.
                    But now we come
To do thee homage—mother of our chief!
Fit homage—such as honoreth him who pays.
Methinks we see thee—as in olden time—
Simple in garb—majestic and serene,

Unmoved by pomp or circumstance—in truth
Inflexible, and with a Spartan zeal
Repressing vice and making folly grave.
Thou didst not deem it woman's part to waste
Life in inglorious sloth—to sport awhile
Amid the flowers, or on the summer wave,
Then fleet, like the ephemeron, away,
Building no temple in her children's hearts,
Save to the vanity and pride of life
Which she had worshipped.

           For the might that clothed
The "Pater Patriæ," for the glorious deeds
That make Mount Vernon's tomb a Mecca shrine
For all the earth, what thanks to thee are due,
Who, 'mid his elements of being, wrought,
We know not—Heaven can tell.

           Rise, sculptured pile!
And show a race unborn who rest below;
And say to mothers what a holy charge
Is theirs—with what a kingly power their love
Might rule the fountains of the new-born mind.
Warn them to wake at early dawn—and sow
Good seed before the world hath sown her tares;
Nor in their toil decline—that angel bands
May put the sickle in, and reap for God,
And gather to his garner.

           Ye, who stand,
With thrilling breast, to view her trophied praise,
Who nobly reared Virginia's godlike chief—
Ye, whose last thought upon your nightly couch,
Whose first at waking, is your cradled son,
What though no high ambition prompts to rear
A second Washington; or leave your name
Wrought out in marble with a nation's tears
Of deathless gratitude;—yet may you raise

A monument above the stars—a soul
Led by your teachings, and your prayers to God.

Our Aborigines

I heard the forests as they cried
Unto the valleys green,
"Where is the red-brow'd hunter-race,
Who lov'd our leafy screen?
Who humbled 'mid these dewy glades
The red deer's antler'd crown,
Or soaring at his highest noon,
Struck the strong eagle down."

Then in the zephyr's voice replied
Those vales, so meekly blest,
"They rear'd their dwellings on our side,
Their corn upon our breast;
A blight came down, a blast swept by,
The cone-roof'd cabins fell,
And where that exil'd people fled,
It is not ours to tell."

Niagara, of the mountains gray,
Demanded, front his throne,
And old Ontario's billowy lake
Prolong'd the thunder tone,
"The chieftains at our side who stood
Upon our christening day,
Who gave the glorious names we bear,
Our sponsors, where are they?"

And then the fair Ohio charg'd
Her many sisters dear,
"Show me once more, those stately forms

61

Within my mirror clear;"
But they replied, "tall barks of pride
Do cleave our waters blue,
And strong keels ride our farthest tide,
But where's their light canoe?"

The farmer drove his plough-share deep
"Whose bones are these?" said he,
"I find them where my browsing sheep
Roam o'er the upland lea."
But starting sudden to his path
A phantom seem'd to glide,
A plume of feathers on his head,
A quiver at his side.

He pointed to the rifled grave
Then rais'd his hand on high,
And with a hollow groan invok'd
The vengeance of the sky.
O'er the broad realm so long his own
Gaz'd with despairing ray,
Then on the mist that slowly curl'd,
Fled mournfully away.

Funeral of Mazeen

The Last of the Royal Line of the Mohegan Nation

'Mid the trodden turf is an open grave,
And a funeral train where the wild flowers wave,
And a manly sleeper doth seek his bed
In the narrow house of the sacred dead,
Yet the soil hath scantily drank of the tear,
For the red-brow'd few are the mourners here.

They have lower'd the prince to his resting spot,
The deep prayer hath swell'd, but they heed it not,
Their abject thoughts 'mid his ashes grope,
And quench'd in their souls is the light of hope;
Know ye their pangs, who turn away
The vassal foot from a monarch's clay?

With the dust of kings in this noteless shade,
The last of a royal line is laid,
In whose stormy veins that current roll'd
Which curb'd the chief and the warrior bold;
Yet pride still burns in their humid clay,
Though the pomp of the sceptre hath pass'd away.

They spake, and the war-dance wheel'd its round,
Or the wretch to the torturing stake was bound;
They lifted their hand, and the eagle fell
From his sunward flight, or his cloud-wrapt cell;
They frown'd, and the tempest of battle arose,
And streams were stain'd with the blood of foes.

Be silent, O Grave! o'er thy hoarded trust,
And smother the voice of the royal dust;
The ancient pomp of their council-fires,
Their simple trust in our pilgrim sires,
The whiles that blasted their withering race,
Hide, hide them deep in thy darkest place.

Till the rending caverns shall yield their dead,
Till the skies as a burning scroll are red,
Till the wondering slave from his chain shall spring,
And to falling mountains the tyrant cling,
Bid all their woes with their relics rest
And bury their wrongs in thy secret breast.

But, when aroused at the trump of doom,
Ye shall start, bold kings, from your lowly tomb,
When some bright-wing'd seraph of mercy shall bend
Your stranger eye on the Sinner's Friend,
Kneel, kneel, at His throne whose blood was spilt,
And plead for your pale-brow'd brother's guilt.

Indian Girl's Burial

"In the vicinity of Montrose, Wisconsin Territory, the only daughter of an Indian woman of the Sac tribe, died of lingering consumption, at the age of eighteen. A few of her own race, and a few of the pale-faces were at the grave, but none wept, save the poor mother."

—HERALD OF THE UPPER MISSISSIPPI.

A voice upon the prairies
A cry of woman's woe,
That mingleth with the autumn blast
All fitfully and low;
It is a mother's wailing;
Hath earth another tone
Like that with which a mother mourns
Her lost, her only one?

Pale faces gather round her,
They mark'd the storm swell high
That rends and wrecks the tossing soul,
But their cold, blue eyes are dry.
Pale faces gaze upon her,
As the wild winds caught her moan,
But she was an Indian mother,
So she wept her tears alone.

Long o'er that wasted idol,
She watch'd, and toil'd, and pray'd,
Though every dreary dawn reveal'd

Some ravage Death had made,
Till the fleshless sinews started,
And hope no opiate gave,
And hoarse, and hollow grew her voice,
An echo from the grave.

She was a gentle creature,
Of raven eye and tress,
And dove-like were the tones that breath'd
Her bosom's tenderness,
Save when some quick emotion,
The warm blood strongly sent,
To revel in her olive-cheek
So richly eloquent.

I said Consumption smote her,
And the healer's art was vain,
But she was an Indian maiden,
So none deplor'd her pain;
None, save that widow's mother,
Who now by her open tomb,
Is writhing like the smitten wretch
Whom judgement marks for doom.

Alas! that lowly cabin,
That bed beside the wall,
That seat beneath the mantling vine,
They're lone and empty all.
What hand shall pluck the tall, green corn
That ripeneth on the plain?
Since she for whom the board was spread
Must ne'er return again.

Rest, rest, thou Indian maiden,
Nor let thy murmuring shade
Grieve that those pale-brow'd ones with scorn

Thy burial rite survey'd;
There's many a king whose funeral
A black-rob'd realm shall see,
For whom no tear of grief is shed
Like that which falls for thee.

Yea, rest thee, forest maiden!
Beneath thy native tree;
The proud may boast their little day
Then sink to dust like thee
But there's many a one whose funeral
With nodding plumes may be
Whom nature nor affection mourn
As here they mourn for thee.

The African Mother at her Daughter's Grave

Some of the pagan Africans visit the burial-places of their departed relatives,
bearing food and drink; and mothers have been known, for a long course
of years, to bring, in an agony of grief, their annual oblation to the tombs
of their children.

"Daughter! I bring thee food;
The rice-cake, pure and white,
The cocoa, with its milky blood,
Dates, and pomegranates bright,
The orange, in its gold,
Fresh from thy favourite tree,
Nuts, in their ripe and husky fold,
Dearest! I spread for thee.
"Year after year, I tread
Thus to thy low retreat,
But now the snow-hairs mark my head,
And age enchains my feet.
O! many a change of woe
Hath dimmed thy spot of birth,

Since first my gushing tears did flow
O'er this thy bed of earth.
There came a midnight cry;
Flames from our hamlet rose
A race of pale-browed men were nigh,
They were our country's foes:
Thy wounded sire was borne
By tyrant force away
Thy brothers from our cabin torn,
While in my blood I lay.
"I watched for their return,
Upon the rocky shore,
Till night's red planets ceased to burn,
And the long rains were o'er.
Till seeds, their hands had sown,
A ripened fruitage bore,
The billows echoed to my moan,
Yet they returned no more.
"But thou art slumbering deep,—
And to my wildest cry,
When, pierced with agony, I weep,
Dost render no reply.
Daughter! my youthful pride,
The idol of my eye;
Why didst thou leave thy mother's side,
Beneath these sands to lie?"
Long o'er the hopeless grave
Where her lost darling slept,
Invoking gods that could not save,
That pagan mourner wept.
O! for some voice of power,
To soothe her bursting sighs:
"There is a resurrection hour;
Thy daughter's dust shall rise!"
Christians! ye hear the cry
From heathen Afric's strand,

Haste! lift salvation's banner high
O'er that benighted land:
With faith that claims the skies,
Her misery control,
And plant the hope that never die
Deep in her tear-wet, soul.

To An Absent Daughter

Where art thou, bird of song?
Brightest one and dearest?
Other groves among,
Other nests thou cheerest;
Sweet thy warbling skill
To each ear that heard thee,
But 'twas sweetest still
To the heart that rear'd thee.

Lamb, where dost thou rest?
On stranger-bosoms lying?
Flowers, thy path that drest,
All uncropp'd are dying;
Streams where thou didst roam
Murmur on without thee,
Lov'st thou still thy home?
Can thy mother doubt thee?

Seek thy Saviour, flock,
To his blest fold going,
Seek that smitten rock
Whence our peace is flowing;
Still should Love rejoice,
Whatsoe'er betide thee,
If that Shepherd's voice
Evermore might guide thee.

Forgotten Flowers to a Bride

We were left behind, but we would not stay,
We found your clue, and have kept the way,
For, sooth to tell, the track was plain
Of a bliss like yours, in a world of pain.
—How little we thought, when so richly we drest,
To go to your wedding, and vie with the best,
When we made our toilette, with such elegant care,
That we might not disgrace an occasion so rare,
To be whirl'd in a coach, at this violent rate,
From county to county, and State to State!
—Though we travell'd incog, yet we trembled with fear,
For the accents of strangers fell hoarse on our ear;
We could hear every word, as we quietly lay
In the snug box of tin, where they stow'd us away:
But how would our friends at a distance have known
If, charm'd by our beauty, they'd made us their own?
—All unus'd to the taverns and roads, as we were,
Our baggage and bones were a terrible care:
Yet we've 'scaped every peril, the journey is o'er,
And hooded and cloak'd, we are safe at your door.
—We bring you a gift from your native skies,
The crystal gem from affection's eyes,
Which tenderly trickles, when dear ones part,
We have wrapp'd it close in the rose's heart:
We are charg'd with a mother's benison kiss,
Will you welcome us in, to your halls, for this?
—We are chill'd with the cold of our wintry way,
Our message is done, we must fade away:
Let us die on your breast, and our prayer shall be
An Eden's wreath, for thy love and thee.

The Bride

I came, but she was gone.
                              In her fair home,
There lay her lute, just as she touch'd it last,
At summer twilight, when the woodbine cups
Fill'd with pure fragrance. On her favorite seat
Lay the still-open work-box, and that book
Which last she read, its pencil'd margin mark'd
By an ill-quoted passage—trac'd, perchance
With hand unconscious, while her lover spake
That dialect, which brings forgetfulness
Of all beside. It was the cherish'd home,
Where from her childhood, she had been the star
Of hope and joy.
                      I came—and she was gone.
Yet I had seen her from the altar led,
With silvery veil but slightly swept aside,
The fresh, young rose-bud deepening in her cheek,
And on her brow the sweet and solemn thought
Of one who gives a priceless gift away.
And there was silence mid the gather'd throng.
The stranger, and the hard of heart, did draw
Their breath supprest, to see the mother's lip
Turn ghastly pale, and the majestic sire
Shrink as with smothered sorrow, when he gave
His darling to an untried guardianship,
And to a far off clime.
                              Haply his thought
Travers'd the grass-grown prairies, and the shore
Of the cold lakes; or those o'erhanging cliffs,
And pathless mountain tops, that rose to bar
Her log-rear'd mansion from the anxious eye
Of kindred and of friend. Even triflers felt
How strong and beautiful is woman's love,
That, taking in its hand its thornless joys,

The tenderest melodies of tuneful years,
Yea! and its own life also—lays them all,
Meek and unblenching, on a mortal's breast,
Reserving nought, save that unspoken hope
Which hath its root in God.

                        Mock not with mirth,
A scene, like this, ye laughter-loving ones;
The licens'd jester's lip, the dancer's heel—
What do they here?

                  Joy, serious and sublime,
Such as doth nerve the energies of prayer,
Should swell the bosom, when a maiden's hand,
Fill'd with life's dewy flow'rets, girdeth on
That harness, which the ministry of Death
Alone unlooseth, but whose fearful power
May stamp the sentence of Eternity.

Death of an Infant

Death found strange beauty on that polish'd brow,
And dash'd it out. There was a tint of rose
On cheek and lip. He touched the veins with ice,
And the rose faded.

                  Forth from those blue eyes
There spake a wishful tenderness, a doubt
Whether to grieve or sleep, which innocence
Alone may wear. With ruthless haste he bound
The silken fringes of those curtaining lids
For ever.

          There had been a murmuring sound
With which the babe would claim its mother's ear,
Charming her even to tears. The spoiler set
The seal of silence.

             But there beam's a smile,
So fix'd, so holy, from that cherub brow,

Death gazed, and left it there. He dar'd not steal
The signet-ring of Heaven.

On The Death of a Sister
While Absent at School

Sweet sister! is it so? And shall I see
Thy face on earth no more? And didst thou breathe
The last sad pang of agonising life
Upon a stranger's pillow? No kind hand,
Of parent or of sister near, to press
Thy throbbing temples, when the shuddering dew
Stood thick upon them? And they say my name
Hung on thy lips 'mid the chill, parting strife.
Ah!—those were hallowed memories that could stir
Thy bosom thus in death. The tender song
Of cradle-nurture—the low, lisping prayer,
Learned at our mother's knee—the childish sport,
The gift divided, and the parted cake—
Our walk to school amid the dewy grass—
Our sweet flower-gatherings—all those cloudless hours
Together shared, did wake a love so strong
That Time must yield it to Eternity
For its full crown. Would it had been my lot
But with one weeping prayer to gird thy heart
For its last conflict. Would that I had seen
That peaceful smile which Death did leave thy clay
After his conquest o'er it. But the turf
On thy lone grave was trodden, while I deemed
Thee meekly musing o'er the classic page,
Loving and loved, amid the studious band
As erst I left thee.
        Sister!—toils and ills
Henceforth are past—for knowledge without pain,

A free translucent, everlasting tide,
O'erflows thy spirit. Thou no more hast need
Of man's protecting arm, for thou may'st lean
On His unchanging throne who was thy trust,
Even from thine early days.
                            'Tis well! 'tis well!
Saviour of souls! I thank thee for her bliss.

School of Young Ladies

How fair upon the admiring sight,
In Learning's sacred fane,
With cheek of bloom, and robe of white,
Glide on yon graceful train.
Blest creatures! to whose gentle eye
Earth's gilded gifts are new,
Ye know not that distrustful sigh
Which deems its vows untrue.

There is a bubble on your cup
By buoyant fancy mus'd,
How high its sparkling foam leaps up!
Ye do not think 'twill burst:
And be it far from me to fling
On budding joys a blight,
Or darkly spread a raven's wing
To shade a path so bright.

Three twines a wreath around your brow,
Blent with the sunny braid;
Love lends its flowers a radiant glow –
Ye do not think 'twill fade:
And yet 'twere safer there to bind
That plant of changeless dye,

Whose root is in the lowly mind,
Whose blossom in the sky.

But who o'er beauty's form can hang,
Nor think how future years
May bring stern sorrow's speechless pang
Or, disappointment's tears,
Unceasing toil, unpitied care,
Cold treachery's serpent moan—
Ills that the tender heart must bear,
Unanswering and alone.

Yet, as the frail and fragrant flower,
Crushed by the sweeping blast,
Doth even in death an essence pour,
The sweetest, and the last,
So woman's deep, enduring love,
Which nothing can appall,
Her steadfast faith, that looks above
For rest, can conquer all.

Benevolence
"The silver is mine, and the gold is mine—saith the Lord of Hosts."

HAGGAI, II. 8.

Whose is the gold that glitters in the mine?
And whose the silver? Are they not the Lord's?
And lo! the cattle on a thousand hills,
And the broad earth with all her gushing springs,
Are they not his who made them?
                    Ye who hold
Slight tenantry therein, and call your lands
By your own names, and lock your gathered gold
From him who in his bleeding Saviour's name
Doth ask a part, whose shall those riches be

When, like the grass-blade from the autumn-frost,
You fall away?
                    Point out to me the forms
That in your treasure-chambers shall enact
Glad mastership, and revel where you toiled
Sleepless and stern. Strange faces are they all.
Oh man! whose wrinkling labor is for heirs
Thou knowest not who, thou in thy mouldering bed,
Unkenned, unchronicled of them, shalt sleep;
Nor will they thank thee, that thou didst bereave
Thy soul of good for them.
                              Now, thou mayest give
The famished food, the prisoner liberty,
Light to the darkened mind, to the lost soul
A place in heaven. Take thou the privilege
With solemn gratitude. Speck as thou art
Upon earth's surface, gloriously exult
To be co-worker with the King of kings.

A Cottage Scene

I saw a cradle at a cottage door,
Where the fair mother, with her cheerful wheel,
Carolled so sweet a song, that the young bird,
Which, timid, near the threshold sought for seeds,
Paused on its lifted foot, and raised its head,
As if to listen. The rejoicing bees
Nestled in throngs amid the wood-bine cups
That o'er the lattice clustered. A clear stream
Came leaping from its sylvan height, and poured
Music upon the pebbles, and the winds
Which gently 'mid the vernal branches played
Their idle freaks, brought showering blossoms down,
Surfeiting earth with sweetness.
                              Sad I came

From weary commerce with the heartless world;
But when I felt upon my withered cheek
My mother Nature's breath, and heard the trump
Of those gay insects at their honied toil,
Shining like winged jewelry, and drank
The healthful odor of the flowering trees
And bright-eyed violets; but, most of all,
When I beheld mild slumbering innocence,
And on that young maternal brow the smile
Of those affections which do purify
And renovate the soul, I turned me back
In gladness, and with added strength, to run
My weary race—lifting a thankful prayer
To Him who showed me some bright tints of Heaven
Here on the earth, that I might safer walk
And firmer combat sin, and surer rise
From earth to Heaven.

Statue of the Spinning Girl
At Chatsworth, the Seat of the Duke of Devonshire

Spin on, most beautiful. There's none to mock
Thy simple labour here. Majestic forms
Of high renown, and brows of classic grace,
Whose sculptured features speak the breathing soul,
Rise in illustrious ranks, but not to scorn thy lowly toil.
Even so it was of old,
That woman's hand, amid the elements
Of patient industry and household good,
Reproachless wrought, twining the slender thread
From the light distaff, or in skilful loom
Weaving rich tissues, or with glowing tints
Of rich embroidery, pleased to decorate
The mantle of her lord. And it was well;
For in such shelter'd and congenial sphere

Content with duty dwelt. Yet few there are,
Sweet Filatrice, who in their earnest task
Find such retreat as thine, mid lordly halls,
And sparkling fountains, and umbrageous trees,
And parks far stretching, where the antler'd deer
Forget the hound and horn. And we, who roam
Mid all this grand enchantment-proud saloons,
And galleries radiant with the gems of art
And genius, ravish'd from the grasp of time
And princely chapel, uttering praise to God
Or lose ourselves amid the wildering maze
Of plants, and flowers, and blossoms, breathing forth
Their eloquence to Him-delighted lay
This slight memorial at thy snowy feet.

Poetry

Morn on her rosy couch awoke,
Enchantment led the hour,
And mirth and music drank the dews
That freshen Beauty's flower.
Then from her bower of deep delight,
I heard a young girl sing,
"Oh, speak no ill of poetry,
For 'tis a holy thing."

The Sun in noon-day heat rose high,
And on with heaving breast,
I saw a weary pilgrim toil,
Unpitied and unblest;
Yet still in trembling measures flow'd
Forth from a broken string,
"Oh, speak no ill of poetry,
For 'tis a holy thing."

'Twas night, and Death the curtains drew,
'Mid agony severe,
While there a willing spirit went
Home to a glorious sphere;
Yet still it sigh'd, even when was spread
The waiting Angel's wing,
"Oh, speak no ill of poetry,
For 'tis a holy thing."

Farewell of the Soul to the Body

Companion dear! the hour draws nigh,
The sentence speeds—*to die, to die.*
So long in mystic union held,
So close with strong embrace compell'd,
How canst thou bear the dread decree,
That strikes thy clasping nerves from me?
—To Him who on this mortal shore,
The same encircling vestment wore,
To Him I look, to Him I bend,
To Him thy shuddering frame commend.
—If I have ever caus'd thee pain,
The throbbing breast, the burning brain.
With cares and vigils turn'd thee pale,
And scorn'd thee when thy strength did fail—
Forgive!—Forgive!—thy task doth cease,
Friend! Lover!—let us part in peace.
If thou didst sometimes check my force,
Or, trifling, stay mine upward course,
Or lure from Heaven my wavering trust,
Or bow my drooping wing to dust –
I blame thee not, the strife is done,
I knew thou wert the weaker one,
The vase of earth, the trembling clod,
Constrained to hold the breath of God.

—Well hast thou in my service wrought,
Thy brow hath mirror'd forth my thought,
To wear my smile thy lip hath glow'd,
Thy tear, to speak my sorrows, flowed,
Thine ear hath borne me rich supplies
Of sweetly varied melodies,
Thy hands my prompted deeds have done,
Thy feet upon mine errands run –
Yes, thou hast mark'd my bidding well,
Faithful and true farewell, farewell.

—Go to thy rest. A quiet bed
Meek mother Earth with flowers shall spread,
Where I no more thy sleep may break
With fever'd dream, nor rudely wake
Thy wearied eye.
                          Oh quit thy hold,
For thou art faint, and chill, and cold,
And long thy gasp and groan of pain
Have bound me pitying in thy chain,
Though angels urge me hence to soar,
Where I shall share thine ills no more.
—Yet we shall meet. To soothe thy pain
Remember—we shall meet again.
Quell with this hope the victor's sting,
And keep it as a signet-ring,
When the dire worm shall pierce thy breast,
And nought but ashes mark thy rest,
When stars shall fall, and skies grow dark,
And proud suns quench their glow-worm spark,
Keep thou that hope, to light thy gloom,
Till the last trumpet rends the tomb.
—Then shalt thou glorious rise, and fair,
Nor spot, nor stain, nor wrinkle bear,
And, I with hovering wing elate,
The bursting of thy bonds shall wait,

And breathe the welcome of the sky—
"No more to part, no more to die,
Co-heir of Immortality."

The Sacred Poet

Art thou a mouth for the immortal mind?
A voice that shall be heard when ages sleep
In cold oblivion? When the rich man's pomp,
And all the ambitious strivings of the crowd
Shall be forgotten? Art thou well convinced
That such a gift is thine? Bow thee to dust,
And take this honour from the hand of God
In deep humility, worm as thou art,
And all unworthy. Ask for naught beside,
Though worldlings scorn thy lot. Prosperity,
Such as earth names, what are its gauds to thee?
Accustom'd to the crystal and the gold
Of poesy, that, like a sea of glass,
Doth compass thee around. Look up! look up!
Baptized and set apart for Heaven's high will,
Search for its lessons. List when trembling dawn
Instructs Aurora; muse when night to night
Doth show forth knowledge; when the folded flower
Taketh its lesson of the dews that steal
Into its bosom, like the mother's hymn
O'er the tired infant; and thine ear shall drink
A music tone to solace every wound
That earth has made. Then strike thy hallow'd harp
For unborn ages, and with trumpet-tone
Wake the immortal mind to highest hopes,
And be the teacher of what cannot die.
Yea, wear thy birthright nobly on thy brow,
And nerve the wing for God.

The Muse

They say that the cell of the poet should be
Like the breast of the shell that remembers the sea,
Quiet and still, save a murmuring sigh
Of the far-rolling wave to the summer-lit sky;
Tasteful and polished, as coralline bowers,
Remote from intrusion, and fragrant with flowers.
'Twould be beautiful, surely, but as for me,
Nothing like this I expect to see,
For I've written my poetry, sooth to say,
In the oddest of places, by night or by day,
Line by line, with a broken chain,
Interrupted, and joined again.
I, if paper were wanting, or pencils had fled,
Some niche in the brain, spread a storehouse instead,
And Memory preserved, in her casket of thought,
The embryo rhymes, till the tablets were brought:
At home or abroad, on the land or the sea,
Wherever it came, it was welcome to me
When first it would steal o'er my infantine hour,
With a buzz or a song, like a bee in a flower,
With its ringing rhythm, and its measured line,
What it was I could scarce divine,
Calling so oft, from my sports and play,
To some nook in the garden, away, away,
To a mound of turf which the daisies crown,
Or a vine-wreathed summer-house, old and brown,
On a lilac's green leaf, with a pin, to grave
The tinkling chime of the words it gave.
At dewy morn, when to school I hied,
Methought like a sister it went by my side,
Well pleased o'er the fresh lanes to gambol and stray,
Or gather the violets that grew by the way,
Or turn my lessons to rhyme, and bask
In a rose, 'till I finished my needle's task.

When Winter in frost did the landscape enfold,
And my own little study was cheerless and cold,
A humble resource from the exigence rose,
And a barn was my favourite place to compose;
A season there was when the viol grew sweet,
And the maze of the dance was a charm to my feet,
For Youth and Joy, with their measures gay,
Beckoned me onward both night and day;
Yet oft in the soul was a secret tone
Winning away to my chamber lone,
And, lingering there, was a form serene
With a mild reproof on her pensive mien;
And though I feigned from her sway to start,
Having music enough in my own merry heart,
Yet her quiet tear on my brow that fell,
Was more dear than the dance or the viol's swell.
When life's mantling pleasures their climax attained,
And the sphere of a wife and a mother was gained,
When that transport awoke, which no language may speak,
As the breath of my first-born stole soft o'er my cheek,
While she slept on my breast, in the nursery fair,
A smothered lyre would arrest me there,
Half complaining of deep neglect,
Half demanding its old respect;
And if I mingled its cadence mild
With the tuneful tones of the rosy child,
Methought 'twas no folly such garlands to twine,
As could brighten life's cares, and its pleasures refine.
And now, though my life from its zenith doth wane,
And the wreaths of its morning grow scentless and vain,
And many a friend who its pilgrimage blest,
Have fallen from my heart and gone down to their rest,
Yet still by my side, unforgetful and true,
Is the being that walked with me all the way through.
She doth cling to the High Rock wherein is my trust,
Let her chant to my soul when I go to the dust;

Hand in hand with the faith that my Saviour hath given
Let her kneel at His feet mid the anthems of Heaven.

The Needle, Pen, and Sword

What hast thou seen, with thy shining eye,
Thou Needle, so subtle and keen?
"I have been in Paradise, stainless and fair,
And fitted the apron of fig-leaves there,
To the form of its fallen queen.
"The mantles and wimples, the hoods and veils,
That the belles of Judah wore,
When their haughty mien and their glance of fire
Enkindled the eloquent prophet's ire,
I help'd to fashion of yore
The beaded belt of the Indian maid
I have deck'd with as true a zeal
As the gorgeous ruff of the knight of old,
Or the monarch's mantle of purple and gold,
Or the satrap's broider'd heel.
I have lent to Beauty new power to reign,
At bridal and courtly hall,
Or wedded to Fashion, have help'd to bind
Those gossamer links, that the strongest mind
Have sometimes held in thrall.
"I have drawn a blood-drop, round and red,
From the finger small and white
Of the startled child, as she strove with care
Her doll to deck with some gewgaw rare,
But wept at my puncture bright.
"I have gazed on the mother's patient brow,
As my utmost speed she plied,
To shield from winter her children dear,
And the knell of midnight smote her ear,
While they slumber'd at her side.

"I have heard in the hut of the pining poor
The shivering inmate's sigh,
When faded the warmth of her last, faint brand,
As slow from her cold and clammy hand
She let me drop, to die!"

What dost thou know, thou gray goose-quill?
And methought, with a spasm of pride,
It sprang from the inkstand, and flutter'd in vain,
Its nib to free from the ebon stain,
As it fervently replied:
"What do I know!—Let the lover tell
When into his secret scroll
He poureth the breath of a magic lyre,
And traceth those mystical lines of fire
That move the maiden's soul.
"What do I know!—The wife can say,
As the leaden seasons move,
And over the ocean's wildest sway,
A blessed missive doth wend its way,
Inspired by a husband's love.
"Do ye doubt my power? Of the statesman ask,
Who buffets ambition's blast,
Of the convict, who shrinks in his cell of care,
A flourish of mine hath sent him there,
And lock'd his fetters fast;
"And a flourish of mine can his prison ope,
From the gallows its victim save,
Break off the treaty that kings have bound,
Make the oath of a nation an empty sound,
And to liberty lead the slave.
"Say, what were History, so wise and old,
And Science that reads the sky?
Or how could Music its sweetness store,
Or Fancy and Fiction their treasures pour,
Or what were Poesy's heaven-taught lore,

Should the pen its aid deny?
"Oh, doubt if ye will, that the rose is fair,
That the planets pursue their way,
Go, question the fires of the noontide sun,
Or the countless streams that to ocean run,
But ask no more what the Pen hath done."
And it scornfully turn'd away.

What are thy deeds, thou fearful thing
By the lordly warrior's side?
And the Sword answer'd, stern and slow,
"The hearth-stone lone and the orphan know,
And the pale and widow'd bride.
"The shriek and the shroud of the battle-cloud,
And the field that doth reek below,
The wolf that laps where the gash is red,
And the vulture that tears ere the life hath fled,
And the prowling robber that strips the dead,
And the foul hyena know.
"The rusted plough, and the seed unsown,
And the grass that doth rankly grow
O'er the rotting limb, and the blood-pool dark,
Gaunt Famine that quenches life's lingering spark,
And the black-wing'd Pestilence know.
"Death with the rush of his harpy-brood,
Sad Earth in her pang and throe,
Demons that riot in slaughter and crime,
And the throng of the souls sent, before their time,
To the bar of the judgment-know."

Then the terrible Sword to its sheath return'd,
While the Needle sped on in peace,
But the Pen traced out from a Book sublime
The promise and pledge of that better time
When the warfare of earth shall cease.

Lucy Larcom:

1824–1893

Introduction

M ost male poets of mid nineteenth-century America are genteel: Longfellow, Oliver Wendell Holmes, Sr., James Russell Lowell, Whittier (although not Poe or Whitman). The women poets are actually less so. They come from a range of backgrounds and situations in which writing stands in various tensions with or against financial and social pressures. Lucy Larcom emerges from what was just then beginning to take shape as a working class—although, as she remarks, in those days "the term was not working class or working people—everybody worked with their hands." Larcom was born in 1824 in the sea-town of Beverly, Massachusetts, the ninth of ten children. The death of her father, a sea captain in the merchant service, in 1830, left the family in need. The mother accordingly moved them to the then new experimental Mills at Lowell, setting up as a boardinghouse-mistress for the girls who came to work there.

Larcom has left an account of the Lowell Mills in her memoir, "A New England Girl" (1889) and her long narrative poem, "An Idyll of Work" (1875). She makes vivid the transition from country-girl to factory worker. Her memoir recounts the original ideals of the Mill project—to create a kind, homelike environment even while answering new needs in factory labor. Mr. Francis Cabot Lowell, the inventor of the power loom, intended, as she puts it, to create a "moral atmosphere" for young women "brought up to earn their own living in the fear and love of God." Looking back on this beginning, Larcom's tone is somewhat sad. This benign vision, she reluctantly records, proved to go unfulfilled. She herself, after some few years of schooling, began at the age of eleven to work in the Mills. She remained there for the next ten years. The work day lasted ten to twelve hours, starting at 5:30 in summer and in winter at daylight, and lasting until 7:30 or 8:00 in the evening. Leisure hours were from 8:00 till lights out at 10:00. On the negative side, the work was confining, repetitive, "in the midst of monotonous noise and a sense of isolation." On the positive side, however, Larcom describes a deep sense of comradeship with the other Mill girls, her admiration for their industry, their resourcefulness and invention, and their self-determination. In her account, the Mills constituted a community combining womanhood, religion, and a republican ethos. It was "homelike" and with "no real poverty," with "no classes in the Old World sense." "Everything about us," she writes, "was educating us to become true children of the republic." For "the members of a republic like ours owe it to one another that every kind of useful labor shall be held respectable with especial emphasis in a Christian republic that womanhood should mean sisterhood." Most girls working in Lowell came from the country and planned to return there, working in the Mills in order to put by money for their futures. The hours of leisure were organized into a wide range of "improvement circles" and classes, lectures, and charitable work of different kinds. It was in this manner that Larcom's older sister with some friends began in 1841 to put together the *Lowell Offering*, a newspaper collecting writings by the Mill girls. Larcom, who had reportedly memorized one hundred hymns by the age of five and had been writing since she was seven, became the youngest contributor. Some of her work drew the notice of John Greenleaf Whittier, who was then conducting a Free-soil paper in Lowell and who was to become a lifelong mentor.

In 1846, Larcom, with her sister's family, went West. At first she found work in a one-room log district school. She was able, however, thereafter to teach and study at the Monticello Female Seminary in Godfrey, Illinois, under the directorship of a charismatic Phildelphia woman named Philena Fobes. In this way she at last fulfilled her desire for the more formal education she had missed working in the Mills. She completed her course at Monticello in three years. At that time, her young man (Frank, her sister's brother-in-law) decided to leave his medical studies and go to California in search of gold. The expectation was for her to join him there. Instead, in 1852 she returned to Massachusetts to visit her family before doing so, and decided to remain. Perhaps her sister's married life of hard, menial labor and year after year of dead babies discouraged her from conformity. She had, in Illinois, undergone a religious conversion experience and this gave her strength, believing that God wanted her for some particular mission. She took up teaching, at first privately and then, in 1854, in the Wheaton Seminary at Norton. She continued there for nine years. But teaching drained her, and left her little time for her writing. She seems also not to have liked people in groups.

While still out West, Larcom had begun to publish poems, several of which appeared in the *National Era*, the abolitionist paper where Alice Cary and Harriet Beecher Stowe had also published. Whittier was the corresponding editor, and he began to promote Larcom's work. He wrote the biographical sketch for the two poems by her that Rufus Griswold included in his 1848 *Female Poets of America*. Her poem, "Hannah Binding Shoes," published in 1857 in a small eastern journal, drew wide attention when the *New York Knickerbocker* accused her of plagiarism. This was followed by a series of invitations and publications, and her increasing circulation in Boston literary circles. Her poem "The Rose Enthroned" appeared in the *Atlantic Monthly* in 1861 and was widely thought to have been written by Emerson until its authorship, as in the practice of the magazine, was later disclosed. She served as editor for the religious newspaper *the Congregationalist* and then, in 1864 and for several years after, as editor of a children's magazine published by her friend James T. Fields, and whose contibutors included Whittier, Longfellow, and Stowe. She was thus able to resign from teaching, supporting herself by writing and lectures, owning her own home. Her first book of *Poems* appeared in 1868. In the 1870s, she collaborated with Whittier in a series of poetry anthologies. Always religious—her father was a strict Calvinist, and she describes her childhood Massachusetts as one where a "grave Puritanism still brooded over the landscape"—her poems became increasingly so. Her religious experience seems to have been rather inward and personal, although in her last years she attended the Episcopal Church, and her final books were written, between 1890 and 1892, in association with it. She died in 1893.

Lucy Larcom's poetry shares many trends and impulses with other women poets of her time. But her particular area or strong terrain may be called the practice of women's voices. This is a thread running through a variety of poems. "An Idyll of Work" is arranged as a dialogue among several Mill girls. A "Lady" poem—a type that recurs throughout the century—the text explores just what it is to be one; that is, what the values of womanhood are, and its truest definition. As is characteristic in Larcom, fashion and ancestral family are rejected as worthy definitions, as is the idle woman of leisure (Venus, one of the mythological goddesses judging the discussion, says: "I married a blacksmith"). Consistent with other Larcom poems such as "Her Choice" and "The Schoolmistress," ordinary daily life of bread-baking (which in "The Idyll" becomes the pivotal image of womanhood) and dignified labor makes the true "lady," a transformation of the term that reflects what seems to be a deep-seated republicanism in Larcom. One Mill girl even dubs herself the "Lady of the Loom." However, here as elsewhere, Larcom is not fully consistent; or rather, is ambivalent about her own elevation of practical labor. "The Idyll" ends with happy news of a days release from the Mills. "Prudence" portrays a child-laborer whose whole "round world" is nothing "But a world for knitting stockings, / Sweeping floors, and baking pies." There is, moreover, here as often in Larcom, a stark sense of men and women living in separate realities: Prudence's "is a world that women work in" while "men grow rich." Here woman's work is alienating from nature and stands in opposition to "beauty." "Prudence" turns out to be not an ideal of feminine virtue but the construction of a "good wife" from a viewpoint not her own.

Yet that is also the poem's art. Larcom's poetic is one that sets out to give voice to feminine figures reluctant or unable to do so themselves. Here, the poet says what Prudence doesn't. This is especially powerful in the poem "Getting Along," where the woman's voice is structured through complex layers. The overt rhetoric consists in the woman's justification of her married life—what she says to her husband or to herself about him and them. Yet, in its course it strongly asserts also what she is not saying—what she suppresses, even to herself, even though she deeply knows what she refuses to acknowledge. As she goes along in the poem, the more she insists they are "Getting Along" the more we understand that they aren't; or rather, that they are only at the cost of her own utter self-suppression and inner dissociation. Her silence is the price she pays in order to sustain or continue in the marriage. In this missed-dialogue form, there is not the remotest possibility that her husband would understand her if she spoke to him directly. Their experience of life is irrevocably unmatching. Yet the poet does name what the woman cannot, including the acute pressure of woman's silencing.

This silencing is the subject of "They Said," where the poet defends and interprets the woman against oppressive misunderstanding. On the other hand, the force of "The Loyal Woman's No" is partly due to an enormous release in finally speaking—although even this poem oddly concludes with a silencing image: "Take my life's silence for your answer: No!" The poem, printed in 1863, has the biographical context of Larcom's having at last broken off her engagement on the grounds of Southern sympathy on her lover's part. Actually, she seems to have abandoned that marriage before this; yet it is interesting, and characteristic of her, to place her romance in an ideological context. In this poem, identity has foundation in such moral and political commitments. Again, the woman poet defies and calls into question the supposed separation of spheres as domestic against the public and political.

Larcom thus characteristically situates herself inside a woman's point of view, giving it voice: whether as a "School Mistress" (a poem that again explores and redefines what it is to be a "lady," although its idealization of teaching stands against the fact that Larcom herself hated the job); or in "Hannah Binding Shoes"—a woman-figure of deep reticence to which the poem at once gives testimony and redeems; or through the figures of "The Light Houses." "Elsie in Illinois," a poem of women's experiences of the West, explores their ambivalence at abandoning their past homes in order to try to build a new one. Larcom's prize-winnng "Call to Kansas" was written after she had herself moved back East. On the other hand, the poem, composed in 1854, has definite political overtones concerning the settlement of "Bloody Kansas" as a violent confrontation between slave and free territory. Larcom's is a call to establish Kansas as a place where "sons, brave and good, / Shall to freemen grow." The series of war poems, which she dates in a way that recalls Melville's "Battle-Pieces," she wrote (as he did not) as patriotic confirmations. These texts interestingly demonstrate the premises of American civil religion—with "Gospels writ in blood" in "The Flag," and Lincoln, as is obsessively the case in this period, the "patriot martyr" in "Tolling." At the same time, Larcom's war poems remain strongly situated in women's experience of war. "Waiting for News" and "Re-enlisted" recount the war from behind the lines, through woman's separation and distressed worry over lovers and sons at the front.

In Larcom, as generally in the American world, public concern binds with religious vision and, as she adds, gendered experience as well. It is the juncture among these three that her poems on public affairs display. Religion is not a private affair, any more than womanhood is. As "The Weeping Prophet" she takes on (although in the guise of a male biblical prophet, Jeremiah) a public voice, speaking to "my dear country's sin" and calling the American Jerusalem back to repentance. As often among women who raise their voices, her strength to do so is drawn from this sense of divine mission: "To be his messenger of wrath I shrank: / I cried, "O Lord, I am a child, so weak! … Then did He touch my lips, His words I speak." In "Heaven's Need," Larcom remarkably adopts a more directly feminized vision. Here heaven is experienced as "Mother-love" and "Sister-love," with these womanly "ties" the heart of redemption.

This sense of woman's community on which she draws and for which she speaks is very strong in Larcom. It reaches into history, most concretely the immediate history of New England surrounding her.

Larcom's poetry is rich in regional detail, with close descriptions of place and also of time. Historical consciousness is particularly strong in "Goody Grunsell's House" and "A Gambrel Roof." The first traces the desolation of a woman betrayed, as she secretly consumes herself in the figure of burning her own house around her, piece by piece. The poem is not least about woman's invisibility in history—here as social ostracism. "A Gambrel Roof" gives a cheerier side. Here the historical memory of women (featuring especially the Salem witch-trials) is rendered in an account of a wife's own house-witty version of the Boston tea-party, in which male and female experience again part ways. "My Name-Aunt" grounds Larcom's own name in her female geneology—with naming an important feminine topos throughout the century in terms of self-formation and identity and having a voice. "Unwedded" and "Weaving" each reflect directly on Larcom's personal experience. "Weaving" is especially self-reflective, and specifi-cally in terms of her self-definition as an artist. Adopting for her art the figure of weaving—a recurrent and even defining women's craft, and recalling her own experience as a Mill girl—she compares herself, with misgivings, to the Lady of Shallott. But her art is saved from this Lady's unreality by direct plunge into her historical and political world. The poem sweeps into the plight of black women slaves, of poor women and prostitute outcasts, all bound together with her in an equality and responsibility of Christian concern. Larcom, apparently never directly drawn to the woman's rights movement, had written in her memoir that the "measure of woman is in the loyalty of her womanhood to the most ennobling instincts and principles of our common humanity." In "Weaving," she affirms: "The world of women haunteth me," and she concludes with a community of sisters.

Poems

Prudence

What is this round world to Prudence,
With her round, black, restless eyes,
But a world for knitting stockings,
Sweeping floors, and baking pies?
'Tis a world that women work in,
Sewing long seams, stitch by stitch:
Barns for hay, and chests for linen;
'Tis a world where men grow rich.
Ten years old is little Prudence;
Ten years older still she seems,
With her busy eyes and fingers,
With her grown-up thoughts and schemes.
Sunset is the time for candles;
Cows are milked at fall of dew;
Beans will grow, and melons ripen,
When the summer skies are blue.
Is there more than work in living?
Yes; a child must go to school,
And to meeting every Sunday;
Not a heathen be, or fool.
Something more has haunted Prudence
In the song of bird and bee,
In the low wind's dreamy whisper
Through the light-leaved poplar-tree.
Something lingers, bends above her,
Leaning at the mossy well;

Some sweet murmur from the meadows;
On the air some gentle spell.
But she will not stop to listen:
Maybe there are witches yet!
So she runs away from beauty;
Tries its presence to forget.
'Tis the way her mother taught her;
Prudence is not much to blame.
Work is good for child or woman;
Childhood's jailer,—'tis a shame!
Gravely at the romping children
Their gray heads the gossips shake;
Saying, with a smile for Prudence,
"What a good wife she will make!"

Getting Along

We trudge on together, my good man and I.
Our steps growing slow as the years hasten by,
Our children are healthy, our neighbors are kind,
And with the world round us we've no fault to find,
'Tis true that he sometimes will choose the worst way
For sore feet to walk in, a weary hot day;
But then my wise husband can scarcely go wrong
And, somehow or other, we're getting along.

There are soft summer shadows beneath our home trees:
How handsome he looks, sitting there at his ease
We watch the flocks coming while sunset grows dim,
His thoughts on the cattle, and mine upon him.
The blackbirds and thrushes come chattering near;
I love the thieves' music, but listen with fear:
He shoots the gay rogues I would pay for their song;
We're different, sure; still, we're getting along.

He seems not to know what I eat, drink, or wear;
He's trim and he's hearty, so why should I care?
No harsh word from him my poor heart ever shocks:
I wouldn't mind scolding, so seldom he talks.
Ah, well! 'tis too much that we women expect:
He only has promised to love and protect.
See, I lean on my husband, so silent and strong;
I'm sure there's no trouble;—we're getting along.

Life isn't so bright as it was long ago,
When he visited me amid tempest and snow;
And would bring me a ribbon or jewel to wear,
And sometimes a rosebud to twist in my hair:
But when we are girls, we can all laugh and sing;
Of course, growing old, life's a different thing;
My good man and I have forgot our May song,
But still we are quietly getting along.

'Tis true I was rich; I had treasures and land;
But all that he asked was my heart and my hand:
Though people do say it, 'tis what they can't prove,
"He married for money; she, poor thing! For love."
My fortune is his, and he saves me its care;
To make his home cheerful's enough for my share.
He seems always happy our broad fields among;
And so I'm contented: we're getting along.

With stocks to look after, investments to find,
It's not very strange that I'm seldom in mind:
He can't stop to see how my time's dragging on,
And oh! would he miss me, if I should be gone?
Should he be called first, I must follow him fast,
For all that's worth living for then will be past.
But I'll not think of losing him; fretting is wrong,
While we are so pleasantly getting along.

"They Said"

They said of her, "She never can have felt
The sorrows that our deeper natures feel":
They said, "Her placid lips have never spelt
Hard lessons taught by Pain; her eyes reveal
No passionate yearning, no perplexed appeal
To other eyes. Love and her heart have dealt
With her but lightly."—When the Pilgrims dwelt
First on these shores, lest savage hands should steal
To precious graves with desecrating tread,
The burial-field was with the ploughshare crossed
And there the maize her silken tresses tossed.
With thanks those Pilgrims ate their bitter bread,
While peaceful harvests hid what they had lost.
—What if her smiles concealed from you her dead?

A Loyal Woman's No

No! is my answer from this cold, bleak ridge,
Down to your valley: you may rest you there
The gulf is wide, and none call build a bridge
That your gross weight would safely hither bear.

Pity me, if you will. I look at you
With something that is kinder far than scorn,
And think, "Ah, well! I might have grovelled, too;
I might have walked there, fettered and forsworn."

I am of nature weak as others are;
I might have chosen comfortable ways;
Once from these heights I shrank, beheld afar,
In the soft lap of quiet, easy days.

I might,—I will not hide it,—once I might
Have lost, in the warm whirlpools of your voice,
The sense of Evil, the stern cry of Right;
But Truth has steered me free, and I rejoice.

Not with the triumph that looks back to jeer
At the poor herd that call their misery bliss;
But as a mortal speaks when God is near,
I drop you down my answer, it is this:

I am not yours, because you prize in me
What is the lowest in my own esteem:
Only my flowery levels can you see,
Nor of my heaven-smit summits do you dream.

I am not yours, because you love yourself:
Your heart has scarcely room for me beside.
I will not be shut in with name and pelf;
I spurn the shelter of your narrow pride!

Not yours, because you are not man enough
To grasp your country's measure of a man.
For such as you, when Freedom's ways are rough,
Cannot walk in them, learn that women can!

Not yours, because, in this the nation's need,
You stoop to bend her losses to your gain,
And do not feel the meanness of your deed;—
I touch no palm defiled with such a stain!

Whether man's thought can find too lofty steeps
For woman's scaling, care not I to know;
But when he falters by her side, or creeps,
She must not clog her soul with him to go.

Who weds me must at least with equal pace
Sometimes move with me at my being's height:
To follow him to his superior place,
His rarer atmosphere, were keen delight.

You lure me to the valley: men should call
Up to the mountains, where the air is clear.
Win me and help me climbing, if at all!
Beyond these peaks great harmonies I hear:

The morning chant of Liberty and Law!
The dawn pours in, to wash out Slavery's blot;
Fairer than aught the bright sun ever saw,
Rises a Nation without stain or spot!

The men and women mated for that time
Tread not the soothing mosses of the plain;
Their hands are joined in sacrifice sublime;
Their feet firm set in upward paths of pain.

Sleep your thick sleep, and go your drowsy way!
You cannot hear the voices in the air!
Ignoble souls will shrivel in that day;
The brightness of its coming can you bear?

For me, I do not walk these hills alone:
Heroes who poured their blood out for the truth,
Women whose hearts bled, martyrs all unknown,
Here catch the sunrise of immortal youth.

On their pale cheeks and consecrated brows:
It charms me not, your call to rest below.
I press their hands, my lips pronounce their vows:
Take my life's silence for your answer: No!

Hannah Binding Shoes

Poor lone Hannah,
Sitting at the window, binding shoes.
Faded, wrinkled,
Sitting, stitching, in a mournful muse.
Bright-eyed beauty once was she,
When the bloom was on the tree:
Spring and winter,
Hannah's at the window, binding shoes.
Not a neighbor,
Passing nod or answer will refuse,
To her whisper,
"Is there from the fishers any news?"
O, her heart's adrift, with one
On an endless voyage gone!
Night and morning,
Hannah's at the window, binding shoes.
Fair young Hannah,
Ben, the sunburnt fisher, gayly woos:
Hale and clever,
For a willing heart and hand he sues.
May-day skies are all aglow,
And the waves are laughing so!
For her wedding
Hannah leaves her window and her shoes.
May is passing:
Mid the apple boughs a pigeon coos.
Hannah shudders,
For the mild southwester mischief brews.
Round the rocks of Marblehead,
Outward bound, a schooner sped:
Silent, lonesome,
Hannah's at the window, binding shoes.
'Tis November,
Now no tear her wasted cheek bedews.

From Newfoundland
Not a sail returning will she lose,
Whispering hoarsely, "Fishermen,
Have you, have you heard of Ben?"
Old with watching,
Hannah's at the window, binding shoes.
Twenty winters
Bleach and tear the ragged shore she views.
Twenty seasons:—
Never one has brought her any news.
Still her dim eyes silently
Chase the white sails o'er the sea:
Hopeless, faithful,
Hannah's at the window, binding shoes.

Her Choice

Strange, strange to herself it seemed, for a moment's time,—no
    more,—
As he turned to smile from his plough in sight of the cottage door,
And she smiled back, and went in under the woodbine leaves,
And sang at her work with the bird that wove a nest in the eaves.

It was not the man of her dreams, out there in his coarse farm-
    frock,
Sturdy and firm on the earth as an oak or a lichen's rock,
With an eye sun-clear in its health, and a cheek red-bronzed with
    tan!—
No; that shadow shrank into mist, and fled from this living man.

She had shaped a pretty ideal, as a child might fashion a doll;
She had clothed it with such perfection as never Heaven let fall
On the shoulders of mortal wight; but slowly, one after one,
From her idol fluttered away the shreds by fantasy spun.

And what of him then was left? There seemed to scatter in air
An eyebrow's curve, a weak lip with a delicate fringe of hair,
And a town-bred curl of contempt for the boors who till the
      land.—
She shuddered, to think how empty sometimes is a wedded hand!

Yet once she had pictured herself that pitiful stripling's bride;
Would have laid her heart on the shrine of a puppet deified!
For the first commands of the ten all maidens are prone to break,
In bowing down to such gods as their own crude fancies make.

And this had been her first love! To her forehead rushed a flame
As memory taunted and laughed,—the blush of a matron's shame
At her girlhood's shallowness. Ah! the poets falsely sing
That the loveliest blossoms of all are gathered in early spring.

Many a May-day past she had found under leafless trees
A crowfoot, perhaps, or a tuft of pallid anemones;
Could these compare with the rose, grown shapely in summer's
      heat,
Or the lily's late-brimmed cup, or the spice of the meadow-sweet?

The high sun deepens the scent and color of slow-blown flowers;
Intense with the white warmth of heaven, glows earth, in her mid-
      noon hours:
The more life, richer the love, else life itself is a lie,
And aspiration and faith on the gusts of April die.

And—there the furrow he turned,—her husband, whose cheerful
      years
Looked out of his eyes with a light that conquered her foolish fears
Of the coming loneliness, when the world would be chill with
      rime;
Stanch friends and honest were he and his elder field-mate, Time.

And Time, laying by his scythe at their hearth, in the evenings
    long,
Would read from his ancient scroll, would charm them with noble
    song:
And life would mellow with love, and the future would open fair
And grand, as the silver of age fell softly upon their hair.

For she had not wedded a clod, whose heart was earthy, of earth,
Whose cattle and acres and crops were the measure of his worth:
He knew the ring of a truth, and the shape of a royal thought,
And how at integrity's mint the wealth of a land is wrought.

He labored with mind and strength, and yet he could wisely rest;
He toiled for his daily bread, and ate it with wholesome zest
At the world-wide human board, the brother and friend of all
With whom he could share a hope, on whom let a blessing fall.

She had chosen a working-man; never idler at heart was she;
And her possible fate had been the fate of a homesick bee
In a butterfly's leash, driven on amid scentless and useless
    bloom,—
What drudgery were not bliss to inanities of that doom?

Woman's lot at the best is hard; but hardest of all to share
No growth into larger thought, no struggle, burden, or prayer.
And again she caught his smile, and silently, proudly said,
"This man, with the love of my heart and the life of my soul, I
    wed."

The Loaf-Giver: From *An Idyll of Work*

"Is there a lady yet
  Under the sun?"
Dames of Olympus
Called down, one by one.

"If a true lady
　Be left, of earth's race,
　Seats of the goddesses
　Offer her place."

Answer came slowly
From hemispheres two:
Dead seemed the Old World,
And heedless the New.

"I am a lady, then!
See! for I wear
Latest of bonnets,
Last twist of hair;
French gloves and laces,—
What more can I need?"

Laughed mighty Juno,
"A lady, indeed!"
"I am a lady born!
I have a name!
An unbroken ancestry
Settles my claim."

"Weak!" said Minerva;
"Irrelevant too!
Substitute ladyhood
Never will do."

"I am a lady!
No token of toil
Is on my fine fingers,—
Vulgarity's soil!

I mix with no workfolk!"
"Ah?" Venus exclaimed;

"*I* wedded a blacksmith,
And was not ashamed:

"What face, bright as Hebe's,
Illumines yon street?
That beautiful maiden
Gives beggars their meat;
Her graceful hand leads them
To honor and peace.

My sigh for lost ladies,"
Said Venus, "I cease."
"I too!" called Minerva;
And pointed to where
In a dreary log school-house,
A girl, young and fair,
Spent life, strength, and beauty.—
"She scatters live seed!
She works in wild thought-fields,
The starved soul to feed."

Cried Juno, "Yon farm-wife,
With white arms like mine,
Round, snowy leaves shaping,
To me seems divine.
She, moulded a goddess,
Who yet can prefer
To be useful and helpful,—
What lady like her?"
Nodded the sky-women,
Glad, one by one.
"Still there are ladies left
Under the sun.
"Counterfeit creatures
May borrow the name;

But the deep-seeing heavens
Accept not their claim."

"Lady is loaf-giver!"
Echoed the three.
"Who stays the world's hunger,
True lady is she!"

"That suits me, Esther," Minta said. "You know
I am Minerva's lady half the year;
That is to say, I deal out learning's pap
To country babes, in District Number Three,
Under Chocorua's shadow. In plain words,
I am a schoolma'am in the summer-time,
As now I am a Lady of the Loom.
Come up and see me, girls! I'll give you bread
White as that Juno-woman's in the song,
Made with my own hands, too. And you may feast
Your eyes on stones,—our mountain-peaks—besides;
All you down-country folks are fond of them."

"How beautiful!" said Esther. "If we could!"
For Esther, born of Puritans by the sea
That washes Plymouth Rock, within the curve
Of the long arm that Cape Cod reaches out
Toward Cape Ann's shoulder, never yet had seen
The mountains, save in glamour of her dreams.
"Come, then, for Eleanor's sake! Her cheeks will bloom
With pinks in place of lilies. Quite too much
Of the fine-lady look her pale face wears
For any working-girl. With yellow cream,
Raspberries, brook-trout, and mountain-blackberries,
We'll make a woman of her," Minta said.

"'Lady' again!" cried Isabel. "Now I know
There's something more in it than feeding folks

With bread or with ideas. Eleanor says
I look a lady; you say she looks one.
I think it's in the dress, the air, the gait—"
"Yes, there's a ladyish drawl and wriggle, too,
Easy enough to catch; and furbelows—
Made usually of silk or satin, though,"
Said Minta, giving Isabel's gown a twitch
Upon its fluttering ruffles, which betrayed
Faint reminiscences of yesterday
Among the looms, in sundry spots of grease.

Strange! Eleanor, in her large coarse apron wrapped,
Walked past the oily wheels immaculate,
As saints have trodden on coals without a smirch;
While Isabel groaned daily over stains
Almost indelible. With Isabel's face
After her reddening like an angry cloud,
Minta retreated; vanishing from sight
In the room's farthest shadow. Esther spoke,
Half to herself, half to the other two:
"Not long ago I read a doleful wail
From some town-dame, that now even factory-girls
Shine with gold watches, and you cannot tell,
Therefore, who are the ladies. Well-a-day!
If one could buy and hang about the neck
The ornament of a meek and quiet spirit,
'Twould make a bauble even of that."

"But say, Esther, whom do you call a lady?"
"She, Dear Isabel, who is so in her mind,—
Harbors no millinery jealousies,
Holds no conventional standards. She may wear
Dainty kid gloves, or wear no gloves at all;
May work at wash-boards or embroidery-frames:
This is her mark,—she lives not for herself.
Our Lord has given us 'service' for a badge.

True ladies, following him, seek not to be
Ministered unto, but to minister."
Then all grew thoughtful; whereat Eleanor,
With gentle tact, called out,—"A hymn! a tune!
Let us sing, sisters, now the preaching's done!
Look! how the slanting sunbeams light the slope
Across the river!" And her voice arose
Clear as an oriole's, in a grand psalm-tune
Married to one of Watts' old-fashioned hymns...

Just then the overseer, passing by them, said,
"A holiday! The river's will is up
To stop the mills, and for a while you are free."
It was a welcome word. The three glad girls
Slipped off work-aprons, bonnets caught, and shawls,
And went out for a walk among green trees,
Like souls released from earth to Paradise.

The Light-Houses

Two pale sisters, all alone,
On an island bleak and bare,
Listening to the breakers' moan,
Shivering in the chilly air
Looking inland towards a hill,
On whose top one aged tree
Wrestles with the storm-wind's will,
Rushing, wrathful, from the sea.
Two dim ghosts at dusk they seem,
Side by side, so white and tall,
Sending one long, hopeless gleam
Down the horizon's darkened wall.
Spectres, strayed from plank or spar,
With a tale none lives to tell,
Gazing at the town afar,

Where unconscious widows dwell.
Two white angels of the sea,
Guiding wave-worn wanderers home;
Sentinels of hope they be,
Drenched with sleet, and dashed with foam,
Standing there in loneliness,
Fireside joys for men to keep;
Through the midnight slumberless
That the quiet shore may sleep.
Two bright eyes awake all night
To the fierce moods of the sea;
Eyes that only close when light
Dawns on lonely hill and tree.
O kind watchers! teach us, too,
Steadfast courage, sufferance long!
Where an eye is turned to you,
Should a human heart grow strong.

Goody Grunsell's House

A weary old face, beneath a black mutch;
Like a flame in a cavern her eye,
Betwixt craggy forehead and cheek-bone high;
Her long, lean fingers hurried to clutch
A something concealed in her rusty cloak,
As a step on the turf the stillness broke,
While a sound—was it curse or sigh?
Smote the ear of the passer-by.

A dreary old house, on a headland slope,
Against the gray of the sea:
Where garden and orchard used to be,
Witch-grass and nettle and rag-weed grope,—
Paupers that eat the earth's riches out,—
Nightshade and henbane are lurking about,

Like demons that enter in
When a soul has run waste to sin.

The house looked wretched and woe-begone;
Its desolate windows wept
With a dew that forever dripped and crept
From the moss-grown eaves; and ever anon
Some idle wind, with a passing slap,
Made rickety shutter or shingle flap,
As who with a jeer should say,
"Why does the old crone stay?"

Goody Grunsell's house,—it was all her own;
There was no one living to chide,
Though she tore every rib from its skeleton side
To kindle a fire when she sat alone
With the ghosts that had leave to go out and in,
Through crevice and rent, to the endless din
Of winds that muttered and moaned,
Of waves that wild ditties droned.

And this was the only booty she hid
Under her threadbare cloak,—
A strip of worn and weather-stained oak:
Then in to her lonesome hearth she slid;
And, inch by inch, as the cold years sped,
She was burning the old house over her head;
Why not, when each separate room
Held more than a lifetime's gloom?

Goody Grunsell's house,—not a memory glad
Illumined bare ceiling or wall;
But cruel shadows would sometimes fall
On the floor, and faces eerie and sad
At dusk would peer in at the broken pane,
While ghostly steps pattered through the rain,

Sending the blood with a start
To her empty, shriveled heart.

For she had not been a forbearing wife,
Nor a loyal husband's mate;
The twain had been one but in fear and hate;
And the horror of that inverted life
Had not spent itself on their souls alone:
From the bitter root evil buds had blown;
There were births that blighted grew,
And died, and no gladness knew.

The house unto nobody home had been,
But a lair of pain and shame:
Could any its withered mistress blame,
Who sought from its embers a spark to win,
A warmth for the body, to soul refused?
Such questioning ran through her thoughts confused,
As she slipped with her spoil from sight:—
Could the dead assert their right?

The splintered board, like a dagger's blade,
Goody Grunsell cowering hid,
As if the house had a voice that chid,
When wound after wound in its side she made;
As if the wraiths of her children cried
From their graves, to denounce her a homicide;
While the sea, up the weedy path,
Groaned, spurning in wordless wrath.

The house, with its pitiful, haunted look,—
Old Goody, more piteous still,
Angry and sad, as the night fell chill,—
They are pictures out of a long-lost book:
But the windows of many a human face
Show tenants that burn their own dwelling-place;

And spectre and fiend will roam
Through the heart which is not love's home.

A Gambrel Roof

How pleasant! This old house looks down
Upon a shady little town,
Whose great good luck has been to stay
Just outside of the modern way
Of tiresome strut and show;
The elm-trees overhead have seen
Two hundred new-born summers green
Up to their tops for sunshine climb;
And, since the old colonial time,
The road has wound just so:

This way through Salem Village; that,
Along the Plains (the place is flat,
And names itself so); toward the tide
Of sea-fed creeks, past Royal-Side,
And round by Folly Hill,
Whose sunken cellar now is all
Memorial of a stately hall
Where yule-logs roared and red wine flowed;
From its lost garden to the road
A gold bloom trickles still:

Wood-waxen gold—a foreign weed,
Spoiling the fields for useful seed,
Yet something to recall the day
When we were under royal sway,
And paid our taxes well.
And from that memory, as a thread,
The shuttle of my rhyme is fed;
Upon this ancient gambrel roof

The warp was spun; behold the woof,
And all there is to tell.

About a hundred years ago,
When Danvers roadsides were aglow
With cardinal flowers and golden-rod;
Months ere in Lexington the sod
Was dewed with soldiers' blood;
Though warlike rumors filled the air,
And red coats loitered here and there,
Eye-sores to every yeoman free;
When from the White Hills to the sea
Swelled Revolution's bud;

In this old house, even then not new,
A Continental Colonel true
Dwelt, with a blithe and willful wife,
The sparkle on his cup of life;—
A man of sober mood,
He felt the strife before it came,
Within him, like a welding flame,
That nerve and sinew changed to steel,
And, at the opening cannon peal,
Ready for fight he stood.

Cheap was the draught, beyond a doubt,
The mother country served us out;
And many a housewife raised a wail,
Hearing of fragrant chest and bale
To thirstless mermaids poured.
And Mistress Audrey's case was hard,
When her tall Colonel down the yard
Called, "Wife, be sure you drink no tea!"
For best Imperial, prime Bohea,
Were in her cupboard stored;

Young Hyson, too, the finest brand;
And here the good wife made a stand:
"Now, Colonel, well enough you know
Our tea was paid for long ago,
Before this cargo came,
With threepence duty on the pound;
It won't be wasted, I'll be bound!
I've asked a friend or two to sup,
And not to offer them a cup
Would be a stingy shame."

Into his face the quick blood flew:
"Wife, I have promised, so must you,
None shall drink tea inside my house;
Your gossips elsewhere must carouse."—
The lady curtsied low
"Husband, your word is law;" she said,
But archly turned her well-set head
With roguish poise toward this old roof,
Soon as she heard his martial hoof
Along the highway go.

"Late dusk will fall ere he comes back
Quick, Dill!" Whereat a figure black,
A strange, grotesque, swift shadow made
Between the silent elm-trees' shade,
Where all was grass and sun
Then maid and mistress passed within
The pantry, hung with glittering tin,
Tiptoeing every sanded floor,
Till, at the china-closet door,
They saw their work begun.

The egg-shell porcelain, crystal-fine,
Was polished to its utmost shine;
The silver teaspoons gleamed as bright,

Upon the damask napkin white;
And many a knowing smile
Flashed from the fair face to the black,
Across the kitchen chimney-back,
While syllabubs and custards grew
To comely shape betwixt the two;
And cakes, a toothsome pile.

But lightly dined the dame that day:
Her guests, in Sunday-best array,
Came, and not one arrived too soon,
In the first slant of afternoon.
An hour or two they sat,
In the low-studded western room,
Where hollyhocks threw rosy bloom
On sampler framed, and quaint Dutch tile.
They knit; they sewed long seams; the while
Chatting of this and that;—

Of horrors scarcely died away
From memory of the heads grown gray
On neighboring farms: how wizard John
And Indian Tituba went on,
When sorcerers were believed;
How Parson Parris tried to make
Poor Mary Sibley's conjuring cake
The leaven of that black witchcraft curse,
That grew and spread, from bad to worse,
And even the elect deceived;

Of apparitions at Cape Ann,
And spectral fights—the story ran;
Of pirate gold in Saugus' caves;
Sea-serpents off Nahant, the waves
Lashing with fearsome trail;
Of armies flashing in the air

Auroral swords, prefiguring there
Some dreadful conflict, bloodshed, death:—
And needles stopped, and well-nigh breath,
As eerier grew the tale.

Dame Audrey said: "The sun gets low;
Good neighbors mine, before you go,
Come to the house-top, pray, with me!
A goodly prospect you shall see,
I promise, spread around.
If we must part ere day decline,
And if no hospitable sign
Appear, of China's cheering drink,
Not niggardly your hostess think!
We all are patriots sound."

They followed her with puzzled air;
But saw, upon the topmost stair,
Out on the railed roof, dark-faced Dill
Guarding the supper-board, as still
As solid ebony.
"A goodly prospect, as I said,
You here may see before you spread
Upon a house is not *within* it;
But now we must not waste a minute;
Neighbors, sit down to tea!"

How Madam then her ruse explained,
What mirth arose as sunset waned,
In the close covert of these trees,
No leaf told the reporter breeze;
But when the twilight fell,
And hoof-beats rang down Salem road,
And up the yard the Colonel strode,
No soul beside the dame and Dill

Stirred in the mansion dim and still
The game was played out well.

Let whoso chooses settle blame
Betwixt the Colonel and his dame,
Or dame and country. That the view
Is from this housetop fine, is true,
And needs but visual proof
And if a woman's will found way
Years since, up here, its pranks to play,
Under Mansards the sport goes on.—
Moral of all here said or done
I like a gambrel roof.

The Schoolmistress

"Why are you so cheerful,
Oh gentle Edith Lane!
Be it bright or cloudy,
Fall of dew or rain,
In that lonely schoolhouse,
Patiently you stay,
Teaching simple children,
All the livelong day."
"Teaching simple children?
I am simple, too:
So we learn together
Lessons plain as true,
From this thumb-worn Bible,
Full of love's best lore;
Or, to read another,
Just unlatch the door.
"Can I but be cheerful
While I bid them look,
Through the sunny pages

Of each opening book?
Showing tracks of angels,
On the footworn sod;
Listening to the music
Nature makes to God."
"Have you then no sorrow,
Smiling Edith Lane?
Where the barberry's coral
Rattles on the pane,
Where, in endless yellow,
Autumn flowers I see,
Working for a living
Were a woe to me."
"Sorrow! I—a woman,
And in years not young?
Of the common chalice,
Drops are on my tongue.
What of that? No whisper
To my heart is lost,
From the barberry-clusters,
Sweetened by the frost;
"From the rooted sunshine,
Golden-rod in bloom,
Lighting up the hillsides,
For November's gloom.
Shall I blot with weeping
Nature's joy and grace?
Rather be her gladness
Mirrored in my face.
"'Working for a living'?
May no worse befall!
Love is always busy;
God works, over all.
Life is worth the earning,
For its daily cheer,
Shared with those who love me,

In yon cottage dear.
"If you can, fair lady,
Go and be a drone!
Leave me with the children,
Dear as if my own.
Leave me to the humming
Of my little hive,
Glad to earn a living,
Glad to be alive!"

A Call To Kansas
Tune of "Nelly Bly"

Yeomen strong, hither throng!
Nature's honest men;
We will make the wilderness
Bud and bloom again.
Bring the sickle, speed the plow,
Turn the ready soil!
Freedom is the noblest pay
For the true man's toil.
Ho, brothers! come, brothers!
Hasten all with me;
We'll sing upon the Kansas plains
A song of liberty.
Father, haste! O'er the waste
Lies a pleasant land.
There your fireside's altar-stones,
Fixed in truth, shall stand.
There your sons, brave and good,
Shall to freemen grow,
Clad in triple mail of right,
Wrong to overthrow.
Ho, brothers! come, brothers!
Hasten all with me;

We'll sing upon the Kansas plains
A song of liberty!
Brother, come! Here's a home
In the waiting West;
Bring the seeds of love and peace,
You who sow them best.

Elsie in Illinois

"At home is home, no matter where!"
Sang a happy, youthful pair,
Journeying westward, years ago,
As they left the April snow
White on Massachusetts' shore;
Left the sea's incessant roar;
Left the Adirondacks, piled
Like the playthings of a child,
On the horizon's eastern bound;
And, the unbroken forests found,
Heard Niagara's sullen call,
Hurrying to his headlong fall,
Like a Titan in distress,
Tearing through the wilderness,
Rending earth apart, in hate
Of the unpitying hounds of fate.
Over Erie's green expanse
Inland wild-fowl weave their dance:
Lakes on lakes, a crystal chain,
Give the clear heaven back again;
Wampum strung by Manitou,
Lightly as the beaded dew.
Is it wave, or is it shore?
Greener gleams the prairie-floor,
West and south, one emerald;
Earth untenanted, unwalled.

There, a thread of silent joy,
Winds the grass-hid Illinois.
Bringing comfort unawares
Out of little daily cares,
Here has Elsie lived a year,
Learning well that home is dear,
By the green breadth measureless
Of the outside wilderness,
So unshadowed, so immense!
Garden without path or fence,
Rolling up its billowy bloom
To her low, one-windowed room.
Breath of prairie-flowers is sweet;
But the baby at her feet
Is the sweetest bud to her,
Keeping such a pleasant stir,
On the cabin hearth at play,
While his father turns the hay,
Loads the grain, or binds the stack,
Until sunset brings him back.
Elsie's thoughts awake must keep,
While the baby lies asleep.
Far Niagara haunts her ears;
Mississippi's rush she hears
Ancient nurses twain, that croon
For her babe their mighty tune,
Lapped upon the prairies wild:
He will be a wondrous child!
Ah! but Elsie's thoughts will stray
Where, a child, she used to play
In the shadow of the pines:
Moss and scarlet-berried vines
Carpeted the granite ledge,
Sloping to the brooklet's edge,
Sweet with violets, blue and white;
While the dandelions, bright

As if Night had spilt her stars,
Shone beneath the meadow-bars.
Could she hold her babe, to look
In that merry, babbling brook,
See it picturing his eye
As the violet's blue and shy,
See his dimpled fingers creep
Where the sweet-breathed May-flowers peep
With pale pink anemones,
Out among the budding trees!
On his soft cheek falls a tear
For the hillside home so dear.
At her household work she dreams;
And the endless prairie seems
Like a broad, unmeaning face
Read through in a moment's space,
Where the smile so fixed is grown,
Better you would like a frown.
Elsie sighs, "We learn too late,
Little things are more than great
Hearts like ours must daily be
Fed with some kind mystery,
Hidden in a rocky nook,
Whispered from a wayside brook,
Flashed on unexpecting eyes,
In a winged, swift surprise:
Small the pleasure is to trace
Boundlessness of commonplace."
But the south wind, stealing in,
Her to happier moods will win.
In and out the little gate
Creep wild roses delicate:
Fragrant grasses hint a tale
Of the blossomed intervale
Left behind, among the hills.
Every flower-cup mystery fills;

Every idle breeze goes by,
Burdened with life's blissful sigh.
Elsie hums a thoughtful air;
Spreads the table, sets a chair
Where her husband first shall see
Baby laughing on her knee;
While she watches him afar,
Coming with the evening star
Through the prairie, through the sky,
Each as from eternity.

Blue-Eyed Grace

Our walk is lonely, blue-eyed Grace,
Down the long forest-road to school,
Where shadows troop, at dismal pace,
From sullen chasm to sunless pool.
Are you not often, little maid,
Beneath the sighing trees afraid?
"Afraid! beneath the tall, strong trees
That bend their arms to shelter me,
And whisper down, with dew and breeze,
Sweet sounds that float on lovingly,
Till every gorge and cavern seems
Thrilled through and through with fairy dreams?
"Afraid,—beside the water dim,
That holds the baby lilies white
Upon its bosom, where a hymn
Ripples forth softly to the light
That now and then comes gliding in,
A lily's budding smile to win?
"Fast to the slippery precipice
I see the nodding harebell cling:
In that blue eye no fear there is;
Its hold is firm,—the frail, free thing!

The harebell's Guardian cares for me,
So I am in safe company.
"The woodbine clambers up the cliff,
And seems to murmur, 'Little Grace,
The sunshine were less welcome, if
It brought not every day your face.'
Red leaves slip down from maples high,
And touch my cheek as they flit by.
"I feel at home with everything
That has its dwelling in the wood;
With flowers that laugh, and birds that sing;
Companions beautiful and good,
Brothers and sisters everywhere;
And over all our Father's care.
"In rose-time or in berry-time;
When ripe seeds fall, or buds peep out;
When green the turf, or white the rime,
There's something to be glad about.
It makes my heart bound just to pass
The sunbeams dancing on the grass.
"And when the bare rocks shut me in
Where not a blade of grass will grow,
My happy fancies soon begin
To warble music rich and low,
And paint what eyes could never see:
My thoughts are company for me.
"What does it mean to be alone?
And how is any one afraid
Who feels the dear God on his throne,
Sending his sunshine through the shade,
Warming the damp sod into bloom,
And smiling off the thicket's gloom?
"At morning, down the woodpath cool,
The fluttering leaves make cheerful talk.
After the stifled day at school,
I hear, along my homeward walk,

The airy wisdom of the wood,
Far easiest to be understood!
"I whisper to the winds; I kiss
The rough old oak, and clasp his bark;
No farewell of the thrush I miss;
I lift the soft veil of the dark,
And say to bird, and breeze, and tree,
'Good night! good friends you are to me!'"

The Nineteenth of April (1861)

This year, till late in April, the snow fell thick and light:
Thy flag of truce, kind Nature, in clinging drifts of white,
Hung over field and city:—now everywhere is seen,
In place of that white quietness, a sudden glow of green.
The verdure climbs the Common, beneath the leaf less trees,
To where the glorious Stars and Stripes are floating on the breeze.
There, suddenly as Spring awoke from Winter's snow-draped
     gloom,
The Passion-Flower of Seventy-Six is bursting into bloom.
Dear is the time of roses, when earth to joy is wed,
And garden-plot and meadow wear one generous flush of red;
But now in dearer beauty, to her ancient colors true,
Blooms the old town of Boston in red and white and blue.
Along the whole awakening North are those bright emblems
     spread;
A summer noon of patriotism is burning overhead.
No party badges flaunting now,—no word of clique or clan;
But "Up for God and Union!" is the shout of every man.
O, peace is dear to Northern hearts; our hard earned homes more
     dear;
But Freedom is beyond the price of any earthly cheer;
And Freedom's flag is sacred; he who would work it harm,
Let him, although a brother, beware our strong right arm!
A brother! ah, the sorrow, the anguish of that word!

The fratricidal strife begun, when will its end be heard?
Not this the boon that patriot hearts have prayed and waited for;
We loved them, and we longed for peace: but they would have it
    war.
Yes; war! on this memorial day, the day of Lexington,
A lightning-thrill along the wires from heart to heart has run.
Brave men we gazed on yesterday, today for us have bled:
Again is Massachusetts blood the first for freedom shed.
For war,—and with our brethren, then, if only this can be!
Life hangs as nothing in the scale against dear Liberty!
Though hearts be torn asunder, for Freedom we will fight:
Our blood may seal the victory, but God will shield the Right!

The Sinking of the Merrimack (May, 1862)

One down in the flood, and gone out in the flame!
What else could she do, with her fair Northern name?
Her font was a river whose last drop is free:
That river ran boiling with wrath to the sea,
To hear of her baptismal blessing profaned,
A name that was Freedom's, by treachery stained.
'Twas the voice of our free Northern mountains that broke
In the sound of her guns, from her stout ribs of oak:
'Twas the might of the free Northern hand you could feel
In her sweep and her moulding, from topmast to keel:
When they made her speak treason (does Hell know of worse?)
How her strong timbers shook with the shame of her curse!
Let her go! Should a deck so polluted again
Ever ring to the tread of our true Northern men?
Let the suicide-ship thunder forth, to the air
And the sea she has blotted, her groan of despair!
Let her last heat of anguish throb out into flame,
Then sink them together,—the ship and the name!

Waiting for News (July 4, 1863)

At the corner of the lane,
Where we stood this time last year,
Droops and waves the ripening grain;
Sounds the meadow-lark's refrain,
Just as sad and clear.
Cornel-trees let blossoms fall
In a white shower at my feet;
Thick viburnums hide the wall;
And behind, the bush-bird's call
Bubbles, summery-sweet,
Now, as then, o'er purple blooms
Veiled by meadow-grasses rare;
Bubbles through the coppice glooms;
Joins the sweetbrier's late perfumes
Wandering through the air.
All returns; your word, your look,
As we stood where now I stand:
With a dread I could not brook,
Well I knew my faint voice shook,
While you held my hand.
Firm you always were, and then
High resolve had made you strong.
Could I bid you linger, when
Freedom called aloud for men
To requite her wrong?
Southrons threw their gauntlet-lie
In the face of God and Truth.
"Go, for love's sake!" was my cry;
"Were not Truth more dear than I,
Thou wert naught, in sooth!"
And you went. The whole year through,
I have felt war's thunder-quake
Rend me hour by hour anew:
Yet I would not call for you,

Though my heart should break.
Only, standing here to-day,
With the sweetbrier's wandering breath,
And the smell of new-mown hay
In the air, "This life," I say,
"Strikes deep root in death."
Death! while here I pass the hours,
Blood is rising round your feet:
I sit ankle-deep in flowers:
On you, red shot falls in showers,
Through the battle-heat.
What if there I saw you lie,
Where the grasses nod and blow,
With your forehead to the sky,
And your wounds—O God! that I,
That I bade you go!
Yet, were that to say once more,
"Go," I'd say, "at any cost!"
Many a heart has bled before.
God his heroes will restore;
No great soul is lost.
And the strife that rages so
Burns out meanness from the land.
Men must fall, and blood must flow,
That our Plants of Honor grow
Unto stature grand.
Aye, today it seems to me,
That yon little straggling rose
Fed by War's red springs must be:
All of fair and good I see,
Out of anguish grows.
Vines that shade the cottage-home;
Laurels for the warrior's wreath;
Lilies of white peace, that bloom
After battle's lurid gloom;—
All are nursed by death.

By our bond, I'm close to-day
As your sword is, to your side.
If your breath stops in the fray,
Watchers from above will say,
Two for freedom died.
Still I loiter in the lane,
If I might but send you, dear,
Sweetbrier scents, the lark's refrain,
They would soothe the battle-pain;
You should feel me near:
And the fresh thought of these fields
With new strength would nerve your arm.
Fearlessly his sword he wields,
Whose whole risk is what it shields,
Home-love, pure and warm.
And you ventured this; you gave
Freely all your wealth of life,
That the Stars and Stripes might wave
Nevermore above a slave.
Cheerfully your wife
Climbs with you great Freedom's pyre
Not as Hindoo widows die.
We to life in Life aspire:
Love's last height is our desire;
Lo! we tread the sky!
Treading with a joyful scorn
Selfish joy beneath our feet:
In a nation's hope new-born,
In a free world's radiant morn,
Breathing bliss complete.
Hark! a jubilee of bells
Pealing through the sunset light,
Shaking out fresh clover-smells!
Parting day to-morrow tells,
Victory's in sight.
Hark, again! the long, shrill blast

Eager throngs are waiting for.
Is it Death's train, sweeping past?
Homeward, Heart! Pain cannot last.
What news from the war?

Re-enlisted (May, 1864)

Did you see him in the street, dressed up in army-blue,
When drums and trumpets into town their storm of music threw,
A louder tune than all the winds could muster in the air,
The Rebel winds, that tried so hard our flag in strips to tear?
You didn't mind him? O, you looked beyond him then, perhaps,
To see the mounted officers rigged out with trooper caps,
And shiny clothes, and sashes, and epaulets and all;
It wasn't for such things as these he heard his country call.
She asked for men; and up he spoke, my handsome, hearty Sam,
"I'll die for the dear old Union, if she'll take me as I am."
And if a better man than he there's mother that can show,
From Maine to Minnesota, then let the nation know.
You would not pick him from the rest by eagles or by stars,
By straps upon his coat-sleeve, or gold or silver bars;
Nor a corporal's strip of worsted, but there's some thing in his face,
And something in his even step, a-marching in his place,
That couldn't be improved by all the badges in the land:
A patriot, and a good, strong man; are generals much more grand?
We rest our pride on that big heart wrapped up in army-blue,
The girl he loves, Mehitabel, and I, who love him too.
He's never shirked a battle yet, though frightful risks he's run,
Since treason flooded Baltimore, the spring of Sixty One;
Through blood and storm he's held out firm, nor fretted once, my
        Sam,
At swamps of Chickahominy, or fields of Antietam.
Though many a time, he's told us, when he saw them lying dead,
The boys that came from Newburyport, and Lynn, and
        Marblehead,

Stretched out upon the trampled turf, and wept on by the sky,
It seemed to him the Commonwealth had drained her life-blood
    dry.
"But then," he said, "the more's the need the country has of me:
To live and fight the war all through, what glory it will be!
The Rebel balls don't hit me; and, mother, if they should,
You'll know I've fallen in my place, where I have always stood."
He's taken out his furlough, and short enough it seemed:
I often tell Mehitabel he'll think he only dreamed
Of walking with her nights so bright you couldn't see a star,
And hearing the swift tide come in across the harbor bar.
The Stars that shine above the Stripes, they light him southward
    now;
The tide of war has swept him back; he's made a solemn vow
He'll build himself no home-nest till his country's work is done;
God bless the vow, and speed the work, my patriot, my son!
And yet it is a pretty place where his new house might be;
An orchard-road that leads your eye straight out upon the sea.
The boy not work his father's farm? it seems almost a shame;
But any selfish plan for him he'd never let me name.
He's re-enlisted for the war, for victory or for death,
A soldier's grave, perhaps! the thought has half way stopped my
    breath,
And driven a cloud across the sun; my boy, it will not be
The war will soon be over; home again you'll come to me!
He's re-enlisted: and I smiled to see him going, too!
There's nothing that becomes him half so well as army-blue.
Only a private in the ranks! but sure I am indeed,
If all the privates were like him, they'd scarcely captains need.
And I and Massachusetts share the honor of his birth,
The grand old State! to me the best in all the peopled earth!
I cannot hold a musket, but I have a son who can;
And I'm proud for Freedom's sake to be the mother of a man!

Tolling (April 15, 1865)

Tolling, tolling, tolling!
All the bells of the land!
Lo! the patriot martyr
Taketh his journey grand;
Travels into the ages,
Bearing a hope how dear!
Into life's unknown vistas,
Liberty's great pioneer.
Tolling, tolling, tolling!
Do the budded violets know
The pain of the lingering clangor
Shaking their bloom out so?
They open into strange sorrow,
The rain of a nation's tears;
Into the saddest April
Twined with the New World's years.
Tolling, tolling, tolling!
See, they come as a cloud,
Hearts of a mighty people,
Bearing his pall and shroud!
Lifting up, like a banner,
Signals of loss and woe!
Wonder of breathless nations,
Moveth the solemn show.
Tolling, tolling, tolling!
Was it, O man beloved,—
Was it thy funeral only,
Over the land that moved?
Veiled by that hour of anguish,
Borne with the Rebel rout,
Forth into utter darkness,
Slavery's corse went out.

The Flag (June 17, 1865)

Let it idly droop, or sway
To the wind's light will;
Furl its stars, or float in day;
Flutter, or be still!
It has held its colors bright,
Through the war-smoke dun;
Spotless emblem of the Right,
Whence success was won.
Let it droop in graceful rest
For a passing hour, Glory's banner, last and best;
Freedom's freshest flower!
Each red stripe has blazoned forth
Gospels writ in blood;
Every star has sung the birth
Of some deathless good.
Let it droop, but not too long!
On the eager wind
Bid it wave, to shame the wrong,
To inspire mankind
With a larger human love;
With a truth as true
As the heaven that broods above
Its deep field of blue.
In the gathering hosts of hope,
In the march of man,
Open for it place and scope,
Bid it lead the van;
Till beneath the searching skies,
Martyr-blood be found,
Purer than our sacrifice,
Crying from the ground:—
Fill a flag with some new light
Out of Freedom's sky,
Kindles, through the gulfs of night,

Glory yet more high.
Let its glow the darkness drown!
Give our banner sway;
Till its joyful stars go down,
In undreamed-of day!

The Secret

What selfishness asked for
Was vain:
What came for that asking
Brought pain.
Heaven's manna in keeping
Was spoiled:
All beauty self-seeking
Hath soiled.
Complacency blazoned
Dull dross.
No gain came of hoarding,
But loss.
Gain! none save the giver
Receives.
Yet who that old gospel
Believes?
Nor pauper nor beggar
Then be;
Nor niggard of bounty
Most free.
But one way is Godlike, to give.
Then pour out thy heart's blood,
And live!

My Angel-Dress

Heavenly Father, I would wear
Angel-garments, white and fair:
Angel-vesture undefiled
Wilt Thou give unto thy child?
Not a robe of many hues,
Such as earthly fathers choose;
Discord weaves the gaudy vest:
Not in such let me be drest.
Take the raiment soiled away
That I wear with shame to-day:
Give my angel-robe to me,
White with heavenly purity.
Take away my cloak of pride,
And the worthless rags 'twould hide:
Clothe me in my angel-dress,
Beautiful with holiness.
Perfume every fold with love,
Hinting heaven where'er I move;
As an Indian vessel's sails
Whisper of her costly bales.
Let me wear my white robes here,
Even on earth, my Father dear,
Holding fast Thy hand, and so
Through the world unspotted go.
Let me now my white robes wear:
Then I need no more prepare,
All apparelled for my home
Whensoe'er Thou callest, "Come!"
Thus apparelled, I shall be
As a signal set for Thee,
That the wretched and the weak
May the same fair garments seek.
"Buy of Me," I hear Thee say:
I have naught wherewith to pay,

But I give myself to Thee;
Clothed, adopted I shall be.

Canticle De Profundis

Glory to Thee, Father of all the Immortal,
Forever belongs:
We bring Thee from our watch by the grave's portal
Nothing but songs.
Though every wave of trouble has gone o'er us,
Though in the fire
We have lost treasures time cannot restore us,
Though all desire
That made life beautiful fades out in sorrow;
Though the strange path
Winding so lonely through the bleak to-morrow,
No comfort hath;
Though blackness gathers round us on all faces,
And we can see
By the red war-flash but Love's empty places;
Glory to Thee!
For, underneath the crash and roar of battle,
The deafening roll
That calls men off to butchery like cattle,
Soul after soul,
Under the horrid sound of chaos seething
In blind, hot strife,
We feel the moving of Thy Spirit, breathing
A better life
Into the air of our long-sickened nation;
A muffled hymn;
The star-sung prelude of a new creation;
Suffusions dim,
The bursting upward of a stifled glory,
That shall arise

To light new pages in the world's great story
For happier eyes.
If upon lips too close to dead lips leaning,
Songs be not found,
Yet wilt Thou know our life's unuttered meaning:
In its deep ground,
As seeds in earth, sleep sorrow-drenched praises,
Waiting to bring
Incense to Thee along thought's barren mazes
When Thou send'st spring.
Glory to Thee! we say, with shuddering wonder,
While a hushed land
Hears the stern lesson syllabled in thunder,
That Truth is grand
As life must be; that neither man nor nation
May soil thy throne
With a soul's life-blood—horrible oblation!
Nor quick be shown
That thou wilt not be mocked by prayer whose nurses
Were Hate and Wrong;
That trees so vile must drop back fruit in curses
Bitter and strong.
Glory to Thee, who wilt not let us smother
Ourselves in sin;
Sending Pain's messengers fast on each other
Us thence to win
Praise for the scourging under which we languish,
So torn, so sore!
And save us strength, if yet uncleansed by anguish,
To welcome more.
Life were not life to us, could they be fables,
Justice and Right:
Scathe crime with lightning, till we see the tables
Of Law burn bright!
Glory to Thee, whose glory and whose pleasure
Must be in good!

By Thee the mysteries we cannot measure
Are understood.
With the abysses of Thyself above us,
Our sins below,
That Thou dost look from Thy pure heaven and love us,
Enough to know.
Enough to lay our praises on Thy bosom;
Praises fresh-grown
Out of our depths, dark root and open blossom,
Up to thy throne.
When choking tears make our Hosannas falter,
The music free!
O keep clear voices singing at Thy altar,
Glory to Thee!

The Weeping Prophet

Woe, woe is me for my dear country's sin!
Woe, that a prophet's torch was given to me
To hold up, hid God's shadowing light within,
Before a people who refuse to see
How guilt draws down that light in burning levin;
How awful is the purity of heaven.
A boy among the hills of Anathoth
I saw the visionary caldron seethe,
The almond-tree its ominous blossoms wreathe,
In token that a righteous God was wroth
With Israel, and in judgment would condemn
The city of His love, Jerusalem.
To be his messenger of wrath I shrank:
I cried, "O Lord, I am a child, so weak!
Who bears a curse, none give God-speed, or thank."
Then did He touch my lips, His words I speak;
And, knowing that His eyes are on the truth,
I cannot answer evil ways with ruth.

Therefore I sit a mourner, and mine eyes
Pour day and night their heavy sorrows down.
My people pass me by, for they despise
His goodness, and with scoffs His warnings drown.
While o'er my head, in cloudy columns low,
The birds of prey that scent their ruin go.
Was ever any sorrow like to mine?
It is no selfish trouble that I weep,
O daughter of my people, but I keep
Vigil for thee, beneath the wrath divine,
The love that reddens into justice, when
God's perfect law is made the mock of men.
For, evermore, the tables of that law,
Broken by man, are back upon him hurled.
O virgin daughter, thee defiled I saw,
Wandering from Him, an outcast in the world,
Filthy without, and vile and crushed within;
A by-word through the ages for thy sin.
Alike in visions of the day and night,
A spectral presence, not to be shut out,
A bleeding shadow, chased by shame and doubt,
Hither and thither past me takes its flight
Into the unsheltering dark of east and west:
A phantom, yet in faded splendors drest.
For thou wert beautiful, Jerusalem!
Celestial colors wrapped thee at thy birth;
Kings pressed from far to kiss thy garment's hem,
Chosen of God, a glory in the earth!
Falling from such a height to such a deep,
To be the prophet of thy doom I weep!

The Rose Enthroned

It melts and seethes, the chaos that shall grow
To adamant beneath the house of life;

In hissing hatred atoms clash, and go
To meet intenser strife.
And ere that fever leaves the granite veins,
Down thunders over them a torrid sea:
Now Flood, now Fire, alternate despot reigns,
Immortal foes to be.
Built by the warring elements, they rise,
The massive earth-foundations, tier on tier,
Where slimy monsters with unhuman eyes
Their hideous heads uprear.
The building of the world is not for you,
That glare upon each other, and devour:
Race floating after race fades out of view,
Till beauty springs from power.
Meanwhile from crumbling rocks and shoals of death
Shoots up rank verdure to the hidden sun;
The gulfs are eddying to the vague, sweet breath
Of richer life begun;
Richer and sweeter far than aught before,
Though rooted in the grave of what has been:
Unnumbered burials yet must heap Earth's floor
Ere she her heir shall win;
And ever nobler lives and deaths more grand,
For nourishment of that which is to come;
While mid the ruins of the work she planned
Sits Nature, blind and dumb.
For whom or what she plans, she knows no more
Than any mother of her unborn child:
Yet beautiful forewarnings murmur o'er
Her desolations wild.
Slowly the clamor and the clash subside;
Earth's restlessness her patient hopes subdue;
Mild oceans shoreward heave a pulse-like tide;
The skies are veined with blue.
And life works through the growing quietness,
To bring some darling mystery into form:

Beauty her fairest Possible would dress
In colors pure and warm.
Within the depths of palpitating seas
A tender tint,—anon a line of grace,
Some lovely thought from its dull atom frees,
The coming joy to trace:
A pencilled moss on tablets of the sand,
Such as shall veil the unbudded maiden-blush
Of beauty yet to gladden the green land;
A breathing, through the hush,
Of some sealed perfume longing to burst out,
And give its prisoned rapture to the air;
A brooding hope, a promise through a doubt,
Is whispered everywhere.
And, every dawn a shade more clear, the skies
A flush as from the heart of heaven disclose:
Through earth and sea and air a message flies,
Prophetic of the Rose.
At last a morning comes, of sunshine still,
When not a dewdrop trembles on the grass,
When all winds sleep, and every pool and rill
Is like a burnished glass
Where a long looked-for guest might lean to gaze;
When Day on Earth rests royally,—a crown
Of molten glory, flashing diamond rays,
From heaven let lightly down.
In golden silence, breathless, all things stand;
What answer waits this questioning repose?
A sudden gush of light and odors bland,
And, lo,—the Rose! the Rose!
The birds break into canticles around;
The winds lift Jubilate to the skies;
For, twin-born with the rose on Eden-ground,
Love blooms in human eyes.
Life's marvellous queen-flower blossoms only so,
In dust of low ideals rooted fast.

Ever the Beautiful is moulded slow
From truth in errors past.
What fiery fields of Chaos must be won,
What battling Titans rear themselves a tomb,
What births and resurrections greet the sun
Before the rose can bloom!
And of some wonder-blossom yet we dream
Whereof the time that is infolds the seed;
Some flower of light, to which the Rose shall seem
A fair and fragile weed.

Heaven's Need

He who, passing, bore away
Best of sunshine from our day,
That rare glory which revives
On the sky of clouded lives,
When, through mists at evening rent,
Rays from inmost heaven are sent,
What of earth to you remains,
Mid imperishable gains?
Mother-love, unchilled by change,
Absence wide, and coldness strange,
Mother-love, that here must yearn
Vainly for its full return
From the shallow heart of youth,
Art requited now, in truth?
Or does thy dumb longing go
Through heaven's happy overflow?
Sister-love, so calm, so wise!
Starlight, risen on darkened skies;
Heart that made its rifled nest
Shelter for the homeless guest,
Of thy tenderness bereft,
Little warmth in life is left.

Has that new world's flood of bliss
Swept apart the ties of this?
None may name a drearier thought;—
Hearts we lean on need us not.
If they ask for us no more,
Gathering in heaven's affluent store,
Life is lonelier than we knew;
Sharper anguish thrills death through.
In this rubbish-heap of earth.
Hides no pearl heaven's saving worth?
God is good. His face they see,
And are glad eternally.
Yet they hear love's wordless prayer,
Sigh that stirs the peaceful air,
And our yearning secret tells
To the bending asphodels.
Lacks one drop their cup to fill;
Still they want us, wait us still.

My Name-Aunt

I can see her, as she grew
By the sea, in spray and dew,
Little girl and woman too.

Childhood soberly she wears,
Taking hold of woman's cares
Through love's outreach, unawares:

Glint of ocean, depth of sky,
Tenderness; intensity.
Blending in her large blue eye.

Fair she must have been, in sooth,
While the freshness of her youth
Blossomed out of inward truth;

Where the pathos of the wave
To her maiden feelings gave
Wistful wonder, sweetness grave.

Everybody called her good,
When, with steady feet, she stood
On the heights of womanhood.

Ere I saw her, locks of brown
Into silvery bands had grown;
Age had placed on her his crown.

Still in dreams her face I view—
Noblest that my childhood knew—
Motherly and saintly too.

Seriously my eyes she read;
Laid her hand upon my head,—
Once—again,—two brief words said:

Liquid syllables, that fell
On my child-heart like a spell:
My name, borne by her so well.

Softly, with a yearning grace,
Said she, searching still my face,—
"Never, dear, the name disgrace!"

Since that hour, I wear a charm
In the charge she gave; her arm
Shields from many an unseen harm.

And I bless her for an aim
Fixed upon the Best, that came
As my portion, with her name:

Name she gave me, that confers
Honor in its characters,
Standing for a life like hers.

And I fain would make it sweet
For the sea-winds to repeat
Where she strayed, with childish feet;

Down the beach, and through the wood,
Where she grew so gently good
In her wild-rose maidenhood.

Unwedded

Behold her there in the evening sun,
That kindles the Indian Summer trees
To a separate burning bush, one by one,
Wherein the Glory Divine she sees!

Mate and nestlings she never had:
Kith and kindred have passed away;
Yet the sunset is not more gently glad,
That follows her shadow, and fain would stay.

For out of her life goes a breath of bliss,
And a sunlike charm from her cheerful eye,
That the cloud and the loitering breeze would miss;
A balm that refreshes the passer-by.

"Did she choose it, this single life?"
Gossip, she saith not, and who can tell?

But many a mother, and many a wife,
Draws a lot more lonely, we all know well.

Doubtless she had her romantic dream,
Like other maidens, in May-time sweet,
That flushes the air with a lingering gleam,
And goldens the grass beneath her feet:

A dream unmoulded to visible form,
That keeps the world rosy with mists of youth.
And holds her in loyalty close and warm,
To her fine ideal of manly truth.

"But is she happy, a woman, alone?"
Gossip, alone in this crowded earth,
With a voice to quiet its hourly moan,
And a smile to heighten its rarer mirth?

There are ends more worthy than happiness:
Who seeks it, is digging joy's grave, we know.
The blessed are they who but live to bless;
She found out that mystery, long ago.

To her motherly, sheltering atmosphere,
The children hasten from icy homes:
The outcast is welcome to share her cheer;
And the saint with a fervent benison comes.

For the heart of woman is large as man's;
God gave her his orphaned world to hold,
And whispered through her His deeper plans
To save it alive from the outer cold.

And here is a woman who understood
Herself, her work, and God's will with her,

To gather and scatter His sheaves of good,
And was meekly thankful, though men demur.

Would she have walked more nobly, think,
With a man beside her, to point the way,
Hand joining hand in the marriage-link?
Possibly, Yes: it is likelier, Nay.

For all men have not wisdom and might:
Love's eyes are tender, and blur the map;
And a wife will follow by faith, not sight,
In the chosen footprint, at any hap.

In the comfort of home who is gladder than she?
Yet, stirred by no murmur of "might have been,"
Her heart as a carolling bird soars free,
With the song of each nest she has glanced within.

Having the whole, she covets no part:
Hers is the bliss of all blessed things.
The tears that unto her eyelids start,
Are those which a generous pity brings;

Or the sympathy of heroic faith
With a holy purpose, achieved or lost.
To stifle the truth is to stop her breath,
For she rates a lie at its deadly cost.

Her friends are good women and faithful men,
Who seek for the True, and uphold the Right;
And who shall proclaim her the weaker, when
Her very presence puts sin to flight?

"And dreads she never the coming years?"
Gossip, what are the years to her?

All winds are fair, and the harbor nears,
And every breeze a delight will stir.

Transfigured under the sunset trees,
That wreathe her with shadowy gold and red,
She looks away to the purple seas,
Whereon her shallop will soon be sped.

She reads the hereafter by the here:
A beautiful Now, and a better To Be:
In life is all sweetness, in death no fear.
You waste your pity on such as she.

Weaving

All day she stands before her loom;
The flying shuttles come and go:
By grassy fields, and trees in bloom,
She sees the winding river flow.
And fancy's shuttle flieth wide,
And faster than the waters glide.

Is she entangled in her dreams,
Like that fair weaver of Shalott,
Who left her mystic mirror's gleams,
To gaze on light Sir Lancelot?
Her heart, a mirror sadly true,
Brings gloomier visions into view.

"I weave, and weave, the livelong day
The woof is strong, the warp is good:
I weave, to be my mother's stay;
I weave, to win my daily food:
But ever as I weave," saith she,
"The world of women haunteth me.

"The river glides along, one thread
In nature's mesh, so beautiful!
The stars are woven in; the red
Of sunrise; and the rain-cloud dull.
Each seems a separate wonder wrought;
Each blends with some more wondrous thought.

"So, at the loom of life, we weave
Our separate shreds, that varying fall,
Some stained, some fair; and, passing, leave
To God the gathering up of all,
In that full pattern, wherein man
Works blindly out the eternal plan.

"In his vast work, for good or ill,
The undone and the done he blends.
With whatsoever woof we fill,
To our weak hands His might He lends,
And gives the threads beneath His eye
The texture of eternity.

"Wind on, by willow and by pine,
Thou blue, untroubled Merrimack!
Afar, by sunnier streams than thine,
My sisters toil, with foreheads black;
And water with their blood this root,
Whereof we gather bounteous fruit.

"There be sad women, sick and poor;
And those who walk in garments soiled:
Their shame, their sorrow, I endure;
By their defect my hope is foiled:
The blot they bear is on my name;
Who sins, and I am not to blame?

"And how much of your wrong is mine,
 Dark women slaving at the South?
 Of your stolen grapes I quaff the wine;
 The bread you starve for fills my mouth:
 The beam unwinds, but every thread
 With blood of strangled souls is red.

"If this be so, we win and wear
 A Nessus-robe of poisoned cloth;
 Or weave them shrouds they may not
 Fathers and brothers falling both
 On ghastly, death-sown fields, that lie
 Beneath the tearless Southern sky.

"Alas! the weft has lost its white.
 It grows a hideous tapestry,
 That pictures war's abhorrent sight:
 Unroll not, web of destiny!
 Be the dark volume left unread,
 The tale untold,—the curse unsaid!"

So up and down before her loom
 She paces on, and to and fro,
 Till sunset fills the dusty room,
 And makes the water redly glow,
 As if the Merrimack's calm flood
 Were changed into a stream of blood.

Too soon fulfilled, and all too true
 The words she murmured as she wrought
 But, weary weaver, not to you
 Alone was war's stern message brought:
 "Woman!" it knelled from heart to heart,
 "Thy sister's keeper know thou art!"

Francis Watkins Harper:
1825–1911

Introduction

Francis Harper is an heroic figure, at once the most radical and the most devout of American women (and men?) poets. Born a free black in Baltimore, Maryland, her mother died when she was three (no record exists of her father). She was taken care of by an aunt, and went to school at her uncle's impressive and demanding Academy—a "school of oratory, literature, and debate"—until the age of thirteen. Despite her education, she could find employment only as a domestic, although the family she worked for owned a bookshop in which she read widely. After the 1850 Compromise and Fugitive Slave Act, her family left Baltimore's worsening conditions to go to Canada, although she herself went to Ohio, where she taught sewing at the Union Seminary, soon moving to another teaching post in Pennsylvania. The 1853 Maryland legislation declaring any free blacks visiting there subject to enslavement closed off her access to her original home, and impelled her into the Underground Railroad (most biographical data about her derives from William Still's account in his *Underground Railroad*). Working first in Philadelphia, she later moved North where her status as a single woman interfered less in her ability to serve. She became a popular and very active lecturer, traveling, most unusually, among white abolitionists, and contributing much of her earnings to the Railroad. A supporter of John Brown, she spent two weeks with his wife before his execution. In 1860 she married Fenton Harper of Cincinnati, living with him on his farm until his death in 1864. She had one child, Mary. During this time, her activism was greatly curtailed, although not stopped completely. On the death of her husband, she returned to active lecturing, traveling, and teaching, now in the cause of the freedmen. Again, almost uniquely, Harper crossed the color line, working with whites in abolition, suffrage, women's education, and temperance. She was active in the American Equal Rights Association, the Christian Temperance Union, the American Women's Suffrage Association, and the National Council of Women, as well as the National Council of Negro Women founded in 1896, and where she was elected vice-president in 1897.

Harper brings into her writing a wide range of black genres and modes. In poetic form she recasts elements from spirituals and hymns, oral traditions, slave narratives, and spiritual autobiography—an important mode of black female testimony, in which religious calling impels and strengthens creative expression, community identity, and political activism. In addition are her writings in prose, short stories, and *Iola Leroy*, a novel of passing and then reaffirmation of black identity (as is her long narrative poem *Moses: A Story of the Nile*, who first passes as Egyptian and then identifies as Hebrew). Although writing in Standard English, hers are among the earliest experiments in colloquial and dialect poetry, as in her Aunt Chloe sequence.

Harper's work takes shape through black, and often female, viewpoints. While her first commitment tends to be to her ethnic identity and community—both as black and as American—many female figures are featured, and not least among them, the figure of the female poet herself. This is constructed not as a solitary singer drawing upon its own transcendent imaginative power, but as a voice deeply embedded in community, speaking for and to it rather than by and of herself. She draws her authoritative power from her sense of participation in an historical destiny, in faith and pledge to a greater power of truth that has called her forth to this devotion. This poetry of calling is not a strategy employed by women in order to gain access to a wider domain, although this is one of its effects. Nor does it oppose private against public spheres. In Harper, religion in particular emerges in all its force as a median space between interiority and public action—with the possibility of public action itself founded in a sense of individual conscience, commitment, and agency. Harper's poems went through many volumes and editions—her first volumes sold overall 50,000 copies; and she included her essay "Christianity" in the many printings of *Poems on Miscellaneous Subjects*. Yet, as her poem "The Present Age" makes clear, her vision is resolutely non-doctrinal and non-dogmatic, a most general embrace of a great range of different spiritual and moral and cultural positions in mutual toleration, respect, and common aid.

This construction of a female poetic voice has wide implications for feminine poetics, even if grounded in Harper's very particular social, historical and ethnic case. It can be seen in "Bury Me in a Free Land." The poem opens not with a claim to personal authority or power, but with the poet putting her self to the side. The poem is in fact anti-monumental. The grave she invokes—from the outset invoking self-sacrifice—may be "where'er you will," among "earth's humblest graves." It is not for her own memorial. And if she conjures not only a "lowly plain" but a "lofty hill," this suggestion of Moses, buried on a hill but still anonymously and as servant to God and his people, affirms Harper's sense of the poet as prophet serving others. Here, as in much prophecy, the message is unpleasant. In a pattern of inversion that is one of her characteristic techniques, the land of the free is exposed as the home of slaves, and liberty comes to the dead, not the living. This is not to repudiate America, but to call it back to its own truest vision. She as poet, even though female, takes this position of leadership; not to have power over others, but to call them back to themselves, and to their true national life.

Harper in her poetry of calling thus speaks in answer to an historical vision and sense of moral commitment, which, however, also impel her into her own speaking voice. In this, she is very concretely set into a biblical tradition that is deeply American. In the ante-bellum period especially, a pervasive and explosive biblical discourse was shrilly central to the terms of American contest. Both

North and South claimed biblical sanction for their cultures—a disturbing circumstance Harper powerfully enacts in "Bible Defense of Slavery." Again through patterns of inversion, Harper shows the (black) "Servants" of biblical truth to be in dark mourning, while false (white) "reverend" men take biblical "light" and make it "dark." Their church becomes altars where truth is sacrificed, while the true worshipers breathe "sorrow" in their songs (in clear reference to the spirituals). At issue for Harper is not relativism. In her view, there is a clear good, and evil is its betrayal. The South, in claiming the Bible to defend slavery, distorts both its message and its authority—a message and authority that, to Harper, ground the very integrity and agency of every individual which slavery violates.

The Bible in Harper infuses her entire view of history, which is in this sense always a sacred history. This can be seen as judgment in "Retribution," and as redemptive in "Deliverance." It is a sacred history that, while measuring from certain moral positions, nevertheless places agency and creative responsibility within each individual soul. On the one hand, Harper does not waver in her belief in divine presence. On the other, it is for each unique and sacred soul to establish him and herself in relation to it. This is true for all. Yet, in Harper there is a particular, although not exclusive, focus through female figures—including those who have been cast to the side in biblical tradition. As in contemporary feminist writing, Harper recovers figures of women from obscurity. Vashti, the scorned queen of the Book of Esther; Rizpah, the suffering concubine of Saul in Second Samuel; Hagar, the repudiated wife of Abraham. Vashti is particularly arresting: treated recurrently by nineteenth-century American women poets (see also Jackson and Wilcox), this Queen at once fulfills a womanly nature (as seen by Harper) by refusing shameful exposure "before the crowd;" yet in doing so affirms her own "spotless name" (naming is a central topic in women's writing), "strong in her earnest womanhood." Ruth and Naomi stand as emblem of "The wealth of woman's love."

These womanly values as firm commitment to a sense of self in moral assertion equally characterizes Harper's poems on slavery. Treatments of slave auctions, of fugitives, of sexual violence and family rupture under slavery appear in much abolitionist writing. Harper represents slavery—"The Slave Mother," "Eliza Harris" (in homage to *Uncle Tom's Cabin*), "The Slave Auction," "The Fugitive's Wife"—through the viewpoints of the slaves, thus asserting their interiority, their inner spiritual and moral life—in itself a major argument against slavery, which would reduce the human to commodity only. By insisting on the sensibility of the slave, and not least enslaved women, Harper is "sentimental" in the recently recognized sense as addressing political topics through personal experience. Here again the line between public and private is challenged by her; where just asserting a private life to slaves is a political act.

Sadly, the denial of personhood to the black continued after emancipation. If "The Freedom Bell" and "The Change" proclaim the reconciliation of heaven and earth, freedom and answered prayer; the "Appeal" to the American people and to American women record the failure of this hope. Harper worked for the freedmen as she had done for the slave. In both efforts, she faced enormous—and, through Reconstruction, increasing—resistance and obstacles. The battle for "freedom's God" has turned post-war into rejection of the black soldier who fought it. Women's missions find worthy souls everywhere but in their own national home. The divine retribution that the war itself represented will not be stilled in this continued sin.

Harper never restricted herself only to slavery. The reduction of the human to economy, the betrayal of moral relationships for social ones, extends deep into America's nineteenth-century course. Harper, like so many other contemporary woman writers, seizes on the double standard not only as sexual, but as broadly cultural. In "The Double Standard" and "The Outcast," the seduced woman is outcast, but the seducer is well-established. In "Going East"—a woman's history of the Westward movement—the woman is wife, but her life is lived in a different dimension than the husband's pursuit of profit. "Simon's Feast" offers a biblical version of this call to recognize the destruction of the person (woman) in social strata disguised as moral criteria.

Harper's poetic is strongly one of viewpoint, address, and call. These, with her womanly focus, come to special and enjoyable form in the "Aunt Chloe" dramatic monologues. Experimental in its natural and near-dialect language, not to mention its identification with a woman ex-slave, the poem also serves as historical document. It faithfully records plantation debt and the impersonal selling-off of slaves to cover it; the destruction, indeed denial, of family, and of the black spirituality that countered with strength; the post-bellum political corruption (and a woman's views of it); the highly significant issue of slave literacy. Frederick Douglass recounts in his slave narrative the immense challenge and triumph it was for him to learn to read, despite the white's purposeful attempts to prevent blacks from doing so—not only on pragmatic grounds of writing their own passes but as undermining slavery itself, opening the mind and spirit to larger worlds. As "Learning to Read" records, this spiritual element of reading was also directly religious, in the reading of the Bible—"The hymns and Testament"—as ground of human dignity and freedom.

Harper's voice of the spiritual black tradition emerges in "Deliverance," as her own written spiritual. This poem shows all the sophistication of the spirituals themselves in its rendering of complex time-frames. Opening in the past, in prophetic call to Israel in Egypt—"Rise up! Rise up!"—the poem overlays biblical narrative with Harper's own immediate history. The poem is structured through a sequence of time-markers of repeated "when"s that point both to past and future: to redemption granted in the past as redemption promised in the future. That this promise had not yet been fulfilled in 1901 when the poem was written, is also attested by the switch to "Then," an aftermath in an as yet unattained future looking back at this very past to pledge to its still incomplete vision—all gathered and enacted within the space of this prophetic text.

Poems

Bury Me in a Free Land

Make me a grave where'er you will,
In a lowly plain, or a lofty hill,
Make it among earth's humblest graves,
But not in a land where men are slaves.

I could not rest if around my grave
I heard the steps of a trembling slave:
His shadow above my silent tomb
Would make it a place of fearful gloom.

I could not rest if I heard the tread
Of a coffle gang to the shambles led,
And the mother's shriek of wild despair
Rise like a curse on the trembling air.

I could not sleep if I saw the lash
Drinking her blood at each fearful gash,
And I saw her babes torn from her breast,
Like trembling doves from their parent nest.

I'd shudder and start if I heard the bay
Of blood-hounds seizing their human prey,
And I heard the captive plead in vain
As they bound afresh his galling chain.

If I saw young girls from their mother's arms
Bartered and sold for their youthful charms,
My eye would flash with a mournful flame,
My death-paled cheek grow red with shame.

I would sleep, dear friends, where bloated might
Can rob no man of his dearest right;
My rest shall be calm in any grave
Where none can call his brother a slave.

I ask no monument, proud and high
To arrest the gaze of the passers-by;
All that my yearning spirit craves,
Is bury me not in a land of slaves.

Bible Defence of Slavery

Take sackcloth of the darkest dye,
And shroud the pulpits round!
Servants of Him that cannot lie,
Sit mourning on the ground.

Let holy horror blanch each cheek,
Pale every brow with fears:
And rocks and stones, if ye could speak,
Ye well might melt to tears!

Let sorrow breathe in every tone,
In every strain ye raise;
Insult not God's majestic throne
With th' mockery of praise.

A reverend man, whose light should be
The guide of age and youth,

Brings to the shrine of slavery
The sacrifice of truth!

For the direst wrong of man imposed,
Since Sodom's fearful cry,
The word of life has been enclosed,
To give your God the lie.

Oh! when we pray for the heathen lands,
And plead for their dark shores,
Remember Slavery's cruel hands
Make heathens at your doors!

Vashti

She leaned her head upon her hand
And heard the the King's decree—
"My lords are feasting in my halls;
Bid Vashti come to me.

"I've shown the treasures of my house,
My costly jewels rare,
But with the glory of her eyes
No rubies can compare.

"Adorn'd and crown'd I'd have her come,
With all her queenly grace,
And, 'mid my lords-and mighty men,
Unveil her lovely face.

"Each gem that sparkles in my crown,
Or glitters on my throne,
Grows poor and, pale when she appears,
My beautiful, my own!"

All waiting stood the chamberlains
To hear the Queen's reply.
They saw her cheek grow deathly pale,
But light flash'd to her eye:

"Go, tell the King," she proudly said,
"That I am Persia's Queen,
And by his crowds of merry men
I never will be seen.

"I'll take the crown from off my head
And tread it 'neath my feet,
Before their rude and careless gaze
My shrinking eyes shall meet.

"A queen unveil'd before the crowd!—
Upon each lip my name!—
Why, Persia's women all would blush
And weep for Vashti's shame!

"Go back!" she cried, and waved her hand,
And grief was in her eye:
"Go, tell the King," she sadly said,
"That I would rather die."

They brought her massage to the King;
Dark flash'd his angry eye;
'Twas as the lightning ere the storm
Hath swept in fury by.

Then bitterly outspoke the King,
Through purple lips of wrath—
"What shall be done to her who dares
To cross your monarch's path?"

Then spoke his wily counsellors—
"O King of this fair land!
From distant Ind to Ethiop,
All bow to thy command.

"But if, before thy servant's eyes,
This thing they plainly see,
That Vashti doth not heed thy will
Nor yield herself to thee,

"The women, restive 'neath our rule,
Would learn to scorn our name,
And from her deed to us would come
Reproach and burning shame.

"Then, gracious King, sign with thy hand
This stern but just decree,
That Vashti lay aside her crown,
Thy Queen no more to be."

She heard again the King's command,
And left her high estate;
Strong in her earnest womanhood,
She calmly met her fate.

And left the palace of the King,
Proud of her spotless name—
A woman who could bend to grief,
But would not bow to shame.

Dedication Poem

Dedication Poem on the reception of the annex to the home for aged colored people, from the bequest of Mr. Edward T. Parker.

Outcast from her home in Syria
In the lonely, dreary wild;
Heavy hearted, sorrow stricken,
Sat a mother and her child.

There was not a voice to cheer her
Not a soul to share her fate;
She was weary, he was fainting,
And life seemed so desolate.

Far away in sunny Egypt
Was lone Hagar's native land;
Where the Nile in kingly bounty
Scatters bread throughout the land.

In the tents of princely Abram
She for years had found a home;
Till the stern decree of Sarah
Sent her forth the wild to roam.

Hour by hour she journeyed onward
From the shelter of their tent
Till her footsteps slowly faltered
And the water all was spent;

Then she veiled her face in sorrow,
Feared her child would die of thirst;
Till her eyes with tears so holden
Saw a sparkling fountain burst.

Oh! how happy was that mother,
What a soothing of her pain;

When she saw her child reviving,
Life rejoicing through each vein.

Does not life repeat this story,
Tell it over day by day?
Of the fountain of refreshment
Ever springing by our way.

Here is one by which we gather,
On this bright and happy day.
Just to bask beside a fountain
Making gladder life's highway.

Bringing unto hearts now aged
Who have borne life's burdens long,
Such a gift of love and mercy
As deserves our sweetest song.

Such a gift that even heaven
May rejoice with us below,
If the pure and holy angels
Join us in our joy and woe.

May the memory of the giver
In this home—where age may rest,
Float like fragrance through the ages,
Ever blessing, ever blest.

When the gates of pearl are opened
May we there this friend behold
Drink with him from living fountains,
Walk with him the streets of gold.

When life's shattered cords of music
Shall again be sweetly sung;

Then our hearts with life immortal,
Shall be young, forever young.

Rizpah, the Daughter of Ai

Tidings! Sad tidings for the daughter of Ai,
They are bearing her prince and loved away,
Destruction falls like a mournful pall
On the fallen house of ill-fated Saul.

And Rizpah hears that her loved must die,
But she hears it all with a tearless eye;
And clasping her hand with grief and dread
She meekly bows her queenly head.

The blood has left her blanching cheek,
Her quivering lips refuse to speak,
Oh! grief like hers has learned no tone—
A world of grief is all its own.

But the deed is done, and the hand is stay'd
That havoc among the brethren made,
And Rizpah takes her lowly seat
To watch the princely dead at her feet.

The jackall crept out with a stealthy tread,
To battern and feast on the noble dead;
The vulture bore down with a heavy wing
To dip his beak in life's stagnant spring.

The hyena heard the jackall's howl,
And he bounded forth with a sullen growl,
When Rizpah's shriek rose on the air
Like a tone from the caverns of despair.

She sprang from her sad and lowly seat,
For a moment her heart forgot to beat,
And the blood rushes up to her marble cheek
And a flash to her eye so sad and meek.

The vulture paused in his downward flight,
As she raised her form to its queenly height,
The hyena's eye had a horrid glare,
As he turned again to his desert lair.

The jackall slunk back with a quickened tread,
From his cowardly search of Rizpah's dead;
Unsated he turned from the noble prey,
Subdued by the glance of the daughter of Ai.

Of grief! that a mother's heart should know,
Such a weary weight of consuming woe,
For seldom if ever earth has known
Such love as the daughter of Ai hath known.

Ruth and Naomi

"Turn my daughters, full of woe,
Is my heart so sad and lone?
Leave me children—I would go
To my loved and distant home.

"From my bosom death has torn
Husband, children, all my stay,
Left me not a single one,
For my life's declining day.

"Want and woe surround my way,
Grief and famine where I tread;

In my native land they say
God is giving Jacob bread."

Naomi ceased, her daughters wept,
Their yearning hearts were filled;
Falling upon her withered neck,
Their grief in tears distill'd.

Like rain upon a blighted tree,
The tears of Orpah fell
Kissing the pale and quivering lip,
She breathed her sad farewell.

But Ruth stood up, on her brow
There lay a heavenly calm;
And from her lips came, soft and low
Words like a holy charm.

"I will not leave thee, on thy brow
Are lines of sorrow, age and care;
Thy form is bent, thy step is slow,
Thy bosom stricken, lone and sear.

"Oh! when thy heart and home were glad,
I freely shared thy joyous lot;
And now that heart is lone and sad,
Cease to entreat—I'll leave thee not.

"Oh! if a lofty palace proud
Thy future home shall be;
Where sycophants around thee crowd,
I'll share that home with thee.

"And if on earth the humblest spot,
Thy future home shall prove;

I'll bring into thy lonely lot
The wealth of woman's love.

"Go where thou wilt, my steps are there,
  Our path in life is one;
Thou hast no lot I will not share,
  'Till life itself be done.

"My country and my home for thee,
  I freely, willingly resign,
Thy people shall my people be,
  Thy God he shall be mine.

"Then, mother dear, entreat me not
  To turn from following thee;
My heart is nerved to share thy lot,
  Whatever that may be."

Burial of Sarah

He stood before the sons of Heth,
  And bowed his sorrowing head;
"I've come," he said, "to buy a place
  Where I may lay my dead.

"I am a stranger in your land,
  My home has lost its light;
Grant me a place where I may lay
  My dead away from sight."

Then tenderly the sons of Heth
  Gazed on the mourner's face,
And said, "Oh, Prince, amid our dead,
  Choose thou her resting-place.

"The sepulchres of those we love,
We place at thy command;
Against the plea thy grief hath made
We close not heart nor hand."

The patriarch rose and bowed his head,
And said, "One place I crave;
'Tis at the end of Ephron's field,
And called Machpelah's cave.

"Entreat him that he sell to me
For her last sleep that cave;
I do not ask for her I loved
The freedom of a grave."

The son of Zohar answered him,
"Hearken, my lord, to me;
Before our sons, the field and cave
I freely give to thee."

"I will not take it as a gift,"
The grand old man then said;
"I pray thee let me buy the place
Where I may lay my dead."

And with the promise in his heart,
His seed should own that land,
He gave the shekels for the field
He took from Ephron's hand.

And saw afar the glorious day
His chosen seed should tread,
The soil where he in sorrow lay
His loved and cherished dead.

Retribution

Judgment slumbered. God in mercy
Stayed his strong avenging hand;
Sent them priests and sent them prophets,
But they would not understand.

Judgment lingered; men, grown bolder,
Gloried in their shame and guilt;
And the blood of God's poor children
Was as water freely spilt.

Then arose a cry to heaven,
Deep and startling, sad and wild,
Sadder than the wail of Egypt,
Mourning for the first-born child.

For the sighing of the needy
God at length did bare his hand,
And the footsteps of his judgments
Echoed through the guilty land.

Oh! the terror, grief and anguish;
Oh! the bitter, fearful strife,
When the judgments of Jehovah
Pressed upon the nation's life.

And the land did reel and tremble
'Neath the terror of his frown,
For its guilt lay heavy on it,
Pressing like an iron crown.

As a warning to the nations,
Bathed in blood and swathed in fire,
Lay the once oppressing nation,
Smitten by God's fearful ire.

Simon's Feast

He is coming, she said, to Simon's feast,
The prophet of Galilee,
Though multitudes around him throng
In longing his face to see.

He enters the home as Simon's guest,
But he gives no welcome kiss;
He brings no water to bathe his feet—
Why is Simon so remiss?

If a prophet, he will surely know
The guilt of my darkened years;
With broken heart I'll see his face,
And bathe his feet with my tears.

No holy rabbi lays his hand
In blessing on my head;
No loving voice floats o'er the path,
The downer path I tread.

Unto the Master's side she pressed,
A penitent, frail and fair,
Rained on his feet a flood of tears,
And then wiped them with her hair.

Over the face of Simon swept
An air of puzzled surprise;
Can my guest a holy prophet be,
And not this woman despise?

Christ saw the thoughts that Simon's heart
Had written upon his face,
Kindly turned to the sinful one
In her sorrow and disgrace.

Where Simon only saw the stains,
Where sin and shame were rife,
Christ looked beneath and saw the perms
Or a fair, outflowering life.

Like one who breaks a galling chain,
And sets a prisoner free,
He rent her fetters with the words,
"Thy sins are forgiven thee."

God be praised for the gracious words
Which came through that woman's touch,
That souls redeemed thro' God's dear Son
May learn to love him so much;

That souls once red with guilt and crime
May their crimson stains outgrow;
The scarlet spots upon their lives
Become whiter than driven snow.

The Slave Auction

The sale began—young girls were there,
Defenceless in their wretchedness,
Whose stifled sobs of deep despair
Revealed their anguish and distress.

And mothers stood with streaming eyes,
And saw their dearest children sold;
Unheeded rose their bitter cries,
While tyrants bartered them for gold.

And woman, with her love and truth—
For these in sable forms may dwell—

Gaz'd on the husband of her youth,
With anguish none may paint or tell.

And men, whose sole crime was their hue,
The impress of their Maker's hand,
And frail and shrinking children, too,
Were gathered in that mournful band.

Ye who have laid your love to rest,
And wept above their lifeless clay,
Know not the anguish of that breast,
Whose lov'd are rudely torn away.

Ye may not know how desolate
Are bosoms rudely forced to part,
And how a dull and heavy weight
Will press the life-drops from the heart.

The Slave Mother

Heard you that shriek? It rose
So wildly on the air,
It seemed as if a burden'd heart
Was breaking in despair.

Saw you those hands so sadly clasped—
The bowed and feeble hand—
The shuddering of that fragile form—
That look of grief and dread?

Saw you the sad, imploring eye?
Its every glance was pain,
As if a storm of agony
Were sweeping through the brain.

She is a mother, pale with fear,
Her boy clings to her side,
And in her kirtle vainly tries
His trembling form to hide.

He is not hers, although she bore
For him a mother's pains;
He is not hers, although her blood
Is coursing through his veins!

He is not hers, for cruel hands
May rudely tear apart
The only wreath of household love
That binds her breaking heart.

His love has been a joyous light
That o'er her pathway smiled,
A fountain gushing ever new,
Amid life's desert wild.

His lightest word has been a tone
Of music round her heart,
Their lives a streamlet blent in one—
Oh, Father! must they part?

They tear him from her circling arms,
Her last and fond embrace.
Oh! never more may her sad eyes
Gaze on his mournful face.

No marvel, then, these bitter shrieks
Disturb the listening air;
She is a mother, and her heart
Is breaking in despair.

Eliza Harris

Like a fawn from the arrow, startled and wild,
A woman swept by us, bearing a child;
In her eyes was the night of a settled despair,
And her brow was o'ershaded with anguish and care.

She was nearing the river—in reaching the brink,
She heeded no danger, she paused not to think;
For she is a mother—her child is a slave—
And she'll give him his freedom, or find him a grave!

It was a vision to haunt us, that innocent face—
So pale in its aspect, so fair in its grace;
As the tramp of the horse and the bay of the hound,
With the fetters that gall, were trailing the ground!

She was nerv'd by despair, and strengthened by woe,
As she leap'd o'er the chasms that yawn'd from below;
Death howl'd in the tempest, and rav'd in the blast,
But she heard not the sound till the danger was past.

Oh! how shall I speak of my proud country's shame
Of the stains on her glory, how give them their name?
How say that her banner in mockery waves—
Her star—spangled banner—o'er millions of slaves?

How say that the lawless may torture and chase
A woman whose crime is the hue of her face?
How the depths of the forest may echo around
With the shrieks of despair, and the bay of the hound?

With her step on the ice, and her arm on her child,
The danger was fearful, the pathway was wild;
But, aided by Heaven, she gained a free shore,
Where the friends of humanity open'd their door.

So fragile and lovely, so fearfully pale,
Like a lily that bends to the breath of the gale,
Save the heave of her breast, and the sway of her hair,
You'd have thought her a statue of fear and despair.

In agony close to her bosom she press'd
The life of her heart, the child of her breast—
Oh! love from its tenderness gathering might,
Had strengthen'd her soul for the dangers of light.

But she's free:—yes, free from the land where the slave
From the hound of oppression must rest in the grave;
Where bondage and torture, where scourges and drains
Have plac'd on our banner indelible stains.

The bloodhounds have miss'd the scent of her way;
The hunter is rifled and foil'd of his prey;
Fierce jargon and cursing, with clanking of chains,
Make sounds of strange discord on Liberty's plains.

With the rapture of love and fullness of bliss,
She plac'd on his brow a mother's fond kiss:—
Oh! poverty, danger and death she can brave,
For the child of her love is no longer a slave!

The Fugitive's Wife

It was my sad and weary lot
To toil in slavery;
But one thing cheered my lowly cot—
My husband was with me.

One evening, as our children played
Around our cabin door,

I noticed on his brow a shade
I'd never seen before;

And in his eyes a gloomy night
Of anguish and despair;—
I gazed upon their troubled light,
To read the meaning there.

He strained me to his heaving heart—
—My own beat wild with fear;
I knew not, but I sadly felt
There might be evil near.

He vainly strove to cast aside
The tears that fell like rain:—
Too frail, indeed, is manly pride,
To strive with grief and pain.

Again he clasped me to his breast,
And said that we must part:
I tried to speak—but, oh! it seemed
An arrow reached my heart.

"Bear not," I cried, "unto your grave,
The yoke you've borne from birth;
No longer live a helpless slave,
The meanest thing on earth!"

The Slave Mother, A Tale of the Ohio

I have but four, the treasures of my soul,
They lay like doves around my heart;
I tremble lest some cruel hand
Should tear my household wreaths apart.

My baby girl, with childish glance,
Looks curious in my anxious eye,
She little knows that for her sake
Deep shadows round my spirit lie.

My playful boys could I forget,
My home might seem a joyous spot,
But with their sunshine mirth I blend
The darkness of their future lot.

And thou my babe, my darling one,
My last, my loved, my precious child,
Oh! when I think upon thy doom
My heart grows faint and then throbs wild.

The Ohio's bridged and spanned with ice,
The northern star is shining bright,
I'll take the nestlings of my heart
And search for freedom by its light.

Winter and night were on the earth,
And feebly moaned the shivering trees,
A sigh of winter seemed to run
Through every murmur of the breeze.

She fled, and with her children all,
She reached the stream and crossed it o'er,
Bright visions of deliverance came
Like dreams of plenty to the poor.

Dreams! vain dreams, heroic mother,
Give all thy hopes and struggles o'er,
The pursuer is on thy track,
And the hunter at thy door.

Judea's refuge cities had power
To shelter, shield and save,
E'en Rome had altars, 'neath whose shade
Might crouch the wan and weary slave.

But Ohio had no sacred fane,
To human rights so consecrate,
Where thou may'st shield thy hapless ones
From their darkly gathering fate.

Then, said the mournful mother,
If Ohio cannot save,
I will do a deed for freedom,
Shalt find each child a grave.

I will save my precious children
From their darkly threatened doom,
I will hew their path to freedom
Through the portals of the tomb.

A moment in the sunlight,
She held a glimmering knife,
The next moment she had bathed it
In the crimson fount of life.

They snatched away the fatal knife,
Her boys shrieked wild with dread;
The baby girl was pale and cold,
They raised it up, the child was dead.

Sends this deed of fearful daring
Through my country's heart no thrill,
Do the icy hands of slavery
Every pure emotion chill?

Oh! if there is any honor,
Truth or justice in the land,
Will ye not, us men and Christians,
On the side of freedom stand?

Ethiopia

Yes! Ethiopia yet shall stretch
Her bleeding hands abroad;
Her cry of agony shall reach
The burning throne of God.

The tyrant's yoke from off her neck,
His fetters from her soul,
The mighty hand of God shall break,
And spurn the base control.

Redeemed from dust and freed from chains,
Her sons shall lift their eyes;
From cloud-capt hills and verdant plains
Shall shouts of triumph rise.

Upon her dark, despairing brow,
Shall play a smile of peace;
For God shall bend unto her woe,
And bid her sorrows cease.

'Neath sheltering vines and stately palms
Shall laughing children play,
And aged sires with joyous psalms
Shall gladden every day.

Secure by night, and blest by day,
Shall pass her happy hours;

Nor human tigers hunt for prey
Within her peaceful bowers.

Then, Ethiopia! stretch, oh! stretch
Thy bleeding hands abroad;
Thy cry of agony shall reach
And find redress from God.

Free Labor

I wear an easy garment,
O'er it no toiling slave
Wept tears of hopeless anguish,
In his passage to the grave.

And from its ample folds
Shall rise no cry to God,
Upon its warp and woof shall be
No stain of tears and blood.

Oh, lightly shall it press my form,
Unladen with a sigh,
I shall not 'mid its rustling hear,
Some sad despairing cry.

This fabric is too light to bear
The weight of bondsmen's tears,
I shall not in its texture trace
The agony of years.

Too light to bear a smother'd sigh,
From some lorn woman's heart,
Whose only wreath of household love
Is rudely torn apart.

Then lightly shall it press my form,
Unburden'd by a sigh;
And from its seams and folds shall rise,
No voice to pierce the sky,

And witness at the throne of God,
In language deep and strong,
That I have nerv'd Oppression's hand,
For deeds of guilt and wrong.

The Freedom Bell

Ring, aye, ring the freedom bell,
And let its tones be loud and clear;
With glad hosannas let it swell
Until it reach the Bondman's ear.

Through pain that wrings the life apart,
And spasms full of deadly strife,
And throes that shake the nation's heart,
The fainting land renews her life.

Where shrieks and groans distract the air,
And sods grow red with crimson rain,
The ransom'd slave shall kneel in prayer
And bury deep his rusty chain.

There cheeks now pale with sickening dread,
And brows grow dark with cruel wrath,
Shall Freedom's banner wide be spread
And Hope and Peace attend her path.

White-robed and pure her feet shall move
O'er rifts of ruin deep and wide;

Her hands shall span with lasting love
The chasms rent by hate and pride.

There waters, blush'd with human gore,
Unsullied streams shall purl along;
Where crashed the battle's awful roar
Shall rise the Freeman's joyful song.

Then ring, aye, ring the freedom bell,
Proclaiming all the nation free;
Let earth with sweet thanksgiving swell
And heaven catch up the melody.

The Change

The blue sky arching overhead,
The green turf 'neath my daily tread,
All glorified by freedom's light,
Grow fair and lovely to my sight.

The very winds that sweep along
Seemed burdened with a lovely song,
Nor shrieks nor groans of grief or fear,
Float on their wings and pain my ear.

No more with dull and aching breast,
Roused by the horn—I rise from rest.
Content and cheerful with my lot,
I greet the sun and leave my cot.

For darling child and loving wife
I toil with newly waken'd life;
The light that lingers round her smile
The shadows from my soul beguile.

The prattle of my darling boy.
Fills my old heart with untold joy;
Before his laughter, mirth and song
Fade out long scores of grief and wrong.

Oh, never did the world appear
So lovely to my eye and ear,
'Till Freedom came, with Joy and Peace,
And bade my hateful bondage cease!

Fifteenth Amendment

Beneath the burden of our joy
Tremble, O wires, from East to West!
Fashion with words your tongues of fire,
To tell the nation's high behest.

Outstrip the winds, and leave behind
The murmur of the restless waves;
Nor tarry with your glorious news,
Amid the ocean's coral caves.

Ring out! ring out! your sweetest chimes,
Ye bells, that call to praise;
Let every heart with gladness thrill,
And songs of joyful triumph raise.

Shake off the dust, O rising race!
Crowned as a brother and a man;
Justice to-day asserts her claim,
And from thy brow fades out the ban.

With freedom's chrism upon thy head,
Her precious ensign in thy hand,

Go place thy once despised name
Amid the noblest of the land.

A ransomed race! Give God the praise,
Who let thee through a crimson sea,
And 'mid the storm of fire and blood,
Turned out the war-cloud's light to thee.

An Appeal to the American People

When a dark and fearful strife
Raged around the nation's life,
And the traitor plunged his steel
Where your quivering hearts could feel,
When your cause did need a friend,
We were faithful to the end.

When we stood with bated breath,
Facing fiery storms of death,
And the war-cloud, red with wrath,
Fiercely swept around our path,
Did our hearts with terror quail?
Or our courage ever fail?

When the captive, wanting bread,
Sought our poor and lowly shed,
And the blood-hounds missed his way,
Did we e'er his path betray?
Filled we not his heart with trust
As we shared with him our crust?

With your soldiers, side by side,
Helped we turn the battle's tide,
Till o'er ocean, stream and shore,
Waved the rebel flag no more,

And above the rescued sod
Praises rose to freedom's God.

But to-day the traitor stands
With crimson on his hands,
Scowling 'neath his brow of hate,
On our weak and desolate,
With the blood-rust on the knife.
Aimed at the nation's life.

Asking you to weakly yield
All we won upon the field,
To ignore, on land and flood,
All the offerings of our blood,
And to write above our slain
"They have fought and died in vain."

To your manhood we appeal,
Lest the traitor's iron heel
Grind and trample in the dust
All our new-born hope and trust,
And the name of freedom be
Linked with bitter mockery.

An Appeal to my Country Women

You can sigh o'er the sad-eyed Armenian
Who weeps in her desolate home.
You can mourn o'er the exile of Russia
From kindred and friends doomed to roam.

You can pity the men who have woven
From passion and appetite chains
To coil with a terrible tension
Around their heartstrings and brains.

You can sorrow o'er little children
Disinherited from their birth,
The wee waifs and toddlers neglected,
Robbed of sunshine, music and mirth.

For beasts you have gentle compassion;
Your mercy and pity they share.
For the wretched, outcast and fallen
You have tenderness, love and care.

But hark! from our Southland are floating
Sobs of anguish, murmurs of pain,
And women heart-stricken are weeping
Over their tortured and their slain.

On their brows the sun has left traces;
Shrink not from their sorrow in scorn.
When they entered the threshold of being
The children of a King were born.

Each comes as a guest to the table
The hands of our God has outspread,
To fountains that ever leap upward,
To share in the soil we all tread.

When we plead for the wrecked and fallen,
The exile from far-distant shores,
Remember that men are still wasting
Life's crimson around our own doors.

Have ye not, oh, my favored sisters,
Just a plea, a prayer or a tear,
For mothers who dwell 'neath the shadows
Of agony, hatred and fear?

Men may tread down the poor and lowly,
May crush them in anger and hate,
But surely the mills of God's justice
Will grind out the grist of their fate.

Oh, people sin-laden and guilty,
So lusty and proud in your prime,
The sharp sickles of God's retribution
Will gather your harvest of crime.

Weep not, oh my well-sheltered sisters,
Weep not for the Negro alone,
But weep for your sons who must gather
The crops which their fathers have sown.

Go read on the, tombstones of nations
Of chieftains who masterful trod,
The sentence which time has engraven,
That they had forgotten their God.

'Tis the judgment of God that men reap
The tares which in madness they sow,
Sorrow follows the footsteps of crime,
And Sin is the consort of Woe.

A Double Standard

Do you blame me that I loved him?
If when standing all alone
I cried for bread a careless world
Pressed to my lips a stone.

Do you blame me that I loved him,
That my heart beat glad and free,

When he told me in the sweetest tones
He loved but only me?

Can you blame me that I did not see
Beneath his burning kiss
The serpent's wiles, nor even hear
The deadly adder hiss?

Can you blame me that my heart grew cold
That the tempted, tempter turned;
When he was feted and caressed
And I was coldly spurned?

Would you blame him, when you draw from me
Your dainty robes aside.
If he with gilded baits should claim
Your fairest as his bride?

Would you blame the world if it should press
On him a civic crown;
And see me struggling in the depth
Then harshly press me down?

Crime has no sex and yet to-day
I wear the brand of shame;
Whilst he amid the gay and proud
Still bears an honored name.

Can you blame me if I've learned to think
Your hate of vice a sham,
When you so coldly crushed me down
And then excused the man?

Would you blame me if to-morrow
The coroner should say,

A wretched girl, outcast, forlorn,
Has thrown her life away?

Yes, blame me for my downward course,
But oh! remember well,
Within your homes you press the hand
That led me down to hell.

I'm glad God's ways are not our ways,
He does not see as man,
Within His love I know there's room
For those whom others ban.

I think before His great white throne,
His throne of spotless light,
That whited sepulchres shall wear
The hue of endless night.

That I who fell, and he who sinned,
Shall reap as we have sown;
That each the burden of his loss
Must bear and bear alone.

No golden weights can turn the scale
Of justice in His sight;
And what is wrong in woman's life
In man's cannot be right.

The Contrast

They scorned her for her sinning,
Spoke harshly of her fall,
Nor let the hand of mercy
To break her hated thrall.

The dews of meek repentance
Stood in her downcast eye:
Would no one heed her anguish?
All pass her coldly by?

From the cold, averted glances
Of each reproachful eye,
She turned aside, heart-broken,
And laid her down to die.

And where was he, who sullied
Her once unspotted name;
Who lured her from life's brightness
To agony and shame?

Who left her on life's billows,
A wrecked and ruined thing;
Who brought the winter of despair
Upon Hope's blooming spring?

Through the halls of wealth and fashion
In gaiety and pride,
He was leading to the altar
A fair and lovely bride!

None scorned him for his sinning,
Few saw it through his gold;
His crimes were only foibles,
And these were gently told.

Before him rose a vision,
A maid of beauty rare;
Then a pale, heart-broken woman,
The image of despair.

Next came a sad procession,
With many a sob and tear;
A widow'd, childless mother
Totter'd by an humble bier.

The vision quickly faded,
The sad, unwelcome sight;
But his lip forgot its laughter,
And his eye its careless light.

A moment, and the flood-gates
Of memory opened wide;
And remorseful recollection
Flowed like a lava tide.

That widow's wail of anguish
Seemed strangely blending there,
And mid the soft lights floated
That image of despair.

The Revel

"He knoweth not that the dead are there."

In yonder halls reclining
Are forms surpassing fair,
And brilliant lights are shining,
But, oh! the dead are there!

There's music, song and dance,
There's banishment of care,
And mirth in every glance,
But, oh! the dead are there!

The wine cup's sparkling glow
Blends with the viands rare,

There's revelry and show,
But still, the dead are there!

'Neath that flow of song and mirth
Runs the current of despair,
But the simple sons of earth
Know not the dead are there!

They'll shudder start and tremble,
They'll weep in wild despair
When the solemn truth breaks on them,
That the dead, the dead are there!

Going East

She came from the East a fair, young bride,
With a light and bounding heart,
To find in the distant West a home
With her husband to make a start.

He builded his cabin far away,
Where the prairie flower bloomed wild;
Her love made lighter all his toil,
And joy and hope around him smiled.

She plied her hands to life's homely tasks,
And helped to build his fortunes up;
While joy and grief, like bitter and sweet,
Were mingled and mixed in her cup.

He sowed in his fields of golden grain,
All the strength of his manly prime;
Nor music of bides, nor brooks, nor bees,
Was as sweet as the dollar's chime.

She toiled and waited through weary years
For the fortune that came at length;
But toil and care and hope deferred,
Had stolen and wasted her strength.

The cabin changed to a stately home,
Rich carpets were hushing her tread;
But light was fading from her eye,
And the bloom from her cheek had fled.

Her husband was adding field to field,
And new wealth to his golden store;
And little thought the shadow of death
Was entering in at his door.

Slower and heavier grew her step,
While his gold and his gains increased;
But his proud domain had not the charm
Of her humble home in the East.

He had no line to sound the depths
Of her tears repressed and unshed;
Nor dreamed 'mid plenty a human heart
Could be starving, but not for bread.

Within her eye was a restless light,
And a yearning that never ceased,
A longing to see the dear old home
She had a left in the distant East.

A longing to clasp her mother's hand,
And nestle close to her heart,
And to feel the heavy cares of life
Like the sun-kissed shadows depart.

The hungry heart was stilled at last;
Its restless, baffled yearning ceased.
A lonely man sat by the bier
Of a corpse that was going East.

The Present Age

Say not the age is hard and cold—
I think it brave and grand;
When men of diverse sects and creeds
Are clasping hand in hand.

The Parsee from his sacred fires
Beside the Christian kneels;
And clearer light to Islam's eyes
The word of Christ reveals.

The Brahmin from his distant home
Brings thoughts of ancient lore;
The Bhuddist breaking bonds of caste
Divides mankind no more.

The meek-eyed sons of far Cathay
Are welcome round the board;
Not greed, nor malice drives away
These children of our Lord.

And Judah from whose trusted hands
Came oracles divine;
Now sits with those around whose hearts
The light of God doth shine.

Japan unbars her long sealed gates
From islands far away;

Her sons are lifting up their eyes
To greet the coming day.

The Indian child from forests wild
Has learned to read and pray;
The tomahawk and scalping knife
From him have passed away.

From centuries of servile toil
The Negro finds release,
And builds the fanes of prayer and praise
Unto the God of Peace.

England and Russia face to face
With Central Asia meet;
And on the far Pacific coast
Chinese and natives greet.

Crusaders once with sword and shield
The Holy Land to save;
From Moslem hands did strive to clutch
The dear Redeemer's grave.

A battle greater, grander far
Is for the present age;
A crusade for the rights of man
To brighten history's page.

Where labor faints and bows her head,
And want consorts with crime;
Or men grown faithless sadly say
That evil is the time.

There is the field, the vantage ground
For every earnest heart;

To side with justice, truth and right
And act a noble part.

To save from ignorance and vice
The poorest, humblest child;
To make our age the fairest one
On which the sun has smiled;

To plant the roots of coming years
In mercy, love and truth;
And bid our weary, saddened earth
Again renew her youth.

Oh! earnest hearts! toil on in hope,
'Till darkness shrinks from light;
To fill the earth with peace and joy,
Let youth and age unite;

To stay the floods of sin and shame
That sweep from shore to shore;
And furl the banners strained with blood,
'Till war shall be no more.

Blame not the age, nor think it full
Of evil and unrest;
But say of every other age,
"This one shall be the best."

The age to brighten every path
By sin and sorrow trod;
For loving hearts to usher in
The commonwealth of God.

God Bless Our Native Land

God bless our native land,
Land of the newly free,
Oh may she ever stand
For truth and liberty.

God bless our native land,
Where sleep our kindred dead,
Let peace at thy command
Above their graves be shed.

God help our native land,
Bring surcease to her strife,
And shower from thy hand
A more abundant life.

God bless our native land,
Her homes and children bless,
Oh may she ever stand
For truth and righteousness.

The Artist

He stood before his finished work;
His heart beat warm and high;
But they who gazed upon the youth
Knew well that he must die.

For many days a fever fierce
Had burned into his life;
But full of high impassioned art,
He bore the fearful strife.

And wrought in ecstasy and hope
The image of his brain;
He felt the death throes at his heart,
But labored through the pain.

The statue seemed to glow with life—
A costly work of art;
For it he paid the fervent blood
From his own eager heart.

With kindling eye and flushing cheek
But slowly laboring breath,
He gazed upon his finished work,
Then sought his couch of death.

And when the plaudits of the crowd
Came like the south wind's breath,
The dreamy, gifted child of art
Had closed his eyes in death.

Songs for the People

Let me make the songs for the people,
Songs for the old and young;
Songs to stir like a battle-cry
Wherever they are sung.

Not for the clashing of sabres,
Nor carnage nor for strife;
But songs to thrill the hearts of men
With more abundant life.

Let me make the songs for the weary,
Amid life's fever and fret,

Till hearts shall relax their tension,
And careworn brows forget.

Let me sing for little children,
Before their footsteps stray,
Sweet anthems of love and duty,
To float o'er life's highway.

I would sing for the poor and aged,
When shadows dim their sight;
Of the bright and restful mansions,
Where there shall be no night.

Our world, so worn and weary,
Needs music, pure and strong,
To hush the jangle and discords
Of sorrow, pain, and wrong.

Music to soothe all its sorrow,
Till war and crime shall cease;
And the hearts of men grown tender
Girdle the world with peace.

Aunt Chloe

I remember, well remember,
That dark and dreadful day,
When they whispered to me, "Chloe,
Your children's sold away!"

It seemed as if a bullet
Had shot me through and through,
And I felt as if my heart-strings
Was breaking right in two.

And I says to cousin Milly,
"There must be some mistake;
Where's Mistus?" "In the great house crying—
Crying like her heart would break.

"And the lawyer's there with Mistus;
Says he's come to 'ministrate,
'Cause when master died he just left
Heap of debt on the estate.

"And I thought 'twould do you good
To bid your boys good-bye—
To kiss them both and shake their hands,
And have a hearty cry.

"Oh! Chloe, I knows how you feel,
'Cause I'se been through it all;
I thought my poor old heart would break,
When master sold my Saul."

Just then I heard the footsteps
Of my children at the door,
And then I rose right up to meet them,
But I fell upon the floor.

And I heard poor Jakey saying,
"Oh, mammy, don't you cry!"
And I felt my children kiss me
And bid me, both, good-bye.

Then I had a mighty sorrow,
Though I nursed it all alone;
But I wasted to a shadow,
And turned to skin and bone.

But one day dear uncle Jacob,
(In heaven he's now a saint)
Said, "Your poor heart is in the fire,
But child you must not faint."

Then I said to uncle Jacob,
"If I was good like you,
When the heavy trouble dashed me
I'd know just what to do."

Then he said to me, "Poor Chloe,
The way is open wide."
And he told me of the Saviour,
And the fountain in His side.

Then he said "Just take your burden
To the blessed Master's feet;
I takes all my troubles, Chloe,
Right unto the mercy-seat."

His words waked up my courage,
And I began to pray,
And I felt my heavy burden
Rolling like a stone away.

And a something seemed to tell me,
"You will see your boys again."
And that hope was like a poultice
Spread upon a dreadful pain.

And it often seemed to whisper,
"Chloe, trust and never fear;
You'll get justice in the kingdom,
If you do not get it here."

Church Building

Uncle Jacob often told us,
Since freedom blessed our race
We ought all to come together
And build a meeting place.

So we pinched, and scraped, and spared,
A little here and there:
Though our wages was but scanty,
The church did get a share.

And, when the house was finished,
Uncle Jacob came to pray;
He was looking mighty feeble,
And his head was awful gray.

But his voice rang like a trumpet;
His eyes looked bright and young;
And it seemed a mighty power
Was resting on his tongue.

And he gave us all his blessing—
'Twas parting words he said,
For soon we got the message
The dear old man was dead.

But I believe he's in the kingdom,
For when we shook his hand
He said, "Children, you must meet me
Right in the promised land;

"For when I done a-moiling
And toiling here below,
Through the gate into the city
Straightway I hope to go."

Aunt Chloe's Politics

Of course, I don't know very much
About these politics,
But I think that some who run 'em,
Do mighty ugly tricks.

I've seen 'em honey-fugle round,
And talk so awful sweet,
That you'd think them full of kindness
As an egg is full of meat.

Now I don't believe in looking
Honest people in the face,
And saying when you're doing wrong,
That 'I haven't sold my race.'

When we want to school our children,
If the money isn't there,
Whether black or white have took it,
The loss we all must share.

And this buying up each other
Is something worse than mean,
Though I thinks a heap of voting,
I go for voting clean.

Learning to Read

Very soon the Yankee teachers
Came down and set up school;
But, oh! how the Rebs did hate it,—
It was agin' their rule.

Our masters always tried to hide
Book learning from our eyes;
Knowledge did'nt agree with slavery—
'Twould make us all too wise.

But some of us would try to steal
A little from the book,
And put the words together,
And learn by hook or crook.

I remember Uncle Caldwell,
Who took pot liquor fat
And greased the pages of his book,
And hid it in his hat.

And had his master ever seen
The leaves upon his head,
He'd have thought them greasy papers,
But nothing to be read.

And there was Mr. Turner's Ben,
Who heard the children spell,
And picked the words right up by heart,
And learned to read 'em well.

Well, the Northern folks kept sending
The Yankee teachers down;
And they stood right up and helped us,
Though Rebs did sneer and frown.

And I longed to read my Bible,
For precious words it said;
But when I begun to learn it,
Folks just shook their heads,

And said there is no use trying,
Oh! Chloe, you're too late;
But as I was rising sixty,
I had no time to wait.

So I got a pair of glasses,
And straight to work I went,
And never stopped till I could read
The hymns and Testament.

Then I got a little cabin
A place to call my own—
And I felt as independent
As the queen upon her throne.

Deliverance

Rise up! rise up! Oh Israel,
Let a spotless lamb be slain;
The angel of death will o'er you bend
And rend your galling chain.

Sprinkle its blood upon the posts
And lintels of your door;
When the angel sees the crimson spots
Unharmed he will pass you o'er.

Gather your flocks and herds to-night,
Your children by your side;
A leader from Arabia comes
To be your friend and your guide.

With girded loins and sandled feet
Await the hour of dread,

When Mizraim shall wildly mourn
Her first-born and her dead.

The sons of Abraham no more
Shall crouch 'neath Pharaoh's hand,
Trembling with agony and dread
He'll thrust you from the land.

And ye shall hold in unborn years
A feast to mark this day,
When joyfully the fathers rose
And cast their chains away.

When crimson tints of morning flush
The golden gates of day,
Or gorgeous hue of even melt
In sombre shades away,

Then ye shall to your children teach
The meaning of this feast,
How from the proud oppressor's hand
Their fathers were released,

And ye shall hold through distant years
This feast with glad accord,
And children's children yet shall learn
To love and trust the Lord.

Ages have passed since Israel trod
In triumph through the sea,
And yet they hold in memory's urn
Their first great jubilee,

When Moses led the ransomed hosts,
And Miriam's song arose,

While ruin closed around the path
Of their pursuing foes.

Shall Israel thro' long varied years
These memories cherish yet,
And we who lately stood redeemed
Our broken chains forget?

Should we forget the wondrous change
That to our people came,
When justice rose and sternly plead
Our cause with sword and flame,

And led us through the storms of war
To freedom's fairer shore,
When slavery sank beneath a flood
Whose waves were human gore?

Oh, youth and maidens of the land,
Rise up with one accord,
And in the names of Christ go forth
To battle for the Lord.

Go forth, but not in crimson fields,
With fratricidal strife,
But in the name of Christ go forth
For freedom, love and life.

Go forth to follow in his steps,
Who came not to destroy,
Till wasteds shall blossom as the rose,
And deserts sing for joy.

Alice and Phoebe Cary:
1820/1824–1871

Introduction

Alice and Phoebe Cary are what might be called documentary poets; although in Phoebe Cary's case there is an additional dimension, almost unique to her among nineteenth-century women poets, of witty reflection back on the materials she records. In this mode she more or less invents her own genre and poetic language, in what can be called humorous counter-poems. But what is mainly found in these sister-poets is a presentation of materials that are in various ways historical, from the specific angle of their own particular biographies and with a steady attention to women's viewpoints, figures, religion, and experience.

Alice and Phoebe Cary represent in the range of women poets the context of the West, of self-made, self-educated women who, like Lincoln, grew up on a farm with almost no schooling, and yet created for themselves a life in the image of their own desire and ambition. They were born in Ohio (Alice in 1820, Phoebe in 1824), eight miles from Cincinnati, of old American stock. The first Cary had come to America in 1630, to the colony at Plymouth. A great-grandfather had been educated at Yale; his son was rewarded for service in the Revolutionary War with a land-grant out West. This is the farm the

Carys' father worked, and where the family of nine grew up, first with an admired and encouraging mother (about her Alice later said: "how she raised a large family and yet found time to read is still a mystery to me"). After the mother's death in 1835 (and the death of two sisters in 1833, whom Alice had ghostly visions of), the father remarried a woman who could see no point in writing or reading, and who begrudged the already literary step-daughters both time and supplies for their creative efforts. They wrote at night by improvised candles. Their formal education consisted of some few stretches at a local, one room district school. Their library was comprised of hymnals, the Bible, a *History of the Jews,* Lewis and Clarke's travels, and Pope's essays. Their introduction to poetry came by way of the Christian Universalist journal, *The Trumpet,* to which their parents subscribed, and which had a poet's corner.

By eighteen Alice had placed her first poem in print, in the local Cincinnati Universalist newspaper, *The Sentinel.* She continued to publish through the 1830s and 40s, finally gaining the notice of Whittier, Griswold, and through Griswold, Poe. Griswold then included both Alice and Phoebe's work in his 1848 *Female Poets of America,* and on his recommendation their poetry was brought out in a volume called *Poems of Alice and Phoebe Carey* (name misspelled) in 1850. This gave Alice the impetus to visit and then settle in New York City. Phoebe and a younger sister, Elmina—already an invalid who eventually died in 1862—joined her the following year, 1851. In 1855 they together bought a house on East 20ᵗʰ street, supporting themselves by writing, and hosting a weekly Sunday evening literary salon throughout the next fifteen years, with especially close ties to Horace Greeley and attended by many New Yorkers on the literary scene.

Alice and Phoebe thus managed to create for themselves a life in their own chosen image, although accompanied by a full share of complex and at times strained allegiances. Although living as writers in the city, they wrote of the country—a "Contradiction" Alice acknowledges in the poem of that title and Phoebe records in "City Life." In their poetry, and in Alice's prose (notably her *Clovernook* stories), they return to Ohio scenes of their youth. This is the first level of documentary which they offer. Alice's "The West Country," and "The Emigrants," for example, portray life in the American West, and specifically from the viewpoints of women, thus recording (and acknowledging the existence of) women's historical experiences. What she depicts is the price they paid in pursuit of the western promise—or rather, the price women paid in what emerges essentially as a male pursuit. "The Washerwoman" inscribes the dignity of this woman's work in figural opposition to the male blacksmith's and the proper ladies who exploit her. "The West Country" concludes optimistically, but in celebration of male achievement. "Growing Rich" is more severe and more split. Here, despite a third person narrative style, the poem divides (in the manner of the missed-dialogue of women's verse) into two voices, one male and one female. They essentially talk past each other, as the husband heartens his wife with a roster of their increasing prosperity while she increasingly grieves. This is a discourse that entirely misses the causes of her concerns in her attachment to her family abandoned in the East and suffering deprivations there.

At issue here is gender, but specifically as situated within and emblematic of trends and major conflicts in nineteenth-century American culture and society. As in other women's poetry of the period, the poetic distributions complicate and challenge the division of gendered-life into "public" and "private" domains. In "Growing Rich," there is a split in experience represented by husband and wife. But this is less a question of public and private than of economic and communal—where economy is in effect private enterprise, while family attachment is a community commitment and in this sense public. This topography of American culture emerges in Alice's poetry in various guises. "The Specter Woman" is one of her many ballads, melodramatic and tragic. But its specific domain is the betrayed and outcast fallen woman, haunting a graveyard with her unwanted child. Here is, that is, in balladic form the question of the double standard so persistent in women's poetry of the period. And here and elsewhere, the double standard is not only sexual but social and cultural, representing a broad bifurcation of values splitting American society into unrestrained economic individualism as against community life.

Alice's poetry directly presents and addresses this broadly

social concern. "The Fourth of July (1864)" is a Jeremiad reproaching America and calling it back to the common good—a fully constituted political paper in fact. The poem (one of very many in the period) on Abraham Lincoln offers him as representative American and indeed redemptive image of America itself—one which concludes with an appeal to his "humble hearth," the very figure of women's life as well. "Revolutionary Story" makes heroic into personal and feminized narrative. "The Poor" shows directly her social conscience; "Past and Present" her social dreams.

Phoebe Cary

Phoebe Cary's work accompanies her sister's through many of its topics and scenes. She too acutely feels America to be falling ever deeper into a double standard—sexual, as in her poem "The Outcast," but also much more broadly as social, cultural, and economic. As in the poetry of Alice and many other women poets, she too poses economy against community, as in "Nobody's Child." "Man Believes the Strong" is a hard-headed exposure of the world's ways. Her "The Wife" oddly matches Alice's "The Washerwoman" as a portrait of woman's place. And she has a set of political poems—on "Our Good President," "John Brown," "Tent Scene," and, quite powerful in its vision of America as haven and welcoming refuge, "Homes for All."

But Phoebe's personal signature and even invention are her counter-poems. Some of these are, as she called them in her volume of poetry, parodies. She re-writes texts by Longfellow, Poe, as well as Wordsworth, Goldsmith ("When Lovely Woman"; cf. T.S. Eliot's "The Waste Land") and Shakespeare, even Isaac Watts (better know through Lewis Carroll's later parody) in her own very funny "Moral Lessons: How doth the little busy flea." Her re-versions tend to follow particular strategies. What she does is socialize—bring down to everyday activities, concerns, relationships, and desires—what are presented as ideal abstractions in the male poems. Longfellow's melancholic "The Day is Done" becomes in Phoebe Cary the practical and earthy matter of eating: "Come, get for me some supper, / A good and regular meal, / That shall soothe this restless feeling, / And banish the pain I feel." Longfellow's idealized "Psalm of Life" becomes the deflated scene of how to capture a man. This is a sustained topic in Phoebe Cary's work, and, really oddly, displaces the pervasive and counterpart topic in male poetry, that of dead women. Poe's gruesome and apocalyptic "Annabelle Lee" becomes social comedy as "Samuel Brown." Poe's coveting angels become Cary's competing ladies; and his necrophiliac sepulchre-bed becomes her casual and triumphant "walk down in Broadway... To our house in the street down town." Wordsworth's dead Lucy in her solitary, shy fascination is deposed by Jacob, "Fair as a man when only one / Is in the neighbourhood." And in "Shakespearean Readings" Cary compares the being and not being of "The weariest and most troubled married life" as against "being an old maid."

These counter male-poet poems take their place beside counter-romance poems and counter-ballads. As against expected moans of undying love, perfect devotion, and ideal matches, she has a poem like "The Annoyer" where love "comes unbidden everywhere, / Like people we don't want." "I Remember," "The Change," and "Worser Moments" all feature the regretful outcomes of successful courtships. "Granny's House" provides a good antidote to Alice's "The Old Homestead," with its own little twist on Washington's Cherry Tree story and a very hardheaded refusal of ungrounded nostalgia. "Dorothy's Dower," "Coming Round" and "Helpless" follow the mode of missed-dialogues, where women and men speak past each other, here in a course of willful feminine delusion. As to counter-ballads, "John Thompson's Daughter," "Dorothy's Dower," and "Kate Ketchem" are raucous exposures of the dance of love as taking place in the counting house. Here is Phoebe Cary's own particular take on the topic that other poets treat as the sexual double standard and Charlotte Gilman as prostitution: the unnerving intersection of America's cultures of economy and community in that most intimate of scenes, love. Phoebe Cary stakes this out as the marriage market (cf. Alice Cary's more predictable "The Unwise Choice"), as courtship become economic calculation.

Both Alice and Phoebe Cary were deeply religious women, with some of their poems, notably Phoebe's "Nearest Home," circulating widely as hymns. Theirs, however, was a liberal, activist religion, connecting them to abolition, women's rights, and a general commitment, as pious as it was political, to equality. Their backgrounds as Universalists pledged them to the ultimate salvation of all human souls. As Phoebe wrote of Alice, "she most firmly believed in human brotherhood as taught by Jesus; and in a God whose loving kindness is so deep and so unchangeable that there can never [be] even the vilest sinner [whose] Father will not see him afar off, and have compassion upon him." Their poetry traces links between this religious faith and political practice. Alice's "The Women at the Sepulchre" poses a question of feminist biblical interpretation, as to why the female figures, central and decisive in their role in the Christian message, never were acknowledged as disciples. Writing in the aftermath of the Lincoln assassination, she prays for her country that "mercy keep her just, / And through her justice, free." Phoebe's "John Brown" has "read God's writing of 'reprieve,' / And grant of endless liberty." Her poem "Equality" grounds equality in the dignity of every human soul before God: "For in all truest wealth, to-day, / I stand an equal by your side!/ No better parentage have you,/ One is our Father, one our Friend."

Alice published her work in *The Era*, which had serialized *Uncle Tom's Cabin* and published Larcom as well. Both sisters were involved in the women's rights movement—Alice as the first president (1868) of the New York Woman's Club, called "Sorosis," founded to help women overcome barriers that denied them opportunities (although she resigned after one year for reasons of ill health). As she said in her inaugural address: "Some of us cannot hope to see great results, for our feet are already on the downhill side of life," but that the joint "loyalty to woman, and her unceasing industry, shall incite us to renewed earnestness of effort, each in our own appointed place, to hasten the time when women shall receive recognition not only as honest and reliable workers, but as a class faithful and true to each other."

Phoebe served for a time as assistant editor to Susan B. Anthony's journal *The Revolution*, and dedicated a poem to her on her fiftieth birthday—again working in her theme of the independent, single woman: for, as she writes, Susan Anthony is one of those women who has "proved by word and carriage, / That one of the United States / Is not the state of marriage." Phoebe's popular "Was She Henpecked," one of a number of animal-fables she wrote, again takes shape as a missed-dialogue between rooster-husband and hen-wife (one thinks of Elizabeth Bishop's "Roosters"), exposing to ridicule the man's arguments against women's suffrage and independence.

Yet, for all their strength of self-formation, of establishing themselves as independent, self-supporting, creative and activist women, their poetry also registers a good deal of strain between their various identities and roles as women and as poets. The poems on poetry they wrote tend to cast the writer as male. Phoebe's support for Susan Anthony and the poem in her honor stands beside her ambivalent "Advice Gratis to Certain Women by a Woman." Here the confusion of definition as to what it is, or is not, to be a woman takes public stage, as the poem advises a professional public appearance even while warning: "'Tis a good thing to write and to rule in the state, / But to be a true womanly woman is great."

Like many women poets, neither Alice nor Phoebe married; although in both cases there is a love story. Alice apparently was engaged to a lover back in Ohio, whose wealthy family prevented him from marrying her. She read of his wedding in the newspapers, and moved to New York City. She saw him again when he visited her on her deathbed. Phoebe is said to have been courted, but to have resisted marriage to devote herself to her sister. Indeed, Phoebe survived Alice by barely a few months, declining quickly after Alice's death in February, 1871, to die in the following July of that year. It was ultimately the shared life of sisters that created their community of support and poetry, making possible their unusual choices and paths of self-formation. Phoebe's own sense of her self-chosen fate as unmarried is glimpsed in the self-reflective poems "Do You Blame Her" (Phoebe doesn't) and her own favorite, "A Woman's Conclusion." Or, as she wrote in "The Lovers," an anti-romance showing that her perhaps deepest love was the sheer joy in word-play:

Wretch, he cried, when she threatened to leave him, and left
How could you deceive me, as you have deceft?
And she answered, I promised to cleave, and I've cleft.

Poems: Alice Cary

Growing Rich

And why are you pale, my Nora?
And why do you sigh and fret?
The black ewe had twin lambs to-day,
And we shall be rich folk yet.

Do you mind the clover-ridge, Nora,
That slopes to the crooked stream?
The brown cow pastured there this week,
And her milk is sweet as cream.

The old gray mare that last year fell
As thin as any ghost,
Is getting a new white coat, and looks
As young as her colt, almost.

And if the corn should do well,
And so, please God, it may,
I'll buy the white-faced bull a bell,
To make the meadows gay.

I know we are growing rich, Johnny,
And that is why I fret,
For my little brother Phil is down
In the dismal coal-pit yet.

And when the sunshine sets in the corn,
The tassels green and gay,
It will not touch my father's eyes,
That are going blind, they say.

But if I were not sad for him,
Nor yet for little Phil,
Why, darling Molly's hand, last year,
Was cut off in the mill.

And so, nor mare nor brown milch-cow,
Nor lambs can joy impart,
For the blind old man and th' mill and mine
Are all upon my heart.

Too much of joy is sorrowful,
So cares must needs abound;
The vine that bears too many flowers
Will trail upon the ground.

The Washerwoman

At the north end of our village stands,
With gable black and high,
A weather-beaten home, I've stopt
Often as I went by,

To see the strip of bleaching grass
Slipped brightly in between
The long straight rows of hollyhocks,
And current-bushes green;

The clumsy bench beside the door,
And oaken washing-tub,

Where poor old Rachel used to stand,
And rub, and rub, and rub!

Her blue-checked apron speckled with
The suds, so snowy white
From morning when I went to school
Till I went home at night,

She never took her sunburnt arms
Out of the steaming tub:
We used to say 'twas weary work
Only to hear her rub.

With sleeves stretched straight upon the grass
The washed shirts used to lie;
By dozens I have counted them
Some days, as I went by.

The burly blacksmith, battering at
His red-hot iron bands,
Would make a joke of wishing that
He had old Rachel's hands!

And when the sharp and ringing strokes
Had doubled up his shoe,
As crooked as old Rachel's back,
He used to say 'twould do.

And every village housewife, with
A conscience clear and light,
Would send for her to come and wash
An hour or two at night!

Her hair beneath her cotton cap
Grew silver-white and thin

And the deep furrows in her face
Ploughed all the roses in.

Yet patiently she kept at work,
We school-girls used to say
The smile about her sunken mouth
Would quite go out some day.

Nobody ever thought the spark
That in her sad eyes shone,
Burned outward from a living soul
Immortal as their own.

And though a tender flush sometimes
Into her cheek would start,
Nobody dreamed old Rachel had
A woman's loving heart!

At last she left her heaps of clothes
One quiet autumn day,
And stript from off her sunburnt arms
The weary suds away;

That night within her moonlit door
She sat alone, her chin
Sunk in her hand, her eyes shut up,
As if to look within.

Her face uplifted to the star
That stood so sweet and low
Against old crazy Peter's house
(He loved her long ago!)

Her heart had worn her body to
A handful of poor dust,

Her soul was gone to be arrayed
In marriage-robes, I trust.

The West Country

Have you been in our wild west country? then
You have often had to pass
Its cabins lying like birds' nests in
The wild green prairie grass.

Have you seen the women forget their wheels
As they sat at the door to spin
Have you seen the darning fall away
From their fingers worn and thin,

As they asked you news of the villages
Where they were used to be,
Gay girls at work in the factories
With their lovers gone to sea!

Ah, have you thought of the bravery
That no loud praise provokes
Of the tragedies acted in the lives
Of poor, hard-working folks!

Of the little more, and the little more
Of hardship which they press
Upon their own tired hands to make
The toil for the children less:

And not in vain; for many a lad
Born to rough work and ways,
Strips off his ragged coat, and makes
Men clothe him with their praise.

The Emigrants

Don't you remember how oft you have said,
Darling Coralin May,
"When the hawthorns are blossoming we shall wed,
And then to the prairie away!"

And now, all over the hills they peep,
Milkwhite, out of the spray,
And sadly you turn to the past and weep,
Darling Coralin May.

When the cricket chirped in the hickory blaze,
You cheerily sung, you know,
"Oh for the sunnier summer days,
And the time when we shall go!"

The corn-blades now are unfolding bright,
While busily calls the crow;
And clovers are opening red and white,
And the time has come to go.

To go to the cabin our love has planned,
On the prairie green and gay,
In the blushing light of the sunset land,
Darling Coralin May.

"How happy our lives will be," you said,
Don't you remember the day?
"When our hands shall be, as our hearts are, wed!"'
Darling Coralin May.

"How sweet," you said, "when my work is o'er,
And your axe yet ringing clear,
To sit and watch at the lowly door
Of our home in the prairie, dear."

The rose is ripe by the window now,
And the cool spring flowing near;
But shadows fall on the heart and brow
From the home we are leaving here.

Written on the Fourth of July, 1864

Once more, despite the noise of wars,
And the smoke gathering fold on fold,
Our daisies set their stainless stars
Against the sunshine's cloth of gold.
Lord, make us feel, if so thou will,
The blessings crowning us to-day,
And the yet greater blessing still,
Of blessings thou hast taken away.
Unworthy of the favors lent,
We fell into apostasy;
And lo! our country's chastisement
Has brought her to herself, and thee!
Nearer by all this grief than when
She dared her weak ones to oppress,
And played away her States to men
Who scorned her for her foolishness.
Oh, bless for us this holiday,
Men keep like children loose from school,
And put it in their hearts, we pray,
To choose them rulers fit to rule.
Good men, who shall their country's pride
And honor to their own prefer;
Her sinews to their hearts so tied
That they can only live through her.
Men sturdy—of discerning eyes,
And souls to apprehend the right;
Not with their little light so wise
They set themselves against Thy light

Men of small reverence for names,
Courageous, and of fortitude
To put aside the narrow aims
Of factor, for the public good.
Men loving justice for the race,
Not for the great ones, and the few
Less studious of outward grace
Than careful to be clean all through.
Men holding state, not self, the first
Ready when all the deep is tossed
With storms, and worst is come to worst,
To save the ship at any cost.
Men upright, and of steady knees,
That only to the truth will bow;
Lord help us choose such men as these,
For only such can save us now.

The Past and Present

The wealth of nations: was she not endowed
With that most perilous gift of beauty-pride?
And spite of all her glories blazoned loud,
Idolatrous, voluptuous, and allied
Closer to vice than virtue? Hark! the sounds
Of tramping thousands in her stony street!
And now the amphitheatre resounds
With acclamations for the engrossing feat!
Draw near, where men of wars and senates stood,
And see the pastime, whence they joyance drank—
The Lybian lion lapping the warm blood
Oozed from the Dacian's bosom. On the bank
Of the sweet Danube, smiling children wait
To greet their sire, unconscious of his fate.
Oh draw the wildering veil a little back,
Ye blind idolaters of things that were;

Who, through the glory trailing in their track,
See but the whiteness of the sepulchre!
Then to the Present turning, ye will see
Even as one, the universal mind
Rousing, like genius from a reverie,
With the exalted aim to serve mankind:
Lo! as my song is closing, I can feel
The spirit of the Present in my heart;
And for the future, with a wiser zeal,
In life's great drama I would act my part:
That they may say, who see the curtain fall
And from the closing scene in silence go,
Haply as some light favour they recall,
Peace to her ashes, she hath lessened woe!

Revolutionary Story

"Good mother, what quaint legend are you reading,
In that old-fashioned book?
Beside your door I've been this half hour pleading
All vainly for one look.
"About your chair the little birds fly bolder
Than in the woods they fly,
With heads dropt slantwise, as if o'er your shoulder
They read as they went by;
"Each with his glossy collar ruffling double
Around his neck so slim,
Even as with that atmosphere of trouble,
Through which our blessings swim.
"Is it that years throw on us chillier shadows,
The longer time they run,
That, with your sad face fronting yonder meadows,
You creep into the sun?
That, all, too mighty to be thwarted by it,
Breaks through into the light."

"Then frosty age may wrap about its bosom
The light of fires long dead?"
Kissing the piece of dust she called a blossom,
She shut the book, and said:
"You see yon ash-tree with its thick leaves, blowing
The blue side out?
(Great Power, keep its head green!)
My sweetheart, in the mowing
Beneath it found my flower.
"A mile off all that day the shots were flying,
And mothers, from the door,
Looked for the sons, who, on their faces lying,
Would come home never more.
"Across the battle-field the dogs went whining;
I saw, from where I stood,
Horses with quivering flanks, and
strained eyes, shining
Like thin skins full of blood.
"Brave fellows we had then: there was my neighbor,
The British lines he saw;
Took his old scythe and ground it to a sabre,
And mowed them down like straw!
"And there were women, then, of giant spirit,
Nay, though the blushes start,
The garments their degenerate race inherit
Hang loose about the heart.
"Where was I, child? how is my story going?"
"Why, where by yonder tree
With leaves so rough your sweetheart, in the mowing,
Gathered your flower!" "Ah me!
My poor lad dreamed not of the red coat devil,
That, just for pastime, drew
To his bright epaulet his musket level,
And shot him through and through.
Beside him I was kneeling the next minute
From the red grass he took

The shattered hand up, and the flower was in it
You saw within my book."
"He died. Then you have seen
some stormy weather?"
"Aye, more of foul than fair;
And all the snows we should have
shared together
Have fallen on my hair."
"And has your life been worth the living, mother,
With all its sorrows?" "Aye,
I'd live it o'er again, were there no other,
For this one memory."
I answered soft,—I felt the place was holy—
One maxim stands approved:
"They know the best of life, however lowly,
Who ever have been loved."

Abraham Lincoln
Foully assassinated, April 1865

No glittering chaplet brought from other lands!
As in his life, this man, in death is ours;
His own loved prairies o'er his "gaunt gnarled hands"
Have fitly drawn their sheet of summer flowers!

What need hath he now of a tardy crown,
His name from mocking jest and sneer to save?
When every ploughman turns his furrow down
As soft as though it fell upon his grave.

He was a man whose like the world again
Shall never see, to vex with blame or praise:
The landmarks that attest his bright, brief reign
Are battles, not the pomps of gala-days.

The grandest leader of the grandest war
That ever time in history gave place;
What were the tinsel flattery of a star
To such a breast! Or what a ribbon's grace!

'Tis to the man, and the man's honest worth,
The nation's loyalty in tears upsprings;
Through him the soil of labor shines henceforth
High o'er the silken broideries of kings.

The mechanism of external forms—
The shrifts that courtiers put their bodies through,
Were alien ways to him—his brawny arms
Had other work than posturing to do.

Born of the people, well he knew to grasp
The wants and wishes of the weak and small;
Therefore we hold him with no shadowy clasp—
Therefore his name is household to us all.

Therefore we love him with a love apart
From any fawning love of pedigree—
His was the royal soul and mind and heart—
Not the poor outward shows of royalty.

Forgive us then, O friends, if we are low
To meet your recognition of his worth—
We're jealous of the very tears that flow
From eyes that never loved a humble hearth.

The Dawn of Peace

The sword we sheathed, our enemy
Has bared, and struck us through;
And heart, and soul, and spirit cry,

What wilt thou have us do!
After the cloud and the whirlwind,
After the long, dark night,
After the dull, slow marches,
And the thick, tumultuous fight,
Thank God, we see the lifting
Of the golden, glorious light!
Be with our country in this grief
That lies across her path,
Lest that she mourn her martyred chief
With an unrighteous wrath.
After the sorrowful partings,
After the sickening fear,
And after the bitter sealing
With blood, of year to year,
Thank God, the light is breaking;
Thank God, the day is here!
Give her that steadfast faith and trust
That look through all, to Thee;
And in her mercy keep her just,
And through her justice, free.
The land is filled with mourning
For husbands and brothers slain,
But a hymn of glad thanksgiving
Rises over the pain;
Thank God, our gallant soldiers
Have not gone down in vain!
The cloud is spent; the whirlwind
That vexed the night is past;
And the day whose blessed dawning
We see, shall surely last,
Till all the broken fetters
To ploughshares shall be cast!
All, all beneath the shining sun
Is vanity and dust;
Help us, O high and holy One,

To fix in thee our trust;
When over the field of battle
The grass grows green, and when
The Spirit of Peace shall have planted
Her olives once again,
Oh, how the hosts of the people
Shall cry, Amen, Amen!

The Spectre Woman

Along the hollow chancel the winds of autumn sung,
And the heavy flitting of the bat was heard the aisles among;
The sky was full of stars that night, the moon was at the full,
And yet about the old gray church the light was something dull.
And in that solemn churchyard, where the mould was freshly
    thrown,
Wrapped in a thin, cold sheet, there sat a lovely maid alone:
The dark and tangled tresses half revealed her bosom's charms,
And a something that lay hidden, like a birdling in her arms.
By that pale, sad brow of beauty, and the locks that fall so low,
And by the burning blushes in that lovely cheek, I know
She hath listened to the tempter, she hath heard his whisper dread,
When the "Get behind me, Satan," hath been all too faintly said.
It was not the willows trailing, as the winds among them stole,
That was heard there at the midnight, nor the digging of the mole
Nor yet the dry leaves dropping where the grass was crushed and
    damp,
And the light that shone so spectral was not the firefly's lamp.
The pale moon veiled her beauty in a lightly passing cloud,
When a voice was heard thrice calling to that woman in the
    shroud!
But whether fiend or angel were for her spirit come,
The lips that could have told it have long been sealed and dumb.
But they say, who pass that churchyard at the dead watch of the
    night,

That a woman in her grave-clothes, when the moon is full and
    bright,
Is seen to bend down fondly, but without a mother's pride,
Over something in her bosom that her tresses cannot hide.

The Women at the Sepulchre

Morn broke on Calvary, and the sun was flinging
The earliest brightness from his locks abroad,
As the meek sisters came in sadness, bringing
Gifts of sweet spices to anoint their Lord.
They who had loved his blessed precepts ever,
And linger'd with him when the earth was gloom,
They were the faithful who reviled him never,
"Last at the cross, and earliest at the tomb!"
I've sometimes thought I never could inherit
A glorious mansion in the skies above:
For, oh! how weak and faltering is my spirit,
Compared with such undying faith and love!
But, Father, cannot all that heavenly meekness,
That deathless love which all things could endure,
Can it not plead before Thee, for the weakness
Of one whose faith is oft so faint and poor?

The Poor

Cradled in poverty, unloved, alone,
Seeing far off the wave of gladness roll;
Sorrow, to happier fortune never known,
Strikes deep its poison-roots within the soul!
What need is there for rhetoric to seek
For the fine phrase of eloquence, to tell
Of the eye sunken, and the hueless cheek,
Where naked want and gnawing hunger dwell?

Down in the lanes and alleys of life's mart
Are beds of anguish that no kind hands tend;
And friendless wanderers, without map or chart,
Urged to despair, or, worse, a nameless end!
Their very smiles are bitter, in whose track
The fountains are with penury made chill;
For by their smiles, their sighs are driven back
To stifle in the heart-strings, and be still!
The poor are criminals! The opulent man
Is unsuspected, and must needs be true;
Such is the popular verdict, such the plan
That gives the loathsome hangman work to do!
If he who treads the convict's gloomy cell,
To soothe Heaven's vengeance with officious prayer,
Had dealt as kindly with him ere he fell,
Haply his presence had been needless there!
Oh there is need of union, firm and strong,
Of effort vigorous and directed well;
To rescue weakness from oppressive wrong
Would shake the deep foundations of dark hell!
Dear are the humble in God's equal sight,
And every hair upon their heads he sees,
Even as the laurel freshening in the light,
That trails along the path of centuries.
Then treat them kindly, for the selfsame hand,
(And with as large an exercise of power,)
That makes the planets in their order stand,
Gives its meek beauty to the desert flower.

A Dying Hymn

And if thy holy will it be,
Keep me alive, once, more to see
The glad and glorious day.
Earth, with its dark and dreadful ills,

Recedes, and fades away;
Lift up your heads, ye heavenly hills:
Ye gates of death, give way.
My soul is full of whispered song;
My blindness is my sight;
The shadows that I feared so long
Are all alive with light.
The while my pulses faintly beat,
My faith doth so abound,
I feel grow firm beneath my feet
The green, immortal ground.
That faith to me a courage gives,
Low as the grave to go:
I know that my Redeemer lives—
That I shall live I know.
The palace walls I almost see
Where dwells my Lord and King;
O grave! where is thy victory?
O death! where is thy sting?

Contradictory

We contradictory creatures
Have something in us alien to our birth,
That doth suffuse us with the infinite,
While downward through our natures
Run adverse thoughts, that only find delight
In the poor perishable things of earth.
Blindly we feel about
Our little circle—ever on the quest
Of knowledge, which is only, at the best,
Pushing the boundaries of our ignorance out.
But while we know all things are miracles,
And that we cannot set
An ear of corn, nor tell a blade of grass

The way to grow, our vanity o'erswells
The limit of our wisdom, and we yet
Audaciously o'erpass
This narrow promontory
Of low, dark land, into the unseen glory,
And with unhallowed zeal
Unto our fellow-men God's judgments deal.

My Poet

Ah, could I my poet only draw
In lines of a living light,
You would say that Shakespeare never saw
In his dreams a fairer sight.

Along the bright crisp grass where by
A beautiful water lay,
We walked—my fancies and I
One morn in the early May.

And there, betwixt the water sweet
And the gay and grassy land,
I found the print of two little feet
Upon the silvery sand.

These following, and following on,
Allured by the place and time,
I, all of a sudden, came upon
This poet of my rhyme.

Betwixt my hands I longed to take
His two cheeks brown with tan,
To kiss him for my true love's sake,
And call him a little man.

A rustic of the rustics he,
By every look and sign,
And I knew, when he turned his face to me,
'Twas his spirit made him fine.

His ignorance he had sweetly turned
Into uses passing words:
He had cut a pipe of corn, and learned
Thereon to talk to the birds.

And now it was the bluebird's trill,
Now the blackbird on the thorn,
Now a speckle-breast, or tawny-bill
That answered his pipe of corn,

And now, though he turned him north and south,
And called upon bird by bird,
There was never a little golden mouth
Would answer him back a word.

For all, from the red bird bold and gay
To the linnet dull and plain
Had fallen on beds of the leafy spray,
To listen in envious pain.

"Ah, do as you like, my golden quill;"
So he said, for his wise share;
"And the same to you, my tawny-bill,
There are pleasures everywhere."

Then his heart fell in him dancing so,
It spun to his cheek the red,
As he spied himself in the wave below
A standing on his head.

Ah, could I but this picture draw
Thus glad by his nature's right,
You would say that Shakespeare never saw
In his dreams a fairer sight.

Secret Writing

Sometimes we find that he who says
The least about his faith,
Has steadfastness and sanctity
To suffer unto death;
And find that he who prays aloud
With ostentatious mien,
Prays only to be heard of men,
And only to be seen.
For when the hearth is kindled,
And the house is hushed at night
Ah, then the secret writing
Of the spirit comes to light.

Who is the Richer

The house that you see underneath the great pine,
With walls that are painted, and doors that are fine,
And meadows and cornfields about it, is mine.

On the stormy side hill of the woodland close by,
In a house that is not half so wide nor so high,
Elijah, my miller, lives, richer than I.

At night, when he ties up the last bag of meal,
And turns the brown oxen away from the wheel,
He sits down with zest at his table of deal.

No bother of notes to be paid on demand,
His girl on his knee, and his boys at each hand,
He is happy and proud as the lord of the land.

Of the meadows about him, he owns not a rod,
No stone of the brook-side, no stick of the wood,
And yet he has shelter, and clothing, and food.

'Tis good in his blue eyes the twinkle to see
That the mill goes wrong never troubles his glee
'Tis I that must pay for the mending, not he.

He laughs when I frown, and he hums, when I sigh,
The pleasant love-ditties of days that are by;
So who is the richer, Elijah or I?

The Old Homestead

When skies are growing warm and bright,
And in the woodland bowers
The Spring-time in her pale, faint robes
Is calling up the flowers,

When all with naked little feet
The children in the morn
Go forth, and in the furrows drop
The seeds of yellow corn;

What a beautiful embodiment
Of ease devoid of pride
Is the good old-fashioned homestead,
With its doors set open wide!

But when the happiest time is come,
That to the year belongs,

When all the vales are filled with gold
And all the air with songs;

When fields of yet unripened grain,
And yet ungarnered stores
Remind the thrifty husbandman
Of ampler threshing-floors,

How pleasant, from the din and dust
Of the thoroughfare aloof,
Stands the old-fashioned homestead,
With steep and mossy roof!

When home the woodsman plods with axe
Upon his shoulder swung,
And in the knotted apple-tree
Are scythe and sickle hung;

When low about her clay-built nest
The mother swallow trills,
And decorously slow, the cows
Are wending down the hills;

What a blessed picture of comfort
In the evening shadows red,
Is the good old-fashioned homestead,
With its bounteous table spread!

And when the winds moan wildly,
When the woods are bare and brown,
And when the swallow's clay-built nest
From the rafter crumbles down;

When all the untrod garden-paths
Are heaped with frozen leaves,

And icicles, like silver spikes,
Are set along the eaves;

Then when the book from the shelf is brought,
And the fire-lights shine and play,
In the good old-fashioned homestead,
Is the farmer's holiday!

But whether the brooks be fringed with flowers,
Or whether the dead leaves fall,
And whether the air be full of songs,
Or never a song at all,

And whether the vines of the strawberries
Or frosts through the grasses run,
And whether it rain or whether it shine
Is all to me as one,

For bright as brightest sunshine
The light of memory streams
Round the old-fashioned homestead,
Where I dreamed my dream of dreams!

Make Believe

Kiss me, though you make believe;
Kiss me, though I almost know
You are kissing to deceive:
Let the tide one moment flow
Backward ere it rise and break,
Only for poor pity's sake!

Give me of your flowers one leaf,
Give me of your smiles one smile,
Backward roll this tide of grief

Just a moment, though, the while,
I should feel and almost know
You are trifling with my woe.

Whisper to me sweet and low;
Tell me how you sit and weave
Dreams about me, though I know
It is only make believe!
Just a moment, though 'tis plain
You are jesting with my pain.

The Bridal Veil

We're married, they say, and you think you have won me,
Well, take this white veil from my head, and look on me:
Here's matter to vex you, and matter to grieve you,
Here's doubt to distrust you, and faith to believe you,
I am all as you see, common earth, common dew;
Be wary, and mould me to roses, not rue!

Ah! shake out the filmy thing, fold after fold,
And see if you have me to keep and to hold,
Look close on my heart—see the worst of its sinning—
It is not yours today for the yesterday's winning—
The past is not mine—I am too proud to borrow—
You must grow to new heights if I love you to-morrow.

We're married! I'm plighted to hold up your praises,
As the turf at your feet does its handful of daisies;
That way lies my honor, my pathway of pride,
But, mark you, if greener grass grow either side,
I shall know it, and keeping in body with you,
Shall walk in my spirit with feet on the dew!

We're married! Oh, pray that our love do not fail!
I have wings flattened down and hid under my veil:
They are subtle as light—you can never undo them,
And swift in their flight—you can never pursue them
And spite of all clasping, and spite of all bands,
Can slip like a shadow, a dream, from your hands.

Nay, call me not cruel, and fear not to take me,
I am yours for my lifetime, to be what you make me,
To wear my white veil for a sign, or a cover,
As you shall be proven my lord, or my lover
A cover for peace that is dead, or a token
Of bliss that can never be written or spoken.

The Unwise Choice

Two young men, when I was poor,
Came and stood at my open door;
One said to me, "I have gold to give;"
And one, "I will love you while I live!"
My sight was dazzled; woe's the day!
And I sent the poor young man away;
Sent him away, I know not where,
And my heart went with him, unaware.
He did not give me any sighs,
But he left his picture in my eyes;
And in my eyes it has always been:
I have no heart to keep it in!
Beside the lane with hedges sweet,
Where we parted, never more to meet,
He pulled a flower of love's own hue,
And where it had been came out two!
And in the grass where he stood, for years,
The dews of the morning looked like tears.
Still smiles the house where I was born

Among its fields of wheat and corn.
Wheat and corn that strangers bind,
I reap as I sowed, and I sowed to the wind:
As one who feels the truth break through
His dream, and knows his dream untrue,
I live where splendors shine, and sigh,
For the peace that splendor cannot buy;
Sigh for the day I was rich tho' poor,
And saw the two young men at my door!

Fame

Fame guards the wreath we call a crown
With other wreaths of fire,
And dragging this or that man down
Will not raise you the higher!
Fear not too much the open seas,
Nor yet yourself misdoubt;
Clear the bright wake of geniuses,
Then steadily steer out.
That wicked men in league should be
To push your craft aside,
Is not the hint of modesty,
But the poor conceit of pride.

Women

'Tis a sad truth, yet 'tis a truth
That does not need the proving:
They give their heats away, unasked,
And are not loved for loving.

Striving to win a little back,
For all they feel they hide it;

And lips that tremble with their love,
In trembling have denied it.

Sometimes they deem the kiss and smile
Is life and love's beginning;
While he who wins the heart away,
Is satisfied with winning.

Sometimes they think they have not found
The right one for their mating;
And go on till the hair is white,
And eyes are blind with waiting.

And if the mortal tarry still,
They fill their lamps, undying;
And till the midnight wait to hear
The "Heavenly Bridegroom" crying.

For while she lives, the best of them
Is less a saint than woman;
And when her lips ask love divine
Her heart asks love that's human.

Contradiction

I love the deep quiet all buried in leaves,
To sit the day long just as idle as air,
Till the spider grows tame at my elbow, and weaves,
And toadstools come up in a row round my chair.

I love the new furrows—the cones of the pine,
The grasshopper's chirp, and the hum of the mote;
And short pasture-grass where the clover-blooms shine
Like red buttons set on a holiday coat.

Flocks packed in the hollows, the droning of bees,–
The stubble so brittle—the damp and flat fen;
Old homesteads I love, in their clusters of trees,
And children and books, but not women nor men.

Yet, strange contradiction! I live in the sound
Of a sea-girdled city—'tis thus that it fell,
And years, oh, how many! have gone since I bound
A sheaf for the harvest, or drank at a well.

And if, kindly reader, one moment you wait
To measure the poor little niche that you fill,
I think you will own it is custom or fate
That has made you the creature you are, not your will.

Poems: Phoebe Cary

The Lovers

Sally Salter, she was a young teacher who taught
And her friend, Charley Church, was a preacher who praught
Though his enemies called him a screecher who scraught

His heart, when he saw her, kept sinking and sunk
And his eyes, when he saw her, began winking and wunk
While she, in her turn, kept thinking and thunk

He hastened to woo her, and sweetly he wooed
For his love grew until to a mountain it grewed
And what he was longing to do then he doed

In secret, he wanted to speak and he spoke
To seek with his lips what his heart long had soke
So he managed to let the truth leak, and it loke.

He asked her to ride to the church, and they rode;
They so sweetly did glide that they both thought they glode,
And they came to the place to be tied, and they toed

Then homeward, he said, let us drive and they drove,
And as soon as they wished to arrive, they arrove,
For whatever he couldn't contrive, she controve.

The kiss he was dying to steal, then he stole;
At the feet that he wanted to kneel, then he knole;
And he said, I feel better than ever I fole.

So they to each other kept clinging, and clung,
While time his swift circuit was winging, and wung;
And this was the thing he was bringing, and brung:

The man Sally wanted to catch, and had caught
That she wanted from others to snatch, and she snaught;
Was the one that she now liked to scratch, and she scraught.

And Charley's warm love began freezing, and froze;
While he took to teasing, and cruelly he toze
The girl he had wished to be squeezing, and squoze.

Wretch, he cried, when she threatened to leave him, and left
How could you deceive me, as you have deceft?
And she answered, I promised to cleave, and I've cleft.

Samuel Brown

'Twas many and many a year ago,
In a dwelling down in town,
That a fellow there lived whom you may know,
By the name of Samuel Brown;
And this fellow lived with no other thought
Than to our house come down.

I was a child, and he was a child,
In that dwelling down in town,
But we loved with a love that was more than love,
I and my Samuel Brown,
With a love that the ladies coveted
Me and Samuel Brown.

And this was the reason that, long ago,
To that dwelling down in town,
A girl came out of her carriage, courting
My beautiful Samuel Brown;
So that her high-bred kinsman came
And bore away Samuel Brown,
And shut him up in a dwelling-house,
In a street quite up in town.

The ladies not half so happy up there,
Went envying me and Brown;
Yes! that was the reason, (as all men know,
In this dwelling down in town),
That the girl came out of the carriage by night,
Coquetting and getting my Samuel Brown.

But our love is more artful by far than the love
Of those who are older than we,
Of many far wiser than we,
And neither the girls that are living above,
Nor the girls that are living in town,
Can ever dissever my soul from the soul
Of the beautiful Samuel Brown.

For the morn never shines without bringing me lines
From my beautiful Samuel Brown;
And the night's never dark, but I sit in the park
With my beautiful Samuel Brown.
And often by day, I walk down in Broadway,
With my darling, my darling, my life and my stay,
To our dwelling down in town,
To our house in the street down town.

The Day is Done

The day is done, and darkness
From the wing of night is loosed,
As a feather is wafted downward
From a chicken going to roost.

I see the lights of the baker
Gleam through the rain and mist,
And a feeling of sadness comes o'er me
That I cannot well resist.

A feeling of sadness and longing,
That is not like being sick,
And resembles sorrow only
As a brick-bat resembles a brick.

Come, get for me some supper,
A good and regular meal,
That shall soothe this restless feeling,
And banish the pain I feel.

Not from the pastry baker's,
Not from the shops for cake,
I wouldn't give a farthing
For all that they can make.

For, like the soup at dinner,
Such things would but suggest
Some dishes more substantial,
And to-night I want the best.

Go to some honest butcher,
Whose beef is fresh and nice
As any they have in the city,
And get a liberal slice.

Such things through days of labor,
And nights devoid of ease,
For sad and desperate feelings
Are wonderful remedies.

They have an astonishing power
To aid and reinforce,
And come like the "Finally, brethren,"
That follows a long discourse.

Then get me a tender sirloin
From off the bench or hook,
And lend to its sterling goodness
The science of the cook.

And the night shall be filled with comfort,
And the cares with which it begun
Shall fold up their blankets like Indians,
And silently cut and run.

Jacob

He dwelt among "apartments jet."
About five stories high,
A man I thought that none would get,
And very few would try.

A boulder, by a larger stone
Half hidden in the mud,
Fair as a man when only one
Is in the neighbourhood.

He lived unknown, and few could tell
When Jacob was not free;

But he has got a wife—and O!
The difference to me!

A Psalm of Life:
What the Heart of the Young Woman
Said to the Old Maid

Tell me not, in idle jingle,
Marriage is an empty dream,
For the girl is dead that's single,
And things are not what they seem.

Married life is real, earnest;
Single blessedness a fib;
Taken from man, to man returnest,
Has been spoken of the rib.

Not enjoyment, and not sorrow,
Is our destined end or way;
But to act, that each to-morrow
Nearer brings the wedding-day.

Life is long and youth is fleeting,
And our hearts, if there we search,
Still like steady drums are beating
Anxious marches to the church.

In the world's broad field of battle,
In the bivouac of life,
Be not like dumb, driven cattle!
Be a woman, be a wife!

Trust no Future, howe'er pleasant!
Let the dead Past bury its dead!
Act, act in the living Present:
Heart within, and MAN ahead!

Lives of married folks remind us
We can live our lives as well,
And, departing, leave behind us
Such examples as will tell;

Such examples, that another,
Sailing far from Hymen's port,
A forlorn, unmarried brother,
Seeing, shall take heart, and court.

Let us then be up and doing,
With the heart and head begin;
Still achieving, still pursuing,
Learn to labor, and to win!

When Lovely Woman

When lovely woman wants a favor,
And finds, too late, that man won't bend,
What earthly circumstance can save her
From disappointment in the end?
The only way to bring him over
The last experiment to try,
Whether a husband or a lover,
If he have feeling, is, to cry!

Shakesperian Readings

Ah, but to fade, and live we know not where,
To be a cold obstruction and to groan!
This sensible, warm woman to become
A prudish clod; and the delighted spirit
To live and die alone, or to reside
With married sisters, and to have the care
Of half a dozen children, not your own;
And driven, for no one wants you,
Round about the pendant world; or worse than worse
Of those that disappointment and pure spite
Have driven to madness: 'Tis too horrible!
The weariest and most troubled married life
That age, ache, penury, or jealousy
Can lay on nature, is a paradise
To being an old maid.

Moral Lessons

How doth the little busy flea
Improve each awful jump;
And mark her progress as she goes,
By many an itchin—lump!
To lively back-biting and sich,
My great ambition tends;
Thus would I make me fat and rich
By living off my friends.

The Wife

Her washing ended with the day,
Yet lived she at its close,
And passed the long, long night away,

In darning ragged hose.
But when the sun in all his state
Illumed the eastern skies,
She passed about the kitchen grate,
And went to making pies.

The Annoyers

"Common as light is love,
And its familiar voice wearies not ever."

—Shelley.

Love knoweth everybody's house,
And every human haunt,
And comes unbidden everywhere,
Like people we don't want.

The turnpike-roads and little creeks
Are written with love's words,
And you hear his voice like a thousand bricks
In the lowing of the herds.

He peeps into the teamster's heart,
From his Buena Vista's rim,
And the cracking whips of many men
Can never frighten him.

He'll come to his cart in the weary night,
When he's dreaming of his craft;
And he'll float to his eye in the morning light,
Like a man on a river raft.

He hears the sound of the cooper's adz,
And makes him, too, his dupe,
For he sighs in his ear from the shaving pile
As he hammers on the loop.

The little girl, the beardless boy,
The men that walk or stand,
He will get them all in his mighty arms,
Like the grasp of your very hand.

The shoemaker bangs above his bench,
And ponders his shining awl,
For love is under the lapstone hid,
And a spell is on the wall.

It heaves the sole where he drives the pegs,
And speaks in every blow,
Till the last is dropped from his crafty hand
And his foot hangs bare below.

He blurs the prints which the shopmen sell,
And intrudes on the hatter's trade,
And profanes the hostler's stable-yard
In the shape of the chamber-maid.

In the darkest night and the bright daylight,
Knowing that lie can win,
In every home of good-looking folks
Will human love come in.

John Thompson's Daughter

A fellow near Kentucky's clime
Cries, "Boatman, do not tarry,
And I'll give thee a silver dime
To row us o'er the ferry."
"Now, who would cross the Ohio,
This dark and stormy water?"
"O, I am this young lady's beau,
And she John Thompson's daughter.

We've fled before her father's spite
With great precipitation,
And should he find us here to-night,
I'd lose my reputation.
"They've missed the girl and purse beside,
His horsemen hard have pressed me,
And who will cheer my bonny bride,
If yet they shall arrest me?"
Out spoke the boatman then in time,
"You shall not fail, don't fear it;
I'll go, not for your silver dime,
But for your manly spirit.
"And by my word, the bonny bird
In danger shall not tarry;
For though a storm is coming on,
I'll row you o'er the ferry."
By this the wind more fiercely rose,
The boat was at the landing,
And with the drenching rain their clothes
Grew wet where they were standing.
But still, as wilder rose the wind,
And as the night grew drearer,
Just back a piece came the police,
Their tramping sounded nearer.
"O, haste thee, haste!" the lady cries,
"It's any thing but funny;
I'll leave the light of loving eyes,
But not my father's money!"
And still they hurried in the face
Of wind and rain unsparing;
John Thompson reached the landing-places
His wrath was turned to swearing.
For by the lightning's angry flash,
His child's lie did discover;
One lovely hand held all the cash,
And one was round her lover!

"Come back, come back," he cried in woe,
Across the stormy water;
"But leave the purse, and you may go,
My daughter, O my daughter!"
'Twas vain; they reached the other shore,
(Such dooms the Fates assign us,)
The gold he piled went with his child,
And he was left there, minus.

Kate Ketchem

Kate Ketchem on a winter's night
Went to a party dressed in white.
Her chinon in a net of gold
Was about as large as they ever sold.
Gayly she went, because her "pap"
Was supposed to be a rich old chap.
But when by chance her glances fell
On a friend who had lately married well,
Her spirits sunk, and a vague unrest
And a nameless longing filled her breast
A wish she wouldn't have had made known
To have an establishment of her own.
Tom Fudge came slowly through the throng
With chestnut hair worn pretty long
And saw Kate Ketchem in the crowd
And knowing her slightly, stopped and bowed,
Then asked her to give him a single flower,
Saying he'd think it a priceless dower.
Out from those with which she was decked
She took the poorest she could select,
And blushed as she gave it, looking down
To draw attention to her gown.
"Thanks," said Fudge; and he thought how dear
Flowers must be at that time of year.

Then several charming remarks be made,
Asked if she sang, or danced, or played;
And being exhausted, inquired whether
She thought it was going to be pleasant weather.
And Kate displayed her "jewelry,"
And dropped her lashes becomingly;
And listened, with no attempt to disguise
The admiration in her eyes.
At last, like one who has nothing to say,
He turned around and walked away.
Kate Ketchem smiled, and said, "You bet
I'll catch that Fudge and his money yet.
"He's rich enough to keep me in clothes,
And I think I could manage him as I chose.
"He could aid my father as well as not,
And buy my brother a splendid yacht.
"My mother for money should never fret,
And all it cried for, the baby should get.
"And after that, with what he could spare,
I'd make a show at a charity fair."
Tom Fudge looked back as he crossed the sill,
And saw Kate Ketchem standing still.
"A girl more suited to my mind
It isn't an easy thing to find;
"And everything that she has to wear
Proves her rich as she is fair.
"Would she were mine, and I to-day
Had the old man's cash my debts to pay!
"No creditors with a long account,
No tradesmen wanting 'that little amount;'
"But all my scores paid up when due
By a father-in-law as rich as a Jew!"
But he thought of her brother not worth a straw
And her mother, that would be his, in law;
So, undecided, he walked along,
And Kate was left alone in the throng.

But a lawyer smiled, whom he sought by stealth,
To ascertain old Ketchem's wealth;
And as for Kate she schemed and planned
Till one of the dancers claimed her hand.
He married her for her father's cash
She married him to cut a dash.
But as to paying his debts, do you know,
The father couldn't see it so;
And at hints for help, Kate's hazel eyes
Looked out in their innocent surprise.
And when Tom thought of the way he had wed,
He longed for a single life instead,
And closed his eyes in a sulky mood,
Regretting the days of his bachelorhood;
And said, in a sort of reckless vein,
"I'd like to see her catch me again,
"If I were free, as on that night
When I saw Kate Ketchem dressed in white!"
She wedded him to be rich and gay;
But husband and children didn't pay.
He wasn't the prize she hoped to draw,
And wouldn't live with his mother-in law.
And oft when she had to coax and pout,
In order to get him to take her out,
She thought how very attentive and bright
He seemed at the party that winter's night;
Of his laugh, as soft as a breeze of the south
('Twas now on the other side of his mouth);
How he praised her dress and gems in his talk
As he took a careful account of stock.
Sometimes she hated the very walls
Hated her friends, her dinners, and calls;
Till her weak affection, to hatred turned,
Like a dying tallow-candle burned.
So she took up her burden with a groan,
Saying only, "I might have known!"

Alas for Kate! and alas for Fudge!
Though I do not owe them any grudge;
And alas for any who find to their shame
That two can play at their little game!
For of all hard things to bear and grin,
The hardest is knowing you're taken in.

Dorothy's Dower: In Three Parts

I.

"My sweetest Dorothy," said John,
  Of course before the wedding,
As metaphorically he stood,
  His gold upon her shedding,
"Whatever thing you wish or want
  Shall be hereafter granted,
For all my worldly goods are yours."
  The fellow was enchanted!
"About that little dower you have,
  You thought might yet come handy,
Throw it away, do what you please,
  Spend it on sugar-candy!
I like your sweet, dependent ways,
  I love you when you tease me;
The more you ask, the more you spend,
  The better you will please me."

II.

"Confound it, Dorothy!" said John,
  "I haven't got it by me.
You haven't, have you, spent that sum,
  The dower from Aunt Jemima?
"No, well that's sensible for you
  This fix is most unpleasant;

But money's tight, so just take yours
And use it for the present.
Now I must go—to meet a man!
By George! I'll have to borrow!
Lend me a twenty—that's all right!
I'll pay you back to-morrow."

III.

"Madam," says John to Dorothy,
And past her rudely pushes,
"You think a man is made of gold,
And money grows on bushes!
Tom's shoes! Your doctor! Can't you now
Get up some new disaster?
You and your children are enough
To break John Jacob Astor.
Where's what you had yourself, when I
Was fool enough to court you?
That little sum, till you got me
'Twas what had to support you!"
"It's lent and gone, not very far;
Pray don't be apprehensive."
"Lent! I've had use enough for it:
My family is expensive.
I didn't, as a woman would,
Spend it on sugar-candy!"
"No, John, I think the most of it
Went for cigars and brandy!"

Granny's House

Comrades, leave me here a little, while as yet 'tis early morn,
Leave me here, and when you want me, sound upon the dinner-
    horn.
'Tis the place, and all about it, as of old, the rat and mouse

Very loudly squeak and nibble, running over Granny's house;
Granny's house, with all its cupboards, and its rooms as neat as
    wax,
And its chairs of wood unpainted, where the old cats rubbed their
    backs,
Many a night from yonder garret window, ere I went to rest,
Did I see the cows and horses come in slowly from the west;
Many a night I saw the chickens, flying upward through the trees,
Roosting on the sleety branches, when I thought their feet would
    freeze;
Here about the garden wandered, nourishing a youth sublime
With the beans, and sweet potatoes, and the melons which were
    prime;
When the pumpkin-vines behind me with their precious fruit
    reposed,
When I clung about the pear-tree, for the promise that it closed,
When I dipt into the dinner far as human eye could see,
Saw the vision of the pie, and all the dessert that would be.

In the spring a fuller crimson comes upon the robin's breast;
In the spring the noisy pullet gets herself another nest;
In the spring a livelier spirit makes the ladies' tongues more glib;
In the spring a young boy's fancy lightly hatches up a fib.
Then her cheek was plump and fatter than should be for one so
    old,
And she eyed my every motion, with a mute intent to scold.
And I said, "My worthy Granny, now I speak the truth to thee,
Better believe it, I have eaten all the apples from one tree."
On her kindling cheek and forehead came a color and a light,
As I have seen the rosy red flashing in one northern night;
And she turned, her fist was shaken at the coolness of the lie;
She was mad, and I could see it, by the snapping of her eye,
Saying "I have hid my feelings, fearing they should do thee wrong,"
Saying, "I shall whip you, Sammy, whipping, I shall go it strong!"
She took me up and turned me pretty roughly, when she'd done,
And every time she shook me, I tried to jerk and run;

She took off my little coat, and struck again with all her might,
And before another minute I was free and out of sight.
Many a morning, just to tease her, did I tell her stories yet,
Though her whisper made me tingle, when she told me what I'd
get;
Many an evening did I see her where the willow sprouts grew
thick,
And I rushed away from Granny at the touching of her stick.

O my Granny, old and ugly, O my Granny's hateful deeds,
O the empty, empty garret, O the garden gone to weeds,
Crosser than all fancy fathoms, crosser than all songs have sung,
I was puppet to your threat, and servile to your shrewish tongue,
Is it well to wish thee happy, having seen thy whip decline
On a boy with lower shoulders, and a narrower back, than mine?
Hark, my merry comrades call me, sounding on the dinner-horn,
They to whom my Granny's whippings were a target for their
scorn;
Shall it not be scorn to me to harp on such a mouldered string?
I am shamed through all my nature to have loved the mean old
thing;
Weakness to be wroth with weakness! woman's pleasure, woman's
spite,
Nature made them quicker motions, a considerable sight.

Woman is the lesser man, and all thy whippings matched with
mine
Are as moonlight unto sunlight, and as water unto wine.
Here at least when I was little, something, ah, for some retreat
Deep in yonder crowded city where my life began to beat,
Where one winter fell my father, slipping on a keg of lard,
I was left a trampled orphan, and my case was pretty hard
Or to burst all links of habit, and to wander far and fleet,
On from farmhouse unto farmhouse till I found my Uncle Pete,

Larger sheds and barns, and newer, and a better neighborhood,
Greater breadth of field and woodland, and an orchard just as
    good.

Never comes my Granny, never cuts her willow switches there;
Boys are safe at Uncle Peter's, I'll bet you what you dare.
Hangs the heavy fruited pear-tree: you may eat just what you like.
'T is a sort of little Eden, about two miles off the pike.
There, methinks, would be enjoyment, more than being quite so
    near
To the place where even in manhood I almost shake with fear.
There the passions, cramped no longer, shall have scope and
    breathing space.
I will 'scape that savage woman, she shall never rear my race;
Iron-jointed, supple-sinewed, they shall dive and they shall run;
She has caught me like a wild goat, but she shall not catch my son.
He shall whistle to the dog, and get the books from off the shelf,
Not, with blinded eyesight, cutting whips to whip himself –
Fool again, the dream of fancy! no, I don't believe it's bliss,
But I'm certain Uncle Peter's is a better place than this.
Let them herd with narrow foreheads, vacant of all glorious gains,
Like the horses in the stables, like the sheep that crop the lanes;
Let them mate with dirty cousins, what to me were style or rank,
I the heir of twenty acres, and some money in the bank?
Not in vain the distance beckons, forward let us urge our load,
Let our cart-wheels spin till sun-down, ringing down tile grooves
    of road;
Through the white dust of the turnpike she can't see to give as
    chase:
Better seven years at uncle's, than fourteen at Granny's place.

O, I see the blessed promise of my spirit hath not set!
If we once get in the wagon, we will circumvent her yet.
Howsoever these things, be a long farewell to Granny's farm:
Not for me she'll cut the willows, not at me she'll shake her arm.
Comes a vapor from the margin, blackening over heath and holt,

Cramming all the blast before it,—guess it holds a thunderbolt:
Wish 'twould fall on Granny's house, with rain, or hail, or fire, or
    snow,
Let me get my horses started Uncle Peteward, and I'll go.

I Remember, I Remember

I remember, I remember,
The house where I was wed,
And the little room from which that night,
My smiling bride was led;
She didn't come a wink too soon,
Nor make too long a stay;
But now I often wish her folks
Had kept the girl away!
I remember, I remember,
Her dresses, red and white,
Her bonnets and her caps and cloaks,
They cost an awful sight!
The "corner lot" on which I built,
And where my brother met
At first my wife, one washing-day,
That man is single yet!
I remember, I remember,
Where I was used to court,
And thought that all of married life
Was just such pleasant sport:
My spirit flew in feathers then,
No care was on my brow;
I scarce could wait to shut the gate,
I'm not so anxious now!
I remember, I remember,
My dear one's smile and sigh;
I used to think her tender heart
Was close against the shy;

It was a childish ignorance,
But now it soothes me not
To know I'm farther off from heaven
Than when she wasn't got!

The Change

In sunset's light o'er Boston thrown,
A young man proudly stood
Beside a girl, the only one
He thought was fair or good;
The one on whom his heart was set,
The one he tried so long to get.
He heard his wife's first loving sound,
A low, mysterious tone,
A music sought, but never found,
By beaux and gallants gone;
He listened and his heart beat high,
That was the song of victory!
The rapture of the conqueror's mood
Rushed burning through his frame,
And all the folks that round him stood
Its torrents could not tame,
Though stillness lay with eve's last smile
Round Boston Common all the while.
Years came with care; across his life
There swept a sudden change,
E'en with the one he called his wife,
A shadow dark and strange,
Breathed from the thought so swift to fall
O'er triumph's hour, and is this all?
No, more than this! what seemed it now
Right by that one to stand?
A thousand girls of fairer brow
Walked his own mountain land;

Whence, far o'er matrimony's track,
Their wild, sweet voices called him back.
They called him back to many a glade
Where once he joyed to rove,
Where often in the beechen shade
He sat and talked of love;
They called him with their mocking sport
Back to the times he used to court.
But, darkly mingling with the thought
Of each remembered scene,
Rose up a fearful vision, fraught
With all that lay between,
His wrinkled face, his altered lot,
His children's wants, the wife he'd got!
Where was the value of that bride
He likened once to pearls?
His weary heart within him died
With yearning for the girls,
All vainly struggling to repress
That rush of painful tenderness
He wept; the wife that made his bed.
Beheld the sad reverse,
Even on the spot where he had said
"For better or for worse."
O happiness! how far we flee
Thine own sweet path in search of thee.

Coming Round

'Tis all right, as I knew it would be by and by;
We have kissed and made up again, Archie and I;
And that quarrel, or nonsense, what ever you will,
I think makes us love more devotedly still.
The trouble was all upon my side, you know;
I'm exacting sometimes, rather foolishly so;

And let any one tell me the veriest lie
About Archie, I'm sure to get angry and cry.
Things will go on between us again just the same,
For as he explains matters he wasn't to blame;
But 'tis useless to tell you; I can't make you see
How it was, quite as plainly as he has made me.
You thought "I would make him come round when we met!"
You thought "there were slights I could never forget!"
Oh you did! let me tell you, my dear, to your face,
That your thinking these things doesn't alter the case!
You "can tell what I said?" I don't wish you to tell!
You know what a temper I have, very well;
That I'm sometimes unjust to my friends who are best;
But you've turned against Archie the same as the rest!
"Why hasn't he written? what kept him so still?"
His silence was sorely against his own will;
He has faults, that I own; but he, he wouldn't deceive;
He was ill, or was busy,—was both, I believe!

Worser Moments

That fellow's voice! how often steals
Its cadence o'er my lonely days!
Like something sent on wagon wheels,
Or packed in an unconscious chaise.
I might forget the words he said
When all the children fret and cry,
But when I get them off to bed,
His gentle tone comes stealing by,
And years of matrimony flee,
And leave me sitting on his knee.
The times he came to court a spell,
The tender things he said to me,
Make me remember mighty well
My hopes that he'd propose to me.

My face is uglier, and perhaps
Time and the comb have thinned my hair,
And plain and common are the caps
And dresses that I have to wear;
But memory is ever yet
With all that fellow's flatteries writ
I have been out at milking-time
Beneath a dull and rainy sky,
When in the barn 'twas time to feed,
And calves were bawling lustily,
When scattered hay, and sheaves of oats,
And yellow corn-ears, sound and hard,
And all that makes the cattle pass
With wilder fleetness through the yard,
When all was hateful, then have I,
With friends who had to help me milk
Talked of his wife most spitefully,
And how he kept her dressed in silk;
And when the cattle, running there,
Threw over me a shower of mud,
That fellow's voice came on the air,
Like the light chewing of the cud
And resting near some speckled cow
The spirit of a woman's spite,
I've poured a low and fervent vow
To make him, if I had the might,
Live all his lifetime just as hard,
And milk his cows in such a yard.
I have been out to pick up wood,
When night was stealing from the dawn
Before the fire was burning good,
Or I had put the kettle on
The little stove—when babes were waking
With a low murmur in the beds,
And melody by fits was breaking
Above their little yellow heads,

And this when I was up perhaps
From a few short and troubled naps,
And when the sun sprang scorchingly
And freely up, and made us stifle,
And fell upon each hill and tree
The bullets from his subtle rifle,
I say a voice has thrilled me then,
Hard by that solemn pile of wood,
Or creeping from the silent glen,
Like something on the unfledged brood,
Hath stricken me, and I have pressed
Close in my arms my load of chips,
And pouring forth the hatefulest
Of words that ever passed my lips,
Have felt my woman's spirit rush
On me, as on that milking night,
And, yielding to the blessed gush
Of my ungovernable spite,
Have risen up, the red, the old,
Scolding as hard as I could scold.

Helpless

You never said a word to me
That was cruel, under the sun;
It isn't the things you do, darling,
But the things you leave undone.

If you could but know a wish or want,
You would grant it joyfully;
Ah! that is the worst of all, darling,
That you cannot know nor see.

For favors free alone are sweet,
Not those that we must seek;

If you loved as I love you, darling,
I would not need to speak.

But today I am helpless as a child
That must be led along;
Then put your hand in mine, darling,
And make me brave and strong.

There's a heavy care upon my mind,
A trouble on my brain;
Now gently stroke my hair, darling,
And take away the pain.

I feel a weight within my breast,
As if all had gone amiss;
Oh kiss me with your lips, darling,
And fill my heart with bliss.

Enough! no deeper joy than this
For souls below is given;
Now take me in your arms, darling,
And lift me up to heaven!

My Lady

As violets, modest, tender-eyed,
The light of their beauty love to hide
In deepest solitudes;
Even thus, to dwell unseen, she chose,
My flower of womanhood, my rose,
My lady of the woods!
Full of the deepest, truest thought,
Doing, the very things she ought,
Stooping to all good deeds:
Her eyes too pure to shrink from such,

And her hands too clean to fear the touch
Of the sinfulest in his needs.
There is no line of beauty or grace
That was not found in her pleasant face,
And no heart can ever stir,
With a sense of human wants and needs,
With promptings unto the holiest deeds,
But had their birth in her.
With never a taint of the world's untruth,
She lived from infancy to youth,
From youth to womanhood:
Taking no soil in the ways she trod,
But pure as she came from the hand of God,
Before His face she stood.
My sweetest darling, my tenderest care!
The hardest thing that I have to bear
Is to know my work is past;
That nothing now I can say or do
Will bring any comfort or aid to you,
I have said and done the last.
Yet I know I never was good enough,
That my tenderest efforts were all too rough
To help a soul so fine;
So the lovingest angel among them all,
Whose touches fell, with the softest fall,
Has pushed my hand from thine!

Equality

Most favored lady in the land,
I well can bear your scorn or pride;
For in all truest wealth, to-day,
I stand an equal by your side!
No better parentage have you,
One is our Father, one our Friend;

The same inheritance awaits
Our claiming, at the journey's end.
No broader flight your thought can take,
Faith on no firmer basis rest;
Nor can the dreams of fancy wake
A sweeter tumult in your breast.
Life may to you bring every good,
Which from a Father's hand can fall;
But if true lips have said to you
"I love you" I have known it all.

Happy Women

Impatient women as you wait
In cheerful homes to-night, to hear
The sound of steps that, soon or late,
Shall come as music to your ear;
Forget yourselves a little while
And think in pity of the pain
Of women who will never smile
To hear a coming step again.
With babes that in their cradle sleep,
Or cling to you in perfect trust;
Think of the mothers left to weep,
Their babies lying in the dust
And when the step you wait for comes,
And all your world is full of light,
O women, safe in happy homes,
Pray for all lonesome souls to-night!

To Miss Susan Anthony,
on her Fiftieth Birthday

We touch our caps, and place to-night
The victor's wreath upon her,
The woman who outranks us all
In courage and in honor.

While others in domestic broils
Have proved by word and carriage,
That one of the United States
Is not the state of marriage.

She, caring not for loss of men,
Nor for the world's confusion,
Has carried on a civil war,
And made a "Revolution."

True, other women have been brave,
When banded or hus-banded,
But she has bravely fought her way
Alone and single-handed.

And think of her unselfish strength,
Her generous disposition,
Who never made a lasting prop
Out of a proposition.

She might have chosen an honored name,
And none have scorned or hissed it
Have written Mrs. Jones or Smith,
But, strange to say, she Missed it.

For fifty years to come may she
Grow rich and ripe and mellow,

Be quoted even above "par,"
Or any other fellow!

And speak the truth from pole to pole,
And keep her light a-burning,
Before she cuts her stick to go
The way there's no returning.

Because her motto grand hath been
The right of every human,
And first and last, and right or wrong
She takes the side of woman

"A perfect woman, nobly planned,"
To aid, not to amuse one,
Take her for all in all we ne'er
Shall see the match for Susan!

Advice Gratis to Certain Women by a Woman

Oh, my strong-minded sisters, aspiring to vote,
And to row with your brothers, all in the same boat,
When you come out to speak to the public your mind,
Leave your tricks, and your airs, and your graces behind!

For instance, when you by the world would be seen
As reporter, or editor (first-class, I mean),
I think just to come to the point in one line—
What you write will be finer, if 'tis not too fine.

Pray, don't let the thread of your subject be strung
With "golden," and "shimmer," "sweet," "filter," and "flung;"
Nor compel, by your style, all your readers to guess
You've been looking up words Webster marks obs.

And another thing: whatever else you may say,
Do keep personalities out of the way;
Don't try every sentence to make people see
What a dear, charming creature the writer must be!

Leave out affectations and pretty appeals;
Don't "drag yourself in by the neck and the heels,"
Your dear little boots, and your gloves; and take heed,
Nor pull your curls over men's eyes while they read.

Don't mistake me; I mean that the public's not home,
You must do as the Romans do, when you're in Rome;
I would have you be womanly, while you are wise;
'Tis the weak and the womanish tricks I despise.

On the other hand: don't write and dress in such styles
As astonish the natives, and frighten the isles;
Do look, on the platform, so folks in the show
Needn't ask, "Which are lions, and which tigers? you know!"

'Tis a good thing to write, and to rule in the state,
But to be a true, womanly woman is great:
And if ever you come to be that, 'twill be when
You can cease to be babies, nor try to be men!

Was He Henpecked?

"I'll tell you what it is, my dear,"
    Said Mrs. Dorking, proudly,
"I do not like that chanticleer
    Who crows o'er us so loudly.

"And since I must his laws obey,
    And have him walk before me,

I'd rather like to have my say
Of who should lord it o'er me."

"You'd like to vote?" he answered slow,
"Why, treasure of my treasures,
What can you, or what should you know
Of public men, or measures?

"Of course, you have ability,
Of nothing am I surer;
You're quite as wise, perhaps, as I;
You're better, too, and purer.

"I'd have you just for mine alone
Nay, so do I adore you,
I'd put you queen upon a throne,
And bow myself before you."

"You'd put me! you? Now that is what
I do not want, precisely;
I want myself to choose the spot
That I can fill most wisely."

"My dear, you're talking like a goose
Unhenly, and improper"
But here again her words broke loose,
In vain he tried to stop her:

"I tell you, though she never spoke
So you could understand her,
A goose knows when she wears a yoke,
As quickly as a gander."

"Why, bless my soul! what would you do?
Write out a diagnosis?

Speak equal rights? join with their crew
And dine with the Sorosis?

"And shall I live to see it, then
My wife a public teacher?
And would you be a crowing hen
That dreadful unsexed creature?"

"Why, as to that, I do not know;
Nor see why you should fear it;
If I can crow, why let me crow,
If I can't, then you won't hear it!"

"Now, why," he said, "can't such as you
Accept what we assign them?
You have your rights, 'tis very true,
But then, we should define them!

"We would not peck you cruelly,
We would not buy and sell you;
And you, in turn, should think, and be,
And do, just what we tell you!

"I do not want you made, my dear,
The subject of rude men's jest;
I like you in your proper sphere,
The circle of a hen's nest!

"I'd keep you in the chicken-yard,
Safe, honored, and respected;
From all that makes us rough and hard,
Your sex should be protected."

"Pray, did it ever make you sick?
Have I gone to the dickens?

Because you let me scratch and pick
Both for myself and chickens?"

"Oh, that's a different thing, you know,
Such duties are parental;
But for some work to do, you'd grow
Quite weak and sentimental."

"Ah! yes, it's well for you to talk
About a parent's duty!
Who keeps your chickens from the hawk?
Who stays in nights, my beauty?"

"But, madam, you may go each hour,
Lord bless your pretty faces!
We'll give you anything, but power
And honor, trust and places.

"We'd keep it hidden from your sight
How public scenes are carried;
Why, men are coarse, and swear, and fight"
"I know it, dear; I'm married!"

"Why, now you gabble like a fool;
But what's the use of talking?
'Tis yours to serve, and mine to rule,
I tell you, Mrs. Dorking!"

"Oh, yes," she said, "you've all the sense;
Your sex are very knowing
Yet some of you are on the fence,
And only good at crowing."

"Ah! preciousest of precious souls,
Your words with sorrow fill me;

To see you voting at the polls
I really think would kill me.

"To mourn my home's lost sanctity;
To feel you did not love me;
And worse, to see you fly so high,
And have you roost above me!"

"Now, what you fear in equal rights
I think you've told precisely;
That's just about the place it lights,"
Said Mrs. Dorking wisely.

Man Believes the Strong

Ah! in this world, where all is fair and bright,
Save human wickedness and human pride,
Marring what else were lovely to the sight,
It is a truth that may not be denied,
However deeply we deplore the wrong,
Man hath believed, and still believes the strong.

When injured and defenceless woman stands,
Haply the child of innocence or youth,
And lifts to heaven her pleading voice and hands
In all the moving eloquence of truth,
Who will believe, in that most trying hour,
Her words who is not strong in wealth or power?

Or let the slave, of all on earth bereft,
Stand up to plead before a human bar;
And though the fetters and the lash have left
Upon his limbs the deep-attesting scar,
Who trusts his tale, or who will rise to save
From wrong and injury the outcast slave?

If a poor, friendless criminal appear,
A criminal which men themselves have made,
By the injustice and oppression here,
Who to pronounce him "guilty" is afraid?
But who, if rank or wealth were doomed thereby,
Would speak that final word as fearlessly?

Oh, where so much of wrong and sorrow are,
There must be need of an unfaltering trust
In His all seeing watchfulness and care,
Whose ways to man below we know are just;
In Him, whose love has numbered every tear
Wrung from his weak, defenceless creatures here.

And there is need of earnest, full belief,
And patient work, to bring that holier day
When there shall be redress for humblest grief,
And equal right and justice shall have sway;
And we will strive, in trustfulness sublime,
Hoping our eyes may see the blessed time!

Moralizings

Hark to the triumph for a victory won,
Shaking the solid earth whereon we stand!
What noble action hath the Nation done,
That thus rejoicing echoes through the land?
Hath she beheld life's inequality
How, still, her stronger sons the weak oppress,
And, in the spirit of philanthropy,
Made the deep sum of human anguish less?
Or hath she risen up, at last to free
The hopeless slave from his captivity?
No, not for these the shout is heard to-night;
Waking its echoes in each vale and glen,

Not that the precepts of the Lord of Light
Have found a dwelling in the hearts of men;
'Tis that a battle hath been fought and won
That the deep cannon's note is heard afar—
Telling us of the bloody conflict done,
That Victory hovers o'er our ranks in war
And that her solidiery their triumph sing
In the broad shadow of her starry wing.
And war is here! Impatient for the fight,
Our Nation in her majesty arose,
Even as the restless lion in his might
Up from the swelling of the Jordan goes,
And, with a trampling noise that shook each hill,
On to this conflict madly hath she rushed,
Vowing to falter not, nor yield, until
The life from out a Nation's heart is crushed;
Until her hapless sons are made to feel
The bloody vengeance of her iron heel!
And what will be our gain, though we return
Proudly victorious from each battle plain?
A weakened Nation will be left to mourn
Her bravest heroes in the conflict slain;
Her treasury drained; our broad and goodly land
Filled with the orphan and the widowed wife;
A soldiery corrupted to disband,
Unfit for useful toil or virtuous life;
And a long train of evils yet to be
Darkly entailed upon posterity!
And this is glory! This is what hath been
To ages back the proudest theme of song,
And, dazzled by its glare, man has not seen
Beneath its pageantry the deadly wrong.
Deeming it fame to tread where heroes trod,
In his career he has not paused, or known
That all are children of the self-same God,
And that our brother's interest is our own;

For man that hardest lesson has to learn,
Still to forgive, and good for ill to return.
But oh! for all will come that solemn hour
When memory calls to mind each deed of sin,
And the world's hollow praise can have no power
To still the voice of conscious guilt within
And grant, O Lord of Love, that it may be
My lot, when on the brink of death I press,
To think of some slight act of charity,
Some pang of human wretchedness made less,
So, that in numbering o'er life's deeds again,
I then may deem I have not lived in vain!

The Outcast

She died at the middle of night:
And brother nor sister, lover nor friend,
Came not near her their aid to lend,
Ere the spirit took its flight.

She died at the middle of night:
Food and raiment she had no more,
And the fire had died on the hearth before,
'Twas a pitiful, pitiful sight.

She died at the middle of night:
Napkin pressed back the parted lips;
Weeper, watching the eyes' eclipse,
Covered them up from sight.

She died at the middle of night:
And there was no taper beside the dead,
But the stars, through the broken roof o'er head,
Shone with a solemn light.

She died at the middle of night:
And the winter snow spread a winding-sheet
Over the body from head to feet,
Dainty, and soft, and white.

She died at the middle of night:
But if she heard, ere her hour was o'er,
"I have not condemned thee—sin no more,"
She lives where the day is bright.

Nobody's Child

Only a newsboy, under the light
Of the lamp-post plying his trade in vain:
Men are too busy to stop to-night,
Hurrying home through the sleet and rain.
Never since dark a paper sold;
Where shall he sleep, or how be fed?
He thinks as he shivers there in the cold,
While happy children are safe abed.
Is it strange if he turns about
With angry words, then comes to blows,
When his little neighbor, just sold out,
Tossing his pennies, past him goes?
"Stop!" some one looks at him, sweet and mild,
And the voice that speaks is a tender one:
"You should not strike such a little child,
And you should not use such words, my son!"
Is it his anger or his fears
That have hushed his voice and stopped his arm?
"Don't tremble," these are the words he hears;
"Do you think that I would do you harm?"
"It isn't that," and the hand drops down;
"I wouldn't care for kicks and blows;
But nobody ever called me son,

Because I'm nobody's child, I s'pose."
O men! as ye careless pass along,
Remember the love that has cared for you;
And blush for the awful shame and wrong
Of a world where such a thing could be true!
Think what the child at your knee had been
If thus on life's lonely billows tossed;
And who shall bear the weight of the sin,
If one of these "little ones" be lost!

The Brothers

We had no home, we only had
A shelter for our head:
How poor we were, how scantily
We all were clothed and fed!
But though a wretched little child,
I know not why or how,
I did not feel it half so much
As I can feel it now!
When mother sat at night and sewed,
My rest was calm and deep;
I did not know that she was tired,
Or that she needed sleep.
She wrapped the covering round our bed,
In many an ample fold;
She had not half so much herself
To keep her from the cold.
I know it now, I know it all,
They knew it then above,
Her life of patient sacrifice,
And never-tiring love.
I know, for then her tasks seemed done,
We all were grown beside,
How glad she must have been to go,

After the baby died!
I do not care to deck me now
With costly robe or gaud,
My mother dressed so plain at home,
And never went abroad.
I do not even want a shroud
Of linen, white and pure,
They made our little baby one
That was so coarse and poor.
I had another brother then,
I prayed that God would save;
I knew not life had darker dooms
Than lying in the grave.
I did not know, when o'er the dead
So bitterly I cried,
I'd live to wish a thousand times
The other, too, had died.

John Brown

Men silenced on his faithful lips
Words of resistless truth and power;
Those words, re-echoing now, have made
The gathering war-cry of the hour.
They thought to darken down in blood
The light of freedom's burning rays
The beacon-fires we tend to-day
Were lit in that undying blaze.
They took the earthly prop and staff
Out of an unresisting hand
God came, and led him safely on,
By ways they could not understand.
They knew not, when from his old eyes
They shut the world for evermore,
The ladder by which angels come

Rests firmly on the dungeon's floor.
They deemed no vision bright could cheer
His stony couch and prison ward;
He slept to dream of Heaven, and rose
To build a Bethel to the Lord!
They showed to his unshrinking gaze
The "sentence" men have paled to see
He read God's writing of "reprieve,"
And grant of endless liberty.

Our Good President

Our sun hath gone down at the noon day,
The heavens are black;
And over the morning, the shadows
Of night-time are back.

Stop the proud boasting mouth of the cannon;
Hush the mirth and the shout;
God is God! and the ways of Jehovah
Are past finding out.

Lo! the beautiful feet on the mountains,
That yesterday stood,
The white feet that came with glad tidings
Are dabbled in blood.

The Nation that firmly was settling
The crown on her head,
Sits like Rizpah, in sackcloth and ashes,
And watches her dead.

Who is dead? who, unmoved by our wailing,
Is lying so low?

O my Land, stricken dumb in your anguish,
Do you feel, do you know,

That the hand which reached out of the darkness
Hath taken the whole;
Yea, the arm and the head of the people,
The heart and the soul?

And that heart, o'er whose dread awful silence
A nation has wept;
Was the truest, and gentlest, and sweetest,
A man ever kept.

Why, he heard from the dungeons, the rice-fields,
The dark holds of ships
Every faint, feeble cry which oppression
Smothered down on men's lips.

In her furnace, the centuries had welded
Their fetter and chain;
And like withes, in the hands of his purpose,
He snapped them in twain.

Who can be what he was to the people,
What he was to the state?
Shall the ages bring to us another
As good and as great?

Our hearts with their anguish are broken,
Our wet eyes are dim;
For us is the loss and the sorrow,
The triumph for him!

For, ere this, face to face with his Father
Our martyr hath stood;

Giving into his hand a white record,
With its great seal of blood!

A Tent Scene

Our generals sat in their tent one night,
On the Mississippi's banks,
Where Vicksburg sullenly still held out
Against the assaulting ranks.
They could hear the firing as they talked,
Long after set of sun
And the blended noise of a thousand guns
In the distance seemed as one.
All at once Sherman started to his feet,
And listened to the roar,
His practiced ear had caught a sound,
That he had not heard before.
They have mounted another gun on the walls;
"'Tis new," he said, "I know;
I can tell the voice of a gun, as a man
Can tell the voice of his foe.
"What! not a soul of you hears but me?
No matter, I am right;
Bring me my horse! I must silence this
Before I sleep to-night!"
He was gone and they listened to the ring
Of hoofs on the distant track;
Then talked and wondered for a while,
In an hour he was back.
"Well, General! what is the news?" they cried,
As he entered flush and worn;
"We have picked their gunners off, and the gun
Will be dislodged at morn!"

Peace

O Land, of every land the best
O Land, whose glory shall increase;
Now in your whitest raiment drest
For the great festival of peace:
Take from your flag its fold of gloom,
And let it float undimmed above,
Till over all our vales shall bloom
The sacred colors that we love.
On mountain high, in valley low,
Set Freedom's living fires to burn;
Until the midnight sky shall show
A redder pathway than the morn.
Welcome, with shouts of joy and pride,
Your veterans from the war-path's track;
You gave your boys, untrained, untried
You bring them men and heroes back!
And shed no tear, though think you must
With sorrow of the martyred band;
Not even for him whose hallowed dust
Has made our prairies holy land.
Though by the places where they fell,
The places that are sacred ground,
Death, like a sullen sentinel,
Paces his everlasting round.
Yet when they set their country free
And gave her traitors fitting doom,
They left their last great enemy,
Baffled, beside an empty tomb.
Not there, but risen, redeemed, they go
Where all the paths are sweet with flowers;
They fought to give us peace, and lo!
They gained a better peace than ours.

Nearer Home

One sweetly solemn thought
Comes to me o'er and o'er;
I am nearer home to-day
Than I ever have been before;
Nearer my Father's house,
Where the many mansions be;
Nearer the great white throne,
Nearer the crystal sea;
Nearer the bound of life,
Where we lay our burdens down;
Nearer leaving the cross,
Nearer gaining the crown!
But lying, darkly between,
Winding down through the night,
Is the silent, unknown stream,
That leads at last to the light.
Closer and closer my steps
Come to the dread abysm:
Closer Death to my lips
Presses the awful chrism.
Oh, if my mortal feet
Have almost gained the brink;
If it be I am nearer home
Even today than I think
Father, perfect my trust;
Let my spirit feel in death,
That her feet are firmly set
On the rock of a living faith!

Burial Hymn

Earth to earth, and dust to dust:
Here, in calm and holy trust,

We have made her quiet bed
With the pale hosts of the dead,
And, with hearts that, stricken weep,
Come to lay her down to sleep.
From life's weary cares set free,
Mother Earth, she comes to thee!
Hiding from its ills and storms
In the shelter of thine arms:
Peaceful, peaceful be her rest,
Here upon thy faithful breast.
And when sweetly from the dust
Heaven's last summons calls the just,
Saviour! when the nations rise
Up to meet thee in the skies,
Gently, gently, by the hand,
Lead her to the better land!

The Spiritual Body

I have a heavenly home,
To which my soul may come,
And where forever safe it may abide;
Firmly and sure it stands,
That house not made with hands,
And garnished as a chamber for a bride!
'Tis such as angels use,
Such as good men would choose;
It hath all fair and pleasant things in sight:
Its walls as white and fine
As polished ivory shine,
And through its windows comes celestial light.
'Tis builded fair and good,
In the similitude
Of the most royal palace of a king;
And sorrow may not come

Into that heavenly home,
Nor pain, nor death, nor any evil thing.
Near it that stream doth pass
Whose waters, clear as glass,
Make glad the city of our God with song;
Whose banks are fair as those
Whereon stray milk-white does,
Feeding among the lilies all day long.
And friends who once were here
Abide in dwellings near;
They went up thither on a heavenly road;
While I, though warned to go,
Yet linger here below,
Clinging to a most miserable abode.
The evil blasts drive in
Through chinks, which time and sin
Have battered in my wretched house of clay;
Yet in so vile a place,
Poor, unadorned with grace
I choose to live, or rather choose to stay.
And here I make my moan
About the days now gone,
About the souls passed on to their reward;
The souls that now have come
Into a better home,
And sit in heavenly places with their Lord.
'Tis strange that I should cling
To this despised thing,
To this poor dwelling crumbling round my head:
Making myself content
In a low tenement
After my joys and friends alike are fled!
Yet I shall not, I know,
Be ready hence to go,
And dwell in my good palace, fair and whole,
Till unrelenting Death

Blows with his icy breath
Upon my naked and unsheltered soul.

Sabbath Thoughts

I am sitting all the while
Looking down the solemn aisle,
Toward the saints and martyrs old,
Standing in their niches cold,
Toward the wing of cherubs fair,
Veiling half their golden hair,
And the painted light that falls
Through the window on the walls.
I can see the revered flow
Of soft garments, white as snow,
And the shade of silver hair
Dropping on the book of prayer.
I can hear the litany,
"Miserable sinners, we!"
And the organ swelling higher,
And the chanting of the choir.
And I marvel if with them,
In the New Jerusalem,
I shall hear the sacred choir
Chant with flaming tongues of fire;
If I e'er shall find a place
With the ransomed, saved by grace;
If my feet shall ever tread
Where the just are perfected?
Not, my soul, as now thou art;
Not with this rebellious heart;
Not with nature unsubdued,
Evil overshadowing good;
Not while I for pardon seek
With a faith so faint and weak;

Not while tempted thus to sin,
From without and from within
Thou whom love did once compel
Down from heaven to sleep in hell;
Thou whose mercy purged from dross
Even the thief upon the cross,
Save me, O thou bleeding Lamb,
Chief of sinners though I am,
When, with clouds about thee furled,
Thou shalt come to judge the world!

The City Life

How shall I know thee in that sphere that keeps
Thee country youth that to the city goes,
When all of thee, that change can wither, sleeps
And perishes among your cast-off clothes?
For I shall feel the sting of ceaseless pain,
If there I met thy one-horse carriage not;
Nor see the hat I love, nor ride again,
When thou art driving on a gentle trot.
Wilt thou not for me in the city seek,
And turn to note each passing shawl and gown?
You used to come and see me once a week,
Shall I be banished from your thought in town?
In that great street I don't know how to find,
In the resplendence of that glorious sphere,
And larger movements of the unfettered mind.
Wilt thou forget the love that joined us here?
The love that lived through all the simple past,
And meekly with my country training bore,
And deeper grew, and tenderer to the last,
Shall it expire in town, and be no more?
A happier lot than mine and greater praise,
Await thee there; for thou, with skill and tact,

Has learnt the wisdom of the world's just ways,
And dressest well, and knowest how to act
For me, the country place in which I dwell
Has made me one of a proscribed band;
And work hath left its scar—that fire of hell
Has left its frightful scar upon my hand.
Yet though thou wear'st the glory of the town,
Wilt thou not keep the same beloved name,
The same black-satin vest, and morning-gown,
Lovelier in New York City, yet the same?
Shalt thou not teach me, in that grander home,
The wisdom that I learned so ill in this,
The wisdom which is fine,—till I become
Thy fit companion in that place of bliss?

Homes for All

Columbia, fairest nation of the world,
Sitting in queenly beauty in the west,
With all thy banners round about thee furled,
Nursing the cherub Peace upon thy breast;
Never did daughter of a kingly line
Look on a lovelier heritage than thine
Thou hast deep forests stretching far away,
The giant growth of the long centuries,
From whose dim shadows to the light of day
Come forth the mighty rivers toward the seas,
To walk like happy lovers, hand in hand,
Down through the green vales of our pleasant land.
Thou liest broad prairies, where the lovely flowers
Blossom and perish with the changing year;
There harvests wave not through the summer hours,
Nor with the autumn ripen in the ear;
And beautiful lakes that toss their milky spray
Where the strong ship hath never cleaved its way.

And yet with all thy broad and fertile land,
Where hands sow not, nor gather in the grain,
Thy children come and round about thee stand,
Asking the blessing of a home in vain,
Still lingering, but with feet that long to press
Through the green windings of the wilderness.
In populous cities do men live and die,
That never breathe the pure and liberal air:
Down where the damp and desolate rice swamps lie,
Wearying the ear of Heaven with constant prayer,
Are souls that never yet have learned to raise
Under God's equal sky the psalm of praise.
Turn not, Columbia! from their pleading eyes;
Give to thy sons that ask of thee a home;
So shall they gather round thee, not with sighs,
But as young children to their mother come;
And brightly to the centuries shall go down
The glory that thou wearest like a crown.

Do You Blame Her?

Ne'er lover spake in tenderer words,
While mine were calm, unbroken;
Though I suffered all the pain I gave
In the No, so firmly spoken.

I marvel what he would think of me,
Who called it a cruel sentence,
If he knew I had almost learned today
What it is to feel repentance.

For it seems like a strange perversity,
And blind beyond excusing,
To lose the thing we could have kept,
And after, mourn the losing.

And this, the prize I might have won,
Was worth a queen's obtaining;
And one, if far beyond my reach,
I had sighed, perchance, for gaining.

And I know—ah! no one knows so well,
Though my heart is far from breaking
'Twas a loving heart, and an honest hand,
I might have had for the taking.

And yet, though never one beside
Has place in my thought above him,
I only like him when he is by,
'Tis when he is gone I love him.

Sadly of absence poets sing,
And timid lovers fear it;
But an idol has been worshiped less
Sometimes when we came too near it.

And for him my fancy throws to-day
A thousand graces o'er him
For he seems a god when he stands afar
And I kneel in my thought before him.

But if he were here, and knelt to me
With a lovers fond persistence
Would the halo brighten to my eyes
That crows him now in the distance?

Could I change the words I have said, and say
Till one of us shall perish,
Forsaking others, I take this man
Alone, to love and to cherish?

Alas! whatever beside to-day
I might dream like a fond romancer,
I know my heart so well that I know
I should give him the self-same answer.

A Woman's Conclusions

I said, if I might go back again
To the very hour and place of my birth;
Might have my life whatever I chose,
And live it in any part of the earth;

Put perfect sunshine into my sky,
Banish the shadow of sorrow and doubt;
Have all my happiness multiplied,
And all my suffering stricken out;

If I could have known, in the years now gone,
The best that a woman comes to know;
Could have had whatever will make her blest,
Or whatever she thinks will make her so:

Have found the highest and purest bliss
That the bridal-wreath and ring in close;
And gained the one out of all the world,
That my heart as well as my reason chose;

And if this had been, and I stood to-night
By my children, lying asleep in their beds,
And could count in my prayers, for a rosary,
The shining row of their golden heads;

Yea! I said, if a miracle such as this
Could be wrought for me, at my bidding, still
I would choose to have my past as it is,

And to let my future come as it will!

I would not make the path I have trod
More pleasant or even, more straight or wide;
Nor change my course the breadth of a hair,
This way or that way, to either side.

My past is mine, and I take it all;
Its weakness, its folly, if you please;
Nay, even my sins, if you come to that,
May have been my helps, not hindrances!

If I saved my body from the flames
Because that once I had burned my hand:
Or kept myself from a greater sin
By doing a less—you will understand;

It was better I suffered a little pain,
Better I sinned for a little time,
If the smarting warned me back from death,
And the sting of sin withheld from crime.

Who knows its strength, by trial, will know
What strength must be set against a sin;
And how temptation is overcome
He has learned, who has felt its power within!

And who knows how a life at the last may show?
Why, look at the moon from where we stand!
Opaque, uneven, you say; yet it shines,
A luminous sphere, complete and grand.

So let my past stand, just as it stands,
And let me now, as I may, grow old;
I am what I am, and my life for me
Is the best—or it had not been, I hold.

Julia Ward Howe:
1819–1910

Introduction

Julia Ward Howe lived major issues and changes in nineteenth-century women's status—in legal, economic, religious and social terms. She comes, as does Emily Dickinson, from elite society. She is also one of the few women poets who attempted to combine—with strain—marriage and writing. The descendent of two governors of Rhode Island, Richard and Samuel Ward, she was born in New York City in 1819 into a wealthy banking family, with private tutors and elite schooling. Her family's Manhattan home had an extensive library and art collection; her brother married into the Astor family. Her mother died in childbirth when Julia was five; and her father, in deep mourning, exercised great restraint on the family, being, as Howe wrote in her "Reminiscences," "a strenuous Protestant evangelical Calvinist of the Episcopal Church." He raised her, as she put it, protected from the evil trinity of "the world, the flesh, and the devil;" warning, in her daughters' account, "against Faust, forbidden Shelley, with Byron carefully administered." On his death, however, the uncle who took up guardianship was more tolerant, and Howe in her young womanhood enjoyed parties, suitors, and singing—she had a beautiful and trained voice. In 1841, she visited Boston, and there met Samuel Gridley Howe, soldier and Chevalier of the Greek War of Independence, social activist, director of the New England (later Perkins) Institute of the Blind, and twenty years her senior. They married in 1843.

Samuel Howe proved, however, to support every reform except women's rights. Their first struggle was over her property—about which nothing is said either in Julia's "Reminiscences" or her daughters' memoir—an account, if possible, still more impersonal than hers is. Before the first property laws for women were passed in New York in 1848 (by wealthy fathers), women had no rights of ownership, whether to inherit, to sell or buy, to sign contracts, own bank accounts, or to bequeath. Julia was granted $3000.00 a year and considerable holdings in New York real estate. Over these her husband demanded control. Her family refused, also insisting that she keep her maiden name as Julia Ward Howe rather than becoming Mrs. Samuel Gridley Howe. She did later sign a power of attorney giving to her husband her annual income. In 1847 he also gained control over her property, already mismanaged by her brother. This included 58th and 60th Streets, parts of downtown Manhattan, and a section east of 8th Avenue. Her husband sold it and invested in South Boston, in what proved to be worthless real estate. By the time Howe inherited her money in 1875 on her husband's death, her financial circumstances were quite straightened. Even her daughters concede that "all through her journals is the note of financial anxiety." As Howe wrote to her sister of Samuel Howe, "His tyrannical instincts more than any direct purpose, have made him illiberal with me in money matters, and if he can possibly place this so I cannot easily use it, he will, only because money is power, and a man never wishes a woman to have any which she does not derive from him."

Samuel Howe also vehemently opposed either public appearances or publication for his wife (the daughters again admit their father was "strongly opposed to her taking any active part in public life"). On their wedding trip to Europe—with Horace Mann and his own new wife, in order to research educational reform—the Howes met Florence Nightingale, who discussed with them her desire to work in hospitals. Samuel Howe's answer (in their daughters' account) that "it would be unusual, and therefore unsuitable, but she should go forth" is one he never extended to his wife. When Julia pointed this out, his reply was, she reports: "if he had been engaged to Florence Nightingale and had loved her ever so dearly, he would have given her up as soon as she commenced her career as a public woman."

Samuel Howe was no less opposed to his wife's publishing. Julia recounts how, on the publication of her first article, her uncle had told her: "This is my little girl who knows about books, and writes articles and has it printed, but I wish she knew more about housekeeping." Her husband shared this view. In 1848 several of her poems were published in two anthologies, to her husband's displeasure. Her collection of poems, *Passion Flowers*, came out anonymously in 1854, but its authorship was soon uncovered ("The authorship is of course no secret now," Howe wrote her family, "and you had best talk openly of it all of you, as it may help the sale of the book in New York"). Hawthorne wrote to publisher George Ticknor that the book seemed "to let out a whole history of domestic unhappiness.... What does her husband think of it?"

Samuel Howe in the event was, as Julia wrote to her sister, "very angry about the book, and I really thought at one time that he would have driven me to insanity, so horribly did he behave." She sums up in her journal: "I have been married twenty years today. In the course of that time I have never known my husband to approve of any act of mine which I myself valued. Books—poems—essays—everything has been contemptible in his eyes because not his way of doing things.... I am much grieved and disconcerted." The argument led to discussion of divorce, but Samuel Howe demanded custody of the children, the legal norm of the time. To this Julia could not consent. She wrote to her sister: "His dream was to marry again—some young girl who would love him supremely.... I thought it my real duty to give up every thing that was dear and sacred to me, rather than be forced to leave two of my children.... I made the greatest sacrifice I can ever be called upon to make." It is no accident that in her later years, she was, as her daughters recount, active in efforts at legal reform, focusing especially on the right of widows to property equal to that of widowers; the criminalization of male frequenters in prostitution;

the effort to make mothers equal as guardians with fathers for minor children; and the rights of women to serve on school boards. And against her husband's opposition, she persisted in publishing. In 1857 she published another book of poems, *Words for the Hour*, and also a play, "The World's Own." She wrote up a trip to Cuba for the *Atlantic Monthly*, served as a newspaper correspondent from Newport, and, in 1866, published her *Later Lyrics*. But by then, the "Battle-Hymn" had happened.

Howe's change from New York socialite to Boston wife was rather a shock, and she tells of her difficult adjustment to keeping a small house on the grounds of the Perkins Institute, remote from Boston society and with poor transportation. Nonetheless, her experience in Boston was enlarging. Samuel Howe was an activist in the anti-slavery cause (indeed, he was one of the five radical backers of John Brown) and Julia joined him, helping, in 1853, to edit the anti-slavery journal *The Commonwealth*. When war broke out, she worked with him on the U.S. Sanitary Commission. This led to their being invited to Washington in 1862 by President Lincoln. Julia, in her memoir, recounts how she heard Union troops singing "John Brown's Body," and that night, inspired and desiring to serve, she wrote the words that came to her—in the dark in order not to awaken her sleeping children. The poem was published in 1863 in the *Atlantic Monthly* (for $5.00), and spread like wildfire. It is an irony of literary history that one of the very few poems by a woman to have remained in circulation and become widely known is altogether public.

The Boston scene was also one of radical religion. Thomas Parker, whose church Howe came to attend, was a leader in the Higher Criticism in America. His message she calls a "two-edged sword of the spirit against foes of religious freedom and against advocates and instruments of political oppression." He was as well the "first minister who addressed God in public prayer as 'Father and Mother of us all.' With this, Emerson's "Divinity School Address," and steady reading on her own, "I studied my way out of all the mental agonies which Calvinism can engender and became a Unitarian." Although never ordained, she preached frequently in Unitarian churches, and her political activism reflected this strong religious base. Her worldwide peace movement called women to "seize and bear about the prophetic word of the hour," in the name of "equal sacredness of rights" with "equal stringency of duties." In the *Woman's Journal*, which she helped edit from 1870 onwards, she writes of "the new domain of true womanhood, woman no longer in her ancillary relation to man, but in direct relation to the divine plan and purpose, as a free agent fully sharing with man every human right and every human responsibility." Or again: "The religion which makes me a moral agent equally with my father and brother, gives me my right and title to the citizenship which I am here to assert."

Howe's post-war life is almost dizzying in its public activities. At first skeptical about the women's rights movement, she was asked by Thomas Wentworth Higginson in 1868 to endorse a Suffrage meeting. She agreed, and by the evening's end, when called upon to speak, she stood up and said: "I am with you." She went on to become founder and president of the New England Women's Club; to help found the New England Woman Suffrage Association (serving as its president 1868–77 and 1893–1910); the American Woman Suffrage Association in 1869 with Lucy Stone; presided over the Massachusetts Suffrage Association, 1870–78 and 1891–93. Besides the Woman's Peace Movement, there was Mother's Day, and a "Woman's Church," which began as a convention of women ministers called by Howe in 1870. It became fully established in 1892, with Howe as president until her death. This "dream of a church of true womanhood" would represent, in Howe's words, "the womanly side of religion" as against "the masculine administration of religious doctrine [that] had overridden us women."

Howe's post Civil-War activism outstripped her poetry. Yet the two are of a piece. Again, against notions of women and women's poetry as private and domestic, Howe's poems, especially after her earliest writing, is solidly public; with a particularly pronounced blend of non-doctrinal religion and politics characteristic of the period's civil religion. "Battle-Hymn" remains her overwhelmingly successful text (as she ruefully recalls, one friend said after it "Mrs. Howe ought to die now," from which she demurred). Its charismatic assertion of prophetic history, at once biblical and immediate, political and cosmic, speaks for a wide contemporary American public. To die "to make men holy" becomes the same as to die "to make men free." That she does so in the voice of a woman, insisting on her own testimony and vision—"Mine eyes have seen," "I have seen," "I have read"—is no less significant. As she wrote in her diary in 1864, her speaking and writing came to her "in obedience to a deep, strong impulse" essentially religious. Other war poems register these forces. "The New Exodus" oddly endorses the first expulsion from Eden as the possibility of human engagement in history, condemning slavery instead as a true Fall. "The Question" speaks in the voice of a slave, accusing America of its own betrayal. "Requital" joins with the many, many devotions to Lincoln-Martyr. But "Our Orders" specifically transposes the war effort to a woman's effort—"Weave no more silks... to deck our girls" but rather "the flag;" while "The First Martyr" recounts the feelings of women left behind while men risk life. This is the ground of her own "Sibyl Arts." The poem "Left Behind" recalls Dickinson's "Success" in its taking on the viewpoint of the defeated in battle, although with justifications Dickinson never offers.

On the other hand, Howe's texts register severe discords regarding gender. "Save the Old South" posits a "manhood's zeal and haste" against woman's "patient hand," man's "gold" against woman's "sympathy" as what can redeem the public world. The contest of gender emerges as a contest of values: of increasing economic obsession as against every other human interest. "Outside the Party" dramatizes this double standard as sexual, written in the voice of a fallen woman. Other poems, such as "The Fine Lady" and "Amanda's Inventory," critique and resist the bourgeois reduction of women as well as men. "The Charitable Visitor" offers a different option of service. A group of texts together explore, with some bewilderment, different images of women, different contexts they inhabit, with Howe's own sense of herself often quite torn and ambivalent. "Woman" inscribes the ideal of her social world, only in the end to dissociate herself from it—whether as failure or rejection. "A Rough Sketch" describes her husband, all praise except again, at the end, in the double-edged suggestion of her failure to be "The woman's soul, to match with his." This ambivalent combination of irony and diffidence defines her politics in

"The Tea Party," a highly conflicted text about woman's rights activism; also her religious identity in "Of Woman," where different biblical models of womanhood are weighed, with Eve strikingly defended, yet claiming to "love the woman with the woman's heart, / Giving, not gathering." Perhaps most ambivalent of all is the figure of the poet. "To my Master" and "The Royal Guest" suggest a difficult position, with a male "muse" figure at once commanding and therefore also inhibiting the poet. But "A Visit to C. H." suggests a sisterhood of poetry. "Sybil" and "Mother Mind" project female muses and poetic resources. What gives the poet strength to create here is not a boldly asserted sense of self, but a very nineteenth-century sense of service. "Mother Mind" insists on her reluctance to write, modest in her claims and providing a model of creativity close to gestation. Yet, in the complexity of the modest and apologetic in women's writing, Howe also offers "An Apology for a Warm Word Spoken" which oddly repeats what it purports to retract. This text emerges more as aggressive defense than effacement, more reassertion than apology. And it reaffirms her political, religious, and moral calling that gives her the strength and authority to speak out, with justice and right as sacred, each grounding and reflecting the other.

Poems

Battle-Hymn of the Republic

Mine eyes have seen the glory of the coming of the Lord:
He is trampling out the vintage where the grapes of wrath are
     stored;
He hath loosed the fateful lightning of his terrible swift sword:
     His truth is marching on.

I have seen Him in the watch-fires of a hundred circling camps;
They have builded Him an altar in the evening dews and damps;
I can read His righteous sentence by the dim and flaring lamps.
     His day is marching on.

I have read a fiery gospel, writ in burnished rows of steel:
"As ye deal with my contemners, so with you my grace shall deal;
Let the Hero, born of woman, crush the serpent with his heel,
     Since God is marching on."

He has sounded forth the trumpet that shall never call retreat;
He is sifting out the hearts of men before his judgment-seat:
Oh! be swift, my soul, to answer Him! be jubilant, my feet!
     Our God is marching on.

In the beauty of the lilies Christ was born across the sea,
With a glory in his bosom that transfigures you and me:
As he died to make men holy, let us die to make men free,
     While God is marching on.

Our Orders

Weave no more silks, ye Lyons looms,
To deck our girls for gay delights!
The crimson flower of battle blooms,
And solemn marches fill the night.

Weave but the flag whose bars to-day
Drooped heavy o'er our early dead,
And homely garments, coarse and gray,
For orphans that must earn their bread!

Keep back your tunes, ye viols sweet,
That poured delight from other lands!
Rouse there the dancer's restless feet:
The trumpet leads our warrior bands.

And ye that wage the war of words
With mystic fame and subtle power,
Go, chatter to the idle birds,
Or teach the lesson of the hour!

Ye Sibyl Arts, in one stern knot
Be all your offices combined!
Stand close, while Courage draws the lot,
The destiny of human kind.

And if that destiny could fail,
The sun should darken in the sky,
The eternal bloom of Nature pale,
And God, and Truth, and Freedom die!

The New Exodus

"Forsake this flowery garden" the frowning Angel said;
"Its vines no more may feed thee, compel from stones thy bread;
Pursue the veins deep buried that hide thy wine and oil:
Fruit shalt thou find with sorrow, and children rear in toil."

Oh! not in heathen vengeance the winged apostle spoke;
Nor savage retribution the blooming fetters broke.
Man had an arm for labor, a strength to conquer pain,
A brain to plot and study, a will to serve and reign.

That will with slow arraying confronts itself with fate,
The pair unconscious twining the arches of the State.
Earth keeps her fairest garlands to crown the tireless spade;
The fields are white with harvest, the hireling's fee is paid.

From tented field to city, to palace, and to throne,
Man builds with work his kingdom, and makes the world his own.
All welded with conditions is empire's golden ring:
The king must keep the peasant, the peasant feed the king.

The word of God once spoken, from truth is never lost;
The high command once given, earth guards jealous cost.
By this perplexing lesson, men build their busy schemes:
"The way of comfort lies not, kind Eden, through thy dreams."

I see a land before me, where manhood in its pride
Forgot the solemn sentence, the wage of toil denied:
"To wealth and lofty station some royal road must be;
Our brother, bound and plundered, shall earn us luxury.

"One half of knowledge give him for service and, for skill,
The nobler half withholding, that moulds the manly Will:
From justice bar his pleadings, from mercy keep his prayers;
His daughters for our pleasure, his sons to serve our heirs."

Again the frowning Angel commandeth to depart,
With fiery scourge of terror, with want and woe of Heart:
"Go forth! the earth is weary to bear unrighteous feet;
Release your false possession; go, work that ye may eat.

"Bring here the light of knowledge, the scale of equal rule;
Bring the Republic's weapons, the forum and the school:
The Dagon of your worship is broken on his shrine;
The palm of Christian mercy brings in the true divine."

So from your southern Eden the flaming sword doth drive;
Your lesson is appointed; go, learn how workmen thrive!
Not sloth has ice of plenty, nor pride of stately crest;
But thou of God beloved, O Labor crowned with rest!

The Question

Tell me, Master am I free?
From the prison land I come,
From a mocked humanity,
From the fable of a home;

From the shambles, where my wife
With my baby at her breast,
Faded from my narrow life,
Rudely bartered, ill-possest.

Will you keep me, for my faith,
From the hound that scents my track,
From the riotous, drunken breath,
From the murder at my back?

Masters, ye are fighting long;
Well your trumpet-blast we know;

Are ye come to right a wrong?
Do we call you friend or foe?

God must come, for whom we pray,
Knowing his deliverance true;
Shall our men be left to say
He must work it free of you?

Fetters of a burning chain
Held the spirit of our braves;
Waiting for the nobler strain,
Silence told him *we* were slaves.

The First Martyr

My five-years' darling, on my knee,
  Chattered and toyed and laughed with me:
"Now tell me, mother mine," quoth she,
"Where you went in the afternoon."
"Alas! my pretty little life,
  I went to see a sorrowing wife,
Who will be widowed soon."

"Now, mother, what is that?" she said,
With wondering eyes and restless head:
"Will, then, her husband soon be dead?
Tell me, why must he die?
Is he like flowers the frost doth sear,
Or like the birds, that, every year,
Melt back into the sky?"

"No, love: the flowers may bloom their time,
The birdlings sing their merry chime,
Till bids them seek another clime
The Winter sharp and cold;

But he who waits with fettered limb,
Nor God nor Nature sends for him,—
He is not weak nor old.

"He lies upon a prison bed
With sabre gashes on his head;
And one short month will see him led
Where Vengeance wields the sword.
Then shall his form be lifted high,
And strangled in the public eye
With horrible accord."

"But, mother, say, what has he done?
Has he not robbed or murdered one?"
"My darling, he has injured none.
To free the wretched slaves
He led a band of chosen men,
Brave, but too few; made captives then,
And doomed to felon graves."

"O mother! let us go this day
To that sad prison, far away;
The cruel governor we'll pray
To unloose the door so stout.
Some comfort we can bring him, sure:
And is he locked up so secure,
We could not get him out?"

"No, darling: he is closely kept."
Then nearer to my heart she crept,
And, hiding there her beauty, wept
For human misery.
Child! it is fit that thou shouldst weep;
The very babe unborn would leap
To rescue such as he.

O babe unborn! O future race!
Heir of our glory and disgrace,
We cannot see thy veilèd face;
But shouldst thou keep our crime,
No new Apocalypse need say
In what, wild woe shall pass away
The falsehood of the time.

April 19

A spasm o'er my heart
Sweeps like a burning flood;
A sentence rings upon mine ears,
Avenge the guiltless blood!

Sit not in health and ease,
Nor reckon loss nor gain,
When men who bear our country's flag
Are set upon and slain,

Not by mistaken hearts
With long oppression wrung,
Filled with great thoughts that ripen late,
And madden, when they're young.

The murderer's wicked lust
Their righteous steps withstood;
The zeal that thieves and pirates know
Brought down the guiltless blood.

From every vein of mine
Its fiery burthen take;
From every drop the burning coin
Of righteous vengeance make.

Low let the city lie
That thus her guests receives;
A smoking ruin to the eye
Be marble walls and eaves!

Thou God of love and wrath,
That watchest on the wing,
Remorseless at those caitiff hearts
Thy bolts of judgment fling!

Blot from the sight of heaven
The city, where she stood,
And with thy might, avenging Right,
Wipe out the guiltless blood!

Requital

He died beneath the uplifted thong
Who spared for us a thousand lives:
He came to sing glad Israel's song;
We gave him Babylonian gyves.

With swelling heart and simple thought
He warned us of the unheeded snare
Our chiefs discovered: vilely caught,
They flung him back to perish there.

Did Pilate seal the Saviour's fate
As still the shuddering Nations say,
When, in that hour of high debate,
With ill-washed hands he turned away?

Sweet Christ, with flagellations brought
To thine immortal martyrdom,

Cancel the bitter treasons wrought
By men who bid thy kingdom come.

Their sinful blood we may not urge
While Mercy stays thy righteous hand;
But take all ours, if that should purge
The wicked patience of the land.

The Battle-Eucharist

Above the seas of gold and glass
The Christ, transfigured, stands to-day;
Below, in troubled currents, pass
The tidal fates of man away.

Through that environed blessedness
Our sorrow cannot wholly rise,
Nor his swift sympathy redress
The anguish that in Nature lies.

Yet Mindful from his banquet sends
The guest of God a cup of wine,
And shares a morsel with his friends,
Who, wondering, wait without the shrine.

Left Behind

The foe is retreating, the field is clear;
My thoughts fly like lightning, my steps stay here;
I'm bleeding to faintness, no help is near;
What, ho! comrades; what, ho!

The battle was deadly, the shots fell thick;
We leaped from our trenches, and charged them quick;

I knew not my wound till my heart grew sick!
So there, comrades; so there.

We charged the left column, that broke and fled;
Poured powder for powder, and lead for lead;
So they must surrender, what matter who's dead?
Who cares, comrades? Who cares?

My soul rises upon the wings of the slain,
A triumph thrills through me that quiets the pain:
If it were yet to do, I would do it again!
Farewell, comrades, farewell!

Harvard Student's Song

Remember ye the fateful gun that sounded
To Sumter's walls from Charleston's treacherous shore?
Remember ye how hearts indignant bounded
When our first dead came back from Baltimore?
The banner feel that every breeze had flattered,
The hum of thrift was hushed with sudden woe;
We raised anew, the emblems shamed and shattered,
And turned a front resolved to meet the foe.

Remember ye how, out of boyhood leaping,
Our gallant mates stood ready for the fray,
As new-fledged eaglets rise, with sudden sweeping,
And meet unscared the dazzling front of day?
Our classic toil became inglorious leisure,
We praised the calm Horatian ode no more,
But answered back with song the martial measure,
That held its throb above the cannon's roar.

"Save the Old South!"

Two hands the God of Nature gave,
One swift to smite, one fond to save,
Betwixt the cradle and the grave.

Where Strength hews out his story stent,
Where woods are felled and metals blent,
The right hand measures his content.

Where Skill sits tireless at her loom,
Where beauty wafts her transient bloom,
The tender saving hand has room.

And Fate, as in a tourney fine,
The differing powers does match and join,
That each may wear the crown divine.

But manhood in its zeal and haste
Leaves cruel overthrow and waste
Upon its pathway, roughly traced.

Then woman comes with patient hand,
With loving heart of high command,
To save the councils of the land.

Round this old church so poor to see,
Record of years that swiftly fell,
She draws the chain of sympathy.

The men who make their gold their weal,
Who guard with powder and with steel,
Have not a weapon she can feel.

Before the venerable pile,
Armed with a reason and a smile,
She stations with benignant wile.

Like Barbara Frietchie in her day,
She has a royal will to say:
"You shall not tear one stone away."

You disavow the spirit need
That avarice may build with heed
The gilded monuments of greed.

What hope, what help can patriots know?
Only this counter mandate slow,
"The mothers will not have it so."

Mothers! The wrongs of ages wait!
Amend them, ministers of fate!
Redeem the church, reform the state!

Outside the Party

Thick throng the snow-flakes, the evening is dreary,
Glad rings the music in yonder gay hall;
On her who listens here, friendless and weary,
Heavier chill than the winter's doth fall.

At yon clear window, light-opened before me,
Glances the face I have worshipped so well:
There's the fine gentleman, grand in his glory;
There, the fair smile by whose sweetness I fell.

This is akin to him, shunned and forsaken,
That at my bosom sobs low, without bread;

Had not such pleading my marble heart shaken,
I had been quiet, long since, with the dead.

Oh! could I enter there, ghastly and squalid,
Stand in men's eyes with my spirit o'erborne,
Show them where roses bloomed, crushed now and pallid,
What he found innocent, leaving forlorn,—

How the fair ladies would fail from their dances,
Trembling, aghast at my horrible tale!
How would he shrink from my words and my glances!
How would they shrink from him, swooning and pale!

This is the hair that was soft to enchain him;
Snakelike, it snarls on my beautiless brow:
These are the hands that were fond to detain him
With a sense—magic then, powerless now!

No: could I come, like a ghost, to affright him,
How should that heal my wound, silence my pain?
Had I the wrath of God's lighting to smite him,
That could not bring me my lost peace again.

Ne'er let him grieve while good fortunes betide him,
Ne'er count again the poor game lost of old;
When he comes forth, with his young bride beside him,
Here shall they find us both, dead in the cold.

The Soul-Hunter

Who hunts so late 'neath evening skies,
A smouldering love-brand in his eyes?
His locks outshame the black of night,
Its stars arc duller than his sight
Who hunts so late, so dark.

A drooping mantle shrouds his form,
To shield him from the winter's storm?
Or is there something at his side,
That, with himself, he strives to hide.
Who hunts so late, so dark?

He hath such promise, silver sweet,
Such silken hands, such fiery feet,
That, where his look has charmed the prey,
His swift-winged passion forces way,
Who hunts so late, so dark.

Sure no one underneath the moon
Can whisper to so soft a tune:
The hours would flit from dusk to dawn
Lighter than dews upon the lawn
With him, so late, so dark.

But, should there break a day of need,
Those hands will try no valorous deed:
No help is in that sable crest,
Nor manhood in that hollow breast
That sighed so late, so dark.

O maiden! of the salt waves make
Thy sinless shroud, for God's dear sake;
Or to the flame commit thy bloom;
Or lock thee, living, in the tomb
So desolate and dark,—

Before thou list one stolen word
Of him who lures thee like a bird.
He wanders with the Devil's bait,
For human souls he lies in wait,
Who hunts so late, so dark.

At a Corner

Here should I meet you, here only, recalling
The soul-drunken look you vouchsafed me one day,
That, like a spark in some hidden mine falling,
Shook my frail senses, and swept me away.

What did that look portend? Dark was its meaning,
Faded in tears the swift gleam of delight;
Ask the deep thoughts of eternity's screening,
Ask the wide stars in the bosom of night.

Like some winged Seraphim, never descending,
That for a moment unveils to our view:
Sudden its ravishment, bitter its ending;
Love flashed a promise that Life never knew.

The Fine Lady

Her heart is set on folly,
An amber gathering straws:
She courts each poor occurrence,
Heeds not the heavenly laws.
Pity her!

She has a little beauty,
And she flaunts it in the day,
While the selfish wrinkles, spreading,
Steal all its charm away.
Pity her!

She has a little money,
And she flings it everywhere:
'Tis a gewgaw on her bosom,

A tinsel in her hair.
Pity her!

She has a little feeling,
She spreads a foolish net
That snares her own weak footsteps,
Not his for whom 'tis set.
Pity her!

Ye harmless household drudges,
Your draggled daily wear
And horny palms of labor
A softer heart may bear.
Pity her!

Ye steadfast ones, whose burthens
Weigh valorous shoulders down,
With hands that cannot idle,
And brows that will not frown,
Pity her!

Ye saints, whose thoughts are folded
As graciously to rest
As a dove's stainless pinions
Upon her guileless breast,
Pity her!

But most, ye helpful angels
That send distress and work,
Hot task and sweating forehead,
To heal man's idle irk,
Pity her!

The Black Coach

In the black coach you must ride,—
You, so dainty once a time.
We who saw your bloom of pride,
Stifle now the crop of crime,
Lest its poisonous, fruitful birth
Scatter monsters o'er the earth.

She had holidays as gay
As the highest you have known,
Lady, flitting fast away,
With your chariot for a throne.
Wild-flowers for a moment please
In the hands of pampered ease.

Lifted, like a summer treasure
In a golden goblet placed,
To decline in mournful leisure,
Scorned, untended, and disgraced;
With the meadow yet in sight
Where the daisies glisten white.

Come, a carriage blacker still,
Narrowed to the form you bear;
Bring the last of good and ill;
Take the leavings of despair.
Death's cold purity condense
Vaporous sin to soul's intense.

Ere the prison-gates unswing,
Let the spirit portals ope;
While the Winter holds the Spring
Shall the grave-mound cover hope;
Come the pang that ends all woe,
God can better pardon so.

Contrasts

I shall not come to the heavenly court
As I enter your ball to-night,
In tissues wreathed with flowery sport,
And jewels of haughty light,

Bearing on shoulders stiff and straight
The marble of my face,
Moving with high and measured gait
To claim my yielded place.

Poor narrow soul! your easy spite
Moves this enforced disdain:
I cannot vanish from the fight
Other than crowned or slain.

The russet garb of penitence
For me were lighter wear
Than all a queen's magnificence,
A prince's minivère

Unloose, unloose your chains of pride,
Set my vexed spirit free,
That I may follow my angel guide
In glad humility.

For I would hearken the sentence deep,
Abide the lifted rod,
And sink, like a chastened child, to weep
In the fatherhood of God.

Amanda's Inventory

This is my hat: behold its upstart Plume,
Soaring like pride, that, even in heaven asks room!
This is my cloak of scarlet splendor rare,
A saucy challenge to the sunset glare.

Behold my coach of state and pony chaise,
A fairy pleasure for the summer days;
The steeds that fly, like lightnings in a leash,
With their rude Jove, subservient to my wish.

Here are my jewels; each a fortune holds;
A starving artist planned file graceful moulds:
Here hang my dresses in composed array,
A rainbow with a hue, for every day.

These are my lovers, registered in date,
Who, with my dowry, seek myself to mate.
The haughtiest wooer wins me for his bride:
Who asks affection? Pride should wed with pride.

These are my friends, who hourly come or send,
Pleased with my notice and a finger-end;
Yonder's my parson, proud to share my feast;
My doctor's there, a sycophantic beast.

This is my villa, where I take my case
With flowers well-ordered, and ambitious trees;
And this—what sudden spectre stays my breath?
Amanda, poor Amanda! this is death.

Lyke-Wake

I saw him at a banquet gay,
Elate with speech and flushed with wine:
Above the revel slaking way,
His eye, unwilling, answered mine.

What his expressed I did not read;
But mine, if I mistake not, said,
"This minds me of their feasts indeed
Who drain the wine-cup o'er their dead;

"Who set the liquid fire to flare
Where late the spirit-flame has flown;
The sorrow still unearthed and bare
The miserable drink should drown."

Bargains

He prest a ruby on her lips, whose burning blood shone through;
Twin sapphires bound above her eyes, to match their fiery blue;
And, where her hair was parted back, an opal gem he set,—
Type of her changing countenance, where all delights were met.

"Will you surrender now," he said, "the ancient grudge you keep
Untiring and unutterèd, like murder in the deep?"
"I thank you for the word," she said; "your gems are fair of form
But when did jewels bind the depths, or splendors still the storm?

"There is no diamond in the mine, nor pearl beneath the wave,
There is no fretted coronet that soothes a princely grave,
There is nor fate nor empire in the wide infinity,
Can stand in grace and virtue with the gift you had from me."

The Charitable Visitor

She carries no flag of fashion, her clothes are but passing plain,
Though she comes from a city palace all jubilant with her reign
She threads a bewildering alley, with ashes and dust thrown out,
And fighting and cursing children, who mock as she moves about.
Why walk you this way, my lady, in the snow and slippery ice?
These are not the shrines of virtue,—here misery lives, and vice:
Rum helps the heart of starvation to a courage bold and bad;
And women are loud and brawling, while men sit maudlin and
    mad.
I see in the corner yonder the boy with a broken arm,
And the mother whose blind wrath did it,—strange guardian from
    childish harm!
That face will grow bright at your coming, but your steward might
    come as well,
Or better the Sunday teacher that helped him to read and spell.
Oh! I do not come of my willing, with froward and restless feet:
I have pleasant tasks in my chamber, and friends well-beloved to
    greet.
To follow the dear Lord Jesus, I walk in the storm and snow;
Where I find the trace of his footsteps, there lilies and roses grow.
He said that to give was blessèd, more blessèd than to receive;
But what could he take, dear angels, of all that we had to give,
Save a little pause of attention, and a little thrill of delight,
When the dead were waked from their slumbers, and the blind
    recalled to sight?
Say, the King came forth with the morning, and opened his palace
    doors,
Thence flinging his gifts like sunbeams that break upon marble
    floors;
But the wind with wild pinions caught them, and carried them
    round about:
Though I looked till mine eyes were dazzled, I never could make
    them out.

But he bade me go far and find them, "go seek them with zeal and
     pain:
The hand is most welcome to me that brings me mine own again;
And those who follow them furthest, with faithful searching and
     sight,
Are brought with joy to my presence, and sit at my feet all night."
So, hither and thither walking, I gather them broadly cast;
Where yonder young face doth sicken, it may be the best and last.
In no void or vague of duty I come to his aid to-day:
I bring God's love to his bedside, and carry God's gift away.

A Thought for Washing Day

The clothes-line is a Rosary
Of household help and care;
Each little saint the Mother loves
Is represented there.

And when across her garden plot
She walks, with thoughtful heed,
I should not wonder if she told
Each garment for a bead.

For Celia's scarlet stockings hang
Beside Amelia's skirt,
And Bilbo's breeches, which of late
Were sadly smeared with dirt.

Yon kerchief small wiped bitter tears
For ill-success at school;
This pinafore was torn in strife
'Twixt Fred and little Jule.

And that device of finer web,
And over-costly lace,

Adorned our Eldest when she danced
At some gay fashion place.

A stranger passing, I salute
The Household in its wear,
And smile to think how near of kin
Are love and toil and prayer.

Of Woman

It was a silken woman of the world
That of fond Herod claimed the Baptist's head:
"If this sad virtue gets to countenance,
   Our dancing's done with, in the quickest way."
And, for a painted toy, the anointed brow
That knew the Christ's significance must fall.
Such deadly power if hid in smallest things:
The Aspic might have chilled from Love's delight
The bosom it assisted to Love's end.
The shaft of death is subtle as a thread,—
The air may bring, the garland's bloom conceal,—
Our desperate finger holds it over us,
Or in a woman's snowy breast it lies.
Teach, then, the woman all the Prophet's worth,
So will she bow the tresses of her head
To yield him passing, homage, and pour out
The treasure of her life to ransom his.
I love the woman with the woman's heart,
Giving, not gathering,—shedding light abroad
As the man glooms it in, for midnight toil.
Better our Hebrew Eve, who shares with love
The guilty glory of her stolen prize,
Than the three haughty Heathen who rose up,
Claiming of man a vain pre-eminence,—
Not his to give,—God's only, and the heart's.

They showed me drawings by a six-years' child
Of beasts incongruous, harnessed to a car:
"Now, on my life, he is artist-born," I said.
"Wherefore? You see the slim camelopard
Rearing her strength up, pulling from the head;
While the swift horses stretch to twice their length,
Spinning themselves to slender threads of speed,
Nay, with their iron sinews knitting up
A belt of haste like that our Shakespeare drew
With Puck's impatient malice, round the world.
The little one has guessed the trick of strength
And action, so is artist-born," I say.
"For your true artist knows how all things work;
Bestows no Zephyrus to prop a pile
Whose angles huge insult his littleness,
Cramping the sympathetic soul with pain,
But the great patient forms whose shoulders broad
Invite such burthens; whose fixed features say,
'This weight contents us; we are glad in strength;'
While the light figure poises at the top,
Holding the heavy network gathered up
To meet the apex of his graciousness.
So, Sisters, leave the weightier tasks of strength,
The underpinnings of society,
And flutter with your graces nearer heaven.
He thinks of yon, the steadfast Caryatid,—
The faithful arches clasp their hands beneath
To keep you in your breathless eminence;
The gloomy cellar way, the weary stair,
Exalt the platform where you reign serene.
Stay there, Beloved, the Angel at the top,
That crowns and lightens all the heavy work.
The very prisoners, entering at the grate,
Perceive an intercession in thine eyes,
And keep their dungeons, waiting for thy sword.
Stay thus, my Angel, seeing over thee

The Heaven that dreamed Mary and her Christ,—
The dream whereat the Baby Earth awoke,
And, smiling, keeps that smile forever more."

Woman

A vestal priestess proudly pure,
But of a meek and quiet spirit;
With soul all dauntless to endure,
And mood so calm that naught can stir it,
Save when a thought most deeply thrilling
Her eyes with gentlest tears is filling,
Which seem with her true words to start
From the deep fountain at her heart.
A mien that neither seeks nor shuns
The homage scattered in her way;
A love that hath few favored ones,
And yet for all can work and pray;
A smile wherein each mortal reads
The very sympathy he needs;
An eye like to a mystic book
Of lays that bard or prophet sings,
Which keepeth for the holiest look
Of holiest love its deepest things.
A form to which a king had bent,
The fireside's dearest ornament—
Known in the dwellings of the poor
Better than at the rich man's door;
A life that ever onward goes,
Yet in itself has deep repose.
A vestal priestess, maid, or wife—
Vestal, and vowed to offer up
The innocence of a holy life
To Him who gives the mingled cup;
With man its bitter sweets to share,

To live and love, to do and dare;
His prayer to breathe, his tears to shed,
Breaking to him the heavenly bread
Of hopes which, all too high for earth,
Have yet in her a mortal birth.
This is the woman I have dreamed,
And to my childish thought she seemed
The woman I myself should be:
Alas! I would that I were she.

The Rough Sketch: Samuel Gridley Howe

A great grieved heart, an iron will,
As fearless blood as ever ran;
A form elate with nervous strength
And fibrous vigor,—all a man.

A gallant rein, a restless spur,
The hand to wield a biting scourge;
Small patience for the tasks of Time,
Unmeasured power to speed and urge.

He rides the errands of the hour,
But sends no herald on his ways;
The world would thank the service done,
He cannot stay for gold or praise.

Not lavishly he casts abroad
The glances of an eye intense,
And did he smile but once a year,
It were a Christmas recompense.

I thank a poet for his name,
The "Down of Darkness," this should be;

A child, who knows no risk it runs,
Might stroke its roughness harmlessly.

One helpful gift the Gods forgot,
Due to the man of lion-mood;
Woman's soul, to match with his
In high resolve and hardihood.

To My Master

Thou who so dear a mediation wert
Between the heavens and my mortality,
Give ear to these faint murmurs of the heart,
Which, upward tending, take their tone from thee.
Follow where'er the wayward numbers run,
And if on my deserving, not my need,
Some boon should wait, vouchsafe this only meed,
Modest, but glorious—say, 'Thou hast well done.'

I've wrought alone—my pleasure was my task:
As I walk onward to Eternity,
It were a trivial thing to stand and ask
That my faint footsteps should remembered be;
Of all Earth's crownings, I would never one
But thine approving hand upon my head,
Dear as the sacred laurels of the dead,
And that high, measured praise, 'Thou hast well done.'

The Royal Guest

They tell me, I am shrewd with other men,
With thee I'm slow and difficult of speech;
With others, I may guide the car of talk,
Thou wing'st it oft to realms beyond my reach.

If other guests should come, I'd deck my hair,
And choose my newest garment from the shelf;
When thou art bidden, I would clothe my heart
With holiest purpose, as for God himself.

For them, I wile the hours with tale or song,
Or web of fancy, fringed with careless rhyme;
But how to find a fitting lay for thee,
Who hast the harmonies of every time?

Oh friend beloved! I sit apart and dumb,
Sometimes in sorrow, oft in joy divine;
My lip will falter, but my prison'd heart
Springs forth, to measure its faint pulse with thine.

Thou art to me most like a royal guest,
Whose travels bring him to some lowly roof,
Where simple rustics spread their festal fare,
And blushing, own it is not good enough.

Bethink thee, then, whene'er thou com'st to me
From high emprise and noble toil to rest,
My thoughts are weak and trivial, matched with thine,
But the poor mansion offers thee its best.

The Tea-Party

I am not with you, sisters, in your talk;
I sit not in your fancied judgment-seat:
Not thus the sages in their council walk,
Not in this wise the calm great spirits meet.

My life has striven for broader scope than yours;
The daring of its failure and its fact

Have taught how deadly difficult it is
To suit the high endeavor with an act.

I do not reel my satire by the yard,
To flout, the fronts of honorable men;
Nor, with poor cunning, underprize the heart
Whose impulse is not open to my ken.

Ah! sisters, but your forward speech comes well
To help the woman's standard, new-unfurled:
In carpet council ye may win the day;
But keep your limits,—do not rule the world.

What strife should come, what discord rule the times,
Could but your pettish will assert its way!
No lengthened wars of reason, but, a rage,
Shown and repented twenty times a day.

You're all my betters,—one in beauty more,
And one in sharpness of the wit and tongue,
And one in trim, decorous piety,
And one with arts and graces ever young.

But well I thank my father's sober house
Where shallow judgment had no leave to be,
And hurrying years, that, stripping much beside,
Turned as they fled, and left me charity.

A Visit to C. H.

Let us sit with you, sister, before the low fire,
The scanty rag-carpet sufficing our feet:
You cannot command, and we need not require,
The window well shaded and soft-cushioned seat.

The children of pride scarcely come to your door,
And we who have entered walk not in their ways;
But experience brings to the rich and the poor
One value abiding in life's changeful days.

You are homely in breeding? Some one of your race
Had a spark of high blood, to immortals akin:
You are loath to be seen in this desolate place?
What honor may lack where the Muse is within?

A presence I feel in the God-lightened air,
The spell of the art I have followed so long:
In your calico garment and rough-twisted hair
Let us speak of your queendom, poor sister of song.

For, well may we know it, the tap that you bear,
When you lay down the needle, and take up the pen,
Is the summons august that the highest revere,
The greatest that visits the children of men.

The fountain of song in your bosom arose
When the small baby pillow was tenantless left?
You share with all mortals life's burthen of woes;
But all have not music, when grieved and bereft.

You dream o'er the wash-tub, strive vainly to fix
Your thought on the small household matter in hand?
Some spices, no doubt, in your condiments mix,
Some flavors your neighbors can scarcely command.

The world is so hard, and the world is so cold?
And the dear-bought deliverance comes scanty and slow?
Say, whether is better,—its frosts to behold,
Or to share its heart winter, and shed no more glow?

I have found a rich blossom astray on the heath;
In sordid surroundings, an altar of love;
Or lashed in a cart, beyond beauty and breath,
The steed that should carry the bidding of Jove.

The town that hums near us has rich folk, besure,—
Its man of the Congress, its Mayor with his state,
Its lords of the spindle who pillage the poor,
Its pampered young people who quarrel and mate.

But not for their scanning I come here to-day;
The rich and the proud are forever the same:
My feet, poet sister, have found out this way,
Unsought and unsummoned, your kinship to claim.

Sybil

Your head is wild with books, Sybil,
But your heart is good and kind—
I feel a new contentment near you,
A pleasure of the mind.

Glad should I be to sit beside you,
And let long hours glide by,
Reading, through all your sweet narrations,
The language of your eye.

Since the maternal saint I worshipped
Did look and love her last,
No woman o'er my wayward spirit
Such gentle spell has cast.

Oh! tell me of your varied fortunes,
For you know not, from your face

Looks out strange sadness, lit with rapture,
And melancholy grace.

You are a gem, whose native brilliance
Could never wholly reign,
An opal, whose prismatic fire
A white cloud doth restrain.

And thus, the mood to which you move me
Is never perfect, quite,
'Tis pity, wonderment, and pleasure,
Opacity and light.

Bear me then in your presence, Sybil,
And leave your hand in mine,
For, though human be my nature,
You've made it half divine.

Mother Mind

I never *made* a poem, dear friend—
I never sat me down, and said,
This cunning brain and patient hand
Shall fashion something to be read.

Men often came to me, and prayed
I should indite a fitting verse
For fast, or festival, or in
Some stately pageant to rehearse.
(As if, than Balaam more endowed,
I of myself could bless or curse.)

Reluctantly I bade them go,
Ungladdened by my poet-mite;

My heart is not so churlish but
It loves to minister delight.

But not a word I breathe is mine
To sing, in praise of man or God;
My Master calls, at noon or night,
I know his whisper and his nod.

Yet all my thoughts to rhythms run,
To rhyme, my wisdom and my wit?
True, I consume my life in verse,
But wouldst thou know how *that* is writ?

'Tis thus—through weary length of days,
I bear a thought within my breast
That greatens from my growth of soul,
And waits, and will not be expressed.

It greatens, till its hour has come,
Not without pain, it sees the light;
'Twixt smiles and tears I view it o'er,
And dare not deem it perfect, quite.

These children of my soul I keep
Where scarce a mortal man may see,
Yet not unconsecrate, dear friend,
Baptismal rites they claim of thee.

An Apology: For a Warm Word Spoken

I spake, perhaps, too sharp a word
For one bred up in modesty,
But base injustice, trivial scorn
On honor heaped, had angered me.

The smile of courtesy forsook
These lips, so timid even for good,
While o'er the paleness of my brow
Flashed crimson, the indignant blood.

Nor could I to the contest bring
The trainèd weapon of the mind,
Snatching from Reason's armory
Such shafts as grief had left behind.

Grief for the faltering of the Age,
Grief for my country and my race,
Grief to sit here with Christian men,
That boast their want of Christian grace.

I say not that the man I praise
By that poor tribute stands more high,
I say not that the man I blame
Be not of purer worth than I;

But when I move reluctant lips
For holy Justice, human Right,
The sacred cause I strive to plead
Lends me its favor and its might.

And I must argue from the faith
Which gave the fervor of my youth,
Or keep such silence as yon stars,
That only look and live God's truth.

Emily Dickinson:
1830–1886

Introduction

Dickinson's poems are strikingly like her life: contracted, secretive, hidden; yet, on entering, opening into corridors and mazes, riddles and sudden turns. In Dickinson, the compact is the explosive. She speaks to us, as she did in her lifetime to those around her, from behind screens or another room. The art of reading her is the art of decipherment.

Her biography is the first barrier, its fascination offering an almost irresistible seduction. Dickinson was born in 1830 in religiously conservative Amherst, Massachusetts—what had been Jonathan Edwards country—to a prominent family, active in civic projects, education, and government. Her grandfather helped found Amherst Academy and College, serving as treasurer of the college, as did her father and brother after him. Her father held elected office on both the state and national level: elected in 1838 to the General Court of Massachusetts (with Melville's father-in-law, Judge Shaw); delegate in 1852 to the National Whig Convention; and in the same year elected Congressman from Massachusetts (sharing offices with T.S. Eliot's grand-uncle). These were the years of crisis culminating in Civil War—a crisis penetrating every aspect of American identity and self-definition, whether historical, religious, or political. Dickinson's own friendships included newspaper and journal editors—Samuel Bowles of the *Springfield Republican*, Josiah Holland of *Scribner's Magazine* and also Lincoln's first biographer; and Thomas Wentworth Higginson, editor of the *Atlantic Monthly* and famous in his own day for extreme radicalism in abolition, women's rights, one of the five funders of John Brown—although known in Dickinson studies as the dolt who advised her not to publish, something in any case she did not wish to do, as Helen Hunt Jackson learned after repeated rebuffs in her efforts to put Dickinson's poems into print. Dickinson's deadline was not publishing but immortality.

Dickinson herself, however, aggressively, defiantly, adamantly faced away from public exposure, even while launching a severe reflection on it in her work. Her reclusion, beginning around 1860—the very time of the Civil War, interestingly enough—extended not only to a refusal to go out, but also to greet or speak directly with visitors, to address her own envelopes, as well as strange habits such as dressing in white (none of which prevented her, however, from continuing in her ordinary domestic and expected chores). She also began intensively to write poetry, which she also recluded: circulating her work privately to a coterie of letter-correspondents, and carefully copying and sewing them into little booklets which she kept in her bureau drawer, to be found on her death by her sister Lavinia; but refusing to publish them herself. In face of all this mystery, we must say of Dickinson what Ben Jonson said of Shakespeare: reader, look not on her picture but her book.

Dickinson's grandeur distances her from other women (and most men) poets of her time. Nevertheless these other writers provide not only contexts but essential windows into her texts. Her extreme abstraction conceals (among many other things) the historical and social address of her writing. This crosses several areas: gender, religion, and history—social and economic. With regard to the first, reading Dickinson's as an utterly self-enclosed, self-defining meditation on eternal truths not only misses the very materially gendered circumstances of her life but how these penetrate her sense of herself as poet, her many representations of womanhood, and especially as these entail distributions of power, authority, and possibility. The very meanings of her words are arenas of contest, as is explicitly marked in her uses of quotations around, for example, the words "wife" ("I'm Wife") or "husband" ("Title Divine"), whose senses she investigates and critiques, often wrenching them in counter-directions. "I Meant To Have But Modest Needs" confronts the centrally defining word of nineteenth-century womanhood—modesty—to systematically and subversively unravel it. The sets of relationships that modesty underwrites, of awe and obedience to greater, male powers in return for care and grace, is exposed instead as a swindle—a doubtful economy of distributive power. "Severer Service of Myself" works in similar ways for the word "service." This is what women performed, in the home, to the family, and, as here, at the deathbed. Dickinson in this text both embraces the familiar role and also rejects it as failing to give her stability in the face of dying.

Dickinson's preoccupation with death is an outstanding feature of her work. Yet it is far from abnormally morbid when read in terms of other women's writing, sentimental and religious; and in the context of history, which meant for her—as indeed for other contemporary women writers—most dramatically war. Dickinson unlike them wrote no tributes to Lincoln as martyr. Yet a surprising number of poems register war, both directly and indirectly: not only as deadly, but as a violent rupture in the fundamental fabric of her understanding of her world. Dickinson's work registers a deep suspicion that reality is unsatisfactory. As in the Christian tradition, she feels an intense need for redemption. Her difficulty resides in her being unable to accept what tradition offered her as to redemption's structure, method, or guarantee. The problem of evil presses upon her, but without the conviction of long-proposed solutions. It is a problem at once intensely intimate and broadly historical. Indeed, in her work can be seen how the question of evil is itself ultimately the question of history, whether personal or communal and national. The Civil War was interpreted by Dickinson's contemporaries as a great travail in punishment for sin, that is slavery; and hence also as a providential purgation and rebirth of the nation into its true destiny (or, conversely in the South, as a providential trial and test by divine power to realize the true, i.e. Southern, American self-definition). Dickinson's poetics engages questions of justification in structure as well as conception, directly in terms of war as well as in intimate, theological, and the most generally philosophical terms. These categories all impinge on one another. "My Triumph Lasted Till The Drums" imagines the poet on the battlefield, to whom victory is little consolation for the carnage surrounding her. Even as she projects reaching beyond the immediate moment in the time-honored theodicean justification of particular evils in terms of their contribution to or place in a larger good, she rejects this generalized perspective as betraying, and failing to address, the particular suffering it is meant to justify. "The Bayonet's contrition / Is nothing to the dead." "Victory Comes Late" again mourns not defeat, but the cost of triumph, turning this historical suffering into bitter questioning of God's providence, as asserted in the Bible.

Dickinson's poetry is in fact as seeded with biblical reference as is the work of so many of her compeers. Hers are strained engagements. The language of the Bible fractures in her hands, as stories of divine involvement are rendered into accusation and critique ("It Always Seemed to Me a Wrong"). Yet this is a contest also against herself. She is deeply divided as to her rejection and her need, her biblical appeal as well as its doubt. The pebble she aims in "I Took My Power In My Hand" both assaults and emulates David, and, as she says, ultimately it was "Myself was all the one that fell."

"It Feels A Shame To Be Alive," a specific war elegy for a dead Amherst soldier, Frazar Stearns, poses the question of theodicy directly: "Are we that wait—Sufficient worth?" War is the ultimate context in which a community requires the sacrificial service of its members. Presumably, for that greater whole, the individual can justly be sacrificed. Dickinson questions this. Even more, she makes overt the economic terms which effectively underwrite it. "The Price is Great, Sublimely Paid / Do We deserve—a Thing / That lives like Dollars—must be piled?" The simile of money is not accidental. Economic imagery is in fact surprisingly pervasive in Dickinson's work—an imagery that comparison with other women poets of her time brings to attention and clarifies. The Civil War was fought in the North in the name of the liberty and dignity of the individual. Yet in the same period the economic reduction of the person to commercial value is advancing apace. Providential trial can look very like banking transactions of payment and exchange. But Dickinson is suspicious of such economy. Like other women poets, she resists the conversion of American life into monetary measure. "Success," written as war approached, combines imagery of war with the problematics of accounts that cancel individual suffering in greater goods, using the ultimate American term for gainful achievement: success. Dickinson looks at success in the poem from the angle of the defeated, whom it does not reach and whose pain it does not redeem.

There is no such thing as a standard selection of Dickinson poems. Too many of her 1775 poems (in the Johnson counting; 1789 in Franklin's, see note below) are great. The most an anthology can afford is to provide narrow window slits into the castle of her imagination. Against the original headings of her work—Nature, Love, Eternity—when they finally began to be published by Mabel Loomis Todd, Dickinson's brother's mistress; and Higginson, at last persuaded to act as her editor (and then some: this first edition of the 1890s 'corrected' Dickinson's odd off-rhymes and strange, intentionally ruptured grammar); we now approach her poems in terms of gender, metaphysical critique, and history. The tendrils of history reach surprisingly deep into Dickinson's poetic. "My Life Had Stood A Loaded Gun" is a poem foremostly about poetic creativity. It is at once powerfully vivid and recalcitrantly unstable. As "Gun," the speaker's "Life" awaits agency. Yet, as "Gun," she will never be her own agent; and her activity will be deadly. The explosive and contradictory yet intricately allied reflection between creativity and violence, agency and obedience, sexuality and complicity, language and power continue in this text unresolved and mutually implicating. Yet the open figural energy of the text is anchored in the fact that its imagery of the gun was written in a time of war; and that its sense of linguistic violence is framed by a public rhetoric, and not least religious rhetoric, that had become violent with widespread and consequential force.

As a poem about writing, "My Life Had Stood" also shows how both the overt violence and implicit conflicts of her time penetrated her language, both as instrument and image. Fractured grammar, disjunctive antecedents, missing referents, volatile image structures with figures often at odds or in highly ambiguous relation to each other: all these enact linguistically Dickinson's uncertainty or critical, conflicted sense of the metaphysical, historical, and social frames available to her in her attempts to negotiate and interpret reality. Her retreat into reclusion is the measure of her need for defense. Yet, as her poems of isolation show, enclosure in the self threatened not liberty but imprisonment, not wholeness but fragmentation. If "The Soul Selects Her Own Society" (in electoral language), apparently sovereign choice contracts into a stonelike entombment. "Renunciation," as in the poem of that title, is immeasurably costly, with gain and loss very uncertainly balanced in endless inner strife. To these strains poetic form may, on the one hand, offer refuge, even at times transcendence. Yet, as in "After Great Pain," it may itself instead render an image of paralyzed fragment, without wider reference or placement. "Circumference," as in "I Saw No Way," may be as dislocating as it is encompassing.

In a fundamental sense, reality in Dickinson emerges as a matter of linguistic relations: implicitly in her contentious poetic forms, explicitly in her reflections on poetry and her linguistic imagery. Her sense of linguistic relation—and of its fragility—extends in many directions. "Prayer" constructs her effort, and her disappointment, at achieving a linguistic relation to God. This poem can serve as commentary on Dickinson's persistent use of the hymnal form, which pervades her work but, as in her uses of the Bible, does so in ways that at once retract the reference to faith that it offers, erasing what it declares, asserting and denying at the same time. "Ended Ere It Begun" makes creation itself linguistic—a text written at a crossroads between the human and the divine, but finally interdicted by God.

Nevertheless, Dickinson inscribes her own language, her own voice: emerging, as did the women poets around her, out of the historical absence of women's voices, in literature as in the record of events. Dickinson peculiarly both fulfills and defies the gender roles which would keep her reticent. Her sense of herself as poet stands in constant reference to that of herself as woman, as also of herself as American and Christian. These various identities stand in differing alignments and tensions with each other. "I Would Not Paint A Picture" records grave difficulties in imagining herself as both woman and poet. "This Was A Poet" declares a poetic office, but in the guise of male gendering, and with ambiguous vocation: "Himself—to Him—a Fortune" can ring quite self-centered, and in an economic language Dickinson treats throughout with suspicion. "Publication Is The Auction Of The Mind of Man" represents Dickinson's dramatic division between writing and (not) publishing. This dilemma extends through the poem's complex figuration of metaphysical, social, and personal turmoil as to being in a (woman's) body or not (as in "I Am Afraid To Own A Body" and "I'm Nobody"); being part of a (sexual) economy ("Auction") or not; being embodied in language, and then in print, or not.

It is the enormous strength of Dickinson's writing not to have evaded the conflict of values and orders around her, metaphysical and social, political and poetic. In her poetry we hear their intense and loud clash. This was not (only) Dickinson's private affair. It is a challenge she offers to her readers, conceived however posthumously. She is of the "Martyr Poets" who figure the difficulty of negotiating an often illegible world, not only for herself, but to "encourage Some" others. Even her "I'm Nobody" is addressed to "you:" against, in brilliant defiance of commercial culture, those who would "advertise;" and creating, in the space of her text, a community in which she is able to name herself.

Note on texts: Dickinson's publication history is a story in itself. After her death, her sister Lavinia found in her bureau drawer hundreds of poems, many of them neatly sewn into 'fascicle' booklets. These she divided, giving half to her brother Austin's wife, Susan Gilbert Dickinson, whose intense and complex friendship with Dickinson had possibly erotic as well as emotional and literary dimensions. The other half went to Mabel Loomis Todd, Austin's mistress. The lack of amity between these two led to a legacy of divided texts. Todd published, with Higginson, a heavily edited *Poems of Emily Dickinson*, First Series, in 1890; followed by *Poems of Emily Dickinson*, Second Series,

1891 and *Poems by Emily Dickinson*, Third Series, 1896. Todd also brought out a *Letters of Emily Dickinson* in 1894. Susan Dickinson's daughter, Martha Dickinson Bianchi, published a selection from her group called *The Single Hound* in 1914; *The Life and Letters of Emily Dickinson* and, edited with Alfred Leete Hampson, *The Complete Poems of Emily Dickinson* in 1924. In 1924, she brought out *Further Poems by Emily Dickinson*. Still further poems and letters were edited and published by Bianchi in 1929, 1932, 1935, 1937; and by Mabel Loomis Todd in 1931, and with her daughter Millicent Todd Bingham (*Bolts of Melody*) in 1945. A complete edition of Dickinson's work did not appear until the Thomas Johnson volumes of 1955, an amazing achievement given the difficulty of access to various manuscripts. In 1998, Bruce Franklin published his own complete poems, altering the numeration of Johnson as well as some of the sequence, formatting, boundaries and spelling of the texts. Hence the double numerations here. I have followed the Franklin edition as the most recent copyright, but have restored the Johnson spellings in the interest of consistency within this anthology and to lessen rather than increase the impression of Dickinson's idiosyncratic differentiation from other women writers. The best edition to consult, to my mind, is the Facsimile Edition, also compiled by Franklin. There, in pictures on the page, each can witness the unfinished quality of Dickinson's manuscripts, which she never prepared for publication: her experimentation with different word choices, her dashes that at once divide and conjoin words and phrases in lieu of conventional punctuation, with the least editorial mediation.

Poems

Success is counted sweetest
By those who ne'er succeed.
To comprehend a nectar
Requires sorest need.

Not one of all the purple Host
Who took the Flag today
Can tell the definition
So clear of Victory

As he defeated—dying—
On whose forbidden ear
The distant strains of triumph
Burst agonized and clear

J 67 / F 112

My Life had stood—a Loaded Gun—
In Corners—till a Day
The Owner passed—identified—
And carried Me away—

And now We roam in Sovereign Woods—
And now We hunt the Doe—
And every time I speak for Him
The Mountains straight reply—

And do I smile, such cordial light
Upon the Valley glow—
It is as a Vesuvian face
Had let it's pleasure through—

And when at Night—Our good Day done—
I guard My Master's Head—
'Tis better than the Eider Duck's
Deep Pillow—to have shared—

To foe of His—I'm deadly foe—
None stir the second time—
On whom I lay a Yellow Eye—
Or an emphatic Thumb—

Though I than He—may longer live
He longer must—than I—
For I have but the power to kill,
Without—the power to die—

J 754 / F 764

It feels a shame to be Alive—
When Men so brave—are dead—
One envies the Distinguished Dust—
Permitted—such a Head—

The Stone—that tells defending Whom
This Spartan put away
What little of Him we—possessed
In Pawn for Liberty—

The price is great—Sublimely paid—
Do we deserve—a Thing—
That lives—like Dollars—must be piled
Before we may obtain?

Are we that wait—sufficient worth—
That such Enormous Pearl
As life—dissolved be—for Us—
In Battle's—horrid Bowl?

It may be—a Renown to live—
I think the Men who die—
Those unsustained—Saviors—
Present Divinity—

J 444 / F 524

My Triumph lasted till the Drums
Had left the Dead alone
And then I dropped my Victory
And chastened stole along
To where the finished Faces
Conclusion turned on me
And then I hated Glory
And wished myself were They.

What is to be is best descried
When it has also been—
Could Prospect taste of Retrospect
The Tyrannies of Men
Were Tenderer, diviner
The Transitive toward—
A Bayonet's contrition
Is nothing to the Dead—

J 1227 / F 1212

Victory comes late—
And is held low to freezing lips—
Too rapt with frost
To take it—
How sweet it would have tasted—
Just a Drop—

Was God so economical?
His Table's spread too high for Us—
Unless We dine on Tiptoe—
Crumbs—fit such little mouths—
Cherries—suit Robins—
The Eagle's Golden Breakfast strangles—Them—
God keep His Oath to Sparrows—
Who of little Love—know how to starve—

                                        J 690 / F 195

It always felt to me—a wrong
To that Old Moses—done—
To let him see—the Canaan—
Without the entering—

And tho' in soberer moments—
No Moses there can be
I'm satisfied—the Romance
In point of injury—

Surpasses sharper stated—
Of Stephen—or of Paul—
For these—were only put to death—
While God's adroiter will

On Moses—seemed to fasten
With tantalizing Play
As Boy—should deal with lesser Boy—
To prove ability—

The fault—was doubtless Israel's—
Myself—had banned the Tribes—
And ushered Grand Old Moses
In Pentateuchal Robes

Upon the Broad Possession
'Twas little—He should see—
Old Man on Nebo! Late as this—
My justice bleeds—for Thee!

J 597 / F 521

I took my Power in my Hand—
And went against the World—
'Twas not so much as David—had—
But I—was twice as bold—

I aimed my Pebble—but Myself
Was all the one that fell –
Was it Goliah—was too large—
Or was myself—too small?

J 540 / F 660

Four Trees—upon a solitary Acre—
Without Design
Or Order, or Apparent Action—
Maintain—

The Sun—upon a Morning meets them—
The Wind—
No nearer Neighbor—have they—
But God—

The Acre gives them—Place—
They—Him—Attention of Passer by—
Of Shadow, or of Squirrel, haply—
Or Boy—

What Deed is Their's unto the General Nature—
What Plan

They severally—retard—or further—
Unknown—

> *J 742 / F 778*

I saw no Way—The Heavens were stitched—
I felt the Columns close—
The Earth reversed her Hemispheres—
I touched the Universe—

And back it slid—and I alone—
A speck upon a Ball—
Went out upon Circumference—
Beyond the Dip of Bell—

> *J 378 / F 633*

Title divine, is mine.
The Wife without the Sign—
Acute Degree conferred on me—
Empress of Calvary—
Royal, all but the Crown—
Betrothed, without the Swoon
God gives us Women—
When You hold Garnet to Garnet—
Gold—to Gold—
Born—Bridalled—Shrouded—
In a Day
Tri Victory—
"My Husband"—Women say
Stroking the Melody—
Is this the way—

> *J 1072 / F 194*

I'm "wife"—I've finished that—
That other state—
I'm Czar—I'm "Woman" now—
It's safer so—

How odd the Girl's life looks
Behind this soft Eclipse—
I think that Earth feels so
To folks in Heaven—now—

This being comfort—then
That other kind—was pain—
But Why compare?
I'm "Wife"! Stop there!

J 199 / F 225

A solemn thing—it was—I said—
A Woman—white—to be—
And wear—if God should count me fit—
Her blameless mystery—

A hallowed thing—to drop a life
Into the purple well—
Too plummetless—that it return—
Eternity—until—

I pondered how the bliss would look—
And would it feel as big—
When I could take it in my hand—
As hovering—seen—through fog—

And then—the size of this "small" life—
The Sages—call it small—
Swelled—like Horizons—in my vest—
And I sneered—softly—"small"!

J 271 / F 307

I meant to have but modest needs—
Such as Content—and Heaven—
Within my income—these could lie
And Life and I—keep even—

369

But since the last—included both—
It would suffice my Prayer
But just for one—to stipulate—
And Grace would grant the Pair—

And so—upon this wise—I prayed—
Great Spirit—Give to me
A Heaven not so large as Your's,
But large enough—for me—

A Smile suffused Jehovah's face—
The Cherubim—withdrew—
Grave Saints stole out to look at me—
And showed their dimples—too—

I left the Place—with all my might—
I threw my Prayer away—
The Quiet Ages picked it up—
And judgment—twinkled—too—
That one so honest—be extant—
It take the Tale for true—
That "Whatsoever Ye shall ask—
Itself be given You"—

But I, grown shrewder—scan the Skies
With a suspicious Air—
As Children—swindled for the first
All Swindlers—be—infer—

                    J 476 / F 711

Severer Service of myself
I hastened to demand
To fill the awful Vacuum
Your life had left behind—

I worried Nature with my Wheels
When Her's had ceased to run—
When she had put away Her Work
My own had just begun—

I strove to weary Brain and Bone—
To harass to fatigue
The glittering Retinue of nerves—
Vitality to clog

To some dull comfort Those obtain
Who put a Head away
They knew the Hair to—
And forget the color of the Day—

Affliction would not be appeased—
The Darkness braced as firm
As all my strategem had been
The Midnight to confirm—

No Drug for Consciousness—can be—
Alternative to die
Is Nature's only Pharmacy
For Being's Malady—

                    J 786 / F 887

He fumbles at your Soul
As Players at the Keys—
Before they drop full Music on—
He stuns you by Degrees—

Prepares your brittle nature
For the etherial Blow
By fainter Hammers—further heard—
Then nearer—Then so—slow—

Your Breath—has time to straighten—
Your Brain—to bubble cool—
Deals One—imperial Thunderbolt—
That scalps your naked soul—

When Winds hold Forests in their Paws—
The Universe—is still—

J 315 / F 521

I would not paint—a picture—
I'd rather be the One
It's bright impossibility
To dwell—delicious—on—
And wonder how the fingers feel
Whose rare—celestial—stir—
Evokes so sweet a torment—
Such sumptuous—Despair—

I would not talk, like Cornets—
I'd rather be the One
Raised softly to the Ceilings—
And out, and easy on—
Through Villages of Ether—
Myself endued Balloon
By but a lip of Metal—
The pier to my Pontoon—

Nor would I be a Poet—
It's finer—Own the Ear—
Enamored—impotent—content—
The License to revere,
A privilege so awful
What would the Dower be,
Had I the Art to stun myself
With Bolts—of Melody!

J 505 / F 348

This was a Poet—
It is That
Distills amazing sense
From Ordinary Meanings—
And Attar so immense

From the familiar species
That perished by the Door—
We wonder it was not Ourselves
Arrested it—before—

Of Pictures, the Discloser—
The Poet—it is He—
Entitles Us—by Contrast—
To ceaseless Poverty—

Of Portion—so unconscious—
The Robbing—could not harm—
Himself—to Him—a Fortune—
Exterior—to Time—

J 448 / F 446

The Soul selects her own Society—
Then—shuts the Door—
To her divine Majority—
Present no more—

Unmoved—she notes the Chariots—pausing—
At her low Gate—
Unmoved—an Emperor be kneeling
Upon her Mat—

I've known her—from an ample nation—
Choose One—

Then—close the Valves of her attention—
Like Stone—

> *J 303 / F 409*

Renunciation—is a piercing Virtue—
The letting go
A Presence—for an Expectation—
Not now—
The putting out of Eyes—
Just Sunrise—
Lest Day—
Day's Great Progenitor—
Outvie
Renunciation—is the Choosing
Against itself—
Itself to justify
Unto itself—
When larger function—
Make that appear—
Smaller—that Covered Vision—Here—

> *J 745 / F 782*

After great pain, a formal feeling comes—
The Nerves sit ceremonious, like Tombs—
The stiff Heart questions 'was it He, that bore,'
And 'Yesterday, or Centuries before'?

The Feet, mechanical, go round—
Of Ground, or Air, or Ought—
A Wooden way
Regardless grown,
A Quartz contentment, like a stone—

This is the Hour of Lead—
Remembered, if outlived,

As Freezing persons, recollect the Snow—
First—Chill—then Stupor—then the letting go—

J 341 / F 372

The Spirit lasts—but in what mode—
Below, the Body speaks,
But as the Spirit furnishes—
Apart, it never talks—
The Music in the Violin
Does not emerge alone
But Arm in Arm with Touch, yet Touch
Alone—is not a Tune—
The Spirit lurks within the Flesh
Like Tides within the Sea
That make the Water live, estranged
What would the Either be?
Does that know—now—or does it cease—
That which to this is done,
Resuming at a mutual date
With every future one?
Instinct pursues the Adamant,
Exacting this Reply,
Adversity if it may be, or wild Prosperity,
The Rumor's Gate was shut so tight
Before my Mind was sown,
Not even a Prognostic's Push
Could make a Dent thereon—

J 1576 / F 1627

I am afraid to own a Body—
I am afraid to own a Soul—
Profound—precarious Property—
Possession, not optional—

Double Estate, entailed at pleasure
Upon an unsuspecting Heir—

375

Duke in a moment of Deathlessness
And God, for a Frontier.

J 1090 / F 1050

Ended, ere it begun—
The Title was scarcely told
When the Preface perished from Consciousness
The story, unrevealed—

Had it been mine, to print!
Had it been your's, to read!
That it was not our privilege
The interdict of God—

J 1088 / F 1048

Prayer is the little implement
Through which Men reach
Where Presence—is denied them—
They fling their Speech

By means of it—in God's Ear—
If then He hear—
This sums the Apparatus
Comprised in Prayer—

J 437 / F 623

The Martyr Poets—did not tell—
But wrought their Pang in syllable—
That when their mortal name be numb—
Their mortal fate—encourage Some—

The Martyr Painters—never spoke—
Bequeathing—rather—to their Work—
That when their conscious fingers cease—
Some seek in Art—the Art of Peace—

J 544 / F 665

Publication—is the Auction
Of the Mind of Man—
Poverty—be justifying
For so foul a thing

Possibly—but We—would rather
From Our Garret go
White—unto the White Creator—
Than invest—Our Snow—

Thought belong to Him who gave it—
Then—to Him Who bear
It's Corporeal illustration—sell
The Royal Air—

In the Parcel—Be the Merchant
Of the Heavenly Grace—
But reduce no Human Spirit
To Disgrace of Price—

                        J 709 / F 788

I'm Nobody! Who are you?
Are you—Nobody—too?
Then there's a pair of us!
Dont tell! they'd advertise—you know!

How dreary—to be—Somebody!
How public—like a Frog—
To tell one's name—the livelong June—
To an admiring Bog!

                J 288 / F 260

Helen Fiske Hunt Jackson: 1830–1885

Introduction

Helen Fiske was born in the same year—1830, and the same place—Amherst, Massachusetts, as Emily Dickinson; and it has been largely her place in literary history to have strongly urged (as against Thomas Wentworth Higginson, from whom she first learned of Dickinson's poetry) Dickinson to publish. Her letters to Dickinson are full of homage, and her efforts to include some Dickinson poems in her "No Name Series" of anonymous writers attest to this community of recognition and support (she did sneak in Dickinson's poem "Success"). The daughter of a professor of languages at Amherst College, Helen, again like Dickinson, began school at Amherst Academy. But both her parents died of tuberculosis, and from the age of eleven she moved between boarding schools, benefiting from the still rather new opportunities for women's education. In 1852 she married Edward Hunt, an army officer and brother to the Governor of New York. He, however, died in an engineering accident on a submarine he was trying to develop in 1863. This was followed by the death of both their children by 1865. In the familiar, inverse pattern of women poets and marriage, she then began writing to support herself—one of the few professional options for educated women of her period. Through personal contacts she gained the support of Higginson, whom she had met at Newport, Rhode Island; as well as Ralph Waldo Emerson, to whom she writes a tribute, and who included five of her poems in his *Parnassus* collection. During the Civil War she did volunteer service in hospitals, and contributed to the U.S. Sanitary Commission. In the 1870s she developed a career as a travel writer covering the far West for Eastern audiences. She remarried in 1875 a wealthy railroad executive and banker whom she had met while in Colorado for reasons of health. Their arrangement, however, was such as not to interfere with her work, her travel, and her writing; and they generally seem to have had little in common. She died in 1885, nine months before Dickinson herself, who was quite shaken at Jackson's death. Ultimately Jackson was best known in her own lifetime for activism in the (doomed) cause of Indian rights, to which she was converted after hearing a lecture by Chief Standing Bear. Especially popular was her novel *Ramona,* dramatizing the plight of Indians, although mostly read as an exotic romance. Her book, *A Century of Dishonor*, collected a roster of betrayed treaties and agreements, violence and confiscation against Indians. She sent a copy to every member of Congress with the accusation on the cover, printed in red: "They are stained with the blood of your relations." Mount Jackson in Colorado is named for her.

Yet there is almost a complete discontinuity between her prose and poetry: in contrast with Lydia Sigourney, who devoted poetry to her Indian causes, or Charlotte Gilman, for whom poetry was entirely of a piece with her other feminist activities. Instead, Jackson's verse can wander into figures of Kings—and especially Queens—rather remote from American social life. Nevertheless, even in this rather stilted manner (matched stylistically by her tendency to somewhat rigid sonnet forms), Jackson's work engages and presents patterns and viewpoints that helped constitute a women's poetic of the period, as well as offering a record of women's experiences, interpretations, and cultural impressions and judgments.

Jackson's poetic strength can be felt in several characteristic constructions. There is repeatedly an interesting feminization of figure and viewpoint, often with the overt claim that she, as woman and poet, is able to understand and see what others cannot. This claim on the part of the poetic speaker becomes a structural and figural center of her texts, as in, for example, "Found Frozen." There, freezing is less an event than an image for the dead woman's whole life, lived in isolation and misunderstanding with the "wintry natures" of those she lives among. The lonely Alpine road where she freezes to death is thus, as the poem states, in fact her home. As against these others, it is the poet "who loved her last and best," who knows her and is able to tell of her. A similar dramatization and privileging of the poetic vision occurs in "In Time of Famine," where, again, a woman is misconstrued and mocked by those around her who misread her strength and self-contained endurance as (unfeminine) harshness. But the poet speaks her deeper knowledge in "words" as "two-edged swords," naming famine as the state of this woman's misunderstood life, which the poet alone can perceive and redeem: "That woman's life I know / Has been all famine. Mock now if ye dare." This sense of women's invisibility, of recovering who women are by penetrating beyond the denial and blindness of others, structures poem after poem: "Memoir of a Queen," "Her Eyes," "A Rose Leaf," "The Loneliness of Sorrow," the poems to the Unknown Lady. In each, the poet is as much at the center of the drama as are the hidden, missed figures; for she is their witness, their knight of rescue and recognition.

Closely linked to poems of invisible women are poems of missed-dialogues. These particularly reward the effort of attention. In them, a woman's voice addresses a man's, but with complete misunderstanding and miscommunication between them, as though they are speaking separate languages. But the woman's voice remains concealed: the man doesn't even hear it or know of it. In "Two Truths," the man has his truth and the woman hers. Hers, however, she does not speak out loud. She instead sacrifices her own voice so as not to be heard by him, in order not to threaten him and their relationship. The third stanza reveals that she keeps her voice nonetheless, retains her viewpoint and judgment, in some hidden recess within her—one, however, the poet has unearthed and brought to light and sound. In "A Woman's Battle," this hidden woman's voice again is heard, even as she suppresses it. Indeed, the poem is about this concealment; a heroic defiance against the unequal odds that doom the woman as against the man—"Fate steers us,—me to deeper night, / And thee to brighter seas and suns." He is not even aware of the damage he is inflicting on her, or her doomed defiance of him.

Jackson's sense of contrasting experience is not only gendered. In "The Prince is Dead," the contrary experiences are by class: royal grief is attended and honored in ways that the grief of the poor are not. Here the recurrent issue in women's writing of the splitting of American society into on the one hand, money, and on the other, everything else, can be felt in Jackson as well. Jackson brings gender into these divisions, as another alignment on this cultural map. "The Money-Seeker" is male. In "No Man's Land," it is specifically no man's land where there is "No greed, no gain; not sold or bought, / Unmarred by name or brand." The poem "Freedom" extends this penetrating, retrieving poetic voice to the slave. Here Jackson offers a defense of the freedman for all his confusion and bewilderment at his sudden release. Perhaps there is a hint of patriarchal critique, associating women with slaves, when she contrasts the sudden freedom of the freedmen against those whose "father's fathers through long lives have reigned / O'er kingdoms which mere heritage attained." Nevertheless, Jackson is on record, at least in her piece "Wanted: A Home," as skeptical about the woman's movement and its demotion of "a woman who cares only for her husband and children." Still, her questioning whether "a higher more imperative thing is that she herself be developed to the utmost" seems not to have applied to herself.

Her poetry, as well as her career, instead belie this stance. Her poem on Charlotte Cushman honors this woman artist as a "queen." Jackson focuses repeatedly on central women figures, a poetic strategy that, far from being invented in the twentieth century, was already in effect in the nineteenth-century, although unbeknownst to the later women writers in their dispersed tradition. She thus devotes a poem to "Oenone," recovering a figure from the mythological past. Of special interest is a set of texts based in the biblical book of Esther. These form a fascinating link with other women's poems on the Bible, with Vashti, the scorned queen of the Esther story, receiving very special attention. In Jackson's treatment, Esther, the heroine of the tradition, is criticized exactly because she subordinates herself to her people rather than asserting her own selfhood: "Thou heldest thy race too dear, thyself too cheap." Vashti, in contrast, is upheld as a queen in her own right, in heroic and correct defiance of the king—something the poet, in her unique and penetrating role, claims to be alone able to grasp and pronounce: "not one knowing thee so well ... that he the world could tell." Yet, her figure of the poet in "Refrain" is male (could the title be some sort of pun?). Jackson's poem "Opportunity" records, as do so many woman's poems on this sort of topic, a deep seated ambivalence about achievement, as the "golden gates" of opportunity crash shut on her approach.

Poems

Two Truths

"Darling," he said, "I never meant
To hurt you;" and his eyes were wet
"I would not hurt you for the world:
Am I to blame if I forget?"

"Forgive my selfish tears!" she cried,
"Forgive! I knew that it was not
Because you meant to hurt me, sweet,
I knew it was that you forgot!"

But all the same, deep in her heart
Rankled this thought, and rankles yet—
"When love is at its best, one loves
So much that he cannot forget"

A Woman's Battle

Dear foe, I know thou'lt win the fight.
I know thou hast the stronger bark,
And thou art sailing in the light,
While I am creeping in the dark.
Thou dost not dream that I am crying,
As I come up with colors flying

I clear away my wounded, slain,
With strength like frenzy, strong and swift;
I do not feel the tug and strain,
Though dead are heavy, hard to lift.
If I looked in their faces dying,
I could not keep my colors flying.

Dear foe, it will be short,—our fight,—
Though lazily thou train'st thy guns;
Fate steers us,—me to deeper night,
And thee to brighter seas and suns;
But thou'lt not dream that I am dying,
As I sail by with colors flying!

Found Frozen

She died, as many travellers have died,
O'ertaken on an Alpine road by night
Numbed and bewildered by the falling snow,
Striving, in spite of failing pulse, and limbs
Which faltered and grew feeble at each step,
To toil up the icy steep, and bear
Patient and faithful to the last, the load
Which, in the sunny morn, seemed light!
And yet 'twas in the place she called her home, she died;
And they who loved her with the all of love
Their wintry natures had to give, stood by
And wept some tears, and wrote above her grave
Some common record which they thought was true;
But I, who loved her last and best, I knew.

In Time of Famine

"She has no heart," they said, and turned away,
Then, stung so that I wished my words might be
Two-edged swords, I answered low: "Have ye
Not read how once when famine held fierce sway
In Lydia, and men died day by day
Of hunger, there were found brave souls whose glee
Scarce hid their pangs, who said, 'Now we
Can eat but once in two days; we will play
Such games on those days when we eat no food
That we forget our pain.' Thus they withstood
Long years of famine; and to them we owe
The trumpets, pipes, and balls which mirth finds good
To-day, and little dreams that of such woe
They first were born. That woman's life I know
Has been all famine. Mock now if ye dare,
To hear her brave sad laughter in the air."

Memoir of a Queen

Her name, before she was a queen, boots not.
When she was crowned, her kingdom said,
"The Queen!" And, after that, all other names too mean
By far had seemed. Perhaps all were forgot,
Save "Queen, sweet Queen." Such pitiable lot
As till her birth her kingdom had, was seen
Never in all fair lands, so torn between
False grasping powers, that toiled and fought, but got
No peace. All curious search is wholly vain
For written page or stone whereon occurs
A mention of the kingdom which obeyed
This sweet queen's rule. But centuries have laid
No dead queen down in royal sepulchres
Whose reign was greater or more blest than hers.

Her Eyes

That they are brown, no man will dare to say
He knows. And yet I think that no man's look
Ever those depths of light and shade forsook,
Until their gentle pain warned him away.
Of all sweet things I know but one which may
Be likened to her eyes. When, in deep nook
Of some green field, the water of a brook
Makes lingering, whirling eddy in its way,
Round soft drowned leaves; and in a flash of sun
They turn to gold, until the ripples run
Now brown, now yellow, changing as by some
Swift spell. I know not with what body come
The saints. But this I know, my Paradise
Will mean the resurrection of her eyes.

A Rose Leaf

A Rose-leaf on the snowy deck,
The high wind whirling it astern;
Nothing the wind could know or reck;
Why did the King's eye thither turn?
"The Queen has walked here!" hoarse he cried.
The courtiers, stunned, turned red, turned white;
No use if they had stammered, lied;
Aghast they fled his angry sight.
Kings' wives die quick, when kings go mad;
To death how fair and grave she goes!
What if the king knew now, she had
Shut in her hand a little rose?
And men die quick when kings have said;
Bleeding, dishonored, flung apart
In outcast field a man lies dead
With rose-leaves warm upon his heart.

The Loneliness of Sorrow

Friends crowd around and take it by the hand,
Intruding gently on its loneliness,
Striving with word of love and sweet caress
To draw it into light and air. Like band
Of brothers, all men gather close, and stand
About it, making half its grief their own,
Leaving it never silent nor alone.
But through all crowds of strangers and of friends,
Among all voices of good-will and cheer,
Walks Sorrow, silently, and does not hear.
Like hermit whom mere loneliness defends
Like one born deaf, to whose still ear sound sends
No word of message; and like one born dumb,
From whose sealed lips complaint can never come.
Majestic in its patience, and more sweet
Than all things else that can of souls have birth,
Bearing the one redemption of this earth
Which God's eternities fulfill, complete,
Down to its grave, with steadfast, tireless feet
It goes uncomforted, serene, alone,
And leaves not even name on any stone.

Renunciation

Wherefore thus, apart with drooping wings
Thou stillest, saddest angel,
With hidden face, as if but bitter things
Thou hadst, and no evangel
Of good tidings?
Thou know'st that through our tears
Of hasty, selfish weeping,
Comes surer sun; and for our petty fears
Of loss, thou hast in keeping

A greater gain than all of which we dreamed.
Thou knowest that in grasping
The bright possessions which so precious seemed,
We lose them; but, if clasping
Thy faithful hand, we tread with steadfast feet
The path of thy appointing,
There waits for us a treasury of sweet
Delight; royal anointing
With oil of gladness and of strength! O, things
Of Heaven, Christ's evangel
Bearing, call us with shining face and poised wings,
Thou sweetest, dearest angel!

To an Unknown Lady

I.

There lived a lady who was lovelier
Than anything that my poor skill may paint,
Though I would follow round the world till faint
I fell, for just one little look at her.
Who said she seemed like this or that did err:
Like her dear self she was, alone, no taint
From touch of mortal or of earth; blest saint
Serene, with many a faithful worshipper!
There is no poet's poesy would not,
When laid against the whiteness of her meek,
Proud, solemn face, make there a pitiful blot.
It is so strange that I can never speak
Of her without a tear. O, I forgot!
This surely may fall blameless on that cheek!

II.

I know a lady—no, I do not know
Her face, her voice; I do not know her name:

And yet such sudden, subtle knowledge came
To me of her one day, that I am slow
To think that if I met her I should go
Amiss in greeting her. Such sweet, proud shame
In every look would tell her hidden fame
Whose poet lover, singing, loves her so
That all his songs unconsciously repeat
The fact of her, no matter what he sings,
The color and the tone of her in things
Remotest, and the presence of her, sweet
And strong to hold him lowest at her feet,
When most he soars on highest sunlit wings.
I bless thee, Lady whom I do not know!
I thank God for thy unseen, beauteous face,
And lovely soul, which make this year of grace
In all our land so full of grace to grow;
As years were, solemn centuries ago,
When lovers knew to set in stateliest place
Their mistresses, and, for their sake, no race
Disdained or feared to run, they loved them so.
Reading the verses which I know are thine,
My heart grows reverent, as on holy ground.
I think of many an unnamed saintly shrine
I saw in Old World churches, hung around
With pictured scrolls and gifts in grateful sign
Of help which sore-pressed souls of men had found.
O sweetest immortality, which pain
Of Love's most bitter ecstasy can buy,
Sole immortality which can defy
Earth's power on earth's own ground, and never wane
All other ways, hearts breaking, try in vain.
All fire and flood and moth and rust outvie
Love's artifice. The sculptor's marbles lie
In shapeless fragments; and to dust again
The painter's hand had scarcely turned, before
His colors faded. But the poet came,

Giving to her from whom he took, his fame,
Placing her than the angels little lower,
And centuries cannot harm her any more
Than they can pale the stars which heard her name.

The Prince is Dead

A room in the palace is shut. The king
And the queen are sitting in black.
All day weeping servants will run and bring,
But the heart of the queen will lack
All things; and the eyes of the king will swim
With tears which must not be shed,
But will make all the air float dark and dim,
As he looks at each gold and silver toy,
And thinks how it gladdened the royal boy,
And dumbly writhes while the courtiers read
How all the nations his sorrow heed.
The Prince is dead.

The hut has a door, but the hinge is weak,
And to-day the wind blows it back;
There are two sitting there who do not speak;
They have begged a few rags of black.
They are hard at work, though their eyes are wet
With tears which must not be shed
They dare not look where the cradle is set;
They hate the sunbeam which plays on the floor,
But will make the baby laugh out no more;
They feel as if they were turning to stone,
They wish the neighbors would leave them alone.
The Prince is dead.

Mazzini

That he is dead the sons of kings are glad;
And in their beds the tyrants sounder sleep.
Now he is dead his martyrdom will reap
Late harvest of the palms it should have had
In life. Too late the tardy lands are sad.
His unclaimed crown in secret they will keep
For ages, while in chains they vainly weep,
And vainly grope to find the roads he bade
Them take. O glorious soul! there is no dearth
Of worlds. There must be many better worth
Thy presence and thy leadership than this.
No doubt, on some great sun to-day, thy birth
Is for a race, the dawn of Freedom's bliss,
Which but for thee it might for ages miss.

The Money-Seekers

What has he in this glorious world's domain
Unreckoned loss which he counts up for gain,
Unreckoned shame, of which he feels no stain,
Unreckoned dead he does not know were slain.
What things does he take with him when he dies?
Nothing of all that he on earth did prize:
Unto his grovelling feet and sordid eyes
How difficult and empty seem the skies!

No Man's Land

Who called it so? What accident
The wary phase devised?
What wandering fancy thither went,
And lingered there surprised?

Ah, no man's land! O sweet estate
Illimitably fair!
No measure, wall, or bar or gate.
Secure as sky or air.
No greed, no gain; not sold or bought,
Unmarred by name or brand,
Not dreamed of or desired or sought,
Nor visioned, "no man's land."
Suns set and rise, and rise and set,
Whole summers come and go;
And winters pay the summer's debt,
And years of west wind blow;
And harvests of wild seed-times fill,
And seed and fill again;
And blossoms bloom at blossoms' will,
By blossoms overlain;
And day and night, and night and day,
Uncounted suns and moons,
By silent shadows mark and stay
Unreckoned nights and noons:
Ah, "no man's land," hast thou a lover,
Thy wild, sweet charm who sees?
The stars look down; the birds fly over;
Art thou alone with these?
Ah, "no man's land," when died thy lover,
Who left no trace to tell?
Thy secret we shall not discover;
The centuries keep it well!

Poppies on the Wheat

Along Ancona's hills the shimmering heat,
A tropic tide of air with ebb and flow
Bathes all the fields of wheat until they glow
Like flashing seas of green, which toss and beat

Around the vines. The poppies lithe and fleet
Seem running, fiery torchmen, to and fro
To mark the shore. The farmer does not know
That they are there. He walks with heavy feet,
Counting the bread and wine by autumn's gain,
But I, I smile to think that days remain
Perhaps to me in which, though bread be sweet
No more, and red wine warm my blood in vain,
I shall be glad remembering how the fleet,
Lithe poppies ran like torchmen with the wheat.

Oenone

"Paris, the son of Priam, was wounded by one of the poisoned arrows of
Hercules that Philoctetes bore to the siege of Troy, whereupon he had
himself borne up into Ida, that he might see the nymph Oenone, whom
he once had loved, because she who knew many secret things alone could
heal him; but when he had seen her and spoken with her, she would deal
with the matter in no wise, whereupon Paris died of that hurt."

Woe to thee, Oenone! stricken blind
And poisoned by a darkness and a pain,
O, woe to thee, Oenone! who couldst find
No love when love lay dying, doubly slain
Slain thus by thee, Oenone! O, what stain,
Of red like this on hands of love was seen
Ever before or since, since love has been!
O, woe to thee, Oenone! Hadst thou said,
"Sweet love, lost love, I know now why I live
And could not die, the days I wished me dead;
O love, all strength of life and joy I give
Thee back! Ah me, that I have dared to strive
With fates that bore me to this one sure bliss,
Thou couldst not rob me, O lost love, of this?"
Hadst thou said this, Oenone, though he went

Bounding with life, thy life, and left thee there
Dying and glad, such sudden pain had rent
His heart, that even beating in the fair
White arms of Helen, hid in her sweet hair,
It had made always moan, in strange unrest,
"Oenone's love was greater love, was best."

Mordecai

Make friends with him! He is of royal line,
Although he sits in rags. Not all of thine
Array of splendor, pomp of high estate,
Can buy him from his place within the gate,
The king's gate of thy happiness, where he,
Yes, even he, the Jew, remaineth free,
Never obeisance making, never scorn
Betraying of thy silver and new-born
Delight. Make friends with him, for unawares
The charmed secret of thy joys he bears.
Be glad, so long as his black sackcloth, late
And early, thwarts thy sun; for if in hate
Thou plottest for his blood, thy own death-cry,
Not his, comes from the gallows, cubits high.

Esther

Face more vivid than he dreamed who drew
Thy portrait in that thrilling tale of old!
Dead queen, we see thee still, thy beauty cold
As beautiful; thy dauntless heart which knew
No fear,—not even of a king who slew
At pleasure; maiden heart which was not sold,
Though all the maiden flesh the king's red gold
Did buy! The loyal daughter of the Jew,

No hour saw thee forget his misery;
Thou wert not queen until thy race went free;
Yet thoughtful hearts, that ponder slow and deep,
Find doubtful reverence at last for thee;
Thou heldest thy race too dear, thyself too cheap;
Honor no second place for truth can keep.

Vashti

In all great Shushan's palaces was there
Not one, O Vashti, knowing thee so well,
Poor uncrowned queen, that he the world could tell
How thou wert pure and loyal-souled as fair?
How it was love which made thee bold to dare
Refuse the shame which madmen would compel?
Not one, who saw the bitter tears that fell
And heard thy cry heart-rending on the air:
"Ah me! My Lord could not this thing have meant!
He well might loathe me ever, if I go
Before these drunken princes as a show.
I am his queen: I come of king's descent.
I will not let him bring our crown so low;
He will but bless me when he doth repent!"

Tribute: R.W.E.

Midway in summer, face to face, a king
I met. No king so gentle and so wise.
He calls no man his subject; but his eyes,
In midst of benediction, questioning,
Each soul compel. A first-fruits offering
Each soul must owe to him whose fair land lies
Wherever God has his. No white dove flies
Too white, no wine too red and rich, to bring.

With sudden penitence for all her waste,
My soul to yield her scanty hoards made haste,
When lo! they shrank and failed me in that need,
Like wizard's gold, by worthless dust replaced.
My speechless grief, the king, with tender heed,
Thus soothed: "These ashes sow. They are true seed."
O king! in other summer may I stand
Before thee yet, the full ear in my hand!

Charlotte Cushman

But yesterday it was. Long years ago
It seems. The world so altered looks to-day
That, journeying idly with my thoughts astray,
I gazed where rose one lofty peak of snow
Above grand tiers on tiers of peaks below.
One moment brief it shone, then sank away,
As swift we reached a point where foot-hills lay
So near they seemed like mountains huge to grow,
And touch the sky. That instant, idly still,
My eye fell on a printed line, and read
Incredulous, with sudden anguished thrill,
The name of this great queen among the dead.
I raised my eyes. The dusty foot-hills near
Had gone. Again the snowy peak shone clear.

II.

Oh! thou beloved woman, soul and heart
And life, thou standest unapproached and grand,
As still that glorious snowy peak doth stand.
The dusty barrier our clumsy art
In terror hath called death holds thee apart
From us. 'Tis but the low foot-hill of sand
Which bars our vision in a mountain-land.
One moment further on, and we shall start

With speechless joy to find that we have passed
The dusky mound which shuts us from the light
Of thy great love, still quick and warm and fast,
Of thy great strengths, heroically cast,
Of thy great soul, still glowing pure and white,
Of thy great life, still pauseless, full, and bright!

Refrain

Of all the songs which poets sing
The ones which are most sweet
Are those which at close intervals
A low refrain repeat;
Some tender word, some syllable,
Over and over, ever and ever,
While the song lasts,
Altering never,
Music if sung, music if said,
Subtle like some golden thread
A shuttle casts,
In and out on a fabric red,
Till it glows all through
With the golden hue.
Oh! of all the songs sung,
No songs are so sweet
As the songs with refrains,
Which repeat and repeat.

Of all the lives lived,
No life is so sweet,
As the life where one thought,
In refrain doth repeat,
Over and over, ever and ever,
Till the life ends,
Altering never,

Joy which is felt, but is not said,
Subtler than any golden thread
Which the shuttle sends
In and out in a fabric red,
Till it glows all through
With a golden hue.
Oh! of all the lives lived,
Can be no life so sweet,
As the life where one thought
In refrain doth repeat,
"Now name for me a thought
To make life so sweet,
A thought of such joy
Its refrain to repeat."
Oh! foolish to ask me. Ever, ever
Who loveth believes,
But telleth never.
It might be a name, just a name not said,
But in every thought; like a golden thread
Which the shuttle weaves
In and out on a fabric red,
Till it glows all through
With a golden hue.
Oh! of all sweet lives,
Who can tell how sweet
Is the life which one name
In refrain doth repeat?

The Poet's Forge

He lies on his back, the idling smith,
A lazy, dreaming fellow is he;
The sky is blue, or the sky is gray,
He lies on his back the livelong day,

Not a tool in sight, say what they may,
A curious sort of smith is he.

The powers of the air are in league with him;
The country around believes it well;
The wondering folk draw spying near;
Never sight nor sound do they see or hear;
No wonder they feel a little fear;
When is it his work is done so well?

Never sight nor sound to see or hear;
The powers of the air are in league with him;
High over his head his metals swing,
Fine gold and silver to shame the king;
We might distinguish their glittering,
If once we could get in league with him.

High over his head his metals swing;
He hammers them idly year by year,
Hammers and chuckles a low refrain:
"A bench and a book are a ball and a chain,
The adze is a better tool than the plane;
What's the odds between now and next year?"

Hammers and chuckles his low refrain,
A lazy, dreaming fellow is he:
When sudden, some day, his bells peal out,
And men, at the sound, for gladness shout;
He laughs and asks what it's all about;
Oh, a curious sort of smith is he.

My Days

Veiled priestess, in a holy place,
Day pause this on her threshold, beckoning;

As infants to the mother's bosom spring
At sound of mother's voice, although her face
Be hid, I leap with sudden joy. No trace
Of fear I feel; I take her hand and fling
Her arm around my neck, and walk and cling
Close to her side. She chooses road and pace;
I feast along the way on her shewbread;
I help an hour or two on her great task
Beyond this honoring, no wage I ask.
Then, ere I know, sweet night slips in her stead,
And, while by sunset fires I rest and bask,
Warm to her faithful breast she folds my head.

Freedom

What freeman knoweth freedom? Never he
Whose father's fathers through long lives have reigned
O'er kingdoms which mere heritage attained.
Though from his youth to age he roam as free
As winds, he dreams not freedom's ecstasy.
But he whose birth was in a nation chained
For centuries; where every breath was drained
From breasts of slaves which knew not there could be
Such thing as freedom, he beholds the light
Burst, dazzling; though the glory blind his sight
He knows the joy. Fools laugh because he reels
And wields confusedly his infant will;
The wise man watching with a heart that feels
Says: "Cure for freedom's harms is freedom still."

Opportunity

I do not know if, climbing some steep hill
Through fragrant wooded pass, this glimpse I bought;

Or whether in some midday I was caught
To upper air, where visions of God's will
In pictures to our quickened sense fulfill
His word. But this I saw: A path I sought
Through wall of rock. No human fingers wrought
The golden gates which opened, sudden, still,
And wide. My fear was hushed by my delight.
Surpassing fair the lands; my path lay plain;
Alas! so spell-bound, feasting on the sight,
I paused, that I but reached the threshold bright,
When, swinging swift, the golden gates again
Were rocky walls, by which I wept in vain!

Emma Lazarus: 1849–1887

Introduction

The notion of nineteenth-century women poets as genteel is surprisingly false. This is the case considering not only economic, but religious and ethnic status. Of the men poets, till the end of the century only Whitman and Poe fall outside the well-to-do classes; and all are white and Protestant. Among women poets there is Harper as freewoman black, Larcom the Mill girl, Sigourney the gardener-handyman's daughter; Wilcox and the Cary sisters as poor western farm girls; Jackson and Gilman, self-made and self-supporting by writing; with Howe and Dickinson alone wealthy. Emma Lazarus was wealthy, but Jewish—and not the sole case of a Jewish woman poet in the nineteenth century. Penina Moise, born in South Carolina (1797–1880), was the first American Jew to publish. Adah Isaacs Menken stands out as an exemplum of complex ethnic self-construction, with continued uncertainty till today as to her origins or intersections as creole, black, and/or Jewish. She adopted Judaism as her identity-claim at her second (third?) marriage, short-lived and one of many, to Alexander Isaac Menken.

Lazarus's work makes conscious and central, for the first time, hybrid American identity; or, American identity as hybrid; with all its multiplication, tension, and transformative power, and with gender an additional dimension and claim. Born in 1849, when there were few Jews in America (6000 in 1830; 150,000 in 1860); into a wealthy New York family of German (her father) and Portuguese (her mother) Jewish descent; Lazarus was tutored at home. By the time of her first published volume—*Poems and Translations*—at the age of seventeen (printed privately by her father), she was well-schooled in classics and modern languages and literatures, including German, Italian and French. Although her family attended the Portuguese Synagogue, they were not devout. Summers were spent in the elite society of Newport, Rhode Island, where she met the Wards, the Hawthornes, and the Emersons.

Lazarus's verse remains throughout structured not only by her extraordinary education, but her sense of cross-cultures derived in this wide-ranging exposure to world languages and literatures, as well as in her own increasingly conscious mixed identities. Her group of poems on poetics, written at different times, reflect these various contexts and cultural encounters. She begins, as do so many in the period, with a residual Emersonianism, as displayed in her early poem "Links" (1865). This was strengthened by her personal association with him, first in his praise of her *Poems* which she sent to him; then in her sense of betrayal at his exclusion of her work from his anthology *Parnassus*: "I cannot resist the impulse of expressing to you my extreme disappointment at finding you have so far modified the enthusiastic estimate you held of my literary labors as to refuse me a place in the large and miscellaneous collection of poems you have just published" [Letter to Emerson, 27 Dec., 1874]. Her tribute "To R.W.E." reflects their eventual reconciliation. Yet even here there sounds a subtle difference, the difference of gender. If the "eagle" soars as the "great," so soars also the "lark," even if as the "little." This figure of the poet suggests, in its diminution yet also venture, a feminine sense of self that takes different guises through Lazarus's career. "Echoes," written much later, makes such feminization central. "Late-born and woman-souled I dare not hope," it opens with the modest apology so characteristic of women, perhaps not only in the nineteenth century. Yet the poem goes on to make its own strong claim as well. Although Lazarus, like

Anne Bradstreet, cannot write "elder lays" or epic "strong-armed warriors," her woman's Muse takes her—"veiled and screened by womanhood"—into an enclosed world of "lake-floored cave." This very Romantic image of interiority and reflection becomes her own space of figural "echoes," a feminized art-realm and ultimately preferred by her. This sort of gendering of poetics recurs in "Assurance," where a female Muse comes to her with erotic power; in "Critic and Poet" (again "An Apologue") where the critic is explicitly masculine, while the poet is figured as the classically feminized "nightingale." In "Life and Art," a female Muse addresses a male poet, but one who must withdraw in order to create. "Acceptance" and "Aspiration" enact the mixed pulls of self-assertion and self-effacement so deeply embedded in women's writing of the period.

It is not quite correct to say that Lazarus had no Jewish involvement through her early life. Her rabbi enticed her, against resistance, to translate Jewish poets from Medieval Spain, working from German versions of Abraham Geiger and Michael Sachs. Her early poem "In the Jewish Synagogue at Newport" attests her interest; yet there is a felt difference between this text and her later writings. A response to Longfellow's "In the Jewish Cemetery at Newport," the poem clearly tries to move the Jews from the cemetery back into the realm of the living. This, however, proves difficult to do. Of the "Synagogue" she writes: "No signs of life here." The Hebrew language of its prayers is "dead." And, in an image that will prove crucial for her later, the "perpetual lamp," instead of casting an "undying radiance," is "spent."

But this changed. A trip to Ward Island transformed this elite and sheltered lady into a witness of the mass immigration of Russian Jews fleeing the murderous pogroms of 1881, and poetically, into a visionary prophetic voice. Lazarus, her sister Josephine reports, wrote her first poems at the age of eleven on the outbreak of the Civil War. In the 1880s, historical events impelled her into an explosion of polemical energy. But these were events not only of American, not only of Jewish history: but of their conjunction, intersection, convergence. The difference can be felt in the move from "In the Jewish Synagogue" to "The Crowing of the Red Cock," "The Banner of the Jew," or "The Feast of Lights." The first is contemplative, a withdrawn space of "softened voices" and "mournful echoes," both as culture and as poetic. The latter are urgent calls, both as poetry and as event—with Lazarus herself wielding "David's lyre" and clashing "cymbals"—to accuse, confront, and shape present and past.

This Lazarus poetry is not only profoundly historical, but intensely historiographic. Lazarus undertakes not only to recover events, but to reconstrue the broad historical map and understanding that frames and configures them. She casts Judaism not only as an ancient, pre-Christian episode, but as an ongoing culture in its own historical right, with its own defining values, claims, and integrity. This active Jewish life has been the case since pre-Christian and Christian times and into the present day, in a course still being pursued and created. But to claim continuous, active, and independent Jewish history is to challenge and reconceive Christian historical and religious understanding of its own Jewish antecedents: not as a prefiguration and precursor long since displaced, absorbed, and superceded; but as a cultural life continuing alongside Christianity's. Such a redrawing of the map of history has massive consequences in the distribution of moral as well as historical meaning. As Lazarus flares in poems such as "The Crowing of the Red Cock," "The Valley of Baca," "The Guardian of the Red Disk," Christians, in persecuting Jews, do more than betray their own moral commitments. They betray Christ himself. Lazarus is among the first to reflect in literature the just then emerging *Wissenschaft* studies on the historical Jesus as Jewish. In her work, Jesus becomes the embodiment of Jewish suffering at the hands of Christians. To persecute Jews is then to crucify Christ. Not Jews, but anti-Semites, are the Christ-killers.

Lazarus's urgency is directed against contemporary anti-Semitism, while it is directed towards the notion of a Jewish national homeland in Palestine, an idea inspired by George Eliot's *Daniel Deronda*. This vision of a renewed Judaism was more national than religious. But above all, it stood in complex relation to her own senses of identity. For Lazarus, the restored homeland was essential for Russian Jews, not for American ones. In affirming and constructing a modern Jewish identity, Lazarus was in no way renouncing her American self. On the contrary, she discovers that to affirm the one is not to betray the other, but to embrace both in a multiplicity which is itself American identity. Her recovery of Jewish history thus involved reimagining American history itself. The poem "1492" identifies the year of the expulsion of the Jews from Spain as the year of the discovery of America, making the latter an event in Jewish history. American culture, conversely, was in fact deeply embedded in Old Testament prophecy and biblical senses of the sacred integrity of the self. Lazarus merges these. In "The New Year," she makes American "freedom to proclaim and worship" a Jewish heritage and fulfillment. In "In Exile," America is the "freedom to love the law that Moses brought / To sing the songs of David;" which is to say, America becomes the site of Jewish cultural rebirth. In fact, it is quite unclear whether America is exile to the Jews or not. "In Exile" traces "Refuge" as a journey from "Egypt" to "Texas." In "The New Year," Jewish exile finds its resolution "In two divided streams," with one "rolling homeward" and the other "rushing sunward;" each at once made up of the free individual who also constitutes the nation: "By each the truth is spread, the law unfurled, / Each separate soul contains the nation's force, / And both embrace the world."

Lazarus's work of recovery and recasting was textual and lin-guistic as well as historical. Translation, which she had been engaged in since girlhood, extended to a variety of documents and materials, styles and genres, as well as histories and places. Her whole work can be called a work of cultural translation—and not least *translatio* from Europe to America. Here the importance of the figure of Heinrich Heine emerges. The German-Jewish poet generally represented for her the possibility of Jewish creativity and participation in world culture. Yet this is not without strain. Her translation of Heine's "Donna Clara" is her contemporary commentary on his German commentary on post-Golden Age Spain, when the Jewish effort to be accepted in Spanish society met with violent defeat. For Heine, who despite his conversion to Christianity finally had to make his home in Paris, this effort to be both part and apart from a surrounding culture remained deeply ironic. "The Venus at the Louvre" records Lazarus's own powerful encounter with classical European culture in her first trip overseas, through the figure of Heine, exiled in Paris and forever a "pale, death-stricken Jew" torn in "One ardent heart, one poet-brain, / For vanished Hellas and Hebraic pain." The multiple identities do not necessarily cohere, and their mutual relation can be painful and destabilizing no less than transformative.

In her later works, Lazarus's identity as a woman is less overt than her senses of herself as Jewish, American, and poet. Yet her very stance as visionary prophet places her as woman in a central and active public role; and the poems offer striking feminine figures, not least in the feminized figure of America itself. This is the case in "1492," where America is "virgin world;" and most potently in "The New Colossus," Lazarus's famous poem which, like Julia Ward Howe's "Battle Hymn," is one of the few by a nineteenth-century woman to have gained public place. This, however, was far from straightforward. The poem was written to help raise money for the pedestal of the Statue of Liberty, which France had donated as an emblem of French-American friendship. But its historical context was also a rising American trend opposing immigration, which was to result in the 1924 legislation establishing immigration quotas and that proved so tragic for European Jewry. Only in 1945 was the poem inscribed on the pedestal (in 1903 it had been placed inside). Lazarus in 1883 envisioned the as yet absent monument as instead announcing an America of welcome, refuge, and plurality. Lazarus's "mighty woman with a torch" stands in opposition against the male Old World Colossus, and as a figure for the century-long efforts of American women in acts of benevolence and community service—the "Mother of Exiles." Her "mild eyes" and "silent lips" recall feminine values of modesty, even as they also "command" while she "cries" out her own specific vision of America. The poem is an ultimate instance of Lazarus's view of literature as event, as actively participating in the creation of history and society through its power of image and utterance. In the poem, Europe is reborn as America, the despised as the welcomed and embraced. That the poem inscribes as well Lazarus's own Jewish identity deeply affirms what the poem asserts as American plurality. Lazarus, in casting Europe as Greek, can align herself in counter to it as at once both American and Hebrew—situated against Greeks as the contrasting culture in her poems of the

Maccabee revolt against Hellenism. Most notable is the final image of the "lamp," which had been, throughout her work, associated with the Menorah of Hebrew freedom, with the "perpetual lamp" of the synagogue, the "Feast of Lights," the "immortal lamp" of Hebraic truth ("Gifts"). In "The New Colussus," the lamp is at once ethnic and American, ethnic as American. As image it enacts and invokes an America of plural integrity.

Poems

Links

The little and the great are joined in one
By God's great force. The wondrous golden sun
Is linked unto the glow-worm's tiny spark;
The eagle soars to heaven in his flight;
And in those realms of space, all bathed in light,
Soar none except the eagle and the lark.

Echoes

Late-born and woman-souled I dare not hope,
The freshness of the elder lays, the might
Of manly, modern passion shall alight
Upon my Muse's lips, nor may I cope
(Who veiled and screened by womanhood must grope)
With the world's strong-armed warriors and recite
The dangers, wounds, and triumphs of the fight;
Twanging the full-stringed lyre through all its scope.
But, if thou ever in some lake-floored cave
O'erbrowed by rocks, a wild voice wooed and heard,
Answering at once from heaven and earth and wave,
Lending elf-music to thy harshest word,
Misprize thou not these echoes that belong
To one in love with solitude and song.

Assurance

Last night I slept, and when I woke her kiss
Still floated on my lips. For we had strayed
Together in my dream, through some dim glade,
Where the shy moonbeams scarce dared light our bliss.
The air was dank with dew, between the trees,
The hidden glow-worms kindled and were spent.
Cheek pressed to cheek, the cool, the hot night-breeze
Mingled our hair, our breath, and came and went,
As sporting with our passion. Low and deep,
Spake in mine ear her voice:
                           "And didst thou dream,
This could be buried? this could be asleep?
And love be thrall to death? Nay, whatso seem,
Have faith, dear heart; this is the thing that is!"
Thereon I woke, and on my lips her kiss.

Acceptance: Epochs VII

Yea, she hath looked Truth grimly face to face,
And drained unto the lees the proffered cup.
This silence is not patience, nor the grace
Of resignation, meekly offered up,
But mere acceptance fraught with keenest pain,
Seeing that all her struggles must be vain.

Her future dear and terrible outlies,—
This burden to be borne through all her days,
This crown of thorns pressed down above her eyes,
This weight of trouble she may never raise.
No reconcilement doth she ask nor wait;
Knowing such things are, she endures her fate.

No brave endeavor of the broken will
To cling to such poor strays as will abide
(Although the waves be wild and angry still)
After the lapsing of the swollen tide.
No fear of further loss, no hope of gain,
Naught but the apathy of weary pain.

Aspiration: Phantasies II
(After Robert Schumann)

Dark lies the earth, and bright with worlds the sky:
That soft, large, lustrous star, that first outshone,
Still holds us spelled with potent sorcery.

Dilating, shrinking, lightening, it hath won
Our spirit with its strange, strong influence,
And sways it as the tides beneath the moon.

What impulse this, o'ermastering heart and sense?
Exalted, thrilled, the freed soul fain would soar
Unto that point of shining prominence,

Craving new fields and some unheard-of shore,
Yea, all the heavens, for her activity,
To mount with daring flight, to hover o'er

Low hills of earth, flat meadows, level sea,
And earthly joy and trouble. In this hour
Of waning light and sound, of mystery,

Of shadowed love and beauty—veilèd power,
She feels her wings: she yearns to grasp her own,
Knowing the utmost good to be her dower.

A dream! A dream! For at a touch 'tis gone.
O mocking spirit! Thy mere fools are me,
Unto the depths from heights celestial thrown.

From these blind gropings toward reality,
This thirst for truth, this most pathetic need
Of something to uplift, to justify,

To help and comfort while we faint and bleed,
May we not draw, wrung from the last despair,
Some argument of hope, some blessed creed,

That we can trust the faith which whispers prayer,
The vanishings, the ecstasy, the gleam,
The nameless aspiration and the dream?

Critic and Poet: An Apologue

('Poetry must be simple, sensuous or impassioned; this man is neither
simple, sensuous nor impassioned; therefore he is not a poet.')

No man had ever heard a nightingale,
When once a keen-eyed naturalist was stirred
To study and define—what is a bird,
To classify by rote and book, nor fail
To mark its structure and to note the scale
Whereon its song might possibly be heard.
Thus far, no farther;—so he spake the word.
When of a sudden,—hark, the nightingale!
Oh deeper, higher than he could divine
That all-unearthly, untaught strain! He saw
The plain, brown warbler, unabashed. 'Not mine'
(He cried) 'the error of this fatal flaw.
No bird is this, it soars beyond my line,
Were it a bird, 'twould answer to my law.'

Life and Art

Not while the fever of the blood is strong,
The heart throbs loud, the eyes are veiled, no less
With passion than with tears, the Muse shall bless
The poet-soul to help and soothe with song.
Not then she bids his trembling lips express
The aching gladness, the voluptuous pain.
Life is his poem then; flesh, sense and brain
One full-stringed lyre, attuned to happiness.
But when the dream is done, the pulses fail,
The day's illusion with the day's sun set,
He, lonely in the twilight, sees the pale
Divine Consoler, featured like Regret,
Enter and clasp his hand and kiss his brow.
Then his lips ope to sing—as mine do now.

To R.W.E.

As, when a father dies, his children draw
About the empty hearth, their loss to cheat
With uttered praise and love, and oft repeat
His own familiar words with whispered awe,
The honored habit of his daily law—
Not for his sake, but theirs, whose feebler feet
Need still his guiding lamp, whose faith, less sweet,
Misses that tempered patience without flaw—
So do we gather 'round thy vacant chair,
In thine own elm-roofed, amber-rivered town,
Master and father! For the love we bear,
Not for thy fame's sake, do we weave this crown,
And feel thy presence in the sacred air,
Forbidding us to weep that thou art gone.

Progress and Poverty

Oh splendid age when Science lights her lamp
At the brief lightning's momentary flame,
Fixing it steadfast as a star, man's name
Upon the very brow of heaven to stamp!
Launched on a ship whose iron-cuirassed sides
Mock storm and wave. Humanity sails free;
Gayly upon a vast untraveled sea,
O'er pathless wastes, to ports undreamed she rides,
Richer than Cleopatra's barge of gold,
This vessel, manned by demi-gods, with freight
Of priceless marvels. But where yawns the hold
In that deep, reeking hell, what slaves be they,
Who feed the ravenous monster, pant and sweat,
Nor know if overhead reign night or day?

In the Jewish Synagogue at Newport

Here, where the noises of the busy town,
The ocean's plunge and roar can enter not,
We stand and gaze around with tearful awe,
And muse upon the consecrated spot.

No signs of life are here: the very prayers
Inscribed around are in a language dead;
The light of the "perpetual lamp" is spent
That an undying radiance was to shed.

What prayers were in this temple offered up,
Wrung from sad hearts that knew no joy on earth,
By these lone exiles of a thousand years,
From the fair sunrise land that gave them birth!

Now as we gaze, in this new world of light,
Upon this relic of the days of old,
The present vanishes, and tropic bloom
And Eastern towns and temples we behold.

Again we see the patriarch with his flocks,
The purple seas, the hot blue sky o'erhead,
The slaves of Egypt,—omens, mysteries,—
Dark fleeing hosts by flaming angels led.

A wondrous light upon a sky-kissed mount,
A man who reads Jehovah's written law,
'Midst blinding glory and effulgence rare,
Unto a people prone with reverent awe.

The pride of luxury's barbaric pomp,
In the rich court of royal Solomon—
Alas! we wake: one scene alone remains,—
The exiles by the streams of Babylon,

Our softened voices send us back again
But mournful echoes through the empty hall;
Our footsteps have a strange unnatural sound,
And with unwonted gentleness they fall.

The weary ones, the sad, the suffering,
All found their comfort in the holy place,
And children's gladness and men's gratitude
Took voice and mingled in the chant of praise.

The funeral and the marriage, now, alas!
We know not which is sadder to recall;
For youth and happiness have followed age,
And green grass lieth gently over all.

Natheless the sacred shrine is holy yet,
With its lone floors where reverent feet once trod.
Take off your shoes as by the burning bush,
Before the mystery of death and God.

The Crowing of the Red Cock

Across the Eastern sky has glowed
The flicker of a blood-red dawn,
Once more the clarion cock has crowed,
Once more the sword of Christ is drawn.
A million burning rooftrees light
The world-wide path of Israel's flight.

Where is the Hebrew's fatherland?
The folk of Christ is sore bested;
The Son of Man is bruised and banned,
Nor finds whereon to lay his head.
His cup is gall, his meat is tears,
His passion lasts a thousand years.

Each crime that wakes in man the beast,
Is visited upon his kind.
The lust of mobs, the greed of priest,
The tyranny of kings, combined
To root his seed from earth again,
His record is one cry of pain.

When the long roll of Christian guilt
Against his sires and kin is known,
The flood of tears, the life-blood spilt
The agony of ages shown,
What oceans can the stain remove,
From Christian law and Christian love?

Nay, close the book; not now, not here,
The hideous tale of sin narrate,
Reëchoing in the martyr's ear,
Even he might nurse revengeful hate,
Even he might turn in wrath sublime,
With blood for blood and crime for crime.

Coward? Not he, who faces death,
Who singly against worlds has fought,
For what? A name he may not breathe,
For liberty of prayer and thought.
The angry sword he will not whet,
His nobler task is—to forget.

The Banner of the Jew

Wake, Israel, wake! Recall to-day
The glorious Maccabean rage,
The sire heroic, hoary-gray,
His five-fold lion-lineage:
The Wise, the Elect, the Help-of-God,
The Burst-of-Spring, the Avenging Rod.

From Mizpeh's mountain-ridge they saw
Jerusalem's empty streets, her shrine
Laid waste where Greeks profaned the Law,
With idol and with pagan sign.
Mourners in tattered black were there,
With ashes sprinkled on their hair.

Then from the stony peak there rang
A blast to ope the graves: down poured
The Maccabean clan, who sang
Their battle-anthem to the Lord.

Five heroes lead, and following, see,
Ten thousand rush to victory!

Oh for Jerusalem's trumpet now,
To blow a blast of shattering power,
To wake the sleepers high and low,
And rouse them to the urgent hour!
No hand for vengeance—but to save,
A million naked swords should wave.

Oh deem not dead that martial fire,
Say not the mystic flame is spent!
With Moses' law and David's lyre,
Your ancient strength remains unbent.
Let but an Ezra rise anew,
To lift the *Banner of the Jew*!

A rag, a mock at first—erelong,
When men have bled and women wept,
To guard its precious folds from wrong,
Even they who shrunk, even they who slept,
Shall leap to bless it, and to save.
Strike! for the brave revere the brave!

The Valley of Baca: Psalm LXXXIV

A brackish lake is there with bitter pools
Anigh its margin, brushed by heavy trees.
A piping wind the narrow valley cools,
Fretting the willows and the cypresses.
Gray skies above, and in the gloomy space
An awful presence hath its dwelling-place.

I saw a youth pass down that vale of tears;
His head was circled with a crown of thorn,

His form was bowed as by the weight of years,
His wayworn feet by stones were cut and torn.
His eyes were such as have beheld the sword
Of terror of the angel of the Lord.

He passed, and clouds and shadows and thick haze
Fell and encompassed him. I might not see
What hand upheld him in those dismal ways,
Wherethrough he staggered with his misery.
The creeping mists that trooped and spread around,
The smitten head and writhing form enwound.

Then slow and gradual but sure they rose,
Those clinging vapors blotting out the sky.
The youth had fallen not, his viewless foes
Discomfited, had left the victory
Unto the heart that fainted not nor failed,
But from the hill tops its salvation hailed.

I looked at him in dread lest I should see,
The anguish of the struggle in his eyes;
And lo, great peace was there! Triumphantly
The sunshine crowned him from the sacred skies.
"From strength to strength he goes," he leaves beneath
The valley of the shadow and of death.

"Thrice blest who passing through that vale of Tears,
Makes it a well," and draws life-nourishment
From those death-bitter drops. No grief, no fears
Assail him further, he may scorn the event.
For naught hath power to swerve the steadfast soul
Within that valley broken and made whole.

The Guardian of the Red Disk

Spoken by a Citizen of Malta—1300

A curious title held in high repute,
One among many honors, thickly strewn
On my lord Bishop's head, his grace of Malta.
Nobly he bears them all,—with tact, skill, zeal,
Fulfills each special office, vast or slight,
Nor slurs the least minutia,—therewithal
Wears such a stately aspect of command,
Broad-checked, broad-chested, reverend, sanctified,
Haloed with white about the tonsure's rim,
With dropped lids o'er the piercing Spanish eyes
(Lynx-keen, I warrant, to spy out heresy);
Tall, massive form, o'ertowering all in presence,
Or ere they kneel to kiss the large white hand.
His looks sustain his deeds—the perfect prelate,
Whose void chair shall be taken, but not filled.

You know not, who are foreign to the isle,
Haply, what this Red Disk may be, he guards.
'Tis the bright blotch, big as the Royal seal,
Branded beneath the beard of every Jew.
These vermin so infest the isle, so slide
Into all byways, highways that may lead
Direct or roundabout to wealth or power,
Some plain, plump mark was needed, to protect
From the degrading contact Christian folk.

The evil had grown monstrous: certain Jews
Wore such a haughty air, had so refined,
With super-subtile arts, strict, monkish lives,
And studious habit, the coarse Hebrew type,
One might have elbowed in the public mart
Iscariot,—nor suspected one's soul-peril.
Christ's blood! it sets my flesh a creep to think!

We may breathe freely now, not fearing taint,
Praise be our good Lord Bishop! He keeps count
Of every Jew, and prints on cheek or chin
The scarlet stamp of separateness, of shame.

No beard, blue-black, grizzled or Judas-colored,
May hide that damning little wafer-flame.
When one appears therewith, the urchins know
Good sport's at hand; they fling their stones and mud,
Sure of their game. But most the wisdom shows
Upon the unbelievers' selves; they learn
Their proper rank; crouch, cringe, and hide,—lay by
Their insolence of self-esteem; no more
Flaunt forth in rich attire, but in dull weeds,
Slovenly donned, would slink past unobserved;
Bow servile necks and crook obsequious knees,
Chin sunk in hollow chest, eyes fixed on earth
Or blinking sidewise, but to apprehend
Whether or not the hated spot be spied.
I warrant my lord Bishop has full hands,
Guarding the Red Disk—lest one rogue escape!

The World's Justice

If the sudden tidings came
That on some far, foreign coast,
Buried ages long from fame,
Had been found a remnant lost
Of that hoary race who dwelt
By the golden Nile divine,
Spake the Pharaohs' tongue and knelt
At the moon-crowned Isis' shrine—
How at reverend Egypt's feet,
Pilgrims from all lands would meet!

If the sudden news were known,
That anigh the desert-place
Where once blossomed Babylon,
Scions of a mighty race
Still survived, of giant build,
Huntsmen, warriors, priest and sage,
Whose ancestral fame had filled,
Trumpet-tongued, the earlier age,
How at old Assyria's feet
Pilgrims from all lands would meet!

Yet when Egypt's self was young,
And Assyria's bloom unworn,
Ere the mythic Homer sung,
Ere the gods of Greece were born,
Lived the nation of one God,
Priests of freedom, sons of Shem,
Never quelled by yoke or rod,
Founders of Jerusalem—
Is there one abides to-day,
Seeker of dead cities, say!

Answer, now as then, they are;
Scattered broadcast o'er the lands,
Knit in spirit nigh and far,
With indissoluble bands.
Half the world adores their God,
They the living law proclaim,
And their guerdon is—the rod,
Stripes and scourgings, death and shame.
Still on Israel's head forlorn,
Every nation heaps its scorn.

The Feast of Lights

Kindle the taper like the steadfast star
Ablaze on evening's forehead o'er the earth,
And add each night a lustre till afar
An eightfold splendor shine above thy hearth.

Clash, Israel, the cymbals, touch the lyre,
Blow the brass trumpet and the harsh-tongued horn;
Chant psalms of victory till the heart take fire,
The Maccabean spirit leap new-born.

Remember how from wintry dawn till night,
Such songs were sung in Zion, when again
On the high altar flamed the sacred light,
And, purified from every Syrian stain,

The foam-white walls with golden shields were hung,
With crowns and silken spoils, and at the shrine,
Stood, midst their conqueror-tribe, five chieftains sprung
From one heroic stock, one seed divine.

Five branches grown from Mattathias' stem,
The Blessed John, the Keen-Eyed Jonathan,
Simon the fair, the Burst-of-Spring, the Gem,
Eleazar, Help-of-God; o'er all his clan

Judah the Lion-Prince, the Avenging Rod,
Towered in warrior-beauty, uncrowned king,
Armed with the breastplate and the sword of God,
Whose praise is: "He received the perishing."

They who had camped within the mountain-pass,
Couched on the rock, and tented neath the sky,
Who saw from Mizpah's heights the tangled grass
Choke the wide Temple-courts, the altar lie

Even they by one voice fired, one heart of flame,
Though broken reeds, had risen, and were men,
They rushed upon the spoiler and o'ercame,
Each arm for freedom had the strength of ten.

Now is their mourning into dancing turned,
Their sackcloth doffed for garments of delight,
Week-long the festive torches shall be burned,
Music and revelry wed day with night.

Still ours the dance, the feast, the glorious Psalm,
The mystic lights of emblem, and the Word.
Where is our Judah? Where our five-branched palm?
Where are the lion-warriors of the Lord?

Clash, Israel, the cymbals, touch the lyre,
Sound the brass trumpet and the harsh-tongued horn,
Chant hymns of victory till the heart take fire,
The Maccabean spirit leap new-born!

Bar Kochba

Weep, Israel! your tardy meed outpour
Of grateful homage on his fallen head,
That never coronal of triumph wore,
Untombed, dishonored, and unchapleted.
If Victory makes the hero, raw Success
The stamp of virtue, unremembered
Be then the desperate strife, the storm and stress
Of the last Warrior Jew. But if the man
Who dies for freedom, loving all things less,
Against world-legions, mustering his poor clan;
The weak, the wronged, the miserable, to send
Their death-cry's protest through the ages' span—
If such an one be worthy, ye shall lend

Eternal thanks to him, eternal praise.
Nobler the conquered than the conqueror's end!

Donna Clara [Translation from Heine]

In the evening through her garden
Wanders the Alcade's daughter,
Festal sounds of drum and trumpet
Ring out hither from the Castle.

"I am weary of the dances,
Honeyed words of adulation
From the knights who still compare me
To the sun with dainty phrases.

"Yes, of all things I am weary,
Since I first beheld by moonlight
Him, my cavalier, whose zither
Nightly draws me to my casement.

"As he stands so slim and daring,
With his flaming eyes that sparkle,
And with nobly pallid features,
Truly, he St. George resembles."

Thus went Donna Clara dreaming,
On the ground her eyes were fastened.
When she raised them, lo! Before her
Stood the handsome knightly stranger.

Pressing hands and whispering passion,
These twain wander in the moonlight,
Gently doth the breeze caress them,
The enchanted roses greet them.

The enchanted roses greet them,
And they glow like Love's own heralds.
"Tell me, tell me, my beloved,
Wherefore all at once thou blushest?"

"Gnats were stinging me, my darling,
And I hate these gnats in summer
E'en as though they were a rabble
Of vile Jews with long, hooked noses."

"Heed not gnats nor Jews, beloved,"
Spake the knight with fond endearments.
From the almond trees dropped downward
Myriad snowy flakes of blossoms.

Myriad snowy flakes of blossoms
Shed around them fragrant odors.
"Tell me, tell me, my beloved,
Looks thy heart on me with favor?"

"Yes, I love thee, O my darling,
And I swear it by our Savior,
Whom the accursed Jews did murder,
Long ago with wicked malice."

"Heed thou neither Jews nor Savior,"
Spake the knight with fond endearments.
Far off waved, as in a vision,
Gleaming lilies bathed in moonlight.

Gleaming lilies bathed in moonlight
Seemed to watch the stars above them.
"Tell me, tell me, my beloved,
Didst thou not erewhile swear falsely?"

"Naught is false in me, my darling,
E'en as in my veins there floweth
Not a drop of blood that's Moorish,
Neither of foul Jewish current."

"Heed not Moors nor Jews, beloved,"
Spake the knight with fond endearments.
Then towards a grove of myrtles
Leads he the Alcade's daughter.

And with Love's slight subtile meshes,
He has trapped her and entangled.
Brief their words, but long their kisses,
For their hearts are overflowing.

What a melting bridal carol
Sings the nightingale, the pure one,
How the fire-flies in the grasses
Trip their sparkling torchlight dances!

In the grove the silence deepens,
Naught is heard save furtive rustling
Of the swaying myrtle branches,
And the breathing of the flowers.

But the sound of drum and trumpet
Burst forth sudden from the castle,
Rudely they awaken Clara,
Pillowed on her Lover's bosom.

"Hark! They summon me, my darling!
But before we part, oh tell me,
Tell me what thy precious name is,
Which so closely thou hast hidden."

Then the knight with gentle laughter,
Kissed the fingers of his Donna,
Kissed her lips and kissed her forehead,
And at last these words he uttered:

"I, Senora, your beloved,
Am the son of the respected,
Worthy, erudite Grand Rabbi,
Israel of Saragossa."

Translations from Hebrew Poets of Medieval Spain

Admonition [Yehuda Halevi]

Long in the lap of childhood didst thou sleep,
Think how thy youth like chaff did disappear,
Shall life's sweet spring for ever last? Look up!
Old age approaches ominously near.

O shake thou off the world, e'en as the bird
Shakes off the midnight dew that clogs his wings;
Soar upward! Seek deliverance from thy chains
And from the earthly dross that round thee clings.

Longing for Jerusalem [Yehuda Halevi]

Oh, city of the world, with sacred splendor blest,
My spirit yearns to thee from out the far-off West,
A stream of love wells forth when I recall thy day,
Now is thy temple waste, thy glory passed away.
Had I an eagle's wings, straight would I fly to thee,
Moisten thy holy dust with wet cheeks streaming free.

Oh, how I long for thee! Albeit thy King has gone,
Albeit where balm once flowed, the serpent dwells alone.
Could I but kiss thy dust, so would I fain expire,
As sweet as honey then, my passion and desire!

On the Voyage to Jerusalem [Yehuda Halevi]

II.

A watery waste the sinful world has grown,
With no dry spot whereon the eye can rest,
No man, no beast, no bird to gaze upon,
Can all be dead, with silent sleep possessed?
Oh how I long the hills and vales to see,
To find myself on barren steppes were bliss.
I peer about, but nothing greeteth me,
Naught save the ship, the clouds, the waves' abyss,
The crocodile which rushes from the deeps;
The flood foams gray; the whirling waters reel,
Now like its prey whereon at last it sweeps,
The ocean swallows up the vessel's keel.
The billows rage—exult, oh soul of mine,
Soon shalt thou enter the Lord's sacred shrine!

III. To The West Wind

O West, how fragrant breathes thy gentle air,
Spikenard and aloes on thy pinions glide.
Thou blow'st from spicy chambers, not from there
Where angry winds and tempests fierce abide.
As on a bird's wings thou dost waft me home,
Sweet as a bundle of rich myrrh to me.
And after thee yearn all the throngs that roam
And furrow with light keel the rolling sea.
Desert her not—our ship—bide with her oft,
When the day sinks and in the morning light.

Smooth thou the deeps and make the billows soft,
Nor rest save at our goal, the sacred height.
Chide thou the East that chafes the raging flood,
And swells the towering surges wild and rude.
What can I do, the elements' poor slave?
Now do they hold me fast, now leave me free;
Cling to the Lord, my soul, for He will save,
Who caused the mountains and the winds to be.

A Degenerate Age
[Solomon Ben Yehuda Gabirol]

Where is the man who has been tried and found strong and sound?
Where is the friend of reason and of knowledge?
I see only sceptics and weaklings.
I see only prisoners in the durance of the senses,
And every fool and every spendthrift
Thinks himself as great a master as Aristotle.
Think'st thou that they have written poems?
Call'st thou that a Song?
I call it the cackling of ravens.
The zeal of the prophet must free poesy
From the embrace of wanton youths.
My song I have inscribed on the forehead of Time,
They know and hate it—for it is lofty.

Solomon Ben Judah Gabirol
[Moses Ben Esra]

"Am I sipping the honey of the lips?
Am I drunk with the wine of a kiss?
Have I culled the flowers of the cheek,

Have I sucked the fresh fragrance of the breath?
Nay, it is the Song of Gabirol that has revived me,
The perfume of his youthful, spring-tide breeze."

Consolation [Al-Harizi]

Oh, were my streaming tears to flow,
According to my grievous woe,
Then foot of man in all his quest,
On no dry spot of earth could rest.
But not to Noah's flood alone,
The Covenant's bright pledge was shown,
For likewise to my tears and woe,
Behold once more revealed—the Bow!

By the Waters of Babylon: Prose Poems

I. The Exodus. (August 3, 1492.)

1. The Spanish noon is a blaze of azure fire, and the dusty pilgrims
    crawl like an endless serpent along treeless plains and bleached
    highroads, through rock-split ravines and castellated, cathedral-
    shadowed towns.
2. The hoary patriarch, wrinkled as an almond shell, bows
    painfully upon his staff. The beautiful young mother, ivory-pale,
    well-nigh swoons beneath her burden; in her large enfolding
    arms nestles her sleeping babe, round her knees flock her little
    ones with bruised and bleeding feet. "Mother, shall we soon be
    there?"
3. The youth with Christ-like countenance speaks comfortably to
    father and brother, to maiden and wife. In his breast, his own
    heart is broken.
4. The halt, the blind, are amid the train. Sturdy pack-horses

laboriously drag the tented wagons wherein lie the sick athirst with fever.

5. The panting mules are urged forward with spur and goad; stuffed are the heavy saddlebags with the wreckage of ruined homes.

6. Hark to the tinkling silver bells that adorn the tenderly-carried silken scrolls.

7. In the fierce noon-glare a lad bears a kindled lamp: behind its network of bronze the airs of heaven breathe not upon its faint purple star.

8. Noble and abject, learned and simple, illustrious and obscure, plod side by side, all brothers now, all merged in one routed army of misfortune.

9. Woe to the straggler who falls by the wayside! no friend shall close his eyes.

10. They leave behind the grape, the olive, and the fig the vines they planted, the corn they sowed, the garden-cities of Andalusia and Aragon, Estremadura and La Mancha, of Granada and Castile; the altar, the hearth. and the grave of their fathers.

11. The townsman spits at their garments, the shepherd quits his flock, the peasant his plow, to pelt with curses and stones; the villager sets on their trail his yelping cur.

12. Oh the weary march, oh the uptorn roots of home, oh the blankness of the receding goal!

13. Listen to their lamentation: *They that ate dainty food are desolate in the streets; they that were reared in scarlet embrace dunghills. They flee away and wander about. Men say among the nations, they shall no more sojourn there; our end is near, our days are full, our doom is come.*

14. Whither shall they turn? for the West hath cast them out, and the East refuseth to receive.

15. O bird of the air, whisper to the despairing exiles, that to-day, to-day, from the many-masted, gayly-bannered port of Palos, sails the world-unveiling Genoese, to unlock the golden gates of sunset and bequeath a Continent to Freedom!

II. Treasures

1. Through cycles of darkness the diamond sleeps in its coal-black prison.
2. Purely incrusted in its scaly casket, the breath-tarnished pearl slumbers in mud and ooze.
3. Buried in the bowels of earth, rugged and obscure, lies the ingot of gold.
4. Long hast thou been buried, O Israel, in the bowels of earth; long hast thou slumbered beneath the over-whelming waves; long hast thou slept in the rayless house of darkness.
5. Rejoice and sing, for only thus couldst thou rightly guard the golden knowledge, Truth, the delicate pearl and the adamantine jewel of the Law.

The Birth of Man: A Legend of the Talmud

I.

When angels visit earth, the messengers
Of God's decree, they come as lightning, wind:
Before the throne, they all are living fire.
There stand four rows of angels—to the right
The hosts of Michael, Gabriel's to the left,
Before, the troop of Ariel, and behind,
The ranks of Raphael; all, with one accord,
Chanting the glory of the Everlasting.
Upon the high and holy throne, there rests,
Invisible, the Majesty of God.
About his brows the crown of mystery
Whereon the sacred letters are engraved
Of the unutterable Name. He grasps
A scepter of keen fire; the universe
Is compassed in His glance; at His right Hand
Life stands, and at His left hand standeth Death.

II.

Lo, the divine idea of making man
Had spread abroad among the heavenly hosts;
And all at once before the immortal throne
Pressed troops of angels and of seraphim,
With minds opposed, and contradicting cried:
"Fulfill, great Father, thine exalted thought!
Create and give unto the earth her king!"
"Cease, cease, Almighty God! Create no more!"
And suddenly upon the heavenly sphere
Deep silence fell; before the immortal throne
The angel Mercy knelt, and thus he spoke:
"Fulfill, great Father, thine exalted thought!
Create the likeness of thyself on earth.
In this new creature I will breathe the spirit
Of a divine compassion; he shall be
Thy fairest image in the universe."
But to his words the angel Peace replied,
With heavy sobs: "My spirit was outspread,
Oh God, on thy creation, and all things
Were sweetly bound in gracious harmony.
But man, this strange new being, everywhere
Shall bring confusion, trouble, discord, war."
"Avenger of injustice and of crime,"
exclaimed the angel Justice, "he shall be
subject to me, and peace shall bloom again.
Create, oh Lord, create!" "Father of truth,"
Implored with tears the angel Truth, "Thou bring'st
Upon the earth the father of all lies!"
And over the celestial faces gloomed
A cloud of grief, and stillness deep prevailed.
Then from the midst of that abyss of light
Whence sprang the eternal throne, these words rang forth:
"Be comforted, my daughter! Thee I send
To be companion unto man on earth."
And all the angels cried, lamenting loud:

"Thou robbest heaven of her fairest gem.
Truth! Seal of all thy thoughts, Almighty God,
The richest jewel that adorns thy crown."
From the abyss of glory rang the voice:
"From heaven to earth, from earth once more to heaven,
Shall Truth, with constant interchange, alight
And soar again, an everlasting link
Between the world and sky."
                                    And man was born.

The Supreme Sacrifice

Well-nigh two thousand years hath Israel
Suffered the scorn of man for love of God;
Endured the outlaw's ban, the yoke, the rod,
With perfect patience. Empires rose and fell,
Around him Nebo was adored, and Bel;
Edom was drunk with victory, and trod
On his high places, while the sacred sod
Was desecrated by the infidel.
His faith proved steadfast without breach or flaw,
But now the last renouncement is required.
His truth prevails, his God is God, his Law
Is found the wisdom most to be desired.
Not his the glory! He, maligned, misknown,
Bows his meek head, and says, "Thy will be done."

Gifts

"O World-God, give me Wealth!" the Egyptian cried.
His prayer was granted. High as heaven, behold
Palace and Pyramid; the brimming tide
Of lavish Nile washed all his land with gold.
Armies of slaves toiled ant-wise at his feet,

World-circling traffic roared through mart and street.
His priests were gods, his spice-balmed kings enshrined,
Set death at naught in rock-ribbed charnels deep.
Seek Pharaoh's race to-day and ye shall find
Rust and the moth, silence and dusty sleep.

"O World-God, give me beauty!" cried the Greek.
His prayer was granted. All the earth became
Plastic and vocal to his sense; each peak,
Each grove, each stream, quick with Promethean flame,
Peopled the world with imaged grace and light.
The lyre was his, and his the breathing might
Of the immortal marble, his the play
Of diamond-pointed thought and golden tongue.
Go seek the sunshine-race, ye find to-day
A broken column and a lute unstrung.

"O World-God, give me Power!" the Roman cried.
His prayer was granted. The vast world was chained
A captive to the chariot of his pride.
The blood of myriad provinces was drained
To feed that fierce, insatiable red heart.
Invulnerably bulwarked every part
With serried legions and with close-meshed Code.
Within, the burrowing worm had gnawed its home.
A roofless ruin stands where once abode
The imperial race of everlasting Rome.

"O Godhead, give me Truth!" the Hebrew cried.
His prayer was granted; he became the slave
Of the Idea, a pilgrim far and wide,
Cursed, hated, spurned, and scourged with none to save.
The Pharoahs knew him, and when Greece beheld,
His wisdom wore the hoary crown of Eld.
Beauty he hath foresworn and wealth and power.
Seek him to-day, and find in every land.

No fire consumes him, neither floods devour,
Immortal through the lamp within his hand.

In Exile

"Since that day till now our life is one unbroken paradise. We live a true
brotherly life. Every evening after supper we take a seat under the mighty
oak and sing our songs."

—Extract from a letter of a Russian refugee in Texas.

Twilight is here, soft breezes bow the grass,
Day's sounds of various toil break slowly off.
The yoke-freed oxen low, the patient ass
Dips his dry nostril in the cool, deep trough.
Up from the prairie the tanned herdsmen pass
With frothy pails, guiding with voices rough
Their udder-lightened kine. Fresh smells of earth,
The rich, black furrows of the glebe send forth.

After the Southern day of heavy toil,
How good to lie, with limbs relaxed, brows bare
To evening's fan, and watch the smoke-wreaths coil
Up from one's pipe-stem through the rayless air.
So deem these unused tillers of the soil,
Who stretched beneath the shadowing oak tree, stare
Peacefully on the star-unfolding skies,
And name their life unbroken paradise.

The hounded stag that has escaped the pack,
And pants at ease within a thick-leaved dell;
The unimprisoned bird that finds the track
Through sun-bathed space, to where his fellows dwell:
The martyr, granted respite from the rack,
The death-doomed victim pardoned from his cell,—
Such only know the joy these exiles gain,—
Life's sharpest rapture is surcease of pain.

Strange faces theirs, wherethrough the Orient sun
Gleams from the eyes and glows athwart the skin.
Grave lines of studious thought and purpose run
From curl-crowned forehead to dark-bearded chin.
And over all the seal is stamped thereon
Of anguish branded by a world of sin,
In fire and blood through ages on their name,
Their seal of glory and the Gentiles' shame.

Freedom to love the law that Moses brought,
To sing the songs of David, and to think
The thoughts Gabirol to Spinoza taught,
Freedom to dig the common earth, to drink
The universal air—for this they sought
Refuge o'er wave and continent, to link
Egypt with Texas in their mystic chain,
And truth's perpetual lamp forbid to wane.

Hark! through the quiet evening air, their song
Floats forth with wild sweet rhythm and glad refrain.
They sing the conquest of the spirit strong,
The soul that wrests the victory from pain;
The noble joys of manhood that belong
To comrades and to brothers. In their strain
Rustle of Palms and Eastern streams one hears,
And the broad prairie melts in mist of tears.

The New-Year: Rosh-Hashanah, 5643

Not while the snow-shroud round dead earth is rolled,
And naked branches point to frozen skies.—
When orchards burn their lamps of fiery gold,
The grape glows like a jewel, and the corn
A sea of beauty and abundance lies,
Then the new year is born.

Look where the mother of the months uplifts
In the green clearness of the unsunned West,
Her ivory horn of plenty, dropping gifts,
Cool, harvest-feeding dews, fine-winnowed light;
Tired labor with fruition, joy and rest
Profusely to requite.

Blow, Israel, the sacred cornet! Call
Back to thy courts whatever faint heart throb
With thine ancestral blood, thy need craves all.
The red, dark year is dead, the year just born
Leads on from anguish wrought by priest and mob,
To what undreamed-of morn?

For never yet, since on the holy height,
The Temple's marble walls of white and green
Carved like the sea-waves, fell, and the world's light
Went out in darkness,—never was the year
Greater with portent and with promise seen,
Than this eve now and here.

Even as the Prophet promised, so your tent
Hath been enlarged unto earth's farthest rim.
To snow-capped Sierras from vast steppes ye went,
Through fire and blood and tempest-tossing wave,
For freedom to proclaim and worship Him,
Mighty to slay and save.

High above flood and fire ye held the scroll,
Out of the depths ye published still the Word.
No bodily pang had power to swerve your soul:
Ye, in a cynic age of crumbling faiths,
Lived to bear witness to the living Lord,
Or died a thousand deaths.

In two divided streams the exiles part,
One rolling homeward to its ancient source,
One rushing sunward with fresh will, new heart.
By each the truth is spread, the law unfurled,
Each separate soul contains the nation's force,
And both embrace the world.

Kindle the silver candle's seven rays,
Offer the firstfruits of the clustered bowers,
The garnered spoil of bees. With prayer and praise
Rejoice that once more tried, once more we prove
How strength of supreme suffering still is ours
For Truth and Law and Love.

The Choice

I saw in dream the spirits unbegot,
Veiled, floating phantoms, lost in twilight space;
For one the hour had struck, he paused; the place
Rang with an awful Voice:
                              "Soul, choose thy lot!
Two paths are offered; that, in velvet-flower,
Slopes easily to every earthly prize.
Follow the multitude and bind thine eyes,
Thou and thy sons' sons shall have peace with power.
This narrow track skirts the abysmal verge,
Here shalt thou stumble, totter, weep and bleed,
All men shall hate and hound thee and thy seed,
Thy portion be the wound, the stripe, the scourge.
But in thy hand I place my lamp for light,
Thy blood shall be the witness of my Law,
Choose now for all the ages!"
                              Then I saw
The unveiled spirit, grown divinely bright,
Choose the grim path. He turned, I knew full well

The pale, great martyr-forehead shadowy-curled,
The glowing eyes that had renounced the world,
Disgraced, despised, immortal Israel.

The Venus of the Louvre

Down the long hall she glistens like a star,
The foam-born mother of love, transfixed to stone,
Yet none the less immortal, breathing on;
Time's brutal hand hath maimed, but could not mar.
When first the enthralled enchantress from afar
Dazzled mine eyes, I saw not her alone,
Serenely poised on her world-worshiped throne,
As when she guided once her dove-drawn car,—
But at her feet a pale, death-stricken Jew,
Her life-adorer, sobbed farewell to love.
Here Heine wept! Here still he weeps anew,
Nor ever shall his shadow lift or move
While mourns one ardent heart, one poet-brain,
For vanished Hellas and Hebraic pain.

The New Ezekiel

What, can these dead bones live, whose sap is dried
By twenty scorching centuries of wrong?
Is this the House of Israel, whose pride
Is as a tale that's told, an ancient song?
Are these ignoble relics all that live
Of psalmist, priest and prophet? Can the breath
Of very heaven bid these bones revive,
Open the graves and clothe the ribs of death?

Yea. Prophesy, the Lord hath said. Again
Say to the wind, Come forth and breathe afresh,

Even that they may live upon these slain.
And bone to bone shall leap, and flesh to flesh.
The Spirit is not dead, proclaim the word,
Where lay dead bones, a host of armed men stand!
I ope your graves, my people, saith the Lord,
And I shall place you living in your land.

1492

Thou two-faced year, Mother of Change and Fate,
Didst weep when Spain cast forth with flaming sword,
The children of the prophets of the Lord,
Prince, priest, and people, spurned by zealot hate.
Hounded from sea to sea, from state to state,
The West refused them, and the East abhorred.
No anchorage the known world could afford,
Close-locked was every port, barred every gate.
Then smiling, thou unveil'dst, O two-faced year,
A virgin world where doors of sunset part,
Saying, "Ho, all who weary, enter here!
There falls each ancient barrier that the art
Of race or creed or rank devised, to rear
Grim bulwarked hatred between heart and heart!"

The New Colossus

Not like the brazen giant of Greek fame,
With conquering limbs astride from land to land;
Here at our sea-washed, sunset gates shall stand
A mighty woman with a torch, whose flame
Is the imprisoned lightning, and her name
Mother of Exiles. From her beacon-hand
Glows world-wide welcome; her mild eyes command
The air-bridged harbor that twin cities frame.

"Keep, ancient lands, your storied pomp!" cries she
With silent lips. "Give me your tired, your poor,
Your huddled masses yearning to breathe free,
The wretched refuse of your teeming shore.
Send these, the homeless, tempest-tosst to me,
I lift my lamp beside the golden door!"

Ella Wheeler Wilcox: 1850–1919

Introduction

Wilcox's enormous popularity in her own time continues to displace her in our own. She appears too positive, too moralistic, too extravagant, too married (her conventionally happy and devoted life with her husband makes her the one case among women poets where marriage and writing happily wed; although with no children—their one son died a few hours after birth). Her prodigious volume of work remains uncollected.

She is in fact a true 'New Woman," which is to say, in her there is a conflicted and inconsistent encounter between the new and the old. Conservative and progressive impulses uneasily reside together in almost mutual ignorance. It is simply incorrect to consider her, as Louise Bogan does, only as the writer "who brought into popular love poetry the element of sin" in a "rather daring verse on the subject of feminine and masculine emotions;" finally dismissing hers as a "thoroughly middle-class 'poetic' genre [that combined] an air of the utmost respectability with the wildest sort of implications." In this sense, Wilcox's initial poetic triumph in the same moment defined her poetic defeat. Her *Poems of Passion*, rejected by a first publisher as immoral—"whose verses out-Swinburned Swinburne and out-Whitmaned Whitman"—was picked up by another publisher happy to advertise the indignation of the first. The volume, printed in 1883, sold 60,000 copies in two years. Yet, while Wilcox's verse does investigate male and female sexuality, it does so in terms of and alongside a vigorous address to a range of highly concrete social topics: the American polity, technological change, social disorders, war, and a varied typology of women in the context of changing norms and political possibilities.

Wilcox's married life was conducted in elite society, with world travel and homes in New York and Connecticut. She was born, however, in 1850 on an impoverished farm in Wisconsin, twelve miles from the nearest town of Madison; to whom writing represented a financial resource for her family and a way of lifting herself out of a life that she, in emulation of her mother, felt to be stifling and small. The family had left, as she recounts in her memoir, "a comfortable and even luxurious home in Vermont" to go west. Her father proved not to be good at business, and they lost all they had. Educated in a district school, with one apparently miserable year 1867–1868 at the University of Wisconsin, Wilcox cannot "remember when I did not expect to be a writer" and was "already a celebrity at eight." Persevering unbelievably through her teens to place her poems, she at thirteen succeeded, earning a subscription to the *New York Mercury*, and by 1884 had earned enough money to rebuild her old home. Neighbors who had scorned her mother for "keeping me out of the kitchen and allowing me to scribble" changed their tune. Until her marriage in 1884 to Robert Wilcox, a silver manufacturer, she lived at home excepting three months in Milwaukee, unhappily editing and writing for a literary column in a trade journal. Her married life was spent traveling and entertaining; as well as writing at breakneck speed, including stories, essays, newspaper poems, letters of advice, and numerous collections of poetry—coming in all to around forty books. Her husband's death in 1916 led her deeper into the theosophy they had explored together (advised by him posthumously to do so in an encounter through a ouija board). She died three years later in 1919 of breast cancer, after a year in France lecturing World War I soldiers on the dangers of venereal disease.

As with all multiple explanations—which attest not answers but uncertainties about them—Wilcox's many poems on the figures of woman, womanhood, lady, girl, show how contested and unstable these notions had become. She wants to assert and defend women against social norms which restrict them. Yet she is caught (as feminism largely continues to be) between grounding new possibilities for women in their equality with men, as against the unique commitments, history, roles and values of womanhood that stand counter to and critical of dominant social structures considered as male. Thus, the poem "Woman" poses a conception of womankind as "brave of heart and broad of soul" as against the "lady" of social etiquette and vanity. "A Man's Ideal" exposes the image of the woman as reflecting more the man's interests than hers, and as contradictory and incoherent. Yet "Womanhood" returns to the stereotypes of Victorian True Womanhood, apparently in Wilcox's own voice. This confusion about who and what it is to be a woman takes a social-political direction in "Sisters of Mine," "The Answer," and "The Women." Wilcox is often said to have been opposed to the woman's rights movement. "Sisters of Mine" poses skeptical questions to women's political organization: in "The battle-cry on lips where once was Love's old song / Are we leaving behind better things than we find." The next poem, however, offers one "Answer" to these questions. The new ways may pose problems, but so did the old. Women do need to make new claims, since their sacrifices to and for men have betrayed not only themselves but the world: sold to the "bold, bright face of the dollar" and where virtue "pines alone." "The Women" is a firmly ironic critique of the social appearances demanded of, and destructive to women, in the concrete materiality of women's dress as this detains women's bodies.

As in many other women poets, gender distributions in fact both cross with and represent broad cultural conflicts and issues. Wilcox approaches this through her own distinctive poetic means. Wilcox's is a conversational poetry, a poetry talking to and between people, including talking (mainly) to herself. The poems are made of answering voices, in dialogue or—a specialty of Wilcox's—in missed-dialogues in which each talk passed each other. "A Holiday," for example, presents a wife's and husband's conversation, which is an exercise in complete mutual misunderstanding, striking in its contemporary echo. The wife pleads for company and relationship. The man defines himself wholly in economic terms, through his capacity to earn and support the family. Here what is represented is not only gender, but two different languages, two separate worlds, two distinct value systems—systems that increasingly characterize American post-Civil War society, and against which Wilcox offers a cultural commentary and critique. That she aligns the reduction to money with the male sphere, and the possibilities of other human experiences to the woman's is typical of nineteenth-century feminism. "A Successful Man" and "The Captive" investigate the clash between economic values and other forms of relationship. "The Captive" rather nicely correlates an older, more overt image of captivity to social role as possession. "A Successful Man" compares conventional marriage with violence against women. "Two Sinners," "Two Women," "Two Voices," and "The Unfaithful Wife" each treats (as so often in nineteenth-century women's writing) the way divided and conflicting values are enacted in the sexual double standard.

Wilcox in these texts gives voice to women, in both their inner and outer experiences—indeed, showing how inner sexual and emotional experience is shaped through and framed by outer social and economic life. "Delilah" places the viewpoint and voice as a man's, Samson's. Yet it continues the missed dialogue between male and female. Samson's voice effectively drowns Delilah's out; yet in doing so he also projects an image of female possession, or rather the possession of the female image by the male. Samson's erotic obsession with Delilah; his desire for her (and in the text, she initiates nothing, but is "indolent") is a way of consuming her and determining her fate. This contrasts radically with "The Revolt of Vashti" (a section in a longer work based on the Book of Esther). Vashti, a biblical figure taken up by Harper and Jackson as well as Wilcox, clearly had special attraction for women of the period. Dialogue in this text becomes overt drama which turns around Vashti asserting her own voice and sense of self against Ahasvueras, the king of Persia. As she declaims, "I will loose my veil and loose my tongue." Vashti's rebellion, in the name of modesty; her refusal to unveil herself before the men at

Ahaesvueras' drunken feast, Wilcox reverses into an exposure and defiance of the female self as mere beautiful possession and emblem of male power. She, instead, will name herself.

Wilcox here treats the Bible, as she does religion in general, as a text for rewriting. She is in this not so much irreverent as exercising a familiar impunity. Women earlier in the century found their sanction in religious calling and vision. Wilcox almost reverses this. It is she, her vision, her intuition, which gives sanction to religious claims and traditions. This takes shape on the one hand as an American civil religion, part of a civic conception of the American polity, as in her rewriting of "The Hymn of the Republic." On the other, religion for her is a deeply interiorized authority, grounding individual initiative in the kind of activism that will create a self and society that is her vision of America. "To Men," for example, reinterprets the creation story—a continuous crux of feminist biblical and religious engagement—making Eve's creation after Adam not a secondary act but the masterwork after "apprentice labor." Wilcox tends to ground her claims for women in an innate female character, but at the last settles for parity: a great gain over the traditional gender rankings. Equality emerges as a religious principle (and vice versa), greatly generalized as inner value and inner divinity. "The Creed" and "The Times" speak of the "divinity which dwells within us," as the (hu)man knows him/herself as "something all divine." "Attainment" shows how this interiorized sense of human value structures and sanctions achievement, even for women, in the name of "universal good."

This is a vision, however, that Wilcox must defend against contrary trends. The bifurcation of American life into economic as against all other values she approaches not only as a moral but as a political problem, about which she writes a political poetry. "Protest" protests silence (again going against standard notions of feminine decorum). America's claim to "independence" and freedom must be challenged as long as there remains "one fettered slave" and until "God's soil is rescued from the clutch of greed." "The Age of Motored Things" and "The Protest" examine the complex contribution but also threat brought by technological change. "What We Want" is an America whose economic power is not merely private wealth but also the commonwealth. "Women and War" and "War Mothers" returns to a view of how gender may contribute to building a more genuine community and public life.

Wilcox tended to name her many, many volumes of poetry in the pattern of: *Poems of Passion, Poems of Pleasure, Poems of Progress, Poems of Reflection.* But in many ways what she wrote were poems of ambivalence. She ventures into new roles for women and for the woman poet. Yet she weaves these new images out of mixed strands. The poems often register forces working at odds or in conflict with each other. Creative work conflicts with woman's traditional roles in "Music in the Flat" and "Individuality." A new, positive embrace of the body and of earthly life continues in tense strain against allegiance to the soul in "A Soul's Farewell to the Body" and "Misalliance," where their relation is very tellingly presented as a bad marriage. "The Cost" aligns these gendered divisions with concrete social and economic reality, criticizing the traditional order as instituted by God and lived by women, yet in deep confusion about whether women's attempt to recreate herself in man's image as ambitious and self-interested does not have too high a cost. "The Tiger," often interpreted as an image of passion released, is in fact a richly open figure. Not only sexual but all desire—for economic gain, political power, personal fame or technological progress—is shown in the poem to have immense energy and attraction, yet also danger.

Poems

To Men

Sirs, when you pity us, I say
You waste your pity. Let it stay,
Well corked and stored upon your shelves,
Until you need it for yourselves.

We do appreciate God's thought
In forming you, before He brought
Us into life. His art was crude,
But oh, so virile in its rude

Large elemental strength: and then
He learned His trade in making men;
Learned how to mix and mould the clay
And fashion in a finer way.

How fine that skilful way can be
You need but lift your eyes to see;
And we are glad God placed you there
To lift your eyes and find us fair.

Apprentice labour though you were,
He made you great enough to stir
The best and deepest depths of us,
And we are glad He made you thus.

Aye! we are glad of many things.
God strung our hearts with such fine strings
The least breath moves them, and we hear
Music where silence greets your ear.

We suffer so? but women's souls,
Like violet powder dropped on coals,
Give forth their best in anguish. Oh,
The subtle secrets that we know,

Of joy in sorrow, strange delights
Of ecstasy in pain-filled nights,
And mysteries of gain in loss
Known but to Christ upon the Cross!

Our tears are pitiful to you!
Look how the heaven-reflecting dew
Dissolves its life in tears. The sand
Meanwhile lies hard upon the strand.

How could your pity find a place
For us, the mothers of the race?
Men may be fathers unaware,
So poor the title is you wear,

But mothers—? who that crown adorns
Knows all its mingled blooms and thorns;
And she whose feet that path hath trod
Has walked upon the heights with God.

No, offer us not pity's cup.
There is no looking down or up
Between us: eye looks straight in eye:
Born equals, so we live and die.

Woman

Give us that grand word "woman" once again,
And let's have done with "lady": one's a term.
Full of fine force, strong, beautiful, and firm,
Fit for the noblest use of tongue or pen;
And one's a word for lackeys. One suggests
The Mother, Wife, and Sister! One the dame
Whose costly robe, mayhap, gives her the name.
One word upon its own strength leans and rests;
The other minces tiptoe. Who would be
The perfect woman must grow brave of heart
And broad of soul to play her troubled part
Well in life's drama. While each day we see
The "perfect lady" skilled in what to do
And what to say, grace in each tone and act
('Tis taught in schools, but needs some native tact),
Yet narrow in her mind as in her shoe.
Give the first place then to the nobler phrase,
And leave the lesser word for lesser praise.

A Man's Ideal

A lovely little keeper of the home,
Absorbed in menu books, yet erudite
When I need, counsel, quick at repartee
And slow to anger. Modest as a flower
Yet scintillant and radiant as a star.
Unmercenary in her mould of mind,
While opulent and dainty in her tastes.
A nature generous and free, albeit
The incarnation of economy.
She must be chaste as proud Diana was,
Yet warm as Venus. To all others cold
As some white glacier glittering in the sun;

To me as ardent as the sensuous rose
That yields its sweetness to the burrowing bee.
All ignorant of evil in the world,
And innocent as any cloistered nun,
Yet wise as Phrynne in the arts of love
When I come thirsting to her nectared lips.
Good as the best, and tempting as the worst,
A saint, a siren, and a paradox.

Womanhood

She must be honest, both in thought and deed,
Of generous impulse, and above all greed;
Not seeking praise, or place, or power, or pelf,
But life's best blessings for her higher self,
Which means the best for all.
She must have faith,
To make good friends of Trouble, Pain and Death,
And understand their Message.
She should be
As redolent with tender sympathy
As is a rose with fragrance.
Cheerfulness
Should be her mantle, even tho' her dress
Maybe of Sorrow's weaving.
On her face
A loyal nature leaves its seal of grace,
And chastity is in her atmosphere.
Not that chill chastity which seems austere—
(Like untrod snow peaks, lovely to behold
Till once attained—then barren, loveless, cold).
But the white flame that feeds upon the soul
And lights the pathway to a peaceful goal.
A sense of humor, and a touch of mirth,
To brighten up the shadowy spots of earth;

And pride that passes evil—choosing good.
All these unite in perfect womanhood.

Sisters of Mine

Sisters, sisters of mine, have we done what we could
In all the old ways, through all the new days,
To better the race and to make life sweet and good?
Have we played the full part that was ours in the start,
Sisters of mine?

Sisters, sisters of mine, as we hurry along
To a larger world, with our banners unfurled,
The battle-cry on lips where once was Love's old song,
Are we leaving behind better things than we find,
Sisters of mine?

Sisters, sisters of mine, through the march in the street,
Through turmoil and din, without, and within,
As we gain something big do we lose something sweet?
In the growth of our might is our grace lost to sight?
As new powers unfold do we love of old,
Sisters of mine?

The Answer

O well have we done the old tasks! in the old, old ways of earth.
We have kept the house in order, we have given the children birth;
And our sons went out with their fathers, and left us alone at the
      hearth.

We have cooked the meats for their table; we have woven their
    cloth at the loom;
We have pulled the weeds from their gardens, and kept the flowers
    in bloom;
And then we have sat and waited, alone in a silent room.

We have borne all the pains of travail in giving life to the race;
We have toiled and saved, for the masters, and helped them to
    power and place;
And when we asked for a pittance, they gave it with grudging
    grace.

On the bold, bright face of the dollar all the evils of earth are
    shown;
We are weary of love that is barter, and of virtue that pines alone,
We are out in the world with the masters: we are finding and
    claiming our own.

The Women

See the women—pallid women, of our land!
See them fainting, dying, dead, on every hand!
See them sinking 'neath a weight
Far more burdensome than Fate
Ever placed upon poor human beings' backs.
See them falling as they go—
By their own hands burdened so—
Paling, failing, sighing, dying, on their tracks!

See the women—ghastly women, on the streets!
With their corset-tortured waists, and pinched up feet!
Hearts and lungs all out of place,
Whalebone forms devoid of grace;
Faces pallid, robbed of Nature's rosy bloom;
Purple-lidded eyes that tell,

With a language known too well,
Of the sick-room, death-bed, coffin, pall and tomb.

See the women —sickly women, everywhere,
See the cruel, killing dresses that they wear!
Bearing round those pounds of jet,
Can you wonder that they fret,
Pale, and pine, and fall the victims of decay!
Is it strange the blooming maid,
All so soon should droop and fade—
Like a beast of burden burdened, day on day!

See the women and their dresses as they go,
Trimmed and retrimmed, line on line and row on row;
Hanging over fragile hips,
Driving color from the lips,
Dragging down their foolish wearers to the grave!
Suicide, and nothing less,
In this awful style of dress!
Who shall rise to women's rescue, who shall save!

See the women—foolish women, dying fast;
What have all their trimmed-up dresses brought at last?
Worry, pain, disease and death,
Loss of bloom and gasping breath;
Doctors' bill, and golden hours thrown away.
They have bartered off for these
Beauty, comfort, health and ease—
All to ape the fleeting fashion of a day.

A Holiday

Wife:
The house is like a garden,
The children are the flowers;

The gardener should come, methinks,
And walk among his bowers.
Oh, lock the door on worry,
And shut your cares away!
Not time of year, but love and cheer,
Will make a holiday.

Husband:
Impossible! You women do not know
The toil it takes to make a business grow.
I cannot join you until very late,
So hurry home, nor let the dinner wait.

Wife:
The feast will be like Hamlet,
Without a Hamlet part.
The home is but a house, dear,
Till you supply the heart.
The Christmas gift I long for,
You need not toil to buy.
Oh, give me back one thing I lack—
The love-light in your eye!

Husband:
Of course I love you, and the children too;
Be sensible, my dear; it is for you
I work so hard to make my business pay.
There now, run home; enjoy your holiday.

Wife (turning away):
He does not mean to wound me,
I know his heart is kind.
Alas, that men can love us,
And be so blind, so blind!
A little time for pleasure,
A little time for play,

A word to prove the life of love
And frighten care away,
Though poor my lot in some small cot—
That were a holiday.

Husband (musing):
She has not meant to wound me or to vex.
Zounds! but 'tis difficult to please the sex.
I've housed and gowned her like a very queen,
Yet there she goes with discontented mien.
I gave her diamonds only yesterday.
Some women are like that, do what you may.

Successful Man

There was a man who killed a loving maid
In some mad mood of passion; and he paid
The price, upon a scaffold. Now his name
Stands only as a synonym for shame.
There was another man, who took to wife
A loving woman. She was full of life,
Of hope, and aspirations; and her pride
Clothed her like some rich mantle.
       First, the wide
Glad stream of life that through her veins had sway
He dammed by rocks, cast in it, day by day.
Her flag of hope, flung gaily to the world,
He placed half mast, and then hauled down, and furled.
The aspirations, breathing in each word,
By subtle ridicule, were made absurd:
The delicate fine mantle of her pride,
With rude unfeeling hands, was wrenched aside:
And by mean avarice, or vulgar show,
Her quivering woman's heart was made to know
That she was but a chattel, bought to fill

Whatever niche might please the buyer's will.
So she was murdered, while the slow years went.
And her assassin, honoured, opulent,
Lived with no punishment, or social ban!
'A good provider, a successful man.'

The Captive

My lady is robed for the ball to-night,
All in a shimmer and silken sheen.
She glides down the stairs like a thing of light,
The ballroom's beautiful queen.

Priceless gems on her bosom glow—
Half hid by laces a queen might wear.
Robed is she, as befits, you know,
The wife of a millionaire.

Gliding along at her liege lord's side,
Out-shining all in that company,
Into the mind of the old man's bride
There creeps a curious simile.

She thinks how once in the Long Ago,
A beautiful captive, all aflame
With jewels that weighed her down like woe,
Close in the wake of her captor came.

All day long in that mocking plight,
She followed him in a dumb despair;
And the people thought her a goodly sight,
Decked in her jewels rare.

And now at her lawful master's side,
With a pain in her heart, as great as then

(So thinks this old man's beautiful bride),
Zenobia walks again.

Two Sinners

There was a man, it was said one time,
Who went astray in his youthful prime.
Can the brain keep cool and the heart keep quiet
When the blood is a river that's running riot?
And boys will be boys the old folks say,
And the man is the better who's had his day.
The sinner reformed; and the preacher told
Of the prodigal son who came back to the fold.
And Christian people threw open the door,
With a warmer welcome than ever before.
Wealth and honour were his to command,
And a spotless woman gave him her hand
And the world strewed their pathway with blossoms abloom,
Crying 'God bless lady, and God bless groom!'

There was a maiden who went astray
In the golden dawn of her life's young day.
She had more passion and heart than head,
And she followed blindly where fond Love led.
And Love unchecked is a dangerous guide
To wander at will by a fair girl's side.
The woman repented and turned from sin,
But no door opened to let her in.
The preacher prayed that she might be forgiven,
But told her to look for mercy in Heaven.
For this is the law of the earth, we know:
That the woman is stoned, while the man may go.
A brave man wedded her after all,
But the world said, frowning, 'We shall not call.'

Two Women

I know two women, and one is chaste
And cold as the snows on a winter waste.
Stainless ever in act and thought
(As a man, born dumb, in speech errs not.)
But she has malice toward her kind,
A cruel tongue and a jealous mind.
Void of pity and full of greed,
She judges the world by her narrow creed:
A brewer of quarrels, a breeder of hate,
Yet she holds the key to "Society's" Gate.

The other woman, with heart of flame,
Went mad for a love that marred her name:
And out of the grave of her murdered faith
She rose like a soul that has passed through death.
Her aims are noble, her pity so broad,
It covers the world like the mercy of God.
A soother of discord, a healer of woes,
Peace follows her footsteps wherever she goes
The worthier life of the two no doubt,
And yet "Society" locks her out.

Two Voices

Virtue: O wanton one, O wicked one, how was it that you came,
Down from the paths of purity, to walk the streets of shame?
And wherefore was that precious wealth, God gave to you in trust,
Flung broadcast for the feet of men to trample in the dust?

Vice: O prudent one, O spotless one, now listen well to me.
The ways that led to where I tread these paths of sin, were three:
And God, and good folks, all combined to make them fair to see.

Virtue: O wicked one, blasphemous one, now how could that
 thing be?

Vice: The first was Nature's lovely road, whereon my life was
 hurled.
I felt the stirring in my blood, which permeates the world.
I thrilled like willows in the spring, when sap begins to flow;
It was young passion in my veins, but how was I to know?
The second was the silent road, where modest mothers dwell,
And hide from eager, curious minds, the truth they ought to tell.
That misnamed road called 'Innocence' should bear the sign 'To
 Hell.'
With song and dance in ignorance I walked that road and fell.

Virtue: O fallen one, unhappy one, but why not rise and go
Back to the ways you left behind, and leave your sins below,
Nor linger in this sink of sin, since now you see, and know?

Vice: The third road was the fair high way, trod by the good and
 great.
I cried aloud to that vast crowd, and told my hapless fate.
They hurried all through door and wall and shut Convention's gate.
I beat it with my bleeding hands: they must have heard me knock.
They must have heard wild sob and word, yet no one turned the
 lock.
Oh, it is very desolate, on Virtue's path to stand,
And see the good folks flocking by, withholding look and hand.
And so with hungry heart and soul, and weary brain and feet,
I left that highway whence you came, and sought the sinful street.
O prudent one, O spotless one, when good folks speak of me,
Go, tell them of the roads I came; the roadways fair, and three.

An Unfaithful Wife to Her Husband

Branded and blackened by my own misdeeds
I stand before you; not as one who pleads
For mercy or forgiveness, but as one,
After a wrong is done,
Who seeks the why and wherefore. Go with me
Back to those early years of love, and see
Just where our paths diverged. You must recall
Your wild pursuit of me, outstripping all
Competitors and rivals, till at last
You bound me sure and fast
With vow and ring.
I was the central thing
In all the Universe for you just then.
Just then for me, there were no other men.
I cared
Only for tasks and pleasures that you shared.
Such happy, happy days. You wearied first.
I will not say you wearied, but a thirst
For conquest and achievement in man's realm
Left love's barque with no pilot at the helm.
The money madness, and the keen desire
To outstrip others, set your heart on fire.
Into the growing conflagration went
Romance and sentiment.
Abroad you were a man of parts and power—
Your double dower
Of brawn and brains gave you a leader's place;
At home you were dull, tired, and commonplace.
You housed me, fed me, clothed me; you were kind;
But oh, so blind, so blind.
You could not, would not, see my woman's need
Of small attentions; and you gave no heed
When I complained of loneliness; you said
"A man must think about his daily bread

And not waste time in empty social life—
He leaves that sort of duty to his wife
And pays her bills, and lets her have her way,
And feels she should be satisfied."
Each day
Our lives that had been one life at the start,
Farther and farther seemed to drift apart.
Dead was the old romance of man and maid.
Your talk was all of politics or trade.
Your work, your club, the mad pursuit of gold
Absorbed your thoughts. Your duty kiss fell cold
Upon my lips. Life lost its zest, its thrill,
Until
One fateful day when earth seemed very dull
It suddenly grew bright and beautiful.
I spoke a little, and he listened much;
There was attention in his eyes, and such
A note of comradeship in his low tone,
I felt no more alone.
There was a kindly interest in his air;
He spoke about the way I dressed my hair,
And praised the gown I wore.
It seemed a thousand, thousand years and more
Since I had been so noticed. Had mine ear
Been used to compliments year after year,
If I had heard you speak
As this man spoke, I had not been so weak.
The innocent beginning
Of all my sinning
Was just the woman's craving to be brought
Into the inner shrine of some man's thought.
You held me there, as sweetheart and as bride;
And then as wife, you left me far outside.
So far, so far, you could not hear me call;
You might, you should, have saved me from my fall.
I was not bad, just lonely, that was all.

A man should offer something to replace
The sweet adventure of the lover's chase
Which ends with marriage, Love's neglected laws
Pave pathways for the "Statutory Cause."

Delilah

In the midnight of darkness and terror,
When I would grope nearer to God,
With my back to a record of error
And the highway of sin I have trod,
There come to me shapes I would banish—
The shapes of the deeds I have done;
And I pray and I plead till they vanish—
All vanish and leave me, save one.

That one, with a smile like the splendor
Of the sun in the middle-day skies—
That one, with a spell that is tender—
That one with a dream in her eyes—
Cometh close, in her rare Southern beauty.
Her languor, her indolent grace;
And my soul turns its back on its duty,
To live in the light of her face.

She touches my cheek, and I quiver—
I tremble with exquisite pains;
She sighs—like an overcharged river
My blood rushes on through my veins;
She smiles—and in mad-tiger fashion,
As a she-tiger fondles her own,
I clasp her with fierceness and passion,
And kiss her with shudder and groan.

Once more, in our love's sweet beginning,
I put away God and the World;
Once more, in the joys of our sinnings,
Are the hopes of eternity hurled.
There is nothing my soul lacks or misses
As I clasp the dream-shape to my breast;
In the passion and pain of her kisses
Life blooms to its richest and best.

O ghost of dead sin unrelenting,
Go back to the dust, and the sod!
Too dear and too sweet for repenting,
Ye stand between me and my God.
If I, by the Throne, should behold you,
Smiling up with those eyes loved so well,
Close, close in my arms I would fold you,
And drop with you down to sweet Hell!

The Revolt of Vashti

Ahasueras:
Is this the way to greet thy loving spouse,
But now returned from scenes of blood and strife?
I pray thee raise thy veil and let me gaze
Upon that beauty which hath greater power
To conquer me than all the arts of war!

Vashti:
My beauty! Aye, my beauty! I do hold,
In thy regard, no more an honored place
Than yonder marble pillar, or the gold
And jeweled wine cup which thy lips caress.
Thou would'st degrade me in the people's sight!

Ahasueras:
Degrade thee, Vashti? Rather do I seek
To show my people who are gathered here
How, as the consort of so fair a queen,
I feel more pride than as the mighty king:
For there be many rulers on the earth,
But only one such queen. Come, raise thy veil!

Vashti:
Aye! only one such queen! A queen is one
Who shares her husband's greatness and his throne.
I am no more than yonder dancing girl
Who struts and smirks before a royal court!
But I will loose my veil and loose my tongue!
Now listen, sire—my master and my king;
And let thy princes and the court give ear!
'Tis time all heard how Vashti feels her shame.

Ahasueras:
Shame is no word to couple with thy name!
Shame and a spotless woman may not meet,
Even in a sentence. Choose another word.

Vashti:
Aye, shame, my lord—there is no synonym
That can give voice to my ignoble state.
To be a thing for eyes to gaze upon,
Yet held an outcast from thy heart and mind;
To hear my beauty praised but not my worth;
To come and go at Pleasure's beck and call,
While barred from Wisdom's conclaves! Think ye that
A noble calling for a noble dame?
Why, any concubine amongst thy train
Could play my royal part as well as I—
Were she as fair!

Ahasueras:
Queen Vashti, art thou mad?
I would behead another did he dare
To so besmirch thee with comparison.

Vashti (to the court):
Gaze now your fill! Behold Queen Vashti's eyes!
How large they gleam beneath her inch of brow!
How like a great white star, her splendid face
Shines through the midnight forest of her hair!
And see the crushed pomegranite of her mouth!
Observe her arms, her throat, her gleaming breasts,
Whereon the royal jewels rise and fall!—

And note the crescent curving of her hips,
And lovely limbs suggested 'neath her robes!
Gaze, gaze, I say, for these have made her queen!
She hath no mind, no heart, no dignity,
Worth royal recognition and regard;
But her fair body approbation meets
And whets the sated appetite of kings!
Now ye have seen what she was bid to show.
The queen hath played her part and begs to go.

Ahasueras:
Aye, Vashti, go and never more return!
Not only hast thou wronged thine own true lord,
And mocked and shamed me in the people's eyes,
But thou hast wronged all princes and all men
By thy pernicious and rebellious ways.
Queens act and subjects imitate. So let
Queen Vashti weigh her conduct and her words,
Or be no more called "queen!"

Vashti:
I was a princess ere I was a queen,

And worthy of a better fate than this!
There lies the crown that made me queen in name!
Here stands the woman—wife in name alone!
Now, no more queen—nor wife—but woman still—
Aye, and a woman strong enough to be
Her own avenger.

The Creed

Whoever was begotten by pure love,
And came desired and welcomed into life,
Is of immaculate conception. He
Whose heart is full of tenderness and truth,
Who loves mankind more than he loves himself,
And cannot find room in his heart for hate,
May be another Christ. We all may be
The Saviours of the world, if we believe
In the Divinity which dwells in us
And worship it, and nail our grosser selves,
Our tempers, greeds, and our unworthy aims,
Upon the cross. Who giveth love to all,
Pays kindness for unkindness, smiles for frowns,
And lends new courage to each fainting heart,
And strengthens hope and scatters joy abroad,
He, too, is a Redeemer, Son of God.

The Times

The times are not degenerate. Man's faith
Mounts higher than of old. No crumbling creed
Can take from the immortal soul the need
Of that supreme Creator, God. The wraith
Of dead beliefs we cherished in our youth
Fades but to let us welcome new-born Truth.

Man may not worship at the ancient shrine
Prone on his face, in self-accusing scorn.
That night is past. He hails a fairer morn,
And knows himself a something all divine;
No humble worm whose heritage is sin,
But, born of God, he feels the Christ within.
Not loud his prayers, as in the olden time,
But deep his reverence for that mighty force,
That occult working of the great all Source,
Which makes the present era so sublime.
Religion now means something high and broad,
And man stood never half so near to God.

Attainment

Use all your hidden forces. Do not miss
The purpose of this life, and do not wait
For circumstance to mould or change your fate.
In your own self lies Destiny. Let this
Vast truth cast out all fear, all prejudice,
All hesitation. Know that you are great,
Great with divinity. So dominate
Environment, and enter into bliss.
Love largely and hate nothing. Hold no aim
That does not chord with universal good.
Hear what the voices of the Silence say,
All joys are yours if you put forth your claim.
Once let the spiritual laws be understood,
Material things must answer and obey.

The Age of Motored Things

The wonderful age of the world I sing—
The age of battery, coil and spring,
Of steam, and storage, and motored thing.

Though faith may slumber and art seem dead,
And all that is spoken has once been said,
And all that is written were best unread;

Though hearts are iron and thoughts are steel,
And all that has value is mercantile,
Yet marvelous truths shall the age reveal.

Aye, greater the marvels this age shall find
Than all the centuries left behind,
When faith was a bigot and art was blind.

Oh, sorry the search of the world for gods,
Through faith that slaughters and art that lauds,
While reason sits on its throne and nods.

But out of the leisure that men will know,
When the cruel things of the sad earth go,
A Faith that is Knowledge shall rise and grow.

In the throb and whir of each new machine
Thinner is growing the veil between
The visible earth and the world's unseen.

The True Religion shall leisure bring;
And Art shall awaken and Love shall sing:
Oh, ho! for the age of the motored thing!

The Hymn of the Republic

I have listened to the sighing of the burdened and the bound,
I have heard it change to crying, with a menace in the sound;
I have seen the money getters pass unheeding on the way,
As they went to forge new fetters for the people day by day.

Then the voice of Labor thundered forth its purpose and its need,
And I marveled, and I wondered, at the cold dull ear of greed;
For as chimes, in some great steeple, tell the passing of the hour,
So the voices of the people tell the death of purchased power.

All the gathered dust of ages, God is brushing from His book;
He is opening up its pages, and He bids His children look;
And in shock and conflagration, and in pestilence and strife,
He is speaking to the nations, of the brevity of life.

Mother Earth herself is shaken by our sorrows and our crimes;
And she bids her sons awaken to the portent of the times;
With her travail pains upon her, she is hurling from their place
All the minions of dishonor, to admit the Coming Race.

By, the voice of justice bidden, she has torn the mask from might.
All the shameful secrets hidden, she is dragging into light;
And whoever wrongs his neighbor must be brought to judgment
    now,
Though he wear the badge of Labor, or a crown upon his brow.

There is growth in Revolution, if the word is understood;
It is one with Evolution, up from self, to brotherhood;
He who utters it unheeding, bent on self, or selfish gain,
His own day of doom is speeding, though he toil, or though he
    reign.

God is calling to the masses, to the peasant, and the peer;
He is calling to all classes, that the crucial hour is near;

For each rotting throne must tremble, and fall broken in the dust,
With the leaders who dissemble, and betray a people's trust.

Still the voice of God is calling; and above the wreck I see,
And beyond the gloom appalling, the great Government-to-Be.
From the ruins it has risen, and my soul is overjoyed,
For the School supplants the prison; and there are no
    "unemployed."

And there are no children's faces at the spindle or the loom;
They are out in sunny places, where the other sweet things bloom;
God has purified the alleys, He has set the white slaves free,
And they own the hills and valleys in this Government-to-Be.

Protest

To sin by silence, when we should protest,
Makes cowards out of men. The human race
Has climbed on protest. Had no voice been raised
Against injustice, ignorance, and lust,
The inquisition yet would serve the law,
And guillotines decide our least disputes.
The few who dare, must speak and speak again
To right the wrongs of many. Speech, thank God,
No vested power in this great day and land
Can gag or throttle. Press and voice may cry
Loud disapproval of existing ills;
May criticize oppression and condemn
The lawlessness of wealth-protecting laws
That let the children and childbearers toil
To purchase ease for idle millionaires.

Therefore I do protest against the boast
Of independence in this mighty land.
Call no chain strong, which holds one rusted link.

Call no land free, that holds one fettered slave.
Until the manacled slim wrists of babes
Are loosed to toss in childish sport and glee
Until the mother bears no burden save
The precious one beneath her heart; until
God's soil is rescued from the clutch of greed
And given back to labor, let no man
Call this the land of freedom.

The Protest

Said the great machine of iron and wood,
'Lo, I am a creature meant for good.
But the criminal clutch of Godless greed
Has made me a monster that scatters need
And want and hunger wherever I go.
I would lift men's burdens and lighten their woe,
I would give them leisure to laugh in the sun,
If owned by the Many—instead of the one.
If owned by the people, the whole wide earth
Should learn my purpose and know my worth.
I would close the chasm that yawns in our soil
'Twixt unearned riches and ill-paid toil.
No man should hunger, and no man labour
To fill the purse of an idle neighbour;
And each man should know when his work was done,
Were I shared by the Many—not owned by one.

'I am forced by the few with their greed for gain,
To forge for the many new fetters of pain.
Yet this is my purpose, and ever will be
To set the slaves of the workshop free.
God hasten the day when, overjoyed,
That desperate host of the unemployed

Shall hear my message and understand,
And hail me friend in an opulent land.'

Woman and War

We women teach our little sons how wrong
And how ignoble blows are; school, a church
Support our precepts, and inoculate
The growing minds with thoughts of love and peace
"Let dogs delight to bark and bite," we say;
But human beings with immortal souls
Must rise above the methods of a brute,
And walk with reason and with self-control.
And then—dear God! you men, you wise, strong men,
Our self-announced superiors in brain,
Our peers in judgment, you go forth to war!
You leap at one another, mutilate
And starve and kill your fellow-men, and ask
The world's applause for such heroic deeds.
You boast and strut; and if no song is sung,
No laudatory epic writ in blood,
Telling how many widows you have made,
Why then, perforce, you say our bards are dead
And inspiration sleeps to wake no more.
And we, the women, we whose lives you are—
What can we do but sit in silent homes,
And wait and suffer? Not for us the blare
Of trumpets and the bugle's call to arms
For us no waving banners, no supreme,
Triumphant hour of conquest. Ours the slow
Dread torture of uncertainty, each day
The bootless battle with the same despair.
And when at best your victories reach our ears,
There reaches with them to our pitying hearts
The thought of countless homes made desolate

And other women weeping for their dead.
O men, wise men, superior beings, say,
Is there no substitute for war in this
Great age and era? If you answer 'No,'
Then let us rear our children to be wolves
And teach them from the cradle how to kill.
Why should we women waste our time and words
In talking peace, when men declare for war?

War Mothers

There is something in the sound of drum and fife
That stirs all the savage instincts into life.
In the old times of peace we went our ways,
Through proper days
Of little joys and tasks. Lonely at times,
When from the steeple sounded wedding chimes,
Telling to all the world some maid was wife—
But taking patiently our part in life
As it was portioned us by Church and State,
Believing it our fate.
Our thoughts all chaste
Held yet a secret wish to love and mate
Ere youth and virtue should go quite to waste.
But men we criticised for lack of strength,
And kept them at arm's length.
Then the war came—
The world was all aflame!
The men we had thought dull and void of power
Were heroes in an hour.
He who had seemed a slave to petty greed
Showed masterful in that great time of need.
He who had plotted for his neighbour's pelf,
Now for his fellows offers up himself.

And we were only women, forced by war
To sacrifice the things worth living for.

Something within us broke,
Something within us woke,
The wild cave-woman spoke.
When we heard the sound of drumming,
As our soldiers went to camp,
Heard them tramp, tramp, tramp;
As we watched to see them coming,
And they looked at us and smiled
(Yes, looked back at us and smiled),
As they filed along by hillock and by hollow,
Then our hearts were so beguiled
That, for many and many a day,
We dreamed we heard them say,
'Oh, follow, follow, follow!'
And the distant, rolling drum
Called us 'Come, come, come!'
Till our virtue seemed a thing to give away.

War had swept ten thousand years away from earth.
We were primal once again.
There were males, not modern men;
We were females meant to bring their sons to birth.
And we could not wait for any formal rite,
We could hear them calling to us, 'Come to-night;
For to-morrow, at the dawn,
We move on!' And the drum
Bellowed, 'Come, come, come!'
And the fife
Whistled, 'Life, life, life!'

So they moved on and fought and bled and died;
Honoured and mourned, they are the nation's pride.
We fought our battles, too, but with the tide

Of our red blood, we gave the world new lives.
Because we were not wives
We are dishonoured. Is it noble, then,
To break God's laws only by killing men
To save one's country from destruction?
We took no man's life but gave our chastity,
And sinned the ancient sin
To plant young trees and fill felled forests in.

Oh, clergy of the land,
Bible in hand,
All reverently you stand,
On holy thoughts intent
While barren wives receive the sacrament!
Had you the open visions you could see
Phantoms of infants murdered in the womb,
Who never knew a cradle or a tomb,
Hovering about these wives accusingly.

Bestow the sacrament! Their sins are not well known—
Ours to the four winds of the earth are blown.

Settle the Question Right

However the battle is ended,
Though proudly the victor comes,
With flaunting flags and neighing nags
And echoing roll of drums;
Still truth proclaims this motto
In letters of living light,
No question is ever settled
Until it is settled right.

Though the heel of the strong oppressor
May grind the weak in the dust,

And the voices of fame with one acclaim
May call him great and just;
Let those who applaud take warning
And keep this motto in sight,
No question is ever settled
Until it is settled right.

Let those who have failed take courage,
Though the enemy seem to have won;
If he be in the wrong, though his ranks are strong,
The battle is not yet done.
For sure as the morning follows
The darkest hour of the night,
No question is ever settled
Until it is settled right.

O men, bowed down with labour,
O women, young yet old,
O heart, oppressed in the toiler's breast
And crushed by the power of gold,
Keep on with your weary battle
Against triumphant might;
No question is ever settled
Until it is settled right.

What We Want

All hail the dawn of a new day breaking,
When a strong-armed nation shall take away
The weary burdens from backs that are aching
Maximum labor and minimum pay;
When no man is honored who hoards his millions
When no man feasts on another's toil.
And God's poor suffering, striving billions
Shall share his riches of sun and soil.

There is gold for all in the earth's broad bosom,
There is food for all in the land's great store;
Enough is provided if rightly divided;
Let each man take what he needs—no more.
Shame on the miser with unused riches,
Who robs the toiler to swell his hoard,
Who beats down the wage of the digger of ditches,
And steals the bread from the poor man's board
Shame on the owner of mines whose cruel
And selfish measures have brought him wealth,
While the ragged wretches who dig his fuel
Are robbed of comfort and hope and health.
Shame on the ruler who rides in his carriage
Bought with the labor of half-paid men
Men who are shut out of home and marriage
And are herded like sheep in a hovel pen.
Let the clarion voice of the nation wake him
To broader vision and fairer play;
Or let the hand of a just law shake him
Till his ill-gained dollars shall roll away.
Let no man dwell under a mountain of plunder,
Let no man suffer with want and cold;
We want right living, not mere alms-giving;
We want just dividing of labor and gold.

Friendship After Love

After the fierce midsummer all ablaze
Has burned itself to ashes, and expires
In the intensity of its own fires,
There come the mellow, mild, St. Martin days
Crowned with the calm of peace, but sad with haze.
So after Love has led us, till he tires
Of his own throes, and torments, and desires,
Comes large-eyed friendship: with a restful gaze,

He beckons us to follow, and across
Cool verdant vales we wander free from care.
Is it a touch of frost lies in the air?
Why are we haunted with a sense of loss?
We do not wish the pain back, or the heat;
And yet, and yet, these days are incomplete.

The Younger Born

The modern English-speaking young girl is the astonishment of the world
and the despair of the older generation. Nothing like her has ever been seen
or heard before. Alike in drawing-rooms and the amusement places of the
people, she defies conventions in dress, speech, and conduct. She is bold,
yet not immoral. She is immodest, yet she is chaste. She has no ideals, yet
she is kind and generous. She is an anomaly and a paradox.

We are the little daughters of Time and the World his wife,
We are not like the children, born in their younger life,
We are marred with our mother's follies and torn with our father's
    strife.
We are the little daughters of the modern world, and Time, her
    spouse.
She has brought many children to our father's house
Before we came, when both our parents were content
With simple pleasures and with quiet homely ways.
Modest and mild
Were the fair daughters born to them in those fair days,
Modest and mild.

But Father Time grew restless and longed for a swifter pace,
And our mother pushed out beside him at the cost of her tender
    grace,
And life was no more living but just a headlong race.
And we are wild—Yea, wild are we, the younger born of the World
Into life's vortex hurled.
With the milk of our mother's breast

We drank her own unrest,
And we learned our speech from Time
Who scoffs at the things sublime.

Time and the World have hurried so
They could not help their younger born to grow;
We only follow, follow where they go.
They left their high ideals behind them as they ran;
There was but one goal, pleasure, for Woman or for Man,
And they robbed the nights of slumber to lengthen the days' brief
   span.

We are the demi-virgins of the modern day;
All evil on the earth is known to us in thought,
But yet we do it not.
We bare our beauteous bodies to the gaze of men,
We lure them, tempt them, lead them on, and then
Lightly we turn away.
By strong compelling passion we are never stirred;
To us it is a word—
A word much used when tragic tales are told;
We are the younger born, yet we are very old
In understanding, and our knowledge makes us bold.
Boldly we look at life,
Loving its stress and strife,
And hating all conventions that may mean restraint,
Yet shunning sin's black taint.

We know wine's taste;
And the young-maiden bloom and sweetness of our lips
Is often in eclipse
Under the brown weed's stain.
Yet we are chaste;
We have no large capacity for joy or pain,
But an insatiable appetite for pleasure.
We have no use for leisure

And never learned the meaning of that word 'repose.'
Life as it goes
Must spell excitement for us, be the cost what may.
Speeding along the way,

We ofttimes pause to do some generous little deed,
And fill the cup of need;
For we are kind at heart,
Though with less heart than head,
Unmoral, not immoral, when the worst is said;
We are the product of the modern day.

We are the little daughters of Time and the World his wife,
We are not like the children, born in their younger life,
We are marred with our mother's follies and torn with our father's
    strife.

The Old Stage Queen

Back in the box by the curtains shaded,
She sits alone by the house unseen;
Her eye is dim, her cheek is faded,
She who was once the people's queen.
The curtain rolls up, and she sees before her
A vision of beauty and youth and grace.
Ah! no wonder all hearts adore her,
Silver-throated and fair of face.
Out of her box she leans and listens;
Oh, is it with pleasure or with despair
That her thin cheek pales and her dim eye glistens,
While that fresh young voice sings the grand old air?
She is back again in the past's bright splendour
When life seemed worth living, and love a truth,
Ere Time had told her she must surrender
Her double dower of fame and youth.

It is she herself who stands there singing
To that sea of faces that shines and stirs;
And the cheers on cheers that go up ringing
And rousing the echoes—are hers—all hers.
Just for one moment the sweet delusion
Quickens her pulses and blurs her sight,
And wakes within her that wild confusion
Of joy that is anguish and fierce delight.
Then the curtain goes down and the lights are gleaming
Brightly o'er circle and box and stall.
She starts like a sleeper who wakes from dreaming
Her past lies under a funeral pall.
Her day is dead and her star descended
Never to rise or shine again;
Her reign is over—her Queenship ended
A new name is sounded and sung by men.
All the glitter and glow and splendour,
All the glory of that lost day,
With the friends that seemed true, and the love that seemed tender,
Why, what is it all but a dead bouquet?
She rises to go. Has the night turned colder?
The new Queen answers to call and shout;
And the old Queen looks back over her shoulder,
Then all unnoticed she passes out.

Music in the Flat

When Tom and I were married, we took a little flat;
I had a taste for singing and playing and all that.
And Tom, who loved to hear me, said he hoped I would not stop
All practice, like so many wives who let their music drop.

So I resolved to set apart an hour or two each day
To keeping vocal chords and hands in trim to sing and play.
The second morning I had been for half an hour or more

At work on Haydn's masses, when a tap came at my door.

A nurse, who wore a dainty cap and apron, and a smile,
Ran down to ask if I would cease my music for awhile.
The lady in the flat above was very ill, she said,
And the sound of my piano was distracting to her head.

A fortnight's exercises lost, ere I began them, when,
The following morning at my door, there came that tap again;
A woman with an anguished face implored me to forego
My music for some days to come a man was dead below.

I shut down my piano till the corpse had left the house,
And spoke to Tom in whispers and was quiet as a mouse.
A week of labor limbered up my stiffened hand and voice,
I stole an extra hour from sleep, to practice and rejoice;

When, ting-a-ling, the door-bell rang a discord in my trill
The baby in the flat across was very, very ill.
For ten long days that infant's life was hanging by a thread,
And all that time my instrument was silent as the dead.

So pain and death and sickness came in one perpetual row,
When babies were not born above, then tenants died below.
The funeral over underneath, some one fell ill on top,
And begged me, for the love of God, to let my music drop.

When trouble went not up or down, it stalked across the hall,
And so in spite of my resolve, I do not play at all.

The Coming Man

Oh, not for the great departed,
Who formed our country's laws,
And not for the bravest-hearted

Who died in freedom's cause,
And not for some living hero
To whom all bend the knee,
My muse would raise her song of praise
But for the man to be.

For out of the strife which woman
Is passing through to-day,
A man that is more than human
Shall yet be born, I say.
A man in whose pure spirit
No dross of self will lurk;
A man who is strong to cope with wrong,
A man who is proud to work.
A man with hope undaunted,
A man with godlike power,
Shall come when he most is wanted,
Shall come at the needed hour.

He shall silence the din and clamor
Of clan disputing with clan,
And toil's long fight with purse-proud might
Shall triumph through this man.
I know he is coming, coming,
To help, to guide, to save.
Though I hear no martial drumming,
And see no flags that wave.
But the great soul travail of woman,
And the bold free thought unfurled,
Are heralds that say he is on the way
The coming man of the world.

Mourn not for vanished ages
With their great heroic men,
Who dwell in history's pages
And live in the poet's pen.

For the grandest times are before us,
And the world is yet to see
The noblest worth of this old earth
In the men that are to be.

The Poet's Theme

"What is the explanation of the strange silence of American poets
concerning America's triumphs on sea and land?"

—*Literary Digest*

Why should the poet of these pregnant times
Be asked to sing of war's unholy crimes?

To laud and eulogize the trade which thrives
On horrid holocausts of human lives.

Man was a fighting beast when earth was young
And war the only theme when Homer sung.

'Twixt might and might the equal contest lay;
Not so the battles of our modern day.

Too often now the conquering hero struts
A Gulliver among the Liliputs.

Success no longer rests on skill or fate
But on the movements of a syndicate.

Of old men fought and deemed it right and just.
To-day the warrior fights because he must,

And in his secret soul feels shame because
He desecrates the higher manhood's laws.

Oh, there are worthier themes for poet's pen
In this great hour, than bloody deeds of men

Or triumphs of one hero (though he be
Deserving song for his humility).

The rights of many—not the worth of one—
The coming issues, not the battle done,

The awful opulence, and awful need—
The rise of brotherhood—the fall of greed.

The soul of man replete with God's own force,
The call "to heights" and not the cry, "to horse"—

Are there not better themes in this great age
For pen of poet, or for voice of sage

Than those old tales of killing? Song is dumb
Only that greater song in time may come.

When comes the bard, he whom the world waits for,
He will not sing of War.

Perfectness

All perfect things are saddening in effect.
The autumn wood robed in its scarlet clothes,
The matchless tinting on the royal rose
Whose velvet leaf by no least flaw is flecked
Love's supreme moment, when the soul unchecked
Soars high as heaven, and its best rapture knows,
These hold a deeper pathos than our woes,
Since they leave nothing better to expect.

Resistless change, when powerless to improve,
Can only mar. The gold will pale to gray—
No thing remains tomorrow as today,—
The rose will not seem quite so fair, and love
Must find its measures of delight made less.
Ah, how imperfect is all Perfectness!

The Soul's Farewell to the Body

So we must part forever; and although
I long have beat my wings and cried to go,
Free from your narrow limiting control,
Forth into space, the true home of the soul,

Yet now, yet now that hour is drawing near,
I pause reluctant, finding you so dear.
All joys await me in the realm of God—
Must you, my comrade, moulder in the sod?

I was your captive, yet you were my slave;
Your prisoner, yet obedience you gave
To all my earnest wishes and commands.
Now to the worm I leave those willing hands

That toiled for me or held the books I read,
Those feet that trod where'er I wished to tread,
Those arms that clasped my dear ones, and the breast
On which one loved and loving heart found rest,

Those lips through which my prayers to God have risen,
Those eyes that were the windows to my prison.
From these, all these, Death's Angel bids me sever;
Dear Comrade Body, fare thee well forever!

I go to my inheritance, and go
With joy that only the freed soul can know;
Yet in my spirit wanderings I trust
I may sometimes pause near your sacred dust.

Misalliance

I am troubled tonight with a curious pain;
It is not of the flesh, it is not of the brain,
Nor yet of a heart that is breaking:
But down still deeper, and out of sight—
In the place where the soul and the body unite—
There lies the seat of the aching.

They have been lovers, in days gone by;
But the soul is fickle, and longs to fly
From the fettering misalliance:
And she tears at the bonds which are binding her so,
And pleads with the body to let her go,
But he will not yield compliance.

For the body loves, as he loved in the past
When he wedded the soul; and he holds her fast,
And swears that he will not loose her;
That he will keep her and hide her away
For ever and ever and for a day
From the arms of Death, the seducer.

Ah! This is the strife that is wearying me—
The strife 'twixt a soul that would be free
And a body that will not let her.
And I say to my soul, "Be calm, and wait;
For I tell ye truly that soon or late
Ye surely shall drop each letter.

And I say to the body, "Be kind, I pray;
For the soul is not of the mortal clay,
But is formed in spirit fashion."
And still through the hours of the solemn night
I can hear my sad soul's plea for flight,
And my body's reply of passion.

The Cost

God finished woman in the twilight hour
And said, "To-morrow thou shalt find thy place:
Man's complement, the mother of the race—
With love the motive power—
The one compelling power."

All night she dreamed and wondered. With the light
Her lover came—and then she understood
The purpose of her being. Life was good
And all the world seemed right—
And nothing was, but right.

She had no wish for any wider sway:
By all the questions of the world unvexed,
Supremely loving and superbly sexed,
She passed upon her way—
Her feminine fair way.

But God neglected, when He fashioned man,
To fuse the molten splendor of his mind
With that sixth sense He gave to womankind.
And so He marred His plan—
Aye, marred His own great plan.

She asked so little, and so much she gave,
That man grew selfish: and she soon became,

To God's great sorrow and the whole world's shame,
Man's sweet and patient slave—
His uncomplaining slave.

Yet in the nights (oh! nights so dark and long)
She clasped her little children to her breast
And wept. And in her anguish of unrest
She thought upon her wrong;
She knew how great her wrong.

And one sad hour, she said unto her heart,
"Since thou art cause of all my bitter pain,
I bid thee abdicate the throne: let brain
Rule now, and do his part—
His masterful strong part."

She wept no more. By new ambition stirred
Her ways led out, to regions strange and vast.
Men stood aside and watched, dismayed, aghast,
And all the world demurred—
Misjudged her, and demurred.

Still on and up, from sphere to widening sphere,
Till thorny paths bloomed with the rose of fame.
Who once demurred, now followed with acclaim:
The hiss died in the cheer—
The loud applauding cheer.

She stood triumphant in that radiant hour,
Man's mental equal, and competitor.
But ah! the cost! from out the heart of her
Had gone love's motive power—
Love's all-compelling power.

Individuality

O yes, I love you, and with all my heart;
Just as a weaker woman loves her own,
Better than I love my beloved art,
Which, till you came, reigned royally, alone,
My king, my master. Since I saw your face
I have dethroned it, and you hold that place.

I am as weak as other women are—
Your frown can make the whole world like a tomb.
Your smile shines brighter than the sun, by far,
Sometimes I think there is not space or room
In all the earth for such a love as mine,
And it soars up to breathe in realms divine.

I know that your desertion or neglect
Could break my heart, as women's hearts do break,
If my wan days had nothing to expect
From your love's splendor all joy would forsake
The chambers of my soul. Yes, this is true.
And yet, and yet—one thing I keep from you.

There is a subtle part of me which went
Into my long pursued and worshiped art;
Though your great love fills me with such content
No other love finds room now, in my heart.
Yet that rare essence was my art's alone.
Thank God, you cannot grasp it; 'tis mine own.

Thank God, I say, for while I love you so,
With that vast love, as passionate as tender,
I feel an exultation as I know
I have not made you a complete surrender.
Here is my body: bruise it, if you will.
And break my heart; I have that something still.

You cannot grasp it. Seize the breath of morn,
Or bind the perfume of the rose as well.
God put it in my soul when I was born;
It is not mine to give away, or sell,
Or offer up on any altar shrine.
It was my art's; and when not art's, 'tis mine.

For love's sake, I can put the art away,
Or anything which stands 'twixt me and you.
But that strange essence God bestowed, I say,
To permeate the work He gave to do:
And it cannot be drained, dissolved, or sent
Through any channel, save the one He meant.

Inspiration

Not like a daring, bold, aggressive boy,
Is inspiration, eager to pursue,
But rather like a maiden, fond, yet coy,
Who gives herself to him who best doth woo.
Once she may smile, or thrice, thy soul to fire,
In passing by, but when she turns her face,
Thou must persist and seek her with desire,
If thou wouldst win the favor of her grace.
And if, like some winged bird she cleaves the air,
And leaves thee spent and stricken on the earth,
Still must thou strive to follow even there,
That she may know thy valor and thy worth.
Then shall she come unveiling all her charms,
Giving thee joy for pain, and smiles for tears;
Then shalt thou clasp her with possessing arms,
The while she murmurs music in thine ears.
But ere her kiss has faded from thy cheek,
She shall flee from thee over hill and glade,

So must thou seek and ever seek and seek
For each new conquest of this phantom maid.

The Tiger

In the still jungle of the senses lay
A tiger soundly sleeping, till one day
A bold young hunter chanced to come that way.

"How calm," he said, "that splendid creature lies,
I long to rouse him into swift surprise!"
The well aimed arrow-shot from amorous eyes

And lo! The tiger rouses up and turns,
A coat of fire his glowing eyeball burns,
His mighty frame with savage hunger yearns.

He crouches for a spring; his eyes dilate –
Alas! Bold hunter, what shall be thy fate?
Thou canst not fly, it is too late, too late.

Once having tasted human flesh, ah! Then
Woe, woe unto the whole rash world of men,
The wakened tiger will not sleep again.

Charlotte Perkins Gilman: 1860–1935

Introduction

As with all nineteenth-century women poets, after prominence in life, Charlotte Gilman suffered literary burial at her death. Since that time, Gilman's resurrection has been in prose: her short story "The Yellow Wallpaper" and her utopian novel *Herland* have gained particular recognition. Yet her poetry is of a piece with her other writings—a strong example of the participation of poetry in American public discourse. Gilman is, of nineteenth-century women poets (and other people), among the most deliberate feminists of her time, both in practice and in theory. Her commitment to women structures all of her involvements, from her personal history to her professional life and writings.

Gilman was born into the Beecher family, a great-niece to Harriet and Catherine. Her father, however, deserted her mother, her brother, and herself in her first year. The mother lived under Beecher charity for the next decade, until deciding to sue for divorce; and then in a variety of irregular households. Gilman's autobiographical account gives a portrait of strain with her mother, and of a determined desire to define an independent place for herself, to achieve and contribute to a larger world than the domestic one. In the event, the contribution she made was to the possibility of women to make contributions, their right to work and participate broadly in society. Women's activism became her cause.

Gilman's own personal contest was set most tensely around marriage. Attracted to and wooed by Charles Stetson, Gilman resisted the courtship for more than two years, suspecting married life to be in conflict with her visions of independence and wide service. "But much as I love you," she wrote him, "I love work better, and I cannot make the two compatible." In a sense, her biography is an emblem of the inverse relation so notable among nineteenth (and many twentieth-century) women poets between marriage and writing. Finally married in 1884, domesticity, pregnancy, and birth led to nervous breakdown. A diary entry of May 9, 1884 reads: "I suggest that he pay me for my services; and he much dislikes the idea. I am grieved at offending him, mutual misery, bed and cry." Her subsequent 'rest cure' with S. Weir Mitchell, forbidding all activity whether physical or intellectual (and grimly critiqued in "The Yellow Wallpaper") almost pushed her, she attests, into complete insanity. What seemed to help instead was distance from her husband and household. After a repeated pattern in which travel away restored her to health and the return to domesticity, her collapse into depression, both husband and wife concluded the marriage was harmful to her and agreed to separation. Gilman's consequent divorce, and her decision to place her daughter with her ex-husband and her best friend, whose marriage to each other she had encouraged, led to notoriety and scandal against her. Nonetheless, Gilman discovered herself as an indefatigable lecturer and writer on women's causes. For a time she lived and worked with Jane Addams. Marrying her younger cousin, George Houghton Gilman, in 1900, Gilman did not establish an ordinary domesticity, instead traveling and working as before. She began to publish her own journal, the *Forerunner*, writing all of its material herself. This is where her novels such as *Herland* appeared in serial, as well as a great deal of her poetry. Her death in 1935 was self-induced with chloroform after years of increasingly virulent breast cancer, a self-determination she strongly supported.

In poetry, Gilman's is an art of rhetoric. Hers is a poetic of stances—not only in ideological terms but as and through the words and phrases which circulate in her society. Her poetic strategy—sometimes artful, sometimes preachy—is to adopt positions and arguments which surround her. By speaking through them, she exposes and subverts the claims they make. At her worst, Gilman lectures, although this is interesting from the viewpoint of historical ideology. At her best, Gilman lifts out the speaking voices around her and skillfully re-presents them, in ways that investigate and call them into question. The result is a complex rhetorical structure: the voices in the poem utter widely accepted and circulated views, which the author, in distance and distinction from them, undercuts and refutes. The words of the text take on multiple and contested meanings, yielding a complex cultural polemic, incisive and passionate.

"Homes: A Sestina" exemplifies this rhetorical complexity. Its speaker is the voice of the separate sphere, of domesticity itself, into which women were officially relegated. This voice makes its claims in accordance with official ideology. Yet the repetitions ordered through the elaborate sestina form (where each stanza ends its lines with the same six words in fixed sequence), allow the words to accumulate power and intensity, emerging into increasing critical light as the poem proceeds. Words pull in opposite directions, as their sense in ordinary social terms contests with an other critical sense that emerges through the poetic pattern woven by the author. If the "Homes" who speak announce that they are where "women end their duties and desires," what they mean as purpose the author questions as dead end. The Homes' claim to be the woman's "perfect world / Prescribed by nature and ordained by God" becomes questionable; men's labor to furnish "comfortable homes" as "life's purpose," rings offensive to men and women alike. This is nothing more than to "Wring dry the world to meet our wide desires!", a betrayal of both man and woman.

"An Old Proverb" is a text that specifically examines and dramatizes this ordinary circulation of language and its power. Proverbs are common knowledge, words in everyone's mouth. Yet they do much to create the situation they encapsulate in motto. Not least, the proverb penetrates into those it sums up and defines, becoming their own internal definition as well as reflecting and defining their external situation. In the case of women, the dominant rhetoric of society becomes internalized into negative self-definition and restricted senses of possibility. That women must "Bear bravely, bear dumbly" what befalls them, with "no escape," is not descriptive but a directive women accept and obey; not to mention God's "infinite curse." Yet Gilman hopes that in dramatizing these voices of society she will be able to extricate women from them. Many of her poems set out to present and question social norms for women. "The "Young Wife" who is "content" to "clean things dirty and to soil things clean" is challenged to remember her girlhood desires to "help the groaning world, to serve the state." Domesticity is a "paltry queenship" whose praise only works as concealment of its reductive nature. "The Departing Housewife" is invited to cast off her role as au pair, which has been justified in the name of duty and love. "An Answer" is Gilman's own bitter commentary on her broken marriage—a companion poem to "The Yellow Wallpaper". "Six Hours a Day" in the kitchen is not the high work of "wife and mother," whatever women are told and repeat to themselves. "Modest Maid," "Anti-Suffragists," "Mothers," "Housewife," Gilman reviews the various roles women have been given to adopt, with their false claims and painful complicities. "Women Do Not Want" to change because of the terms, the very language, they have been taught and have accepted.

Gilman's social critique is most fun in her parodies. These are a mode of rhetorical kidnapping. In light of Gilman's mocking imitation of claims made against women, how can anyone take them seriously? Animal fable not only makes the point, but asserts Gilman's evolutionary view that the only species to restrict the female from working and acting are humans ("Females"). In "Wedded Bliss" female self-sacrifice becomes murderous and suicidal, as each wife is coupled with a husband who is her predator. The rhetoric of female unemployment becomes absurd in the dialogue of bees. The fear of women becomes aggressive projection in light of natural history ("More Females").

Gilman's feminism is firmly situated in her specific nineteenth-century context. As such, she emphasizes less personal liberation and self-interest than social service ("Two Callings"). Unusually for the nineteenth century, in Gilman this no longer has much to do with religious context. Pretty thoroughly secular, Gilman is skeptical of Christian institutions ("To the Preacher," "Christian Values") and of creeds in general ("Another Creed"). She refers to the Bible rarely, although "To Man," which she included as her introduction to *Women and Economics*, offers her re-reading of the creation story, that crucible of gender definition. Her "Real Religion" tends to posit an "essential" womanhood against an "essential" manhood, something she does (in a very nineteenth-century way) in her Mother poems as well. But what is positively offered is Gilman's vision of what a moral society would look like (as in *Herland*). Life would be devoted to this world, not the next; to birth, not afterlife; to growth, not eternity; to teaching, not warfare. She sums this up in "Matriatism" as "Fatherland" against "Mother Earth."

Not religion, but economics, is Gilman's committed forum. *Women and Economics* critiques women's unequal work and restricted possibilities; but more centrally, it presents work as the foundation of human dignity and creative possibility. The denial to women of productive labor is the pivot of her social restriction to Gilman, and has the paradoxical result of reducing the woman herself to no more than an economic unit, owned by men. There is in *Women and Economics* little to choose between wifehood and prostitution, a topic Gilman took up in her poetry, in "One Girl of Many" and also in "Unmentionable" (which she mentions), with scandalous result. Prostitution is fueled by the unjust distribution of power and money, masquerading as morality. But women are subject to economic law in other ways as well. In an almost Foucauldian mode, Gilman attacks women's dress as a bodily discipline that curtails their movements, penetrating into their senses of space and possibility of selfhood ("This is a Lady's Hat," "The Cripple;" cf. Wilcox "The Women"). The discipline begins at birth, in a double standard that from the outset defines for women what they cannot do and who they cannot be ("A Protest"). The double standard is sexual, but as such extends to general bodily comportment as social role; and ultimately, as in other women poets of the century, into an extensive system of competing values, where economic self-interest threatens community commitments. Gilman's

own value structure was what today might be called strongly com-
munitarian, which she called "Nationalism" after Bellamy's movement.
Her book, *The Home*, remains ahead of most arrangements today
in its imagining of day-care, pooled laundry and cooking done by
professionals, and other means of releasing women (and men) from
duplicative and confining domestic labor in order to pursue their
own talents in productive activity. Work for her is creativity and
contribution, not the pursuit of personal profit.

Poetry, with her other writings, is Gilman's own work of service.
The role of the "Artist" is to be a lens to focus light for others. Or,
as she writes in her "Lecture Verse," "don't look for wild delight—/
this lecture isn't funny." With or without irony, Gilman's poetry is
always addressed to her passionate commitments, to giving women
back their voices against efforts to silence them.

Poems

Homes: A Sestina

We are the smiling comfortable homes
With happy families enthroned therein,
Where baby souls are brought to meet the world,
Where women end their duties and desires,
For which men labor as the goal of life,
That people worship now instead of God.

Do we not teach the child to worship God?—
Whose soul's young range is bounded by the homes
Of those he loves, and where he learns that life
Is all constrained to serve the wants therein,
Domestic needs and personal desires,—
These are the early limits of his world.

And are we not the woman's perfect world,
Prescribed by nature and ordained of God,
Beyond which she can have no right desires,
No need for service other than in homes?
For doth she not bring up her young therein?
And is not rearing young the end of life?

And man? What other need hath he in life
Than to go forth and labor in the world,
And struggle sore with other men therein?
Not to serve other men, nor yet his God,

But to maintain these comfortable homes,—
The end of all a normal man's desires.

Shall not the soul's most measureless desires
Learn that the very flower and fruit of life
Lies all attained in comfortable homes,
With which life's purpose is to dot the world
And consummate the utmost will of God,
By sitting down to eat and drink therein.

Yea, in the processes that work therein—
Fulfillment of our natural desires—
Surely man finds the proof that mighty God
For to maintain and reproduce his life
Created him and set him in the world;
And this high end is best attained in homes.

Are we not homes? And is not all therein?
Wring dry the world to meet our wide desires!
We crown all life! We are the aim of God!

An Old Proverb

"As much pity to see a woman weep as to see a goose go barefoot."

No escape, little creature! The earth hath no place
For the woman who seeketh to fly from her race.
Poor, ignorant, timid, too helpless to roam,
The woman must bear what befalls her, at home.
Bear bravely, bear dumbly—it is but the same
That all others endure who live under the name.
No escape, little creature!

No escape under heaven! Can man treat you worse
After God has laid on you his infinite curse?
The heaviest burden of sorrow you win

Cannot weigh with the load of original sin;
No shame be too black for the cowering face
Of her who brought shame to the whole human race!
No escape under heaven!

Yet you feel, being human. You shrink from the pain
That each child, born a woman, must suffer again.
From the strongest of bonds heart can feel, man can shape,
You cannot rebel, or appeal, or escape.
You must bear and endure. If the heart cannot sleep,
And the pain groweth bitter,—too bitter,—then—weep!
For you feel, being human.

And she wept, being woman. The numberless years
Have counted her burdens and counted her tears;
The maid wept forsaken, the mother forlorn
For the child that was dead, and the child that was born.
Wept for joy—as a miracle!—wept in her pain!
Wept aloud, wept in secret, wept ever in vain!
Still she weeps, being woman.

She Walketh Veiled and Sleeping

She walketh veiled and sleeping,
For she knoweth not her power;
She obeyeth but the pleading
Of her heart, and the high leading
Of her soul, unto this hour.
Slow advancing, halting, creeping,
Comes the Woman to the hour!—
She walketh veiled and sleeping,
For she knoweth not her power.

To the Young Wife

Are you content, you pretty three-years' wife?
Are you content and satisfied to live
On what your loving husband loves to give,
And give to him your life?

Are you content with work,—to toil alone,
To clean things dirty and to soil things clean;
To be a kitchen-maid, be called a queen,—
Queen of a cook-stove throne?

Are you content to reign in that small space—
A wooden palace and a yard fenced land—
With other queens abundant on each hand,
Each fastened in her place?

Are you content to rear your children so?
Untaught yourself, untrained, perplexed, distressed,
Are you so sure your way is always best?
That you can always know?

Have you forgotten how you used to long
In days of ardent girlhood, to be great,
To help the groaning world, to serve the state,
To be so wise—so strong?

And are you quite convinced this is the way,
The only way a woman's duty lies—
Knowing all women so have shut their eyes?
Seeing the world to-day?

Have you no dream of life in fuller store?
Of growing to be more than that you are?
Doing the things you now do better far,
Yet doing others—more?

Losing no love, but finding as you grew
That as you entered upon nobler life
You so became a richer, sweeter wife,
A wiser mother too?

What holds you? Ah, my dear, it is your throne,
Your paltry queenship in that narrow place,
Your antique labors, your restricted space,
Your working all alone!

Be not deceived! 'Tis not your wifely bond
That holds you, nor the mother's royal power,
But selfish, slavish service hour by hour—
A life with no beyond!

An Answer

A maid was asked in marriage. Wise as fair,
She gave her answer with deep thought and prayer,

Expecting in the holy name of wife
Great work, great pain, and greater joy in life.

Such work she found as brainless slaves might do;
By day and night, long labor, never through.

Such pain—no language can such pain reveal;
It had no limit but her power to feel.

Such joy life left in her sad soul's employ
Neither the hope nor memory of joy.

Helpless she died, with one despairing cry
"I thought it good! How could I tell the lie!"

And answered Nature, merciful and stern,
"I teach by killing. Let the others learn."

Six Hours a Day

Six hours a day the woman spends on food!
Six mortal hours a day.
With fire and water toiling, heat and cold;
Struggling with laws she does not understand
Of chemistry and physics, and the weight
Of poverty and ignorance besides.
Toiling for those she loves, the added strain
Of tense emotion on her humble skill,
The sensitiveness born of love and fear,
Making it harder to do even work.
Toiling without release, no hope ahead
Of taking up another business soon,
Of varying the task she finds too hard—
This, her career, so closely interknit
With holier demands as deep as life
That to refuse to cook is held the same
As to refuse her wife and motherhood.
Six mortal hours a day to handle food,—
Prepare it, serve it, clean it all away,—
With allied labors of the stove and tub,
The pan, the dishcloth, and the scrubbing-brush.
Developing forever in her brain
The power to do this work in which she lives;
While the slow finger of Heredity
Writes on the forehead of each living man,
Strive as he may, "His mother was a cook!"

The Departing Housemaid

The housewife is held to her labors
By three great powers—
Love, that poureth like water
Through hours and hours.

Duty, high as the heavens,
Deep as the sea—
These, and the great compeller,
Necessity.

Duty holds her to housework,
Sin to be free;
These are the bonds of the housewife—
They bind not me!

The man is spurred to his labors
Of plow or sword,
By two of the great incentives—
Pride and Reward.

He in his work finds glory,
Height after height;
He in his work finds riches,
Gain and delight.

Triumph of world-wide conquest—
Profit in fee;
These spur man to his labors—
They spur not me!

I am the lowest of labor,
Ignorant, strong.
They on my ignorance reckoned,
Held me thus long.

Lately I grow to discover
Life's broader way:
Nothing to hold me or spur me—
Why should I stay?

Women Do Not Want It

When the woman suffrage argument first stood upon its legs,
They answered it with cabbages, they answered it with eggs,
They answered it with ridicule, they answered it with scorn,
They thought it a monstrosity that should not have been born.

When the woman suffrage argument grew vigorous and wise,
And was not to be silenced by these apposite replies,
They turned their opposition into reasoning severe
Upon the limitations of our God-appointed sphere.

We were told of disabilities,—a long array of these,
Till one would think that womanhood was merely a disease;
And "the maternal sacrifice" was added to the plan
Of the various sacrifices we have always made—to man.

Religionists and scientists, in amity and bliss,
However else they disagreed, could all agree on this,
And the gist of all their discourse, when you got down to it,
Was—we could not have the ballot because we were not fit!

They would not hear to reason, they would not fairly yield,
They would not own their arguments were beaten in the field;
But time passed on, and someway, we need not ask them how,
Whatever ails those arguments—we do not hear them now!

You may talk of woman suffrage now with an educated man,
And he agrees with all you say, as sweetly as he can;

'Twould be better for us all, of course, if womanhood was free;
But "the women do not want it"—and so it must not be!

'Tis such a tender thoughtfulness! So exquisite a care!
Not to pile on our fair shoulders what we do not wish to bear!
But, oh, most generous brother! Let us look a little more—
Have we women always wanted what you gave to us before?

Did we ask for veils and harems in the Oriental races?
Did we beseech to be "unclean," shut out of sacred places?
Did we beg for scolding bridles and ducking stools to come?
And clamor for the beating stick no thicker than your thumb?

Did we seek to be forbidden from all the trades that pay?
Did we claim the lower wages for a man's full work to-day?
Have we petitioned for the laws wherein our shame is shown
That not a woman's child—nor her own body—is her own?

What women want has never been a strongly acting cause
When woman has been wronged by man in churches, customs,
        laws;
Why should he find this preference so largely in his way
When he himself admits the right of what we ask to-day?

The Modest Maid

I am a modest San Francisco maid,
Fresh, fair, and young,
Such as the painters gladly have displayed,
The poets sung.

Modest?—Oh, modest as a bud unblown,
A thought unspoken;
Hidden and cherished, unbeheld, unknown,
In peace unbroken.

Far from the holy shades of this my home,
The coarse world raves,
And the New Woman cries to heaven's dome
For what she craves.

Loud, vulgar, public, screaming from the stage,
Her skirt divided,
Riding cross-saddled on the dying age,
Justly derided.

I blush for her, I blush for our sweet sex
By her disgraced.
My sphere is home. My soul I do not vex
With zeal misplaced.

Come then to me with happy heart, O man!
I wait your visit.
To guide your footsteps I do all I can,
Am most explicit.

As veined flower-petals teach the passing bee
The way to honey,
So printer's ink displayed instructeth thee
Where lies my money.

Go see! In type and cut across the page,
Before the nation,
There you may read about my eyes, my age,
My education,

My fluffy golden hair, my tiny feet,
My pet ambition,
My well-developed figure, and my sweet,
Retiring disposition.

All, all is there, and now I coyly wait.
Pray don't delay.
My address does the Blue Book plainly state,
And mamma's "day."

Women of To-Day

You women of to-day who fear so much
The women of the future, showing how
The dangers of her course are such and such—
What are you now?

Mothers and Wives and Housekeepers, forsooth!
Great names! you cry, full scope to rule and please!
Room for wise age and energetic youth!—
But are you these?

Housekeepers? Do you then, like those of yore,
Keep house with power and pride, with grace and ease?
No, you keep servants only! What is more,
You don't keep these!

Wives, say you? Wives! Blessed indeed are they
Who hold of love the everlasting keys,
Keeping their husbands' hearts! Alas the day!
You don't keep these!

And mothers? Pitying Heaven! Mark the cry
From cradle death beds! Mothers on their knees!
Why, half the children born—as children die!
You don't keep these!

And still the wailing babies come and go,
And homes are waste, and husbands' hearts fly far,

There is no hope until you dare to know
The thing you are!

The Anti-Suffragists

Fashionable women in luxurious homes,
With men to feed them, clothe them, pay their bills,—
Bow, doff the hat, and fetch the handkerchief;
Hostess or guest, and always so supplied
With graceful deference and courtesy;
Surrounded by their servants, horses, dogs,—
These tell us they have all the rights they want.

Successful women who have won their way
Alone, with strength of their unaided arm,
Or helped by friends, or softly climbing up
By the sweet aid of "woman's influence;"
Successful any way, and caring naught
For any other woman's unsuccess,—
These tell us they have all the rights they want.

Religious women of the feebler sort,—
Not the religion of a righteous world,
A free, enlightened, upward-reaching world,
But the religion that considers life
As something to back out of!—whose ideal
Is to renounce, submit, and sacrifice,
Counting on being patted on the head
And given a high chair when they get to heaven,—
These tell us they have all the rights they want.

Ignorant women—college-bred sometimes,
But ignorant of life's realities
And principles of righteous government,
And how the privileges they enjoy

Were won with blood and tears by those before—
Those they condemn, whose ways they now oppose;
Saying, "Why not let well enough alone?
Our world is very pleasant as it is,"—
These tell us they have all the rights they want.

And selfish women,—pigs in petticoats,—
Rich, poor, wise, unwise, top or bottom round,
But all sublimely innocent of thought,
And guiltless of ambition, save the one
Deep, voiceless aspiration—to be fed!
These have no use for rights or duties more.
Duties to-day are more than they can meet,
And law insures their right to clothes and food,—
These tell us they have all the rights they want.

And, more's the pity, some good women, too;
Good conscientious women, with ideas;
Who think—or think they think—that woman's cause
Is best advanced by letting it alone;
That she somehow is not a human thing,
And not to be helped on by human means,
Just added to humanity—an "L"—
A wing, a branch, an extra, not mankind,—
These tell us they have all the rights they want.

And out of these has come a monstrous thing,
A strange, down-sucking whirlpool of disgrace,
Women uniting against womanhood,
And using that great name to hide their sin!
Vain are their words as that old king's command
Who set his will against the rising tide.
But who shall measure the historic shame
Of these poor traitors—traitors are they all—
To great Democracy and Womanhood!

Two Callings

I hear a deep voice through uneasy dreaming,
A deep, soft, tender, soul-beguiling voice;
A lulling voice that bids the dreams remain,
That calms my restlessness and dulls my pain,
That thrills and fills and holds me till in seeming
There is no other sound on earth—no choice.

"Home!" says the deep voice, "Home!" and softly singing
Brings me a sense of safety unsurpassed;
So old! So old! The piles above the wave—
The shelter of the stone-blocked shadowy cave—
Security of sun-kissed treetops swinging—
Safety and Home at last!

"Home" says the sweet voice, and warm Comfort rises,
Holding my soul with velvet-fingered hands;
Comfort of leafy lair and lapping fur,
Soft couches, cushions, curtains, and the stir
Of easy pleasures that the body prizes,
Of soft swift feet to serve the least commands.

I shrink—half rise—and then it murmurs "Duty!"
Again the past rolls out—a scroll unfurled:
Allegiance and long labor due my lord—
Allegiance in an idleness abhorred—
I am the squaw—the slave—the harem beauty—
I serve and serve, the handmaid of the world.

My soul revels—but hark! a new note thrilling,
Deep, deep, past finding—I protest no more;
The voice says "Love!" and all those ages dim
Stand glorified and justified in him,
I bow—I kneel—the woman soul is willing—
"Love is the law. Be still! Obey! Adore!"

And then—ah then! The deep voice murmurs "Mother!"
And all life answers from the primal sea;
A mingling of all lullabies, a peace
That asks no understanding; the release
Of nature's holiest power—who seeks another?
Home? Home is Mother—Mother, Home, to me.

"Home!" says the deep voice; "Home and Easy Pleasure!
Safety and Comfort, Laws of Life well kept!"
"Love!" and my heart rose thrilling at the word;
"Mother!" it nestled down and never stirred;
"Duty and Peace and Love beyond all measure!
Home! Safety! Comfort! Mother!"—and I slept.

II.

A bugle call! A clear keen ringing cry
Relentless—eloquent—that found the ear
Through fold on fold of slumber, sweet, profound—
A widening wave of universal sound,
Piercing the heart—filling the utmost sky—
I wake—I must wake! Hear—for I must hear!

"The World! The World is crying! Hear its needs!"
Home is a part of life—I am the whole!
Home is the cradle—shall a whole life stay
Cradled in comfort through the working day?
I too am Home—the Home of all high deeds—
The only Home to hold the human soul!

"Courage!—the front of conscious life!" it cried;
"Courage that dares to die and dares to live!
Why should you prate of safety? Is life meant
In ignominious safety to be spent?
Is Home best valued as a place to hide?—
Come out, and give what you are here to give!

"Strength and Endurance! of high action born!"
And all that dream of Comfort shrank away,
Turning its fond, beguiling face aside—
So Selfishness and Luxury and Pride
Stood forth revealed, till I grew fierce with scorn,
And burned to meet the dangers of the day.

"Duty! Ah Duty! Duty! Mark the word!"
I turned to my old standard. It was sent
From hem to hem, and through the gaping place
I saw at last its meaning and its place
I saw my undone duties to the race
Of man—neglected—spurned—how had I heard
That word and never dreamed of what it meant!

"Duty! Unlimited—eternal—new!"
And I? My idol on a petty shrine
Fell as I turned, and Cowardice and Sloth
Fell too, unmasked, false Duty covering both—
While the true Duty, all-embracing, high,
Showed the clear line of noble deed to do.

And then the great voice rang out to the sun,
And all my terror left me, all my shame,
While every dream of joy from earliest youth
Came back and lived!—that joy unhoped was truth,
All joy, all hope, all truth, all peace grew one,
Life, opened clear, and Love? Love was its name!

So when the great word "Mother!" rang once more,
I saw at last its meaning and its place,
Not the blind passion of the brooding past,
But Mother—the World's Mother—came at last,
To love as she had never loved before—
To feed and guard and teach the human race.

The world was full of music clear and high!
The world was full of light! The world was free!
And I? Awake at last, in joy untold
Saw Love and Duty broad as life unrolled—
Wide as the earth—unbounded as the sky—
Home was the World—the World was Home to me!

To Mothers

In the name of your ages to anguish!
In the name of the curse and the stain!
By the strength of your sorrow I call you
By the power of your pain!

We are mothers. Through us in our bondage,
Through us with a brand in the face,
Be we fettered with gold or with iron,
Through us comes the race.

With the weight of all sin on our shoulders,
Midst the serpents of shame ever curled,
We have sat, unresisting, defenseless,—
Making the men of the world!

We were ignorant long, and our children
Were besotted and brutish and blind,
King-driven, priest-ridden,—who are they
Our children—mankind.

We were kept for our beauty, our softness,
Our sex,—what reward do ye find?
We transmit, must transmit, being mothers,
What we are to mankind!

As the mother so follow the children!
No nation, wise, noble and brave,
Ever sprang,—though the father had freedom,—
From the mother,—a slave.

Look now at the world as ye find it!
Blench not! Truth is kinder than lies!
Look now at the world—see it suffer!
Listen now to its cries!

See the people who suffer, all people!
All humanity wasting its powers!
In a hand to hand struggle—death dealing—
All children of ours!

The blind millionaire—the blind harlot—
The blind preacher leading the blind—
Only think of the pain, how it hurts them!
Our little blind babies—mankind!

Shall we bear it? We mothers who love them.
Can we bear it? We mothers who feel
Every pang of our babes and forgive them
Every sin when they kneel?

Little stumbling world! You have fallen!
You are crying in darkness and fear!
Wait, darling, your mother is coming!
Hush, darling, your mother is here!

We are here like an army with banners
The great flag of our freedom unfurled!
With us rests the fate of the nations,
For we make the world!

Dare ye sleep while your children are calling?
Dare ye wait while they clamor unfed?
Dare ye pray in the proud pillared churches
While they suffer for bread?

If the farmer hath sinned he shall answer,
If he check thee laugh back at his powers!
Shall a mother be kept from her children?
These people are ours!

They are ours! He is ours, for we made him!
In our arms he has nestled and smiled!
Shall we, the world-mothers, be hindered
By the freaks of a child?

Rise now in the power of The Woman!
Rise now in the power of our need!
The world cries in hunger and darkness!
We shall light! We shall feed!

In the name of our ages of anguish!
In the name of the curse and the slain!
By the strength of our sorrow we conquer!
In the power of our pain!

The Housewife

Here is the House to hold me—cradle of all the race;
Here is my lord and my love, here are my children dear—
Here is the House enclosing, the dear-loved dwelling place;
Why should I ever weary for aught that I find not here?

Here for the hours of the day and the hours of the night;
Bound with the bands of Duty, rivetted tight;

Duty older than Adam—Duty that saw
Acceptance utter and hopeless in the eyes of the serving squaw.

Food and the serving of food—that is my daylong care;
What and when we shall eat, what and how we shall wear;
Soiling and cleaning of things—that is my task in the main—
Soil them and clean them and soil them—soil them and clean
    them again.

To work at my trade by the dozen and never a trade to know;
To plan like a Chinese puzzle—fitting and changing so;
To think of a thousand details, each in a thousand ways;
For my own immediate people and a possible love and praise:

My mind is trodden in circles, tiresome, narrow and hard,
Useful, commonplace, private—simply a small back-yard;
And I the Mother of Nations!—Blind their struggle and vain!—
I cover the earth with my children—each with a housewife's brain.

Ode to the Cook

O Cook! Domestic Cook! no exhumed stone
In ancient dignity can match thine own.
Crete or Abydos fail to throw their light
So far adown our pro-social night.
Behind the bronze—behind chipped stone we look—
With first discovered fire we find the cook!
That fire, from hearthstone winning wide its place,
Now world-encircling service gives our race;
But thou alone remainest, all unmoved, alone
Tending thy pots around that primal stone
Where once the squaw made, moccasins of hide.
We web the world in fabrics woven wide;
Where toiled she her poor shelter to erect
Now plans the engineer and architect;

Where the lone crone o'er naked babes held rule
Our children know the college and the school;
Art has arisen, science lights and leads;
Labor enriches life with wondrous deeds;
But while the ages urge us, shock on shock,
Thou standest, changeless as primeval rock—
Unchangeable, immovable—we see
Our race's earliest infancy in thee!
Deaf patience and blind habit; and the dumb
Submission of long ages—these have come
To thee instead of progress. Must thou last
Forever?—type of Paleolithic past!

Wedded Bliss

"O come and be my mate!" said the Eagle to the Hen;
"I love to soar, but then
I want my mate to rest
Forever in the nest!"
Said the Hen, "I cannot fly,
I have no wish to try,
But I joy to see my mate careering through the sky!"
They wed, and cried, "Ah, this is Love, my own!"
And the Hen sat, the Eagle soared, alone.

"O come and be my mate!" said the Lion to the Sheep;
"My love for you is deep!
I slay, a Lion should,
But you are mild and good!"
Said the Sheep, "I do no ill—
Could not, had I the will—
But I joy to see my mate pursue, devour, and kill."
They wed, and cried, "Ah, this is Love, my own!"
And the Sheep browsed, the Lion prowled, alone.

"O come and be my mate!" said the Salmon to the Clam;
"You are not wise, but I am.
I know sea and stream as well;
You know nothing but your shell."
Said the Clam, "I'm slow of motion,
But my love is all devotion,
And I joy to have my mate traverse lake and stream and ocean!"
They wed, and cried, "Ah, this is Love, my own!"
And the Clam sucked, the Salmon swam, alone.

Unsexed

It was a wild rebellious drone
That loudly did complain;
He wished he was a worker bee
With all his might and main.

"I want to work," the drone declared.
Quoth they, "The thing you mean
Is that you scorn to be a drone
And long to be a queen.

"You long to lay unnumbered eggs,
And rule the waiting throng;
You long to lead our summer flight,
And this is rankly wrong."

Cried he, "My life is pitiful!
I only eat and wed,
And in my marriage is the end—
Thereafter I am dead.

"I would I were the busy bee
That flits from flower to flower;

I long to share in work and care
And feel the worker's power."

Quoth they, "The life you dare to spurn
Is set before you here
As your one great, prescribed, ordained,
Divinely ordered sphere!

"Without your services as drone,
We should not be alive;
Your modest task, when well fulfilled,
Preserves the busy hive.

"Why underrate your blessed power?
Why leave your rightful throne
To choose a field of life that's made
For working bees alone?"

Cried he, "But it is not enough,
My momentary task!
Let me do that and more beside:
To work is all I ask!"

Then fiercely rose the workers all,
For sorely were they vexed;
"O wretch!" they cried, "should this betide,
You would become *unsexed!*"

And yet he had not sighed for eggs,
Nor yet for royal mien;
He longed to be a worker bee,
But not to be a queen.

Females

The female fox she is a fox;
The female whale a whale;
The female eagle holds her place
As representative of race
As truly as the male.

The mother hen doth scratch for her chicks,
And scratch for herself beside;
The mother cow doth nurse her calf,
Yet fares as well as her other half
In the pasture free and wide.

The female bird doth soar in air;
The female fish doth swim;
The fleet-foot mare upon the course
Doth hold her own with the flying horse—
Yea, and she beateth him!

One female in the world we find
Telling a different tale.
It is the female of our race,
Who holds a parasitic place
Dependent on the male.

Not so, saith she, ye slander me!
No parasite am I!
I earn my living as a wife;
My children take my very life.
Why should I share in human strife.
To plant and build and buy?

The human race holds highest place
In all the world so wide,
Yet these inferior females wive,

And raise their little ones alive,
And feed themselves beside.

The race is higher than the sex,
Though sex be fair and good;
A Human Creature is your state,
And to be human is more great
Than even womanhood!

The female fox she is a fox;
The female whale a whale;
The female eagle holds her place
As representative of race
As truly as the male.

More Females of the Species (After Kipling)

When the traveller in the pasture meets the he-bull in his pride,
He shouts to scare the monster, who will often turn aside;
But the milch cow, thus accosted, pins the traveller to the rail—
For the female of the species is deadlier than the male.

When Nag, the raging stallion, meets a careless man on foot,
He will sometimes not destroy him, even if the man don't shoot;
But the mare, if he should meet one, makes the bravest cowboy
    pale—
For the female of the species is more deadly than the male.

When our first colonial settlers met the Hurons and Choctaws,
They were burned and scalped and slaughtered by the fury-
    breathing squaws;
'Twas the women, not the warriors, who in war-paint took the
    trail—
For the female of the species is more deadly than the male.

Man's timid heart is bursting with the things he must not say
As to women, lest in speaking he should give himself away;
But when he meets a woman—see him tremble and turn pale—
For the female of the species is more deadly than the male.

Lay your money on the hen-fight! On the dog-fight fought by shes!
On the gory Ladies Prize-fight—there are none so fierce as these!
See small girls each other pounding, while their peaceful brothers
    wail—
For the female of the species is more deadly than the male.

So, in history they tell us how all China shrieked and ran
Before the wholesale slaughter dealt by Mrs. Genghis Khan.
And Attila, the Scourage of God, who made all Europe quail,
Was a female of the species and more deadly than the male.

Red war with all its million dead is due to female rage,
The names of women murderers monopolize the page,
The pranks of a Napoleon are nothing to the tale
Of destruction wrought by females, far more deadly than the male.

In the baleful female infant this ferocity we spy,
It glares in bloodshot fury from the maiden's dewy eye,
But the really deadly female, when you see her at her best,
Has two babies at her petticoat and a suckling at her breast.

Yet hold! there is Another! A monster even worse!
The Terror of Humanity! Creation's direst curse!
Before whom men in thousands must tremble, shrink and fail—
A sanguinary Grandma—more deadly than the male!

This is a Lady's Hat (a Trio of Triolets)

This is a lady's hat—
To cover the seat of reason;

It may look like a rabbit or bat,
Yet this is a lady's hat;
May be ugly, ridiculous, that
We never remark, 'twould be treason.
This is a lady's hat,
To cover the seat of reason.

These are a lady's shoes,
Ornaments, curved and bended,
But feet are given to use,
Not merely to show off shoes,
To stand, walk, run if we choose,
For which these were never intended.
These are a lady's shoes.
Ornaments, curved and bended.

This is a lady's skirt,
Which limits her locomotion;
Her shape is so smooth-begirt
As to occupy all the skirt,
Of being swift and alert
She has not the slightest notion;
This is a lady's skirt,
Which limits her locomotion.

The Cripple

There are such things as feet, human feet,
But these she does not use;
Firm and supple, white and sweet,
Softly graceful, lightly fleet,
For comfort, beauty, service meet—
These are feet, human feet,
These she doth with scorn refuse—
Preferring shoes.

There are such things as shoes, human shoes,
Though scant and rare the proof;
Serviceable, soft and strong,
Pleasant, comely, wearing long,
Easy as a well known song—
These are shoes, human shoes,
But from these she holds aloof—
Prefers the hoof!

There are such things as hoofs, sub-human hoofs,
High-heeled sharp anomalies;
Small and pinching, hard and black,
Shiny as a beetle's back,
Cloven, clattering on the track,
These are hoofs, sub-human hoofs,
She cares not for truth, nor ease—
Preferring these!

A Protest

O mother! mother! cried the babe,
Why must I lie so warm?
With woolens thick
That clog and stick
All round my feeble form?

I want to stretch and feel myself
I want to wiggle there—
Why don't you pull
This heap of wool?
Why don't you warm the air?

O mother! cried the little maid,
Why must my dress be fine?
While brother goes

In knicks and hose,
Why are these ruffles mine?

I want to run and roll and climb,
To play, perhaps to fight!
He tumbles down,
Unblamed, in brown—
Why must I mince in white?

His cap is easy on his head,
Alert and free his face—
Why must I wear
O'er eyes and hair
This cauliflower of lace?

Why trail these yards of lengthening skirt
By his brief trouser line?
If I'm so weak
O mother, speak!
Why must the weight be mine?

The mother answered never a word,
But from her eyes shone through
The primal pride
Of the savage bride
In a veil of rich tattoo.

No mercy had she on herself,
No mercy on the child;
As gods to her
Are plume and fur,
By beads is she beguiled.

Exiles

Exiled from home. The far sea rolls
Between them and the country of their birth;
The childhood-turning impulse of their souls
Pulls half across the earth.

Exiled from home. No mother to take care
That they work not too hard, grieve not too sore;
No older brother nor small sister fair;
No father any more.

Exiled from home; from all familiar things;
The low-browed roof, the grass-surrounded door;
Accustomed labors that gave daylight wings;
Loved steps on the worn floor.

Exiled from home. Young girls sent forth alone
When most their hearts need close companioning;
No love and hardly friendship may they own,
No voice of welcoming.

Blinded with homesick tears the exile stands;
To toil for alien household gods she comes;
A servant and a stranger in our lands,
Homeless within our homes.

Where Women Meet

Where women meet!—The village well
Was once their place; the convent cell
For centuries asleep and slow,
Gave all the grouping they could know
Or market-place, to buy and sell.

Now year by year their numbers swell
In crowded halls, 'neath chairman's bell;
To aid the weak, to lift the low,
To urge the right—these efforts show
Where women meet.

New light, our shadows to dispel—
New power beyond all parallel
From motherhood combined shall flow
Helping our stumbling race to grow,—
And a clean happy world will tell
Where women meet.

One Girl of Many

One girl of many. Hungry from her birth
Half-fed. Half-clothed. Untaught of woman's worth.
In joyless girlhood working for her bread.
At each small sorrow wishing she were dead,
Yet gay at little pleasures. Sunlight seems.
Most bright and warm where it most seldom gleams.

One girl of many. Tawdry dress and old;
And not enough beneath to bar the cold.
The little that she had misspent because
She had no knowledge of our nature's laws.
Thinking in ignorance that it was best
To wear a stylish look, and—bear the rest.

One girl of many. With a human heart.
A woman's too; with nerves that feel the smart
Of each new pain as keenly as your own.
The old ones, through long use, have softer grown.
And yet in spite of use she holds the thought
Of might-be joys more than, perhaps, she ought.

One girl of many. But the fault is here;
Though she to all the others was so near;
One difference there was, which made a change.
No wrong thing, surely. Consequence most strange!
Alike in birth. Alike in life's rough way.
She, through no evil, was more fair than they.

So came the offer, "Leave this story cold
Where you may drudge and starve till you are old.
Come! I will give you rest. And food. And fire.
And fair apparel to your heart's desire;
Shelter. Protection. Kindness. Peace and Love.
Has your life anything you hold above?"

And she had not. In all her daily sight
There shone no vestige of the color White.
She had seen nothing in her narrow life
To make her venerate the title "Wife."
She knew no reason why the thing was wrong;
And instinct grows debased in ages long.

All things that she had ever yet desired
All dreams that her starved girlhood's heart had fired
All that life held of yet unknown delight
Shone, to her ignorance, in colors bright.
Shone near at hand and sure. If she had *known!*
But she was ignorant. She was alone.

And so she—sinned. I think we call it sin.
And found that every step she took therein
Made sinning easier and conscience weak.
And there was never one who cared to speak
A word to guide and warn her. If there were
I fear such help were thrown away on her.

Only one girl of many. Of the street.
In lowest depths. The story grows unmeet
For wellbred ears. Sorrow and sin and shame
Over and over till the blackened name
Sank out of sight without a hand to save.
Sin, shame, and sorrow. Sickness, and the grave.

Only one girl of many. 'Tis a need
Of man's existence to repeat the deed.
Social necessity. Men cannot live
Without what these disgraceful creatures give.
Black shame. Dishonor. Misery and Sin.
And men find needed health and life therein.

Unmentionable

There is a thing of which I fain would speak,
Yet shun the deed;
Lest hot disgust flush the averted cheek
Of those who read.

And yet it is as common in our sight
As dust or grass;
Loathed by the lifted skirt, the tiptoe light,
Of those who pass.

We say no word, but the big placard rests
Frequent in view,
To sicken those who do not with requests
Of those who do.

"Gentlemen will not," the mild placards say.
They read with scorn.
"Gentlemen must not"—they defile the way
Of those who warn.

On boat and car the careful lady lifts
Her dress aside;
If careless—think, fair traveller, of the gifts
Of those who ride!

On every hall and sidewalk, floor and stair,
Where man's at home,
This loathsomeness is added to the care
Of those who come.

As some foul slug his trail of slime displays
On leaf and stalk,
These street-beasts make a horror in the ways
Of those who walk.

We cannot ask reform of those who do—
They can't or won't.
We can express the scorn, intense and true,
Of those who don't.

A Social Puzzle

Society sat musing, very sad,
Upon her people's conduct, which was bad.
Said she, "I can't imagine why they sin,
With all the education I put in!
For instance, why so many maimed and sick
After their schooling in arithmetic?
Why should they cheat each other beyond telling
When they were so well grounded in good spelling?
They learned geography by land and tribe,
And yet my statesmen can't refuse a bribe!
Ought not a thorough knowledge of old Greek
To lead to that wide peace the nations seek?
And grammar! With their grammar understood

Why should they still shed one another's blood?
Then, lest these ounces of prevention fail,
I've pounds and tons of cure—of no avail.
I punish terribly, and I have cause,
When they so sin against my righteous laws."

"Of grammar?" I enquired. She look perplexed.
"For errors in their spelling?" She grew vexed.
"Failure in mathematics?" "You young fool!"
She said, "The law don't meddle with the school.
I teach with care and cost, but never ask
What conduct follows from the early task.
My punishment, for all the law's wide reach,
Is in the lines I don't pretend to teach."

I meditated. Does one plant him corn—
Then weep because no oranges are born?

The Holy Stove

O the soap-vat is a common thing!
The pickle-tub is low!
The loom and wheel have lost their grace
In falling from the dwelling-place
To mills where all may go!
The bread-tray needeth not your love;
The wash-tub wide doth roam;
Even the oven free may rove;
But bow ye down to the Holy Stove,
The Altar of the Home!

Before it bend the worshippers,
And wreaths of parsley twine;
Above it still the incense curls,
And a passing train of hired girls

Do service at the shrine.
We toil to keep the altar crowned
With dishes new and nice,
And Art and Love, and Time and Truth,
We offer up, with Health and Youth,
In daily sacrifice.

Speak not to us of a fairer faith,
Of a lifetime free from pain.
Our fathers always worshipped here,
Our mothers served this altar drear,
And still we serve amain.
Our earliest dreams around it cling,
Bright hopes that childhood sees,
And memory leaves a vista wide
Where Mother's Doughnuts rank beside
The thought of Mother's Knees.

The wood-box hath no sanctity;
No glamour gilds the coal;
But the Cook-Stove is a sacred thing
To which a reverent faith we bring
And serve with heart and soul.
The Home's a temple all divine,
By the Poker and the Hod!
The Holy Stove is the altar fine,
The wife the priestess at the shrine—
Now who can be the god?

Christian Virtues

Oh dear!
The Christian virtues will disappear!
Nowhere on land or sea
Will be room for charity!

Nowhere, in field or city,
A person to help or pity!
Better for them, no doubt,
Not to need helping out
Of their old miry ditch.
But, alas for us, the rich!
For we shall lose, you see,
Our boasted charity!—
Lose all the pride and joy
Of giving the poor employ,
And money, and food, and love
(And making stock thereof!).
Our Christian virtues are gone,
With nothing to practice on!

It don't hurt them a bit,
For they can't practice it;
But it's our great joy and pride—
What virtue have we beside?
We believe, as sure as we live,
That it is more blessed to give
Than to want, and waste, and grieve,
And occasionally receive!
And here are the people pressing
To rob us of our pet blessing!
No chance to endow or bedizen
A hospital, school, or prison,

And leave our own proud name
To Gratitude and Fame!
No chance to do one good deed,
To give what we do not need,
To leave what we cannot use
To those whom we deign to choose!
When none want broken meat,
How shall our cake be sweet?

When none want flannels and coals,
How shall we save our souls?
Oh, dear! Oh, dear!
The Christian virtues will disappear!

The poor have their virtues rude,—
Meekness and gratitude,
Endurance, and respect
For us, the world's elect;
Economy, self-denial,
Patience in every trial,
Self-sacrifice, self-restraint,—
Virtues enough for a saint!
Virtues enough to bear
All this life's sorrow and care!
Virtues by which to rise
To a front seat in the skies!
How can they turn from this
To common earthly bliss,—
Mere clothes, and food, and drink,
And leisure to read and think,
And art, and beauty, and ease,—
There is no crown for these!
True, if their gratitude
Were not for fire and food,
They might still learn to bless
The Lord for their happiness!
And, instead of respect for wealth,
Might learn from beauty, and health,
And freedom in power and pelf,
Each man to respect himself!
And, instead of scraping and saving,
Might learn from using and having
That man's life should be spent
In a grand development!
But this is petty and small;

These are not virtues at all;
They do not look as they should;
They don't do *us* any good!
Oh, dear! Oh, dear! Oh, dear!
The Christian virtues will disappear!

Another Creed

Another creed! We're all so pleased!
A gentle tentative new creed. We're eased
Of all those things we couldn't quite believe
But would not give the lie to. Now perceive
How charmingly this suits us! Science even
Has naught against our modern views of Heaven;
And yet the most emotional of women
May find this creed a warm deep sea to swim in.

Here's something now so loose and large of fit
That all the churches may come under it,
And we may see upon the earth once more
A church united—as we had before!
Before so much of precious blood was poured
That each in his own way might serve the Lord.
All wide divergence in sweet union sunk—
Like branches growing up into a trunk!

And in our intellectual delight
In this sweet formula that sets us right;
And controversial exercises gay
With those who still prefer a differing way;
And our glad effort to make known this wonder
And get all others to unite thereunder—
We, joying in this newest, best of creeds,
Continue still to do our usual deeds!

To Man

In dark and early ages, through the primal forests faring,
Ere the soul came shining into prehistoric night,
Two-fold man was equal; they were comrades dear and daring,
Living wild and free together in unreasoning delight.

Ere the soul was born and consciousness came slowly,
Ere the soul was born, to man and woman too,
Ere he found the Tree of Knowledge, that awful tree and holy,
Ere he knew he felt, and knew he knew.
Then said he to Pain, "I am wise now, and I know you!
No more will I suffer while power and wisdom last!"
Then said he to Pleasure," I am strong, and I will show you
That the will of man can seize you; aye, and hold you fast!"
Food he ate for pleasure, and wine he drank for gladness,
And woman? Ah, the woman! the crown of all delight!—
His now—he knew it! He was strong to madness
In that early dawning after prehistoric night.
His—his forever! That glory sweet and tender!
Ah, but he would love her! And she should love but him!
He would work and struggle for her, he would shelter and defend
    her;
She should never leave him, never, till their eyes in death were dim.
Close, close he bound her, that she should leave him never;
Weak still he kept her, lest she be strong to flee;
And the fainting flame of passion he kept alive forever
With all the arts and forces of earth and sky and sea.

And, ah, the long journey! The slow and awful ages
They have labored up together, blind and crippled, all astray!
Through what a mighty volume, with a million shameful pages,
From the freedom of the forest to the prisons of to-day!
Food he ate for pleasure, and it slew him with diseases!
Wine he drank for gladness, and it led the way to crime!

And woman? He will hold her—he will have her when he
　　pleases—
And he never once hath seen her since the pre-historic time!

Gone the friend and comrade of the day when life was younger,
She who rests and comforts, she who helps and saves;
Still he seeks her vainly, with a never-dying hunger;
Alone beneath his tyrants, alone above his slaves!

Toiler, bent and weary with the load of thine own making!
Thou who art sad and lonely, though lonely all in vain!
Who hast sought to conquer Pleasure and have her for the taking,
And found that Pleasure only was another name for Pain,—
Nature, hath reclaimed thee, forgiving dispossession!
God hath not forgotten, though man doth still forget!
The woman-soul is rising, in despite of thy transgression!
Loose her now—and trust her! She will love thee yet!

Love thee? She will love thee as only freedom knoweth;
Love thee? She will love thee while Love itself doth live!
Fear not the heart of woman! No bitterness it showeth!
The ages of her sorrow have but taught her to forgive!

To the Preacher

Preach about yesterday, Preacher!
The time so far away:
When the hand of Deity smote and slew,
And the heathen plagued the stiff-necked Jew;
Or when the Man of Sorrows came,
And blessed the people who cursed his name—
Preach about yesterday, Preacher!
Not about to-day!

Preach about to-morrow, Preacher!
Beyond this world's decay:
Of the sheepfold Paradise we priced
When we pinned our faith to Jesus Christ;
Of those hot depths that shall receive
The goats who would not so believe—
Preach about to-morrow, Preacher,
Not about to-day!

Preach about the old sins, Preacher!
And the old virtues, too:
You must not steal nor take man's life,
You must not covet your neighbor's wife,
And woman must cling at every cost
To her one virtue, or she is lost—
Preach about the old sins, Preacher!
Not about the new!

Preach about the other man, Preacher!
The man we all can see!
The man of oaths, the man of strife,
The man who drinks and beats his wife,
Who helps his mates to fret and shirk
When all they need is to keep at work—
Preach about the other man, Preacher!
Not about me!

The Real Religion

Man, the hunter, Man, the warrior;
Slew for gain and slew for safety,
Slew for rage, for sport, for glory—
Slaughter was his breath:
So the man's mind, searching inward,
Saw in all one red reflection,

Filled the world with dark religions
Built on Death.

Death and The Fate of The Soul;—
The soul, from the body dissevered;
Through the withering failure of age,
Through the horror and pain of disease,
Through raw wounds and destruction and fear:—
In fear, black fear of the dark,
Red fear of terrible gods,
Sent forth on its journey, alone,
To eternity, fearful, unknown—
Death, and The Fate of the Soul.

Woman, bearer; Woman, teacher;
Overflowing love and labor,
Service of the tireless mother
Filling all the earth;—
Now her mind, awakening, searching,
Sees a fair world, young and growing,
Sees at last our real religion—
Built on Birth.

Birth, and the Growth of The Soul;—
The Soul, in the body established;
In the ever-new beauty of childhood,
In the wonder of opening power,
Still learning, improving, achieving;
In hope, new knowledge and light,
Sure faith in the world's fresh Spring,—
Together we live, we grow,
On the earth that we love and know—
Birth, and the Growth of the Soul.

Body of Mine

Body of mine! That once was fair—
Soft, smooth, and fair—
Glad was my soul in its garment fine,
Glad of the crown of shining hair.
Color of roses, eyes of the sea—
Glad and proud was my soul of thee,
Body of mine!

Body of mine! That once was young,
Slim, swift, and young.
Glad was my heart with youth's rich wine,
Spring in the footstep—song on the tongue,
Joylight and lovelight shining on me—
Glad and gay was my heart in thee,
Body of mine!

Body of mine that now grows old—
Thin, dry, and old—
Flowers may wither and pets may pine,
Fire of passion grow palely cold—
But the living world is the frame of me—
Heart and soul are not found in thee—
Body of mine!

The world, the sky, and the work of our hands,
Wonderful work of our hands!
Clothe my soul in a form divine
Young forever to all demands
Ageless and deathless and boundless and free
Glory and joy do I find in thee,
Body of mine!

Nationalism

The nation is a unit. That which makes
You an American of our to-day
Requires the nation and its history,
Requires the sum of all our citizens,
Requires the product of our common toil,
Requires the freedom of our common laws,
The common heart of our humanity.
Decrease our population, check our growth,
Deprive us of our wealth, our liberty,
Lower the nation's conscience by a hair,
And you are less than that you were before!
You stand here in the world the man you are
Because your country is America.
Our liberty belongs to each of us;
The nation guarantees it; in return
We serve the nation, serving so ourselves.
Our education is a common right;
The state provides it, equally to all,
Each taking what he can, and in return
We serve the state, so serving best ourselves.
Food, clothing, all necessities of life,—
These are a right as much as liberty!
The nation feeds its children. In return
We serve the nation, serving still ourselves—
Nay, not ourselves—ourself! We are but parts,
The unit is the state,—America.

Matriatism

Small is the thought of "Fatherland,"
With all its pride and worth;
With all its history of death;
Of fire and sword and wasted breath—

By the great new thought which quickeneth—
The thought of "Mother Earth."
Man fights for wealth and rule and pride,
For the "name" that is his alone;
Comes woman, wakening to her power,
Comes woman, opening the hour
That sees life as one growing flower,
All children as her own.

Fathers have fought for their Fatherland
With slaughter and death and dearth,
But mothers, in service and love's increase,
Will labor together for our release,
From a war-stained past to a world at peace,
Our fair, sweet Mother Earth.

The Artist

Here one of us is born, made as a lens,
Or else to lens-shape cruelly smooth-ground,
To gather light, the light that shines on all,
In concentrated flame it glows, pure fire,
With light a hundredfold, more light for all.

Come and receive, take with the eye or ear,
Take and be filled, illumined, overflowed;
Then go and shine again, your whole work lit,
Your whole heart warm and luminous and glad;
Go shine again—and spread the gladness wide;

Happy the lens! To gather skies of light
And focus it, making the splendor there!
Happy all we who are enriched therewith,
And redistribute ever, swift and far.

The artist is the intermediate lens
Of God, and so best gives Him to the world,
Intensified, interpreted, to us.

Lecture Verse [No. 1]

To all you friends who've gathered here tonight,
And paid for this address with solid money,
I want to say—don't look for wild delight—
This lecture isn't funny!

It is an earnest lecture, written straight
From out one woman's heart to enter many;
And if you ask excuse for facts, I state—
Alas! I haven't any!

For facts are stubborn things, and it is true,
In spite of chivalry and poem and story,
That so far, in the race of which are you—
Man has the glory.

The glory and the shame! He did the deeds
Which fill the world with beauty, power, and wonder;
He kept supplied the wider human needs,—
And kept us under!

And what I wish to urge, to thinking minds,
Is that the race will thrive, both man and woman,
When every baby in its parents find,
That *both* are Human!

S hira Wolosky received her Ph.D. from Princeton University, and was an Associate Professor of English at Yale University before moving to the Hebrew University of Jerusalem, where she is a Professor of English and American Literature. She has written *Emily Dickinson: A Voice of War; Language Mysticism; The Art of Poetry;* and *Poetry and Public Discourse: Nineteenth-Century American Poetry; The Cambridge History of American Literature Vol. 4,* forthcoming.

Articles focusing on nineteenth-century American Women's poetry include: "Public Woman, Private Man: American Women Poets and the Common Good," *Signs,* Winter 2003 Vol. 28, no. 2, 665–694; "Women's Bibles," *Feminist Studies,* Vol. 28, no. 1, Spring 2002, 191–211; "Charlotte Gilman's Public Poetry," *Sources,* Spring No. 12, 2002, pp. 11–28.

"Public and Private in Emily Dickinson's War Poetry," ed. Vivian Pollack, *Oxford Historical Readings of Emily Dickinson,* forthcoming 2004; "Being in the Body," *Cambridge Companion to Emily Dickinson,* ed. Wendy Martin, New York: Cambridge University Press, 2002, 129–141; "The Metaphysics of Language in Emily Dickinson and Paul Celan," *Trajectories of Mysticism,* ed. Philip Leonard, New York, St. Martin's Press, 2000, 25–45.

Further Reading

Listed here are only book length studies, for background and discussion of nineteenth-century women poets and their surrounding historical contexts.

Baym, Nina. *Feminism and American Literary History*. New Brunswick: Rutgers University Press, 1992.

Nancy Cott, *The Bonds of Womanhood: "Women's Sphere" in New England 1780–1835*. New Haven: Yale University Press, 1977.

Degler, Carl. *At Odds: Women and the Family in America from the Revolution to the Present*. New York: Oxford University Press, 1980.

Dickson, Jr. Bruce. *Black American Writing from the Nadir*. Baton Rouge: Louisiana State University Press, 1989.

Dobson, Joanne. *Dickinson and the Strategies of Reticence*. Bloomington: Indiana University Press, 1989.

Douglas, Ann. *The Feminization of American Culture*. New York: Anchor Books, 1977.

Du Bois, W.E.B. *The Souls of Black Folk.* New York: Bantam Books, 1989.

Gilbert, Sandra and Susan Gubar. *The Madwoman in the Attic.* New Haven: Yale University Press, 1979.

Ginzberg, Lori. *Women and the Work of Benevolence.* New Haven: Yale University Press, 1990.

Higginson, Thomas Wentworth. *Army Life in a Black Regiment.* Detroit: Michigan State University Press, 1960.

Higham, John. *Send These To Me.* New York: Atheneaum, 1975.

Homans, Margaret. *Women Writers and Poetic Identity.* Princeton: Princeton University Press, 1980.

Juhasz, Suzanne. *Naked and Fiery Forms.* New York: Harper and Row, 1976.

Kasson, John F. *Rudeness and Civility.* New York: Hill and Wang, 1990.

Kerber, Linda. *Women of the Republic.* Chapel Hill, NC: University of North Carolina Press, 1980.

Michaels, Walter Benn and Donald Pease, eds. *The American Renaissance Reconsidered.* Baltimore: Johns Hopkins University Press, 1985.

McPherson, James. *Battle-Cry of Freedom,* New York: Ballantine Books, 1988.

Macpherson, C.B. *The Political Theory of Possessive Individualism,* London: Oxford University Press, 1962.

Mary Beth Norton. *Liberty's Daughters: The Revolutionary Experience of American Women.* Boston: Little, Brown and Company, 1980.

Ostriker, Alicia. *Stealing the Language.* Boston: Beacon Press, 1986.

Smith-Rosenberg, Carroll. *Disorderly Conduct: Visions of Gender in Victorial America.* New York: Alfred A. Knopf, 1985.

Ruether, Rosemary Radford and Rosemary Skinner Keller, eds. *Women and Religion in America*. Vol. 1. San Francisco: Harper and Row, 1981.

Ryan, Mary. *Womanhood in America*. New York: New Viewpoints, 1975.

Stanton, Elizabeth Cady. *The Woman's Bible*. Seattle: Coalition Task Force on Women and Religion, 1974.

Sundquist, Eric. *To Wake the Nations*. Cambridge, Mass.: Harvard University Press, 1993.

Toqueville, Alexis De. *Democracy in America*. New York: Vintage Books, 1945.

Trachtenberg, Alan. *The Incorporation of America*. New York: Hill and Wang, 1982

Tuveson, Ernest Lee. *Redeemer Nation*. Chicago: The University of Chicago Press, 1968.

Walker, Cheryl. *The Nightingale's Burden*. Bloomington, Indiana: Indiana University Press, 1986.

The fonts used in this book are from the Garamond family

Best Ever
Three & Four
Ingredient
Cookbook

Best Ever

Three & Four Ingredient

Cookbook

400 Fuss-free and fast recipes — breakfasts, appetizers, lunches, suppers and desserts using only four ingredients or less

JENNY WHITE & JOANNA FARROW

HERMES
HOUSE

This edition is published by Hermes House

Hermes House is an imprint of Anness Publishing Ltd
Hermes House, 88–89 Blackfriars Road, London SE1 8HA
tel. 020 7401 2077; fax 020 7633 9499; info@anness.com

A CIP catalogue record for this book is available from the British Library.

Publisher: Joanna Lorenz
Editorial Director: Judith Simons
Senior Editor: Doreen Gillon
Copy-editors: Bridget Jones and Sally Somers
Photography: Tim Auty, Martin Brigdale, Nicky Dowey, Gus Filgate, Michelle Garrett, Amanda
Heywood, William Lingwood, Craig Robertson, Simon Smith
Home Economist: Jenny White
Home Economist's Assistant: Fergul Connolly
Stylist: Helen Trent
Designer: Paul Oakley
Additional Recipes: Pepita Aris, Alex Barker, Georgina Campbell, Jacqueline Clark, Joanna Farrow,
Brian Glover, Christine Ingram, Becky Johnson, Jane Milton, Jennie Shapter, Marlena Spieler, Linda
Tubby, Kate Whiteman, Jeni Wright
Production Controller: Pedro Nelson

Previously published as *The Three Ingredient Cookbook* and *200 Four Ingredient Recipes*

10 9 8 7 6 5 4 3 2 1

NOTES
Bracketed terms are intended for American readers.

For all recipes, quantities are given in both metric and imperial measures and, where appropriate,
measures are also given in standard cups and spoons. Follow one set, but not a mixture, because
they are not interchangeable.

Standard spoon and cup measures are level.
1 tsp = 5ml, 1 tbsp = 15ml, 1 cup = 250ml/8fl oz

Australian standard tablespoons are 20ml. Australian readers should use 3 tsp in place of 1 tbsp for
measuring small quantities of gelatine, flour, salt etc.

Medium (US large) eggs are used unless otherwise stated.

Contents

Cooking with Three and Four Ingredients

Just because a dish includes only a few ingredients, it doesn't mean you need to compromise on taste and enjoyment. Reducing the number of ingredients you use in a dish has many benefits. Not only does it make shopping easier and quicker, it also means spending less time on preparation because there's less measuring, peeling, scrubbing and chopping to be done. It also allows you to really enjoy the flavours of the few ingredients used. Fresh food tastes fantastic, so why not let the flavours of a few truly fabulous ingredients shine through rather than masking them with the taste of other ingredients?

Keeping it quick, keeping it simple

In today's busy world, time is of the essence – and no one ever seems to have enough of it. When you're trying to cram as much as possible into a single day, often the first thing that falls by the wayside is cooking. When you're busy, the last thing you feel like doing is spending an hour in the supermarket shopping for ingredients, then going home and preparing them before finally cooking a meal. The temptation is to grab a ready-prepared meal to heat up when you get home, or to pick up a takeaway – but sometimes, when you've had a hectic day at work or your kids have been running you ragged, what you really want is to sit down and relax with a tasty home-cooked meal. This book is devoted to helping you do just this.

The idea of making a dish that requires a huge list of ingredients can often put you off before you've even started – the shopping and preparation alone seeming like an unmanageable task. But the good news is that cooking doesn't need to be this way. It's incredibly easy to make delicious dishes using just a few simple ingredients – but the key to success lies in the ingredients you choose, and how you prepare and cook them.

Above and opposite: *You need only three ingredients to make this fabulous dish of spaghetti with broccoli and spicy chilli. It tastes delicious and can be made in less than 15 minutes.*

Using the right ingredients

The recipes in this book combine basic ingredients such as fruit, vegetables, meat, fish, herbs and spices, but they also make good use of ready-made or pre-prepared products such as curry pastes and pastry. Using these convenient products is a great way to save time, both on preparation and shopping, and can sometimes enhance the final dish in a way that the home-made version may not. For example, puff pastry is enormously difficult to make, while the bought varieties are easy to use, give great results and taste delicious.

When buying basic ingredients, always try to buy the freshest, best quality ones you can to get the maximum flavour. Really fresh ingredients also have the benefit of having a higher nutritional content. If you can buy organic produce, do so. The flavour will be better and you will have the knowledge that they do not contain chemical fertilizers and pesticides.

It is also a good idea to buy fruits and vegetables when they're in season. Although most are available all year round, you can really notice the difference between those that have been ripened naturally and those that have been grown out of season. Strawberries may be available in the middle of winter, but when you cut them open they are often white inside with a slightly waxy texture and none of the sweet, juicy, almost perfumed flavour of the summer fruits. There are so many fabulous ingredients at their peak in their own season that you don't have to buy unseasonal ones. Why buy tired-looking asparagus in autumn when there are plenty of mushrooms, squashes and root vegetables around – all of which can be made into a huge number of delicious, varied meals.

When buying pre-prepared or ready-made ingredients such as stocks for soups or custard to make ice cream, try to buy really good-quality, fresh varieties. When an ingredient is playing an intregral part in a dish, it needs to be well flavoured with a good texture and consistency. If you use a less good product with an inferior flavour, it will really show in the final dish. The same is true of flavouring ingredients such as curry pastes and spicy sauces – go for quality every time and you will reap the benefits.

About this book

Whether you're an experienced cook or an absolute beginner, you'll find the recipes in this book will suit you perfectly. There are dishes for every occasion: juices to quench your thirst; healthy breakfasts and light lunches to make when time is short. There are also fabulous meat, fish and vegetarian dishes to cook when you have more time on your hands or if you're entertaining guests. There is a selection of divine dishes to eat outside when the weather's sunny, and when you need a sweet treat, there are whole chapters devoted to cookies and cakes and sumptuous hot, cold and iced desserts. No matter what the occasion, how much time you have, how many people you need to feed, or what you're in the mood for – you are sure to find the perfect dish within these pages.

Every recipe has an ingredients list of four items or fewer, and the only other things you will need will come from the storecupboard (pantry): oil or butter to cook with and salt and freshly ground black pepper to season the food. In some cases flavoured oils such as garlic-, lemon-, or herb-infused olive oil are used for cooking or drizzling, so it's well worth keeping a small selection of these oils in the storecupboard.

The Minimalist Kitchen

WHEN YOU'RE USING ONLY THREE OR FOUR INGREDIENTS TO MAKE A DISH, EACH ONE NEEDS TO BE A STAR PLAYER. THIS CHAPTER GUIDES YOU THROUGH THE INTRICACIES OF CHOOSING, PREPARING AND COOKING INGREDIENTS TO ACHIEVE THE BEST RESULTS AND OFFERS TIPS ON MAXIMIZING FLAVOUR USING SIMPLE COOKING TECHNIQUES. THERE ARE RECIPES FOR MAKING BASIC INGREDIENTS SUCH AS FLAVOURED OILS, STOCKS AND SAUCES, PLUS SUGGESTIONS FOR SIMPLE ACCOMPANIMENTS AS WELL AS ADVICE ON MENU PLANNING TO ENSURE SUCCESS EVERY TIME.

Equipment

You don't need a kitchen full of equipment to be a spontaneous and versatile cook. It is quality, not quantity, that counts when you're preparing and cooking food, particularly when choosing essential pieces of equipment such as pans and knives. As long as you look after them, these items should last for many years so are well worth the investment. The following section guides you through the essential items that make cooking as simple and enjoyable as possible, and also offers suggestions on how to improvise if you don't have the right piece of equipment.

Pans and bakeware

Always choose good-quality pans with a solid, heavy base: they retain heat better and are less likely to warp or buckle. Heatproof glass lids are useful because they allow you to check cooking progress without having to uncover the pan repeatedly.

Pans: small, medium and large When cooking large quantities of food, such as pasta or rice, that need to be boiled in a large amount of water, the bigger the pan the better. It does not matter whether the pan is non-stick, but it is useful to have heatproof handles and lids so that the pan can double as a large ovenproof cookpot. A medium-size pan is ideal for cooking sauces and similar mixtures. Ideally, choose a non-stick pan, which will help to prevent thickened sauces sticking and burning. It also makes washing-up easier. The same guidelines apply to a small pan, which is ideal for small quantities.

Above: *Choose good-quality, heavy baking sheets because lightweight sheets tend to buckle in the oven.*

Frying pan Select a non-stick pan that is shallow enough that you can easily slide a fish slice or metal spatula into it. A pan with an ovenproof handle and lid can be placed in the oven and used as a shallow casserole dish.

Baking sheets Having one or two non-stick baking sheets in the kitchen is invaluable. They can be used for a multitude of tasks such as baking cookies and bread, or they can be placed under full dishes in the oven to catch any drips if the mixture overflows.

Roasting pan A good, heavy roasting pan is essential for roasting large cuts of meat and vegetables. Choose a large pan; you will achieve better results if there is room for heat to circulate as the food cooks. Potatoes, for example, will not crisp well if they are crammed together in a small pan.

Left: *It is wise to invest in three good-quality pans of different sizes. Treat them with care and you will get maximum use from them.*

Cutting and grinding

Chopping, slicing, cutting, peeling and grinding are all essential aspects of food preparation so it's important to have the right tools for the job.

Chopping board Essential in every kitchen, these may be made of wood or plastic. Wooden boards tend to be heavier and more stable, but they must be thoroughly scrubbed in hot soapy water and properly dried. Plastic boards are easier to clean and better for cutting meat, poultry and fish.

Knives: cook's, vegetable and serrated When buying knives, choose the best ones you can afford. They should feel comfortable in your hand, so try several different types and practise a cutting action before you buy. You will need three different knives. A cook's knife is a good multi-purpose knife. The blade is usually about 18cm/7in long, but you may find that you prefer a slightly longer or shorter blade. A vegetable knife is a small version of the cook's knife and is used for finer cutting. A large serrated knife is essential for slicing bread and ingredients such as tomatoes, which have a hard-to-cut skin compared to the soft flesh underneath.

Vegetable peelers These may have a fixed or swivel blade. Both types will make quick work of peeling vegetables and fruit, with less waste than a small knife.

Graters These come in various shapes and sizes. Box graters have several different cutting blades and are easy to handle. Microplane graters have razor-sharp blades that retain their sharp edges.

Left: The traditional box grater is solid, reliable and easy to handle – with several different grating blades.

Pepper mill Freshly ground black pepper is essential for seasoning. It is worth buying a good pepper mill with strong blades that will not blunt easily.

Measuring equipment

Accurate measuring equipment is essential, particularly when making breads and cakes, which need very precise quantities of ingredients.

Weighing scales These are good for measuring dry ingredients. Digital scales are the most accurate but balance scales that use weights or a sliding weight are also a good choice. Spring scales with a scoop and dial are not usually as precise.

Measuring cups Suitable for dry or liquid ingredients, these standard measures usually come in a set of separate cups for different fractions or portions of a full cup.

Measuring jug/pitcher This is essential for liquids. A heatproof glass jug is useful because it allows hot liquids to be measured and it is easy to check the quantity.

Measuring spoons Table cutlery varies in size, so a set of standard measuring spoons is extremely useful for measuring small quantities.

Below: A heatproof measuring jug and a set of measuring spoons are invaluable for measuring liquids and small quantities.

Looking after knives

Although it may seem like a contradiction, the sharper the knife, the safer it is to use. It takes far more effort to use a blunt knife and this often results in accidents. Try to get into the habit of sharpening your knives regularly because the blunter they become, the more difficult they are to use and the longer it will take to sharpen them. Always wash knives carefully after use and dry them thoroughly to prevent them from discolouring or rusting.

Mixing, rolling and draining

Bowls, spoons, whisks and strainers are all important kitchen items that you can rarely do without.

Mixing bowls You will need one large and one small bowl. Heatproof glass bowls are a good choice because they can be placed over a pan of simmering water to heat delicate sauces and to melt chocolate.

Wooden spoons Inexpensive and essential for stirring and beating, every kitchen should have two or three wooden spoons.

Metal slotted spoon This large spoon with draining holes is very useful for lifting food out of cooking liquid.

Fish slice/metal spatula This is invaluable for lifting delicate fish fillets and other foods out of a pan.

Rolling pin A heavy wooden or marble rolling pin is useful for rolling out pastry. If you don't have one, use a clean, dry, tall glass bottle (such as a wine bottle) instead.

Above: *Metal ballon whisks are great for beating out lumps from mixtures such as sauces.*

Balloon whisk A metal whisk is great for softly whipping cream and whisking sauces to a smooth consistency. Whisks are available in all shapes and sizes. Do not buy an enormous whisk that is difficult to use and will not fit into pans; mini-whisks are not essential – you can use a fork instead.

Sieve/Strainer For sifting flour, icing (confectioners') sugar, cocoa and other dry ingredients, a stainless steel sieve is essential. It can also be used for straining small quantities of cooked vegetables, pasta and rice. Wash and dry a sieve well after use to prevent it becoming clogged and damp.

Colander Choose a free-standing metal colander with feet on the base. This will keep the base of the colander above the liquid that is being drained off. A free-standing design also has the advantage of leaving both hands free to empty heavy pans.

Below: *No kitchen should be without a good selection of wooden cooking utensils for mixing and stirring.*

Electrical appliances

Although not always essential, these can speed up food preparation.

Food processor This fabulous invention can make life a lot easier. It is perfect for processing soft and hard foods and is more versatile than a blender, which is best suited to puréeing very soft foods or liquids.

Hand-held electric whisk A small, hand-held electric whisk or beater is very useful for making cakes, whipping cream and whisking egg whites. Choose an appliance with a powerful motor that will last.

Below: *A food processor is good for chopping and blending.*

Extra equipment

As well as the essential items, some recipes require other items such as tart tins (pans) and cookie cutters. The following are some items you may find you need.

Above: *Cookie cutters come in all kinds of shapes and sizes.*

Cookie cutters These make quick work of cutting out pastry and cookie dough. Metal ones have a sharper cutting edge so are usually preferable to plastic ones. If you don't have cutters, you can use a cup or glass and cut around it, but this takes more time.

Above: *A pastry brush is useful when baking or grilling.*

Pastry brush Made of bristle, with a wooden or plastic handle, this is useful for brushing food lightly with liquid – for example, brushing meat or fish with oil or marinade while grilling (broiling), or brushing pastry with beaten egg or milk.

Cake tins/pans These may have loose bottoms or spring-clip sides to allow easy removal of the cake. Be sure to use the size specified in the recipe.

Muffin tins/pans These consist of six or twelve fairly deep cups in a tray. They can be used for baking muffins, cupcakes, buns, bread rolls and deep tartlets.

Tart or tartlet tins/pans Available with straight or fluted sides, these are not as deep as muffin tins (pans). They come in a variety of sizes, from individual containers to very large tins. They are useful for baking all kinds of sweet and savoury tarts. Loose-bottomed tins are best because the contents are easier to remove.

Skewers These are used for kebabs and other skewered foods. Metal skewers are reusable and practical if you cook over the barbecue frequently, or cook kebabs that need lengthy cooking. Bamboo skewers are disposable and useful for foods that cook quickly – soak them in cold water for 20 minutes before use to stop them burning.

Palette knife/metal spatula This large, flat, round-bladed, blunt knife is great for spreading icing and fillings on cakes, as well as lifting delicate biscuits (cookies) off baking sheets and flipping pancakes.

Griddle pan A good quality, heavy griddle pan is useful for cooking meat and fish. The pan should be very hot before food is placed on it and the surface of the food should be brushed with a little oil to prevent it from sticking, rather than adding oil to the pan.

Wok This traditional Asian pan is larger and deeper than a frying pan, often with a rounded base and curved sides.

Below: *The ridges in the griddle pan allow fat to drain away and create attractive markings on the surface of the food.*

Below: *Double- and single-handled woks are versatile and make a useful addition to any kitchen. They are great for stir-frying, deep-frying, steaming and braising.*

Minimalist Cooking Techniques

When cooking with a limited number of ingredients, the trick is to bring out the flavour of each one. The choice of cooking method is important because it can affect the flavour quite dramatically. Seasonings and aromatics are used to complement and bring out the flavours of the main ingredients, while marinating or macerating help to intensify the relationship between the basic ingredient and the condiments or seasoning. The result is a full, rich flavour.

Cooking methods to maximize flavour

How you cook food can make a real difference to the end result. For example, long-boiled vegetables become soggy and insipid, devoid of nutrients and flavour. In contrast, lightly steaming vegetables, baking fish wrapped in paper or foil parcels, and dry-frying spices are simple techniques that trap and enhance the natural flavour of the food. Some methods also add other flavours during cooking: for example, sprinkling smoking chips on a barbecue gives the food an extra smoky flavour.

Cooking on a barbecue Good-quality lumpwood charcoal will impart its characteristic smoky flavour to the food. A variety of natural or synthetic aromatics can also be added, including hickory, oak, mesquite or applewood chips; woody herbs, such as thyme or rosemary – just the stalks will do; or shells from almonds or walnuts. Soak nutshells in cold water for about 30 minutes before adding them to the barbecue to help them smoke.

Below: *Cooking vegetables, fish or meat over charcoal can help to give the food a wonderful, rich, smoky flavour.*

Above: *Roasting vegetables in the oven really helps to bring out their sweet flavour as the natural sugars caramelize.*

Roasting This is a good method for cooking meat, poultry, fish and vegetables. Long, slow roasting transforms sweet vegetables such as (bell) peppers and parsnips, bringing out a rich, caramelized flavour.

Grilling/broiling This method adds flavour by browning or charring the surface of the food. To achieve a good result the grill (broiler) must be preheated before cooking so that it is as hot as possible when the food is placed under the heat. Grilling is excellent for cheese, fish, poultry and lean meat, such as steak.

Dry-frying Frying with no fat or oil is a useful technique for certain ingredients. Fatty meats such as bacon and pancetta release fat as the meat cooks, providing fat in which to cook the meat and any other ingredients added to the pan. Dry-frying whole spices, such as coriander or cumin seeds, enhances their taste, taking the raw edge off their flavour while making it more intense and rounded. This technique is also known as roasting.

Shallow frying Meat, poultry, fish and vegetables are all delicious pan-fried with a little oil or butter. They can be cooked quickly over a high heat to seal in the flavours, or slowly over a low heat to achieve tender, juicy results.

Deep-frying Meat, poultry, fish, vegetables and even fruit are delicious cooked in hot oil. It is a very quick method and gives rich results. The outside of the food is sealed almost as soon as it hits the oil, forming a crisp exterior that encloses the flavour and juices of the ingredients. Most foods need to be dipped in a protective coating such as batter or breadcrumbs before frying.

Steaming This healthy cooking method is excellent for quick-cooking foods such as vegetables and fish. The natural flavours and nutrients of the food are retained giving moist, tasty results. Few additional ingredients or flavourings are needed when steaming.

Below: *Steaming is a delicate cooking method that is perfect for foods such as dumplings, vegetables and fish.*

Above: *Deep-frying is a quick way of cooking that produces richly flavoured food with a crisp yet succulent texture.*

Microwaving Vegetables, such as peas and green beans, can be cooked successfully in a microwave. The result is similar to steaming, and traps all the flavour and nutrients. Place the vegetables in a suitable covered container with a little added water, then cook on full power.

Baking in parcels Traditionally known as cooking *en papillote*, this cooking method is a form of steaming. It is perfectly suited to foods such as fish and vegetables. The food is wrapped in baking parchment or foil to make a neat parcel, then baked. The steam and juices from the food are trapped within the parcel as it cooks, capturing the full flavour. Be sure to fold or crumple the edges of the parcel well to ensure that all the steam and juices are retained.

Below: *Fish, such as salmon, is delicious wrapped in a paper parcel with simple flavourings, then baked in the oven.*

Dry-frying whole spices

1 Heat a small frying pan over a medium heat and add the spices. Cook, stirring occasionally, until the spices give off their aroma – take care not to let them burn.

2 Tip the toasted spices into a mortar and roughly crush them with a pestle. (Dry-fry spices freshly, as and when you need them.)

Simple ways of introducing flavour

As well as selecting the cooking method best suited to the ingredients, there are several quick and simple methods of adding flavour using herbs, spices and aromatics. Match the seasoning to the ingredient and go for simple techniques such as marinating, stuffing or coating with a dry spice rub, which will help to intensify the flavours.

Flavours for fish Classic aromatics used for flavouring fish and shellfish include lemon, lime, parsley, dill, fennel and bay leaves. These flavours all have a fresh, intense quality that complements the delicate taste of fish and shellfish without overpowering it. All work well added before, during or after cooking.

• To flavour whole fish, such as trout or mackerel, stuff a few lemon slices and some fresh parsley or basil into the body cavity before cooking. Season with plenty of salt and freshly ground black pepper, then wrap the fish in foil or baking parchment, ensuring the packet is well sealed. Place the fish in an ovenproof dish or on a baking tray and bake until cooked through.

• To marinate chunky fillets of fish, such as cod or salmon, arrange the fish fillets in a dish in a single layer. Drizzle the fish with olive oil, then sprinkle over a little crushed garlic and grated lime rind and squeeze over the lime juice. Cover the dish in clear film (plastic wrap) and leave to marinate in the refrigerator for at least 30 minutes. Grill (broil) lightly until just cooked through.

• To make an unusual, yet delicious, marinade for salmon, arrange the salmon fillets in a single layer in an overproof dish. Drizzle the fillets with a little light olive oil and add a split vanilla pod. Cover and marinate in the refrigerator for a couple of hours before cooking in the oven.

Pepping up meat and poultry Meat and poultry suit both delicate and punchy seasonings. Dry rubs, marinades and sticky glazes are all perfect ways to introduce flavour into the meat and poultry. Marinating the tougher cuts of meat, such as stewing steak, also helps to tenderize them.

• To make a fragrant Cajun spice rub for pork chops, steaks and chicken, mix together 5ml/1 tsp each of dried thyme, dried oregano, finely crushed black peppercorns, salt, crushed cumin seeds and hot paprika. Rub the Cajun spice mix into the raw meat or poultry, then cook over a barbecue or bake until cooked through.

• To marinate red meat, such as beef, lamb or venison, prepare a mixture of two-thirds red wine to one-third olive oil in a shallow non-metallic dish. Stir in some chopped garlic and bruised fresh rosemary sprigs. Add the meat and turn to coat it in the marinade. Cover and chill for at least 2 hours or overnight before cooking.

• To make a mild-spiced sticky mustard glaze for chicken, pork or red meat, mix 45ml/3 tbsp each of Dijon mustard, clear honey and demerara sugar, 2.5ml/^{1}/$_2$ tsp chilli powder, 1.5ml/^{1}/$_4$ tsp ground cloves, and salt and freshly ground black pepper. Cook the poultry or meat over the barbecue or under the grill (broiler) and brush with the glaze about 10 minutes before the end of cooking time.

Below: *Brush on sticky glazes towards the end of cooking time; if the glaze is cooked for too long, it will burn.*

Above: *Adding a drizzle of sesame oil to stir-fried vegetables gives them a wonderfully rich, smoky, nutty flavour.*

Vibrant vegetables Most fresh vegetables have a subtle flavour that needs to be brought out and enhanced. When using delicate cooking methods such as steaming and stir-frying, go for light, fresh flavourings that will enhance the taste of the vegetables. When using more robust cooking methods, such as roasting, choose richer flavours such as garlic and spices.

• To make fragrant, Asian-style steamed vegetables, add a bruised stalk of lemon grass and/or a few kaffir lime leaves to the steaming water, then cook vegetables such as pak choi (bok choy) over the water until just tender. Alternatively, place the aromatics in the steamer under the vegetables and steam as before until just tender.

• To add a rich flavour to stir-fried vegetables, add a splash of sesame oil just before the end of cooking time. (Do not use more than about 5ml/1 tsp because sesame oil has a very strong flavour and can be overpowering.)

• To enhance the taste of naturally sweet vegetables, such as parsnips and carrots, glaze them with honey and mustard before roasting. Mix together 30ml/2 tbsp wholegrain mustard and 45ml/3 tbsp clear honey, and season with salt and ground black pepper. Brush the glaze over the prepared vegetables to coat completely, then roast until sweet and tender.

Fragrant rice and grains Classic accompaniments, such as rice and couscous, can be enhanced by the addition of simple flavourings. Adding herbs, spices and aromatics can help to perk up the rice and grains' subtle flavour. Choose flavourings that will complement the dish that the rice or grains will be served with.

• To make exotic fragrant rice to serve with Asian-style stir-fries and braised dishes, add a whole star anise or a few cardamom pods to a pan of rice before cooking. The rice will absorb the flavour during cooking.

• To make zesty herb rice or couscous, heat a little chopped fresh tarragon and grated lemon rind in olive oil or melted butter until warm, then drizzle the flavoured oil and herbs over freshly cooked rice or couscous.

• To make simple herb rice or couscous, fork plenty of chopped fresh parsley and chives through the cooked grains and drizzle over a little oil just before serving.

Below: *Snipping fresh chives into a bowl of couscous not only adds flavour, but also adds a decorative finish to the side dish.*

Fruit

Widely used in both sweet and savoury dishes, fruit can be used either as a main ingredient or as a flavouring to complement and enhance the taste of other ingredients. The many different varieties offer the cook ample opportunity to create fabulous dishes – whether it's cod fillets with a squeeze of lime juice, a stew of lamb and tangy apricots or a sumptuous dessert made with soft, juicy summer berries.

Orchard fruit

This family of fruit includes apples, pears and quinces, which, depending on the variety, are in season from early summer to late autumn (fall). Choose firm, unblemished fruit and store in a cool dry place.

Apples There are two main categories of apples – eating and cooking. Eating apples have sweet flesh and taste good raw. Many can also be used for cooking; they remain firm making them ideal for pan-frying and open tarts. Cooking apples have a tart flavour and are too sharp to eat raw. When cooked, their flesh tends to break down and become pulpy, making them ideal for sauces and purées.

Pears Most commercially available pears are dessert fruits, just as good for eating as for cooking. They can be pan-fried or used in tarts and pies. They are also excellent poached, especially in a wine syrup.

Quinces Related to the pear, quinces have hard, sour flesh. Cooking and sweetening brings out their delicious, scented flavour. They are worth buying when you find them, and are often used in jellies and sauces.

Stone fruit

Peaches, nectarines, plums, apricots and cherries all belong to this family of fruit which contain a stone (pit) in the

Above: *Sweet, juicy peaches are delicious served fresh in salads or poached in wine.*

middle. Most stone fruits are at their best through the summer months but some, such as plums, are best through the autumn. Choose firm, smooth-skinned fruit without any blemishes and store in a cool, dry place, preferably the refrigerator. They are used raw or cooked. When eating raw, eat at room temperature.

Above: *Fresh raspberries are perfect for breakfast and dessert dishes.*

Soft fruit

These delicate fruits, which include strawberries, raspberries, blackberries, blackcurrants, redcurrants and white currants, need careful handling and storing. Choose brightly coloured fruit and check for signs of grey mould or overripe specimens. Store in the refrigerator for up to 2 days. They are rich in vitamin C.

Citrus fruit

Oranges, lemons, limes, grapefruit, mandarins and satsumas are popular citrus fruits; but there are also hybrids such as clementines. The lemon is probably the most versatile member of the citrus family, with many uses in both savoury and sweet cooking. Citrus fruits are available all year round, with satsumas and clementines at their best in winter. Choose plump fruit that feels heavy. The skin should be bright and not shrivelled. Most citrus fruit is coated with wax to prevent moisture loss, so buy unwaxed fruit when using the rind in a recipe, or scrub the fruit well before use.

Segmenting oranges

1 Cut a slice off the top and bottom of the orange to remove the peel and pith. Stand the fruit on a board and cut off the peel and pith, working around the orange in strips.

2 Hold the orange over a bowl to catch the juices. Cut through one side of a segment, between the flesh and membrane, then cut through the other side of the segment to remove the flesh. Continue removing the segments in this way, leaving behind the clutch of membranes.

Exotic fruit

Once expensive and rarely available, these wonderful fruits are now widely available in supermarkets throughout the year. Eat them fresh or use them in recipes.

Mangoes There are many varieties of this sweet, fragrant, juicy fruit, which are delicious eaten on their own with a squeeze of lime juice, or used in recipes. Choose mangoes that have a fragrant smell, even through the skin, and give slightly when gently squeezed. Store in a cool place, but not the refrigerator, for up to a week.

Pineapple These sweet, tangy, juicy fruits are delicious in fruit salads and desserts. When choosing a pineapple, pull off one of the green leaves at the top – if it comes away easily, the pineapple should be ripe. Store in a cool place, but not the refrigerator, for up to a week.

Kiwi fruit The pale green flesh of kiwi fruit is full of sweet-sharp flavour that goes well with other fruit in salads and is good in various desserts and savoury cooking. Kiwi fruit are rich in vitamin C. Choose fruit with smooth, plump skin and store in the refrigerator for up to 4 days.

Passion fruit These small round fruit have a tough, wrinkled purple-brown skin. A passion fruit should feel heavy if it is nice and juicy. Store in the refrigerator.

Below: *Perfectly ripe pineapples have sweet, tangy flesh with a crisp bite and wonderful fragrance that is quite irresistible.*

Above: *Watermelon has bright pink flesh and a light, delicate flavour that is sweet yet refreshing.*

Other fruit

There are a few fruits that are delicious and very versatile but that don't fit into any particular group.

Rhubarb Tart, pink rhubarb is used in pies, tarts, crumbles and mousses. The stalks are edible but the leaves are poisonous so should be removed before cooking. Rhubarb is available from early spring to mid-summer. Pale, finer-textured pink forced rhubarb is available in January. It has a good colour and flavour, and is considered the best. Choose crisp, firm stalks and store in the refrigerator.

Melons There are two types of melon – dessert melon and watermelon. Charentais, Ogen, cantaloupe, Galia and honeydew melon are all dessert melons, which are in season from summer to winter. Slice them, remove the seeds and enjoy their fragrant flesh. Watermelons have crisp, juicy flesh, studded with dark seeds. They are best served chilled, and are in season from summer to autumn.

Figs Fresh figs with their dense, sweet red flesh are still considered a luxury outside the areas where they are grown. Available in summer, they are delicious raw or cooked and can be used in savoury or sweet dishes. Handle figs carefully and store in the refrigerator for up to 2 days.

Grapes At their best in late summer, there are many varieties of grape, but the seedless ones are popular. Grapes can be used in many ways – served on their own as an accompaniment to cheese; used in fruit salads; or combined with savoury ingredients in salads.

Vegetables

Used in salads and savoury dishes, vegetables are delicious served as the main ingredient in a side dish, or as a flavouring ingredient within a main dish. Take your time when choosing vegetables, selecting healthy-looking specimens that are in season for maximum flavour – you'll really notice the difference.

Root vegetables and potatoes

Grown underground, these vegetables include carrots, parsnips, beetroot and turnips and many varieties of potato. They are very versatile: good for roasting, boiling, steaming and deep-frying. Choose firm vegetables with unblemished skins; avoid withered specimens and green-tinged potatoes, or ones with shoots. Store in a cool, dark place for up to 2 weeks. Scrub well if cooking in their skins.

Cabbages, broccoli and cauliflower

Members of the brassica family, these vegetables are packed with nutrients and good served in many ways.

Cabbage Regardless of variety, cabbage has a distinctive flavour and can be steamed, stir-fried or boiled. The white and red varieties are tight-leafed and ideal for shredding, and can be enjoyed raw in salads such as coleslaw. Green cabbage can be loose or close-leafed, smooth or crinkly and is best cooked. Buy bright, fresh-looking specimens and store in the refrigerator for up to 10 days.

Above: *Fresh, leafy purple sprouting broccoli is delicious steamed, boiled or stir-fried.*

Broccoli With a delicious flavour and crisp texture, broccoli and purple sprouting broccoli can be boiled, steamed and stir-fried. Choose specimens with bright green heads and no sign of yellowing. Store in the refrigerator and use within 4–5 days.

Cauliflower Good cut into florets and served raw with dips, cauliflower can also be boiled or steamed, and is delicious coated in cheese sauce. To ensure even cooking, remove the hard central core, or cut into florets. Choose densely packed heads, avoiding specimens with any black spots, and store in the refrigerator where they will keep for 5–10 days.

Above: *Plump juicy tomatoes have a rich, sweet flavour and are tasty used in salads or cooked in stews and sauces.*

Vegetable fruits

Tomatoes, aubergines, peppers and chillies are actually fruit, although they are generally used as vegetables. They all have a robust flavour and lovely texture and are widely used in Mediterranean-style cooking.

Tomatoes There are numerous varieties of tomatoes, including cherry, plum and beefsteak. They are eaten raw or cooked. Choose plump, bright-red specimens, ideally on the vine, and store in the refrigerator for 5–8 days.

Aubergines/eggplants These can be fried, stewed, brushed with oil and grilled (broiled), or stuffed and baked. Choose firm, plump, smooth-skinned specimens and store in the refrigerator, where they will keep for 5–8 days.

Peppers/bell peppers These may be red, yellow, orange or green, with the green specimens having a fresher, less sweet flavour. Peppers can be grilled, roasted, fried and stewed. Choose firm, unblemished specimens and store in the refrigerator for 5–8 days.

Chillies There are many types of chilli, all with a different taste and heat. As a general rule, the bigger the chilli, the milder it is; green chillies tend to be hotter than red ones.

Leafy green vegetables

There is a wide selection of leafy greens available, which may be used raw in salads or cooked.

Salad leaves There are many different salad leaves, including many types of lettuce. They are delicate and need to be stored in the refrigerator, where most will keep for a few days. Prepare salad leaves at the last minute.

Spinach Tender young spinach leaves are tasty raw. Mature spinach leaves can be fried, boiled or steamed until just wilted; they overcook very easily. Store spinach in the refrigerator for 2–3 days, and wash well before use.

Leafy Asian vegetables Asian vegetables, such as pak choi (bok choy), can be used raw in salads or cooked. Prepare in the same way as cabbage or spinach.

The onion family

This family includes onions, shallots, spring onions (scallions), leeks and garlic. All can be used as flavouring ingredients or cooked on their own. Roasting produces a rich, sweet flavour. Choose firm, unblemished specimens. Store onions in a cool, dry place for up to 2 weeks; store leeks and spring onions in the refrigerator for 2–3 days.

Beans, peas and corn

These are good boiled or steamed and served as a side dish, or used in braised dishes and stir-fries.

Green beans Many varieties of green beans are available throughout the year. Choose firm, fresh-looking beans with a bright green colour; avoid yellowish ones. Store in the refrigerator, where they will keep for up to 5 days.

Above: *Fresh green peas are delightfully sweet and tender.*

Peas Fresh peas are generally only available in their pods in the summer. Only buy really fresh ones because their natural sugar content quickly turns to starch, giving them a mealy texture. Frozen peas are often better than fresh ones because they are frozen within a short time of picking and retain all their natural sweetness.

Above: *Butternut squash has bright orange flesh, a lovely sweet flavour and smooth texture. Roasting brings out its flavour.*

Corn Large corn cobs are good boiled and served with butter, while baby corn are better added to stir-fries. Buy only the freshest specimens when they are in season because stale vegetables can be starchy.

Squashes

These vegetables come in many different shapes and sizes and include courgettes (zucchini); butternut, acorn and spaghetti squashes; and pumpkins and marrows (large zucchini). With the exception of courgettes, all need peeling and seeding before use. They can be cut up and boiled or baked whole. Select smooth, unblemished vegetables with unbroken skin. Most squashes can be stored in a cool place for 1 week, although courgettes should be stored in the refrigerator for 4–5 days.

Mushrooms

Freshly picked mushrooms have a rich, earthy flavour, but are rarely available to most cooks. Chestnut mushrooms are a good alternative; they have more flavour than cultivated mushrooms. Shiitake mushrooms are full-flavoured and delicious in Chinese- and Asian-style dishes.

There are many types of edible wild fungi or mushrooms of different flavours and textures. They tend to have a more intense flavour than cultivated mushrooms and are also more expensive and more difficult to find. Wild mushrooms are seasonal and can generally be found in late summer, autumn (fall) and winter. Choose firm, fleshy specimens and store them in paper bags in a cool place.

Dairy Produce

Milk and milk products, such as yogurt, milk and cheese, are widely used in cooking and can add a delicious richness to many sweet and savoury dishes. Strong-tasting cheeses, such as Gorgonzola or Parmesan, not only contribute a wonderful texture, but also add real bite to many savoury dishes.

Milk, cream and yogurt

These products are widely used in both sweet and savoury dishes, adding a rich, creamy taste and texture.

Milk Full-fat (whole) milk and lower-fat semi-skimmed and skimmed milk is pasteurised and available fresh or in long-life cartons. Buttermilk is a by-product of the butter-making process and is often used in baking.

Cream There are many different types of cream. Double (heavy) cream has a high fat content and can be poured, whipped and heated without curdling. Whipping cream has a lower fat content and can be whipped to give a lighter, less firm texture. Single (light) cream has a lower fat content still and cannot be whipped; it is used for pouring. Clotted cream is very thick and has the highest fat content. Sour cream has the same fat content as single cream, but it is cultured, giving it a thick texture and slightly sour, fresh taste. Créme fraîche is cultured fresh cream, which gives it a slightly sharp, acid taste. It has a fairly thick, spooning texture but it cannot be whipped. It can be heated.

Yogurt Varying in fat content, yogurt may be set or runny, with a thin or creamy texture. It tends to curdle when heated, although Greek (US strained plain) yogurt can be used for cooking.

Above:
Parmesan cheese is
very good for cooking and is also excellent grated
or shaved over pasta, risotto and other dishes.

Butter

There are two main types of butter – salted and unsalted (sweet). Unsalted is better for baking cakes and cookies.

Hard cheeses

These firm, tasty cheeses are good for cooking. They should have a dry rind. Store wrapped in baking parchment in the refrigerator for up to 2 weeks.

Cheddar There are many varieties of this classic sharp cheese – some strong, some mild. Its high fat content and good melting properties make it a great choice for cheese sauces.

Parmesan This cheese comes from the area around Parma in Italy and only cheeses with Parmigiano Reggiano stamped on the rind have this designation. It is a hard, dry cheese with a full, sweet flavour.

Gruyère This Swiss cheese with a dry texture and nutty flavour is good in cooking and for melting over dishes.

Manchego This Spanish ewe's milk cheese has a dry texture and a nutty, buttery taste.

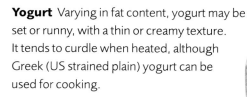

Above: *There are many different types of cream, from thick to pourable.*

Semi-hard cheeses

These vary in softness depending on the type. Choose cheeses that feel springy and have firm rinds. Wrap in waxed paper and store in the refrigerator for 1–2 weeks.

Fontina This deep golden yellow Italian cheese has a pale brown rind and lots of little holes throughout the cheese. It melts fairly well but is not good for sauces.

Halloumi This salty Greek cheese has a firm, slightly rubbery texture and is perfect for grilling (broiling).

Blue cheese

These strong, often sharp, cheeses usually melt well and are good for cooking and flavouring sauces.

Stilton This strong, sharp cheese melts well into sauces and complements chicken and more robust meats.

Gorgonzola This Italian blue cheese has a rich, piquant flavour with a firm but creamy texture. It melts smoothly and can be used in a wide range of dishes.

Dolcelatte This Italian blue cheese has a milder flavour than Gorgonzola and a soft, creamy texture. It is good with summer fruit and can be used in cooking.

Soft and fresh cheeses

These mild, unripened cheeses should smell fresh. Store in a covered container in the refrigerator for up to 1 week.

Mozzarella This Italian cheese has a soft, elastic texture and mild, milky flavour and is good when melted. Baby balls of mozzarella (bocconcini) are also available.

Above: *Stilton has a sharp, tangy flavour and creamy texture. It is good served on its own or used in salads and cooking.*

Feta This white, firm Greek cheese has a crumbly texture and sharp, salty flavour. Feta does not melt easily and is not ideal for general cooking but is good used in salads.

Mascarpone This creamy, mild cheese has a high fat content and can be used in sweet and savoury recipes.

White rind cheeses

These creamy cheeses with a firm, white mould rind are delicious used fresh in salads or cooked.

Brie This French cheese is one of the best of the white rind cheeses. The flavour can be mild or extremely strong, tangy and creamy when ripe. Brie can be grilled (broiled), baked or coated in breadcrumbs and deep-fried.

Firm goat's cheese One of the most popular types is shaped in a log, often sold sliced into a white ring. It is excellent for slicing and melting. Soft goat's cheese, without the rind, has a milder flavour.

Eggs

Widely used in sweet and savoury cooking, eggs are incredibly versatile and are perfect for making simple meals such as omelettes or baked eggs.
Hens' eggs These can be boiled, poached, fried, scrambled or baked. They are widely used for baking. Buy the best you can afford – hens reared in better conditions produce better-tasting eggs.
Quails' eggs These small speckled eggs are similar in flavour to hens' eggs. They can be fried, poached or boiled and are useful for canapés.

Left: *Mild, milky mozzarella is great used fresh in salads or melted in cooked dishes.*

Fish and Shellfish

Full of flavour and quick to cook, fish and shellfish are delicious cooked simply. Always buy really fresh specimens: look for bright-eyed fish with plump flesh and bright, undamaged skin; they should not smell "fishy" but should have a faint aroma of the sea. Good fishmongers will scale, cut and fillet the fish for you. Choose lobsters and crabs that feel heavy for their size. Store fish and shellfish, covered, towards the bottom of the refrigerator, and use within a day of purchase.

Above: *Fresh anchovies are tasty marinated in lemon juice.*

Oily fish

The rich flesh of oily fish is extremely tasty and very good for you. Oily fish are rich in omega 3 fatty acids, which are an essential part of a healthy diet and are said to be good for the heart. Oily fish also contain less fat than most meat or poultry, and the fat is generally unsaturated.

Anchovies When available fresh, anchovies are delicious grilled (broiled) and served with a squeeze of lemon juice. Good-quality salted anchovies are versatile and delicious in many dishes, particularly pasta sauces.

Mackerel These fish have iridescent skin and quite firm, brownish flesh. They can be baked whole, wrapped in baking parchment, with lemon and herbs, or marinated and grilled. The robust flavour of mackerel is enhanced by pungent spices, such as coriander and cumin.

Herring Smaller than mackerel, herring can be treated in much the same way. They are also delicious pickled.

Sardines These small fish are delicious fresh, cooked over a barbecue with lime or lemon juice and herbs.

Rich, meaty fish

This group of firm fish have a meaty texture. Some have a mild flavour, while others such as tuna are more robust.

Monkfish Tasty baked, pan-fried and grilled, this fish is usually sold prepared as monkfish tails, which have a firm, meaty texture and a delicate flavour. Ask the fishmonger to remove all traces of skin and membrane around the fish, as this turns very rubbery on cooking.

Sea bass This is an expensive fish but its flavour is well worth the cost. Try fillets pan-fried in a little butter and served with a squeeze of lime juice.

Tuna Fresh tuna is now more widely available – bluefin is the most prized, followed by yellowfin. It is best served rare. Steaks are best pan-fried for 1–2 minutes each side.

Swordfish Pink-tinged, meaty swordfish is excellent cooked over a barbecue, but be sure not to overcook it because the flesh becomes dry.

Red mullet You can recognise red mullet by the yellow stripe that runs along the body. It is an attractive fish with fine, delicious white flesh. The fillets are good pan-fried with the skin on and served with creamy mashed potato.

White fish

These fish have a firm yet delicate white flesh, excellent cooked simply with subtle or piquant flavouring.

Cod Stocks of cod in the sea are diminishing due to overfishing resulting in a rise in price. Large cod fillet has a firm texture and an almost milky quality to its flesh.

Plaice Cooked whole or as fillets, plaice can be fried, grilled, steamed or baked. It can be slightly bland, so add a piquant sauce or herbs and olive oil to perk it up.

Below: *Tuna steaks are great marinated in oil and lime juice and then grilled.*

Left: Fresh mussels are delicious steamed with white wine and garlic, but be sure that they are absolutely fresh and have been prepared and cleaned thoroughly.

Crab These crustaceans are cooked live, plunged into a pan of boiling water, which many people find off-putting. However, crab is also available ready-cooked. A crab yields a small amount of meat for its size, so allow 500g/1¼lb weight of whole crab per person.

Lobster Like crabs, lobsters should be cooked live, so buy ready-cooked lobsters and split in half lengthways to extract the meat. Crack the claws with a hammer to extract the meat in the same way as for crab claws.

Prawns/shrimp There are many types of prawns of different sizes, cooked or raw, in the shell, or peeled. They are delicious pan-fried with chopped garlic and chilli. When large prawns are peeled, the black vein that runs along the back has to be removed and discarded. Brown shrimps must be used for potted shrimps.

Haddock This flaky fish can be used instead of cod or in recipes calling for white fish. Smoked haddock is delicious but avoid the bright yellow dyed variety and go for the paler, undyed version.

Skate This fish has a hard, cartilaginous skeleton and no bones. It is sold as flat wings. Piquant capers are the perfect companion seasoning.

Shellfish

There are several different types of shellfish. Molluscs have either one or two shells. Once dead, they deteriorate rapidly and can cause food poisoning. Because of this, they must always be perfectly fresh and cooked alive. Crustaceans, including crabs, lobsters and prawns (shrimp) have a protective shell that is shed occasionally as the creature grows. Store shellfish in the refrigerator and always use within 1–2 days.

Mussels Sweet, mild-tasting mussels need to be cleaned thoroughly before cooking. Wash or scrub in cold water and pull off any black hairs (the beard) protruding from the shell. Tap any open mussels on a work surface and discard any that do not close straight away, along with any broken shells. When cooked, discard any unopened mussels.

Scallops Tender, delicately flavoured scallops need very little cooking. Simply pan-fry for 1–2 minutes on each side over high heat. Choose scallops with a sweet smell; this indicates freshness. To open, hold the scallop shell, curved side down, and insert the tip of an oyster knife between the two shells. Twist to prise the shells apart, then cut through the muscle holding the scallop in the shell, and remove any muscle and membrane from the meat and coral.

Extracting meat from a cooked crab

1 Lay the crab on its back and twist off the legs and claws. Use a hammer to break open the claws and legs, and pick out the meat.

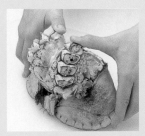

2 There is a flap or opening on the body – carefully lift this up and twist it off, gently pulling the crab out of its shell.

3 Discard the gills from the side of the body and spoon the brown meat from the main body section and from the shell.

Meat and Poultry

If possible, buy organic meat and poultry. It is better to eat less meat of better quality than a larger quantity of cheaper meat. Animals and birds that have been raised in a good environment and fed on quality feed produce better-tasting meat than mass-reared, unhappy livestock. When you are cooking with only a few ingredients, each one needs to have an excellent flavour and texture.

Pork

Comparatively inexpensive, pork is a very versatile meat. It is generally tender and has an excellent flavour.

Shoulder, leg and loin The shoulder or leg is the best cut for roasting. To make good crackling, ensure that the rind is thoroughly dry and rub it generously with sea salt. Loin or shoulder chops are suited to pan-frying or braising.

Belly Traditionally quite fatty, belly pork is good roasted and braised. It is especially tasty with Asian flavourings.

Spare ribs Meaty pork ribs can be delicious marinated and then roasted or barbecued with a sticky glaze.

Pork tenderloin A lean, long piece of meat, the tenderloin can dry out during cooking. Wrap it in bacon to keep it moist before roasting.

Bacon Available smoked or unsmoked. If possible, buy dry-cured bacon. Streaky (fatty) bacon has a higher percentage of fat than back bacon, and can be cooked to a crisp-fried texture. Back bacon has larger rashers (strips) and a balance of lean to fatty areas.

Above: *Entrecôte steaks are cut from beef sirloin, have a rich colour and are delicious pan-fried or grilled.*

Gammon This smoky meat is available in a whole piece or as steaks. Whole gammon may need soaking before cooking. Steaks can be pan-fried or grilled (broiled).

Pancetta This traditional Italian cured bacon comes in rashers (strips) or cut into dice. It can be pan-fried.

Prosciutto This dry-cured ham is eaten raw, cut into very thin slices. It can be cooked, usually as a topping on dishes or to enclose other ingredients before grilling or roasting.

Beef

This well-flavoured, versatile meat is good for stewing, roasting, grilling (broiling), pan-frying and stir-frying.

Fillet/beef tenderloin, forerib, topside and silverside/pot roast These are best roasted. To make the most of the flavour, serve medium, not well-done.

Steaks Sirloin, T-bone, porterhouse, fillet (beef tenderloin) and sirloin are best pan-fried over a high heat.

Shin or leg/shank, chuck and brisket These cuts can be quite tough and are best stewed slowly to tenderize them and bring out their excellent flavour.

Mince/ground meat This is a very versatile ingredient for meat sauces, chilli con carne, meatballs, pasta dishes, samosas, pies and many other dishes.

Left: *Rolled belly of pork is a fatty joint that is succulent either slowly roasted or pot-roasted. Serve with piquant flavours, which go well with the fatty meat.*

Lamb

Delicious in roasts and superb grilled (broiled), pan-fried and stewed, lamb is one of the best-loved of all meats.

Best end of neck, leg, shoulder and saddle These are the best cuts for roasting. Best end of neck can be cut into chops. Shoulder contains more fat than leg but it has an excellent flavour. Spring lamb has the best taste.

Chump chops and leg steaks These have a full flavour and can be either grilled (broiled) or pan-fried.

Sausages and offal

Offal refers to all offcuts from the carcass but in everyday use, this usually means liver and kidneys.

Sausages There are many types of fresh sausage from around the world. Depending on the variety, they may be fried, grilled (broiled) or baked.

Liver Pigs', lambs' or calves' liver has a strong flavour and is good pan-fried, with bacon and mashed potato.

Kidneys Lambs' kidneys are lighter in flavour than pigs'. They should be halved and the central core discarded before they are pan-fried or used in stews and pies.

Poultry and game birds

Many people prefer the lighter flavour of poultry and game birds to that of red meat.

Chicken Buy organic or free-range chicken. Choose smooth-skinned, unblemished plump birds.

Carving a roast chicken

1 Leave the bird to rest for 10 minutes, then remove the legs and cut through the joints to make the thigh and drumstick portions.

2 Remove the wings, then carve the meat off the breasts, working down on either side of the breastbone. Use a gentle sawing action.

Poussin These baby chickens are perfect roasted or spatchcocked , then cooked over the barbecue.

Duck Traditionally, duck can be very fatty with a fairly small amount of meat. An average duck will serve two or three people. Duck breasts and legs are a good choice for simple cooking.

Pheasant One pheasant will serve two. The breast meat is fairly dry and needs constant basting during roasting. Choose pheasants that are no older than six months; older birds are tough.

Below from left: *Corn-fed, free-range and organic chickens have a good flavour.*

Herbs

Invaluable in a huge number of sweet and savoury recipes, herbs add flavour, colour and contrast to many dishes. Fresh herbs are widely available and their flavour is superior to that of dried herbs. Many are easy to grow yourself at home – either in the garden or in a pot on the windowsill. You can grow them from seed, or buy them already growing in pots from supermarkets and garden stores.

Robust herbs

These strong-tasting, often pungent herbs are good with meat and well-flavoured dishes. Use in moderation.

Bay leaves These shiny, aromatic leaves can be added to meat dishes, roasts, casseroles and stews before cooking. Roughly tear the leaves before you add them, then remove before serving. They are an essential part of a bouquet garni.

Rosemary This pungent herb is delicious with lamb – insert a few sprigs into slits in the skin of a leg of lamb and the flavour will really penetrate the meat during roasting. For other recipes, use whole leaves or chop them finely.

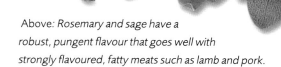

Above: *Rosemary and sage have a robust, pungent flavour that goes well with strongly flavoured, fatty meats such as lamb and pork.*

Freezing herbs

This is a great way of preserving fresh herbs because it retains their natural flavour. Use in cooked dishes only. Chop the herbs and place about one tablespoonful in each compartment of an ice cube tray. Pour over water to cover and freeze. To use, simply add a herb ice cube to the pan and stir.

Making a bouquet garni

This classic flavouring for stews, casseroles and soups is very easy to make. Using a piece of string, tie together a fresh bay leaf and a sprig each of parsley and thyme. Alternatively, tie the herbs in a square of muslin (cheesecloth).

Thyme One of the traditional herbs used in a bouquet garni, thyme has small leaves and some types have woody stems. It has a strong, pungent flavour. Add whole sprigs to meat dishes or strip the leaves and use in pasta sauces.

Sage Peppery tasting sage has large, slightly furry leaves. It is a great companion for pork and is excellent with potatoes and also in tomato and garlic pasta dishes. Ravioli served with a little melted butter and warmed sage leaves is particularly delicious. Use in moderation because its flavour can be overpowering if used in excess.

Chives Long slender chives have a distinct onion-like flavour. Chives are best snipped with scissors. They are good in potato salads and egg and dairy dishes.

Oregano One of the few herbs that responds well to drying, oregano is great for tomato-based sauces and with other vegetables. It is also good with chicken.

Lavender This can be used sparingly to complement chicken dishes and also in sweet recipes such as drinks and desserts. The stalks and leaves can be used as well as the flowers, which make a pretty garnish.

Leafy herbs

These delicate, soft-leafed herbs have a fragrant flavour. Use in salads or add towards the end of cooking time.

Basil Widely used in Italian cookery, basil has delicate leaves and should be added at the end of cooking. It has a slightly aniseed flavour that goes well with chicken, fish, all types of vegetables and pasta. It is one of the main ingredients of pesto.

Coriander/cilantro The deep, almost woody, flavour of coriander is superb in spicy dishes. It is good in Thai-style soups and curries, meat and egg dishes, as well as more robustly flavoured fish dishes.

Parsley Flat or curly leafed, parsley is one of the most versatile herbs and adds flavour to most savoury dishes. The flat-leafed variety has a stronger flavour and it can be used as an ingredient in its own right to make soup.

Mint There are many different varieties of mint, including apple mint and spearmint.It grows easily and goes well with lamb, desserts and drinks.

Tarragon This fragrant herb has a strong aniseed flavour and is most often paired with chicken and fish.

Chervil This pretty herb has a mild aniseed flavour that goes well with fish, chicken, cheese and creamy savoury dishes. It is also good in salads.

Below: *Mint has a cool and refreshing flavour and is used in both sweet and savoury dishes.*

Below: *Dill has a sweet, aromatic fragrance and is particularly good used in fish and egg dishes.*

Left: *Delicate, fragrant basil is the perfect flavouring to use with tomatoes.*

Fragrant herbs

These distinctive herbs have a strong, aromatic scent and flavour and suit many different kinds of dishes.

Kaffir lime leaves These dark green leaves are used to impart a citrus flavour to many South-east Asian soups and curries. Add the leaves whole, torn or finely shredded.

Lemon balm With a distinctive lemon flavour and fragrance, this herb complements all ingredients that go well with citrus fruit or juice. Lemon balm makes a good addition to fish, chicken and vegetable dishes as well as sweet drinks and desserts. Use in moderation.

Dill This pretty, feathery herb has a distinctive flavour that is perfect with fish, chicken and egg dishes. It also goes very well with potatoes, courgettes (zucchini) and cucumber. It should be added to dishes just before serving because its mild flavour diminishes with cooking.

Spices and Aromatics

These flavourings play a very important role when cooking with a limited number of ingredients, adding a warmth and roundness of flavour to simple dishes. It is difficult to have every spice to hand, but a few key spices will be enough to create culinary magic. Black pepper is an essential seasoning in every storecupboard; cumin seeds, coriander seeds, dried chillies and turmeric are also good basics.

Above: *Saffron has a delicate fragrance and imparts a pale golden colour to both sweet and savoury dishes.*

Dried spices

Store spices in airtight jars or containers in a cool, dark place. Buy small quantities that will be used up fairly quickly because flavours diminish with age. Check the sell-by dates of the spices in your store cupboard (pantry) and throw away any spices that are old or no longer fragrant; there is little point in using old, tasteless spices to flavour food because the results will not be satisfactory.

Pepper Black pepper is one of the most commonly used spices. It should always be freshly ground because, once ground, it loses its flavour quickly. It is used in almost all savoury recipes but can also be used to flavour shortbread and to bring out the flavour of fruit such as pineapple and strawberries. Green peppercorns have a mild flavour. They are available dried or preserved in brine and are excellent for flavouring pâtés and meat dishes. White pepper is hotter than green, but less aromatic than black.

Chilli flakes Crushed dried red chillies can be added to, or sprinkled over, all kinds of dishes – from stir-fries and grilled (broiled) meats to pasta sauces and pizza.

Cayenne pepper This fiery, piquant spice is made from a dried hot red chilli, so use sparingly. It is excellent in cheese dishes and creamy soups and sauces.

Paprika An essential seasoning for Hungarian goulash and used in many Spanish dishes, paprika is available in a mild and hot form. It has a slightly sweet flavour.

Saffron This expensive spice is the dried stigma of a crocus flower, and is available in strands or ground. Saffron strands have a superior flavour and are best infused in a little hot liquid, such as milk or water, before being added to a recipe. Saffron has a distinct but delicate flavour. It is used sparingly in all kinds of dishes, including paella, curry, risotto, rice pudding and baking. Be wary of very cheap saffron because it is probably not the true spice and will not offer the rich, rounded flavour of the real thing.

Below: *Sweet paprika is the mildest of all the chilli powders and can be used to add a rich flavour and colour to savoury dishes.*

Mustard seeds These may be black, brown or white. They are used to make the condiment mustard and are also used as a flavouring in cooking. Black mustard seeds are added to Indian dishes, for their crunchy texture as well as flavour. Try adding a few mustard seeds to bread dough to give it a spicy kick.

Cumin This warm, pungent spice is widely used in Indian and North African cooking. Cumin works well with meats and a variety of vegetables, particularly robust-tasting sweet potatoes, squashes and cabbage.

Caraway seeds These small dark seeds have a fennel-like flavour. They are very versatile and make a lively addition to savoury breads and sweet cakes, while also complementing strongly flavoured sausage dishes and vegetables such as cabbage.

Fennel seeds These pretty little green seeds have a sweet, aniseed-like flavour that pairs well with chicken and robust fish dishes. It also tastes good in breads.

Coriander Available whole or ground, this warm, aromatic spice is delicious with most meats, particularly lamb. It is widely used in Indian and Asian cooking and is frequently paired with cumin. When combined, ground coriander and cumin make an excellent spice rub.

Below: Turmeric root is hard and must be ground to make the familiar bright yellow spice used in Indian cooking.

Above: *Mustard seeds and cumin seeds have a warm, spicy aroma. Buy them whole, then grind them as you need them.*

Turmeric Made from dried turmeric root, the ground spice is bright yellow with a peppery, slightly earthy flavour. It is used in many Indian recipes.

Garam masala This Indian mixture of ground roasted spices is usually made from cumin, coriander, cardamom and black pepper. Ready mixed garam masala is widely available, although the flavour is better when the spices are freshly roasted and ground.

Chinese five spice This is a mixture of ground spices, including anise pepper, cassia, fennel seeds, star anise and cloves. It is used in Chinese cookery, particularly to season pork and chicken dishes. Chinese five spice is a powerful mixture and should be used sparingly.

Salt

Probably the most important of all seasonings, salt is an essential ingredient in almost every cuisine. It has been used for many years, not only to flavour and bring out the taste of other foods, but to preserve them as well. Cured fish and meat, such as salt cod, prosciutto, salt beef and bacon, are preserved in salt to draw out moisture and prevent them from decomposing.

The type of salt used is important – rock salt or sea salt does not have added chemicals, which are often found in table salt. Rock salt is available in crystal form and can be ground in a mill, or refined to cooking salt. Sea salt has a strong, salty taste and it is used in smaller amounts.

Above: *Cinnamon sticks can be used whole in hot drinks, stews and casseroles to add a warm, spicy flavour.*

Green cardamom This fragrant spice is widely used in Indian and North African cooking to flavour both sweet and savoury dishes. The papery green pods enclose little black seeds that are easily scraped out and can be crushed in a mortar with a pestle if required.

Cinnamon This warm spice is available in sticks and ground into powder and has many uses in savoury and sweet recipes. Add sticks to stews, casseroles and other liquid dishes, then remove them before serving. Use ground cinnamon in baking, desserts and drinks.

Ginger The ground, dried spice is particularly useful for baking. For a fresher flavour in savoury recipes and drinks, it is best to use fresh root ginger.

Nutmeg This large aromatic seed has a spicy flavour, which adds a warm spiciness to milk, egg and cream dishes and enhances the flavour of spinach. Nutmeg is available ready ground, but the flavour is far better when the spice is freshly grated. Try sprinkling a little grated nutmeg over milk-based soups before serving.

Mace This spice is the casing of the nutmeg – it has a similar flavour but is slightly milder. Mace is great for flavouring butter for savoury dishes and is an essential ingredient in potted shrimps.

Star anise This pretty, star-shaped spice has a strong aniseed flavour. It is widely used in Chinese and Asian cooking and is a great partner for pork and chicken. It is also good for flavouring rice – simply add a single star anise to the cooking water. It can be used to flavour sweet dishes such as ice creams and jellies.

Allspice This berry has a warm, slightly cinnamon-clove flavour. It is more readily available in its ground form and can be used in both savoury and sweet cooking. It goes particularly well in winter recipes and fruit cake.

Cloves Available whole or ground these dried flower buds are used in savoury and sweet dishes. Ham is particularly tasty studded with whole cloves before baking, while the ground spice is suitable for cakes and cookies. Ground cloves are strong, so use sparingly.

Juniper berries These small, dark-purple berries are the main flavouring in gin. Add a few juniper berries to meaty stews and casseroles to give a fragrant, spicy kick.

Vanilla Dried vanilla pods (beans) are long and black, encasing hundreds of tiny black seeds. Warm the whole pod in milk, or place in a jar of sugar, to allow the flavour to infuse (steep), or split the pods, scrape out the seeds and add to cakes, desserts and ice cream. Natural vanilla extract is distilled from vanilla pods and is a useful alternative to pods. Vanilla extract tends to have a better flavour than vanilla essence, which can be quite overpowering. Some flavourings are not actually vanilla, but a synthetic alternative.

Above: *For the best flavour, grate whole nutmegs as and when you need the spice, using a special small grater.*

Fresh spices and aromatics

These wonderful flavourings are widely used in many dishes and add a rich, round, aromatic taste.

Fresh root ginger This pale-brown root should be peeled and then sliced, shredded, finely chopped or grated as required. It is used in curries, stir-fries, and grilled (broiled) and braised dishes. Choose plump roots and store in the refrigerator for up to 6 weeks. Preserved and crystallized ginger can be used in sweet dishes.

Galangal Similar in appearance to fresh root ginger, but often slimmer and with a pink-purple tinge, galangal is used in Thai and Indonesian cooking. Treat as for fresh root ginger, but store for a maximum of 3 weeks.

Above: *Fresh root ginger has a pungent, zesty flavour that is delicious used in savoury dishes – either raw or cooked.*

Above: *Fresh lemon grass is widely used in Thai cooking.*

Lemon grass This woody pale green stalk is excellent with fish and chicken, and can be used to flavour sweet dishes such as ice cream. Either bruise the bulbous end of the stalk and add whole to curries and soups, or finely slice or chop the end of the stalk and stir into the dish.

Garlic A member of the onion family and therefore often included as a vegetable, garlic also deserves mention as an aromatic for its role in flavouring all kinds of savoury dishes, raw or cooked. The potency of garlic depends on how it has been prepared. Crushed garlic gives the most powerful flavour, while finely chopping, shredding or slicing gives a slightly less strong result. Use garlic to flavour salad dressings or dips, or use whole, peeled cloves to flavour oils or vinegars. (Garlic is renowned for lingering on the breath after consumption; chewing fresh parsley is said to help counteract this.)

Ready-made spice mixes

There is an excellent selection of ready-made spice mixes available that make great short-cut flavouring ingredients for savoury dishes.

Harissa This North Arfrican spice paste is made of chillies, garlic, coriander, caraway, olive oil and other spices. It is delicious with oily fish as well as meat.

Chermoula This is another North African spice paste, which includes coriander, parsley, chilli and saffron.

Cajun seasoning This spice mixture made of black and white pepper, garlic, cumin and paprika is good for rubbing into meat before cooking over a barbecue.

Jerk seasoning This Caribbean spice blend is made of dry spices and goes well with chicken and pork.

Above: *Harissa paste can be used to flavour savoury dishes, such as soups and stews, or as a marinade for meat and fish.*

Other Flavourings

As well as herbs, spices and aromatics, there are a number of basic flavourings that are widely used in both sweet and savoury cooking. Sweeteners, such as sugar and honey, and flavourings, such as chocolate and alcohol, are mainly used in sweet dishes, but they can also be used in savoury dishes. Sauces and condiments, such as soy sauce, can be used to enhance the taste of savoury ingredients.

Sugars and sweet spreads

Refined and raw sugars and sweet spreads such as honey and marmalade can all be used to sweeten and flavour.

Granulated This refined white sugar has large crystals. It is used for sweetening drinks and everyday cooking; it can also be used as a crunchy cookie or cake topping, or stirred into crumble mixtures for extra texture.

Caster/Superfine sugar This fine-grained white sugar is most frequently used in baking. Its fine texture is particularly well suited to making cakes and cookies.

Icing/Confectioners' sugar The finest of all the refined sugars, this sugar has a light, powdery texture. It is used for making icing and sweetening flavoured creams. It is also good for dusting on cakes, desserts and cookies as a decoration.

Below: Sugar cubes and rock sugar are most frequently used to sweeten drinks.

Demerara sugar This golden sugar consists of large crystals with a rich, slightly honeyish flavour. It is great for adding a crunchy texture to cookies.

Brown sugars These dark, unrefined sugars have a rich, caramel flavour. There are different types including light and dark muscovado (brown) sugar and dark brown molasses sugar. The darker the sugar, the more intense its flavour. Always check you are buying unrefined sugar because "brown" sugars are often actually white sugar that has been coloured after refining.

Left: Granulated sugar has larger crystals than caster sugar but both are good for making cakes and desserts.

Below: Golden demerara sugar and soft brown sugar have a moist texture and rich, more rounded flavour.

Honey Clear honey is used to flavour desserts, cakes and cookies as well as savoury dressings. It also makes a good base for barbecue sauces and glazes for chicken or meat.

Above: *Sweet, golden honey is perfect for flavouring sweet and savoury dishes.*

Marmalade Most often served as a sweet spread, marmalade can also make an interesting ingredient. Try orange marmalade as the base for a quick sauce to serve with duck.

Chocolate

There are many different types of chocolate, each with its own unique flavour. They can all be used in many ways – grated, chopped or melted, and stirred into ice creams, or used for desserts, sauces or in baking. Always choose plain (semisweet) chocolate with at least 70 per cent cocoa solids for a good flavour. Children often prefer the milder flavour of milk chocolate. White chocolate has a low cocoa solids content and is sweet with a very mild flavour. Chocolate spread is also a useful ingredient. It can be melted and stirred into ice cream, custard or drinks, or used in many desserts.

Below: *White, dark and milk chocolate are all popularly used in desserts, cookies, cakes, drinks and sweet sauces.*

Edible flowers

Many flowers are edible and can be used as ingredients. Roses and violets look delightful frosted and are used to decorate cakes and desserts. Simply brush the clean flower heads or petals with a little egg white, sprinkle with caster (superfine) sugar and leave to dry. Plain rose petals can be used to flavour sugar syrups; rosewater and orange flower water are readily available and convenient and easy to use. Fragrant lavender heads can be left to infuse in cream for about 30 minutes, imparting their flavour.

Flowers can also be used in savoury dishes. Nasturtiums, pansies, marigolds and herb flowers, such as chives, are used to flavour salads.

Coffee

To achieve a strong coffee flavour, use good-quality espresso. You do not need an espresso machine for this because espresso coffee is sold for use in cafetières or filter machines. Make a double-strength brew to flavour desserts, sauces, cakes and cookies.

Almond essence/extract

This distinctive-tasting flavouring is perfect for cakes, cookies and desserts, and is also used for flavouring cream that will be served with fruit desserts. It is very strong, so use sparingly.

Above: *Buy good quality espresso coffee beans and grind them freshly to make a really strong brew for flavouring desserts and cakes. Alternatively, use ready-ground espresso coffee.*

Alcohol

Wine, spirits, beer and cider add body to both sweet and savoury dishes. Wines and spirits can be used to perk up cooked dishes and to macerate fruits and enliven desserts. Beer and cider are more widely used in savoury dishes such as stews and casseroles.

Wine Fruity red wines can be used to enrich meat dishes, tomato sauces and gravies. Dry white wine goes well with chicken or fish dishes. Sweet white wines and sparkling wines can be used to make jellies and sweet sauces.

Port Ruby port can be added to sauces for red meats – it is richer and sweeter than red wine, so use more sparingly. Port is also suitable for macerating summer fruits.

Sherry Dry, medium or sweet sherry can be used in savoury and sweet recipes. Add a dash to gravies and meat sauces or add a couple of spoonfuls to a rich fruit cake or dessert.

Marsala This Italian fortified wine is used to flavour desserts such as tiramisu and is also good in meat dishes.

Spirits Use rum and brandy for flavouring meat sauces, ice creams and cakes. Clear spirits, such as vodka and gin, can be used for sorbets; add a splash of vodka to tomato-based pasta dishes and fish dishes to give an extra kick. Irish cream liqueurs have a velvet-like texture that is excellent in creams, ice creams and cake fillings. Sweet fruit liqueurs are great used in desserts.

Right: *Almond-flavoured amaretto is delicious in creams and ice creams.*

Above: *Sherry and Marsala are classic flavourings for desserts such as trifle and Italian tiramisu. They are also used in meat dishes and can add a rich, round flavour to meat sauces.*

Preserved fruit and nuts

Above: *Preserved lemons have an intense flavour.*

Preserved lemons A classic in North African cooking, the lemons are preserved whole or in large pieces in a mixture of salt and spices. The chopped peel is usually added to chicken dishes to add an intense, sharp, citrus flavour.

Dried fruit Dried apricots, prunes, figs, currants, sultanas (golden raisins) and raisins can be added to savoury dishes and meat stews to impart a rich, sweet flavour. They are also good for adding flavour and body to sweet desserts, cakes and cookies.

Nuts Almonds, walnuts and pine nuts are useful for savoury dishes such as salads, vegetable dishes, pastes and dips, as well as in desserts and baking.

Coconut milk Thin, creamy coconut milk is made from pulped coconut and is widely used in Thai and Asian cooking, particularly in curries and soups.

Sauces and condiments

Not only are sauces and condiments perfect for serving with main dishes at the table, they are also great for adding extra flavour and bite to simple dishes during cooking.

Mustard Wholegrain mustard containing whole mustard seeds has a sweet, fruity taste and makes a mild, flavourful salad dressing. French Dijon mustard has a fairly sharp, piquant flavour which complements red meat and makes a sharply flavoured dressing. English mustard may be purchased as a dry powder or ready prepared and is excellent added to cheese dishes, or used to enliven bland creamy sauces.

Tomato purée/paste This concentrated purée is an essential in every storecupboard (pantry). It is great for adding flavour, and sometimes body, to sauces and stews.

Passata/bottled strained tomatoes This Italian product, made of sieved tomatoes, has a fairly thin consistency and makes a good base for a tomato sauce.

Tomato ketchup Add a splash of this strong table condiment to tomato sauces for a sweet-sour flavour.

Worcestershire sauce This thin, brown, very spicy sauce brings a piquant flavour to casseroles, stews and soups. It can also be used to perk up cheese dishes.

Below: Wholegrain mustard can be used in dressings and cheese sauces – adding real bite and interest to their flavour.

Right: Dark and light soy sauce are the perfect flavourings for Chinese and Asian dishes.

Below: Sun-dried tomato paste can add extra flavour to tomato sauces, and meat and vegetable soups and stews.

Curry paste There are many ready-made curry pastes, including those for classic Indian and Thai curries. They can also be used to spice up dishes such as burgers.

Sweet chilli sauce You can add this sweet, spicy dipping sauce to stir-fries and braised chicken dishes, and it can be used as a glaze for chicken or prawns before grilling (broiling) or cooking over a barbecue.

Soy sauce Made from fermented soy beans, soy sauce is salty and a little adds a rich, rounded flavour to Asian-style stir-fries, glazes and sauces.

Teriyaki marinade This Japanese marinade has a sweet, salty flavour. Use it to marinate meat, chicken and fish before frying; the leftover marinade will cook down to make a delicious, sticky sauce.

Oyster sauce Add this thick Chinese sauce with a sweet, meaty taste to stir-fries and braised dishes.

Pesto Use fresh pesto, made with basil, garlic, pine nuts and Parmesan cheese, on pasta or to flavour sauces, soups, stews and dressings. There are also variations such as red pesto made with roasted red (bell) peppers.

Kitchen Basics

Keep a well-stocked storecupboard (pantry) and you will be able to cook almost anything at any time. However, this does not mean overloading your storage space with a vast range of ingredients. A selection of well-chosen, essential ingredients is more important than a cupboard full of obscure, out-of-date items that have been used once and then forgotten. The following are some useful basic ingredients that will be invaluable in every kitchen; try to remember to check cupboards regularly and be vigilant about throwing away out-of-date ingredients and replenishing them with fresh ones.

Flour

This is an essential ingredient in every kitchen. There are many different types, which serve many purposes in both sweet and savoury cooking – from baking cakes to thickening gravy and making cheese sauce.

Wheat flours Plain (all-purpose) flour can be used in most recipes, including sauces. Self-raising (self-rising) flour has a raising agent added and is useful for cakes and other baking recipes. Wholemeal flour is available as plain (all-purpose) or self-raising (self-rising). Strong bread flour contains more gluten than plain flour, making it more suitable for making breads.

Right: *(Clockwise from top) There are many different types of flour for different purposes, including strong bread flour, French bread flour, self-raising flour and plain flour. For general kitchen use, plain flour is probably the most versatile.*

Gluten-free flours For those with an allergy to gluten, which is found in wheat and other grains, gluten-free flour is an invaluable ingredient. It is widely available from most large supermarkets and health food stores.

Cornflour/cornstarch This very fine white flour is useful for thickening sauces and stabilizing egg mixtures, such as custard, to prevent them curdling. A little cornflour is first blended with cold water or another liquid to make a smooth, runny paste, which is then stirred into a hot sauce, soup or stew and boiled until it thickens.

Raising agents Self-raising flour contains raising agents, normally baking powder, which give a light texture to cakes and cookies. You can add baking powder to plain flour to achieve the same result. The baking powder reacts with liquids and heat during cooking and produces carbon-dioxide bubbles, which make the mixture rise.

Oils

Essential both for cooking and adding flavour, there are many different types of oil, all of which have their own character and use in the kitchen. Every cook should have a bottle of oil for cooking, and also oils for drizzling and flavouring.

Olive oil Extra virgin olive oil, made from the first pressing of the olives, has the best, most pronounced flavour and is the most expensive type. It is best reserved for condiments or salad dressings. Ordinary olive oil is generally the third or fourth pressing of the oil and is better used in cooking. Light olive oil is paler and milder in flavour than ordinary olive oil and is ideal for making lightly flavoured salad dressings.

Groundnut/peanut oil This virtually flavourless oil is used for frying, baking and making dressings.

Corn oil Golden-coloured corn oil has a fairly strong flavour and can be used in most types of cooking.

Below: Flavoured oils are invaluable in the minimalist kitchen – providing extra taste without having to add extra ingredients.

Left: Rich, dark sesame oil and spicy chilli oil can be added to stir-fries and dressings to add flavour.

Vegetable oil This is a blend of oils, usually including corn oil and other vegetable oils. It is quite flavourless and useful in most types of cooking.

Sesame oil Sesame and toasted sesame seed oils both have strong flavours and should be used sparingly when cooking.

Hazelnut and walnut oils Both are quite strongly flavoured and useful as dressings rather than for cooking. They are delicious drizzled over cooked fish, poultry or vegetables, or used in salad dressings.

Flavoured oils There are many types and brands of flavoured oils. Look out for those using a good-quality olive oil as the base.

Chilli oil This is available in various styles – it adds a pleasing spicy kick to all sorts of dishes such as pasta, fish and salads. Add a drizzle just before serving the food.

Garlic oil This is a good alternative to fresh garlic. It has a fairly strong flavour so it should be used with care.

Lemon-infused oil
This is excellent with fish, chicken and pasta, and for salad dressings.

Right: Extra virgin olive oil has a rich, fruity taste and is perfect for drizzling over dishes and making dressings.

Pasta and noodles

These are invaluable storecupboard (pantry) ingredients that can be used as the base of many hot and cold dishes.

Pasta Dried pasta keeps for months in an airtight container – check the packet for information on keeping quality. There is a wide variety of pasta in all shapes and

sizes. Egg pasta is enriched with egg yolks and it has a richer flavour than plain pasta. Generally, the choice depends on personal taste – use whichever type you have in the cupboard. Cook pasta at a rolling boil in plenty of salted water. Fresh pasta cooks very quickly and is available chilled. It can be stored in the refrigerator for several days, or in the freezer for several months.

Above: *Dried pasta is a handy kitchen standby and can be used to make hot, hearty dishes or light, tasty salads.*

Egg noodles Made from wheat flour and eggs, these may be thick, medium or thin. Use them for stir-fries or as an accompaniment to Chinese and Asian dishes.

Below: *Egg noodles have a nutty taste and can be served hot in Asian-style stir-fries and soups, and cold in salads.*

Above:

Polenta is widely used in Italian-style dishes and makes a good alternative to pasta. It can be served as an accompaniment or made into a main dish.

Rice noodles These transluscent white noodles are a good alternative to wheat noodles – particularly for those on a gluten-free diet. They are available as broad flat or thin noodles that can be added to stir-fries and soups as well as used cold as the base for salads. Rice noodles are easy to prepare because they don't need to be cooked. Simply soak in boiling water for about 5 minutes, then stir-fry, add to soups or toss with salad ingredients.

Couscous and polenta

Like pasta and noodles, couscous and polenta can be served as an accompaniment or can act as the base of many dishes. They have a mild flavour, and go particularly well with strongly flavoured ingredients.

Couscous Made from durum wheat, couscous is often regarded as a type of pasta. Traditional couscous needed long steaming before serving, but the majority of brands available in supermarkets today are "instant" and need only brief soaking in water. It is the classic accompaniment to Moroccan tagines, but also goes well with all kinds of meat, fish and vegetable stews. It makes an excellent base for salads.

Polenta This is made from finely ground cornmeal. It is cooked with water and either served soft (rather like mashed potato) or left to set and then cut into pieces that can be grilled (broiled) or fried. Quick-cook and ready-made polenta are available in most supermarkets and can be made into simple, hearty dishes. It is best served with flavourful ingredients.

Rice

This versatile grain can be served as an accompaniment, or form the base of both sweet and savoury dishes.

Long-grain rice The narrow grains of white rice cook to a light, fluffy texture and are generally served as an accompaniment to main dishes. They also make a perfect base for other dishes such as stir-fries and salads.

Short-grain rice There are several types of short, stubby, polished rice such as pudding rice and sushi rice. These usually have a high starch content and cook into tender grains that cling together and can be shaped easily.

Thai Jasmine rice This white, slightly sticky rice has a scented flavour. Serve with Thai curries or in stir-fries.

Risotto rice This rice has medium-length polished grains. The grains can absorb a great deal of liquid while still retaining their shape. There are several types of risotto rice, including the popular arborio and carnaroli. When cooking risotto rice, it is imperative to stir it regularly. Liquid or stock should be added periodically throughout cooking to prevent the rice sticking to the pan and burning.

Basmati rice This long-grain rice is widely used in Indian cooking. It is aromatic and cooks to give separated, fluffy grains. Brown basmati rice is also available.

Below: *Canned beans are nutritious and versatile and can be used in hearty stews, healthy salads or tasty dips and pâtés.*

Vegetables, beans and lentils

Dried, canned and bottled vegetables, beans and lentils are very versatile and are a useful storecupboard standby.

Above: *Canned tomatoes are a real storecupboard standby.*

Canned tomatoes
Available chopped or whole, canned tomatoes are an essential item in every kitchen. They are very versatile and can be used to make sauces, pasta dishes, pizza toppings, soups and stews. Look out for canned Italian pomodorino tomatoes in a thick juice; they make a superbly rich sauce.

Dried mushrooms Dried wild mushrooms such as porcini and morels are a useful alternative to fresh, seasonal mushrooms, which are not always available. They add a rich flavour to pasta dishes and casseroles.

Bottled antipasti Red (bell) peppers, aubergines (eggplant), mushrooms and artichoke hearts preserved in olive oil with garlic and herbs are a classic Italian appetizer but can make a tasty addition to salads and pasta dishes.

Above: *Juicy black olives add bite to sauces and salads.*

Olives Black and green, olives bring a rich flavour to salads and pasta dishes; they also make a quick and easy appetizer when served with salami and bread.

Red lentils Compared to most other dried beans, red lentils have a relatively short cooking time and are ideal for making a quick and tasty Indian-style dhal.

Canned pulses Dried pulses such as flageolet beans, chickpeas, red kidney beans, cannellini beans and butter (lima) beans have a long shelf-life but require lengthy preparation: soaking overnight and then long boiling. The canned alternatives simply need to be rinsed in cold water, and can then be used in hot dishes or used to make salads.

Short-cut Ingredients

There are some useful products available in supermarkets and food stores that can help you save valuable time in the kitchen. These ingredients are usually pre-prepared in some way, taking the time and effort out of preparation. They provide a quick base for dishes so you will need fewer ingredients and can spend less time on shopping and cooking, and more time relaxing and eating.

Pastry Ready-made pastry is widely available in supermarkets and can make quick work of tarts, pies and filled pastries. Shortcrust, sweet shortcrust, puff and filo pastry can all be purchased frozen or chilled and ready to use. They are usually of excellent quality, giving delicious results. Some pastries are even ready-rolled so all you have to do is open the packet, cut, fold and fill the pastry, and then bake it in the oven until crisp and golden.

Cookie dough Cartons of chocolate chip cookie dough can be useful for many sweet recipes. It can be shaped and baked to make plain cookies or, more imaginatively, they could be coated with a topping or sandwiched together with a chocolate filling or ice cream to make a decadent treat or a sumptuous dessert. The dough can also be rolled thinly and used to line muffin tins (pans) to make a crisp cookie cup to fill with ice cream for dessert. Bitesize pieces of the cookie dough can be stirred into a vanilla ice cream mix to make cookie dough ice cream.

Marzipan Good quality marzipan is available in most supermarkets. It is perfect for decorating cakes, but it can be used in many other ways as well. Try rolling it out thinly and using it as a tart base under fruit, or chop it into small pieces and add to cookies and cakes.

Right (from top to bottom): Ready-made filo, shortcrust, puff and flaky pastries are available fresh and frozen. They can save time when making tarts and pies and give reliably good results.

Custard Fresh ready-made custard is great served hot as an accompaniment to desserts, but it also makes a useful base for ice creams, sauces and soufflés.

Frozen fruit Mixed frozen fruit has already been prepared, ready for making into desserts and sauces. It is available all year round, which means that you can enjoy the sweet taste of summer fruits during the winter when they are out of season. Frozen fruit is often cheaper than fresh.

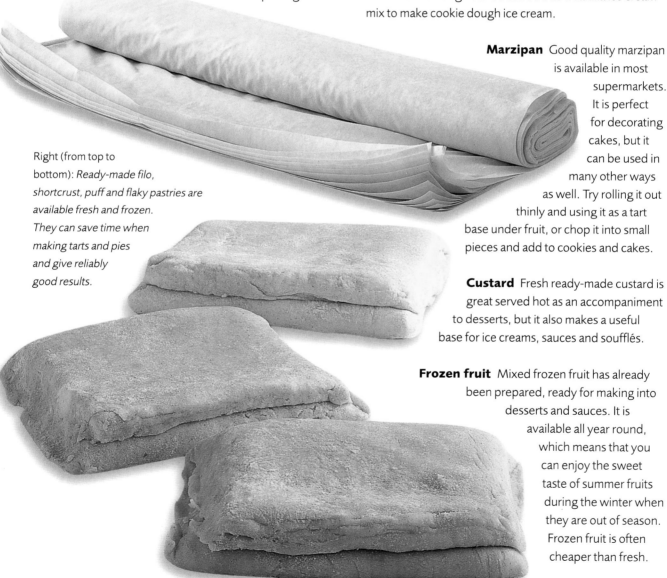

Above: *Good quality fresh custards are widely available in most supermarkets and make an ideal base for many sweet dishes.*

Above: *Frozen summer berries are available all year round and make a handy alternative to fresh ones in most cooked dishes.*

Cake mixes With the simple addition of an egg and water, these easy-to-use mixes can be turned into a freshly baked cake in no time at all. Scattering the cake mixture with chopped nuts before baking, or sandwiching the cake with cream and fresh summer fruits once it has cooled can transform these simple mixes from an "emergency" storecupboard (pantry) item into a fabulous tea-time treat or delicious dessert with almost no effort.

Above: *Crisp ginger cookies can be roughly broken or finely crushed and used as the base for simple desserts such as trifle.*

Cakes and cookies Store-bought cakes and cookies can often be used as the base for simple desserts. Dark chocolate brownies can be combined with cream and macerated fruit to create a rich, indulgent dessert, or blended with milk and ice cream to make a decadent milkshake. Broken ginger cookies or sponge fingers can be used as the base for many creamy desserts.

Batter mixes These are another useful "emergency" product. Simply combine with an egg and water and use to make pancakes for breakfast or dessert, or to coat food before deep-frying.

Pizza base mixes and bread mixes Whereas ready-baked pizza bases tend to be rather cardboard-like, these mixes are excellent and take very little effort to make.

Pasta sauces Both bottled and fresh pasta sauces are widely available in most supermarkets. Simple tomato and herb sauces are useful for tossing with pasta, spreading over a pizza base or as the base for a quick soup. Ready-made cheese sauces are also versatile – not only good for serving with pasta, but also for topping vegetable gratins, or combining with whisked egg whites and extra grated cheese to make a quick and simple soufflé.

Microwave rice mixes A fairly recent invention, these come in a variety of flavours, including mushroom and pilau. They are extremely useful as the base for quick rice dishes such as kedgeree.

Bags of mixed salad These save time selecting and preparing a variety of leaves. For maximum flavour, choose a bag that includes baby leaves and herbs.

Making the Basics

Having a few ready-made basics, such as stocks, pasta sauces and flavoured oils, can really help with everyday cooking. They can all be bought ready-made in the supermarket, but they are easy to make at home. Stocks take time to prepare, but they can be stored in the freezer for several months. Flavoured oils are easy to make and keep in the same way as ordinary oils so it's well worth having a few in the cupboard. All the basic sauces, dressings, marinades and flavoured creams in this section are simple to make and can be made fresh or in advance.

Flavoured oils

Good quality olive oil can be flavoured with herbs, spices and aromatics to make rich-tasting oils that are perfect for drizzling, making dressings and cooking. Make a couple of different flavoured oils and store in a cool, dark place.

Herb-infused oil Half-fill a jar with washed and dried fresh herbs such as rosemary or basil. Pour over olive oil to cover, then seal the jar and place in a cool, dark place for 3 days. Strain the herb-flavoured oil into a clean jar or bottle and discard the herbs.

Lemon oil Finely pare the rind from 1 lemon, place on kitchen paper, and leave to dry for 1 day. Add the dried rind to a bottle of olive oil and leave to infuse for up to 3 days. Strain the oil into a clean bottle and discard the rind.

Chilli oil Add several dried chillies to a bottle of olive oil and leave to infuse for about 2 weeks before using. If the flavour is not sufficiently pronounced, leave for another week. The chillies can be left in the bottle and give a very decorative effect.

Garlic oil Add several whole garlic cloves to a bottle of olive oil and leave to infuse for about 2 weeks before using. If the flavour is not sufficiently pronounced, leave the oil to infuse for another week, then strain the oil into a clean bottle and store in a cool, dark place.

Stock

You cannot beat the flavour of good home-made stock so it's worth making a large batch and freezing it. To freeze, pour the cooled stock into 600ml/1 pint/2^1/2 cup containers and freeze for up to 2 months.

Chicken stock Put a 1.3kg/3lb chicken carcass into a large pan with 2 peeled and quartered onions, 2 halved carrots, 2 roughly chopped celery sticks, 1 bouquet garni, 1 peeled garlic clove and 5 black peppercorns. Pour in 1.2 litres/2 pints/5 cups cold water to cover the chicken and vegetables and bring to the boil. Reduce the heat, cover and simmer for 4–5 hours, regularly skimming off any scum from the surface. Strain the stock through a sieve lined with kitchen paper and leave to cool.

Beef stock Preheat the oven to 230°C/450°F/Gas 8. Put 1.8kg/4lb beef bones in a roasting pan and roast for 40 minutes, until browned, turning occasionally. Transfer the bones and vegetables to a large pan. Cover with water, add 2 chopped tomatoes and cook as for chicken stock.

Fish stock Put 2 chopped onions, 1.3kg/3lb fish bones and heads, 300ml/^{1}/2 pint/1^1/4 cups white wine, 5 black peppercorns and 1 bouquet garni in a large pan. Pour in 2 litres/3^1/2 pints/9 cups water. Bring to the boil and simmer for 20 minutes, skimming often. Strain the stock.

Vegetable stock
Put 900g/2lb chopped vegetables, including onions, leeks, tomatoes, carrots, parsnips and cabbage, in a large pan. Pour in 1.5 litres/2^1/2 pints/ 6^1/4 cups water. Bring to the boil and simmer for 30 minutes, then strain.

Marinades

These strong-tasting mixes are perfect for adding flavour to meat, poultry, fish and vegetables. Most ingredients should be left to marinate for at least 30 minutes.

Ginger and soy marinade This is perfect for use with chicken and beef. Peel and grate a 2.5cm/1in piece of fresh root ginger and peel and finely chop a large garlic clove. In a small bowl, whisk together 60ml/ 4 tbsp olive oil with 75ml/ 5 tbsp dark soy sauce. Season with freshly ground black pepper and stir in the ginger and garlic.

Rosemary and garlic marinade This is ideal for robust fish, lamb and chicken. Roughly chop the leaves from 3 fresh rosemary sprigs. Finely chop 2 garlic cloves and whisk together with the rosemary, 75ml/5 tbsp olive oil and the juice of 1 lemon.

Lemon grass and lime marinade Use with fish and chicken. Finely chop 1 lemon grass stalk. Whisk together the grated rind and juice of 1 lime with 75ml/5 tbsp olive oil, salt and black pepper and the lemon grass.

Red wine and bay marinade This is ideal for red meat, particularly tougher cuts. Whisk together 150ml/^{1}/$_4$ pint/ ^{2}/$_3$ cup red wine, 1 chopped garlic clove, 2 torn fresh bay leaves and 45ml/3 tbsp olive oil. Season with black pepper.

Below: *Marinades containing red wine are particularly good for tenderizing tougher cuts of meat such as stewing steak.*

Dressings

Freshly made dressings are delicious drizzled over salads but are also tasty served with cooked vegetables and simply cooked fish, meat and poultry. You can make these dressings a few hours in advance and store them in a sealed container in the refrigerator until ready to use. Give them a quick whisk before drizzling over the food.

Honey and wholegrain mustard dressing

Drizzle this sweet, peppery dressing over leafy salads, fish, chicken and red meat dishes or toss with warm new potatoes. Whisk together 15ml/1 tbsp wholegrain mustard, 30ml/2 tbsp white wine vinegar, 15ml/1 tbsp honey and 75ml/5 tbsp extra virgin olive oil and season with salt and ground black pepper.

Orange and tarragon dressing

Serve this fresh, tangy dressing with salads and grilled (broiled) fish. In a small bowl, whisk together the rind and juice of 1 large orange with 45ml/ 3 tbsp olive oil and 15ml/1 tbsp chopped fresh tarragon. Season with salt and plenty of freshly ground black pepper to taste.

Toasted coriander and cumin dressing

Drizzle this warm, spicy dressing over grilled chicken, lamb or beef. Heat a small frying pan and sprinkle in 15ml/1 tbsp each of coriander and cumin seeds. Dry-fry until the seeds release their aromas and start to pop, then crush the seeds using a mortar and pestle. Add 45ml/3 tbsp olive oil, whisk to combine, then leave to infuse for 20 minutes. Season with salt and freshly ground black pepper to taste.

Savoury sauces

Hot and cold savoury sauces lie at the heart of many dishes or can be the finishing touch that makes a meal – tomato sauce tossed with pasta, cheese sauce poured over a vegetable gratin, apple sauce to accompany pork, or a spoonful of mayonnaise with poached salmon. This section covers all the basic sauces: from tomato and pesto sauces to toss with pasta and rich, fruity sauces to serve with meat and poultry to creamy ones such as mayonnaise.

Easy tomato sauce

This versatile sauce can be tossed with pasta, used on a pizza base or served with chicken or fish. Heat 15ml/ 1 tbsp olive oil in a pan, add 1 chopped onion and fry for 3–4 minutes until soft. Add 1 chopped garlic clove and cook for about 1 minute more. Pour in 400g/14oz chopped canned tomatoes and stir in 15ml/1 tbsp tomato purée (paste). Add 30ml/2 tbsp dried oregano and simmer for about 15 minutes, until thickened. Season with salt and pepper.

Mustard cheese sauce

Toss this rich, creamy sauce with pasta, or serve with boiled vegetables or baked white fish. Melt 25g/1oz/2 tbsp butter in a medium pan and stir in 25g/1oz/¼ cup plain (all-purpose) flour. Remove the pan from the heat and stir in 5ml/1 tsp prepared English mustard, then gradually add 200ml/7fl oz/scant 1 cup milk, stirring well to remove any lumps. (If the sauce becomes lumpy, whisk until smooth.) Return the pan to the heat and bring to the boil, stirring

constantly. Remove from the heat and stir in 115g/4oz/ 1 cup grated Gruyère or Cheddar cheese. Season to taste with salt and freshly ground black pepper.

Quick satay sauce

Serve this spicy Asian-style sauce with grilled (broiled) chicken, beef or prawns, or toss with freshly cooked egg noodles. Put 30ml/ 2 tbsp crunchy peanut butter in a pan and stir in 150ml/¼ pint/⅔ cup coconut milk, 45ml/3 tbsp hot water, a pinch of chilli powder and 30ml/2 tbsp light soy sauce. Heat gently and simmer for 1 minute.

Apple sauce Serve with pork. Peel, core and slice 450g/ 1lb cooking apples and place in a pan. Add a splash of water, 15ml/1 tbsp caster (superfine) sugar and a few whole cloves. Cook the apples over a gentle heat, stirring occasionally, until the fruit becomes pulpy.

Quick cranberry sauce Serve with roast chicken or turkey. Put 225g/8oz/2 cups cranberries in a pan with 75g/3oz/scant ½ cup light muscovado (brown) sugar, 45ml/3 tbsp port and 45ml/3 tbsp orange juice. Bring to the boil, then simmer, uncovered, for 10 minutes, or until the fruit is tender. Stir occasionally to stop it from sticking.

Gooseberry relish Serve this tart relish with oily fish, such as mackerel, or fatty meat such as pork. Put 225g/ 8oz fresh or frozen gooseberries in a pan with 225g/8oz/ generous 1 cup caster (superfine) sugar and 1 star anise. Add a splash of water and a little white wine if desired. Bring to the boil and simmer, uncovered, for 10 minutes, stirring occasionally, until the fruit is soft and pulpy.

Below: *Sauces made from tart fruit, such as cranberries, are excellent served with mild or fatty roast poultry and meat.*

Traditional pesto This classic Italian sauce is made with basil, garlic, pine nuts and Parmesan cheese but there are many variations. Toss with pasta, stir into mashed potatoes or plain boiled rice, or use to flavour sauces and dressings. Put 50g/2oz fresh basil leaves in a food processor and blend to a paste with 25g/1oz/^{1}/$_4$ cup toasted pine nuts and 2 peeled garlic cloves. With the motor still running, drizzle in 120ml/4fl oz/^{1}/$_2$ cup extra virgin olive oil until the mixture forms a paste. Spoon the pesto into a bowl and stir in 25g/1oz/^{1}/$_3$ cup freshly grated Parmesan cheese. Season to taste with salt and freshly ground black pepper.

Parsley and walnut pesto Put 50g/2oz fresh parsley leaves in a food processor and blend to a paste with 25g/1oz/^{1}/$_4$ cup walnuts and 2 peeled garlic cloves. With the motor still running, drizzle in 120ml/4fl oz/^{1}/$_2$ cup extra virgin olive oil until the mixture forms a paste. Spoon the pesto into a bowl and stir in 25g/1oz/^{1}/$_3$ cup freshly grated Parmesan cheese. Season to taste with salt and freshly ground black pepper.

Gravy

This classic sauce for roast poultry and meat is quick and easy to make. Remove the cooked poultry or meat from the roasting pan, transfer to a serving platter, cover with foil and leave to rest. Spoon off all but about 30ml/2 tbsp of the cooking fat and juices, leaving the sediment in the pan. Place the pan over a low heat and add a splash of white wine for poultry or red wine for meat, stirring in any sediment from the roasting pan. Stir in 30ml/2 tbsp plain (all-purpose) flour and mix to a paste. Remove from the heat and gradually pour in 450ml/^{3}/$_4$ pint/scant 2 cups stock. Return to the heat and stir over a medium heat until the gravy comes to the boil. Simmer for 2–3 minutes, until thickened. Adjust the seasoning and serve.

Rocket pesto Put 50g/2oz fresh rocket (arugula) leaves into a food processor and blend to a paste with 25g/1oz/^{1}/$_4$ cup toasted pine nuts and 2 peeled garlic cloves. With the motor still running, drizzle in 120ml/4fl oz/^{1}/$_2$ cup extra virgin olive oil until the mixture forms a paste. Spoon the pesto into a bowl and stir in 25g/1oz/^{1}/$_3$ cup freshly grated Parmesan cheese. Season to taste with salt and freshly ground black pepper.

Asian-style pesto Try this Asian version of Italian pesto tossed with freshly cooked egg noodles. Put 50g/2oz fresh coriander (cilantro) leaves into a food processor and add 25g/1oz/^{1}/$_4$ cup toasted pine nuts, 2 peeled garlic cloves and 1 roughly chopped, seeded red chilli. Blend until smooth. With the motor still running, drizzle in 120ml/4fl oz/^{1}/$_2$ cup extra virgin olive oil until the mixture forms a paste. Spoon the pesto into a bowl and season to taste with salt and freshly ground black pepper.

Mayonnaise Once you have made your own mayonnaise you will never want to buy it again. Put 2 egg yolks, 10ml/2 tsp lemon juice, 5ml/1 tsp Dijon mustard and some salt and ground black pepper in a food processor. Process briefly to combine, then, with the motor running, drizzle in about 350ml/12fl oz/1^1/$_2$ cups olive oil. The mayonnaise will become thick and pale. Scrape the mayonnaise into a bowl, taste and add more lemon juice and salt and pepper if necessary.

Aioli This classic French garlic mayonnaise is particularly good served with piping hot chips (French fries). Make the mayonnaise as described above, adding 2 peeled garlic cloves to the food processor with the egg yolks.

Lemon mayonnaise This zesty, creamy mayonnnaise complements cold poached fish perfectly. Make the mayonnaise as described above, adding the grated rind of 1 lemon to the food processor with the egg yolks.

Herb mayonnaise Make the plain mayonnaise as described above. Finely chop a handful of fresh herbs, such as basil, coriander (cilantro) and tarragon, then stir into the freshly made mayonnaise.

Savoury dips

These richly flavoured dips are delicious served with tortilla chips, crudités or small savoury crackers, but can also be served as an accompaniment to grilled (broiled) or poached chicken and fish. The creamy dips also make flavourful dressings for salads; you may need to thin them slightly with a squeeze of lemon juice or a little cold water.

Blue cheese dip This sharp, tangy mixture is best served with crunchy crudites. Put 200ml/ 7fl oz/scant 1 cup crème fraîche in a large bowl and add 115g/4oz/1 cup crumbled blue cheese such as stilton. Stir well until the mixture is smooth and creamy. Season with salt and freshly ground black pepper and fold in 30ml/2 tbsp chopped fresh chives.

Sour cream and chive dip This tasty dip is a classic combination and goes particularly well with crudités and savoury crackers. Put 200ml/ 7fl oz/scant 1 cup sour cream in a bowl and add 30ml/2 tbsp snipped fresh chives and a pinch of caster (superfine) sugar. Stir well to mix, then season with salt and plenty of freshly ground black pepper to taste.

Avocado and cumin salsa Serve this spicy Mexican-style salsa with tortilla chips; they're the perfect shape for scooping up the chunky salsa. Peel, stone (pit) and roughly chop 1 ripe avocado. Transfer to a bowl and gently stir in 1 finely chopped fresh red chilli, 15ml/1 tbsp toasted crushed cumin seeds, 1 chopped ripe tomato, the juice of 1 lime, 45ml/3 tbsp olive oil and 30ml/2 tbsp chopped fresh coriander (cilantro). Season and serve immediately.

Sweet sauces

These luscious sauces are perfect spooned over ice cream and can turn a store-bought dessert into an indulgent treat.

Chocolate fudge sauce Put 175ml/6fl oz/$^3/_4$ cup double (heavy) cream in a small pan with 45ml/3 tbsp golden (light corn) syrup, 200g/7oz/scant 1 cup light muscovado (brown) sugar and a pinch of salt. Heat gently, stirring, until the sugar has dissolved. Add 75g/3oz/$^1/_2$ cup chopped plain (semisweet) chocolate and stir until melted. Simmer the sauce gently for about 20 minutes, stirring occasionally, until thickened. To keep warm until ready to use, pour into a heatproof bowl, cover and place over a pan of simmering water.

Toffee chocolate sauce Roughly chop 2 Mars bars (chocolate toffee bars) and put them in a pan with 300ml/ $^1/_2$ pint/1$^1/_4$ cups double (heavy) cream. Stir over a gentle heat until the chocolate bars have melted.

Raspberry and vanilla sauce Scrape the seeds from a vanilla pod into a food processor. Add 200g/7oz/1 cup raspberries and 30ml/2 tbsp icing (confectioners') sugar. Process to a purée, adding a little water to thin, if necessary.

Below: *Blended fruit sauces are quick and simple to make and are great drizzled over ice cream and many other desserts.*

Flavoured creams

Cream is the perfect accompaniment for any dessert – whether it's a healthy fruit salad, a sumptuous plum tart or a warming baked apple. Flavoured creams are even better and can transform a tasty dessert into a truly luscious one. The ideas below are all incredibly simple and can be prepared in advance and stored in the refrigerator until you are ready to serve.

Rosemary and almond cream This fragrant cream has a lovely texture and is good served with fruit compotes, pies and tarts. Pour 300ml/^{1}/$_2$ pint/ 1^1/$_4$ cups double (heavy) cream into a pan and add 2 fresh rosemary sprigs. Heat the mixture until just about to boil, then remove the pan from the heat and leave the mixture to infuse for 20 minutes. Remove the rosemary from the pan and discard. Pour the cream into a bowl and chill until cold. Whip the cold cream into soft peaks and stir in 30ml/2 tbsp chopped toasted almonds.

Rum and cinnamon cream You can serve this versatile cream with most desserts. It goes particularly well with coffee, chocolate and fruit. Pour 300ml/^{1}/$_2$ pint/1^1/$_4$ cups double (heavy) cream into a pan and add 1 cinnamon stick. Heat the mixture until just about to boil, then remove the pan from the heat and leave to infuse for about 20 minutes. Strain the cream through a fine sieve (strainer) and place in the refrigerator until cold. Whip the cold cream until it stands in soft peaks, then stir in 30ml/2 tbsp rum and 15ml/1 tbsp icing (confectioners') sugar.

Marsala mascarpone This rich, creamy Italian cheese is perfect for serving with grilled (broiled) fruit, tarts and hot desserts. Spoon 200g/7oz/scant 1 cup mascarpone into a large bowl and add 30ml/2 tbsp icing (confectioners') sugar and 45ml/3 tbsp Marsala. Beat the mixture well until smooth and thoroughly combined.

Cardamom cream Warm, spicy cardamom pods make a wonderfully subtle, aromatic cream that is delicious served with fruit salads, compôtes, tarts and pies. It goes particularly well with tropical fruits such as mango. Pour 300ml/ ^{1}/$_2$ pint/1^1/$_4$ cups double (heavy) cream into a pan and add 3 green cardamom pods. Heat the mixture gently until just about to boil, then remove the pan from the heat and leave to infuse for about 20 minutes. Strain the cream through a fine sieve (strainer) and place in the refrigerator until cold. Whip the cold cream until it stands in soft peaks.

Praline cream

1 Put 115g/4oz/^{1}/$_2$ cup sugar and 75ml/5 tbsp water in a small, heavy pan. Stir over a gentle heat until the sugar has dissolved, then boil (not stirring) until golden.

2 Remove from the heat and stir in 50g/2oz/ ^{1}/$_3$ cup whole blanched almonds and tip on to a lightly oiled baking sheet. Leave until hard.

3 Break the hardened nut mixture into smaller pieces and put in a food processor. Process for about 1 minute until finely chopped.

4 In a large bowl, whip 300ml/^{1}/$_2$ pint/1^1/$_4$ cups double (heavy) cream into soft peaks, then stir in the praline and serve immediately.

Making Simple Accompaniments

When you've made a delicious main meal, you need to serve it with equally tasty accompaniments. The following section is full of simple, speedy ideas for fabulous side dishes – from creamy mashed potatoes, fragrant rice and spicy noodles to Italian-style polenta and simple, healthy vegetables.

Mashed potatoes

Potatoes go well with just about any main dish. They can be cooked simply – boiled, steamed, fried or baked – but they are even better mashed with milk and butter to make creamy mashed potatoes. To make even more enticing side dishes, try stirring in different flavourings.

Perfect mashed potatoes Peel 675g/ 1¹/₂lb floury potatoes and cut them into large chunks. Place in a pan of salted boiling water. Return to the boil, then simmer for 15–20 minutes, or until completely tender. Drain the potatoes and return to the pan. Leave over a low heat for a couple of minutes, shaking the pan to drive off any excess moisture. Take the pan off the heat and, using a potato masher, mash the potatoes until smooth. Beat in 45–60ml/3–4 tbsp warm milk and a large knob (pat) of butter, then season with salt and freshly ground black pepper to taste.

Pesto mash This is a simple way to dress up plain mashed potatoes. It gives them real bite and a lovely green-specked appearance. Make mashed potatoes as described above, then stir in 30ml/ 2 tbsp pesto sauce until thoroughly combined.

Mustard mash Make mashed potatoes as above, then stir in 15–30ml/1–2 tbsp wholegrain mustard.

Parmesan and parsley mash Make mashed potatoes as above, then stir in 30ml/2 tbsp freshly grated Parmesan and 15ml/1 tbsp chopped fresh flat leaf parsley.

Apple and thyme mash Serve with pork. Make mashed potatoes as above. Heat 25g/1oz/2 tbsp butter in a pan and add 2 peeled, cored and sliced eating apples. Fry for 4–5 minutes, turning. Roughly mash, then fold into the potatoes, with 15ml/1 tbsp fresh thyme leaves.

Crushed potatoes

This chunky, modern version of mashed potatoes tastes delicious and can be flavoured in different ways.

Crushed potatoes with parsley and lemon Cook 675g/1¹/₂lb new potatoes in salted boiling water for 15–20 minutes, until tender. Drain the potatoes and crush roughly, using a fork. Stir in 30ml/ 2 tbsp extra virgin olive oil, the grated rind and juice of 1 lemon and 30ml/2 tbsp chopped fresh flat leaf parsley. Season with freshly ground black pepper to taste.

Crushed potatoes with garlic and basil Cook 675g/1¹/₂lb new potatoes in a pan of boiling salted water for 15–20 minutes until tender. Drain and crush roughly, using the back of a fork. Stir in 30ml/ 2 tbsp extra virgin olive oil, 2 finely chopped garlic cloves and a handful of torn basil leaves until well combined, then season with ground black pepper to taste.

Crushed potatoes with pine nuts and Parmesan Cook 675g/1¹/₂lb new potatoes in boiling salted water for 15–20 minutes until tender. Drain and crush using a fork. Stir in 30ml/2 tbsp extra virgin olive oil, 30ml/2 tbsp grated Parmesan cheese and 30ml/2 tbsp toasted pine nuts.

Rice

This versatile grain is the staple in many diets around the world. It can be served simply – either boiled or steamed – or can be flavoured or stir-fried with different ingredients to make a tasty, exciting accompaniment to curries, stir-fries, stews and grilled (broiled) meat or fish.

Easy egg-fried rice
Cook 115g/4oz/generous ½ cup long-grain rice in a large pan of boiling water for 10–12 minutes, until tender. Drain well and refresh under cold running water. Spread out on a baking sheet and leave until completely cold. Heat 30ml/2 tbsp sunflower oil in a large frying pan and add 1 finely chopped garlic clove. Cook for 1 minute, then add the rice and stir-fry for 1 minute. Push the rice to the side of the pan and pour 1 beaten egg into the pan. Cook the egg until set, then break up with a fork and stir into the rice. Add a splash of soy sauce, and mix well.

Star anise and cinnamon rice Add 225g/8oz/generous 1 cup basmati rice to a large pan of salted boiling water. Return to the boil, then reduce the heat and add a cinnamon stick and 2 star anise and simmer gently for 10–15 minutes, until the rice is tender. Drain well and remove the star anise and cinnamon before serving.

Coconut rice Put 225g/8oz/generous 1 cup basmati rice in a pan and pour in a 400ml/14oz can coconut milk. Cover with water, add some salt and bring to the boil. Simmer for 12 minutes, or until the rice is tender. Drain well and serve.

Coriander and spring onion rice Cook 225g/8oz/generous 1 cup basmati rice in a large pan of salted boiling water for about 12 minutes, or until tender. Drain the rice well and return to the pan. Stir in 3 finely sliced spring onions (scallions) and 1 roughly chopped bunch of fresh coriander (cilantro) until well mixed, then serve immediately.

Noodles

There are many different types of noodles, all of which are quick to cook and make the perfect accompaniment to Chinese- and Asian-style stir-fries and curries. Serve them on their own, or toss them with a few simple flavourings. They can also be served cold as a simple salad.

Spicy peanut noodles
Cook a 250g/9oz packet of egg noodles according to the instructions on the packet, then drain. Heat 15ml/1 tbsp sunflower oil in a wok and add 30ml/2 tbsp crunchy peanut butter. Add a splash of cold water and a dash of soy sauce and stir the mixture over a gentle heat until thoroughly combined. Add the noodles to the pan and toss to coat in the peanut mixture. Sprinkle with fresh coriander (cilantro) to serve.

Chilli and spring onion noodles Soak 115g/4oz flat rice noodles in cold water for 30 minutes, until softened. Drain well. Heat 30ml/2 tbsp olive oil in a wok or large frying pan. Add 2 finely chopped garlic cloves and 1 seeded and finely chopped red chilli and fry gently for 2 minutes. Slice a bunch of spring onions (scallions) and add to the pan. Cook for a minute or so, then stir in the rice noodles. Season with salt and freshly ground black pepper before serving.

Soy and sesame egg noodles Cook a 250g/9oz packet of egg noodles according to the instructions on the packet. Drain well and tip the noodles into a large bowl. Drizzle over 30ml/2 tbsp dark soy sauce and 10ml/2 tsp sesame oil, then sprinkle over 15ml/1 tbsp toasted sesame seeds and toss well until thoroughly combined. Serve the noodles hot, or cold as a salad.

Polenta

This classic Italian dish made from cornmeal makes a delicious accompaniment to many dishes and is a useful alternative to the usual potatoes, bread or pasta. It can be served in two ways – either soft, or set and cut into wedges and grilled (broiled) or fried. Soft polenta is rather like mashed potatoes, while the grilled or fried variety has a much firmer texture and lovely crisp shell. Both types can be enjoyed plain, or flavoured with other ingredients such as cheese, herbs and spices. Traditional polenta requires lengthy boiling and constant attention during cooking, but the quick-cook varieties, which are widely available in most large supermarkets, give excellent results and are much simpler and quicker to prepare.

Soft polenta Cook 225g/8oz/2 cups quick-cook polenta according to the instructions on the packet. As soon as the polenta is cooked, stir in about 50g/2oz/¼ cup butter. Season with salt and black pepper to taste, then serve immediately.

Soft polenta with Parmesan and sage
Cook 225g/8oz/2 cups quick-cook polenta according to the instructions on the packet. As soon as the polenta is cooked, stir in 115g/4oz/1¹/₃ cups freshly grated Parmesan cheese and a handful of chopped fresh sage. Stir in a large knob (pat) of butter and season with salt and freshly ground black pepper to taste before serving.

Soft polenta with Cheddar cheese and thyme
Cook 225g/8oz/2 cups quick-cook polenta according to the instructions on the packet. As soon as the polenta is cooked, stir in 50g/2oz/¹/₂ cups grated Chedar cheese and 30ml/2 tbsp chopped fresh thyme until thoroughly combined. Stir a large knob (pat) of butter into the cheesy polenta and season with salt and plenty of freshly ground black pepper to taste before serving.

Fried chilli polenta triangles Cook 225g/8oz/2 cups quick-cook polenta according to the instructions on the packet. Stir in 5ml/1 tsp dried chilli flakes, check the seasoning, adding more if necessary, and spread the mixture out on an oiled baking sheet to a thickness of about 1cm/¹/₂in. Leave the polenta until cold and completely set, then chill for about 20 minutes. Turn the polenta out on to a board and cut it into large squares, then cut each square into 2 triangles. Heat 30ml/2 tbsp olive oil in a large frying pan. Fry the triangles in the olive oil for 2–3 minutes on each side, until golden, then lift out and briefly drain on kitchen paper before serving.

Grilled polenta with Gorgonzola Cook 225g/8oz/2 cups quick-cook polenta according to the instructions on the packet. Check the seasoning, adding more if necessary, and spread the mixture out on an oiled baking sheet to a thickness of about 1cm/¹/₂in. Leave the polenta until cold and completely set, then chill for about 20 minutes. Turn the polenta out on to a board and cut it into large squares, then cut each square into 2 triangles. Pre-heat the grill (broiler) and arrange the polenta triangles on the grill pan. Cook for about 5 minutes, or until golden brown, then turn over and top each triangle with a sliver of Gorgonzola. Cook for a further 5 minutes, or until bubbling.

Below: *Wedges of set polenta are great fried and served as an accompaniment to stews, casseroles and other main dishes.*

Quick and simple vegetables

Fresh vegetables are an essential part of your everyday diet. They are delicious cooked on their own but they can also be stir-fried with other ingredients. This can be an interesting way of adding flavour and creating colourful, enticing and heathy vegetable dishes.

Stir-fried cabbage with hazelnuts Heat 30ml/2 tbsp sunflower oil in a wok or large frying pan and add 4 roughly chopped rashers (strips) smoked streaky (fatty) bacon. Stir-fry for about 3 minutes, until the bacon starts to turn golden, then add ¹/₂ shredded green cabbage to the pan. Stir-fry for 3–4 minutes, until the cabbage is just tender. Season with salt and freshly ground black pepper, and stir in 25g/1oz/ ¹/₄ cup roughly chopped toasted hazelnuts.

Creamy stir-fried Brussels sprouts Heat 15ml/1 tbsp sunflower oil in a wok or large frying pan. Add 1 chopped garlic clove and stir-fry for about 30 seconds. Shred 450g/ 1lb Brussels sprouts and add to the pan. Stir-fry for 3–4 minutes, until just tender. Season with salt and pepper and stir in 30ml/2 tbsp crème fraîche. Warm through for 1 minute before serving.

Honey-fried parsnips and celeriac Peel 250g/ 8oz parsnips and 115g/ 4oz celeriac. Cut both into matchsticks. Heat 30ml/ 2 tbsp olive oil in a wok or large frying pan and add the parsnips and celeriac. Fry over a gentle heat for 6–7 minutes, stirring occasionally, until golden and tender. Season with salt and ground black pepper and stir in 15ml/1 tbsp clear honey. Allow to bubble for 1 minute before serving.

Flavoured breads

Bread makes a simple accompaniment to many meals and is the perfect ready-made side dish when time is short. Look out for part-baked breads that you can finish off in the oven, so you can enjoy the taste of freshly baked bread in a few minutes.

Ciabatta This chewy Italian bread is long and oval in shape and is commonly available in ready-to-bake form. Look out for ciabatta with added sun-dried tomatoes or olives.

Focaccia This flat, dimpled Italian bread is made with olive oil and has a softer texture than ciabatta. It is available plain but is also often flavoured with fresh rosemary and garlic.

Naan Traditionally cooked in a clay oven, this Indian bread is easy to find in supermarkets and makes a tasty accompaniment to curries. It is available plain, and also flavoured with spices.

Chapati This Indian flatbread is less heavy than naan and makes a good alternative. The small, round breads can be a little more difficult to find but are worth searching for.

Above: *Rosemary focaccia has a crumbly texture and is perfect for sandwiches and serving with Italian dishes.*

Planning a Menu

Getting together with friends and family to enjoy good food is one of life's most enjoyable experiences. There's nothing better than inviting friends over to enjoy a leisurely lunch, relaxing dinner or summer barbecue and making sure that everyone has a great time. But just because you are the host, it doesn't mean that you can't enjoy yourself too. Cooking and entertaining should be fun for everybody – including the cook. Try following the suggestions below to ensure your party goes smoothly and that you enjoy the occasion as much as your guests. The key to success is always to plan ahead.

- Make a list of the people you have invited and work out how many you need to cater for. Remember to check if anyone is vegetarian or has special dietary requirements such as an allergy to nuts or dairy products.

- Decide what you are going to make, then make sure you have all the equipment you need. If necessary, buy or borrow the items from a friend. When planning the menu, choose dishes you can cook with confidence and avoid being too adventurous. There's no point in cooking to impress if you can't pull it off.

- Ensure you have enough space in the refrigerator for drinks, ingredients and dishes that need to be chilled. If necessary, have a clear-out and remove any unnecessary items to make space.

- Don't leave shopping for ingredients to the last minute. Buy everything you need the day before. This gives you plenty of time for preparation, and also gives you time to track down ingredients elsewhere if the supermarket or food store is out of stock.

- Try to prepare as much as you can in advance. If some dishes can be made or part-prepared the day before, then it's well worth doing.

- On the day, don't leave everything to the last minute. Prepare in good time, leaving yourself time to relax before your guests arrive.

Healthy breakfast

This healthy breakfast is the perfect way to give your system a boost. It's low in fat, packed with health-giving vitamins and nutrients and offers slow-release energy to keep you going throughout the morning.

Beetroot, ginger and orange juice
This refreshing blend of juices is full of vitamins and nutrients to cleanse and boost the system. Make sure you drink the juice as soon as you've made it because the vitamin content will begin to deplete soon after making.

Zingy papaya, lime and ginger salad
A refreshing fruit salad is the perfect way to start your day. Papaya and ginger are beneficial for the digestion and the tangy flavours of ginger and lime will wake you up with a zing.

Cranachan
The oats in this creamy breakfast dish are packed with slow-release carbohydrates that will sustain you until lunchtime. If you want to be really healthy, use low-fat Greek (US strained plain) yogurt.

Indulgent breakfast

This fabulous combination of dishes is perfect for a lazy weekend breakfast or brunch. You can even prepare the apricot turnovers the night before so you can really take it easy and just enjoy.

Cardamom hot chocolate
This rich, spiced hot chocolate is the perfect way to start a lazy weekend morning. It's particularly good in winter when you want something piping hot.

Apricot turnovers
Make these the night before and keep them in the refrigerator to bake in the morning. If you prefer, you can use rhubarb or raspberry compote in place of apricot.

Smoked salmon and chive omelette
Smoked salmon is a real treat for breakfast and you can buy small packets of smoked salmon quite cheaply. If you don't like fish, try serving Eggs Benedict instead.

Supper for two

For an intimate dinner for two, keep the tone informal. Prepare as much as you can in advance
so that you can relax and enjoy your friend's company when he or she arrives.

Potted shrimps with cayenne pepper
These can be made the day before and kept in the refrigerator – but remember to order fresh shrimps from your fishmonger.

Crème fraîche and coriander chicken
Delicious and quick so your guest will not sit alone while you are cooking!

Green salad
Choose a mixed bag of leaves with plenty of herbs for extra flavour. Whether you dress it or not is up to you.

Coffee Mascarpone creams
These luscious creams can be made ahead and kept in the refrigerator until ready to serve.

Formal entertaining

Although you're taking a more formal approach, it doesn't mean you can't enjoy yourself. To get the party going,
serve a tasty aperitif, such as Quick Bloody Mary, when your guests arrive.

Chicken liver and brandy pâté
This simple appetizer is best made the day before to allow its flavours to develop. Serve with crusty bread or Melba toast.

Sea bass with parsley and lime butter
Remember to order the fish to avoid disappointment and last-minute panic. Ask the fishmonger to fillet and scale it for you.

Green beans with almond and lemon butter
Lightly cook the beans in advance, then warm them through with the almond butter at the last minute.

Crushed potatoes with parsley and lemon

Roast peaches with amaretto
*These peaches make the perfect end to a meal. For the more daring cook, try making passion fruit soufflés.
They need to be made at the last minute, but you can prepare the ramekin dishes in advance.*

Barbecue for 12

When the weather is good, it is fun to go outdoors and cook over the coals. Make everything in advance and keep it in the refrigerator, ready to be cooked on the grill. Serve salads in bowls and let everyone help themselves.

Barbecued sardines with orange and parsley

Ask your fishmonger to get you the freshest sardines possible. Even people who don't think they like sardines will adore these!

Cumin- and coriander-rubbed lamb

Prepare the lamb several hours ahead to let the flavours develop. Let the coals get hot before putting the lamb on the barbecue.

Spring onion flatbreads

These can be made ahead of time if you prefer and served warm or at room temperature.

Roast aubergines with feta and coriander

These are perfect for vegetarian guests but they will also be a hit with meat eaters. You can use different types of cheese such as goat's cheese or halloumi if you prefer.

Potato and caraway seed salad

A potato salad is a barbecue must – caraway seeds give this one a slight edge.

Butter bean, tomato and red onion salad

This is quite a substantial salad, so serve a leafy mix as well. Toss everything together in advance and leave the flavours to develop.

Cuba Libre

Make a big jug with plenty of ice – but remember to offer soft drinks too.

Sunday lunch

This is probably one of the most relaxed and informal meals of the week and is surprisingly easy to make. Get everyone to help out in the kitchen to make it more relaxing for you.

Roast chicken with black pudding and sage
Nobody will expect the surprise black pudding stuffing, but it is so delicious they will be back for second helpings. If you have invited a lot of guests, you will need to roast two chickens.

Crisp and golden roast potatoes with goose fat and garlic
Sunday lunch is not Sunday lunch without roast potatoes. Remember to fluff up the outside of the potatoes when you drain them to get a really crispy result.

Cheesy creamy leeks
These make a tasty alternative to plain boiled or steamed vegetables. Use sliced large leeks, or whole baby ones.

Plum and almond tart
This impressive tart is easy to make and can be prepared in advance. Serve it warm with generous dollops of clotted cream.

Picnic

Picnics are great fun. Take lots of paper napkins, plates, plastic cups and cutlery. A cool box is invaluable for transporting food and keeping it fresh so if you don't have one, try to borrow one from a friend.

Artichoke and cumin dip
Take this tasty dip in a plastic container and pack breadsticks and raw vegetable crudités for dipping.

Cannellini bean pâté
Serve this as a second dip or spread on wedges of fresh soda bread. Alternatively, use it as a sandwich filling with slices of fresh tomato.

Marinated feta with lemon and oregano
Make this the day before and transport it in a container with a well-fitting lid.

Traditional Irish soda bread
This delicious bread is superb with the feta and the cannellini bean pâté. If you have time, make it on the morning of the picnic.

Pasta with fresh tomatoes and basil
Use small pasta shapes, which are easier to eat. Take a small bottle of olive oil so that you can add an extra drizzle before serving.

Blueberry cake
To make serving easier, cut the cake into wedges before you go, and take along a pot of cream or crème fraîche to serve with it.

Summer al fresco lunch

Al fresco simply means outdoors – and there are few things so enjoyable as eating outside when the sun is shining.

Peperonata
Make this the night before to allow the flavours to develop, and serve with bread and olives.

Fresh crab sandwiches
Little preparation is needed for these glorious sandwiches – but do remember to order the crabs from the fishmonger.

Halloumi and fennel salad
This richly flavoured salad is the perfect partner for crab sandwiches and is ideal if you have the barbecue out.

Watermelon ice
This refreshing, fruity dessert is the perfect way to round off a summer lunch.

Breakfasts and Brunches

NO ONE WANTS THE BOTHER OF LOTS OF INGREDIENTS

AND LENGTHY PREPARATION FOR THEIR FIRST MEAL OF

THE DAY. THIS COLLECTION OF WONDERFULLY SIMPLE

YET DELICIOUS DISHES HAS BEEN CREATED WITH THAT

IN MIND. WHETHER YOU WANT A HEALTHY, VITAMIN-

PACKED FRUIT SALAD FOR BREAKFAST OR AN

INDULGENT SERVING OF EGGS BENEDICT FOR A LAZY

WEEKEND BRUNCH, YOU'RE SURE TO FIND THE PERFECT

RECIPE TO SET YOU UP FOR THE DAY.

Zingy Papaya, Lime and Ginger Salad

This refreshing, fruity salad makes a lovely light breakfast, perfect for the summer months. Choose really ripe, fragrant papayas for the best flavour.

SERVES FOUR

1 Cut the papaya in half lengthways and scoop out the seeds, using a teaspoon. Using a sharp knife, cut the flesh into thin slices and arrange on a platter.

2 Squeeze the lime juice over the papaya and sprinkle with the sliced stem ginger. Serve immediately.

2 large ripe papayas

juice of 1 fresh lime

2 pieces preserved stem ginger, finely sliced

VARIATION *This refreshing fruit salad is delicious made with other tropical fruit. Try using 2 ripe peeled stoned mangoes in place of the papayas.*

Cantaloupe Melon with Grilled Strawberries

If strawberries are slightly underripe, sprinkling them with a little sugar and grilling them will help bring out their flavour.

SERVES FOUR

1 Preheat the grill (broiler) to high. Hull the strawberries and cut them in half. Arrange the fruit in a single layer, cut side up, on a baking sheet or in an ovenproof dish and dust with the icing sugar.

2 Grill (broil) the strawberries for 4–5 minutes, or until the sugar starts to bubble and turn golden.

3 Meanwhile, scoop out the seeds from the half melon using a spoon. Using a sharp knife, remove the skin, then cut the flesh into wedges and arrange on a serving plate with the grilled strawberries. Serve immediately.

115g/4oz/1 cup strawberries

15ml/1 tbsp icing (confectioners') sugar

$^{1}/_{2}$ cantaloupe melon

Crunchy Oat Cereal

Serve this tasty crunchy cereal simply with milk or, for a real treat, with yogurt and fresh fruit such as raspberries or blueberries.

SERVES SIX

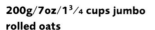

200g/7oz/1³⁄₄ cups jumbo rolled oats

150g/5oz/1¹⁄₄ cups pecan nuts, roughly chopped

90ml/6 tbsp maple syrup

FROM THE STORECUPBOARD

75g/3oz/6 tbsp butter, melted

1 Preheat oven to 160°C/325°F/Gas 3. Mix all the ingredients together and spread on to a large baking tray.

2 Bake for 30–35 minutes, or until golden and crunchy. Leave to cool, then break up into clumps and serve.

COOK'S TIPS
• *This crunchy oat cereal will keep in an airtight container for up to two weeks. Store in a cool, dry place.*
• *You can use other types of nuts if you prefer. Try roughly chopped almonds or hazelnuts instead of pecan nuts, or use a mixture.*

Cranachan

This lovely, nutritious breakfast dish is a traditional Scottish recipe, and is delicious served with a generous drizzle of heather honey. It is also absolutely wonderful served with fresh blueberries or blackberries in place of the raspberries.

SERVES FOUR

75g/3oz crunchy oat cereal

600ml/1 pint/2¹/₂ cups Greek (strained plain) yogurt

250g/9oz/1¹/₃ cups raspberries

1 Preheat the grill (broiler) to high. Spread the oat cereal on a baking sheet and place under the hot grill for 3–4 minutes, stirring regularly. Set aside to cool.

2 When the cereal has cooled completely, fold it into the Greek yogurt, then gently fold in 200g/7oz/generous 1 cup of the raspberries, being careful not to crush the berries too much.

3 Spoon the yogurt mixture into four serving glasses or dishes, top with the remaining raspberries and serve immediately.

Porridge

One of the oldest breakfast foods, porridge remains a favourite way to start the day, especially during winter. Brown sugar or honey, cream and a tot of whiskey are treats added for weekend breakfasts and to spoil guests.

SERVES FOUR

1 litre/1³/₄ pints/4 cups water

115g/4oz/1 cup pinhead oatmeal

FROM THE STORECUPBOARD

good pinch of salt

1 Put the water, pinhead oatmeal and salt into a heavy pan and bring to the boil over a medium heat, stirring with a wooden spatula. When the porridge is smooth and beginning to thicken, reduce the heat to a simmer.

2 Cook gently for about 25 minutes, stirring occasionally, until the oatmeal is cooked and the consistency smooth.

3 Serve hot with cold milk and extra salt, if required.

VARIATION

Modern rolled oats can be used, in the proportion 115g/4oz/1 cup rolled oats to 750ml/1¹/₄ pints/3 cups water, plus a sprinkling of salt. This cooks more quickly than pinhead oatmeal. Simmer, stirring to prevent sticking, for about 5 minutes. Either type of oatmeal can be left to cook overnight in the slow oven of a range.

Eggy Bread Panettone

Thickly sliced stale white bread is usually used for eggy bread, but the slightly dry texture of panettone makes a great alternative. Serve with a selection of fresh summer fruits such as strawberries, raspberries and blackcurrants.

SERVES FOUR

2 large (US extra large) eggs

4 large panettone slices

30ml/2 tbsp caster (superfine) sugar

FROM THE STORECUPBOARD

50g/2oz/¹/₄ cup butter or 30ml/2 tbsp sunflower oil

1 Break the eggs into a bowl and beat with a fork, then tip them into a shallow dish. Dip the panettone slices in the beaten egg, turning them to coat evenly.

2 Heat the butter or oil in a large non-stick frying pan and add the panettone slices. (You will probably have to do this in batches, depending on the size of the pan.) Fry the panettone slices over a medium heat for 2–3 minutes on each side, until golden brown.

3 Remove the panettone slices from the pan and drain on kitchen paper. Cut the slices in half diagonally and dust with the sugar. Serve immediately.

Chocolate Brioche Sandwiches

This luxury breakfast sandwich is a bit of a twist on the classic *pain au chocolat* and beats a boring slice of toast any day. The pale green pistachio nuts work really well with the chocolate spread, adding a satisfying crunch as well as a lovely contrast in colour.

SERVES FOUR

1 Toast the brioche slices until golden on both sides. Spread four of the slices thickly with the chocolate spread and sprinkle over the chopped pistachio nuts in an even layer.

2 Place the remaining brioche slices on top of the chocolate and nuts and press down gently. Using a sharp knife, cut the sandwiches in half diagonally and serve immediately.

COOK'S TIP *Brioche is a classic butter-enriched bread from France. It has a wonderful golden colour and slightly sweet taste. It is available in most supermarkets but you can use ordinary white bread if you can't get hold of brioche. Use an uncut loaf rather than a pre-sliced one so that you can cut thick slices.*

8 thick brioche bread slices

120ml/8 tbsp chocolate spread

30ml/2 tbsp shelled pistachio nuts, finely chopped

Roast Bananas with Greek Yogurt and Honey

Roasting bananas like this brings out their natural sweetness. If you are watching the calories, use low-fat Greek yogurt and omit the nuts. Use ripe bananas for maximum flavour. You can also cook bananas in this way over a barbecue and serve them as a simple barbecue dessert drizzled with a little honey.

SERVES FOUR

2 ripe bananas, peeled

500ml/17fl oz/2¼ cups Greek (US strained plain) yogurt with honey

30ml/2 tbsp toasted hazelnuts, roughly chopped

1 Preheat the oven to 200°C/400°F Gas 6. Wrap the bananas in foil and bake for 20 minutes. Leave the bananas to cool completely, then unwrap, place in a small bowl and mash roughly with a fork.

2 Pour the yogurt into a large bowl, add the mashed bananas and gently fold them into the yogurt. Sprinkle with the hazelnuts and serve.

Apricot Turnovers

These sweet and succulent pastries are delicious served with a big cup of milky coffee for a late breakfast or mid-morning treat.

SERVES FOUR

1 Preheat the oven to 190°C/375°F/Gas 5. Roll out the pastry on a lightly floured surface to a 25cm/10in square. Using a sharp knife, cut the pastry into four 13cm/5in squares.

2 Place a tablespoon of the apricot conserve in the middle of each square of pastry. Using a pastry brush, brush the edges of the pastry with a little cold water and fold each square over to form a triangle. Gently press the edges together to seal.

3 Carefully transfer the turnovers to a baking sheet and bake for 15–20 minutes, or until risen and golden. Using a metal spatula, remove the pastries to a wire rack to cool, then dust generously with icing sugar and serve.

225g/8oz ready-made puff pastry, thawed if frozen

60ml/4 tbsp apricot conserve

30ml/2 tbsp icing (confectioners') sugar

Warm Pancakes
with Caramelized Pears

If you can find them, use Williams pears for this recipe because they are juicier than most other varieties. For a really indulgent breakfast, top with a generous spoonful of crème fraîche or fromage frais.

SERVES FOUR

8 ready-made pancakes

4 ripe pears, peeled, cored and thickly sliced

30ml/2 tbsp light muscovado (brown) sugar

FROM THE STORECUPBOARD

50g/2oz/¼ cup butter

1 Preheat the oven to 150°C/330°F/Gas 2. Tightly wrap the pancakes in foil and place in the oven to warm through.

2 Meanwhile, heat the butter in a large frying pan and add the pears. Fry for 2–3 minutes, until the undersides are golden. Turn the pears over and sprinkle with sugar. Cook for a further 2–3 minutes, or until the sugar dissolves and the pan juices become sticky.

3 Remove the pancakes from the oven and take them out of the foil. Divide the pears among the pancakes, placing them in one quarter. Fold each pancake in half over the filling, then into quarters and place two folded pancakes on each plate. Drizzle over any remaining juices and serve immediately.

Smoked Salmon and Chive Omelette

The addition of a generous portion of chopped smoked salmon gives a really luxurious finish to this simple, classic dish. You can use this omelette recipe as the basis of endless variations. Simply replace the salmon and chives with other ingredients such as chopped ham and parsley or grated Cheddar and torn basil leaves.

SERVES TWO

1 Beat the eggs until just combined, then stir in the chives and season with salt and pepper.

2 Heat the butter in a medium-sized frying pan until foamy. Pour in the eggs and cook over a medium heat for 3–4 minutes, drawing the cooked egg from around the edge into the centre of the pan from time to time.

3 At this stage, you can either leave the top of the omelette slightly soft or finish it off under the grill (broiler), depending on how you like your omelette. Top with the smoked salmon, fold the omelette over and cut in half to serve.

4 eggs

15ml/1 tbsp chopped fresh chives

50g/2oz smoked salmon, roughly chopped

FROM THE STORECUPBOARD

knob (pat) of butter

salt and ground black pepper

Quick Kedgeree

Kedgeree is a rice, lentil and onion dish that originally came from India. Fish and eggs were added by the British to make the breakfast dish we know and love today. A garnish of fresh coriander (cilantro) leaves adds extra flavour and colour.

SERVES FOUR

175g/6oz undyed smoked haddock fillet

4 eggs

2 x 250g/9oz packets microwave pilau rice

FROM THE STORECUPBOARD

salt and ground black pepper

1 Preheat the grill (broiler) to medium. Place the smoked haddock on a baking sheet and grill for about 10 minutes, or until cooked through.

2 Meanwhile, place the eggs in a pan of cold water and bring to the boil. Cook for 6–7 minutes, then drain and place under cold running water until cool enough to handle.

3 While the eggs and haddock are cooking, cook the rice according to the instructions on the packet. Shell the eggs and cut into halves or quarters. Flake the fish and gently mix into the rice, with the eggs, taking care not to break up the eggs too much. Spoon on to serving plates, and serve immediately.

Jugged Kippers

The demand for naturally smoked kippers is ever increasing. They are most popular for breakfast, served with scrambled eggs, but they're also good at an old-fashioned high tea. Jugging is the same as poaching, except that the only equipment needed is a jug and kettle. Serve with freshly made bread or toast and a wedge of lemon, if you like.

SERVES FOUR

4 kippers (smoked herrings), preferably naturally smoked, whole or filleted

FROM THE STORECUPBOARD

25g/1oz/2 tbsp butter

ground black pepper

1 Select a jug (pitcher) tall enough for the kippers to be immersed when the water is added. If the heads are still on, remove them.

2 Put the fish into the jug, tails up, and then cover them with boiling water. Leave for about 5 minutes, until tender.

3 Drain well and serve on warmed plates with a knob (pat) of butter and a little black pepper on each kipper.

Scotch Pancakes with Bacon and Maple Syrup

Also known as drop scones, Scotch pancakes are available in most supermarkets. Raisin varieties also work well in this recipe.

SERVES FOUR

8 ready-made Scotch pancakes

8 dry-cured smoked back (lean) bacon rashers (strips)

30ml/2 tbsp maple syrup

1 Preheat the oven to 150°C/330°F/Gas 2. Wrap the pancakes in a sheet of foil and place them in the oven to warm through.

2 Meanwhile, preheat the grill (broiler) and arrange the bacon on a grill pan. Grill (broil) for 3–4 minutes on each side, until crisp.

3 Divide the warmed pancakes between four warmed serving plates and top with the grilled bacon rashers. Drizzle with the maple syrup and serve immediately.

Croque-monsieur

This classic French toastie is delicious served at any time of day, but with a foaming cup of milky coffee it makes a particularly enjoyable brunch dish. Gruyère is traditionally used, but you could use mild Cheddar instead. Prosciutto and Gorgonzola, served with a smear of mustard, also make a fabulous alternative to the classic ham and Gruyère combination.

SERVES FOUR

8 white bread slices

4 large lean ham slices

175g/6oz Gruyère cheese, thinly sliced

FROM THE STORECUPBOARD

a little softened butter

ground black pepper

1 Preheat the grill (broiler). Arrange the bread on the grill rack and toast four slices on both sides and the other four slices on one side only.

2 Butter the slices of bread that have been toasted on both sides and top with the ham, then the cheese, and season with plenty of ground black pepper.

3 Lay the remaining, half-toasted bread slices on top of the cheese, with the untoasted side uppermost. Grill the tops of the sandwiches until golden brown, then cut them in half using a sharp knife and serve immediately.

Eggs Benedict

Use a good quality bought hollandaise sauce for this recipe because it will make all the difference to the end result. Eggs Benedict are delicious served on half a toasted English muffin. Always use organic eggs – they have a superior flavour to eggs from battery hens.

SERVES FOUR

1 Pour cold water into a medium pan to a depth of about 5cm/2in and bring to a gentle simmer. Crack two eggs into the pan and bring back to the simmer. Simmer for 2–3 minutes, until the white is set, but the yolk is still soft.

2 Meanwhile, arrange the ham slices on four serving plates (or on top of four toasted, buttered muffin halves if using). Remove the eggs from the pan using a slotted spoon and place on top of the ham on two of the plates. Cook the remaining eggs in the same way.

3 Spoon the hollandaise sauce over the eggs, sprinkle with salt and pepper and serve immediately.

4 large (US extra large) eggs

4 lean ham slices

60ml/4 tbsp hollandaise sauce

FROM THE STORECUPBOARD

salt and ground black pepper

VARIATION *If you prefer eggs cooked all the way through, scramble them instead of poaching. Then spoon over the ham and top with hollandaise sauce as before.*

Appetizers

WHEN A SNACK IS CALLED FOR, OR A LITTLE
SOMETHING TO WHET THE APPETITE BEFORE A MAIN
MEAL, YOU WON'T FIND ANYTHING SIMPLER OR MORE
TASTY THAN THE FOLLOWING RECIPES. FROM
MOUTHWATERING DIPS TO DELICIOUS LITTLE EGGS
MIMOSA, THIS CHAPTER IS PACKED WITH SIMPLE, FUSS-
FREE IDEAS THAT YOU WON'T BE ABLE TO RESIST.

Hummus

This classic Middle Eastern chickpea dip is flavoured with garlic and tahini (sesame seed paste).
A little ground cumin can also be added, and olive oil can be stirred in to enrich the hummus, if you like.
It is delicious served with wedges of toasted pitta bread or crudités.

SERVES FOUR TO SIX

1 Using a potato masher or fork, coarsely mash the chickpeas in a mixing bowl. If you like a smoother purée, process the chickpeas in a food processor or blender until a smooth paste is formed.

2 Mix the tahini into the bowl of chickpeas, then stir in the chopped garlic cloves and lemon juice. Season to taste with salt and freshly ground black pepper, and if needed, add a little water. Serve the hummus at room temperature.

400g/14oz can chickpeas, drained

60ml/4 tbsp tahini

2–3 garlic cloves, chopped

juice of $^{1}/_{2}$–1 lemon

FROM THE
STORECUPBOARD

salt and ground black pepper

Baba Ghanoush

Adjust the amount of aubergine, garlic and lemon juice in this richly flavoured Middle Eastern aubergine dip depending on how creamy, garlicky or tart you want it to be. The dip can served with a garnish of chopped fresh coriander leaves, olives or pickled cucumbers. Hot pepper sauce or a little ground coriander can be added, too.

1 large or 2 medium aubergines (eggplant)

2–4 garlic cloves, chopped

90–150ml/6–10 tbsp tahini

juice of 1 lemon, or to taste

SERVES TWO TO FOUR

1 Place the aubergine(s) directly over the flame of a gas stove or on the coals of a barbecue. Turn the aubergine(s) fairly frequently until deflated and the skin is evenly charred. Remove from the heat with tongs. Alternatively, place under a hot grill (broiler), turning frequently, until charred.

2 Put the aubergine(s) in a plastic bag and seal the top tightly, or place in a bowl and cover with crumpled kitchen paper. Leave to cool for 30–60 minutes.

3 Peel off the blackened skin from the aubergine(s), reserving the juices. Chop the aubergine flesh, either by hand for a coarse texture or in a food processor for a smooth purée. Put the aubergine in a bowl and stir in the reserved juices.

4 Add the garlic and tahini to the aubergine and stir until smooth. Stir in the lemon juice. If the mixture becomes too thick, add 15–30ml/1–2 tbsp water. Spoon into a serving bowl. Serve at room temperature.

Cannellini Bean Pâté

Serve this simple pâté with melba toast or toasted wholegrain bread as an appetizer or snack. A dusting of paprika gives an extra kick. You can also use other types of canned beans such as kidney beans.

SERVES FOUR

2 x 400g/14oz cans cannellini beans, drained and rinsed

50g/2oz mature Cheddar cheese, finely grated

30ml/2 tbsp chopped fresh parsley

FROM THE STORECUPBOARD

45ml/3 tbsp olive oil

salt and ground black pepper

1 Put the cannellini beans in a food processor with the olive oil, and process to a chunky paste.

2 Transfer to a bowl and stir in the cheese, parsley and some salt and pepper. Spoon into a serving dish and sprinkle a little paprika on top, if you like.

COOK'S TIP *Canned beans are usually in a sugar, salt and water solution so always drain and rinse them thoroughly before use – otherwise the finished pâté may be rather too salty.*

Chicken Liver and Brandy Pâté

This pâté really could not be simpler to make, and tastes so much better than anything you can buy ready-made in the supermarkets. Serve with crispy Melba toast for an elegant appetizer.

SERVES FOUR

1 Heat the butter in a large frying pan until foamy. Add the chicken livers and cook over a medium heat for 3–4 minutes, or until browned and cooked through.

2 Add the brandy and allow to bubble for a few minutes. Let the mixture cool slightly, then tip into a food processor with the cream and some salt and pepper.

3 Process the mixture until smooth and spoon into ramekin dishes. Level the surface and chill overnight to set. Serve garnished with sprigs of parsley to add a little colour.

350g/12oz chicken livers, trimmed and roughly chopped

30ml/2 tbsp brandy

30ml/2 tbsp double (heavy) cream

FROM THE STORECUPBOARD

50g/2oz/¼ cup butter

salt and ground black pepper

Peperonata

This richly flavoured spicy tomato and sweet red pepper dip is delicious served with crisp Italian-style bread sticks – enjoy it with drinks or as a snack while watching television. It also makes a tasty relish served with grilled chicken and fish dishes. It is delicious served either hot, cold or at room temperature and can be stored in the refrigerator for several days.

SERVES FOUR

1 Heat the oil in a large pan over a low heat and add the sliced peppers. Cook very gently, stirring occasionally for 3–4 minutes.

2 Add the chilli flakes to the pan and cook for 1 minute, then pour in the tomatoes and season. Cook gently for 50 minutes to 1 hour, stirring occasionally.

> **COOK'S TIP**
> Long, slow cooking helps to bring out the sweetness of the peppers and tomatoes, so don't be tempted to cheat on the cooking time by cooking over a higher heat.

2 large red (bell) peppers, halved, seeded and sliced

pinch dried chilli flakes

400g/14oz can pomodorino tomatoes

FROM THE STORECUPBOARD

60ml/4 tbsp garlic-infused olive oil

salt and ground black pepper

Artichoke and Cumin Dip

This dip is so easy to make and is unbelievably tasty. Serve with olives, hummus and wedges of pitta bread to make a summery snack selection. Grilled artichokes bottled in oil have a fabulous flavour and can be used instead of canned artichokes. You can also vary the flavourings – try adding chilli powder in place of the cumin and add a handful of basil leaves to the artichokes before blending.

SERVES FOUR

1 Put the artichoke hearts in a food processor with the garlic and ground cumin, and a generous drizzle of olive oil. Process to a smooth purée and season with plenty of salt and ground black pepper to taste.

2 Spoon the purée into a serving bowl and serve with an extra drizzle of olive oil swirled on the top and slices of warm pitta bread for dipping.

2 x 400g/14oz cans artichoke hearts, drained

2 garlic cloves, peeled

2.5ml/¹⁄₂ tsp ground cumin

FROM THE STORECUPBOARD

olive oil

salt and ground black pepper

Sweet and Salty Vegetable Crisps

This delightfully simple snack is perfect to serve with pre-dinner drinks as an informal appetizer. Serve them with a bowl of aioli or a creamy dip such as hummus or taramasalata, and use the crisps to scoop it up. You can cook other sweet root vegetables, such as carrots and sweet potatoes, in the same way. Make a pretty, appetizing snack by making several different types of vegetable crisps, then pile them together in a bowl.

SERVES FOUR

1 Peel the beetroot and, using a mandolin or a vegetable peeler, cut it into very thin slices. Lay the slices on kitchen paper and sprinkle them with sugar and fine salt.

2 Heat 5cm/2in oil in a pan, until a bread cube dropped into the pan turns golden in 1 minute. Cook the slices, in batches, until they float to the surface and turn golden at the edge. Drain on kitchen paper and sprinkle with salt when cool.

1 small fresh beetroot (beet)

caster (superfine) sugar

FROM THE STORECUPBOARD

salt, for sprinkling

olive oil, for frying

Sizzling Prawns

These richly flavoured prawns (shrimp) are a classic Spanish tapas dish, but they also make a perfect appetizer. Traditionally they are brought to the table in little individual earthenware dishes, sizzling frantically in the hot oil with garlic. The addition of fiery chillies gives them an additional kick, but if you prefer a milder appetizer, simply omit the chillies.

SERVES FOUR

1 Split the chillies lengthways and discard the seeds. (Wash your hands with soap and water immediately.)

2 Heat the olive oil in a large frying pan and stir-fry the garlic and chillies for 1 minute, until the garlic begins to turn brown.

3 Add the whole prawns and stir-fry for 3–4 minutes, coating them well with the flavoured oil.

4 Remove the pan from the heat and divide the prawns among four dishes. Spoon over the flavoured oil and serve immediately. (Remember to provide a plate for the heads and shells, plus plenty of napkins.)

1–2 dried chillies (to taste)

3 garlic cloves, finely chopped

16 large raw prawns (shrimp), in the shell

FROM THE STORECUPBOARD

60ml/4 tbsp olive oil

Potted Shrimps
with Cayenne Pepper

Cayenne pepper adds a hint of spiciness to this traditional English seaside favourite. Serve with crusty bread or brown toast. The potted shrimps can be stored in the refrigerator for up to 3 days.

SERVES SIX

2 blades of mace

a pinch of cayenne pepper

600ml/1 pint/2½ cups peeled brown shrimps

FROM THE STORECUPBOARD

115g/4oz/½ cup butter, plus extra for greasing

90ml/6 tbsp clarified butter

1 Put the butter, mace and cayenne pepper into a small pan and warm over a gentle heat until melted.

2 Add the peeled shrimps and stir gently until warmed through. Butter six small ramekin dishes.

3 Remove the mace from the shrimp mixture and divide the shrimps and butter evenly between the six ramekins, patting down gently with the back of a spoon. Chill until set.

4 When the butter in the shrimp mixture has set, put the clarified butter in a small pan and melt over a gentle heat. Pour a layer of clarified butter over the top of each ramekin to cover the shrimps and chill again to set.

Marinated Feta
with Lemon and Oregano

The longer the cheese is left to marinate, the better the flavour will be. Serve with tomato and red onion salad and some crisp flatbreads.

SERVES FOUR

200g/7oz Greek feta cheese

1 lemon, cut into wedges

a small handful of fresh oregano sprigs

FROM THE STORECUPBOARD

300ml/½ pint/1¼ cups extra virgin olive oil

1 Drain the feta and pat dry with kitchen paper. Cut it into cubes and arrange in a non-metallic bowl or dish with the lemon wedges and oregano sprigs.

2 Pour the olive oil over the top and cover with clear film (plastic wrap). Chill for at least 3 hours, then serve with a selection of flat breads and salads.

> **COOK'S TIP** *Feta cheese is a salty, crumbly Greek cheese that is usually bought packed in brine. Use a good quality brand and drain thoroughly before using.*

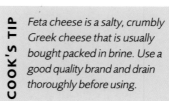

Mushroom Caviar

The name caviar refers to the dark colour and texture of this dish of chopped mushrooms. Serve the mushroom mixture in individual serving dishes with toasted rye bread rubbed with cut garlic cloves, to accompany. Chopped hard-boiled egg, spring onion and parsley, the traditional garnishes for caviar, can be added as a garnish.

SERVES FOUR

1 Heat the oil in a large pan, add the mushrooms, shallots and garlic, and cook, stirring occasionally, until browned. Season with salt, then continue cooking until the mushrooms give up their liquor.

2 Continue cooking, stirring frequently, until the liquor has evaporated and the mushrooms are brown and dry.

3 Put the mixture in a food processor or blender and process briefly until a chunky paste is formed. Spoon the mushroom caviar into dishes and serve.

450g/1lb mushrooms, coarsely chopped

5–10 shallots, chopped

4 garlic cloves, chopped

FROM THE STORECUPBOARD

45ml/3 tbsp olive or vegetable oil

EXTRAS *For a rich wild mushroom caviar, soak 10–15g/¼–½oz dried porcini in about 120ml/4fl oz/ ½ cup water for about 30 minutes. Add the porcini and their soaking liquid to the browned mushrooms in step 2. Continue as in the recipe. Serve with wedges of lemon, for their tangy juice.*

Brandade of Salt Cod

There are many versions of this creamy French salt cod purée: some contain mashed potatoes, others truffles. Serve the brandade with warmed crispbread or crusty bread for a tasty appetizer, or for a light lunch serve the brandade and bread with a tomato and basil salad. You can omit the garlic from the brandade, if you prefer, and serve toasted slices of French bread rubbed with garlic instead.

SERVES SIX

200g/7oz salt cod

250ml/8fl oz/1 cup extra virgin olive oil

4 garlic cloves, crushed

250ml/8fl oz/1 cup double (heavy) or whipping cream

1 Soak the fish in cold water for 24 hours, changing the water frequently. Drain the fish well. Cut the fish into pieces, place in a shallow pan and pour in enough cold water to cover. Heat the water until it is simmering and poach the fish for 8 minutes, until it is just cooked. Drain the fish, then remove the skin and bones.

2 Combine the extra virgin olive oil and crushed garlic cloves in a small pan and heat gently. In another pan, heat the double cream until it just starts to simmer.

3 Put the cod into a food processor, process it briefly, then gradually add alternate amounts of the garlic-flavoured olive oil and cream, while continuing to process the mixture. The aim is to create a purée with the consistency of mashed potato.

4 Season to taste with freshly ground black pepper, then scoop the brandade into a serving bowl or on to individual serving plates and serve with crispbread or crusty bread.

Chopped Egg and Onions

This dish is one of the oldest dishes in Jewish culinary history. It is delicious served sprinkled with chopped parsley and onion rings on crackers, piled on toast, or used as a sandwich or bagel filling. Serve chopped egg and onion as part of a buffet with a selection of dips and toppings.

SERVES FOUR TO SIX

1 Put the eggs in a large pan and cover with cold water. Bring the water to the boil and when it boils, reduce the heat and simmer over a low heat for 10 minutes.

2 Hold the boiled eggs under cold running water (if too hot to handle, place the eggs in a strainer and hold under the running water). When cool, remove the shells from the eggs and discard. Dry the eggs and chop coarsely.

3 Place the chopped eggs in a large bowl, add the onions, season generously with salt and black pepper and mix well. Add enough mayonnaise or chicken fat to bind the mixture together. Stir in the mustard, if using, and chill before serving.

8–10 eggs

6–8 spring onions (scallions) and/or 1 yellow or white onion, very finely chopped, plus extra to garnish

60–90ml/4–6 tbsp mayonnaise or rendered chicken fat

mild French wholegrain mustard, to taste (optional if using mayonnaise)

FROM THE STORECUPBOARD

salt and ground black pepper

Israeli Cheese with Green Olives

In Israel, mild white cheeses spiked with seasonings, such as this one that is flavoured with piquant green olives, are served with drinks and little crackers or toast. It is also very good served for brunch – spread generously on chunks of fresh, crusty bread or bagels.

SERVES FOUR

175–200g/6–7oz soft white (farmer's) cheese

65g/2½ oz feta cheese, preferably sheep's milk, lightly crumbled

20–30 pitted green olives, some chopped, the rest halved or quartered

2–3 large pinches of fresh thyme, plus extra to garnish

1 Place the soft white cheese in a mixing bowl and stir with the back of a spoon or a fork until soft and smooth. Add the crumbled feta cheese and stir the two cheeses together until they are thoroughly combined.

2 Add the chopped, halved and quartered olives and the pinches of fresh thyme to the cheese mixture and mix thoroughly.

3 Spoon the mixture into a bowl, sprinkle with thyme and serve with crackers, toast, chunks of bread or bagels.

Bacon-rolled Enokitake Mushrooms

The Japanese name for this dish is *Obimaki enoki*: an *obi* (belt or sash) is made from bacon and wrapped around enokitake mushrooms before they are grilled. The strong, smoky flavour of the bacon complements the subtle flavour of mushrooms. Small heaps of ground white pepper can be offered with these savouries, if you like.

450g/1lb fresh enokitake mushrooms

6 rindless smoked streaky (fatty) bacon rashers (strips)

4 lemon wedges

SERVES FOUR

1 Cut off the root part of each enokitake cluster 2cm/¾in from the end. Do not separate the stems. Cut the bacon rashers in half lengthways.

2 Divide the enokitake into 12 equal bunches. Take one bunch, then place the middle of the enokitake near the edge of one bacon rasher, with 2.5–4cm/1–1½in of enokitake protruding at each end.

3 Carefully roll up the bunch of enokitake in the bacon. Tuck any straying short stems into the bacon and slide the bacon slightly upwards at each roll to cover about 4cm/1½in of the enokitake. Secure the end of the bacon roll with a cocktail stick (toothpick). Repeat using the remaining enokitake and bacon to make 11 more rolls.

4 Preheat the grill (broiler) to high. Place the enokitake rolls on an oiled wire rack. Grill (broil) both sides until the bacon is crisp and the enokitake start to char. This takes 10–13 minutes.

5 Remove the enokitake rolls and place on a board. Using a fork and knife, chop each roll in half in the middle of the bacon belt. Arrange the top part of the enokitake roll standing upright, the bottom part lying down next to it. Add a wedge of lemon to each portion and serve.

Walnut and Goat's Cheese Bruschetta

The combination of toasted walnuts and melting goat's cheese is lovely in this simple appetizer, served with a pile of salad leaves. Toasting the walnuts helps to enhance their flavour. Walnut bread is readily available in most large supermarkets and makes an interesting alternative to ordinary crusty bread, although this can be used if walnut bread is unavailable.

SERVES FOUR

1 Preheat the grill (broiler). Lightly toast the walnut pieces, then remove and set aside. Put the walnut bread on a foil-lined grill rack and toast on one side. Turn the slices over and drizzle each with 15ml/1 tbsp of the French dressing.

2 Cut the goat's cheese into twelve slices and place three on each piece of bread. Grill (broil) for about 3 minutes, until the cheese is melting and beginning to brown.

3 Transfer the bruschetta to serving plates, sprinkle with the toasted walnuts and drizzle with the remaining French dressing. Serve the bruschetta immediately with salad leaves.

50g/2oz/¹⁄₂ cup walnut pieces

4 thick slices walnut bread

120ml/4fl oz/¹⁄₂ cup French dressing

200g/7oz chèvre or other semi-soft goat's cheese

COOK'S TIP *Use walnut bread slices from a slender loaf, so that the portions are not too wide. If you can buy only a large loaf, cut the slices in half to make neat, chunky pieces.*

Party Snacks

WHEN YOU WANT LITTLE PARTY SNACKS WITH THE
MINIMUM OF FUSS, THINK SIMPLICITY. FROM
MOUTHWATERING CANAPES SUCH AS BLINIS WITH
CAVIAR AND CRÈME FRAÎCHE TO MOREISH SALT COD
AND POTATO FRITTERS, THIS CHAPTER IS PACKED WITH
FUSS-FREE IDEAS THAT YOU WON'T BE ABLE TO RESIST.
SERVE GOLDEN, MELT-IN-THE-MOUTH PARMESAN
TUILES OR GOLDEN GRUYÈRE AND BASIL TORTILLAS
WITH DRINKS, OR ENJOY CRAB AND WATER-CHESTNUT
WONTONS AS AN APPETIZER.

Spanish Salted Almonds

Served with a glass of chilled dry sherry, these delicious salted nuts make a perfect tapas dish or pre-dinner snack.

SERVES FOUR TO SIX

1 Preheat the oven 200°C/400°F/Gas 6. Whisk the egg white in a bowl until it forms stiff peaks.

2 Add the almonds to the egg white, and stir until the nuts are thoroughly coated. Tip the mixture on to a baking sheet and spread out evenly in a single layer.

3 Sprinkle the salt over the almonds and bake for about 15 minutes, or until the egg white and salt are crusty. Leave to cool completely, then serve in bowls with a selection of other nibbles, dips and pâtés.

1 egg white

200g/7oz/generous 1 cup shelled unblanched almonds

a good handful of flaked sea salt

Golden Gruyère and Basil Tortillas

These simple fried tortilla wedges make a great late-night snack with sweet chilli sauce. If you have a few slices of ham or salami in the refrigerator, add these to the tortillas as well.

SERVES TWO

1 Heat the oil in a frying pan, over a medium heat. Add one of the tortillas, arrange the Gruyère cheese slices and basil leaves on top and season with salt and pepper.

2 Place the remaining tortilla on top to make a sandwich and flip the whole thing over with a metal spatula. Cook for a few minutes, until the underneath is golden.

3 Slide the tortilla sandwich on to a chopping board or plate and cut into wedges. Serve immediately.

2 soft flour tortillas

115g/4oz Gruyère cheese, thinly sliced

a handful of fresh basil leaves

FROM THE STORECUPBOARD

15ml/1 tbsp olive oil

salt and ground black pepper

Polenta Chips

These tasty Parmesan-flavoured batons are best served warm from the oven with a spicy, tangy dip. A bowl of Thai chilli dipping sauce or a creamy, chilli-spiked guacamole are perfect for dipping into.

MAKES ABOUT EIGHTY

1 Put 1.5 litres/2½ pints/6¼ cups water into a large heavy pan and bring to the boil. Reduce the heat, add the salt and pour in the polenta in a steady stream, stirring constantly with a wooden spoon. Cook over a low heat for about 5 minutes, stirring, until the mixture thickens and comes away from the sides of the pan.

2 Remove the pan from the heat and add the cheese and butter. Season to taste. Stir well until the mixture is smooth. Pour on to a smooth surface, such as a marble slab or a baking sheet.

3 Using a metal spatula, spread out the polenta to a thickness of 2cm/¾in and shape into a rectangle. Leave to stand for at least 30 minutes until cold. Meanwhile preheat the oven to 200°C/400°F/Gas 6 and lightly oil two or three baking sheets.

4 Cut the polenta slab in half, then carefully cut into even-size strips. Bake for 40–50 minutes, or until dark golden brown and crunchy, turning from time to time. Serve warm.

375g/13oz/3¼ cups instant polenta

150g/5oz/1½ cups freshly grated Parmesan cheese

FROM THE STORECUPBOARD

10ml/2 tsp salt, plus extra

90g/3½oz/7 tbsp butter

10ml/2 tsp cracked black pepper

olive oil, for brushing

Parmesan Tuiles

These lacy tuiles look very impressive and make splendid nibbles for a party, but they couldn't be easier to make. Believe or not, they use only a single ingredient – Parmesan cheese.

MAKES EIGHT TO TEN

1 Preheat the oven to 200°C/400°F/Gas 6. Line two baking sheets with baking parchment. Grate the cheese using a fine grater, pulling it down slowly to make long strands.

2 Spread the grated cheese in 7.5–9cm/3–3½in rounds on the baking parchment, forking it into shape. Do not spread the cheese too thickly; it should just cover the parchment. Bake for 5–7 minutes, or until bubbling and golden brown.

3 Leave the tuiles on the baking sheet for about 30 seconds and then carefully transfer, using a metal spatula, to a wire rack to cool completely. Alternatively, drape over a rolling pin to make a curved shape.

115g/4oz Parmesan cheese

COOK'S TIP *Tuiles can be made into little cup shapes by draping over an upturned egg cup. These little cups can be filled to make tasty treats to serve with drinks. Try a little cream cheese flavoured with herbs.*

Yogurt Cheese in Olive Oil

In Greece, sheep's yogurt is hung in muslin to drain off the whey before being patted into balls of soft cheese. Here the cheese is bottled in extra virgin olive oil with dried chillies and fresh herbs to make a wonderful gourmet gift or aromatic appetizer. It is delicious spread on thick slices of toast as a snack or a light lunch.

FILLS TWO 450G/1LB JARS

1 Sterilize a 30cm/12in square of muslin (cheesecloth) by soaking it in boiling water. Drain and lay it over a large plate. Season the yogurt with salt and tip on to the centre of the muslin. Bring up the sides of the muslin and tie with string.

2 Hang the bag on a kitchen cupboard handle or suitable position where it can be suspended over a bowl to catch the whey. Leave for 2–3 days until the yogurt stops dripping.

3 Sterilize two 450g/1lb glass preserving jars by heating them in the oven at 150 C/300 F/Gas 2 for 15 minutes.

4 Mix the crushed dried chillies and herbs. Take teaspoonfuls of the cheese and roll into balls with your hands. Lower into the jars, sprinkling each layer with the herb mixture.

5 Pour the oil over the cheese until completely covered. Store in the refrigerator for up to 3 weeks. To serve, spoon the cheese out of the jars with a little of the flavoured olive oil and spread on slices of lightly toasted bread.

1 litre/1³⁄₄ pints/4 cups Greek sheep's (US strained plain) yogurt

10ml/2 tsp crushed dried chillies or chilli powder

30ml/2 tbsp chopped fresh herbs, such as rosemary, and thyme or oregano

FROM THE STORECUPBOARD

about 300ml/¹⁄₂ pint/ 1¹⁄₄ cups extra virgin olive oil, preferably garlic-flavoured

salt and ground black pepper

Eggs Mimosa

Mimosa describes the fine yellow and white grated egg in this dish, which looks very similar to the flower of the same name. The eggs taste delicious when garnished with black pepper and basil leaves. Grated egg yolk can also be used as a garnish for a variety of other savoury dishes, such as sauces, soups and rice dishes.

MAKES TWENTY

1 Reserve two of the hard-boiled eggs and halve the remainder. Carefully remove the yolks with a teaspoon and blend them with the avocados, garlic and oil, adding freshly ground black pepper and salt to taste. Spoon or pipe the mixture into the halved egg whites using a piping (pastry) bag with a 1cm/½in or pipe star nozzle.

2 Sieve the remaining egg whites and sprinkle over the filled eggs. Sieve the yolks and arrange on top. Arrange the filled egg halves on a serving platter.

12 eggs, hard-boiled and peeled

2 ripe avocados, halved and stoned (pitted)

1 garlic clove, crushed

FROM THE STORECUPBOARD

15ml/1 tbsp olive oil

Marinated Smoked Salmon with Lime and Coriander

If you want an elegant appetizer that is really quick to put together, then this is the one for you. The tangy lime juice and aromatic coriander leaves contrast perfectly with the delicate yet distinct flavour of the salmon. Serve with thinly sliced brown bread and butter.

SERVES SIX

200g/7oz smoked salmon

a handful of fresh coriander (cilantro) leaves

grated rind and juice of 1 lime

FROM THE STORECUPBOARD

15ml/1 tbsp extra virgin olive oil

ground black pepper

1 Using a sharp knife or pair of kitchen scissors, cut the salmon into strips and arrange on a serving platter.

2 Sprinkle the coriander leaves and lime rind over the salmon and squeeze over the lime juice. Drizzle with the olive oil and season with black pepper. Cover with clear film (plastic wrap) and chill for 1 hour before serving.

COOK'S TIP *You can make this dish up to 1 hour before serving. However, do not leave it for longer than this because the lime juice will discolour the salmon and spoil the look of the dish.*

Blinis with Caviar and Crème Fraîche

Classic Russian blinis are made with buckwheat flour, which gives them a very distinctive taste. They are available ready-made in large supermarkets and make a tasty first course or snack to serve with drinks, topped with crème fraîche and caviar. Caviar is expensive, but a very small amount goes a long way and the exquisite flavour is well worth it.

SERVES TWELVE

1 Put the crème fraîche in a bowl and season with salt and ground black pepper to taste. Place a teaspoonful of the mixture on each blini.

2 Top each spoonful of crème fraîche with a teaspoon of caviar and serve immediately.

200g/7oz/scant 1 cup crème fraîche

12 ready-made blinis

60ml/4 tbsp caviar

FROM THE STORECUPBOARD

salt and ground black pepper

VARIATION *For a stunning effect, top half the blinis with orange salmon or trout roe and the other half with black caviar.*

Marinated Anchovies

These tiny fish tend to lose their freshness very quickly so marinating them in garlic and lemon juice is the perfect way to enjoy them. It is probably the simplest way of preparing these fish, because it requires no cooking. Serve them scattered with parsley for a decorative finish.

SERVES FOUR

225g/8oz fresh anchovies, heads and tails removed, and split open along the belly

juice of 3 lemons

2 garlic cloves, finely chopped

FROM THE STORECUPBOARD

30ml/2 tbsp extra virgin olive oil

flaked sea salt

1 Turn the anchovies on to their bellies, and press down along their spine with your thumb. Using the tip of a small knife, carefully remove the backbones from the fish, and arrange the anchovies skin side down in a single layer on a large plate.

2 Squeeze two-thirds of the lemon juice over the fish and sprinkle them with the salt. Cover and leave to stand for 1–24 hours, basting occasionally with the juices, until the flesh is white and no longer translucent.

3 Transfer the anchovies to a serving plate and drizzle with the olive oil and the remaining lemon juice. Scatter the fish with the chopped garlic, then cover with clear film (plastic wrap) and chill until ready to serve.

Chilli Prawn Skewers

Try to get the freshest prawns you can for this recipe. If you buy whole prawns, you will need to remove the heads and shells, leaving the tail section intact. Serve with extra lime wedges.

SERVES FOUR

16 giant raw prawns (shrimp), shelled with the tail section left intact

1 lime, cut into 8 wedges

60ml/4 tbsp sweet chilli sauce

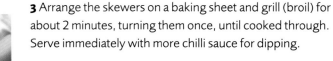

1 Place eight bamboo skewers in cold water and leave to soak for at least 10 minutes, then preheat the grill (broiler) to high.

2 Thread a prawn on to each skewer, then a lime wedge, then another prawn. Brush the sweet chilli sauce over the prawns and lime wedges.

3 Arrange the skewers on a baking sheet and grill (broil) for about 2 minutes, turning them once, until cooked through. Serve immediately with more chilli sauce for dipping.

450g/1lb salt cod fillets

500g/1¹/₄lb floury potatoes, unpeeled

plain (all-purpose) flour, for coating

FROM THE STORECUPBOARD

vegetable oil, for deep-frying

salt and ground black pepper

Salt Cod and Potato Fritters

These little fritters are extremely easy to make and taste delicious. Serve them simply with a wedge of fresh lemon and some watercress or green salad. Offer a bowl of garlic mayonnaise for dipping.

MAKES ABOUT TWENTY FOUR

1 Put the salt cod in a bowl, pour over cold water and leave to soak for 24 hours, changing the water every 6–8 hours. Drain, rinse and place in a pan of cold water. Slowly bring to the boil and simmer for 5 minutes, then drain and cool. When cooled, remove any bones and skin and mash the fish with a fork.

2 Cook the potatoes in their skins in a pan of salted boiling water for 20–25 minutes, or until just tender. Peel and mash.

3 Add the fish to the potatoes and mix well. Season to taste with salt and pepper. Break off walnut-sized pieces of the mixture and roll into balls. Place on a floured plate, cover and chill for 20–30 minutes. Roll each ball lightly in flour, dusting off any excess.

4 Heat enough oil for deep-frying in a large pan and fry the balls for 5–6 minutes, or until golden. Remove with a slotted spoon and drain on kitchen paper. Serve hot or warm.

Asian-style Crab Cakes

You could serve these patties as a simple supper, or an appetizer for eight people. Use a mixture of white and brown crab meat, as the dark adds a depth of flavour and texture. Serve with sweet chilli sauce.

MAKES SIXTEEN

450g/1lb/2²/₃ cups fresh crab meat, white and brown

15ml/1 tbsp grated fresh root ginger

15–30ml/1–2 tbsp plain (all-purpose) flour

FROM THE STORECUPBOARD

60ml/4 tbsp sunflower oil

salt and ground black pepper

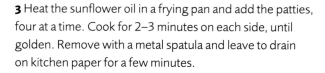

1 Put the crab meat in a bowl and add the ginger, some salt and ground black pepper and the flour. Stir well until thoroughly mixed.

2 Using floured hands, divide the mixture into 16 equal-sized pieces and shape roughly into patties.

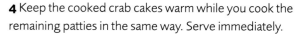

3 Heat the sunflower oil in a frying pan and add the patties, four at a time. Cook for 2–3 minutes on each side, until golden. Remove with a metal spatula and leave to drain on kitchen paper for a few minutes.

4 Keep the cooked crab cakes warm while you cook the remaining patties in the same way. Serve immediately.

Crab and Water-chestnut Wontons

Serve these mouthwatering parcels as part of a dim sum selection or with a bowl of soy sauce for dipping as a first course for a Chinese meal. They are also perfect for serving as snacks with drinks at parties as they can be prepared in advance, then steamed at the last minute. Wonton wrappers are available in most Asian food stores and need to be soaked in cold water for a few minutes before use.

SERVES FOUR

1 Finely chop the water chestnuts, mix them with the crab meat and season with salt and pepper.

2 Place about a teaspoonful of the mixture along the centre of each wonton wrapper. Roll up the wontons, tucking in the sides as you go to form a neat parcel.

3 Fill the bottom part of a steamer with boiling water and place the wontons, seam down, in the steamer basket. Sit the basket on top of the water and cover with a tight-fitting lid. Steam for 5–8 minutes, or until the wonton wrappers are tender. Serve hot or warm.

50g/2oz/¹⁄₃ cup drained, canned water chestnuts

115g/4oz/generous ¹⁄₂ cup fresh or canned white crab meat

12 wonton wrappers

FROM THE STORECUPBOARD

salt and ground black pepper

Chilli-spiced Chicken Wings

These crispy chicken wings are always the perfect snack for parties and go incredibly well with cold beer! If you like your food spicy, use red hot cayenne pepper in place of the chilli powder. To make a milder version that will be a hit with kids, use sweet paprika in place of the chilli powder. Serve with a fresh tomato and onion salsa for dipping.

SERVES FOUR

12 chicken wings

30ml/2 tbsp plain (all-purpose) flour

15ml/1 tbsp chilli powder

FROM THE STORECUPBOARD

a pinch of salt

sunflower oil, for deep-frying

1 Pat the chicken wings dry with kitchen paper. Mix the flour, chilli powder and salt together and put into a large plastic bag. Add the chicken wings, seal the bag and shake well to coat the chicken wings in the seasoned flour.

2 Heat enough sunflower oil for deep-frying in a large pan and add the chicken wings, three or four at a time. Fry for 8–10 minutes, or until golden and cooked through.

3 Remove the chicken wings with a slotted spoon and drain on kitchen paper. Keep warm in a low oven. Repeat with the remaining chicken wings and serve hot.

Vietnamese Spring Rolls with Pork

You will often find these little spring rolls on the menu in Vietnamese restaurants, called "rice paper rolls". Serve with a chilli dipping sauce.

SERVES FOUR

1 Heat the oil in a frying pan and add the pork. Fry for 5–6 minutes, or until browned. Season well with salt and pepper, stir in the oyster sauce and remove from the heat. Leave to cool.

2 Lay the rice paper wrappers on a clean work surface. Place one-eighth of the pork mixture down one edge of each wrapper. Roll up the wrappers, tucking in the ends as you go to form a roll, and then serve immediately.

350g/12oz/1½ cups minced (ground) pork

30ml/2 tbsp oyster sauce

8 rice-paper roll wrappers

FROM THE STORECUPBOARD

15ml/1 tbsp sunflower oil

salt and ground black pepper

Curried Lamb Samosas

Filo pastry is perfect for making samosas. Once you've mastered folding them, you'll be amazed how quick they are to make.

MAKES TWELVE SAMOSAS

225g/8oz/1 cup minced (ground) lamb

30ml/2 tbsp mild curry paste

12 filo pastry sheets

FROM THE STORECUPBOARD

25g/1oz/2 tbsp butter

salt and ground black pepper

1 Heat a little of the butter in a large pan and add the lamb. Fry for 5–6 minutes, stirring occasionally until browned. Stir in the curry paste and cook for 1–2 minutes. Season and set aside. Preheat the oven to 190°C/375°F/Gas 5.

2 Melt the remaining butter in a pan. Cut the pastry sheets in half lengthways. Brush one strip of pastry with butter, then lay another strip on top and brush with more butter.

3 Place a spoonful of lamb in the corner of the strip and fold over to form a triangle at one end. Keep folding over in the same way to form a triangular package. Brush with butter and place on a baking sheet. Repeat using the remaining pastry. Bake for 15–20 minutes until golden. Serve hot.

Soups

SOUP IS ONE OF THE MOST VERSATILE DISHES AROUND AND
CAN BE SERVED AS AN ELEGANT APPETIZER OR A LIGHT
MEAL. FROM CHILLED SUMMER SOUPS TO WARMING
WINTER BROTHS, THEY ARE INCREDIBLY EASY TO MAKE
AND ONLY NEED A FEW INGREDIENTS AND FLAVOURINGS
TO CREATE FABULOUS, MOUTHWATERING RESULTS.

Avocado Soup

This delicious soup has a fresh, delicate flavour and a wonderful colour. For added zest, add a generous squeeze of lime juice or spoon 15ml/1 tbsp salsa into the soup just before serving. Choose ripe avocados for this soup – they should feel soft when gently pressed. Keep very firm avocados at room temperature for 3–4 days until they soften. To speed ripening, place in a brown paper bag.

SERVES FOUR

1 Cut the avocados in half, remove the peel and lift out the stones (pits). Chop the flesh coarsely and place it in a food processor with 45–60ml/3–4 tbsp of the sour cream. Process until smooth.

2 Heat the chicken stock in a pan. When it is hot, but still below simmering point, stir in the rest of the cream.

3 Gradually stir the avocado mixture into the hot stock. Heat but do not let the mixture approach boiling point.

4 Chop the coriander. Ladle the soup into individual heated bowls and sprinkle each portion with chopped coriander and black pepper. Serve immediately.

2 large ripe avocados

300ml/¹/₂ pint/1¹/₄ cups sour cream

1 litre/1³/₄ pints/4 cups well-flavoured chicken stock

small bunch of fresh coriander (cilantro)

FROM THE STORECUPBOARD

ground black pepper

Vichyssoise

This classic, chilled summer soup of leeks and potatoes was first created in the 1920s by Louis Diat, chef at the New York Ritz-Carlton. He named it after Vichy near his home in France. The soup can be sharpened with lemon juice, enriched with swirls of cream and garnished with chives.

SERVES FOUR TO SIX

1 Melt the unsalted butter in a heavy pan and cook the leeks, covered, for 15–20 minutes, until they are soft but not browned.

2 Add the potato chunks and cook over a low heat, uncovered, for a few minutes.

3 Stir in the stock or water and milk, with salt and pepper to taste. Bring to the boil, then reduce the heat and partly cover the pan. Simmer for 15 minutes, or until the potatoes are soft.

4 Cool, then process the soup until smooth in a blender or food processor. Sieve the soup into a bowl. Taste and adjust the seasoning and add a little iced water if the consistency of the soup seems too thick.

5 Chill the soup for at least 4 hours or until very cold. Taste the chilled soup for seasoning again before serving. Pour the soup into bowls and serve.

600g/1lb 5oz leeks, white parts only, thinly sliced

250g/9oz floury potatoes (such as King Edward or Maris Piper), peeled and cut into chunks

1.5 litres/2¹⁄₂ pints/6¹⁄₂ cups half and half light chicken stock or water and milk

FROM THE STORECUPBOARD

50g/2oz/¹⁄₄ cup unsalted (sweet) butter

salt and ground black pepper

EXTRAS

To make a fabulous chilled leek and sorrel or watercress soup, add about 50g/2oz/1 cup shredded sorrel to the soup at the end of cooking. Finish and chill as in the main recipe, then serve the soup garnished with a little pile of finely shredded sorrel. The same quantity of watercress can also be used.

Avgolemono

The name of this popular Greek soup means egg and lemon, the two essential ingredients that produce a light, nourishing soup. The soup also contains orzo, which is Greek, rice-shaped pasta, but you can use any small shape. Serve the soup with thin slices of lightly toasted bread and add a garnish of very thin lemon slices for a pretty appearance on special occasions.

SERVES FOUR TO SIX

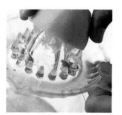

1 Pour the chicken stock into a large pan and bring to the boil. Add the orzo pasta or other small pasta shapes and cook for 5 minutes, or according to the packet instructions.

2 Beat the eggs until they are frothy, then add the lemon juice and a tablespoon of cold water. Slowly stir in a ladleful of the hot chicken stock, then add one or two more. Remove the pan from the heat, then pour in the egg mixture and stir well. Season to taste with salt and freshly ground black pepper and serve immediately. (Do not let the soup boil once the egg, lemon juice and stock mixture has been added, or it will curdle.)

1.75 litres/3 pints/ 7½ cups chicken stock

115g/4oz/½ cup orzo pasta

3 eggs

juice of 1 large lemon

FROM THE STORECUPBOARD

salt and ground black pepper

Simple Cream of Onion Soup

This wonderfully soothing soup has a deep, buttery flavour that is achieved with only a few ingredients and the minimum of fuss. It makes delicious comfort food on a cold day. Use home-made stock if you have it, or buy fresh stock for the best flavour. Crisp croûtons or chopped chives complement the smooth soup when sprinkled over just before serving.

SERVES FOUR

1kg/2¼lb yellow onions, sliced

1 litre/1¾ pints/4 cups good chicken or vegetable stock

150ml/¼ pint/⅔ cup double (heavy) cream

FROM THE STORECUPBOARD

115g/4oz/ ½ cup unsalted (sweet) butter

salt and ground black pepper

1 Melt 75g/3oz/6 tbsp of the unsalted butter in a large, heavy pan. Set about 200g/7oz of the onions aside and add the rest to the pan. Stir to coat in the butter, then cover and cook very gently for about 30 minutes. The onions should be very soft and tender, but not browned.

2 Add the chicken or vegetable stock, 5ml/1 tsp salt and freshly ground black pepper to taste. Bring to the boil, reduce the heat and simmer for 5 minutes, then remove from the heat.

3 Leave the soup to cool, then process it in a blender or food processor. Return the soup to the rinsed pan.

4 Meanwhile, melt the remaining butter in another pan and cook the remaining onions over a low heat, covered, until soft but not browned. Uncover and continue to cook the onions gently until they turn golden yellow.

5 Add the cream to the soup and reheat it gently until hot, but do not allow it to boil. Taste and adjust the seasoning. Add the buttery onions and stir for 1–2 minutes, then ladle the soup into bowls. Serve the soup immediately.

Cappelletti in Broth

This soup is traditionally served in northern Italy on Santo Stefano (St Stephen's Day, the day after Christmas) and on New Year's Day as a welcome light change from all the special celebration food. Cappelletti are little stuffed pasta shapes that resemble hats.

SERVES FOUR

1 Pour the chicken stock into a large pan and bring to the boil. Drop in the pasta.

2 Stir well and bring back to the boil. Lower the heat to a simmer and cook according to the instructions on the packet, until the pasta is *al dente*, that is, tender but still firm to the bite.

3 Swirl in the finely chopped fresh flat leaf parsley, if using, then taste and adjust the seasoning, if necessary. Ladle into four warmed soup plates, then sprinkle with the freshly grated Parmesan cheese and serve immediately.

1.2 litres/2 pints/ 5 cups chicken stock

90–115g/3½–4oz/ 1 cup fresh or dried cappelletti

about 45ml/3 tbsp finely chopped fresh flat leaf parsley (optional)

about 30ml/2 tbsp freshly grated Parmesan cheese

COOK'S TIP *If you don't have home-made stock use two 300g/11oz cans of condensed beef consommé, adding water as instructed, or chilled commercial stock.*

Tiny Pasta in Broth

This Italian soup is ideal for a light supper served with ciabatta bread and also makes a delicious first course for an *al fresco* supper. A wide variety of different types of *pastina* or soup pasta are available including stellette (stars), anellini (tiny thin rounds), risoni (rice-shaped) and farfalline (little butterflies). Choose just one shape or a combination of different varieties for an interesting result.

SERVES FOUR

1.2 litres/2 pints/ 5 cups beef stock

75g/3oz/¾ cup dried tiny soup pasta

2 pieces bottled roasted red (bell) pepper, about 50g/2oz

coarsely shaved Parmesan cheese

1 Bring the beef stock to the boil in a large pan. Drop in the dried soup pasta. Stir well and bring the stock back to the boil.

2 Reduce the heat so that the soup simmers and cook for 7–8 minutes, or according to the packet instructions, until the pasta is *al dente*, that is, tender but still firm to the bite.

3 Drain the pieces of roasted pepper and dice them finely. Place them in the base of four warmed soup plates. Taste the soup for seasoning before ladling it into the soup plates. Serve immediately, topped with shavings of Parmesan.

Potato and Roasted Garlic Broth

Roasted garlic takes on a mellow, sweet flavour that is subtle, not overpowering, in this delicious vegetarian soup. Choose floury potatoes for this soup, such as Maris Piper, Estima, Cara or King Edward – they will give the soup a delicious velvety texture. Serve the broth piping hot with melted Cheddar or Gruyère cheese on French bread, as the perfect winter warmer.

SERVES FOUR

1 Preheat the oven to 190°C/375°F/Gas 5. Place the unpeeled garlic bulbs or bulb in a small roasting pan and bake for 30 minutes until soft in the centre.

2 Meanwhile, par-boil the potatoes in a large pan of boiling water for 10 minutes.

3 Simmer the stock in another pan for 5 minutes. Drain the potatoes and add them to the stock.

4 Squeeze the garlic pulp into the soup, reserving a few whole cloves and stir. Simmer for 15 minutes and serve topped with whole garlic cloves and parsley.

2 small or 1 large whole head of garlic (about 20 cloves)

4 medium potatoes (about 500g/1¼lb in total), diced

1.75 litres/3 pints/ 7½ cups good-quality hot vegetable stock

chopped flat leaf parsley, to garnish

Winter Squash Soup with Tomato Salsa

Creamy butternut squash makes good soup with very few additional ingredients. Select a really good bought salsa for this soup and add a sprinkling of chopped fresh oregano or marjoram as a garnish.

1 butternut squash

2 onions, chopped

60–120ml/4–8 tbsp tomato salsa

FROM THE STORECUPBOARD

75ml/5 tbsp garlic-flavoured olive oil

SERVES FOUR TO FIVE

1 Preheat the oven to 220°C/425°F/Gas 7. Halve and seed the butternut squash and place it on a baking sheet and brush with some of the oil and roast for 25 minutes. Reduce the temperature to 190°C/375°F/Gas 5 and cook for 20–25 minutes more, or until it is tender.

2 Heat the remaining oil in a large, heavy pan and cook the chopped onions over a low heat for about 10 minutes, or until softened.

3 Meanwhile, scoop the squash out of its skin, adding it to the pan. Pour in 1.2 litres/ 2 pints/5 cups water and stir in 5ml/1 tsp salt and plenty of black pepper. Bring to the boil, cover and simmer for 10 minutes.

4 Cool the soup slightly, then process it in a blender or food processor to a smooth purée. Alternatively, press the soup through a fine sieve with the back of a spoon. Reheat without boiling, then ladle it into warmed bowls. Top each serving with a spoonful of salsa and serve.

Butter Bean, Sun-dried Tomato and Pesto Soup

This soup is so quick and easy to make: the key is to use a good-quality home-made or bought fresh stock for the best result. Using plenty of pesto and sun-dried tomato purée (paste) gives it a rich, minestrone-like flavour. As an alternative to butter beans, haricot (navy) or cannellini beans will make good substitutes.

SERVES FOUR

1 Put the stock in a pan with the butter beans and bring just to the boil. Reduce the heat and stir in the tomato purée and pesto. Cook gently for 5 minutes.

2 Transfer six ladlefuls of the soup to a blender or food processor, scooping up plenty of the beans. Process until smooth, then return the purée to the pan.

3 Heat gently, stirring frequently, for 5 minutes. Ladle into four warmed soup bowls and serve with warm crusty bread or breadsticks.

**900ml/1¹⁄₂ pints/
3³⁄₄ cups chicken or
vegetable stock**

**2 x 400g/14oz cans
butter (lima) beans,
drained and rinsed**

**60ml/4 tbsp sun-dried
tomato purée (paste)**

75ml/5 tbsp pesto

Stilton and Watercress Soup

A good creamy Stilton and plenty of peppery watercress bring maximum flavour to this rich, smooth soup, which is superlative in small portions. Rocket (arugula) can be used as an alternative to watercress – both leaves are an excellent source of iron. When choosing any salad leaves, look for crisp, fresh leaves and reject any wilted or discoloured greens.

SERVES FOUR TO SIX

1 Pour the stock into a pan and bring almost to the boil. Remove and discard any very large stalks from the watercress. Add the watercress to the pan and simmer gently for 2–3 minutes, until tender.

2 Crumble the cheese into the pan and simmer for 1 minute more, until the cheese has started to melt. Process the soup in a blender or food processor, in batches if necessary, until very smooth. Return the soup to the pan.

3 Stir in the cream and check the seasoning. The soup will probably not need any extra salt, as the blue cheese is already quite salty. Heat the soup gently, without boiling, then ladle it into warm bowls.

600ml/1 pint/2¹⁄₂ cups chicken or vegetable stock

225g/8oz watercress

150g/5oz Stilton or other blue cheese

150ml/¹⁄₄ pint/²⁄₃ cup single (light) cream

Curried Cauliflower Soup

This spicy, creamy soup is perfect for lunch on a cold winter's day served with crusty bread and garnished with fresh coriander (cilantro). You can also make broccoli soup in the same way, using the same weight of broccoli in place of the cauliflower.

SERVES FOUR

750ml/1¼ pints/3 cups milk

1 large cauliflower

15ml/1 tbsp garam masala

FROM THE STORECUPBOARD

salt and ground black pepper

1 Pour the milk into a large pan and place over a medium heat. Cut the cauliflower into florets and add to the milk with the garam masala and season with salt and pepper.

2 Bring the milk to the boil, then reduce the heat, partially cover the pan with a lid and simmer for about 20 minutes, or until the cauliflower is tender.

3 Let the mixture cool for a few minutes, then transfer to a food processor and process until smooth (you may have to do this in two batches). Return the purée to the pan and heat through gently, checking and adjusting the seasoning, and serve immediately.

Tuscan Bean Soup

Cavolo nero is a very dark green cabbage with a nutty flavour from Tuscany and southern Italy. It is ideal for this traditional recipe. It is available in most large supermarkets, but if you can't get it, use Savoy cabbage instead. Serve with ciabatta bread.

SERVES FOUR

2 x 400g/14oz cans chopped tomatoes with herbs

250g/9oz cavolo nero leaves

400g/14oz can cannellini beans

FROM THE STORECUPBOARD

60ml/4 tbsp extra virgin olive oil

salt and ground black pepper

1 Pour the tomatoes into a large pan and add a can of cold water. Season with salt and pepper and bring to the boil, then reduce the heat to a simmer.

2 Roughly shred the cabbage leaves and add them to the pan. Partially cover the pan and simmer gently for about 15 minutes, or until the cabbage is tender.

3 Drain and rinse the cannellini beans, add to the pan and warm through for a few minutes. Check and adjust the seasoning, then ladle the soup into bowls and drizzle each one with a little olive oil and serve.

Pea Soup with Garlic

If you keep peas in the freezer, you can rustle up this delicious soup in minutes. It has a wonderfully sweet taste and smooth texture and is great served with crusty bread and garnished with mint.

SERVES FOUR

1 garlic clove, crushed

900g/2lb/8 cups frozen peas

1.2 litres/2 pints/5 cups chicken stock

FROM THE STORECUPBOARD

25g/1oz/2 tbsp butter

salt and ground black pepper

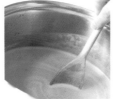

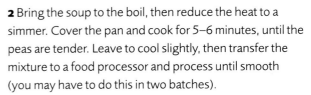

1 Heat the butter in a large pan and add the garlic. Fry gently for 2–3 minutes, until softened, then add the peas. Cook for 1–2 minutes more, then pour in the stock.

2 Bring the soup to the boil, then reduce the heat to a simmer. Cover the pan and cook for 5–6 minutes, until the peas are tender. Leave to cool slightly, then transfer the mixture to a food processor and process until smooth (you may have to do this in two batches).

3 Return the soup to the rinsed pan and heat through gently. Season with salt and pepper.

Star-gazer Vegetable Soup

If you have the time, it is worth making your own stock for this recipe.

SERVES FOUR

**1 yellow (bell) pepper and
2 large courgettes (zucchini)**

2 large carrots

**900ml/1¹/₂ pints/3³/₄ cups
well-flavoured vegetable stock**

50g/2oz rice vermicelli

FROM THE STORECUPBOARD

salt and ground black pepper

> **COOK'S TIP** *Sauté the leftover vegetable pieces in a little oil and mix with cooked brown rice to make a tasty risotto.*

1 Cut the pepper into quarters, removing the seeds and core. Cut the courgettes and carrots lengthways into 5mm/¹/₄in slices.

2 Using tiny pastry cutters, stamp out shapes from the vegetables or use a very sharp knife to cut the sliced vegetables into stars and other decorative shapes.

3 Place the vegetables and stock in a pan and simmer for 10 minutes, until the vegetables are tender. Season to taste with salt and pepper.

4 Meanwhile, place the vermicelli in a bowl, cover with boiling water and set aside for 4 minutes. Drain, then divide among four warmed soup bowls. Ladle over the soup and serve with fresh bread.

Light Lunches

WHAT COULD BE BETTER THAN A TASTY MEAL IN THE

MIDDLE OF THE DAY THAT HAS TAKEN ONLY MINUTES

TO PREPARE AND NEEDS JUST THREE OR FOUR

INGREDIENTS? WHATEVER YOU'RE IN THE MOOD FOR,

WHETHER IT'S A HEALTHY SALAD, A GOURMET

SANDWICH OR A BOWL OF PASTA, THERE'S SOMETHING

HERE FOR YOU. THE RECIPES ARE ALL SO SIMPLE THAT

YOU CAN EASILY REDUCE OR INCREASE THE

PROPORTIONS TO MAKE A QUICK LUNCH FOR ONE,

OR A HEALTHY MEAL FOR THE WHOLE FAMILY.

Baked Eggs with Creamy Leeks

This simple but elegant appetizer is perfect for last-minute entertaining or quick dining. Garnish the baked eggs with crisp, fried fresh sage leaves and serve with warm, fresh crusty bread for a special meal. Small- to medium-sized leeks (less than 2.5cm/1in in diameter) are best for this dish as they have the most tender flavour and only require a short cooking time.

SERVES FOUR

1 Preheat the oven to 190°C/375°F/Gas 5. Generously butter the base and sides of four ramekins.

2 Melt the butter in a frying pan and cook the leeks over a medium heat, stirring frequently, for 3–5 minutes, until softened and translucent, but not browned.

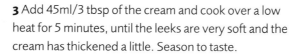

3 Add 45ml/3 tbsp of the cream and cook over a low heat for 5 minutes, until the leeks are very soft and the cream has thickened a little. Season to taste.

4 Place the ramekins in a small roasting pan and divide the leeks among them. Break an egg into each, spoon over the remaining cream and season.

5 Pour boiling water into the roasting pan to come about halfway up the sides of the ramekins. Transfer the pan to the oven and bake in the preheated oven for about 10 minutes, until just set. Serve piping hot.

225g/8oz small leeks, thinly sliced

75–90ml/5–6 tbsp whipping cream

4 small–medium (US medium–large) eggs

FROM THE STORECUPBOARD

15g/$^{1}/_{2}$oz/1 tbsp butter, plus extra for greasing

salt and ground black pepper

Red Onion and Olive Pissaladière

For a taste of the Mediterranean, try this French-style pizza – it makes a delicious and easy snack. Cook the sliced red onions slowly until they are caramelized and sweet before piling them into the pastry cases. To prepare the recipe in advance, pile the cooled onions on to the pastry round and chill the pissaladière until you are ready to bake it.

SERVES SIX

1 Preheat the oven to 220°C/425°F/Gas 7. Heat the oil in a large, heavy frying pan and cook the onions gently, stirring frequently, for 15–20 minutes, until they are soft and golden. Season to taste.

2 Roll out the pastry thinly on a floured surface. Cut out a 33cm/13in round and transfer it to a lightly dampened baking sheet.

3 Spread the onions over the pastry in an even layer to within 1cm/½in of the edge. Sprinkle the olives on top. Bake the tart for 20–25 minutes, until the pastry is risen and deep golden. Cut into wedges and serve warm.

500g/1¼lb small red onions, thinly sliced

500g/1¼lb puff pastry, thawed if frozen

75g/3oz/¾ cup small pitted black olives

FROM THE STORECUPBOARD

75ml/5 tbsp extra virgin olive oil

Figs with Prosciutto and Roquefort

Fresh figs are a delicious treat, whether you choose dark purple, yellowy green or green-skinned varieties. When they are ripe, you can split them open with your fingers to reveal the soft, sweet flesh full of edible seeds. In this easy, stylish dish figs and honey balance the richness of the ham and cheese. Serve with warm bread for a simple appetizer before any rich main course.

SERVES FOUR

1 Preheat the grill (broiler). Quarter the figs and place on a foil-lined grill rack. Tear each slice of prosciutto into two or three pieces and crumple them up on the foil beside the figs. Brush the figs with 15ml/1 tbsp of the clear honey and cook under the grill until lightly browned.

2 Crumble the Roquefort cheese and divide among four plates, setting it to one side. Add the honey-grilled figs and ham and pour over any cooking juices caught on the foil. Drizzle the remaining honey over the figs, ham and cheese, and serve seasoned with plenty of freshly ground black pepper.

8 fresh figs

75g/3oz prosciutto

**45ml/3 tbsp
clear honey**

75g/3oz Roquefort cheese

FROM THE STORECUPBOARD

ground black pepper

Pea and Mint Omelette

Serve this deliciously light omelette with crusty bread and a green salad for a fresh and tasty lunch. If you're making the omelette for a summer lunch when peas are in season, use freshly shelled peas instead of frozen ones.

SERVES TWO

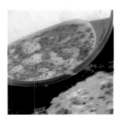

1 Cook the peas in a large pan of salted boiling water for 3–4 minutes until tender. Drain well and set aside. Break the eggs into a large bowl and beat with a fork. Season well with salt and pepper, then stir in the peas and chopped mint.

2 Heat the butter in a medium frying pan until foamy. Pour in the egg mixture and cook over a medium heat for 3–4 minutes, drawing in the cooked egg from the edges from time to time, until the mixture is nearly set.

3 Finish off cooking the omelette under a hot grill (broiler) until set and golden. Carefully fold the omelette over, cut it in half and serve immediately.

50g/2oz/¹/₂ cup frozen peas

4 eggs

30ml/2 tbsp chopped fresh mint

FROM THE STORECUPBOARD

knob (pat) of butter

salt and ground black pepper

Warm Penne with Fresh Tomatoes and Basil

This dish is fresh, healthy and ready in minutes. It is the perfect way to use up a glut of ripe summer tomatoes.

SERVES FOUR

500g/1¼lb dried penne

5 very ripe plum tomatoes

1 small bunch of fresh basil

FROM THE STORECUPBOARD

60ml/4 tbsp extra virgin olive oil

salt and ground black pepper

1 Cook the pasta in plenty of salted, boiling water according to the instructions on the packet. Meanwhile, roughly chop the tomatoes, pull the basil leaves from their stems and tear up the leaves.

2 Drain the pasta thoroughly and toss with the tomatoes, basil and olive oil. Season with salt and freshly ground black pepper and serve immediately.

COOK'S TIP *If you cannot find ripe tomatoes, roast them to bring out their flavour. Put the tomatoes in a roasting pan, drizzle with oil and roast at 190°C/375°F/ Gas 5 for 20 minutes, then mash roughly.*

Broccoli and Chilli Spaghetti

The contrast between the hot chilli and the mild broccoli is delicious and goes perfectly with spaghetti. To add extra flavour and texture, sprinkle the spaghetti and broccoli with toasted pine nuts and grated or shaved Parmesan cheese just before serving.

SERVES FOUR

350g/12oz dried spaghetti

450g/1lb broccoli, cut into small florets

1 fat red chilli, seeded and finely chopped

FROM THE STORECUPBOARD

150ml/¼ pint/⅔ cup garlic-infused olive oil

salt and ground black pepper

1 Bring a large pan of lightly salted water to the boil. Add the spaghetti and broccoli and cook for 8–10 minutes, until both are tender. Drain thoroughly.

2 Using the back of a fork crush the broccoli roughly, taking care not to mash the spaghetti strands at the same time.

3 Meanwhile, warm the oil and finely chopped chilli in a small pan over a low heat and cook very gently for 5 minutes.

4 Pour the chilli and oil over the spaghetti and broccoli and toss together to combine. Season to taste. Divide between four warmed bowls and serve immediately.

Grilled Aubergine, Mint and Couscous Salad

Packets of flavoured couscous are available in most supermarkets – you can use whichever you like, but garlic and coriander is particularly good for this recipe. Serve with a crisp green salad.

SERVES TWO

1 large aubergine (eggplant)

115g/4oz packet garlic-and-coriander (cilantro) flavoured couscous

30ml/2 tbsp chopped fresh mint

FROM THE STORECUPBOARD

30ml/2 tbsp olive oil

salt and ground black pepper

1 Preheat the grill (broiler) to high. Cut the aubergine into large chunky pieces and toss them with the olive oil. Season with salt and pepper to taste and spread the aubergine pieces on a non-stick baking sheet. Grill for 5–6 minutes, turning occasionally, until golden brown.

2 Meanwhile, prepare the couscous according to the instructions on the packet. Stir the grilled aubergine and chopped mint into the couscous, toss thoroughly and serve immediately.

Marinated Courgette and Flageolet Bean Salad

Serve this healthy salad as a light lunch or as an accompaniment to meat and chicken dishes. It has a wonderful bright green colour and is perfect for a summer lunch.

SERVES FOUR

2 courgettes (zucchini), halved lengthways and sliced

400g/14oz can flageolet beans, drained and rinsed

grated rind and juice of 1 unwaxed lemon

FROM THE STORECUPBOARD

45ml/3 tbsp garlic-infused olive oil

salt and ground black pepper

1 Cook the courgettes in boiling salted water for 2–3 minutes, or until just tender. Drain well and refresh under cold running water.

2 Transfer the drained courgettes into a bowl with the beans and stir in the oil, lemon rind and juice and some salt and pepper. Chill for 30 minutes before serving.

VARIATION *To add extra flavour to the salad add 30ml/2 tbsp chopped fresh herbs before chilling. Basil and mint both have fresh, distinctive flavours that will work very well.*

Roasted Pepper and Hummus Wrap

Wraps make a tasty change to sandwiches and have the bonus that they can be made a few hours in advance without going soggy in the way that bread sandwiches often can. You can introduce all kinds of variation to this basic combination. Try using roasted aubergine (eggplant) in place of the red peppers, or guacamole in place of the hummus. As well as plain flour tortillas, you can also buy flavoured tortillas from most supermarkets.

SERVES TWO

1 large red (bell) pepper, halved and seeded

4 tbsp hummus

2 soft flour tortillas

FROM THE STORECUPBOARD

15ml/1 tbsp olive oil

salt and ground black pepper

1 Preheat the grill (broiler) to high. Brush the pepper halves with the oil and place cut side down on a baking sheet. Grill for 5 minutes, until charred. Put the pepper halves in a sealed plastic bag and leave to cool.

2 When cooled, remove the peppers from the bag and carefully peel away the charred skin and discard. Thinly slice the flesh using a sharp knife.

3 Spread the hummus over the tortillas in a thin, even layer and top with the roasted pepper slices. Season with salt and plenty of ground black pepper, then roll them up and cut in half to serve.

Focaccia with Sardines and Roast Tomatoes

Fresh sardines not only have a lovely flavour and texture, but they are also cheap to buy – so make an economical yet utterly delicious lunch.

SERVES FOUR

20 cherry tomatoes

12 fresh sardine fillets

1 focaccia loaf

FROM THE STORECUPBOARD

45ml/3 tbsp herb-infused olive oil

salt and ground black pepper

1 Preheat the oven to 190°C/375°F/Gas 5. Put the cherry tomatoes in a small roasting pan and drizzle 30ml/2 tbsp of the oil over the top. Season with salt and pepper and roast for 10–15 minutes, or until tender and slightly charred. Remove from the oven and set aside.

2 Preheat the grill (broiler) to high. Brush the sardine fillets with the remaining oil and lay them on a baking sheet. Grill for 4–5 minutes on each side, until cooked through.

3 Split the focaccia in half horizontally and cut each piece in half to give four equal pieces. Toast the cut side under the grill until golden. Top with the sardines and tomatoes and an extra drizzle of oil. Season with black pepper then serve.

Jansson's Temptation

This traditional Swedish gratin is utterly moreish. The name probably does not refer to a specific Jansson but means "everyone's temptation", as Jansson is a common Swedish surname.

SERVES FOUR TO SIX

1 Preheat the oven to 200°C/400°F/Gas 6. Cut the potatoes into thin slices, then cut the slices into matchstick strips. Sprinkle half of them in the base of a greased shallow 1.5 litre/2½ pint/6¼ cup baking dish.

2 Lay half of the onions on top of the potatoes, and season with black pepper. Lay the anchovies on top of the onions, then add the remaining onions and potatoes.

3 Mix the cream with 30ml/2 tbsp cold water and pour over the potatoes and onions. Cover with foil and bake for 1 hour, then reduce the oven temperature to 180°C/350°F/Gas 4 and uncover the dish. Bake for a further 40–50 minutes, or until the potatoes are golden and tender when tested with a knife.

900g/2lb potatoes

2 large, sweet onions, sliced

2 x 50g/2oz cans anchovies in olive oil, drained

450ml/¾ pint/scant 2 cups whipping cream or half and half double (heavy) and single (light) cream

Crisp Fried Whitebait

This must be one of the simplest of all classic fish dishes and it is absolutely delicious with lemon wedges and thinly sliced brown bread and butter. If you prefer, serve the whitebait with a simple lemon and herb dip – mix 150ml/¼ pint/⅔ cup natural (plain) yogurt with the rind of one lemon and 45ml/ 3 tbsp chopped fresh herbs. Serve chilled.

SERVES FOUR

150ml/¹/₄ pint/²/₃ cup milk

115g/4oz/1 cup plain (all-purpose) flour

450g/1lb whitebait

FROM THE STORECUPBOARD

oil, for deep-frying

<table>
<tr><td>COOK'S TIP</td><td>Most whitebait are sold frozen. Thaw them before use and dry them thoroughly on kitchen paper before flouring.</td></tr>
</table>

1 Heat the oil in a large pan or deep-fryer. Put the milk in a shallow bowl and spoon the flour into a paper bag. Season the flour well with salt and pepper.

2 Dip a handful of the whitebait into the bowl of milk, drain them well, then put them into the paper bag. Shake to coat them evenly in the seasoned flour, then transfer to a plate. Repeat until all the fish have been coated. Don't add too many whitebait at once to the bag, or they will stick together.

3 Heat the oil for deep-frying to 190°C/375°F or until a cube of stale bread, dropped into the oil, browns in about 20 seconds. Add a batch of whitebait, preferably in a frying basket, and deep-fry for 2–3 minutes, until crisp and golden brown. Drain and keep hot while you cook the rest. Serve very hot.

Seared Tuna Niçoise

A traditional tuna Niçoise consists of tuna, olives, green beans, potatoes and eggs, but this modern version using fresh tuna is a simplified one – although just as tasty. Serve it with a green salad.

SERVES FOUR

4 tuna steaks, about 150g/ 5oz each

30ml/2 tbsp sherry vinegar

2 eggs

FROM THE STORECUPBOARD

45ml/3 tbsp garlic-infused olive oil

salt and ground black pepper

1 Put the tuna steaks in a shallow non-metallic dish. Mix the oil and vinegar together and season with salt and pepper.

2 Pour the mixture over the tuna steaks and turn them to coat in the marinade. Cover and chill for up to 1 hour.

3 Heat a griddle pan until smoking hot. Remove the tuna steaks from the marinade and lay them on the griddle pan. Cook for 2–3 minutes on each side, so that they are still pink in the centre. Remove from the pan and set aside.

4 Meanwhile, cook the eggs in a pan of boiling water for 5–6 minutes, then cool under cold running water. Shell the eggs and cut in half lengthways.

5 Pour the marinade on to the griddle pan and cook until it starts to bubble. Divide the tuna steaks among four serving plates and top each with half an egg. Drizzle the marinade over the top and serve immediately.

Creamy Parmesan-Baked Eggs

These eggs are delicious as they are but can easily be "dressed up" with additional ingredients. Try adding chopped smoked ham and parsley before you cook them. Serve with thinly sliced bread and butter.

SERVES TWO

1 Preheat the oven to 160°C/325°F/Gas 3. Break the eggs into four ramekin dishes and spoon the cream over the top. Season with salt and ground black pepper and sprinkle the Parmesan cheese on top.

2 Bake the eggs for about 10 minutes, or until they are just set, and serve immediately.

4 large (US extra large) eggs

60ml/4 tbsp double (heavy) cream

30ml/2 tbsp freshly grated Parmesan cheese

FROM THE STORECUPBOARD

salt and ground black pepper

COOK'S TIPS *Serve these rich and creamy eggs with a leafy green salad flavoured with fresh tarragon. For the best results, be sure to serve the eggs as soon as they are cooked.*

Toasted Sourdough with Goat's Cheese

Choose a good-quality, firm goat's cheese for this recipe because it needs to keep its shape during cooking. Serve with fresh rocket leaves.

SERVES TWO

2 thick sourdough bread slices

30ml/2 tbsp chilli jam

2 firm goat's cheese slices, about 90g/3½oz each

FROM THE STORECUPBOARD

30ml/2 tbsp garlic-infused olive oil

ground black pepper

1 Preheat the grill (broiler) to high. Brush the sourdough bread on both sides with the oil, and grill (broil) one side until golden. Spread the un-toasted side of each slice with the chilli jam and top with the goat's cheese.

2 Return the bread to the grill and cook for 3–4 minutes, or until the cheese is beginning to melt and turn golden and bubbling. Season with ground black pepper and serve immediately with rocket (arugula) leaves.

Steak and Blue Cheese Sandwiches

Many people like their rib eye steaks cooked quite rare in the centre, but how you like yours is up to you. Add a couple of minutes to the cooking time if you prefer them more well done.

SERVES TWO

1 Bake the ciabatta according to the instructions on the packet. Remove from the oven and leave to rest for a few minutes. Cut the loaf in half and split each half horizontally.

2 Heat a griddle pan until hot. Brush the steaks with the olive oil and lay them on the griddle pan. Cook for 2–3 minutes on each side, depending on the thickness of the steaks.

3 Remove the steaks from the pan and set aside to rest for a few minutes. Cut them in half and place in the sandwiches with the cheese. Season with salt and pepper, and serve.

1 ready-to-bake ciabatta bread

2 rib eye steaks, about 200g/7oz each

115g/4oz Gorgonzola cheese, sliced

FROM THE STORECUPBOARD

15ml/1 tbsp olive oil

salt and ground black pepper

Spicy Chorizo Sausage and Spring Onion Hash

Use up leftover boiled potatoes for this recipe. Fresh chorizo sausages are available from good butchers and Spanish delis.

SERVES FOUR

1 Heat a large frying pan over a medium heat and add the sausages. Cook for 8–10 minutes, turning occasionally, until cooked through. Remove from the pan and set aside.

2 Add the olive oil to the sausage fat in the pan and then add the potatoes. Cook over a low heat for 5–8 minutes, turning occasionally until golden. Meanwhile, cut the sausages into bite-size chunks and add to the pan.

3 Add the spring onions to the pan and cook for a couple more minutes, until they are piping hot. Season with salt and pepper, and serve immediately.

450g/1lb fresh chorizo sausages

450g/1lb cooked potatoes, diced

1 bunch of spring onions (scallions), sliced

FROM THE STORECUPBOARD

15ml/1 tbsp olive oil

salt and ground black pepper

Baked Sweet Potatoes with Leeks and Gorgonzola

This dish tastes wonderful and looks stunning if you buy the beautiful orange-fleshed sweet potatoes.

SERVES FOUR

4 large sweet potatoes, scrubbed

2 large leeks, washed and sliced

115g/4oz Gorgonzola cheese, sliced

FROM THE STORECUPBOARD

30ml/2 tbsp olive oil

salt and ground black pepper

1 Preheat the oven to 190°C/375°F/Gas 5. Dry the sweet potatoes with kitchen paper and rub them all over with 15ml/ 1 tbsp of the oil. Place them on a baking sheet and sprinkle with salt. Bake for 1 hour, or until tender.

2 Meanwhile, heat the remaining oil in a frying pan and add the sliced leeks. Cook for 3–4 minutes, or until softened and just beginning to turn golden.

3 Cut the potatoes in half lengthways and place them cut side up on the baking sheet. Top with the cooked leeks and season.

4 Lay the cheese slices on top and grill (broil) under a hot grill for 2–3 minutes, until the cheese is bubbling. Serve immediately.

Fish and Shellfish

THE DELICATE TASTE OF FISH AND SHELLFISH IS PERFECTLY

SUITED TO SUBTLE, SIMPLE FLAVOURINGS SUCH AS FRESH

HERBS, CITRUS JUICE, SUCCULENT TOMATOES OR SMOKY

BACON. THE FABULOUS RECIPES IN THIS CHAPTER MAKE

THE MOST OF SIMPLE, SEASONAL INGREDIENTS TO ACHIEVE

TRULY WONDERFUL DISHES.

Mussels in White Wine

This simple yet delicious dish is perfect for informal entertaining. Serve with a big bowl of chips (US fries) to share. To make a variation, cook the mussels in beer instead of wine – they taste fantastic.

SERVES TWO

300ml/^{1}/$_2$ pint/1^1/$_4$ cups dry white wine

1kg/2^1/$_4$lb mussels, cleaned

45ml/3 tbsp chopped fresh parsley

FROM THE STORECUPBOARD

25g/1oz/2 tbsp butter

salt and ground black pepper

1 Heat the butter in a large pan until foaming, then pour in the wine. Bring to the boil. Discard any open mussels that do not close when sharply tapped, and add the remaining ones to the pan. Cover with a tight-fitting lid and cook over a medium heat for 4–5 minutes, shaking the pan every now and then. By this time, all the mussels should have opened. Discard any that are still closed.

2 Line a large sieve with kitchen paper and strain the mussels and their liquid through it. Transfer the mussels to warmed serving bowls. Pour the liquid into a small pan and bring to the boil. Season with salt and pepper and stir in the parsley. Pour over the mussels and serve immediately.

Crab and Cucumber Wraps

This dish is a modern twist on the ever-popular Chinese classic, crispy Peking duck with pancakes. In this quick and easy version, crisp, refreshing cucumber and full-flavoured dressed crab are delicious with spicy-sweet hoisin sauce in warm tortilla wraps. Serve the wraps as an appetizer for four people, or as a main course for two.

SERVES TWO

1 Cut the cucumber into small even-sized batons. Scoop the dressed crab into a small mixing bowl, add a little freshly ground black pepper and mix lightly to combine.

2 Heat the tortillas gently, one at a time, in a heavy frying pan until they begin to colour on each side.

3 Spread a tortilla with 30ml/2 tbsp hoisin sauce, then sprinkle with one-quarter of the cucumber. Arrange one-quarter of the seasoned crab meat down the centre of each tortilla and roll up. Repeat with the remaining ingredients. Serve immediately.

¹/₂ cucumber

1 medium dressed crab

4 small wheat tortillas

120ml/8 tbsp hoisin sauce

FROM THE STORECUPBOARD

ground black pepper

Scallops with Fennel and Bacon

This dish is a delicious combination of succulent scallops and crispy bacon, served on a bed of tender fennel and melting mascarpone. If you can't get large scallops (known as king scallops), buy the smaller queen scallops and serve a dozen per person. If you buy scallops in the shell, wash and keep the pretty fan-shaped shells to serve a range of fish dishes in.

SERVES TWO

1 Trim, halve and slice the fennel, reserving and chopping any feathery tops. Blanch the slices in boiling water for about 3 minutes, until softened, then drain.

2 Preheat the grill (broiler) to moderate. Place the fennel in a shallow flameproof dish. Dot with the mascarpone and grill (broil) for about 5 minutes, until the cheese has melted and the fennel is lightly browned.

3 Meanwhile, pat the scallops dry on kitchen paper and season lightly. Cook the bacon in a large, heavy frying pan, until crisp and golden, turning once. Drain and keep warm. Fry the scallops in the bacon fat for 1–2 minutes on each side, until cooked through.

4 Transfer the fennel to serving plates and crumble or snip the bacon into bite size pieces over the top. Pile the scallops on the bacon and sprinkle with any reserved fennel tops.

2 small fennel bulbs

130g/4¹/₂oz/ generous ¹/₂ cup mascarpone cheese

8 large scallops, shelled

75g/3oz thin smoked streaky (fatty) bacon rashers (strips)

Prawn and New Potato Stew

New potatoes with plenty of flavour, such as Jersey Royals, Maris Piper or Nicola, are essential for this effortless stew. Use a good quality jar of tomato and chilli sauce; there are now plenty available in the supermarkets. For a really easy supper dish, serve with warm, crusty bread to mop up the delicious sauce, and a mixed green salad.

SERVES FOUR

675g/1½lb small new potatoes, scrubbed

15g/½oz/½ cup fresh coriander (cilantro)

350g/12oz jar tomato and chilli sauce

300g/11oz cooked peeled prawns (shrimp), thawed and drained if frozen

1 Cook the potatoes in boiling water for 15 minutes, until tender. Drain and return to the pan.

2 Finely chop half the coriander and add to the pan with the tomato and chilli sauce and 90ml/6 tbsp water. Bring to the boil, reduce the heat, cover and simmer gently for 5 minutes.

3 Stir in the prawns and heat briefly until they are warmed through. Do not overheat the prawns or they will quickly shrivel, becoming tough and tasteless. Spoon into shallow bowls and serve sprinkled with the remaining coriander, torn into pieces.

Haddock with Fennel Butter

Fresh fish tastes fabulous cooked in a simple herb butter. Here the liquorice flavour of fennel complements the haddock beautifully to make a simple dish ideal for a dinner party. If you can buy only small haddock fillets, fold them in half before baking, or use cod as an alternative. Serve tiny new potatoes and a herb salad with the fish to make a light, summery main course.

SERVES FOUR

1 Preheat the oven to 220°C/425°F/Gas 7. Season the fish on both sides with salt and pepper. Melt one-quarter of the butter in a frying pan, preferably non-stick, and cook the fish over a medium heat briefly on both sides.

2 Transfer the fish to a shallow ovenproof dish. Cut four wafer-thin slices from the lemon and squeeze the juice from the remainder over the fish. Place the lemon slices on top and then bake for 15–20 minutes, or until the fish is cooked.

3 Meanwhile, melt the remaining butter in the frying pan and add the fennel and a little seasoning.

4 Transfer the cooked fish to plates and pour the cooking juices into the herb butter. Heat gently for a few seconds, then pour the herb butter over the fish. Serve immediately.

675g/1¹/₂ lb haddock fillet, skinned and cut into 4 portions

1 lemon

45ml/3 tbsp coarsely chopped fennel

FROM THE STORECUPBOARD

50g/2oz/¹/₄ cup butter

salt and ground black pepper

Baked Salmon with Caraway Seeds

This classic Czech way of cooking salmon is very easy and gives excellent results. The fish cooks in its own juices, taking on the lovely warm flavour of the caraway seeds. Serve sprinkled with flat leaf parsley and wedges of lemon for squeezing over the fish.

SERVES FOUR

1.8kg/4lb whole salmon, cleaned

2.5–5ml/¹/₂–1 tsp caraway seeds

45ml/3 tbsp lemon juice

FROM THE STORECUPBOARD

115g/4oz/¹/₂ cup butter, melted

1 Preheat the oven to 180°C/350°F/Gas 4. Scale the salmon, remove the head and tail and slice off the fins with a sharp knife, then cut the fish in half lengthways.

2 Place the salmon, skin-side down, in a lightly greased roasting pan. Brush with the melted butter. Season with salt and pepper, sprinkle over the caraway seeds and drizzle with lemon juice.

3 Cover the salmon loosely with foil and bake for 25 minutes. Remove it from the oven, lift off the foil and test the fish. (The flesh should be opaque and flake easily. Return to the oven if necessary.)

4 Remove the foil and carefully lift the fish on to a serving plate. It may be served hot or cold.

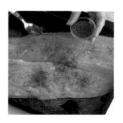

Sea Bass in a Salt Crust

Baking fish in a crust of sea salt seals in and enhances its flavour. Any firm fish can be cooked in this way. Decorate with a garnish of seaweed or blanched samphire and lemon slices, and break open the crust at the table to release the glorious aroma. Serve the fish with baby new potatoes roasted with olive oil and a sprinkling of dried rosemary, and steamed green vegetables such as broccoli or green beans.

SERVES FOUR

1 Preheat the oven to 240°C/475°F/Gas 9. Fill the cavity of the fish with the sprigs of fresh fennel, rosemary and thyme, and grind over some of the mixed peppercorns.

2 Spread half the salt in an ovenproof dish (ideally oval) and lay the sea bass on it. Cover the fish all over with a 1cm/½in layer of salt, pressing it down firmly. Moisten the salt lightly by spraying with water from an atomizer. Bake the fish for 30–40 minutes, until the salt crust is just beginning to colour.

3 Bring the sea bass to the table in its salt crust. Use a sharp knife to break open the crust and cut into four portions.

1 sea bass, about 1kg/2¹⁄₄lb, cleaned and scaled

1 sprig each of fresh fennel, rosemary and thyme

mixed peppercorns

2kg/4¹⁄₂lb coarse sea salt

Roast Cod Wrapped in Prosciutto with Vine Tomatoes

Wrapping chunky fillets of cod in wafer-thin slices of prosciutto keeps the fish succulent and moist, at the same time adding flavour and visual impact. Serve with baby new potatoes and a herb salad for a stylish supper or lunch dish.

SERVES FOUR

1 Preheat the oven to 220°C/425°F/Gas 7. Pat the fish dry on kitchen paper and remove any stray bones. Season.

2 Place one fillet in an ovenproof dish and drizzle 15ml/ 1 tbsp of the oil over it. Cover with the second fillet, laying the thick end on top of the thin end of the lower fillet to create an even shape. Lay the ham over the fish, overlapping the slices to cover the fish in an even layer. Tuck the ends of the ham under the fish and tie it in place at intervals with fine string.

3 Using kitchen scissors, snip the vines into four portions and add to the dish. Drizzle the tomatoes and ham with the remaining oil and season lightly. Roast for 35 minutes, until the tomatoes are lightly coloured and the fish is cooked through. Test the fish by piercing one end of the parcel with the tip of a knife to check that it flakes easily.

4 Slice the fish and transfer the portions to warm plates, adding the tomatoes. Spoon over the cooking juices from the dish and serve immediately.

2 thick skinless cod fillets, each weighing about 375g/13oz

75g/3oz prosciutto, thinly sliced

400g/14oz tomatoes, on the vine

FROM THE STORECUPBOARD

75ml/5 tbsp extra virgin olive oil

salt and ground black pepper

Grilled Hake with Lemon and Chilli

Choose firm hake fillets, as thick as possible. This is an ideal recipe if you are counting the calories, because it is low in fat. Serve with new potatoes and steamed fine green beans. Or, if you're not counting calories, serve with creamy mashed potatoes with plenty of butter stirred in.

SERVES FOUR

4 hake fillets, each 150g/5oz

finely grated rind and juice of 1 unwaxed lemon

15ml/1 tbsp crushed chilli flakes

FROM THE STORECUPBOARD

30ml/2 tbsp olive oil

salt and ground black pepper

1 Preheat the grill (broiler) to high. Brush the hake fillets all over with the olive oil and place them skin side up on a baking sheet.

2 Grill (broil) the fish for 4–5 minutes, until the skin is crispy, then carefully turn them over using a metal spatula.

3 Sprinkle the fillets with the lemon rind and chilli flakes and season with salt and ground black pepper.

4 Grill the fillets for a further 2–3 minutes, or until the hake is cooked through. (Test using the point of a sharp knife; the flesh should flake.) Squeeze over the lemon juice just before serving.

Trout with Grilled Serrano Ham

Traditionally in this Spanish recipe, the trout would have come from mountain streams and been stuffed and wrapped in locally cured ham. One of the beauties of this method is that the skins come off in one piece, leaving the succulent, moist flesh to be eaten with the crisped, salt ham.

SERVES FOUR

1 Extend the belly cavity of each trout, cutting up one side of the backbone. Slip a knife behind the rib bones to loosen them (sometimes just flexing the fish makes them pop up). Snip these off from both sides with scissors, and season the fish well inside.

2 Preheat the grill (broiler) to high, with a shelf in the top position. Line a baking tray with foil and butter it.

3 Working with the fish on the foil, fold a piece of ham into each belly. Use smaller or broken bits of ham for this, and reserve the eight best slices.

4 brown or rainbow trout, about 250g/9oz each, cleaned

16 thin slices Serrano ham, about 200g/7oz

buttered potatoes, to serve (optional)

FROM THE STORECUPBOARD

50g/2oz/¹/₄ cup melted butter, plus extra for greasing

salt and ground black pepper

4 Brush each trout with a little butter, seasoning the outside lightly with salt and pepper. Wrap two ham slices round each one, crossways, tucking the ends into the belly. Grill (broil) the trout for 4 minutes, then carefully turn them over with a metal spatula, rolling them across on the belly so the ham doesn't come loose, and grill for a further 4 minutes.

5 Serve the trout very hot, with any spare butter spooned over the top. Diners should open the trout on their plates, and eat them from the inside, pushing the flesh off the skin.

Tonno con Piselli

This Jewish Italian dish of fresh tuna and peas is especially enjoyed at Passover, which falls in spring. Before the days of the freezer, little peas were only eaten at this time of year when they were in season. At other times of the year chickpeas were used instead – they give a heartier result.

SERVES FOUR

1 Preheat the oven to 190°C/375°F/Gas 5. Sprinkle the tuna steaks on each side with salt and plenty of freshly ground black pepper and place in a shallow ovenproof dish, in a single layer.

2 Bring the tomato sauce to the boil, then add the fresh shelled or frozen peas and chopped fresh flat leaf parsley. Pour the sauce and peas evenly over the fish steaks in the ovenproof dish and bake in the preheated oven, uncovered, for about 20 minutes, or until the fish is tender. Serve the fish, sauce and peas immediately, straight from the dish.

350g/12oz tuna steaks

600ml/1 pint/2¹/₂ cups fresh tomato sauce

350g/12oz/3 cups fresh shelled or frozen peas

45ml/3 tbsp chopped fresh flat leaf parsley

FROM THE STORECUPBOARD

salt and ground black pepper

Filo-wrapped Fish

Select a chunky variety of tomato sauce for this simple but delicious recipe. The choice of fish can be varied according to what is in season and what is freshest on the day of purchase. When working with filo pastry, keep it covered with clear film (plastic wrap) or a damp dishtowel, as once it's exposed to air it dries out quickly and is difficult to handle.

SERVES THREE TO FOUR

130g/4¹/₂oz filo pastry (6–8 large sheets)

about 30ml/2 tbsp 450g/1lb salmon or cod steaks or fillets

550ml/18fl oz/2¹/₂ cups tomato sauce

FROM THE STORECUPBOARD

olive oil, for brushing

1 Preheat the oven to 200°C/400°F/Gas 6. Take a sheet of filo pastry, brush with a little olive oil and cover with a second sheet of pastry. Place a piece of fish on top of the pastry, towards the bottom edge, then top with 1–2 spoonfuls of the tomato sauce, spreading it in an even layer.

2 Roll the fish in the pastry, taking care to enclose the filling completely. Brush with a little olive oil. Arrange on a baking sheet and repeat with the remaining fish and pastry. You should have about half the sauce remaining, to serve with the fish.

3 Bake for 10–15 minutes, or until golden. Meanwhile, reheat the remaining sauce. Serve immediately with the remaining sauce.

Poached Fish in Spicy Tomato Sauce

A selection of white fish fillets are used in this Middle-Eastern dish – cod, haddock, hake or halibut are all good. Serve the fish with flat breads, such as pitta, and a spicy tomato relish. It is also good with couscous or rice and a green salad with a refreshing lemon juice dressing.

SERVES EIGHT

1 Heat the tomato sauce with the harissa and coriander in a large pan. Add seasoning to taste and bring to the boil.

2 Remove the pan from the heat and add the fish to the hot sauce. Return to the heat and bring the sauce to the boil again. Reduce the heat and simmer very gently for about 5 minutes, or until the fish is tender. (Test with a fork: if the flesh flakes easily, then it is cooked.)

3 Taste the sauce and adjust the seasoning, adding more harissa if necessary. Serve hot or warm.

600ml/1 pint/2¹/₂ cups fresh tomato sauce

2.5–5ml/¹/₂–1 tsp harissa

60ml/4 tbsp chopped fresh coriander (cilantro) leaves

1.5kg/3¹/₄lb mixed white fish fillets, cut into chunks

FROM THE STORECUPBOARD

salt and ground black pepper

COOK'S TIP *Harissa is a chilli paste spiced with cumin, garlic and coriander. It is fiery and should be used with care until you are familiar with the flavour. Start by adding a small amount and then add more after tasting the sauce.*

Fish with Tomato and Pine Nuts

Whole fish marinated in lemon juice and cooked with pine nuts in a spicy tomato sauce is a speciality of Jewish cooking, particularly as a festival treat for Rosh Hashanah, the Jewish New Year. The fish may be cooked and served with head and tail on, as here, or if you like, with these removed. A simple garnish of flat leaf parsley improves the appearance of this delicious dish.

SERVES SIX TO EIGHT

1–1.5kg/2^1/$_4$–3^1/$_4$lb fish, such as snapper, cleaned, with head and tail left on

juice of 2 lemons

65g/2^1/$_2$oz/scant ^{3}/$_4$ cup pine nuts, toasted

350ml/12fl oz/1^1/$_2$ cups spicy tomato sauce

FROM THE STORECUPBOARD

salt and ground black pepper

1 Prick the fish all over with a fork and rub with 2.5ml/ ½ tsp salt. Put the fish in a roasting pan or large dish and pour over the lemon juice. Leave to stand for 2 hours.

2 Preheat the oven to 180°C/350°F/Gas 4. Sprinkle half of the pine nuts over the base of an ovenproof dish, top with half of the sauce, then add the fish and its marinade. Add the remaining tomato sauce and the remaining pine nuts.

3 Cover the ovenproof dish tightly with a lid or foil and bake in the preheated oven for 30 minutes, or until the fish is tender. Serve the fish immediately, straight from the dish.

Baked Salmon with Green Sauce

When buying whole salmon, there are several points to consider – the skin should be bright and shiny, the eyes should be bright and the tail should look fresh and moist. Baking the salmon in foil produces a moist result, rather like poaching, but with the ease of baking. Garnish the fish with thin slices of cucumber and dill to conceal any flesh that may look ragged after skinning and serve with lemon wedges.

SERVES SIX TO EIGHT

2–3kg/4^1/$_2$–6^3/$_4$lb salmon, cleaned with head and tail left on

3–5 spring onions (scallions), thinly sliced

1 lemon, thinly sliced

600ml/1 pint/2^1/$_2$ cups watercress sauce or herb mayonnaise

FROM THE STORECUPBOARD

salt and ground black pepper

1 Preheat the oven to 180°C/350°F/Gas 4. Rinse the salmon and lay it on a large piece of foil. Stuff the fish with the sliced spring onions and layer the lemon slices inside and around the fish, then sprinkle with plenty of salt and ground black pepper.

2 Loosely fold the foil around the fish and fold the edges over to seal. Bake for about 1 hour.

3 Remove the fish from the oven and leave to stand, still wrapped in the foil, for about 15 minutes, then unwrap the parcel and leave the fish to cool.

4 When the fish is cool, carefully lift it on to a large plate, retaining the lemon slices. Cover the fish tightly with clear film (plastic wrap) and chill for several hours.

5 Before serving, discard the lemon slices from around the fish. Using a blunt knife to lift up the edge of the skin, carefully peel the skin away from the flesh, avoiding tearing the flesh, and pull out any fins at the same time.

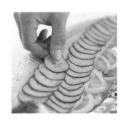

6 Chill the watercress sauce or herb mayonnaise before serving. Transfer the fish to a serving platter, garnish with thin cucumber slices if desired, and serve the sauce separately.

VARIATION *Instead of cooking a whole fish, prepare 6–8 salmon steaks. Place each fish steak on an individual square of foil, then top with a slice of onion and a slice of lemon and season generously with salt and ground black pepper. Loosely wrap the foil up around the fish, fold the edges to seal and place the parcels on a baking sheet. Bake the steaks for 10–15 minutes, or until the flesh is opaque. Serve the fish cold with the chilled watercress sauce or herb mayonnaise.*

Teriyaki Salmon

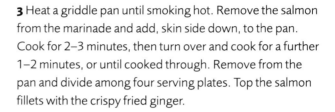

Bottles of teriyaki sauce – a lovely rich Japanese glaze – are available in most large supermarkets and Asian stores. Serve the salmon with sticky rice or soba noodles.

SERVES FOUR

4 salmon fillets, 150g/5oz each

75ml/5 tbsp teriyaki marinade

5cm/2in piece of fresh root ginger, peeled and cut into matchsticks

FROM THE STORECUPBOARD

150ml/¹/₄ pint/²/₃ cup sunflower oil

1 Put the salmon in a shallow, non-metallic dish and pour over the teriyaki marinade. Cover and chill for 2 hours.

2 Meanwhile, heat the sunflower oil in a small pan and add the ginger. Fry for 1–2 minutes, or until golden and crisp. Remove with a slotted spoon and drain on kitchen paper.

3 Heat a griddle pan until smoking hot. Remove the salmon from the marinade and add, skin side down, to the pan. Cook for 2–3 minutes, then turn over and cook for a further 1–2 minutes, or until cooked through. Remove from the pan and divide among four serving plates. Top the salmon fillets with the crispy fried ginger.

4 Pour the marinade into the pan and cook for 1–2 minutes. Pour over the salmon and serve.

Roast Mackerel with Spicy Chermoula Paste

Chermoula is a spice mix used widely in Moroccan and North African cooking. It is now readily available in most large supermarkets.

SERVES FOUR

1 Preheat the oven to 190°C/375°F/Gas 5. Place each mackerel on a large sheet of baking parchment. Using a sharp knife, slash each fish several times.

2 In a small bowl, mix the chermoula with the olive oil, and spread over the mackerel, rubbing the mixture into the cuts.

3 Scatter the red onions over the mackerel, and season with salt and pepper. Scrunch the ends of the paper together to seal the fish and place on a baking tray. Bake for 20 minutes, until the mackerel is cooked through. Serve in the paper parcels, to be unwrapped at the table.

4 whole mackerel, cleaned and gutted

2–3 tbsp chermoula

2 red onions, sliced

FROM THE STORECUPBOARD

75ml/5 tbsp olive oil

salt and ground black pepper

Pan-fried Skate Wings with Capers

This sophisticated way of serving skate is perfect for a dinner party. Serve with a light, green salad.

SERVES SIX

1 Heat the butter in a large frying pan and add one of the skate wings. Fry for 4–5 minutes on each side, until golden and cooked through.

6 small skate wings

grated rind and juice of 2 limes

30ml/2 tbsp salted capers, rinsed and drained

FROM THE STORECUPBOARD

50g/2oz/¹⁄₄ cup butter

salt and ground black pepper

2 Using a fish slice (metal spatula) carefully transfer the cooked skate wing to a warmed serving plate and keep warm while you cook each of the remaining skate wings in the same way.

3 Return the pan to the heat and add the lime rind and juice, and capers. Season with salt and freshly ground black pepper to taste and allow to bubble for 1–2 minutes. Spoon a little of the juices and the capers over each skate wing and serve immediately.

Sea Bass with Parsley and Lime Butter

The delicate but firm, sweet flesh of sea bass goes beautifully with citrus flavours. Serve with roast fennel and sautéed diced potatoes.

SERVES SIX

6 sea bass fillets, about 150g/5oz each

grated rind and juice of 1 large lime

30ml/2 tbsp chopped fresh parsley

FROM THE STORECUPBOARD

50g/2oz/¼ cup butter

salt and ground black pepper

1 Heat the butter in a large frying pan and add three of the sea bass fillets, skin side down. Cook for 3–4 minutes, or until the skin is crisp and golden. Flip the fish over and cook for a further 2–3 minutes, or until cooked through.

2 Remove the fillets from the pan with a metal spatula. Place each on a serving plate and keep them warm. Cook the remaining fish in the same way and transfer to serving plates.

3 Add the lime rind and juice to the pan with the parsley, and season with salt and black pepper. Allow to bubble for 1–2 minutes, then pour a little over each fish portion and serve immediately.

Meat

WITH THE SIMPLE ADDITION OF A FEW WELL-CHOSEN
INGREDIENTS, MEAT DISHES CAN BE TRANSFORMED INTO
EXCITING, INNOVATIVE DISHES. FROM STEAK TO PORK,
THIS CHAPTER INCLUDES A WONDERFUL SELECTION OF
DISHES THAT ARE EQUALLY SUITED TO A QUICK FAMILY
SUPPER, A LONG SUNDAY LUNCH OR AN INSPIRED
DINNER PARTY.

Beef Patties with Onions and Peppers

This is a firm family favourite. It is easy to make and delicious, and it can be varied by adding other vegetables, such as sliced red peppers, broccoli or mushrooms. These patties are very versatile and can be served in a variety of ways – with chunky home-made chips (French fries), with crusty bread, or with rice and a ready-made tomato sauce.

SERVES FOUR

1 Place the minced beef, chopped onion and 15ml/1 tbsp garlic-flavoured oil in a bowl and mix well. Season well and form into four large or eight small patties.

2 Heat the remaining oil in a large non-stick pan, then add the patties and cook on both sides until browned. Sprinkle over 15ml/1 tbsp water and add a little seasoning.

3 Cover the patties with the sliced onions and peppers. Sprinkle in another 15ml/1 tbsp water and a little seasoning, then cover the pan. Reduce the heat to very low and braise for 20–30 minutes.

4 When the onions are turning golden brown, remove the pan from the heat. Serve with onions and peppers.

500g/1¼lb lean minced (ground) beef

4 onions, 1 finely chopped and 3 sliced

2–3 green (bell) peppers, seeded and sliced lengthways into strips

FROM THE STORECUPBOARD

30ml/2 tbsp garlic-flavoured olive oil or olive oil

salt and ground black pepper

Steak with Warm Tomato Salsa

A refreshing, tangy salsa of tomatoes, spring onions and balsamic vinegar makes a colourful topping for chunky, pan-fried steaks. Choose rump, sirloin or fillet – whichever is your favourite – and if you do not have a non-stick pan, grill the steak instead for the same length of time. Serve with potato wedges and a mixed leaf salad with a mustard dressing.

SERVES TWO

1 Trim any excess fat from the steaks, then season on both sides with salt and pepper. Heat a non-stick frying pan and cook the steaks for about 3 minutes on each side for medium rare. Cook for a little longer if you like your steak well cooked.

2 Meanwhile, put the tomatoes in a heatproof bowl, cover with boiling water and leave for 1–2 minutes, until the skins start to split. Drain and peel the tomatoes, then halve them and scoop out the seeds. Dice the tomato flesh. Thinly slice the spring onions.

3 Transfer the steaks to plates and keep warm. Add the vegetables, balsamic vinegar, 30ml/2 tbsp water and a little seasoning to the cooking juices in the pan and stir briefly until warm, scraping up any meat residue. Spoon the salsa over the steaks to serve.

2 steaks, about 2cm/³/₄ in thick

4 large plum tomatoes

2 spring onions (scallions)

30ml/2 tbsp balsamic vinegar

FROM THE STORECUPBOARD

salt and ground black pepper

Meatballs in Tomato Sauce

Cook meatballs in their sauce, rather than frying them first, because this helps keep them nice and moist. Serve in the traditional way with spaghetti and shavings of Parmesan cheese.

SERVES FOUR

225g/8oz/1 cup minced (ground) beef

4 Sicilian-style sausages

2 x 400g/14oz cans pomodorino tomatoes

FROM THE STORECUPBOARD

salt and ground black pepper

1 Put the minced beef in a bowl and season with salt and pepper. Remove the sausages from their skins and mix thoroughly into the beef.

2 Shape the mixture into balls about the size of large walnuts and arrange in a single layer in a shallow baking dish. Cover and chill for 30 minutes.

3 Preheat the oven to 180ºC/350ºF/Gas 4. Process the tomatoes in a food processor until just smooth, and season. Pour over the meatballs, making sure they are all covered.

4 Bake the meatballs for 40 minutes, stirring once or twice until they are cooked through, then serve.

Beef Cooked in Red Wine

Shin of beef is traditionally quite a tough cut that needs long, slow cooking, and marinating the beef in red wine gives a tender result. Sprinkle the stew with rosemary and serve with mashed potatoes.

SERVES FOUR TO SIX

1 Put the beef in a casserole dish with the garlic and some black pepper, and pour over the red wine. Stir to combine, then cover and chill for at least 12 hours.

2 Preheat the oven to 160°C/325°F/Gas 3. Cover the casserole with a tight-fitting lid and transfer to the oven. Cook for 2 hours, or until the beef is very tender. Season with salt and pepper to taste, and serve piping hot.

675g/1¹/₂lb boned and cubed shin of beef

3 large garlic cloves, finely chopped

1 bottle fruity red wine

FROM THE STORECUPBOARD

salt and ground black pepper

VARIATION

Marinate the beef in a mixture of half port and half beef stock instead of the red wine. Port cooks down to produce a lovely rich sauce, but be sure to dilute it with stock because it can be quite overpowering on its own. A half-and-half mixture will give the perfect balance of taste.

Pan-fried Gaelic Steaks

A good steak is always popular and top quality raw materials plus timing are the keys to success. Choose small, thick steaks rather than large, thin ones if you can. Traditional accompaniments include potato chips, fried onions, mushrooms and peas.

SERVES FOUR

4 x 225–350g/8–12oz sirloin steaks, at room temperature

50ml/2fl oz/¼ cup Irish whiskey

300ml/½ pint/1¼ cups double (heavy) cream

FROM THE STORECUPBOARD

15g/1/2oz/1 tbsp butter

5ml/1 tsp oil

salt and ground black pepper

1 Season the steaks with pepper. Heat a heavy pan, over high heat. When it is hot, add the oil and butter. Add the steaks one at a time, to seal the meat quickly. Lower the heat to moderate. Allowing 3–4 minutes for rare, 4–5 minutes for medium or 5–6 minutes for well-done steaks, leave undisturbed for half of the specified cooking time; thick steaks will take longer than thin ones. Turn only once.

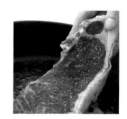

2 When the steaks are cooked to your liking, transfer them to warmed plates to keep warm. Pour off the fat from the pan and discard. Add the whiskey and stir to remove the sediment at the base of the pan. Allow the liquid to reduce a little, then add the cream and simmer over low heat for a few minutes, until the cream thickens. Season to taste, pour the sauce around or over the steaks, as preferred, and serve immediately.

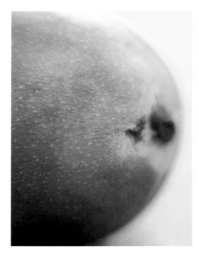

Thai-style Rare Beef and Mango Salad

This simplified version of Thai beef salad is especially tasty served with little bowls of fresh coriander (cilantro) leaves, chopped spring onions (scallions) and peanuts for sprinkling at the table.

450g/1lb sirloin steak

45ml/3 tbsp soy sauce

2 mangoes, peeled, stoned (pitted) and finely sliced

FROM THE STORECUPBOARD

45ml/3 tbsp garlic-infused olive oil

ground black pepper

SERVES FOUR

1 Put the steak in a shallow, non-metallic dish and pour over the oil and soy sauce. Season with pepper and turn the steaks to coat in the marinade. Cover and chill for 2 hours.

2 Heat a griddle pan until hot. Remove the steak from the marinade and place on the griddle pan. Cook for 3–5 minutes on each side, moving the steak halfway through if you want a criss-cross pattern.

3 Transfer the steak to a board and leave to rest for 5–10 minutes. Meanwhile, pour the marinade into the pan and cook for a few seconds, then remove from the heat. Thinly slice the steak and arrange on four serving plates with the mangoes. Drizzle over the pan juices to serve.

North African Lamb

This dish is full of contrasting flavours that create a rich, spicy and fruity main course. For best results, use lamb that still retains some fat, as this will help keep the meat moist and succulent during roasting. Serve the lamb with couscous or mixed white and wild rice, sprinkled with chopped coriander (cilantro). Roasted chunks of red and yellow (bell) peppers, aubergine (eggplant) and courgettes (zucchini), cooked in the oven with the lamb, complete the meal.

SERVES FOUR

1 Preheat the oven to 200°C/400°F/Gas 6. Heat a frying pan, preferably non-stick, and cook the lamb on all sides until beginning to brown. Transfer to a roasting pan, reserving any fat in the frying pan.

2 Peel the onions and cut each into six wedges. Toss with the lamb and roast for about 30-40 minutes, until the lamb is cooked through and the onions are deep golden brown.

3 Tip the lamb and onions back into the frying pan. Mix the harissa with 250ml/8fl oz/1 cup boiling water and add to the roasting pan. Scrape up any residue in the pan and pour the mixture over the lamb and onions. Stir in the prunes and heat until just simmering. Cover and simmer for 5 minutes, then serve.

675g/1¹/₂lb lamb fillet or shoulder steaks, cut into chunky pieces

5 small onions

7.5ml/1¹/₂ tsp harissa

115g/4oz ready-to-eat pitted prunes, halved

Lamb Steaks with Redcurrant Glaze

This classic, simple dish is absolutely delicious and is an excellent, quick recipe for cooking on the barbecue. The tangy flavour of redcurrants is a traditional accompaniment to lamb. It is good served with new potatoes and fresh garden peas tossed in butter.

SERVES FOUR

1 Reserve the tips of the rosemary and chop the remaining leaves. Rub the chopped rosemary, salt and pepperall over the lamb.

2 Preheat the grill (broiler). Heat the redcurrant jelly gently in a small pan with 30ml/2 tbsp water. Stir in the vinegar.

3 Place the steaks on a foil-lined grill (broiler) rack and brush with a little of the redcurrant glaze. Cook for about 5 minutes on each side, until deep golden, brushing with more glaze.

4 Transfer the lamb to warmed plates. Tip any juices from the foil into the remaining glaze and heat through. Pour the glaze over the lamb and serve, garnished with the reserved rosemary.

4 large fresh rosemary sprigs

4 lamb leg steaks

75ml/5 tbsp redcurrant jelly

30ml/2 tbsp raspberry or red wine vinegar

FROM THE STORECUPBOARD

salt and ground black pepper

Lamb Chops with a Mint Jelly Crust

Mint and lamb are classic partners, and the breadcrumbs used here add extra texture. Serve the chops with sweet potatoes baked in their skins and some steamed green vegetables.

SERVES FOUR

1 Preheat the oven to 190°C/375°F/Gas 5. Place the lamb chops on a baking sheet and season with plenty of salt and ground black pepper.

2 Put the breadcrumbs and mint jelly in a bowl and mix together to combine. Spoon the breadcrumb mixture on top of the chops, pressing down firmly with the back of a spoon making sure they stick to the chops.

3 Bake the chops for 20–30 minutes, or until they are just cooked through. Serve immediately.

8 lamb chops, about 115g/4oz each

50g/2oz/1 cup fresh white breadcrumbs

30ml/2 tbsp mint jelly

FROM THE STORECUPBOARD

salt and ground black pepper

Marinated Lamb with Oregano and Basil

Lamb leg steaks are chunky with a sweet flavour and go well with oregano and basil. However, you could also use finely chopped rosemary or thyme. Serve with couscous.

SERVES FOUR

1 Put the lamb in a shallow, non-metallic dish. Mix 45ml/3 tbsp of the oil with the oregano, basil and some salt and pepper, reserving some of the herbs for garnish. Pour over the lamb and turn to coat in the marinade. Cover and chill for up to 8 hours.

2 Heat the remaining oil in a large frying pan. Remove the lamb from the marinade and fry for 5–6 minutes on each side, until slightly pink in the centre. Add the marinade and cook for 1–2 minutes until warmed through. Garnish with the reserved herbs and serve.

4 large or 8 small lamb leg steaks

1 small bunch of fresh oregano, roughly chopped

1 small bunch of fresh basil, torn

FROM THE STORECUPBOARD

60ml/4 tbsp garlic-infused olive oil

salt and ground black pepper

Roast Shoulder of Lamb with Whole Garlic Cloves

The potatoes catch the lamb fat as it cooks, giving garlicky, juicy results. Return the potatoes to the oven to keep warm while you leave the lamb to rest before carving. Serve with seasonal vegetables.

SERVES FOUR TO SIX

675g/1¹/₂lb waxy potatoes, peeled and cut into large dice

12 garlic cloves, unpeeled

1 whole shoulder of lamb

FROM THE STORECUPBOARD

45ml/3 tbsp olive oil

salt and ground black pepper

1 Preheat the oven to 180°C/350°F/Gas 4. Put the potatoes and garlic cloves into a large roasting pan and season with salt and pepper. Pour over 30ml/2 tbsp of the oil and toss the potatoes and garlic to coat.

2 Place a rack over the roasting pan, so that it is not touching the potatoes. Place the lamb on the rack and drizzle over the remaining oil. Season with salt and pepper.

3 Roast the lamb and potatoes for 2–2¹/₂ hours, or until the lamb is cooked through. Halfway through the cooking time, carefully take the lamb and the rack off the roasting pan and turn the potatoes to ensure even cooking.

Roast Leg of Lamb with Rosemary and Garlic

This is a classic combination of flavours, and always popular. Serve as a traditional Sunday lunch with roast potatoes and vegetables. Leaving the lamb to rest before carving ensures a tender result.

SERVES FOUR TO SIX

1 leg of lamb, approx 1.8kg/4lb

2 garlic cloves, finely sliced

leaves from 2 sprigs of fresh rosemary

FROM THE STORECUPBOARD

30ml/2 tbsp olive oil

salt and ground black pepper

1 Preheat the oven to 190°C/375°F/Gas 5. Using a small sharp knife, make slits at 4cm/1½in intervals over the lamb, deep enough to hold a piece of garlic. Push the garlic and rosemary leaves into the slits.

2 Drizzle the olive oil over the top of the lamb and season with plenty of salt and ground black pepper. Roast for 25 minutes per 450g/1lb of lamb, plus another 25 minutes.

3 Remove the lamb from the oven and leave to rest for about 15 minutes before carving.

Sweet-and-sour Lamb

Buy lamb loin chops from your butcher and ask him to French trim them for you. Serve with steamed carrots or green beans.

SERVES FOUR

8 French-trimmed lamb loin chops

90ml/6 tbsp balsamic vinegar

30ml/2 tbsp caster (superfine) sugar

FROM THE STORECUPBOARD

30ml/2 tbsp olive oil

salt and ground black pepper

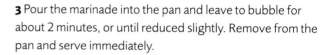

1 Put the lamb chops in a shallow, non-metallic dish and drizzle over the balsamic vinegar. Sprinkle with the sugar and season with salt and black pepper. Turn the chops to coat in the mixture, then cover with clear film (plastic wrap) and chill for 20 minutes.

2 Heat the olive oil in a large frying pan and add the chops, reserving the marinade. Cook for 3–4 minutes on each side.

3 Pour the marinade into the pan and leave to bubble for about 2 minutes, or until reduced slightly. Remove from the pan and serve immediately.

Roast Lamb with Figs

Lamb fillet is an expensive cut of meat, but because it is very lean there is very little waste. To make a more economical version of this dish, use leg of lamb instead. It has a stronger flavour but is equally good. Serve with steamed green beans.

SERVES SIX

1kg/2¹/₄lb lamb fillet

9 fresh figs

150ml/¹/₄ pint/²/₃ cup ruby port

FROM THE STORECUPBOARD

30ml/2 tbsp olive oil

salt and ground black pepper

1 Preheat the oven to 190⁰/375⁰F/Gas 5. Heat the oil in a roasting pan over a medium heat. Add the lamb fillet and sear on all sides until evenly browned.

2 Cut the figs in half and arrange around the lamb. Season the lamb with salt and ground black pepper and roast for 30 minutes. Pour the port over the figs.

3 Return the lamb to the oven and roast for a further 30–45 minutes. The meat should still be slightly pink in the middle so be careful not to overcook.

4 Transfer the lamb to a board and leave to rest for about 5 minutes. Carve into slices and serve.

Paprika Pork

This chunky, goulash-style dish is rich with peppers and paprika. Grilling the peppers before adding them to the meat really brings out their sweet, vibrant flavour. Rice or buttered boiled potatoes go particularly well with the rich pork.

SERVES FOUR

2 red, 1 yellow and 1 green (bell) pepper, seeded

500g/1¼lb lean pork fillet (tenderloin)

45ml/3 tbsp paprika

300g/11oz jar or tub of tomato sauce with herbs or garlic

FROM THE STORECUPBOARD

salt and ground black pepper

1 Preheat the grill (broiler). Cut the peppers into thick strips and sprinkle in a single layer on a foil-lined grill rack. Cook under the grill for 20–25 minutes, until the edges of the strips are lightly charred.

2 Meanwhile, cut the pork into chunks. Season and cook in a frying pan for about 5 minutes, until beginning to brown.

3 Transfer the meat to a heavy pan and add the paprika, tomato sauce, 300ml/½ pint/1¼ cups water and a little seasoning. Bring to the boil, reduce the heat, cover and simmer gently for 30 minutes.

4 Add the grilled (broiled) peppers and cook for a further 10–15 minutes, until the meat is tender. Taste for seasoning and serve immediately.

Pork Kebabs

The word kebab comes from Arabic and means on a skewer. Use pork fillet (tenderloin) for these kebabs because it is lean and tender, and cooks very quickly. They are good served with rice, or stuffed into warmed pitta bread with some shredded lettuce leaves.

SERVES FOUR

500g/1¹⁄₄lb lean pork fillet (tenderloin)

8 large, thick spring onions (scallions), trimmed

120ml/4fl oz/¹⁄₂ cup barbecue sauce

1 lemon

1 Cut the pork into 2.5cm/1in cubes. Cut the spring onions into 2.5cm/1in long sticks.

2 Preheat the grill (broiler) to high. Oil the wire rack and spread out the pork cubes on it. Grill (broil) the pork until the juices drip, then dip the pieces in the barbecue sauce and put back on the grill. Grill for 30 seconds on each side, repeating the dipping process twice more. Set aside and keep warm.

3 Gently grill (broil) the spring onions until soft and slightly brown outside. Do not dip in the barbecue sauce. Thread about four pieces of pork and three spring onion pieces on to each of eight bamboo skewers.

4 Arrange the skewers on a platter. Cut the lemon into wedges and squeeze a little lemon juice over each skewer. Serve immediately, offering the remaining lemon wedges separately.

COOK'S TIP
If you are cooking the pork on a barbecue, soak the skewers overnight in water. This prevents them burning. Keep the skewer handles away from the fire and turn them frequently.

Fragrant Lemon Grass and Ginger Pork Patties

Lemon grass lends a fragrant citrus flavour to pork, enhanced by the fresh zing of ginger. Serve the patties in burger buns with thick slices of juicy tomato, crisp, refreshing lettuce and a splash of chilli sauce.

SERVES FOUR

450g/1lb/2 cups minced (ground) pork

15ml/1 tbsp fresh root ginger, grated

1 lemon grass stalk

FROM THE STORECUPBOARD

30ml/2 tbsp sunflower oil

salt and ground black pepper

1 Put the pork in a bowl and stir in the ginger. Season with salt and pepper. Remove the tough outer layers from the lemon grass stalk and discard. Chop the centre part as finely as possible and mix into the pork. Shape into four patties and chill for about 20 minutes.

2 Heat the oil in a large, non-stick frying pan and add the patties. Fry for 3–4 minutes on each side over a gentle heat, until cooked through. Remove from the pan with a metal spatula and drain on kitchen paper, then serve.

Pan-fried Gammon with Cider

Gammon and cider are a delicious combination with the sweet, tangy flavour of cider complementing the gammon perfectly. Serve with mustard mashed potatoes.

4 gammon steaks (smoked or cured ham), 225g/8oz each

150ml/¹/₄ pint/²/₃ cup dry (hard) cider

45ml/3 tbsp double (heavy) cream

FROM THE STORECUPBOARD

30ml/2 tbsp sunflower oil

salt and ground black pepper

SERVES FOUR

1 Heat the oil in a large frying pan until hot. Neatly snip the rind on the gammon steaks to stop them curling up and add them to the pan.

2 Cook the steaks for 3–4 minutes on each side, then pour in the cider. Allow to boil for a couple of minutes, then stir in the cream and cook for 1–2 minutes, or until thickened. Season with salt and pepper, and serve immediately.

Caramelized Onion and Sausage Tarte Tatin

Toulouse sausages have a garlicky flavour and meaty texture that is delicious with fried onions. Serve with a green salad of bitter leaves.

SERVES FOUR

450g/1lb Toulouse sausages

2 large onions, sliced

250g/9oz ready-made puff pastry, thawed if frozen

FROM THE STORECUPBOARD

45ml/3 tbsp sunflower oil

salt and ground black pepper

1 Heat the oil in a 23cm/9in non-stick frying pan with an ovenproof handle, and add the sausages. Cook over a gentle heat, turning occasionally, for 7–10 minutes, or until golden and cooked through. Remove from the pan and set aside.

2 Preheat the oven to 190°C/375°F/Gas 5. Pour the remaining oil into the frying pan and add the onions. Season with salt and pepper and cook over a gentle heat for 10 minutes, stirring occasionally, until caramelized and tender.

3 Slice each sausage into four or five chunks and stir into the onions. Remove from the heat and set aside.

4 Roll out the puff pastry and cut out a circle slightly larger than the frying pan. Lay the pastry over the sausages and onions, tucking the edges in all the way around. Bake for 20 minutes, or until the pastry is risen and golden. Turn out on to a board, pastry side down, cut into wedges and serve.

Roast Pork with Juniper Berries and Bay

Juniper berries have a strong, pungent taste and are a great flavouring for rich, fatty meats such as pork, while bay leaves add a lovely aroma. Serve with roast potatoes and lightly cooked leafy green vegetables.

SERVES FOUR TO SIX

1kg/2¼lb boned leg of pork

5 fresh bay leaves

6 juniper berries

FROM THE STORECUPBOARD

15ml/1 tbsp olive oil

salt and ground black pepper

1 Preheat the oven to 180°C/350°F/Gas 4. Open out the pork and season with plenty of salt and black pepper.

2 Lay the bay leaves on the pork and sprinkle over the juniper berries. Carefully roll up the pork to enclose the bay leaves and juniper berries and tie with string to secure.

3 Rub the skin with the oil and then rub in plenty of salt. Roast the pork for 20 minutes per 450g/1lb, plus an extra 20 minutes.

4 Remove the pork from the oven and leave to rest for about 10 minutes before carving, then serve immediately.

Sticky Glazed Pork Ribs

These spare ribs have a lovely sweet-and-sour flavour and are always as popular with children as they are with adults, making them the perfect choice for a family meal. They're also great for cooking over a barbecue; make sure you leave them to marinate for at least 30 minutes before cooking. To enjoy sticky ribs at their best you need to get stuck in and eat them with your fingers, so make sure you serve them with plenty of paper napkins.

SERVES FOUR

1 Preheat the oven to 190°C/375°F/Gas 5. Put the spare ribs in a roasting pan and season well with plenty of salt and ground black pepper.

2 In a small bowl, mix together the honey and soy sauce and pour over the ribs. Turn the ribs several times, spooning over the mixture until thoroughly coated.

3 Bake the spare ribs for 30 minutes, then increase the oven temperature to 220°C/425°F/Gas 7 and cook for a further 10 minutes, or until the honey and soy sauce marinade turns into a thick, sticky glaze.

900g/2lb pork spare ribs

75ml/5 tbsp clear honey

75ml/5 tbsp light soy sauce

FROM THE STORECUPBOARD

salt and ground black pepper

Chinese Spiced Pork Chops

Five-spice powder is a fantastic ingredient for perking up dishes and adding a good depth of flavour. The five different spices – Szechuan pepper, cinnamon, cloves, fennel seeds and star anise – are perfectly balanced, with the aniseed flavour of star anise predominating. Serve the chops with lightly steamed pak choi (bok choy) and plain boiled rice.

SERVES FOUR

4 large pork chops, about 200g/7oz each

15ml/1 tbsp Chinese five-spice powder

30ml/2 tbsp soy sauce

FROM THE STORECUPBOARD

30ml/2 tbsp garlic-infused olive oil

1 Arrange the pork chops in a single layer in a non-metallic roasting pan or baking dish.

2 Sprinkle the five-spice powder over the chops, then drizzle over the soy sauce and garlic infused oil. (Alternatively, mix together the garlic-infused olive oil, soy sauce and five-spice powder, and pour over the chops.)

3 Using your hands, rub the mixture into the meat. Cover the dish with clear film (plastic wrap) and chill for 2 hours.

4 Preheat the oven to 160°C/325°F/Gas 3. Uncover the dish and bake for 30–40 minutes, or until the pork is cooked through and tender. Serve immediately.

Poultry and Game

WITH THE SIMPLE ADDITION OF A FEW WELL-CHOSEN
INGREDIENTS, POULTRY CAN BE TRANSFORMED INTO
EXCITING, INNOVATIVE DISHES. FROM DUCK TO PHEASANT,
THIS CHAPTER INCLUDES A WONDERFUL SELECTION OF
DISHES THAT ARE EQUALLY SUITED TO A QUICK FAMILY
SUPPER OR A DINNER PARTY.

Pot-roasted Chicken with Preserved Lemons

Roasting chicken and potatoes in this way gives an interesting variety of textures. The chicken and potatoes on the top crisp up, while underneath they stay soft and juicy. Serve with steamed carrots or curly kale.

SERVES FOUR TO SIX

675g/1¹⁄₂lb potatoes, unpeeled and cut into chunks

6–8 pieces of preserved lemon

1.3kg/3lb corn-fed chicken, jointed

FROM THE STORECUPBOARD

30ml/2 tbsp olive oil

salt and ground black pepper

1 Preheat the oven to 190°C/375°F/Gas 5. Drizzle the olive oil into the bottom of a large roasting pan. Spread the chunks of potato in a single layer in the pan and tuck in the pieces of preserved lemon.

2 Pour about 1cm/¹⁄₂in of cold water into the roasting pan. Arrange the chicken pieces on top and season with plenty of salt and black pepper. Roast for 45 minutes–1 hour, or until the chicken is cooked through, and serve.

Honey Mustard Chicken

Chicken thighs have a rich flavour, but if you want to cut down on fat, use four chicken breast portions instead and cook for 20–25 minutes. Serve with a chunky tomato and red onion salad.

SERVES FOUR

1 Preheat the oven to 190°C/375°F/Gas 5. Put the chicken thighs in a single layer in a roasting pan.

2 Mix together the mustard and honey, season with salt and ground black pepper to taste and brush the mixture all over the chicken thighs.

3 Cook for 25–30 minutes, brushing the chicken with the pan juices occasionally, until cooked through. (To check the chicken is cooked through, skewer it with a sharp knife; the juices should run clear.)

8 chicken thighs

60ml/4 tbsp wholegrain mustard

60ml/4 tbsp clear honey

FROM THE STORECUPBOARD

salt and ground black pepper

Drunken Chicken

In this traditional Chinese dish, cooked chicken is marinated in sherry, fresh root ginger and spring onions for several days. Because of the lengthy preparation time, it is important to use a very fresh bird from a reputable supplier. Fresh herbs can be added as an additional garnish, if you like.

SERVES FOUR TO SIX

1 chicken, about
1.3kg/3lb

1cm/¹/₂ in piece of
fresh root ginger, thinly
sliced

2 spring onions
(scallions), trimmed,
plus extra to garnish

300ml/¹/₂ pint/1¹/₄
cups dry sherry

FROM THE
STORECUPBOARD

salt

1 Rinse and dry the chicken inside and out. Place the ginger and spring onions in the body cavity. Put the chicken in a large pan or flameproof casserole and just cover with water. Bring to the boil, skim off any scum and cook for 15 minutes.

2 Turn off the heat, cover the pan or casserole tightly and leave the chicken in the cooking liquid for 3–4 hours, by which time it will be cooked. Drain well, reserving the stock. Pour 300ml/¹/₂ pint/1¹/₄ cups of the stock into a jug (pitcher).

3 Remove the skin and cut the chicken into neat pieces. Divide each leg into a drumstick and thigh. Make two more portions from the wings and some of the breast. Finally, cut away the remainder of the breast pieces (still on the bone) and divide each piece into two even-size portions.

4 Arrange the chicken portions in a shallow dish. Rub salt into the chicken and cover with clear film (plastic wrap). Leave in a cool place for several hours or overnight in the refrigerator.

5 Later, lift off any fat from the stock, add the sherry and pour over the chicken. Cover again and leave in the refrigerator to marinate for 2–3 days, turning occasionally.

6 When ready to serve, cut the chicken through the bone into chunky pieces and arrange on a large serving platter. Garnish the chicken with spring onion shreds.

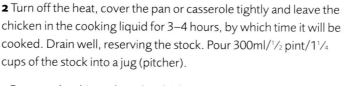

VARIATION
To serve as a cocktail snack, take the meat off the bones, cut it into bitesize pieces, then spear each piece on a cocktail stick (toothpick).

Soy-marinated Chicken

Two simple flavours, soy sauce and orange, combine to make this mouthwatering dish. Serving the chicken on a bed of asparagus turns the dish into a special treat. Wilted spinach or shredded greens work well as an everyday alternative. Boiled egg noodles or steamed white rice make a good accompaniment.

SERVES FOUR

4 skinless, chicken breast fillets

1 large orange

30ml/2 tbsp dark soy sauce

400g/14oz medium asparagus spears

1 Slash each chicken portion diagonally and place them in a single layer in a shallow, ovenproof dish. Halve the orange, squeeze the juice from one half and mix it with the soy sauce. Pour this over the chicken. Cut the remaining orange into wedges and place these on the chicken. Cover and leave to marinate for several hours.

2 Preheat the oven to 180°C/350°F/Gas 4. Turn the chicken over and bake, uncovered, for 20 minutes. Turn the chicken over again and bake for a further 15 minutes, or until cooked through.

3 Meanwhile, cut off any tough ends from the asparagus and place in a frying pan. Pour in enough boiling water just to cover and cook gently for 3–4 minutes, until just tender. Drain and arrange on warmed plates, then top with the chicken and orange wedges. Spoon over the cooking juices. Serve immediately.

Stir-fried Chicken with Thai Basil

Thai basil, sometimes called holy basil, has purple-tinged leaves and a more pronounced, slightly aniseedy flavour than the usual varieties. It is available in most Asian food stores but if you can't find any, use a handful of ordinary basil instead. Serve this fragrant stir-fry with plain steamed rice or boiled noodles and soy sauce on the side.

SERVES FOUR

1 Using a sharp knife, slice the chicken breast portions into strips. Halve the peppers, remove the seeds, then cut each piece of pepper into strips.

2 Heat the oil in a wok or large frying pan. Add the chicken and red peppers and stir-fry over a high heat for about 3 minutes, until the chicken is golden and cooked through. Season with salt and ground black pepper.

3 Roughly tear up the basil leaves, add to the chicken and peppers and toss briefly to combine. Serve immediately.

4 skinless chicken breast fillets, cut into strips

2 red (bell) peppers

1 small bunch of fresh Thai basil

FROM THE STORECUPBOARD

30ml/2 tbsp garlic-infused olive oil

salt and ground black pepper

Crème Fraîche and Coriander Chicken

Boneless chicken thighs are used for this recipe but you can substitute breast portions if you like. Be generous with the coriander leaves, as they have a wonderful fragrant flavour, or use chopped parsley instead. Serve with creamy mashed potatoes. To make a lower fat version of this dish, use chicken breast portions and low-fat crème fraîche.

SERVES FOUR

6 skinless chicken thigh fillets

60ml/4 tbsp crème fraîche

1 small bunch of fresh coriander (cilantro), roughly chopped

FROM THE STORECUPBOARD

15ml/1 tbsp sunflower oil

salt and ground black pepper

1 Cut each chicken thigh into three or four pieces. Heat the oil in a large frying pan, add the chicken and cook for about 6 minutes, turning occasionally, until cooked through.

2 Add the crème fraîche to the pan and stir until melted, then allow to bubble for 1–2 minutes.

3 Add the chopped coriander to the chicken and stir to combine. Season with salt and ground black pepper to taste, and serve immediately.

Chicken Escalopes with Lemon and Serrano Ham

Chicken escalopes are flattened chicken breast fillets – they cook quicker than normal breast portions and absorb flavours more readily. In this light summery dish, the chicken absorbs the delicious flavours of the ham and lemon. It can be assembled in advance, so is good for entertaining.

SERVES FOUR

1 Preheat the oven to 180°C/350°F/Gas 4. Beat the butter with plenty of freshly ground black pepper and set aside. Place the chicken portions on a large sheet of clear film (plastic wrap), spacing them well apart. Cover with a second sheet, then beat with a rolling pin until the portions are half their original thickness.

2 Transfer the chicken to a large, shallow ovenproof dish and crumple a slice of ham on top of each. Cut eight thin slices from the lemon and place two on each slice of ham.

3 Dot with the pepper butter and bake for about 30 minutes, until the chicken is cooked. Transfer to serving plates and spoon over any juices from the dish.

4 skinless chicken breast fillets

4 slices Serrano ham

1 lemon

FROM THE STORECUPBOARD

40g/1¹⁄₂oz/3 tbsp butter, softened

salt and ground black pepper

Roast Chicken with Herb Cheese, Chilli and Lime Stuffing

Whether you are entertaining guests or cooking a family meal, a tasty chicken is a sure winner every time. This is a modern twist on the classic roast chicken – the stuffing is forced under the chicken skin, which helps to produce a wonderfully flavoured, succulent flesh.

SERVES FIVE TO SIX

1 Preheat the oven to 200°C/400°F/Gas 6. Using first the point of a knife and then your fingers, separate the skin from the meat across the chicken breast and over the tops of the legs. Use the knife to loosen the first piece of skin, then carefully run your fingers underneath, taking care not to tear the skin.

2 Grate the lime and beat the rind into the cream cheese together with the chopped chilli. Pack the cream cheese stuffing under the skin, using a teaspoon, until fairly evenly distributed. Push the skin back into place, then smooth your hands over it to spread the stuffing in an even layer.

3 Put the chicken in a roasting pan and squeeze the juice from the lime over the top. Roast for 1½ hours, or until the juices run clear when the thickest part of the thigh is pierced with a skewer. If necessary, cover the chicken with foil towards the end of cooking if the top starts to become too browned.

4 Carve the chicken and arrange on a warmed serving platter. Spoon the pan juices over it and serve immediately.

1.8kg/4lb chicken

1 lime

115g/4oz/½ cup cream cheese with herbs and garlic

1 mild fresh red chilli, seeded and finely chopped

Tandoori Chicken

If you have time, prepare this dish when you get up in the morning, so that it's ready to cook for supper. Serve with a red onion and cucumber salad and warmed naan bread.

SERVES FOUR

4 skinless chicken breast fillets and 4 skinless chicken thigh fillets

200ml/7fl oz/scant 1 cup Greek (US strained plain) yogurt

45ml/3 tbsp tandoori curry paste

FROM THE STORECUPBOARD

salt and ground black pepper

1 Using a sharp knife, slash the chicken breasts and thighs and place in a shallow, non-metallic dish.

2 Put the curry paste and yogurt in a bowl and mix together. Season with salt and pepper, then pour over the chicken and toss to coat well. Cover the dish with clear film (plastic wrap) and chill for at least 8 hours.

3 Preheat the oven to 190°C/375°F/Gas 5. Remove the clear film from the chicken and transfer the dish to the oven. Bake for 20–30 minutes, or until the chicken is cooked through. Serve immediately.

Roast Chicken with Black Pudding and Sage

The combination of juicy roast chicken and black pudding is wonderful. Serve as part of a Sunday roast or simply with a salad.

SERVES FOUR

1 medium oven-ready chicken

115g/4oz black pudding (blood sausage), skinned

30ml/2 tbsp fresh sage leaves

FROM THE STORECUPBOARD

25g/1oz/2 tbsp softened butter

salt and ground black pepper

1 Preheat the oven to 190°C/375°F/Gas 5. Carefully push your fingers between the skin and the flesh at the neck end of the bird to loosen it, making sure you don't tear the skin.

2 Shape the black pudding into a flat, roundish shape, to fit the space between the skin and the breast meat. Push it under the skin with half the sage leaves.

3 Smooth the skin back and tuck underneath. Tie the legs together and place the chicken in a roasting pan. Spread the butter over the breast and thighs, and season. Sprinkle over the remaining sage leaves and roast for 1$\frac{1}{2}$ hours, or until the chicken is cooked through. Remove to a board and leave to rest for 10 minutes before carving.

Spatchcock Poussins with Herb Butter

Spatchcock is said to be a distortion of an 18th-century Irish expression "dispatch cock" for providing an unexpected guest with a quick and simple meal. A young chicken was prepared without frills or fuss by being split, flattened and fried or grilled.

SERVES TWO

2 poussins, each weighing about 450g/1lb

2 garlic cloves, crushed

45ml/3 tbsp chopped mixed fresh herbs, such as flat leaf parsley, sage, rosemary and thyme

FROM THE STORECUPBOARD

75g/3oz/6 tbsp butter, softened

salt and ground black pepper

1 To spatchcock a poussin, place it breast down on a chopping board and split it along the back. Open out the bird and turn it over, so that the breast side is uppermost. Press the bird as flat as possible, then thread two metal skewers through it, across the breast and thigh, to keep it flat. Repeat with the second poussin and place the skewered birds on a large grill pan.

2 Add the crushed garlic and chopped mixed herbs to the butter with plenty of seasoning, and then beat well. Dot the butter over the spatchcock poussins.

3 Preheat the grill to high and cook the poussins for 30 minutes, turning them over halfway through. Turn again and baste with the cooking juices, then cook for a further 5–7 minutes on each side.

Chilli-spiced Poussin

When you are short of time these spicy poussins make a quick alternative to a traditional roast. Serve with a leafy salad.

2 poussins, 675g/1¹/₂lb each

15ml/1 tbsp chilli powder

15ml/1 tbsp ground cumin

FROM THE STORECUPBOARD

45ml/3 tbsp olive oil

salt and ground black pepper

SERVES FOUR

1 Spatchcock one poussin: remove the wishbone and split the bird along each side of the backbone and remove it. Press down on the breastbone to flatten the bird. Push a metal skewer through the wings and breast to keep the bird flat, then push a second skewer through the thighs and breast. Spatchcock the second poussin in the same way.

2 Combine the chilli, cumin, oil and seasoning. Brush over the poussins. Preheat the grill (broiler). Lay the birds, skin side down, on a grill rack and grill (broil) for 15 minutes. Turn over and grill for a further 15 minutes until cooked through.

3 Remove the skewers and split each bird in half along the breastbone. Serve drizzled with the pan juices.

Turkey Patties

So much better than store-bought burgers, these light patties are delicious served hamburger-style in split and toasted buns with relish, salad leaves and chunky fries. They can also be made using minced chicken, lamb, pork or beef. If you are making them for children, shape the mixture into 12 equal-sized rounds and serve in mini-rolls or in rounds stamped out from sliced bread.

SERVES SIX

1 Mix together the turkey, onion, thyme, 15ml/1 tbsp of the oil and seasoning. Cover and chill for up to 4 hours to let the flavours infuse (steep), then divide the mixture into six equal portions and shape into round patties.

2 Preheat a griddle pan. Brush the patties with half of the remaining lime-flavoured olive oil, then place them on the pan and cook for 10–12 minutes. Turn the patties over, brush with more oil, and cook for 10–12 minutes on the second side, or until cooked right through. Serve the patties immediately.

675g/1¹/₂lb minced (ground) turkey

1 small red onion, finely chopped

small handful of fresh thyme leaves

FROM THE STORECUPBOARD

30ml/2 tbsp lime-flavoured olive oil

Guinea Fowl with Whisky Sauce

Served with creamy, sweet mashed potato and lightly boiled whole baby leeks, guinea fowl is magnificent with a rich, creamy whisky sauce. If you don't like the flavour of whisky, then substitute brandy, Madeira or Marsala. Or, to make a non-alcoholic version, use freshly squeezed orange juice instead. Garnish with fresh thyme sprigs or other fresh herbs.

SERVES FOUR

2 guinea fowl, each weighing about 1kg/2^{1}/4lb

90ml/6 tbsp whisky

150ml/^{1}/4 pint/^{2}/3 cup well-flavoured chicken stock

150ml/^{1}/4 pint/^{2}/3 cup double (heavy) cream

FROM THE STORECUPBOARD

salt and ground black pepper

1 Preheat the oven to 200°C/400°F/Gas 6. Brown the guinea fowl on all sides in a roasting pan on the hob (stove-top), then turn it breast uppermost and transfer the pan to the oven. Roast for about 1 hour, until the guinea fowl are golden and cooked through. Transfer the guinea fowl to a warmed serving dish, cover with foil and keep warm.

2 Pour off the excess fat from the pan, then heat the juices on the hob and stir in the whisky. Bring to the boil and cook until reduced. Add the stock and cream and simmer again until reduced slightly. Strain and season to taste.

3 Carve the guinea fowl and serve on individual plates, arranged around the chosen vegetable accompaniments. Sprinkle with plenty of freshly ground black pepper. Spoon a little of the sauce over each portion and serve the rest separately.

Pheasant Cooked in Port with Mushrooms

This warming dish is delicious served with mashed root vegetables and shredded cabbage or leeks. Marinating the pheasant in port helps to moisten and tenderize the meat, which can often be slightly dry. If you prefer, marinate the pheasant in a full-bodied red wine and use button (white) mushrooms.

SERVES FOUR

2 pheasants, cut into portions

300ml/^{1}/$_2$ pint/1^1/$_4$ cups port

300g/11oz chestnut mushrooms, halved if large

FROM THE STORECUPBOARD

50g/2oz/^{1}/$_4$ cup butter

salt and ground black pepper

1 Place the pheasant in a bowl and pour over the port. Cover and marinate for 3–4 hours or overnight, turning the portions occasionally.

2 Drain the meat thoroughly, reserving the marinade. Pat the portions dry on kitchen paper and season lightly with salt and pepper. Melt three-quarters of the butter in a frying pan and cook the pheasant portions on all sides for about 5 minutes, until deep golden. Drain well, transfer to a plate, then cook the mushrooms in the fat remaining in the pan for 3 minutes.

3 Return the pheasant to the pan and pour in the reserved marinade with 200ml/7fl oz/scant 1 cup water. Bring to the boil, reduce the heat and cover, then simmer gently for about 45 minutes, until the pheasant is tender.

4 Using a slotted spoon, carefully remove the pheasant portions and mushrooms from the frying pan and keep warm. Bring the cooking juices to the boil and boil vigorously for 3–5 minutes, until they are reduced and slightly thickened. Strain the juices through a fine sieve and return them to the pan. Whisk in the remaining butter over a gentle heat until it has melted, season to taste, then pour the juices over the pheasant and mushrooms and serve.

Roast Pheasant with Sherry and Mustard Sauce

Use only young pheasants for roasting – older birds are too tough and only suitable for casseroles. Serve with potatoes braised in wine with garlic and onions, Brussel sprouts and bread sauce.

SERVES FOUR

2 young oven-ready pheasants

200ml/7fl oz/scant 1 cup sherry

15ml/1 tbsp Dijon mustard

FROM THE STORECUPBOARD

50g/2oz/¹/₄ cup softened butter

salt and ground black pepper

1 Preheat the oven to 200°C/400°F/Gas 6. Put the pheasants in a roasting pan and spread the butter all over both birds. Season with salt and pepper.

2 Roast the pheasants for 50 minutes, basting often to stop the birds from drying out. When the pheasants are cooked, take them out of the pan and leave to rest on a board, covered with foil.

3 Meanwhile, place the roasting pan over a medium heat. Add the sherry and season with salt and pepper. Simmer for 5 minutes, until the sherry has slightly reduced, then stir in the mustard. Carve the pheasants and serve with the sherry and mustard sauce.

Marmalade and Soy Roast Duck

Sweet-and-sour flavours, such as marmalade and soy sauce, complement the rich, fatty taste of duck beautifully. Serve these robustly flavoured duck breast portions with simple accompaniments such as steamed sticky rice and lightly cooked pak choi (bok choy).

SERVES SIX

6 duck breast portions

45ml/3 tbsp fine-cut marmalade

45ml/3 tbsp light soy sauce

FROM THE STORECUPBOARD

salt and ground black pepper

1 Preheat the oven 190°C/375°F/Gas 5. Place the duck breasts skin side up on a grill (broiler) rack and place in the sink. Pour boiling water all over the duck. This shrinks the skin and helps it crisp during cooking. Pat the duck dry with kitchen paper and transfer to a roasting pan.

2 Combine the marmalade and soy sauce, and brush over the duck. Season with a little salt and some black pepper and roast for 20–25 minutes, basting occasionally with the marmalade mixture in the pan.

3 Remove the duck breasts from the oven and leave to rest for 5 minutes. Slice the duck breasts and serve drizzled with any juices left in the pan.

Duck with Plum Sauce

Sharp plums cut the rich flavour of duck wonderfully well in this updated version of an old English dish. Duck is often considered to be a fatty meat but modern breeding methods have made leaner ducks widely available. For an easy dinner party main course, serve the duck with creamy mashed potatoes and celeriac and steamed broccoli.

SERVES FOUR

4 duck quarters

1 large red onion, finely chopped

500g/1¼lb ripe plums, stoned (pitted) and quartered

30ml/2 tbsp redcurrant jelly

1 Prick the duck skin all over with a fork to release the fat during cooking and help give a crisp result, then place the portions in a heavy frying pan, skin side down.

2 Cook the duck pieces for 10 minutes on each side, or until golden brown and cooked right through. Remove the duck from the frying pan using a slotted spoon and keep warm.

3 Pour away all but 30ml/2 tbsp of the duck fat, then stir-fry the onion for 5 minutes, or until golden. Add the plums and cook for 5 minutes, stirring frequently. Add the jelly and mix well.

4 Replace the duck portions and cook for a further 5 minutes, or until thoroughly reheated. Serve immediately.

COOK'S TIP *It is important that the plums used in this dish are very ripe, otherwise the mixture will be too dry and the sauce will be extremely sharp.*

Pasta and Rice

PASTA AND RICE ARE THE PERFECT STAPLES UPON WHICH

TO BASE SIMPLE, TASTY MEALS. YOU NEED ONLY A FEW

INGREDIENTS TO RUSTLE UP DELICIOUS DISHES, FROM A

SIMPLE MIDWEEK SUPPER TO MORE ELEGANT DISHES FOR

ENTERTAINING. WHETHER YOU CHOOSE A SUBSTANTIAL

BOWL OF PASTA OR A FRAGRANT SEAFOOD RISOTTO –

THE RECIPES IN THIS CHAPTER ARE SURE TO DELIGHT.

Minty Courgette Linguine

Sweet, mild courgettes and refreshing mint are a great combination and are delicious with pasta. Dried linguine has been used here but you can use any type of pasta you like. Couscous also works well in place of pasta if you prefer.

SERVES FOUR

450g/1lb dried linguine

4 small courgettes (zucchini), sliced

1 small bunch of fresh mint, roughly chopped

FROM THE STORECUPBOARD

75ml/5 tbsp garlic-infused olive oil

salt and ground black pepper

1 Cook the linguine in plenty of salted, boiling water according to the instructions on the packet.

2 Meanwhile, heat 45ml/3 tbsp of the oil in a large frying pan and add the courgettes. Fry for 2–3 minutes, stirring occasionally, until they are tender and golden.

3 Drain the pasta well and toss with the courgettes and chopped mint. Season with salt and pepper, drizzle over the remaining oil and serve immediately.

Pasta with Roast Tomatoes and Goat's Cheese

Roasting tomatoes brings out their flavour and sweetness, which contrasts perfectly with the sharp taste and creamy texture of goat's cheese. Serve with a crisp green salad flavoured with herbs.

SERVES FOUR

8 large ripe tomatoes

450g/1lb any dried pasta shapes

200g/7oz firm goat's cheese, crumbled

FROM THE STORECUPBOARD

60ml/4 tbsp garlic-infused olive oil

salt and ground black pepper

1 Preheat the oven to 190°C/375°F/Gas 5. Place the tomatoes in a roasting pan and drizzle over 30ml/2 tbsp of the oil. Season well with salt and pepper and roast for 20–25 minutes, or until soft and slightly charred.

2 Meanwhile, cook the pasta in plenty of salted, boiling water, according to the instructions on the packet. Drain well and return to the pan.

3 Roughly mash the tomatoes with a fork, and stir the contents of the roasting pan into the pasta. Gently stir in the goat's cheese and the remaining oil and serve.

Linguine with Anchovies and Capers

This is a fantastic storecupboard recipe. Use salted capers if you can find them, as they have a better flavour than the bottled ones, but remember that you need to rinse them thoroughly before using. Be sure to chop the anchovies finely so that they "melt" into the sauce.

SERVES FOUR

450g/1lb dried linguine

8 anchovy fillets, drained

30ml/2 tbsp salted capers, thoroughly rinsed and drained

FROM THE STORECUPBOARD

75ml/5 tbsp garlic-infused olive oil

salt and ground black pepper

1 Cook the linguine in plenty of salted, boiling water according to the instructions on the packet.

2 Meanwhile, finely chop the anchovy fillets and place in a small pan with the oil and some black pepper. Heat very gently for 5 minutes, stirring occasionally, until the anchovies start to disintegrate.

3 Drain the pasta thoroughly and toss with the anchovies, oil and capers. Season with a little salt and plenty of black pepper to taste. Divide between warmed bowls and serve immediately.

Home-made Potato Gnocchi

These classic Italian potato dumplings are very simple to make – it just requires a little patience when it comes to shaping them. Serve them as soon as they are cooked, tossed in melted butter and fresh sage leaves, sprinkled with grated Parmesan cheese and plenty of black pepper. They make a fabulous alternative to pasta.

SERVES TWO

900g/2lb floury potatoes, cut into large chunks

2 eggs, beaten

150–175g/5–6oz/1¼–1½ cups plain (all-purpose) flour

FROM THE STORECUPBOARD

10ml/2 tsp salt

1 Cook the potatoes in salted, boiling water for 15 minutes, until tender. Drain well and return to the pan, set it over a low heat and dry the potatoes for 1–2 minutes.

2 Mash the potatoes until smooth, then gradually stir in the eggs and salt. Work in enough flour to form a soft dough.

3 Break off small pieces of the dough and roll into balls, using floured hands. Press the back of a fork into each ball to make indentations. Repeat until all the dough has been used. Leave the gnocchi to rest for 15–20 minutes before cooking.

4 Bring a large pan of water to a gentle boil. Add the gnocchi, about ten at a time, and cook for 3–4 minutes, or until they float to the surface. Drain thoroughly and serve as soon as all the gnocchi have been cooked.

VARIATION *To make herb-flavoured gnocchi, add 45ml/3 tbsp chopped fresh herbs, such as basil, parsley and sage, to the potato and flour dough and combine well. Serve with butter and grated Parmesan.*

Spaghettini with Roasted Garlic

If you have never tried roasting garlic, then this is the recipe that will convert you to its delicious mellowed sweetness. Spaghettini is very fine spaghetti, but any long thin pasta can be used in this dish – try spaghetti, linguine, tagliatelle or capellini. This simple pasta dish is very good served with a mixed leaf salad dressed with lemon juice and extra virgin olive oil.

SERVES FOUR

1 Preheat the oven to 180°C/350°F/Gas 4. Place the garlic in an oiled roasting pan and roast it for 30 minutes.

2 Leave the garlic to cool, then lay it on its side and slice off the top one-third with a sharp knife.

3 Hold the garlic over a bowl and dig out the flesh from each clove with the point of the knife. When all the flesh has been added to the bowl, pour in the oil and add plenty of black pepper. Mix well.

4 Cook the pasta in a pan of salted boiling water according to the instructions on the packet. Drain the pasta and return it to the clean pan. Pour in the oil and garlic mixture and toss the pasta vigorously over a medium heat until all the strands are thoroughly coated. Serve immediately, with shavings of Parmesan.

1 whole head of garlic

400g/14oz fresh or dried spaghettini

coarsely shaved Parmesan cheese

FROM THE STORECUPBOARD

120ml/4fl oz/¹/₂ cup extra virgin olive oil

salt and ground black pepper

Spaghetti with Lemon

This is the dish to make when you get home and find there's nothing to eat. If you keep spaghetti and olive oil in the store cupboard (pantry), and garlic and lemons in the vegetable rack, you can prepare this delicious meal in minutes. You can also add some freshly grated Parmesan cheese if you have some.

SERVES FOUR

1 Cook the pasta in a pan of salted boiling water according to the instructions on the packet, then drain well and return to the pan.

2 Pour the olive oil and lemon juice over the cooked pasta, sprinkle in the slivers of garlic and add seasoning to taste. Toss the pasta over a medium to high heat for 1–2 minutes. Serve immediately in four warmed bowls.

350g/12oz dried spaghetti

juice of 1 large lemon

2 garlic cloves, cut into very thin slivers

FROM THE STORECUPBOARD

90ml/6 tbsp extra virgin olive oil

salt and ground black pepper

COOK'S TIP *Spaghetti is the best type of pasta for this recipe, because the olive oil and lemon juice cling to its long thin strands. If you are out of spaghetti, use another dried long pasta shape instead, such as spaghettini, linguine or tagliatelle.*

Linguine with Rocket

This fashionable first course is very quick and easy to make at home. Rocket has an excellent peppery flavour which combines beautifully with the rich, creamy tang of fresh Parmesan cheese. Fresh Parmesan keeps well in the refrigerator for up to a month – the dried variety is a very poor substitute and bears little resemblance to the real thing.

SERVES FOUR

1 Cook the pasta in a large pan of boiling water according to the instructions on the packet, then drain thoroughly.

2 Heat about 60ml/4 tbsp of the olive oil in the pasta pan, then add the drained pasta, followed by the rocket. Toss over a medium to high heat for 1–2 minutes, or until the rocket is just wilted, then remove the pan from the heat.

3 Tip the pasta and rocket into a large, warmed bowl. Add half the freshly grated Parmesan and the remaining olive oil. Add a little salt and black pepper to taste.

4 Toss the mixture quickly to mix. Serve immediately, sprinkled with the remaining Parmesan.

350g/12oz fresh or dried linguine

1 large bunch rocket (arugula), about 150g/5oz, stalks removed, shredded or torn

75g/3oz/1 cup freshly grated Parmesan cheese

FROM THE STORECUPBOARD

120ml/4fl oz/½ cup extra virgin olive oil

salt and ground black pepper

Tagliatelle with Vegetable Ribbons

Narrow strips of courgette and carrot mingle well with tagliatelle to resemble coloured pasta. Serve as a side dish, or sprinkle with freshly grated Parmesan cheese for a light appetizer or vegetarian main course. Garlic flavoured olive oil is used in this dish – flavoured oils such as rosemary, chilli or basil are widely available and are a quick way of adding flavour to pasta.

SERVES FOUR

2 large courgettes (zucchini)

2 large carrots

250g/9oz fresh egg tagliatelle

FROM THE STORECUPBOARD

60ml/4 tbsp garlic flavoured olive oil

salt and ground black pepper

1 With a vegetable peeler, cut the courgettes and carrots into long thin ribbons. Bring a large pan of salted water to the boil, then add the courgette and carrot ribbons. Bring the water back to the boil and boil for 30 seconds, then drain and set aside.

2 Cook the tagliatelle according to the instructions on the packet. Drain the pasta and return it to the pan. Add the vegetable ribbons, garlic flavoured oil and seasoning and toss over a medium to high heat until the pasta and vegetables are glistening with oil. Serve the pasta immediately.

Spaghetti with Raw Tomato and Ricotta Sauce

This wonderfully simple uncooked sauce goes well with many different kinds of freshly cooked pasta, both long strands such as spaghetti, tagliatelle or linguini, and short shapes such as macaroni, rigatoni or penne. It is always at its best in summer when made with rich, sweet plum tomatoes that have ripened on the vine in the sun and have their fullest flavour.

SERVES FOUR

500g/1¼lb ripe Italian plum tomatoes

350g/12oz dried spaghetti or pasta of your choice

115g/4oz ricotta salata cheese, diced

FROM THE STORECUPBOARD

75ml/5 tbsp garlic-flavoured olive oil

salt and ground black pepper

1 Coarsely chop the plum tomatoes, removing the cores and as many of the seeds as you can.

2 Put the tomatoes and oil in a bowl, adding salt and pepper to taste, and stir well. Cover and leave at room temperature for 1–2 hours to let the flavours mingle.

3 Cook the spaghetti or your chosen pasta according to the packet instructions, then drain well.

4 Taste the sauce to check the seasoning before tossing it with the hot pasta. Sprinkle with the cheese and serve immediately.

Farfalle with Tuna

Bought tomato sauce and canned tuna are endlessly versatile for making weekday suppers. A variety of herbs can be added to simple pasta dishes like this one – choose from basil, marjoram or oregano – and use fresh herbs, as the short cooking time does not allow the flavour of dried herbs to develop fully. Add a garnish of fresh oregano to this dish if you happen to have some.

SERVES FOUR

1 Cook the pasta in a large pan of lightly salted boiling water according to the instructions on the packet. Meanwhile, heat the tomato sauce in a separate pan and add the olives.

2 Drain the canned tuna and flake it with a fork. Add the tuna to the sauce with about 60ml/4 tbsp of the hot water used for cooking the pasta. Taste and adjust the seasoning.

3 Drain the pasta thoroughly and tip it into a large, warmed serving bowl. Pour the tuna sauce over the top and toss lightly to mix. Serve immediately.

400g/14oz/3^1/$_2$ cups dried farfalle

600ml/1 pint/2^1/$_2$ cups tomato sauce

175g/6oz can tuna in olive oil

8–10 pitted black olives, cut into rings

FROM THE STORECUPBOARD

salt and ground black pepper

Fettuccine all'Alfredo

This simple recipe was invented by a Roman restaurateur called Alfredo, who became famous for serving it with a gold fork and spoon. Today's busy cooks will find cartons of long-life cream invaluable for this type of recipe. If you can't get fettucine, any long ribbon-like pasta can be used in this dish – try tagliatelle or slightly wider pappardelle instead.

SERVES FOUR

1 Melt the butter in a large pan. Add the cream and bring it to the boil. Simmer for 5 minutes, stirring constantly, then add the Parmesan cheese, with salt and freshly ground black pepper to taste, and turn off the heat under the pan.

2 Bring a large pan of salted water to the boil. Drop in the pasta all at once and quickly bring the water back to the boil, stirring occasionally. Cook the pasta for 2–3 minutes, or according to the instructions on the packet. Drain well.

3 Turn on the heat under the pan of cream to low, add the cooked pasta all at once and toss until it is well coated in the sauce. Taste the sauce for seasoning. Serve immediately, with extra grated Parmesan handed around separately.

200ml/7fl oz/scant 1 cup double (heavy) cream

50g/2oz/²/₃ cup freshly grated Parmesan cheese, plus extra to serve

350g/12oz fresh fettuccine

FROM THE STORECUPBOARD

50g/2oz/¹/₄ cup butter

salt and ground black pepper

Pansotti with Walnut Sauce

Walnuts and cream make a rich and luscious sauce for stuffed pasta, particularly the types filled with cheese and herbs. Serve this indulgent dish with warm walnut bread and a light, fruity white wine.

SERVES FOUR

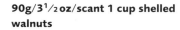

1 Put the walnuts and garlic oil in a food processor and process to a paste, adding up to 120ml/4fl oz/½ cup warm water through the feeder tube to slacken the consistency. Spoon the mixture into a large bowl and add the cream. Beat well to mix, then season to taste with salt and black pepper.

2 Cook the pansotti or stuffed pasta in a large pan of salted boiling water for 4–5 minutes, or according to the instructions on the packet. Meanwhile, put the walnut sauce in a large warmed bowl and add a ladleful of the pasta cooking water to thin it.

3 Drain the pasta and tip it into the bowl of walnut sauce. Toss well, then serve immediately.

90g/3¹/₂oz/scant 1 cup shelled walnuts

120ml/4fl oz/¹/₂ cup double (heavy) cream

350g/12oz cheese and herb-filled pansotti or other stuffed pasta

FROM THE STORECUPBOARD

60ml/4 tbsp garlic-flavoured olive oil

salt and ground black pepper

Fettuccine with Butter and Parmesan

Very few ingredients are needed to make up this incredibly simple dish. It comes from northern Italy, where butter and cheese are the most popular ingredients for serving with pasta. Children love it.

SERVES FOUR

1 Cook the pasta in a pan of salted boiling water according to the instructions on the packet. Drain thoroughly, then tip into a warmed bowl.

2 Add the butter and Parmesan a third at a time, tossing the pasta after each addition until it is evenly coated. Season to taste and serve.

400g/14oz fresh or dried fettuccine

115g/4oz/1¹/₃ cups freshly grated Parmesan cheese

FROM THE STORECUPBOARD

50g/2oz/¹/₄ cup unsalted butter, cubed

salt and ground black pepper

Penne with Cream and Smoked Salmon

This modern way of serving pasta is popular all over Italy and in many Italian restaurants. The three essential ingredients combine beautifully, and the dish is very quick and easy to make.

SERVES FOUR

1 Cook the pasta in a saucepan of salted boiling water according to the instructions on the packet.

2 Meanwhile, using kitchen scissors, cut the smoked salmon into thin strips, about 5mm/¼in wide. Strip the leaves from the thyme sprigs.

3 Melt the butter in a large saucepan. Stir in the cream with about a quarter of the salmon and thyme leaves, then season with pepper. Heat gently for 3–4 minutes, stirring all the time. Do not allow to boil. Taste the sauce for seasoning.

4 Drain the pasta and toss it in the cream and salmon sauce. Divide among four warmed bowls and top with the remaining salmon and thyme leaves. Serve immediately.

350g/12oz/3 cups dried penne

115g/4oz thinly sliced smoked salmon

2–3 fresh thyme sprigs

150ml/¼ pint/⅔ cup extra-thick single cream

FROM THE STORECUPBOARD

25g/1oz/2 tbsp butter

salt and ground black pepper

Oven-baked Porcini Risotto

This risotto is easy to make because you don't have to stand over it stirring constantly as it cooks, as you do with a traditional risotto.

SERVES FOUR

25g/1oz/¹/₂ cup dried porcini mushrooms

1 onion, finely chopped

225g/8oz/generous 1 cup risotto rice

FROM THE STORECUPBOARD

30ml/2 tbsp garlic-infused olive oil

salt and ground black pepper

1 Put the mushrooms in a heatproof bowl and pour over 750ml/1¹/₄ pints/3 cups boiling water. Leave to soak for 30 minutes. Drain the mushrooms through a sieve lined with kitchen paper, reserving the soaking liquor. Rinse the mushrooms thoroughly under running water to remove any grit, and dry on kitchen paper.

2 Preheat the oven to 180°C/350°F/Gas 4. Heat the oil in a roasting pan on the hob and add the onion. Cook for 2–3 minutes, or until softened but not coloured.

3 Add the rice and stir for 1–2 minutes, then add the mushrooms and stir. Pour in the mushroom liquor and mix well. Season with salt and pepper, and cover with foil.

4 Bake in the oven for 30 minutes, stirring occasionally, until all the stock has been absorbed and the rice is tender. Divide between warm serving bowls and serve immediately.

Persian Baked Rice

In this Persian-style dish, rice is cooked slowly over a low heat so that a crust forms on the bottom. The mild flavours of saffron and almonds go perfectly together. This dish is an ideal accompaniment for lamb.

SERVES FOUR

450g/1lb basmati rice

a good pinch of saffron strands

50g/2oz/¹/₂ cup flaked (sliced) almonds

FROM THE STORECUPBOARD

50g/2oz/¹/₄ cup butter

salt and ground black pepper

1 Cook the rice in a pan of boiling salted water for 5 minutes, then drain thoroughly. Meanwhile, put the saffron in a small bowl with 30ml/2 tbsp warm water and leave to infuse for at least 5 minutes.

2 Heat the butter in a large flameproof pan and add the almonds. Cook over a medium heat for 2–3 minutes, or until golden, stirring occasionally. Add the rice and stir well, then stir in the saffron and its liquid, plus 1 litre/1³/₄ pints/ 4 cups water. Season and cover with a tight-fitting lid.

3 Cook over a very low heat for 30 minutes, or until the rice is tender and a crust has formed on the bottom of the pan. Fork up the rice to mix in the crust before serving.

Rosemary Risotto with Borlotti Beans

Select a high-quality risotto in a subtle flavour as the base for this recipe. The savoury beans, heady rosemary and creamy mascarpone will transform a simple product into a feast. For an even more authentic risotto flavour, substitute half the water with dry white wine. Serve with a simple salad of rocket (arugula) and Parmesan shavings dressed with balsamic vinegar and plenty of freshly ground black pepper.

SERVES THREE TO FOUR

400g/14oz can
borlotti beans

275g/10oz packet
vegetable or
chicken risotto

60ml/4 tbsp
mascarpone cheese

5ml/1 tsp finely
chopped fresh
rosemary

1 Drain the beans, rinse under cold water and drain again. Process about two-thirds of the beans to a fairly coarse purée in a food processor or blender. Set the remaining beans aside.

2 Make up the risotto according to the packet instructions, using the suggested quantity of water.

3 Immediately the rice is cooked, stir in the bean purée. Add the reserved beans, with the mascarpone and rosemary. Stir thoroughly, then cover and leave to stand for about 5 minutes so that the risotto absorbs the flavours fully.

VARIATION

Fresh thyme or marjoram could be used for this risotto instead of rosemary, if you like. One of the great virtues of risotto is that it lends itself well to many variations. Experiment with plain or saffron risotto and add different herbs to make your own speciality dish.

Pancetta and Broad Bean Risotto

This moist risotto makes a satisfying, balanced meal, especially when served with cooked fresh seasonal vegetables or a mixed green salad. Add some chopped fresh herbs and Parmesan shavings as a garnish, if you like. Pancetta is dry cured pork and is the Italian equivalent of streaky (fatty) bacon – either can be used in this recipe.

SERVES FOUR

175g/6oz smoked pancetta, diced

350g/12oz/1³/₄ cups risotto rice

1.5 litres/2¹/₂ pints/ 6¹/₄ cups simmering herb stock

225g/8oz/2 cups frozen baby broad (fava) beans

FROM THE STORECUPBOARD

salt and ground black pepper

1 Place the pancetta in a non-stick or heavy pan and cook gently, stirring occasionally, for about 5 minutes, until the fat runs.

2 Add the risotto rice to the pan and cook for 1 minute, stirring constantly. Add a ladleful of the simmering stock and cook, stirring constantly, until the liquid has been absorbed.

3 Continue adding the simmering stock, a ladleful at a time, until the rice is tender, and almost all the liquid has been absorbed. This will take 30–35 minutes.

4 Meanwhile, cook the broad beans in a pan of lightly salted, boiling water for about 3 minutes until tender. Drain well and stir into the risotto. Season to taste. Spoon into a bowl and serve.

COOK'S TIP
If the broad beans are large, or if you prefer skinned beans, remove the outer skin after cooking them.

Mussel Risotto

The addition of freshly cooked mussels, aromatic coriander and a little cream to a packet of instant risotto can turn a simple meal into a decadent treat. Serve with a side salad for a splendid supper. Other types of cooked shellfish, such as clams or prawns (shrimp), can be used instead of mussels.

SERVES THREE TO FOUR

1 Scrub the mussels, discarding any that do not close when sharply tapped. Place in a large pan. Add 120ml/4fl oz/½ cup water and seasoning, then bring to the boil. Cover the pan and cook the mussels, shaking the pan occasionally, for 4–5 minutes, until they have opened. Drain, reserving the liquid and discarding any that have not opened. Shell most of the mussels, reserving a few in their shells for garnish. Strain the mussel liquid.

2 Make up the packet risotto according to the instructions, using the cooking liquid from the mussels and making it up to the required volume with water.

3 When the risotto is about three-quarters cooked, add the mussels to the pan. Add the coriander and re-cover the pan without stirring in these ingredients.

4 Remove the risotto from the heat, stir in the cream, cover and leave to rest for a few minutes. Spoon into a warmed serving dish, garnish with the reserved mussels in their shells, and serve.

900g/2lb fresh mussels

275g/10oz packet risotto

30ml/2 tbsp chopped fresh coriander (cilantro)

30ml/2 tbsp double (heavy) cream

FROM THE STORECUPBOARD

salt and ground black pepper

COOK'S TIP *For a super-quick mussel risotto, use cooked mussels in their shells – the type sold vacuum packed ready to reheat. Just reheat them according to the packet instructions and add to the made risotto with the coriander and cream.*

Crab Risotto

This simple risotto has a subtle flavour that makes the most of delicate crab. It makes a tempting main course or appetizer. It is important to use a good quality risotto rice, which will give a deliciously creamy result, but the cooked grains are still firm to the bite.

SERVES THREE TO FOUR

2 large cooked crabs

275g/10oz/1¹/₂ cups risotto rice

1.2 litres/2 pints/5 cups simmering fish stock

30ml/2 tbsp mixed finely chopped fresh herbs such as chives, tarragon and parsley

FROM THE STORECUPBOARD

salt and ground black pepper

1 One at a time, hold the crabs and hit the underside with the heel of your hand. This should loosen the shell from the body. Using your thumbs, push against the body and pull away from the shell. Remove and discard the intestines and the grey gills.

2 Break off the claws and legs, then use a hammer or crackers to break them open. Using a pick, remove the meat from the claws and legs. Place the meat on a plate.

3 Using a skewer, pick out the white meat from the body cavities and place with the claw and leg meat, reserving a little white meat to garnish. Scoop out the brown meat from the shell and add to the rest of the crab meat.

4 Place the rice in a pan and add one-quarter of the stock. Bring to the boil and cook, stirring, until the liquid has been absorbed. Adding a ladleful of stock at a time, cook, stirring, until about two-thirds of the stock has been absorbed. Stir in the crab meat and herbs, and continue cooking, adding the remaining stock.

5 When the rice is almost cooked, remove it from the heat and adjust the seasoning. Cover and leave to stand for 3 minutes. Serve garnished with the reserved white crab meat.

Coconut Rice

This rich dish is usually served with a tangy papaya salad to balance the sweetness of the coconut milk and sugar. It is one of those comforting treats that everyone enjoys.

SERVES FOUR TO SIX

1 Place the measured water, coconut milk, salt and sugar in a heavy pan. Wash the rice in cold water until it runs clear.

2 Add the jasmine rice, cover tightly with a lid and bring to the boil over a medium heat. Reduce the heat to low and simmer gently, without lifting the lid unnecessarily, for 15–20 minutes, until the rice is tender and cooked through. Test it by biting a grain.

3 Turn off the heat and leave the rice to rest in the pan, still covered with the lid, for a further 5–10 minutes.

4 Gently fluff up the rice grains with chopsticks or a fork before transferring it to a warmed dish and serving.

250ml/8fl oz/1 cup water

475ml/16fl oz/2 cups coconut milk

30ml/2 tbsp granulated sugar

450g/1lb/2²/₃ cups jasmine rice

FROM THE STORECUPBOARD

2.5ml/¹/₂ tsp salt

COOK'S TIP *For a special occasion serve in a halved papaya and garnish with thin shreds of fresh coconut.*

Savoury Ground Rice

Savoury ground rice is often served as an accompaniment to soups and stews in West Africa.

SERVES FOUR

1 Place the water in a saucepan. Pour in the milk, bring to the boil and add the salt and parsley.

2 Add the butter or margarine and the ground rice, stirring with a wooden spoon to prevent the rice from becoming lumpy.

3 Cover the pan and cook over a low heat for about 15 minutes, beating the mixture every 2 minutes to prevent the formation of lumps.

4 To test if the rice is cooked, rub a pinch of the mixture between your fingers: if it feels smooth and fairly dry, it is ready. Serve hot.

300ml/¹/₂ pint/1¹/₄ cups water

300ml/¹/₂ pint/1¹/₄ cups milk

15ml/1 tbsp chopped fresh parsley

25g/1oz/2 tbsp butter or margarine

275g/10oz/1²/₃ cups ground rice

FROM THE STORECUPBOARD

salt

COOK'S TIP *Ground rice is a creamy white colour, with a grainy texture. Although often used in sweet dishes, it is a tasty grain to serve with savoury dishes too. The addition of milk gives a creamier flavour if preferred.*

Vegetarian Dishes

FRESH-TASTING VEGETABLES, MILD EGGS,

RICH AND CREAMY CHEESES AND AROMATIC HERBS

AND SPICES ARE GREAT PARTNERS AND CAN BE COMBINED

TO MAKE A DELICIOUS ARRAY OF VEGETARIAN MAIN

MEALS. ENJOY WONDERFUL DISHES SUCH AS BAKED

STUFFED VEGETABLES, RICHLY FLAVOURED TARTS

AND LIGHT-AS-AIR SOUFFLÉS.

Aubergines with Cheese Sauce

This wonderfully simple dish of aubergines in cheese sauce is delicious hot and the perfect dish to assemble ahead of time ready for baking at the last minute. Kashkaval cheese is particularly good in this recipe – it is a hard yellow cheese made from sheep's milk and is originally from the Balkans. Serve with lots of crusty bread to mop up the delicious aubergine-flavoured cheese sauce.

SERVES FOUR TO SIX

1 Layer the aubergine slices in a bowl or colander, sprinkling each layer with salt, and leave to drain for at least 30 minutes. Rinse well, then pat dry with kitchen paper.

2 Heat the oil in a frying pan, then cook the aubergine slices until golden brown on both sides. Remove from the pan and set aside.

3 Preheat the oven to 180°C/350°F/Gas 4. Mix most of the grated cheese into the savoury white or béchamel sauce, reserving a little to sprinkle on top of the finished dish.

4 Arrange a layer of the aubergines in an ovenproof dish, then pour over some sauce. Repeat, ending with sauce. Sprinkle with the reserved cheese. Bake for 35–40 minutes until golden.

2 large aubergines (eggplants), cut into 5mm/¼ in thick slices

400g/14oz/3½ cups grated cheese, such as kashkaval, Gruyère, or a mixture of Parmesan and Cheddar

600ml/1 pint/2½ cups savoury white sauce or béchamel sauce

FROM THE STORECUPBOARD

about 60ml/4 tbsp olive oil

salt and ground black pepper

Mushroom Stroganoff

This creamy mixed mushroom sauce is ideal for a dinner party. Serve it with toasted buckwheat, brown rice or a mixture of wild rices and garnish with snipped chives. For best results, choose a variety of different mushrooms – wild mushrooms such as chanterelles, ceps and morels add a delicious flavour and texture to the stroganoff, as well as adding colour and producing a decorative appearance.

SERVES FOUR

900g/2lb mixed mushrooms, cut into bitesize pieces, including ²/₃ button (white) mushrooms and ¹/₃ assorted wild or unusual mushrooms

350ml/12fl oz/1¹/₂ cups white wine sauce

250ml/8fl oz/1 cup sour cream

FROM THE STORECUPBOARD

25g/1oz/2 tbsp butter

salt and ground black pepper

1 Melt the butter in a pan and quickly cook the mushrooms, in batches, over a high heat, until brown. Transfer the mushrooms to a bowl after cooking each batch.

2 Add the sauce to the juices remaining in the pan and bring to the boil, stirring. Reduce the heat and replace the mushrooms with any juices from the bowl. Stir well and heat for a few seconds, then remove from the heat.

3 Stir the sour cream into the cooked mushroom mixture and season to taste with salt and lots of freshly ground black pepper. Heat through gently for a few seconds, if necessary, then transfer to warm plates and serve immediately.

Red Onion and Goat's Cheese Pastries

These attractive little tartlets couldn't be easier to make. Garnish them with fresh thyme sprigs and serve with a selection of salad leaves and a tomato and basil salad for a light lunch or quick supper. A wide variety of different types of goat's cheeses are available – the creamy log-shaped types without a rind are most suitable for these pastries. Ordinary onions can be used instead of red, if you prefer.

SERVES FOUR

1 Heat the oil in a large, heavy frying pan, add the onions and cook over a gentle heat for 10 minutes, or until softened, stirring occasionally to prevent them from browning. Add seasoning to taste and cook for a further 2 minutes. Remove the pan from the heat and leave to cool.

2 Preheat the oven to 220°C/425°F/Gas 7. Unroll the puff pastry and using a 15cm/6in plate as a guide, cut out four rounds. Place the pastry rounds on a dampened baking sheet and, using the point of a sharp knife, score a border, 2cm/¾in inside the edge of each pastry round.

3 Divide the onions among the pastry rounds and top with the goat's cheese. Bake for 25–30 minutes until golden brown.

450g/1lb red onions, sliced

425g/15oz packet ready-rolled puff pastry

115g/4oz/1 cup goat's cheese, cubed

FROM THE STORECUPBOARD

15ml/1 tbsp olive oil

salt and ground black pepper

EXTRAS *To make richer-flavoured pastries ring the changes by spreading the pastry base with red or green pesto or tapenade before you top with the goat's cheese and cooked onions.*

Baked Leek and Potato Gratin

Potatoes baked in a creamy cheese sauce make the ultimate comfort dish, whether served as an accompaniment to pork or fish dishes or, as here, with plenty of leeks and melted cheese as a main course. When preparing leeks, separate the leaves and rinse them thoroughly under cold running water, as soil and grit often get caught between the layers.

SERVES FOUR TO SIX

1 Preheat the oven to 180°C/350°F/Gas 4. Cook the potatoes in plenty of lightly salted, boiling water for 3 minutes, until slightly softened, then drain. Cut the leeks into 1cm/½in lengths and blanch them in boiling water for 1 minute, until softened, then drain.

2 Turn half the potatoes into a shallow, ovenproof dish and spread them out to the edge. Cover with two-thirds of the leeks, then add the remaining potatoes. Tuck the slices of cheese and the remaining leeks in among the top layer of potatoes. Season and pour the cream over.

3 Bake for 1 hour, until tender and golden. Cover with foil if the top starts to overbrown before the potatoes are tender.

900g/2lb medium potatoes, thinly sliced

2 large leeks, trimmed

200g/7oz ripe Brie or Camembert cheese, sliced

450ml/¾ pint/scant 2 cups single (light) cream

FROM THE STORECUPBOARD

salt and ground black pepper

Mushroom Polenta

This simple recipe uses freshly made polenta, but for an even easier version you can substitute ready-made polenta and slice it straight into the dish, ready for baking. The cheesy mushroom topping is also delicious on toasted herb or sun-dried tomato bread as a light lunch or supper. Any combination of mushrooms will work – try a mixture of button (white) and wild mushrooms as an alternative.

SERVES FOUR

1 Line a 28 x 18cm/11 x 7in shallow baking tin (pan) with baking parchment. Bring 1 litre/1¾ pints/4 cups water with 5ml/1 tsp salt to the boil in a large pan. Add the polenta in a steady stream, stirring constantly. Bring back to the boil, stirring, and cook for 5 minutes, until thick and smooth. Turn the polenta into the prepared tin and spread it out into an even layer. Leave to cool.

2 Preheat the oven to 200°C/400°F/Gas 6. Melt the butter in a frying pan and cook the mushrooms for 3–5 minutes, until golden. Season with salt and lots of freshly ground black pepper.

3 Turn out the polenta on to a chopping board. Peel away the parchment and cut the polenta into large squares. Pile the squares into a shallow, ovenproof dish. Sprinkle with half the cheese, then pile the mushrooms on top and pour over their buttery juices. Sprinkle with the remaining cheese and bake for about 20 minutes, until the cheese is melting and pale golden.

250g/9oz/1¹/₂ cups quick-cook polenta

50g/2oz/¹/₄ cup butter

400g/14oz chestnut mushrooms, sliced

175g/6oz/1¹/₂ cups grated Gruyère cheese

FROM THE STORECUPBOARD

salt and ground black pepper

Tomato and Tapenade Tarts

These delicious individual tarts look and taste fantastic, despite the fact that they demand very little time or effort. The mascarpone cheese topping melts as it cooks to make a smooth, creamy sauce. Cherry tomatoes have a delicious sweet flavour with a low acidity, but plum tomatoes or vine-ripened tomatoes are also suitable for these tarts and will give delicious results. Red pesto can be used instead of the tapenade if you prefer a subtler flavour.

SERVES FOUR

1 Preheat the oven to 220°C/425°F/Gas 7. Lightly grease a large baking sheet and sprinkle it with water. Roll out the pastry on a lightly floured surface and cut out four 16cm/6½in rounds, using a bowl or small plate as a guide.

2 Transfer the pastry rounds to the prepared baking sheet. Using the tip of a sharp knife, mark a shallow cut 1cm/½in in from the edge of each round to form a rim.

3 Reserve half the tapenade and spread the rest over the pastry rounds, keeping the paste inside the marked rim. Cut half the tomatoes in half. Pile all the tomatoes, whole and halved, on the pastry, again keeping them inside the rim. Season lightly.

4 Bake for 20 minutes, until the pastry is well risen and golden. Dot with the remaining tapenade. Spoon a little mascarpone on the centre of the tomatoes and season with black pepper. Bake for a further 10 minutes, until the mascarpone has melted to make a sauce. Serve the tarts warm.

500g/1¼lb puff pastry, thawed if frozen

60ml/4 tbsp black or green olive tapenade

500g/1¼lb cherry tomatoes

90g/3½oz/scant ½ cup mascarpone cheese

FROM THE STORECUPBOARD

salt and ground black pepper

Stuffed Baby Squash

It is worth making the most of baby squash while they are in season. Use any varieties you can find and do not worry too much about choosing vegetables of uniform size, as an assortment of different types and sizes looks attractive. The baked vegetables can easily be shared out at the table. Serve with warm sun-dried tomato bread and a ready-made spicy tomato sauce for a hearty autumn supper.

SERVES FOUR

1 Preheat the oven to 190°C/375°F/Gas 5. Pierce the squash in with the tip of a knife. Bake for 30 minutes, until the squash are tender. Leave until cool enough to handle.

2 Meanwhile, cook the rice in salted, boiling water for 12 minutes, until tender, then drain. Slice a lid off the top of each squash and scoop out and discard the seeds. Scoop out and chop the flesh.

3 Heat the oil in a frying pan and cook the chopped squash for 5 minutes. Reserve 60ml/4 tbsp of the cheese, add the remainder to the pan with the rice and a little salt. Mix well.

4 Pile the mixture into the squash shells and place in a dish. Sprinkle with the remaining cheese and bake for 20 minutes.

4 small squash, each about 350g/12oz

200g/7oz/1 cup mixed wild and basmati rice

150g/5oz/1¹/₄ cups grated Gruyère cheese

FROM THE STORECUPBOARD

60ml/4 tbsp chilli and garlic oil

salt and ground black pepper

Roasted Peppers with Halloumi and Pine Nuts

Halloumi cheese is creamy-tasting and has a firm texture and salty flavour that contrast well with the succulent sweet peppers. This is a good dish to assemble in advance. Halloumi is usually served cooked and lends itself well to barbecuing, frying or grilling (broiling). When heated the exterior hardens while the interior softens and is similar to mozzarella cheese.

SERVES FOUR

1 Preheat the oven to 220°C/425°F/Gas 7. Halve the red peppers, leaving the stalks intact, and discard the seeds. Seed and coarsely chop the orange or yellow peppers. Place the red pepper halves on a baking sheet and fill with the chopped peppers. Drizzle with half the garlic or herb olive oil and bake for 25 minutes, until the edges of the peppers are beginning to char.

2 Dice the cheese and tuck in among the chopped peppers. Sprinkle with the pine nuts and drizzle with the remaining oil. Bake for a further 15 minutes, until well browned. Serve warm.

4 red and 2 orange or yellow (bell) peppers

250g/9oz halloumi cheese

50g/2oz/¹/₂ cup pine nuts

FROM THE STORECUPBOARD

60ml/4 tbsp garlic or herb olive oil

salt and ground black pepper

Spicy Chickpea Samosas

A blend of crushed chickpeas and coriander sauce makes an interesting alternative to the more familiar meat or vegetable fillings in these little pastries. The samosas look pretty garnished with fresh coriander leaves and finely sliced onion and are delicious served with a simple dip made from Greek (US strained plain) yogurt and chopped fresh mint leaves.

MAKES EIGHTEEN

1 Preheat the oven to 220°C/425°F/Gas 7. Process half the chickpeas to a paste in a food processor. Tip the paste into a bowl and add the whole chickpeas, the hara masala or coriander sauce, and a little salt. Mix until well combined.

2 Lay a sheet of filo pastry on a work surface and cut into three strips. Brush the strips with a little of the oil. Place a dessertspoon of the filling at one end of a strip. Turn one corner diagonally over the filling to meet the long edge. Continue folding the filling and the pastry along the length of the strip, keeping the triangular shape. Transfer to a baking sheet and repeat with the remaining filling and pastry.

3 Brush the pastries with any remaining oil and bake for 15 minutes, until the pastry is golden. Cool before serving.

2 x 400g/14oz cans chickpeas, drained and rinsed

120ml/4fl oz/¹/₂ cup hara masala or coriander (cilantro) sauce

275g/10oz filo pastry

FROM THE STORECUPBOARD

60ml/4 tbsp chilli and garlic oil

salt and ground black pepper

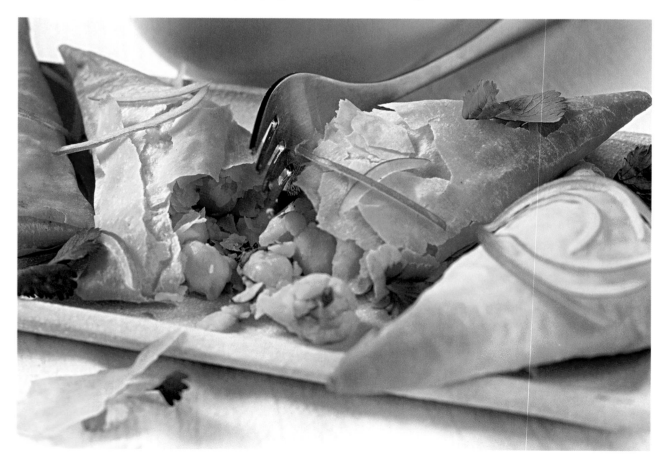

Tofu and Pepper Kebabs

A simple coating of ground, dry-roasted peanuts pressed on to cubed tofu provides plenty of additional flavour along with the peppers. Use metal or bamboo skewers for the kebabs – if you use bamboo, then soak them in cold water for 30 minutes before using to prevent them from scorching during cooking. The kebabs can also be cooked on a barbecue, if you prefer.

SERVES FOUR

1 Pat the tofu dry on kitchen paper and then cut it into small cubes. Grind the peanuts in a blender or food processor and transfer to a plate. Turn the tofu cubes in the ground nuts to coat.

2 Preheat the grill (broiler) to moderate. Halve and seed the peppers, and cut them into large chunks. Thread the chunks of pepper on to four large skewers with the tofu cubes and place on a foil-lined grill rack.

3 Grill (broil) the kebabs, turning frequently, for 10–12 minutes, or until the peppers and peanuts are beginning to brown. Transfer the kebabs to plates and serve with the dipping sauce.

250g/9oz firm tofu

50g/2oz/¹/₂ cup dry-roasted peanuts

2 red and 2 green (bell) peppers

60ml/4 tbsp sweet chilli dipping sauce

FROM THE STORECUPBOARD

salt and ground black pepper

Mixed Bean and Tomato Chilli

Here, mixed beans, fiery red chilli and plenty of freshly chopped coriander are simmered in a tomato sauce to make a delicious vegetarian chilli. Always a popular dish, chilli can be served with a variety of accompaniments – choose from baked potatoes, baked rice, crusty bread or tortillas. Garnish with slices of tomato, chopped celery or sweet (bell) pepper and top with natural (plain) yogurt.

SERVES FOUR

1 Pour the tomato sauce and mixed beans into a pan. Seed and thinly slice the chilli, then add it to the pan. Reserve a little of the coriander, chop the remainder and add it to the pan.

2 Bring the mixture to the boil, reduce the heat, cover and simmer gently for 10 minutes. Stir the mixture occasionally and add a dash of water if the sauce starts to dry out.

3 Ladle the chilli into warmed individual serving bowls and top with a spoonful of yogurt to serve.

400g/14oz jar tomato and herb sauce

2 x 400g/14oz cans mixed beans, drained and rinsed

1 fresh red chilli

large handful of fresh coriander (cilantro)

FROM THE STORECUPBOARD

salt and ground black pepper

Cheese and Tomato Soufflés

Using a ready-made cheese sauce takes the effort out of soufflé making. The key to success when making soufflés is to whisk the egg whites thoroughly to incorporate as much air as possible. During the cooking time don't open the oven door – the cold draught could cause the delicate mixture to collapse.

SERVES SIX

1 Preheat the oven to 200°C/400°F/Gas 6. Turn the cheese sauce into a bowl. Thinly slice the sun-dried tomatoes and add to the bowl with 90g/3½oz/generous 1 cup of the Parmesan, the egg yolks and seasoning. Stir until well combined.

2 Brush the base and sides of six 200ml/7fl oz/scant 1 cup ramekins with the oil and then coat the insides of the dishes with half the remaining cheese, tilting them until evenly covered.

3 Whisk the egg whites in a clean bowl until stiff. Use a large metal spoon to stir one-quarter of the egg whites into the sauce, then fold in the remainder. Spoon the mixture into the prepared dishes and sprinkle with the remaining Parmesan cheese. Place on a baking sheet and bake for 15–18 minutes, until well risen and golden. Serve the soufflés as soon as you remove them from the oven.

350g/12oz tub fresh cheese sauce

50g/2oz sun-dried tomatoes in olive oil, drained, plus 10ml/ 2 tsp of the oil

130g/4½oz/1⅓ cups grated Parmesan cheese

4 large (US extra large) eggs, separated

FROM THE STORECUPBOARD

salt and ground black pepper

Classic Margherita Pizza

Bought pizza base mixes are a great storecupboard stand-by. A Margherita Pizza makes a lovely simple supper, but of course you can add any extra toppings you like. Prosciutto and rocket (arugula) make a great addition – just add them to the pizza after it is cooked.

SERVES TWO

half a 300g/11oz packet pizza base mix

45ml/3 tbsp ready-made tomato and basil sauce

150g/5oz mozzarella, sliced

FROM THE STORECUPBOARD

15ml/1 tbsp herb-infused olive oil

salt and ground black pepper

1 Make the pizza base mix according to the instructions on the packet. Brush the base with a little of the olive oil and spread over the tomato and basil sauce, not quite to the edges.

2 Arrange the slices of mozzarella on top of the pizza and bake for 25–30 minutes, or until golden.

3 Drizzle the remaining oil on top of the pizza, season with salt and black pepper and serve immediately, garnished with fresh basil leaves.

Cheesy Leek and Couscous Cake

The tangy flavour of sharp Cheddar cheese goes perfectly with the sweet taste of leeks. The cheese melts into the couscous and helps it stick together, making a firm cake that's easy to cut into wedges. Serve with a crisp green salad.

SERVES FOUR

300g/11oz couscous

2 leeks, sliced

200g/7oz mature Cheddar or Monterey Jack, grated

FROM THE STORECUPBOARD

45ml/3 tbsp olive oil

salt and ground black pepper

VARIATION
There are endless variations on this tangy, tasty cake but choose a cheese that melts well because it will help the cake to stick together. Try using caramelized onions and blue cheese in place of the leeks and Cheddar.

1 Put the couscous in a large heatproof bowl and pour over 450ml/³/₄ pint/scant 2 cups boiling water. Cover and set aside for about 15 minutes, or until all the water has been absorbed.

2 Heat 15ml/1 tbsp of the oil in a 23cm/9in non-stick frying pan. Add the leeks and cook over a medium heat for 4–5 minutes, stirring occasionally, until tender and golden.

3 Remove the leeks with a slotted spoon and stir them into the couscous. Add the grated cheese and some salt and pepper and stir through. Heat the remaining oil in the pan and tip in the couscous and leek mixture. Pat down firmly to form a cake and cook over a fairly gentle heat for 15 minutes, or until the underside is crisp and golden.

4 Slide the couscous cake onto a plate, then invert it back into the pan to cook the other side. Cook for a further 5–8 minutes, or until golden, then remove from the heat. Slide on to a board and serve cut into wedges.

Potato and Onion Tortilla

This deep-set omelette with sliced potatoes and onions is the best-known Spanish tortilla and makes a deliciously simple meal when served with a leafy salad and crusty bread. Tortilla are often made with a variety of ingredients – chopped red or yellow (bell) peppers, cooked peas, corn, or grated Cheddar or Gruyère cheese can all be added to the mixture in step 2, if you like.

SERVES FOUR TO SIX

800g/1³/₄ lb medium potatoes

2 onions, thinly sliced

6 eggs

FROM THE STORECUPBOARD

100ml/3¹/₂ fl oz/scant ¹/₂ cup extra virgin olive oil

salt and ground black pepper

1 Thinly slice the potatoes. Heat 75ml/5 tbsp of the oil in a frying pan and cook the potatoes, turning frequently, for 10 minutes. Add the onions and seasoning, and continue to cook for a further 10 minutes, until the vegetables are tender.

2 Meanwhile, beat the eggs in a large bowl with a little seasoning. Tip the potatoes and onions into the eggs and mix gently. Leave to stand for 10 minutes.

3 Wipe out the pan with kitchen paper and heat the remaining oil in it. Pour the egg mixture into the pan and spread it out in an even layer. Cover and cook over a very gentle heat for 20 minutes, until the eggs are just set. Serve cut into wedges.

Spiced Lentils

The combination of lentils, tomatoes and cheese is widely used in Mediterranean cooking. The tang of feta cheese complements the slightly earthy flavour of the attractive dark lentils. True Puy lentils come from the region of France, Le Puy, which has a unique climate and volcanic soil in which they thrive.

SERVES FOUR

250g/9oz/1¹/₂ cups Puy lentils

200g/7oz feta cheese

75ml/5 tbsp sun-dried tomato purée (paste)

small handful of fresh chervil or flat leaf parsley, chopped, plus extra to garnish

FROM THE STORECUPBOARD

salt and ground black pepper

1 Place the lentils in a heavy pan with 600ml/1 pint/2½ cups water. Bring to the boil, reduce the heat and cover the pan. Simmer gently for about 20 minutes, until the lentils are just tender and most of the water has been absorbed.

2 Crumble half the feta cheese into the pan. Add the sun-dried tomato purée, chopped chervil or flat leaf parsley and a little salt and freshly ground black pepper. Heat through for 1 minute.

3 Transfer the lentil mixture and juices to warmed plates or bowls. Crumble the remaining feta cheese on top and sprinkle with the fresh herbs to garnish. Serve hot.

Roast Acorn Squash with Spinach and Gorgonzola

Roasting squash brings out its sweetness, here offset by tangy cheese. Acorn squash has been used here, but any type of squash will give delicious results.

SERVES FOUR

4 acorn squash

250g/9oz baby spinach leaves, washed

200g/7oz Gorgonzola cheese, sliced

FROM THE STORECUPBOARD

45ml/3 tbsp garlic-infused olive oil

salt and ground black pepper

1 Preheat the oven to 190°C/375°F/Gas 5. Cut the tops off the squash, and scoop out and discard the seeds. Place the squash, cut side up, in a roasting pan and drizzle with 30ml/2 tbsp of the oil. Season with salt and pepper and bake for 30–40 minutes, or until tender.

2 Heat the remaining oil in a large frying pan and add the spinach leaves. Cook over a medium heat for 2–3 minutes, until the leaves are just wilted. Season with salt and pepper and divide between the squash halves.

3 Top with the Gorgonzola and return to the oven for 10 minutes, or until the cheese has melted. Season with ground black pepper and serve.

Creamy Red Lentil Dhal

This makes a tasty winter supper for vegetarians and meat eaters alike. Serve with naan bread, coconut cream and fresh coriander (cilantro) leaves. The coconut cream gives this dish a really rich taste.

SERVES FOUR

500g/1¼lb/2 cups red lentils

15ml/1 tbsp hot curry paste

FROM THE STORECUPBOARD

15ml/1 tbsp sunflower oil

salt and ground black pepper

1 Heat the oil in a large pan and add the lentils. Fry for 1–2 minutes, stirring continuously, then stir in the curry paste and 600ml/1 pint/2½ cups boiling water.

2 Bring the mixture to the boil, then reduce the heat to a gentle simmer. Cover the pan and cook for 15 minutes, stirring occasionally, until the lentils are tender and the mixture has thickened.

3 Season the dhal with plenty of salt and ground black pepper to taste, and serve piping hot.

Wild Mushroom and Fontina Tart

Use any types of wild mushrooms you like in this tart – chanterelles, morels, horns of plenty and ceps all have wonderful flavours. It makes an impressive vegetarian main course, served with a green salad.

SERVES SIX

225g/8oz ready-made shortcrust pastry, thawed if frozen

350g/12oz/5 cups mixed wild mushrooms, sliced if large

150g/5oz Fontina cheese, sliced

FROM THE STORECUPBOARD

50g/2oz/¼ cup butter

salt and ground black pepper

1 Preheat the oven to 190°C/375°F/Gas 5. Roll out the pastry and use to a line a 23cm/9in loose-bottomed flan tin (tart pan). Chill the pastry for 30 minutes, then bake blind for 15 minutes. Set aside.

2 Heat the butter in a large frying pan until foaming. Add the mushrooms and season with salt and ground black pepper. Cook over a medium heat for 4–5 minutes, moving the mushrooms about and turning them occasionally with a wooden spoon, until golden.

3 Arrange the mushrooms in the cooked pastry case with the Fontina. Return the tart to the oven for 10 minutes, or until the cheese is golden and bubbling. Serve hot.

Parmigiana di Melanzane

This flavoursome Italian dish can be served as a vegetarian main course, or as an accompaniment to meat or chicken dishes. For a delicious variation, layer a few artichoke hearts between the slices of aubergine.

SERVES EIGHT

900g/2lb aubergines (eggplants), sliced lengthways

600ml/1 pint/2¹/₂ cups garlic and herb passata (bottled strained tomatoes)

115g/4oz/1¹/₄ cups freshly grated Parmesan cheese

FROM THE STORECUPBOARD

60ml/4 tbsp olive oil

salt and ground black pepper

1 Preheat the grill (broiler) to high. Brush the aubergine slices with the oil and season with salt and pepper to taste. Arrange them in a single layer on a grill pan and grill (broil) for 4–5 minutes on each side, until golden and tender. (You will have to do this in batches.)

2 Preheat the oven to 190°C/375°F/Gas 5. Spoon a little passata into a large baking dish. Arrange a single layer of aubergine slices over the top and sprinkle with some grated Parmesan cheese. Repeat the layers of passata, aubergine and Parmesan until all the ingredients have been used up, finishing with a good sprinkling of Parmesan. Bake for 20–25 minutes, or until golden and bubbling.

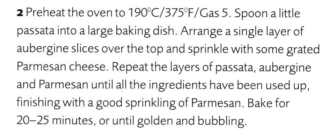

Vegetables and Side Dishes

A FEW CAREFULLY CHOSEN INGREDIENTS CAN BE BROUGHT

TOGETHER TO CREATE MOUTHWATERING SIDE DISHES

AND ACCOMPANIMENTS THAT WILL COMPLEMENT AND

ENHANCE ANY MAIN DISH. THIS COLLECTION OF TASTY

AND COLOURFUL COMBINATIONS OF VEGETABLES MAKES

HEALTHY EATING A TEMPTING TREAT.

Japanese-style Spinach with Toasted Sesame Seeds

This Japanese speciality, known as *O-hitashi*, has been served as a side dish on dining tables in Japan for centuries. Seasonal green vegetables are simply blanched and cooled and formed into little towers. With a little help from soy sauce and sesame seeds, they reveal their true flavour. Serve the spinach towers with simply cooked chicken, or fish such as salmon or tuna.

SERVES FOUR

1 Blanch the spinach leaves in boiling water for 15 seconds. For Japanese-type spinach, hold the leafy part and slip the stems into the pan. After 15 seconds, drop in the leaves and cook for 20 seconds.

2 Drain immediately and place the spinach under running water. Squeeze out all the excess water by hand. Now what looked like a large amount of spinach has become a ball, roughly the size of an orange. Mix the shoyu and water, then pour on to the spinach. Mix well and leave to cool.

3 Meanwhile, put the sesame seeds in a dry frying pan and stir or toss until they start to pop. Remove from the heat and leave to cool.

4 Drain the spinach and squeeze out the excess sauce with your hands. Form the spinach into a log shape of about 4cm/1½in in diameter on a chopping board. Squeeze again to make it firm. With a sharp knife, cut it across into four cylinders.

5 Place the spinach cylinders on a large plate or individual dishes. Sprinkle with the toasted sesame seeds and serve.

450g/1lb fresh young spinach

30ml/2 tbsp shoyu

30ml/2 tbsp water

15ml/1 tbsp sesame seeds

COOK'S TIP *Japanese spinach, the long-leaf type with the stalks and pink root intact, is best, but you can use ordinary young spinach leaves, or any soft and deep-green salad leaves – such as watercress, rocket (arugula) or lamb's lettuce.*

Braised Lettuce and Peas with Spring Onions

This light vegetable dish is based on the classic French method of braising peas with lettuce and spring onions in butter, and is delicious served with simply grilled fish or roast or grilled duck. A sprinkling of chopped fresh mint makes a fresh, flavoursome and extremely pretty garnish. Other legumes such as broad (fava) beans, mangetouts (snow peas) and sugar snap peas can be used instead of peas to create a delicious variation.

SERVES FOUR

1 Melt half the butter in a wide, heavy pan over a low heat. Add the lettuces and spring onions.

2 Turn the vegetables in the butter, then sprinkle in salt and plenty of freshly ground black pepper. Cover, and cook the vegetables very gently for 5 minutes, stirring once.

3 Add the peas and turn them in the buttery juices. Pour in 120ml/4fl oz/½ cup water, then cover and cook over a gentle heat for a further 5 minutes. Uncover and increase the heat to reduce the liquid to a few tablespoons.

4 Stir in the remaining butter and adjust the seasoning. Transfer to a warmed serving dish and serve immediately.

50g/2oz/¹/₄ cup butter

4 Little Gem (Bibb) lettuces, halved lengthways

2 bunches spring onions (scallions), trimmed

400g/14oz shelled peas (about 1kg/2¹/₄lb in pods)

FROM THE STORECUPBOARD

salt and ground black pepper

EXTRA *Braise about 250g/9oz baby carrots with the lettuce.*

Asparagus with Lemon Sauce

Sometimes less is more: here a simple egg and lemon dressing brings out the best in asparagus. Serve the asparagus as an appetizer or side dish; alternatively, enjoy it for a light supper, with bread and butter to mop up the juices. When buying asparagus, look for bright coloured firm spears with tight buds – avoid those with tough woody stems. Choose roughly even-sized spears for uniform cooking.

SERVES FOUR

1 Cook the bundle of asparagus in a tall pan of lightly salted, boiling water for 7–10 minutes.

2 Drain well and arrange the asparagus in a serving dish. Reserve 200ml/7fl oz/scant 1 cup of the cooking liquid.

3 Blend the cornflour with the cooled, reserved cooking liquid and place in a pan. Bring to the boil, stirring constantly, and cook over a gentle heat until the sauce thickens slightly. Remove the pan from the heat and leave to cool.

4 Beat the egg yolks with the lemon juice and stir into the cooled sauce. Cook over a low heat, stirring constantly, until the sauce is thick. Be careful not to overheat the sauce or it may curdle. As soon as the sauce has thickened, remove the pan from the heat and continue stirring for 1 minute. Taste and season with salt. Leave the sauce to cool slightly.

5 Stir the cooled lemon sauce, then pour a little over the cooked asparagus. Cover and chill in the refrigerator for at least 2 hours before serving with the rest of the sauce.

675g/1¹/₂lb asparagus, tough ends removed, and tied in a bundle

15ml/1 tbsp cornflour (cornstarch)

2 egg yolks

juice of 1¹/₂ lemons

FROM THE STORECUPBOARD

salt and ground black pepper

COOK'S TIP *For a slightly less tangy sauce, add a little caster (superfine) sugar with the salt in step 4.*

Caramelized Shallots

Sweet, golden shallots are good with all sorts of main dishes, including poultry or meat. Shallots have a less distinctive aroma than common onions and a milder flavour; they are also considered to be easier to digest. These caramelized shallots are also excellent with braised or roasted chestnuts, carrots or chunks of butternut squash. You may like to garnish the shallots with sprigs of fresh thyme before serving.

SERVES FOUR TO SIX

1 Heat the butter or oil in a large frying pan and add the shallots or onions in a single layer. Cook gently, turning occasionally, until they are lightly browned.

2 Sprinkle the sugar over the shallots and cook gently, turning the shallots in the juices, until the sugar begins to caramelize. Add the wine or port and let the mixture bubble for 4–5 minutes.

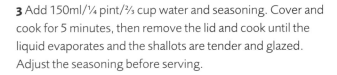

3 Add 150ml/¼ pint/⅔ cup water and seasoning. Cover and cook for 5 minutes, then remove the lid and cook until the liquid evaporates and the shallots are tender and glazed. Adjust the seasoning before serving.

500g/1¼lb shallots or small onions, peeled with root ends intact

15ml/1 tbsp golden caster (superfine) sugar

30ml/2 tbsp red or white wine or port

FROM THE STORECUPBOARD

50g/2oz/¼ cup butter or 60ml/4 tbsp olive oil

salt and ground black pepper

Green Beans with Almond Butter and Lemon

The mild flavour of the almonds in this dish makes it a perfect accompaniment for baked or grilled oily fish such as trout or mackerel.

SERVES FOUR

350g/12oz green beans, trimmed

50g/2oz/¹/₃ cup whole blanched almonds

grated rind and juice of 1 unwaxed lemon

FROM THE STORECUPBOARD

50g/2oz/¹/₄ cup butter

salt and ground black pepper

1 Cook the beans in a pan of salted boiling water for about 3 minutes, or until just tender. Drain well. Meanwhile, melt the butter in a large frying pan until foamy.

2 Add the almonds to the pan and cook, stirring occasionally, for 2–3 minutes, or until golden. Remove from the heat and toss with the beans, lemon rind and juice, and season.

VARIATION This salad is delicious made with different types of nuts. Use the same quantity of roughly chopped shelled walnuts or blanched hazelnuts in place of the almonds.

Garlicky Green Salad with Raspberry Dressing

Adding a splash of raspberry vinegar to the dressing enlivens a simple green salad, turning it into a sophisticated side dish.

SERVES FOUR

2 garlic cloves, finely sliced

4 handfuls of green salad leaves

15ml/1 tbsp raspberry vinegar

FROM THE STORECUPBOARD

45ml/3 tbsp olive oil

salt and ground black pepper

1 Heat the oil in a small pan and add the garlic. Fry gently for 1–2 minutes, or until just golden, being careful not to burn the garlic. Remove the garlic with a slotted spoon and drain on kitchen paper. Pour the oil into a small bowl.

2 Arrange the salad leaves in a serving bowl. Whisk the raspberry vinegar into the reserved oil and season with salt and ground black pepper.

3 Pour the garlic dressing over the salad leaves and toss to combine. Sprinkle over the fried garlic slices and serve.

Cauliflower with Garlic Crumbs

This simple dish makes a great accompaniment to any meat or fish dish. When buying cauliflower look for creamy white coloured florets with the inner green leaves curled round the flower. Discard cauliflowers with discoloured patches or yellow leaves. As an alternative, try using broccoli florets instead of the cauliflower. Broccoli should have a fresh appearance: avoid yellowing specimens and those that feel soft or are wilting.

SERVES FOUR TO SIX

1 Steam or boil the cauliflower in salted water until just tender. Drain and leave to cool.

2 Heat 60–75ml/4–5 tbsp of the olive or vegetable oil in a pan, add the breadcrumbs and cook over a medium heat, tossing and turning, until browned and crisp. Add the garlic, turn once or twice, then remove from the pan and set aside.

3 Heat the remaining oil in the pan, then add the cauliflower, mashing and breaking it up a little as it lightly browns in the oil. (Do not overcook but just cook until lightly browned.)

4 Add the garlic breadcrumbs to the pan and cook, stirring, until well combined, with some of the cauliflower still holding its shape. Season and serve hot or warm.

1 large cauliflower, cut into bitesize florets

130g/4¹/₂oz/2¹/₄ cups dry white or wholemeal (whole-wheat) breadcrumbs

3–5 garlic cloves, thinly sliced or chopped

FROM THE STORECUPBOARD

90–120ml/6–8 tbsp olive or vegetable oil

salt and ground black pepper

COOK'S TIP
Serve this garlicky cauliflower dish as they do in Italy, with cooked pasta, such as spaghetti.

Summer Squash and Baby New Potatoes in Warm Dill Sour Cream

Fresh vegetables and fragrant dill are delicious tossed in a simple sour cream or yogurt sauce. Choose small squash with bright skins that are free from blemishes and bruises. To make a simpler potato salad, pour the dill sour cream over warm cooked potatoes. Serve either version of the potato salad with poached salmon or chargrilled chicken.

SERVES FOUR

1 Cut the squash into pieces about the same size as the potatoes. Put the potatoes in a pan and add water to cover and a pinch of salt. Bring to the boil, then simmer for about 10 minutes, until almost tender. Add the squash and continue to cook until the vegetables are just tender, then drain.

2 Put the vegetables into a wide, shallow pan and gently stir in the finely chopped fresh dill and chives.

3 Remove the pan from the heat and stir in the sour cream or yogurt. Return to the heat and heat gently until warm. Season and serve.

400g/14oz mixed squash, such as yellow and green courgettes (zucchini), and green patty pan

400g/14oz baby new potatoes

1 large handful mixed fresh dill and chives, finely chopped

300ml/^{1}/$_2$ pint/1^1/$_4$ cups sour cream or Greek (US strained plain) yogurt

FROM THE STORECUPBOARD

salt and ground black pepper

Minty Broad Beans with Lemon

Young, tender broad beans have a sweet, mild taste and are delicious served in a simple salad. Take advantage of them when they're in season and make them into this fresh, zesty dish. Green peas – either fresh or frozen – are also delicious served in the same way, but you don't need to peel off their already tender skins.

SERVES FOUR

450g/1lb broad (fava) beans, thawed if frozen

grated rind and juice of 1 unwaxed lemon

1 small bunch of fresh mint, roughly chopped

FROM THE STORECUPBOARD

30ml/2 tbsp garlic-infused olive oil

salt and ground black pepper

1 Using your fingers, slip the grey skins off the broad beans and discard – this takes a little time but the result is well worthwhile. Cook the beans in salted boiling water for 3–4 minutes, or until just tender.

2 Drain well and toss with the oil, lemon rind and juice, and mint. Season with salt and pepper, and serve immediately.

COOK'S TIP *When using fresh broad beans, it is easier to cook them first, then run them under cold water before slipping off their skins. Quickly blanch the skinned beans in boiling water to re-heat them.*

Gingered Carrot Salad

This fresh and zesty salad is ideal served as an accompaniment to simple grilled chicken or fish. Some food processors have an attachment that can be used to cut the carrots into batons, which makes quick work of the preparation, but even cutting them by hand doesn't take too long. Fresh root ginger goes perfectly with sweet carrots, and the tiny black poppy seeds not only add taste and texture, but also look stunning against the bright orange of the carrots.

SERVES FOUR

350g/12oz carrots, peeled and cut into fine matchsticks

2.5cm/1in piece of fresh root ginger, peeled and grated

15ml/1 tbsp poppy seeds

FROM THE STORECUPBOARD

30ml/2 tbsp garlic-infused olive oil

salt and ground black pepper

1 Put the carrots in a bowl and stir in the oil and grated ginger. Cover and chill for at least 30 minutes, to allow the flavours to develop.

2 Season the salad with salt and pepper to taste. Stir in the poppy seeds just before serving.

VARIATION *To make a parsnip and sesame seed salad, replace the carrots with parsnips and blanch in boiling salted water for 1 minute before combining with the oil and ginger. Replace the poppy seeds with the same quantity of sesame seeds.*

Baked Winter Squash with Tomatoes

Acorn, butternut or Hubbard squash can all be used in this simple recipe. Serve the squash as a light main course, with warm crusty bread, or as a side dish for grilled meat or poultry. Canned chopped tomatoes with herbs are used in this recipe. A variety of flavoured canned tomatoes are now available including garlic, onion and olive – they are ideal for adding a combination of flavours when time is short.

SERVES FOUR TO SIX

1 Preheat the oven to 160°C/325°F/Gas 3. Heat the oil in a pan and cook the pumpkin or squash slices, in batches, until golden brown, removing them from the pan as they are cooked.

2 Add the tomatoes and cook over a medium-high heat until the mixture is of a sauce consistency. Stir in the rosemary and season to taste with salt and pepper.

3 Layer the pumpkin slices and tomatoes in an ovenproof dish, ending with a layer of tomatoes. Bake for 35 minutes, or until the top is lightly glazed and beginning to turn golden brown, and the pumpkin is tender. Serve immediately.

1kg/2¼lb pumpkin or orange winter squash, peeled and sliced

2 x 400g/14oz cans chopped tomatoes with herbs

2–3 rosemary sprigs, stems removed and leaves chopped

FROM THE STORECUPBOARD

45ml/3 tbsp garlic-flavoured olive oil

salt and ground black pepper

Stewed Okra with Tomatoes and Coriander

This is a favourite Middle-Eastern way to prepare okra. Add wedges of lemon as a garnish so that their juice can be squeezed over the vegetables to taste. Okra, also known as lady's fingers, are narrow green lantern-shaped pods. They contain a row of seeds that ooze a viscous liquid when cooked. This liquid acts as a natural thickener in a variety of curries and soups.

SERVES FOUR TO SIX

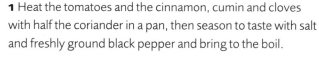

1 Heat the tomatoes and the cinnamon, cumin and cloves with half the coriander in a pan, then season to taste with salt and freshly ground black pepper and bring to the boil.

2 Add the okra and cook, stirring constantly, for 1–2 minutes. Reduce the heat to low, then simmer, stirring occasionally, for 20–30 minutes, until the okra is tender.

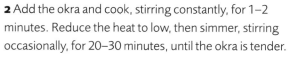

3 Taste for spicing and seasoning, and adjust if necessary, adding more of any one spice, salt or pepper to taste. Stir in the remaining coriander. Serve hot, warm or cold.

400g/14oz can chopped tomatoes with onions and garlic

generous pinch each of ground cinnamon, cumin and cloves

90ml/6 tbsp chopped fresh coriander (cilantro) leaves

800g/1³/₄lb okra

FROM THE STORECUPBOARD

salt and ground black pepper

Roast Asparagus with Crispy Prosciutto

Choose tender, fine asparagus for this recipe, as it cooks through quickly in the oven without losing its flavour or texture.

SERVES FOUR

350g/12oz fine asparagus spears, trimmed

1 small handful of fresh basil leaves

4 prosciutto slices

FROM THE STORECUPBOARD

30ml/2 tbsp olive oil

salt and ground black pepper

1 Preheat the oven to 190°C/375°F/Gas 5. Put the asparagus in a roasting pan and drizzle with the olive oil. Sprinkle over the basil and season with salt and ground black pepper. Gently stir to coat in the oil, then spread the asparagus in a single layer.

2 Lay the slices of prosciutto on top of the asparagus and cook for 10–15 minutes, or until the prosciutto is crisp and the asparagus is just tender. Serve immediately.

Garlicky Roasties

Potatoes roasted in their skins retain a deep, earthy taste (and, as a bonus, absorb less fat too) while the garlic mellows on cooking to give a pungent but not overly-strong taste to serve alongside or squeezed over as a garnish.

SERVES FOUR

1 Preheat the oven to 240°C/475°F/Gas 9. Place the potatoes in a pan of cold water and bring to the boil. Drain.

2 Combine the oils in a roasting tin and place in the oven to get really hot. Add the potatoes and garlic and coat in oil.

3 Sprinkle with salt and roast for 10 minutes. Reduce the heat to 200°C/400°F/Gas 6. Continue roasting, basting occasionally, for 30–40 minutes.

4 Serve each portion with several cloves of garlic.

1kg/2¼lb small floury potatoes

10ml/2 tsp walnut oil

2 whole garlic bulbs, unpeeled

FROM THE STORECUPBOARD

60–75ml/4–5 tbsp sunflower oil

salt and ground black pepper

Leek Fritters

These crispy fried morsels are best served at room temperature, with a good squeeze of lemon juice and a sprinkling of salt and freshly grated nutmeg. Matzo meal, a traditional Jewish ingredient, is used in these fritters: it is made from crumbled matzo, an unleavened bread, similar to water biscuits. Matzo meal is used in a similar way to breadcrumbs, which can also be used to make these fritters.

SERVES FOUR

1 Cook the leeks in salted boiling water for 5 minutes, or until just tender and bright green. Drain well and leave to cool.

2 Chop the leeks coarsely. Put in a bowl and combine with the matzo meal, eggs and seasoning.

3 Heat 5mm/¼in oil in a frying pan. Using two tablespoons, carefully spoon the leek mixture into the hot oil. Cook over a medium-high heat until golden brown on the underside, then turn and cook the second side. Drain on kitchen paper. Add more oil if needed and heat before cooking more mixture.

4 large leeks, total weight about 1kg/2¼lb, thickly sliced

120–175ml/4–6fl oz/½–¾ cup coarse matzo meal

2 eggs, lightly beaten

FROM THE STORECUPBOARD

olive or vegetable oil, for shallow frying

salt and ground black pepper

Deep-fried Artichokes

This is an Italian speciality, named *carciofi alla giudia*. The artichokes are baked, then pressed to open them and plunged into hot oil, where their leaves twist and brown, turning the artichokes into crispy flowers. Serve with lamb or pork steaks.

SERVES FOUR

2–3 lemons, halved

4–8 small young globe artichokes

olive or vegetable oil, for deep-frying

1 Fill a large bowl with cold water and stir in the juice of one or two of the lemons. Trim and discard the stems of the artichokes, then trim off their tough ends and remove all the tough outer leaves until you reach the pale pointed centre. Carefully open the leaves of one of the artichokes by pressing it against the table or poking them open. Trim the tops if they are sharp.

2 If there is any choke inside the artichoke, remove it with a melon baller or small pointed spoon. Put the artichoke in the acidulated water and prepare the remaining artichokes in the same way.

3 Put the artichokes in a large pan and pour over water to cover. Bring to the boil, reduce the heat and simmer for 10–15 minutes, or until partly cooked. If they are small, cook them for only 10 minutes. Drain the artichokes and leave upside down until cool enough to handle. Press them open gently, being careful not to break them apart.

4 Fill a pan with oil to a depth of 5–7.5cm/2–3in and heat. Add one or two artichokes at a time, with the leaves uppermost, and press down with a spoon to open up the leaves. Fry for 5–8 minutes, turning, until golden and crisp. Remove from the pan, and drain on kitchen paper. Serve immediately, with the remaining lemon cut into wedges.

COOK'S TIP *Select immature artichokes, before their chokes have formed. If you like, you can prepare and boil them ahead and deep-fry just before serving.*

Stir-fried Broccoli with Soy Sauce and Sesame Seeds

Purple sprouting broccoli has been used for this recipe, but when it is not available an ordinary variety of broccoli, such as calabrese, will also work very well.

SERVES TWO

225g/8oz purple sprouting broccoli

15ml/1 tbsp soy sauce

15ml/1 tbsp toasted sesame seeds

FROM THE STORECUPBOARD

15ml/1 tbsp olive oil

salt and ground black pepper

1 Using a sharp knife, cut off and discard any thick stems from the broccoli and cut the broccoli into long, thin florets.

2 Heat the olive oil in a wok or large frying pan and add the broccoli. Stir-fry for 3–4 minutes, or until tender, adding a splash of water if the pan becomes too dry.

3 Add the soy sauce to the broccoli, then season with salt and ground black pepper to taste. Add sesame seeds, toss to combine and serve immediately.

Stir-fried Brussels Sprouts with Bacon and Caraway Seeds

This is a great way of cooking Brussels sprouts, helping to retain their sweet flavour and crunchy texture. Stir-frying guarantees that there will not be a single soggy sprout in sight, which is often what puts people off these fabulous vegetables.

SERVES FOUR

1 Using a sharp knife, cut the Brussels sprouts into fine shreds and set aside. Heat the oil in a wok or large frying pan and add the bacon. Cook for 1–2 minutes, or until the bacon is beginning to turn golden.

2 Add the shredded sprouts to the wok or pan and stir-fry for 1–2 minutes, or until lightly cooked.

3 Season the sprouts with salt and ground black pepper to taste and stir in the caraway seeds. Cook for a further 30 seconds, then serve immediately.

450g/1lb Brussels sprouts, trimmed and washed

2 streaky (fatty) bacon rashers (strips), finely chopped

10ml/2 tsp caraway seeds, lightly crushed

FROM THE STORECUPBOARD

30ml/2 tbsp sunflower oil

salt and ground black pepper

Bocconcini with Fennel and Basil

These tiny balls of mozzarella are best when they're perfectly fresh. They should be milky and soft when you cut into them. Buy them from an Italian delicatessen or a good cheese shop.

SERVES SIX

1 Drain the bocconcini well and place in a bowl. Stir in the olive oil, fennel seeds and basil, and season with salt and pepper. Cover and chill for 1 hour.

2 Remove the bowl from the refrigerator and leave to stand for about 30 minutes for the cheese to return to room temperature before serving.

COOK'S TIP *Bocconcini are mini mozzarella balls, each one hand-stretched and rolled, then preserved in brine. If you can't find bocconcini, use ordinary mozzarella cut into bitesize pieces.*

450g/1lb bocconcini mozzarella

5ml/1 tsp fennel seeds, lightly crushed

a small bunch of fresh basil leaves, roughly torn

FROM THE STORECUPBOARD

45ml/3 tbsp extra virgin olive oil

salt and ground black pepper

Noodles with Sesame - roasted Spring Onions

You can use any kind of noodles for this Asian-style dish. Rice noodles look and taste particularly good, but egg noodles work very well too. Serve with fish and chicken dishes.

SERVES FOUR

1 bunch of spring onions (scallions), trimmed

225g/8oz flat rice noodles

30ml/2 tbsp oyster sauce

FROM THE STORECUPBOARD

30ml/2 tbsp sesame oil

salt and ground black pepper

1 Preheat the oven to 200°C/400°F/Gas 6. Cut the spring onions into three pieces, then put them in a small roasting pan and season with salt and pepper.

2 Drizzle the sesame oil over the spring onions and roast for 10 minutes, until they are slightly charred and tender. Set aside.

3 Cook the noodles according to the instructions on the packet and drain thoroughly. Toss with the spring onions and oyster sauce, and season with ground black pepper. Serve immediately.

Spicy Potato Wedges

These wedges are easy to make and can be served on their own with a garlic mayonnaise dip or as an accompaniment to meat or fish dishes. To make extra-hot potato wedges, use chilli powder instead of paprika.

SERVES FOUR

675g/1¹/₂lb floury potatoes, such as Maris Piper

10ml/2 tsp paprika

5ml/1 tsp ground cumin

FROM THE STORECUPBOARD

45ml/3 tbsp olive oil

salt and ground black pepper

1 Preheat the oven to 190°C/375°F/Gas 5. Using a sharp knife, cut the potatoes into chunky wedges and place in a roasting pan.

2 In a small bowl, combine the olive oil with the paprika and cumin and season with plenty of salt and ground black pepper. Pour the mixture over the potatoes and toss well to coat thoroughly.

3 Spread the potatoes in a single layer in the roasting pan and bake for 30–40 minutes, or until golden brown and tender. Serve immediately.

Crisp and Golden Roast Potatoes with Goose Fat and Garlic

Goose fat gives the best flavour to roast potatoes and is now widely available in cans in supermarkets. However, if you can't find goose fat, or you want to make a vegetarian version of these potatoes, use a large knob (pat) of butter or 15ml/1 tbsp olive oil instead. If you like, add a couple of bay leaves to the potatoes before roasting; they impart a lovely flavour.

SERVES FOUR

675g/1¹/₂lb floury potatoes, such as Maris Piper, peeled

30ml/2 tbsp goose fat

12 garlic cloves, unpeeled

FROM THE STORECUPBOARD

salt and ground black pepper

1 Preheat the oven to 190°C/375°F/Gas 5. Cut the potatoes into large chunks and cook in a pan of salted, boiling water for 5 minutes. Drain well and give the colander a good shake to fluff up the edges of the potatoes. Return the potatoes to the pan and place it over a low heat for 1 minute to steam off any excess water.

2 Meanwhile, spoon the goose fat into a roasting pan and place in the oven until hot, about 5 minutes. Add the potatoes to the pan with the garlic and turn to coat in the fat. Season well with salt and ground black pepper and roast for 40–50 minutes, turning occasionally, until the potatoes are golden and tender.

Tomato and Aubergine Gratin

This colourful, Mediterranean dish makes the perfect partner to grilled, pan-fried or baked meat or poultry. If you prefer, thinly sliced courgettes (zucchini) can be used in this dish instead of the aubergines. Grill the courgettes for 10–15 minutes. Choose plum tomatoes if you can – they have fewer seeds than most round tomatoes, so are less watery and are ideal for cooking.

SERVES FOUR TO SIX

1 Preheat the grill (broiler). Thinly slice the aubergines and arrange them in a single layer on a foil-lined grill rack. Brush the aubergine slices with some of the oil and grill (broil) for 15–20 minutes, turning once, until golden on both sides. Brush the second side with more oil after turning the slices.

2 Preheat the oven to 200°C/400°F/Gas 6. Toss the aubergine and tomato slices together in a bowl with a little seasoning, then pile them into a shallow, ovenproof dish. Drizzle with any remaining olive oil and sprinkle with the grated Parmesan cheese. Bake for 20 minutes, until the cheese is golden and the vegetables are hot. Serve the gratin immediately.

2 medium aubergines (eggplants), about 500g/1¼lb

400g/14oz ripe tomatoes, sliced

40g/1½oz/½ cup freshly grated Parmesan cheese

FROM THE STORECUPBOARD

90ml/6 tbsp olive oil

salt and ground black pepper

Bubble and Squeak

Whether you have leftovers or cook this old-fashioned classic from fresh, be sure to give it a really good "squeak" in the pan so it turns a rich honey brown. Serve as an accompaniment to grilled pork chops or fried eggs, or simply serve with warm bread for a quick supper. If you prefer, cook the bubble and squeak in individual-sized portions – divide into four and form into patties before cooking.

SERVES FOUR

1 Heat 30ml/2 tbsp of the bacon fat or oil in a heavy frying pan. Add the onion and cook over a medium heat, stirring frequently, until softened but not browned.

2 In a bowl, mix together the potatoes and cooked cabbage or sprouts and season with salt and plenty of pepper to taste.

3 Add the vegetables to the pan with the cooked onions, stir well, then press the vegetable mixture into a large, even cake.

4 Cook over a medium heat for about 15 minutes, until the cake is browned underneath.

5 Invert a large plate over the pan, and, holding it tightly against the pan, turn them both over together. Lift off the frying pan, return it to the heat and add the remaining bacon fat or oil. When hot, slide the cake back into the pan, browned side uppermost.

6 Cook over a medium heat for 10 minutes, or until the underside is golden brown. Serve hot, in wedges.

60ml/4 tbsp bacon fat or vegetable oil

1 medium onion, chopped

450g/1lb floury potatoes, cooked and mashed

225g/8oz cooked cabbage or Brussels sprouts, chopped

FROM THE STORECUPBOARD

salt and ground black pepper

Cheesy Creamy Leeks

This is quite a rich accompaniment that could easily be served as a meal in itself with brown rice or couscous. Cheddar cheese has been used here for a slightly stronger flavour, but you could use a milder Swiss cheese, such as Gruyère, if you like.

SERVES 4

4 large leeks or 12 baby leeks, trimmed and washed

150ml/¹/₄ pint/²/₃ cup double (heavy) cream

75g/3oz mature Cheddar or Monterey Jack cheese, grated

FROM THE STORECUPBOARD

15ml/1 tbsp olive oil

salt and ground black pepper

1 Preheat the grill (broiler) to high. If using large leeks, slice them lengthways. Heat the oil in a large frying pan and add the leeks. Season with salt and pepper and cook for about 4 minutes, stirring occasionally, until starting to turn golden.

2 Pour the cream into the pan and stir until well combined. Allow to bubble gently for a few minutes.

3 Preheat the grill (broiler). Transfer the creamy leeks to a shallow ovenproof dish and sprinkle with the cheese. Grill for 4–5 minutes, or until the cheese is golden brown and bubbling and serve immediately.

Creamy Polenta with Dolcelatte

Soft-cooked polenta is a tasty accompaniment to meat dishes and makes a delicious change from the usual potatoes or rice. It can also be enjoyed on its own as a hearty snack.

SERVES FOUR TO SIX

900ml/1¹/₂ pints/3³/₄ cups milk

115g/4oz/1 cup instant polenta

115g/4oz Dolcelatte cheese

FROM THE STORECUPBOARD

60ml/4 tbsp extra virgin olive oil

salt and ground black pepper

1 Pour the milk into a large pan and bring to the boil, then add a good pinch of salt. Remove the pan from the heat and pour in the polenta in a slow, steady stream, stirring constantly to combine.

2 Return the pan to a low heat and simmer gently, stirring constantly, for 5 minutes. Remove the pan from the heat and stir in the olive oil.

3 Spoon the polenta into a serving dish and crumble the cheese over the top. Season with more ground black pepper and serve immediately.

Fennel, Potato and Garlic Mash

This flavoursome mash of potato, fennel and garlic goes well with practically all main dishes, whether fish, poultry or meat. Floury varieties of potato such as Pentland Squire, King Edward or Marfona are best for mashing as they produce a light fluffy result. Waxy potatoes are more suitable for baking, or for salads, as they produce a dense, rather starchy mash.

SERVES FOUR

1 Boil the potatoes in water for 20 minutes, until tender.

2 Meanwhile, trim and chop the fennel, reserving any feathery tops. Chop the tops and set them aside. Heat 30ml/ 2 tbsp of the oil in a pan. Add the fennel, cover and cook over a low heat for 20–30 minutes, until soft but not browned.

3 Drain and mash the potatoes. Purée the fennel in a food mill or blender and beat it into the potato with the remaining oil.

4 Warm the milk or cream and beat sufficient into the potato and fennel to make a creamy, light mixture. Season to taste and reheat gently, then beat in any chopped fennel tops. Serve immediately.

800g/1³/₄lb potatoes, cut into chunks

2 large fennel bulbs

120–150ml/4–5fl oz/ ¹/₂–²/₃ cup milk or single (light) cream

FROM THE STORECUPBOARD

90ml/6 tbsp garlic-flavoured olive oil

salt and ground black pepper

Champ

This traditional Irish dish of potatoes and green or spring onions is enriched with a wickedly indulgent amount of butter – for complete indulgence, replace 60ml/4 tbsp of the milk with crème fraîche or buttermilk. Serve the champ as an accompaniment to beef or lamb stew for a warming and hearty winter meal.

SERVES FOUR

1 Boil the potatoes in lightly salted water for 20–25 minutes, or until they are tender. Drain and mash the potatoes with a fork until smooth.

2 Place the milk, spring onions and half the butter in a small pan and set over a low heat until just simmering. Cook for 2–3 minutes, until the butter has melted and the spring onions have softened.

3 Beat the milk mixture into the mashed potato using a wooden spoon until the mixture is light and fluffy. Reheat gently, adding seasoning to taste.

4 Turn the potato into a warmed serving dish and make a well in the centre with a spoon. Place the remaining butter in the well and let it melt. Serve immediately, sprinkled with extra spring onion.

1kg/2¹/₄ lb potatoes, cut into chunks

300ml/¹/₂ pint/1¹/₄ cups milk

1 bunch spring onions (scallions), thinly sliced, plus extra to garnish

115g/4oz/¹/₂ cup salted butter

FROM THE STORECUPBOARD

salt and ground black pepper

EXTRAS *To make colcannon, another Irish speciality, follow the main recipe, using half the butter. Cook about 500g/1¹/₄ lb finely shredded green cabbage or kale in a little water until just tender, drain thoroughly and then beat into the creamed potato. This is delicious served with sausages and grilled (broiled) ham or bacon. The colcannon may also be fried in butter and then browned under the grill (broiler).*

Salads

WHETHER SERVED AS A MAIN COURSE OR AN
ACCOMPANIMENT, SALADS ARE ALWAYS A REFRESHING
AND WELCOME CHANGE. THE MOST SUCCESSFUL ARE
COMPOSED OF ONLY A FEW INGREDIENTS – COOKED OR
RAW – WHOSE COLOURS, TEXTURES AND FLAVOURS
COMPLEMENT AND BALANCE PERFECTLY.

Sour Cucumber with Fresh Dill

This is half pickle, half salad, and totally delicious served with pumpernickel or other coarse, dark, full-flavoured bread, as a light meal or an appetizer. Choose smooth-skinned, smallish cucumbers for this recipe as larger ones tend to be less tender, with tough skins and bitter indigestible seeds. If you can only buy a large cucumber, peel it before slicing.

SERVES FOUR

1 In a large mixing bowl, combine together the thinly sliced cucumbers and the thinly sliced onion. Season the vegetables with salt and toss together until they are thoroughly combined. Leave the mixture to stand in a cool place for 5–10 minutes.

2 Add the cider vinegar, 30–45ml/2–3 tbsp water and the chopped fresh dill to the cucumber and onion mixture. Toss all the ingredients together until well combined, then chill in the refrigerator for a few hours, or until ready to serve.

2 small cucumbers, thinly sliced

3 onions, thinly sliced

75–90ml/5–6 tbsp cider vinegar

30–45ml/2–3 tbsp chopped fresh dill

FROM THE STORECUPBOARD

salt and ground black pepper

Beetroot with Fresh Mint

This simple and decorative beetroot salad can be served as part of a selection of salads, as an appetizer, or as an accompaniment to grilled or roasted pork or lamb. Balsamic vinegar is a rich, dark vinegar with a mellow, deep flavour. It can be used to dress a variety of salad ingredients and is particularly good drizzled over a tomato and basil salad.

SERVES FOUR

1 Slice the beetroot or cut into even-size dice with a sharp knife. Put the beetroot in a bowl. Add the balsamic vinegar, olive oil and a pinch of salt and toss together to combine.

2 Add half the thinly shredded fresh mint to the salad and toss lightly until thoroughly combined. Place the salad in the refrigerator and chill for about 1 hour. Serve garnished with the remaining thinly shredded mint leaves.

EXTRAS *To make Tunisian beetroot, add a little harissa to taste and substitute chopped fresh coriander (cilantro) for the shredded mint.*

4–6 cooked beetroot (beet)

15–30ml/1–2 tbsp balsamic vinegar

1 bunch fresh mint, leaves stripped and thinly shredded

FROM THE STORECUPBOARD

30ml/2 tbsp olive oil

salt and ground black pepper

Globe Artichokes with Green Beans and Garlic Dressing

Piquant garlic dressing or creamy aioli go perfectly with these lightly-cooked vegetables. Serve lemon wedges with the artichokes so that their juice may be squeezed over to taste. The vegetables can also be garnished with finely shredded lemon rind. Artichokes should feel heavy for their size – make sure that the inner leaves are wrapped tightly round the choke and the heart inside.

SERVES FOUR TO SIX

225g/8oz green beans

3 small globe artichokes

250ml/8fl oz/1 cup garlic dressing or aioli

FROM THE STORECUPBOARD

15ml/1 tbsp lemon-flavoured olive oil

salt and ground black pepper

1 Cook the beans in boiling water for 1–2 minutes, until slightly softened. Drain well.

2 Trim the artichoke stalks close to the base. Cook them in a large pan of salted water for about 30 minutes, or until you can easily pull away a leaf from the base. Drain well.

3 Using a sharp knife, halve them lengthways and ease out their chokes using a teaspoon.

4 Arrange the artichokes and beans on serving plates and drizzle with the oil. Season with coarse salt and a little pepper. Spoon the garlic dressing or aioli into the hearts and serve warm.

5 To eat the artichokes, pull the leaves from the base one at a time and use to scoop a little of the dressing. It is only the fleshy end of each leaf that is eaten as well as the base, bottom or "fond".

Halloumi and Grape Salad

Firm and salty halloumi cheese is a great standby ingredient for turning a simple salad into a special dish. In this recipe it is tossed with sweet, juicy grapes, which complement its flavour and texture. Fresh young thyme leaves and dill taste especially good mixed with the salad. Serve with a crusty walnut or sun-dried tomato bread for a light lunch.

SERVES FOUR

1 Toss together the salad leaves and fresh herb sprigs and the green and black grapes, then transfer to a large serving plate.

2 Thinly slice the halloumi cheese. Heat a large non-stick frying pan. Add the sliced halloumi cheese and cook briefly until it just starts to turn golden brown on the underside. Turn the cheese with a fish slice or metal spatula and cook the other side until it is golden brown.

3 Arrange the fried cheese over the salad on the plate. Pour over the oil and lemon juice or vinegar dressing and serve immediately while the cheese is still hot.

150g/5oz mixed salad leaves and tender fresh herb sprigs

175g/6oz mixed seedless green and black grapes

250g/9oz halloumi cheese

75ml/5 tbsp oil and lemon juice or vinegar dressing

Watermelon and Feta Salad

The combination of sweet watermelon with salty feta cheese is inspired by Turkish tradition. The salad may be served plain and light, on a leafy base, or with a herbed vinaigrette dressing drizzled over. It is perfect served as an appetizer. Feta cheese is salty because it is preserved in brine – but the salt is not supposed to overpower the taste of the cheese.

SERVES FOUR

4 slices watermelon, chilled

130g/4¹/₂oz feta cheese, preferably sheep's milk feta, cut into bitesize pieces

handful of mixed seeds, such as lightly toasted pumpkin seeds and sunflower seeds

10–15 black olives

1 Cut the rind off the watermelon and remove as many seeds as possible. Cut the flesh into triangular-shaped chunks.

2 Mix the watermelon, feta cheese, mixed seeds and black olives. Cover and chill the salad for 30 minutes before serving.

COOK'S TIP *The best choice of olives for this recipe are plump black Mediterranean ones, such as kalamata, other shiny, brined varieties or dry-cured black olives.*

Tomato, Bean and Fried Basil Salad

Infusing basil in hot oil brings out its wonderful, aromatic flavour, which works so well in almost any tomato dish. Various canned beans or chickpeas can be used instead of mixed beans in this simple dish, as they all taste good and make a wholesome salad to serve as an accompaniment or a satisfying snack with some warm, grainy bread.

SERVES FOUR

1 Reserve one-third of the basil leaves for garnish, then tear the remainder into pieces. Pour the olive oil into a small pan. Add the torn basil and heat gently for 1 minute, until the basil sizzles and begins to colour.

2 Place the halved cherry tomatoes and beans in a bowl. Pour in the basil oil and add a little salt and plenty of freshly ground black pepper. Toss the ingredients together gently, cover and leave to marinate at room temperature for at least 30 minutes. Serve the salad sprinkled with the remaining basil leaves.

15g/¹/₂oz/¹/₂ cup fresh basil leaves

300g/11oz cherry tomatoes, halved

400g/14oz can mixed beans, drained and rinsed

FROM THE STORECUPBOARD

75ml/5 tbsp extra virgin olive oil

salt and ground black pepper

Moroccan Date, Orange and Carrot Salad

Take exotic fresh dates and marry them with everyday ingredients, such as carrots and oranges, to make this deliciously different salad. The salad looks really pretty arranged on a base of sweet Little Gem (Bibb) lettuce leaves. This fruity salad is excellent served with chargrilled lamb steaks, or with skewered lamb.

SERVES FOUR

3 carrots

3 oranges

115g/4oz fresh dates, stoned (pitted) and cut lengthways into eighths

25g/1oz/¹/₄ cup toasted whole almonds, chopped

FROM THE STORECUPBOARD

salt and ground black pepper

1 Grate the carrots and place in a mound in a serving dish, or on four individual plates.

2 Peel and segment two of the oranges and arrange the orange segments around the carrot. Season with salt and freshly ground black pepper. Pile the dates on top, then sprinkle with the chopped, toasted almonds.

3 Squeeze the juice from the remaining orange and sprinkle it over the salad. Chill in the refrigerator for an hour before serving.

Pink Grapefruit and Avocado Salad

Smooth, creamy avocado and zesty citrus fruit are perfect partners in an attractive, refreshing salad. Pink grapefruit are tangy but not too sharp, or try large oranges for a sweeter flavour. Avocados turn brown quickly when exposed to the air: the acidic grapefruit juice will prevent this from occurring, so combine the ingredients as soon as the avocados have been sliced.

SERVES FOUR

1 Slice the top and bottom off a grapefruit, then cut off all the peel and pith from around the side. Working over a small bowl to catch the juices, cut out the segments from between the membranes and place them in a separate bowl. Squeeze any juices remaining in the membranes into the bowl, then discard them. Repeat with the remaining grapefruit.

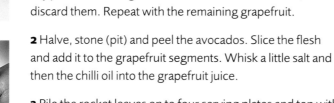

2 Halve, stone (pit) and peel the avocados. Slice the flesh and add it to the grapefruit segments. Whisk a little salt and then the chilli oil into the grapefruit juice.

3 Pile the rocket leaves on to four serving plates and top with the grapefruit segments and avocado. Pour over the dressing and serve.

2 pink grapefruit

2 ripe avocados

90g/3^{1}/$_{2}$oz rocket (arugula)

FROM THE STORECUPBOARD

30ml/2 tbsp chilli oil

salt and ground black pepper

Turnip Salad in Sour Cream

Usually served cooked, raw young tender turnips have a tangy, slightly peppery flavour. Serve this as an accompaniment for grilled poultry or meat. It is also delicious as a light appetizer, garnished with parsley and paprika, and served with warmed flat breads such as pitta or naan. Garnish the salad with fresh flat leaf parsley and paprika, if you like.

SERVES FOUR

1 Thinly slice or coarsely grate the turnips. Alternatively, thinly slice half the turnips and grate the remaining half. Put in a bowl.

2 Add the onion and vinegar and season to taste with salt and plenty of freshly ground black pepper. Toss together, then stir in the sour cream. Chill well before serving.

VARIATIONS Large white radishes can be used instead of turnips and crème fraîche can be substituted for the sour cream. The salad is good with a selection of salads and cold dishes for a light lunch or long and leisurely supper.

2–4 young, tender turnips, peeled

¹/₄–¹/₂ onion, finely chopped

2–3 drops white wine vinegar, or to taste

60–90ml/4–6 tbsp sour cream

FROM THE STORECUPBOARD

salt and ground black pepper

Moroccan Carrot Salad

In this intriguing salad from North Africa, the carrots are lightly cooked before being tossed in a cumin and coriander vinaigrette. Cumin is widely used in Indian and Mexican cooking, as well as North African cuisines. It has a strong and spicy aroma and a warm pungent flavour that goes particularly well with root vegetables. This salad is a perfect accompaniment for both everyday or special meals.

SERVES FOUR TO SIX

3–4 carrots, thinly sliced

1.5ml/¼ tsp ground cumin, or to taste

60ml/4 tbsp garlic-flavoured oil and vinegar dressing

30ml/2 tbsp chopped fresh coriander (cilantro) leaves or a mixture of coriander and parsley

FROM THE STORECUPBOARD

salt and ground black pepper

1 Cook the thinly sliced carrots by either steaming or boiling in lightly salted water until they are just tender but not soft. Drain the carrots, leave for a few minutes to dry and cool, then put into a mixing bowl.

2 Add the cumin, garlic dressing and herbs. Season to taste and chill well before serving. Check the seasoning just before serving and add more ground cumin, salt or black pepper, if required.

Warm Chorizo and Spinach Salad

Spanish chorizo sausage contributes an intense spiciness to any ingredient with which it is cooked. In this hearty warm salad, spinach has sufficient flavour to compete with the chorizo. Watercress or rocket (arugula) could be used instead of the spinach, if you prefer. For an added dimension use a flavoured olive oil – rosemary, garlic or chilli oil would work perfectly. Serve the salad with warm crusty bread to soak up all the delicious cooking juices.

SERVES FOUR

1 Discard any tough stalks from the spinach. Pour the oil into a large frying pan and add the sausage. Cook gently for 3 minutes, until the sausage slices start to shrivel slightly and colour.

2 Add the spinach leaves and remove the pan from the heat. Toss the spinach in the warm oil until it just starts to wilt. Add the sherry vinegar and a little seasoning. Toss the ingredients briefly, then serve immediately, while still warm.

225g/8oz baby spinach leaves

150g/5oz chorizo sausage, very thinly sliced

30ml/2 tbsp sherry vinegar

FROM THE STORECUPBOARD

90ml/6 tbsp olive oil

salt and ground black pepper

Potato and Olive Salad

This delicious salad is simple and zesty – the perfect choice for lunch, as an accompaniment, or as an appetizer. Similar in appearance to flat leaf parsley, fresh coriander has a distinctive pungent, almost spicy flavour. It is widely used in India, the Middle and Far East and in eastern Mediterranean countries. This potato salad is particularly good served as part of a brunch.

SERVES FOUR

8 large new potatoes

45–60ml/3–4 tbsp garlic-flavoured oil and vinegar dressing

60–90ml/4–6 tbsp chopped fresh herbs, such as coriander (cilantro) and chives

10–15 dry-fleshed black Mediterranean olives

FROM THE STORECUPBOARD

salt and ground black pepper

1 Cut the new potatoes into chunks. Put them in a pan, pour in water to cover and add a pinch of salt. Bring to the boil, then reduce the heat and cook gently for about 10 minutes, or until the potatoes are just tender. Drain well and leave in a colander to dry thoroughly and cool slightly.

2 When they are cool enough to handle, chop the potatoes and put them in a serving bowl.

3 Drizzle the garlic dressing over the potatoes. Toss well and sprinkle with the coriander and chives, and black olives. Chill in the refrigerator for at least 1 hour before serving.

EXTRAS *Add a pinch of ground cumin or a sprinkling of roasted whole cumin seeds to spice up the salad.*

Asparagus, Bacon and Leaf Salad

This excellent salad turns a plain roast chicken or simple grilled fish into an interesting meal, especially when served with buttered new potatoes. It also makes an appetizing first course or light lunch. A wide range of different salad leaves are readily available – frisée has feathery, curly, slightly bitter tasting leaves and is a member of the chicory family. Frisée leaves range in colour from yellow-white to yellow-green.

SERVES FOUR

1 Trim off any tough stalk ends from the asparagus and cut the spears into three, setting the tender tips aside. Heat a 1cm/½in depth of water in a frying pan until simmering. Reserve the asparagus tips and cook the remainder of the spears in the water for about 3 minutes, until almost tender. Add the tips and cook for 1 minute more. Drain and refresh under cold, running water.

2 Dry-fry the bacon until crisp and then set it aside to cool. Use kitchen scissors to snip it into bitesize pieces. Place the frisée or mixed leaf salad in a bowl and add the bacon.

3 Add the asparagus and a little black pepper to the salad. Pour the dressing over and toss the salad lightly, then serve.

500g/1¼lb medium asparagus spears

130g/4½oz thin-cut smoked back (lean) bacon

250g/9oz frisée lettuce leaves or mixed leaf salad

100ml/3½fl oz/scant ½ cup French dressing

FROM THE STORECUPBOARD

salt and ground black pepper

Anchovy and Roasted Pepper Salad

Sweet peppers, salty anchovies and plenty of garlic make an intensely flavoured salad that is delicious with meat, poultry or cheese. It also makes a tasty snack with olive bread. If you find that canned anchovies are too salty for your liking, you can reduce their saltiness by soaking them in milk for 20 minutes. Drain off the oil first and after soaking drain and rinse them in cold water.

SERVES FOUR

2 red, 2 orange and 2 yellow (bell) peppers, halved and seeded

50g/2oz can anchovies in olive oil

2 garlic cloves

45ml/3 tbsp balsamic vinegar

FROM THE STORECUPBOARD

salt and ground black pepper

1 Preheat the oven to 200°C/400°F/Gas 6. Place the peppers, cut side down, in a roasting pan. Roast for 30-40 minutes, until the skins are charred. Transfer the peppers to a bowl, cover with clear film (plastic wrap) and leave for 15 minutes.

2 Peel the peppers, then cut them into chunky strips. Drain the anchovies and halve the fillets lengthways.

3 Slice the garlic as thinly as possible and place it in a large bowl. Stir in the olive oil, vinegar and a little pepper. Add the peppers and anchovies and use a spoon and fork to fold the ingredients together. Cover and chill until ready to serve.

Al Fresco

EATING OUTSIDE, WHETHER IT'S A PICNIC, A FAMILY
LUNCH IN THE GARDEN OR A BARBECUE, IS ONE OF THE
GREAT PLEASURES OF SUMMER. THERE'S SOMETHING
QUINTESSENTIALLY RELAXING ABOUT EATING OUT IN
THE OPEN AND THIS CHAPTER IS PACKED WITH SIMPLE,
NO-FUSS RECIPES THAT ARE PERFECT FOR HOT, LAZY
DAYS AND BALMY EVENINGS. TAKE A SELECTION OF
SALADS, MAIN DISHES AND BREADS AND LET
EVERYONE HELP THEMSELVES.

Merguez Sausages with Iced Oysters

This is a truly wonderful taste sensation – revel in the French Christmas tradition of munching on a little hot sausage, then quelling the burning sensation with an ice-cold oyster. Merguez sausages come from North Africa and owe their flavour and colour to harissa, a hot chilli paste with subtle hints of coriander, caraway and garlic.

SERVES SIX

675g/1¹/₂lb merguez sausages

crushed ice for serving

24 oysters

2 lemons, cut into wedges, for squeezing

1 Prepare the barbecue. Once the flames have died down, position a lightly oiled grill rack over the coals to heat. When the coals are medium-hot, place the sausages on the rack. Grill them for 8 minutes, or until cooked through and golden, turning often.

2 Meanwhile, spread out the crushed ice on a platter and keep it chilled while you ready the oysters. Make sure all the oysters are closed, and discard any that aren't. Place them on the grill rack, a few at a time, with the deep-side down, so that as they open the juices will be retained in the lower shell. They will ease open after 3–5 minutes and must be removed from the heat immediately, so they don't start to cook.

3 Lay the oysters on the ice. When they have all eased open, get to work with a sharp knife, opening them fully if need be. Remove the oysters and place them with the juices on the deep half shells. Discard any oysters that fail to open. Serve immediately, with the hot, cooked sausages and with the lemon wedges.

Grilled Corn on the Cob

Keeping the husks on the corn protects the corn kernels and encloses the butter, so the flavours are contained. Fresh corn with husks intact are perfect, but banana leaves or a double layer of foil are also suitable.

SERVES SIX

3 dried chipotle chillies

7.5ml/1¹/₂ tsp lemon juice

45ml/3 tbsp chopped fresh flat leaf parsley

6 corn on the cob, with husks intact

FROM THE STORECUPBOARD

250g/9oz/generous 1 cup butter, softened

1 Heat a frying pan. Add the dried chillies and roast them by stirring them for 1 minute without letting them scorch. Put them in a bowl with almost boiling water to cover. Use a saucer to keep them submerged, and leave them to rehydrate for up to 1 hour. Drain, remove the seeds and chop the chillies finely. Place the butter in a bowl and add the chillies, lemon juice and parsley. Season to taste and mix well.

2 Peel back the husks from each cob without tearing them. Remove the silk. Smear about 30ml/2 tbsp of the chilli butter over each cob. Pull the husks back over the cobs, ensuring that the butter is well hidden. Put the rest of the butter in a pot, smooth the top and chill to use later. Place the cobs in a bowl of cold water and leave in a cool place for 1–3 hours; longer if that suits your work plan better.

3 Prepare the barbecue. Remove the corn cobs from the water and wrap in pairs in foil. Once the flames have died down, position a lightly oiled grill rack over the coals to heat. When the coals are medium-hot, or have a moderate coating of ash, grill the corn for 15–20 minutes. Remove the foil and cook them for about 5 minutes more, turning them often to char the husks a little. Serve hot, with the rest of the butter.

Butter Bean, Tomato and Red Onion Salad

Serve this salad with toasted pitta bread for a fresh summer lunch, or as an accompaniment to meat cooked on a barbecue.

SERVES FOUR

2 x 400g/14oz cans butter (lima) beans, rinsed and drained

4 plum tomatoes, roughly chopped

1 red onion, finely sliced

FROM THE STORECUPBOARD

45ml/3 tbsp herb-infused olive oil

salt and ground black pepper

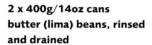

1 Mix together the beans, tomatoes and onion in a large bowl. Season with salt and pepper, and stir in the oil.

2 Cover the bowl with clear film (plastic wrap) and chill for 20 minutes before serving.

VARIATIONS
- *To make a tasty tuna salad, drain a 200g/7oz can tuna, flake the flesh and stir into the bean salad.*
- *For extra flavour and colour, stir in a handful of pitted black olives and a handful of chopped fresh parsley.*
- *To make a wholesome version of the Italian salad Panzanella, tear half a loaf of ciabatta into bite-size pieces and stir into the salad. Leave to stand for 20 minutes before serving.*

Potato, Caraway Seed and Parsley Salad

Leaving the potatoes to cool in garlic-infused oil with the caraway seeds helps them to absorb plenty of flavour.

SERVES FOUR TO SIX

675g/1¹⁄₂lb new potatoes, scrubbed

15ml/1 tbsp caraway seeds, lightly crushed

45ml/3 tbsp chopped fresh parsley

FROM THE STORECUPBOARD

45ml/3 tbsp garlic-infused olive oil

salt and ground black pepper

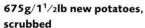

1 Cook the potatoes in salted, boiling water for about 10 minutes, or until just tender. Drain thoroughly and transfer to a large bowl.

2 Stir the oil, caraway seeds and some salt and pepper into the hot potatoes, then set aside to cool. When the potatoes are almost cold, stir in the parsley and serve.

VARIATION
This recipe is also delicious made with sweet potatoes instead of new potatoes. Peel and roughly chop the sweet potatoes, then follow the recipe as before.

Warm Halloumi and Fennel Salad

The firm texture of halloumi cheese makes it perfect for the barbecue, as it keeps its shape very well. It is widely available in most large supermarkets and Greek delicatessens.

SERVES FOUR

200g/7oz halloumi cheese, thickly sliced

2 fennel bulbs, trimmed and thinly sliced

30ml/2 tbsp roughly chopped fresh oregano

FROM THE STORECUPBOARD

45ml/3 tbsp lemon-infused olive oil

salt and ground black pepper

1 Put the halloumi, fennel and oregano in a bowl and drizzle over the lemon-infused oil. Season with salt and black pepper to taste. (Halloumi is a fairly salty cheese, so be very careful when adding extra salt.)

2 Cover the bowl with clear film (plastic wrap) and chill for about 2 hours to allow the flavours to develop.

3 Place the halloumi and fennel on a griddle pan or over the barbecue, reserving the marinade, and cook for about 3 minutes on each side, until charred.

4 Divide the halloumi and fennel among four serving plates and drizzle over the reserved marinade. Serve immediately.

Pear and Blue Cheese Salad

A juicy variety of pear, such as a Williams, is just perfect in this dish. You can use any other blue cheese, such as Stilton or Gorgonzola, in place of the Roquefort if you prefer.

SERVES FOUR

1 Cut the pears into quarters and remove the cores. Thinly slice each pear quarter and arrange on a serving platter.

2 Slice the Roquefort as thinly as possible and place over the pears. Mix the oil and vinegar together and drizzle over the pears. Season with salt and pepper and serve.

COOK'S TIP

Rich, dark balsamic vinegar has an intense yet mellow flavour. It is produced in Modena in the north of Italy and is widely available in most supermarkets.

4 ripe pears

115g/4oz Roquefort cheese

15ml/1 tbsp balsamic vinegar

FROM THE STORECUPBOARD

30ml/2 tbsp olive oil

salt and ground black pepper

Fresh Crab Sandwiches

There's not much to beat the taste of freshly cooked crab, but if you can't face dealing with live crabs, buy fresh cooked ones. Serve the crab meat with a bowl of rocket (arugula) and let everyone get in a mess cracking open the claws and making their own sandwiches.

SERVES SIX

3 live crabs, about 900g/
2lb each

1 crusty wholegrain loaf, sliced

2 lemons, cut into quarters

FROM THE STORECUPBOARD

butter, for spreading

salt and ground black pepper

1 Lower the live crabs into a pan of cold water, then slowly bring to the boil. (This method is considered more humane than plunging the crabs into boiling water.) Cook the crabs for 5–6 minutes per 450g/1lb, then remove from the pan and set aside to cool.

2 Break off the claws and legs, then use your thumbs to ease the body out of the shell. Remove and discard the grey gills from the body and put the white meat in a bowl. Scrape the brown meat from the shell and add to the white meat.

3 Serve the crab meat, and the claws and legs with crab crackers, with slices of brown bread, butter and lemon wedges and let everyone make their own sandwiches.

Warm Pasta with Crushed Tomatoes and Basil

It doesn't matter which type of pasta you use for this recipe – any kind you have in the storecupboard will work well.

SERVES FOUR

6 small ripe tomatoes, halved

a small handful of fresh basil leaves

450g/1lb dried pasta shapes

FROM THE STORECUPBOARD

45ml/3 tbsp extra virgin olive oil

salt and ground black pepper

1 Put the halved tomatoes in a bowl and, using your hands, gently squash them until the juices start to run freely. Stir in the olive oil and tear in the basil leaves.

2 Season the tomatoes with salt and pepper and mix well to combine. Cover the bowl with clear film (plastic wrap) and chill for 2–3 hours, to allow the flavours to develop.

3 Remove the tomatoes from the refrigerator and allow them to return to room temperature.

4 Meanwhile, cook the pasta according to the instructions on the packet. Drain well, toss with the crushed tomato and basil mixture and serve immediately.

Roast Shallot Tart with Thyme

Tarts are perfect for a summer lunch or picnic, and sheets of ready-rolled puff pastry make tart-making incredibly easy.

SERVES FOUR

450g/1lb shallots, peeled and halved

30ml/2 tbsp fresh thyme leaves

375g/13oz packet ready-rolled puff pastry, thawed if frozen

FROM THE STORECUPBOARD

25g/1oz/2 tbsp butter

salt and ground black pepper

1 Preheat the oven to 190°C/375°F/Gas 5. Heat the butter in a large frying pan until foaming, then add the shallots. Season with salt and pepper and cook over a gentle heat for 10–15 minutes, stirring occasionally, until golden. Stir in the thyme, then remove from the heat and set aside.

2 Unroll the puff pastry on to a large baking sheet. Using a small, sharp knife, score a border all the way around, about 2.5cm/1in from the edge, without cutting all the way through the pastry.

3 Spread the shallots over the pastry, inside the border. Bake for 20–25 minutes, or until the pastry is golden and risen around the edges. Cut into squares and serve hot or warm.

Roasted Aubergines with Feta and Coriander

Aubergines take on a lovely smoky flavour when grilled on a barbecue. Choose a good quality Greek feta cheese for the best flavour.

SERVES SIX

3 medium aubergines (eggplants)

400g/14oz feta cheese

a small bunch of coriander (cilantro), roughly chopped

FROM THE STORECUPBOARD

60ml/4 tbsp extra virgin olive oil

salt and ground black pepper

1 Prepare a barbecue. Cook the aubergines for 20 minutes, turning occasionally, until charred and soft. Remove from the barbecue and cut in half lengthways.

2 Carefully scoop the aubergine flesh into a bowl, reserving the skins. Mash the flesh roughly with a fork.

3 Crumble the feta cheese, then stir into the mashed aubergine with the chopped coriander and olive oil. Season with salt and ground black pepper to taste.

4 Spoon the aubergine and feta mixture back into the skins and return to the barbecue for 5 minutes to warm through. Serve immediately.

Barbecued Sardines with Orange and Parsley

Sardines are ideal for the barbecue – the meaty flesh holds together, the skin crisps nicely and there are no lingering indoor cooking smells. Serve them with a selection of salads.

SERVES SIX

6 whole sardines, gutted

1 orange, sliced

a small bunch of fresh flat leaf parsley, chopped

FROM THE STORECUPBOARD

60ml/4 tbsp extra virgin olive oil

salt and ground black pepper

1 Arrange the sardines and orange slices in a single layer in a shallow, non-metallic dish. Sprinkle over the chopped parsley and season with salt and pepper.

2 Drizzle the olive oil over the sardines and orange slices and gently stir to coat well. Cover the dish with clear film (plastic wrap) and chill for 2 hours.

3 Meanwhile, prepare the barbecue. Remove the sardines and orange slices from the marinade and cook the fish over the barbecue for 7–8 minutes on each side, until cooked through. Serve immediately.

Soy Sauce and Star Anise Chicken

The pungent flavour of star anise penetrates the chicken breasts and adds a wonderful aniseedy kick to the smoky flavour of the barbecue. Serve with a refreshing salad.

SERVES FOUR

1 Put the chicken breast fillets in a shallow, non-metallic dish and add the star anise.

2 In a small bowl, whisk together the oil and soy sauce and season with black pepper to make a marinade.

3 Pour the marinade over the chicken and stir to coat each breast fillet all over. Cover the dish with clear film (plastic wrap) and chill for up to 8 hours.

4 Prepare a barbecue. Remove the chicken breasts from the marinade and cook for 8–10 minutes on each side, spooning over the marinade from time to time, until the chicken is cooked through. Serve immediately.

4 skinless chicken breast fillets

2 whole star anise

30ml/2 tbsp soy sauce

FROM THE STORECUPBOARD

45ml/3 tbsp olive oil

ground black pepper

Harissa-spiced Koftas

Serve these spicy koftas in pitta breads with sliced tomatoes, cucumber and mint leaves, with a drizzle of natural yogurt.

SERVES FOUR

450g/1lb/2 cups minced (ground) lamb

1 small onion, finely chopped

10ml/2 tsp harissa paste

FROM THE STORECUPBOARD

salt and ground black pepper

1 Place eight wooden skewers in a bowl of cold water and leave to soak for at least 10 minutes.

2 Put the lamb in a large bowl and add the onion and harissa. Mix well to combine, and season with plenty of salt and ground black pepper.

3 Using wet hands, divide the mixture into eight equal pieces and press on to the skewers in a sausage shape to make the koftas.

4 Prepare a barbecue. Cook the skewered koftas for about 10 minutes, turning occasionally, until cooked through. Serve immediately.

Cumin- and Coriander-rubbed Lamb

Rubs are quick and easy to prepare and can transform everyday cuts of meat such as chops into exciting and more unusual meals. Serve with a chunky tomato salad.

SERVES FOUR

30ml/2 tbsp ground cumin

30ml/2 tbsp ground coriander

8 lamb chops

FROM THE STORECUPBOARD

30ml/2 tbsp olive oil

salt and ground black pepper

1 Mix together the cumin, coriander and oil, and season with salt and pepper. Rub the mixture all over the lamb chops, then cover and chill for 1 hour.

2 Prepare a barbecue. Cook the chops for 5 minutes on each side, until lightly charred but still pink in the centre.

VARIATION *To make ginger- and garlic-rubbed pork, use pork chops instead of lamb chops and substitute the cumin and coriander with ground ginger and garlic granules. Increase the cooking time to 7–8 minutes each side.*

Hot Desserts

A HOT DESSERT MAKES THE PERFECT END TO A MEAL
AND CAN TAKE VERY LITTLE TIME TO PREPARE. A FEW
WELL-CHOSEN INGREDIENTS CAN BE TURNED INTO A
SUMPTUOUS, MOUTHWATERING TREAT WITH THE MINIMUM
OF EFFORT. MANY OF THE RECIPES IN THIS CHAPTER CAN
BE PREPARED IN ADVANCE AND SIMPLY POPPED IN THE
OVEN TO COOK WHILE YOU SERVE THE MAIN COURSE.

Plum and Almond Tart

To transform this tart into an extravagant dessert, dust with a little icing (confectioners') sugar and serve with a dollop of crème fraîche.

SERVES FOUR

1 Preheat the oven to 190°C/375°F/Gas 5. Unroll the pastry on to a large baking sheet. Using a small, sharp knife, score a border 5cm/2in from the edge of the pastry, without cutting all the way through.

2 Roll out the marzipan into a rectangle, to fit just within the pastry border, then lay it on top of the pastry, pressing down lightly with the tips of your fingers.

3 Scatter the sliced plums on top of the marzipan in an even layer and bake for 20–25 minutes, or until the pastry is risen and golden brown.

4 Carefully transfer the tart to a wire rack to cool slightly, then cut into squares or wedges and serve.

375g/13oz ready-rolled puff pastry, thawed if frozen

115g/4oz marzipan

6–8 plums, stoned and sliced

Baked Apples with Marsala

The Marsala cooks down with the juice from the apples and the butter to make a rich, sticky sauce. Serve these delicious apples with a spoonful of extra-thick cream.

SERVES SIX

1 Preheat the oven to 180°C/350°F/Gas 4. Using an apple corer, remove the cores from the apples and discard.

2 Place the apples in a small, shallow baking pan and stuff the figs into the holes in the centre of each apple.

3 Top each apple with a quarter of the butter and pour over the Marsala. Cover the pan tightly with foil and bake for about 30 minutes.

4 Remove the foil from the apples and bake for a further 10 minutes, or until the apples are tender and the juices have reduced slightly. Serve immediately with any remaining pan juices drizzled over the top.

4 medium cooking apples

50g/2oz/^{1}/$_3$ cup ready-to-eat dried figs

150ml/^{1}/$_4$ pint/^{2}/$_3$ cup Marsala

FROM THE STORECUPBOARD

50g/2oz/^{1}/$_4$ cup butter, softened

Grilled Peaches with Meringues

Ripe peaches take on a fabulous scented fruitiness when grilled with brown sugar, and mini meringues are the perfect accompaniment. Serve with crème fraîche flavoured with a little grated orange rind. When buying peaches or nectarines, choose fruit with an attractive rosy bloom, avoiding any that have a green-tinged skin or feel hard. Nectarines have a smoother skin than peaches and are actually a type of peach native to China.

SERVES SIX

2 egg whites

115g/4oz/^{1}/$_2$ cup soft light brown sugar, reserving 5ml/1 tsp for the peaches

pinch of ground cinnamon

6 ripe peaches, or nectarines

1 Preheat the oven to 140°C/275°F/Gas 1. Line two large baking sheets with baking parchment.

2 Whisk the egg whites until they form stiff peaks. Gradually whisk in the sugar and ground cinnamon until the mixture is stiff and glossy. Pipe 18 very small meringues on to the trays and bake for 40 minutes. Leave in the oven to cool.

3 Meanwhile, halve and stone (pit) the peaches or nectarines, sprinkling each half with a little sugar as it is cut. Grill (broil) for 4–5 minutes, until just beginning to caramelize.

4 Arrange the grilled peaches on serving plates with the meringues and serve immediately.

COOK'S TIP *Use leftover egg whites to make these little cinnamon-flavoured meringues. The meringues can be stored in an airtight container for about 2 weeks. Serve them after dinner with coffee or with desserts in place of biscuits (cookies).*

Summer Berries in Sabayon Glaze

This luxurious combination of summer berries under a light and fluffy liqueur sauce is lightly grilled to form a crisp, caramelized topping. Fresh or frozen berries can be used in this dessert. If you use frozen berries, defrost them in a sieve over a bowl to allow the juices to drip. Stir a little juice into the fruit before dividing among the dishes.

SERVES FOUR

1 Arrange the mixed summer berries or soft fruit in four individual flameproof dishes. Preheat the grill (broiler).

2 Whisk the yolks in a large bowl with the sugar and liqueur or wine. Place over a pan of hot water and whisk constantly until the mixture is thick, fluffy and pale.

3 Pour equal quantities of the yolk mixture into each dish. Place under the grill for 1–2 minutes, until just turning brown. Add an extra splash of liqueur, if you like, and serve immediately.

450g/1lb/4 cups mixed summer berries, or soft fruit

4 egg yolks

50g/2oz/¼ cup vanilla sugar or caster (superfine) sugar

120ml/4fl oz/½ cup liqueur, such as Cointreau or Kirsch, or a white dessert wine

Baked Ricotta Cakes with Red Sauce

These honey-flavoured desserts take only minutes to make from a few ingredients. The fragrant fruity sauce provides a contrast of both colour and flavour. The red berry sauce can be made a day in advance and chilled until ready to use. Frozen fruit doesn't need extra water, as it usually yields its juice easily on thawing.

SERVES FOUR

250g/9oz/generous 1 cup ricotta cheese

2 egg whites, beaten

60ml/4 tbsp scented honey, plus extra to taste

450g/1lb/4 cups mixed fresh or frozen fruit, such as strawberries, raspberries, blackberries and cherries

1 Preheat the oven to 180°C/350°F/Gas 4. Place the ricotta cheese in a bowl and break it up with a wooden spoon. Add the beaten egg whites and honey, and mix thoroughly until smooth and well combined.

2 Lightly grease four ramekins. Spoon the ricotta mixture into the prepared ramekins and level the tops. Bake for 20 minutes, or until the ricotta cakes are risen and golden.

3 Meanwhile, make the fruit sauce. Reserve about one-quarter of the fruit for decoration. Place the rest of the fruit in a pan, with a little water if the fruit is fresh, and heat gently until softened. Leave to cool slightly and remove any stones (pits) if using cherries.

4 Press the fruit through a sieve, then taste and sweeten with honey if it is too tart. Serve the sauce, warm or cold, with the ricotta cakes. Decorate with the reserved berries.

Apricot and Ginger Gratin

Made with tangy fresh apricots, this quick and easy dessert has a comforting, baked cheesecake-like flavour. For an even easier version of this delicious gratin, use 400g/14oz canned apricots in juice. Use juice from the can to beat into the cream cheese.

SERVES FOUR

1 Put the apricots in a pan with the sugar. Pour in 75ml/5 tbsp water and heat until barely simmering. Cover and cook very gently for 8–10 minutes, until they are tender but still holding their shape.

2 Preheat the oven to 200°C/400°F/Gas 6. Drain the apricots, reserving the syrup, and place in a large dish or divide among four individual ovenproof dishes. Set aside 90ml/6 tbsp of the syrup and spoon the remainder over the fruit.

3 Beat the cream cheese until softened, then gradually beat in the reserved syrup until smooth. Spoon the cheese mixture over the apricots. Sprinkle the biscuit crumbs over the cream cheese and juice mixture. Bake for 10 minutes, until the crumb topping is beginning to darken and the filling has warmed through. Serve immediately.

500g/1¹/₄ lb apricots, halved and stoned (pitted)

75g/3oz/scant ¹/₂ cup caster (superfine) sugar

200g/7oz/scant 1 cup cream cheese

75g/3oz gingernut biscuits (gingersnaps), crushed to crumbs

Deep-fried Cherries

Fresh fruit coated with a simple batter and then deep-fried is delicious and makes an unusual dessert. These succulent cherries are perfect sprinkled with sugar and cinnamon and served with a classic vanilla ice cream.

SERVES FOUR TO SIX

450g/1lb ripe red cherries, on their stalks

225g/8oz batter mix

1 egg

FROM THE STORECUPBOARD

vegetable oil, for deep-frying

1 Gently wash the cherries and pat dry with kitchen paper. Tie the stalks together with fine string to form clusters of four or five cherries.

2 Make up the batter mix according to the instructions on the packet, beating in the egg. Pour the vegetable oil into a deep-fat fryer or large, heavy pan and heat to 190°C/375°F.

3 Working in batches, half-dip each cherry cluster into the batter and then carefully drop the cluster into the hot oil. Fry for 3–4 minutes, or until golden. Remove the deep-fried cherries with a wire-mesh skimmer or slotted spoon and drain on a wire rack placed over crumpled kitchen paper, and serve immediately.

Hot Blackberry and Apple Soufflé

The deliciously tart flavours of blackberry and apple complement each other perfectly to make a light, mouthwatering and surprisingly low-fat, hot dessert. Running a table knife around the inside edge of the soufflé dishes before baking helps the soufflés to rise evenly without sticking to the rim of the dish. Make this dish in early autumn, when there are plentiful supplies of blackberries.

MAKES SIX

1 Preheat the oven to 200°C/400°F/Gas 6. Put a baking sheet in the oven to heat. Cook the blackberries and apple in a pan for 10 minutes, or until the juice runs from the blackberries and the apple has pulped down well. Press through a sieve into a bowl. Stir in 50g/2oz/¼ cup caster sugar. Set aside to cool.

2 Put a spoonful of the fruit purée into each of six 150ml/¼ pint/⅔ cup greased and sugared individual soufflé dishes and smooth the surface. Set the dishes aside.

3 Whisk the egg whites in a large bowl until they form stiff peaks. Gradually whisk in the remaining caster sugar. Fold in the remaining fruit purée and spoon the flavoured meringue into the prepared dishes. Level the tops with a palette knife (metal spatula) and run a table knife around the edge of each dish.

4 Place the dishes on the hot baking sheet and bake for 10–15 minutes, until the soufflés have risen well and are lightly browned. Dust the tops with a little sugar and serve immediately.

350g/12oz/3 cups blackberries

1 large cooking apple, peeled and finely diced

3 egg whites

150g/5oz/³/₄ cup caster (superfine) sugar, plus extra caster or icing (confectioners') sugar for dusting

Peach Pie

Fruit pies do not have to be restricted to the chunky, deep-dish variety. Here, juicy, ripe peaches are encased in crisp pastry to make a glorious puffed dome – simple but delicious. For a really crispy crust, glaze the pie with beaten egg yolk thinned with a little water before sprinkling with sugar. Serve the pie with good quality vanilla ice cream or clotted cream.

SERVES EIGHT

1 Blanch the peaches for 30 seconds. Drain, refresh in cold water, then peel. Halve, stone (pit) and slice the peaches.

2 Melt the butter in a large frying pan. Add the peach slices, then sprinkle with 15ml/1 tbsp water and the sugar. Cook for about 4 minutes, shaking the pan frequently, or until the sugar has dissolved and the peaches are tender. Set the pan aside to cool.

3 Cut the pastry into two pieces, one slightly larger than the other. Roll out on a lightly floured surface and, using plates as a guide, cut a 30cm/12in round and a 28cm/11in round. Place the pastry rounds on baking sheets lined with baking parchment, cover with clear film (plastic wrap) and chill for 30 minutes.

4 Preheat the oven to 200°C/400°F/Gas 6. Remove the clear film from the pastry rounds. Spoon the peaches into the middle of the larger round and spread them out to within 5cm/2in of the edge. Place the smaller pastry round on top. Brush the edge of the larger pastry round with water, then fold this over the top round and press to seal. Twist the edges together.

5 Lightly brush the pastry with water and sprinkle evenly with a little sugar. Make five or six small crescent-shape slashes on the top of the pastry. Bake the pie for about 45 minutes and serve warm.

6 large, firm ripe peaches

75g/3oz/6 tbsp caster (superfine) sugar, plus extra for glazing

450g/1lb puff pastry

FROM THE STORECUPBOARD

40g/1½oz/ 3 tbsp butter

EXTRAS *Brandy, peach liqueur or peach schnapps would be superb with the peaches in this pie: add 45ml/3 tbsp instead of the water in step 2.*

Treacle Tart

The best chilled commercial shortcrust pastry makes light work of this old-fashioned favourite, with its sticky filling and twisted lattice topping. Smooth creamy custard is the classic accompaniment, but it is also delicious served with cream or ice cream. For a more textured filling, use wholemeal (whole-wheat) breadcrumbs or crushed cornflakes instead of the white breadcrumbs.

SERVES FOUR TO SIX

1 On a lightly floured surface, roll out three-quarters of the pastry to a thickness of 3mm/⅛in. Transfer to a 20cm/8in fluted flan tin (quiche pan) and trim off the overhang. Chill the pastry case (pie shell) for 20 minutes. Reserve the pastry trimmings.

2 Put a baking sheet in the oven and preheat to 200°C/400°F/ Gas 6. To make the filling, warm the syrup in a pan until it melts. Grate the lemon rind and squeeze the juice.

3 Remove the syrup from the heat and stir in the breadcrumbs and lemon rind. Leave to stand for 10 minutes, then add more crumbs if the mixture is too thin and moist. Stir in 30ml/2 tbsp of the lemon juice, then spread the mixture evenly in the pastry case.

4 Roll out the reserved pastry and cut into 10–12 thin strips. Twist the strips into spirals, then lay half of them on the filling. Arrange the remaining strips at right angles to form a lattice. Press the ends on to the rim.

5 Place the tart on the hot baking sheet and bake for 10 minutes. Lower the oven temperature to 190°C/375°F/Gas 5. Bake for 15 minutes more, until golden. Serve warm.

350g/12oz (unsweetened) shortcrust pastry

260g/9¹/₂oz/generous ³/₄ cup golden (light corn) syrup

1 lemon

75g/3oz/1¹/₂ cups fresh white breadcrumbs

Caramelized Upside-down Pear Pie

In this gloriously sticky dessert, which is almost like the French classic *tarte tatin*, the pastry is baked on top of the fruit, which gives it a crisp and flaky texture. When inverted, the pie looks wonderful. Look for good-quality chilled pastry that you can freeze for future use. Serve with whipped cream, ice cream or just plain for a gloriously sticky dessert.

SERVES EIGHT

1 Peel, quarter and core the pears. Toss with some of the sugar in a bowl.

2 Melt the butter in a 27cm/10½in heavy, ovenproof omelette pan. Add the remaining sugar. When it changes colour, arrange the pears in the pan.

3 Continue cooking, uncovered, for 20 minutes, or until the fruit has completely caramelized.

4 Leave the fruit to cool in the pan. Preheat the oven to 200°C/400°F/Gas 6. Meanwhile, on a lightly floured surface, roll out the pastry to a round that is slightly larger than the diameter of the pan. Lay the pastry on top of the pears and then carefully tuck it in around the edge.

5 Bake for 15 minutes, then lower the oven temperature to 180°C/350°F/Gas 4. Bake for a further 15 minutes, or until the pastry is golden.

6 Let the pie cool in the pan for a few minutes. To unmould, run a knife around the pan's edge, then, using oven gloves, invert a plate over the pan and quickly turn the two over together.

7 If any pears stick to the pan, remove them gently with a palette knife (metal spatula) and replace them on the pie. The pie is best served warm.

5–6 firm, ripe pears

175g/6oz/scant 1 cup caster (superfine) sugar

225g/8oz (unsweetened) shortcrust pastry

FROM THE STORECUPBOARD

115g/4oz/¹/₂ cup butter

VARIATIONS *To make caramelized upside-down apple pie, replace the pears with eight or nine firm, full-flavoured eating apples – Cox's Orange Pippins would be a good choice. You will need more apples than pears, as they shrink during cooking.*

Nectarines or peaches also work well, as does rhubarb. Rhubarb is tart, so you may need to add more sugar.

Blueberry and Almond Tart

This is a cheat's version of a sweet almond tart and the result is superb. Whisked egg whites and grated marzipan cook to form a light sponge under a tangy topping of contrasting blueberries. When whisking the egg whites for the filling, ensure all traces of yolk are removed – otherwise you won't be able to whisk them to their maximum volume.

SERVES SIX

250g/9oz (unsweetened) shortcrust pastry

175g/6oz/generous 1 cup white marzipan

4 large (US extra large) egg whites

130g/4¹/₂oz/ generous 1 cup blueberries

1 Preheat the oven to 200°C/400°F/Gas 6. Roll out the pastry and use to line a 23cm/9in round, loose-based flan tin (quiche pan). Line with greaseproof (waxed) paper and fill with baking beans, then bake for 15 minutes. Remove the beans and greaseproof paper and bake for a further 5 minutes. Reduce the oven temperature to 180°C/350°F/Gas 4.

2 Grate the marzipan. Whisk the egg whites until stiff. Sprinkle half the marzipan over them and fold in. Then fold in the rest.

3 Turn the mixture into the pastry case (pie shell) and spread it evenly. Sprinkle the blueberries over the top and bake for 20–25 minutes, until golden and just set. Leave to cool for 10 minutes before serving.

Baked Bananas with Ice Cream and Toffee Sauce

Bananas make one of the easiest of all desserts, just as welcome as a comforting winter treat as they are to follow a barbecue. For an extra sweet finishing touch, grate some plain (semisweet) chocolate on the bananas, over the sauce, just before serving. If baking on a barbecue, turn the bananas occasionally to ensure even cooking.

SERVES FOUR

4 large bananas

75g/3oz/scant ¹/₂ cup light muscovado (brown) sugar

75ml/5 tbsp double (heavy) cream

4 scoops good-quality vanilla ice cream

1 Preheat the oven to 180°C/350°F/Gas 4. Put the unpeeled bananas in an ovenproof dish and bake for 15–20 minutes, until the skins are very dark and the flesh feels soft when squeezed.

2 Meanwhile, heat the light muscovado sugar in a small, heavy pan with 75ml/5 tbsp water until dissolved. Bring to the boil and add the double cream. Cook for 5 minutes, until the sauce has thickened and is toffee coloured. Remove from the heat.

3 Transfer the baked bananas in their skins to serving plates and split them lengthways to reveal the flesh. Pour some of the sauce over the bananas and top with scoops of vanilla ice cream. Serve any remaining sauce separately.

Roast Peaches with Amaretto

This is an excellent dessert to serve in summer, when peaches are at their juiciest and most fragrant. The apricot and almond flavour of the amaretto liqueur subtly enhances the sweet, fruity taste of ripe peaches. Serve with a spoonful of crème fraîche or whipped cream.

SERVES FOUR

1 Preheat the oven 190°C/375°F/Gas 5. Cut the peaches in half and prise out the stones (pits) with the point of the knife.

2 Place the peaches cut side up in a roasting pan. In a small bowl, mix the amaretto liqueur with the honey, and drizzle over the halved peaches, covering them evenly.

3 Bake the peaches for 20–25 minutes, or until tender. Place two peach halves on each serving plate and drizzle with the pan juices. Serve immediately.

4 ripe peaches

45ml/3 tbsp Amaretto di Sarone liqueur

45ml/3 tbsp clear honey

COOK'S TIP *You can cook these peaches over a barbecue. Place them on sheets of foil, drizzle over liqueur, then scrunch the foil around them to seal. Cook for 15–20 minutes.*

Passion Fruit Soufflés

These simplified soufflés are so easy and work beautifully. The passion fruit adds a tropical note to a favourite classic. The soufflés look very pretty sprinkled with icing (confectioners') sugar.

SERVES FOUR

200ml/7fl oz/scant 1 cup ready-made fresh custard

3 passion fruits, halved

2 egg whites

FROM THE STORECUPBOARD

knob (pat) of softened butter, for greasing

1 Preheat the oven to 200°C/400°F/Gas 6. Grease four 200ml/7fl oz/scant 1 cup ramekin dishes with the butter.

2 Pour the custard into a large mixing bowl. Scrape out the seeds and juice from the halved passion fruit and stir into the custard until well combined.

3 Whisk the egg whites until stiff, and fold a quarter of them into the custard. Carefully fold in the remaining egg whites, then spoon the mixture into the ramekin dishes.

4 Place the dishes on a baking sheet and bake for 8–10 minutes, or until the soufflés are well risen. Serve immediately.

Zabaglione

Light as air and wonderfully heady, this warm, wine egg custard is a much-loved Italian dessert. Traditionally made with Sicilian Marsala, other fortified wines such as Madeira or sweet sherry can be used.

SERVES FOUR

1 Place the egg yolks and sugar in a large heatproof bowl and whisk with an electric beater until the mixture is pale and thick.

2 Gradually add the Marsala, Madeira or sweet sherry to the egg mixture, 15ml/1 tbsp at a time, whisking well after each addition.

3 Place the bowl over a pan of gently simmering water and whisk for 5–7 minutes, until thick: when the beaters are lifted, they should leave a thick trail on the surface of the mixture. Do not be tempted to give up when beating the mixture, as the zabaglione will be too runny and will be likely to separate if it is underbeaten.

4 Pour into four warmed, stemmed glasses and serve immediately, with amaretti for dipping.

4 egg yolks

50g/2oz/¹/₄ cup caster (superfine) sugar

60ml/4 tbsp Marsala, Madeira or sweet sherry

amaretti biscuits, to serve

EXTRAS *Marinate chopped strawberries in a little extra Marsala, Madeira or sweet sherry for an hour or so. Sweeten with sugar, if you like, and spoon into glasses before you add the zabaglione.*

Grilled Pineapple and Rum Cream

The sweeter and juicier the pineapple, the more delicious the pan juices will be in this tropical dessert. To test whether the pineapple is ripe, gently pull the green spiky leaves at the top of the fruit. If they come away easily, the fruit is ripe and ready to use.

SERVES FOUR

1 Heat the butter in a frying pan and add the pineapple. Cook over a moderate to high heat until the pineapple is starting to turn golden. Add the rum and allow to bubble for 1–2 minutes. Remove the pan from the heat and set aside to cool completely.

2 Whip the cream until it is soft but not stiff. Fold the pineapple and rum mixture evenly through the cream, then divide it between four glasses and serve.

115g/4oz pineapple, roughly chopped

45ml/3 tbsp dark rum

300ml/^{1}/$_2$ pint/1^1/$_4$ cups double (heavy) cream

FROM THE STORECUPBOARD

25g/1oz/2 tbsp butter

Warm Chocolate Zabaglione

Once you've tasted this sensuous dessert, you'll never regard cocoa in quite the same way again. The zabaglione can be dusted with icing (confectioners') sugar instead of extra cocoa, if you like. Serve with mini amaretti or other small, crisp biscuits (cookies).

SERVES SIX

6 egg yolks

150g/5oz/³/₄ cup caster (superfine) sugar

45ml/3 tbsp (unsweetened) cocoa powder, plus extra for dusting

200ml/7fl oz/scant 1 cup Marsala

1 Prepare a pan of simmering water and a heatproof bowl to fit on top. Place the egg yolks and sugar in the bowl and whisk, off the heat, until the mixture is pale and all the sugar has dissolved.

2 Add the cocoa and Marsala, then place the bowl over the simmering water. Beat with a hand-held electric mixer until the mixture is smooth, thick and foamy.

3 Pour quickly into tall glasses, dust lightly with cocoa and serve immediately, with amaretti or other dessert biscuits, if you like.

Hot Chocolate Rum Soufflés

Light as air, melt-in-the-mouth soufflés are always impressive, yet they are often based on the simplest store-cupboard ingredients. Serve them as soon as they are cooked for a fantastic finale to a special dinner party. For an extra indulgent touch, serve the soufflés with whipped cream flavoured with dark rum and grated orange rind.

SERVES SIX

50g/2oz/½ cup (unsweetened) cocoa powder

65g/2½oz/5 tbsp caster (superfine) sugar, plus extra caster or icing (confectioners') sugar for dusting

30ml/2 tbsp dark rum

6 egg whites

1 Preheat the oven to 190°C/375°F/Gas 3. Place a baking sheet in the oven to heat up.

2 Mix 15ml/1 tbsp of the cocoa with 15ml/1 tbsp of the sugar in a bowl. Grease six 250ml/8fl oz/1 cup ramekins. Pour the cocoa and sugar mixture into each of the dishes in turn, rotating them so that they are evenly coated.

3 Mix the remaining cocoa powder with the dark rum.

4 Whisk the egg whites in a clean, grease-free bowl until they form stiff peaks. Whisk in the remaining sugar. Stir a generous spoonful of the whites into the cocoa mixture to lighten it, then fold in the remaining whites.

5 Divide the mixture among the dishes. Place on the hot baking sheet, and bake for 13–15 minutes, or until well risen. Dust with caster or icing sugar before serving.

COOK'S TIP *When serving the soufflés at the end of a dinner party, prepare them just before the meal is served. Put them in the oven when the main course is finished and serve steaming hot.*

Cold Desserts

BECAUSE THEY CAN BE MADE IN ADVANCE, COLD DESSERTS
ARE THE PERFECT CHOICE FOR ENTERTAINING. ALL THE
RECIPES IN THIS CHAPTER HAVE AN ELEGANT SIMPLICITY
THAT GUARANTEES SUCCESS WITH EVEN THE MOST
SOPHISTICATED DINNER GUESTS. HOWEVER, THESE
DESSERTS ARE SO EASY TO PREPARE THAT YOU WILL WANT
TO SERVE THEM FOR EVERYDAY MEALS TOO.

Tropical Scented Fruit Salad

With its special colour and exotic flavour, this fresh fruit salad is perfect after a rich, heavy meal. For fabulous flavour and colour, try using three small blood oranges and three ordinary oranges. Other fruit that can be added include pears, kiwi fruit and bananas. Serve the fruit salad with whipping cream flavoured with 15g/½oz finely chopped drained preserved stem ginger.

SERVES FOUR TO SIX

1 Put the hulled and halved strawberries and peeled and segmented oranges into a serving bowl. Halve the passion fruit and using a teaspoon scoop the flesh into the bowl.

2 Pour the wine over the fruit and toss gently. Cover and chill in the refrigerator until ready to serve.

350–400g/12–14oz/
3–3¹⁄₂ cups
strawberries, hulled
and halved

6 oranges, peeled
and segmented

1–2 passion fruit

120ml/4fl oz/¹⁄₂ cup
medium dry or
sweet white wine

Juniper-scented Pears in Red Wine

More often used in savoury dishes than sweet, juniper berries have a dark blue, almost black colour with a distinct gin-like flavour. In this fruity winter dessert crushed juniper berries give the classic partnership of pears and red wine a slightly aromatic flavour. These pears are particularly good sprinkled with toasted almonds and whipped cream.

SERVES FOUR

1 Lightly crush the juniper berries using a pestle and mortar or with the end of a rolling pin. Put the berries in a pan with the sugar and wine and heat gently until the sugar dissolves.

2 Meanwhile, peel the pears, leaving them whole. Add them to the wine and heat until just simmering. Cover the pan and cook gently for about 25 minutes, until the pears are tender. Turn the pears once or twice to make sure they cook evenly.

3 Use a slotted spoon to remove the pears. Boil the syrup hard for a few minutes, until it is slightly reduced and thickened. If serving the pears hot, reheat them gently in the syrup, otherwise arrange them in a serving dish and spoon the syrup over.

30ml/2 tbsp juniper berries

50g/2oz/¼ cup caster (superfine) sugar

600ml/1 pint/2½ cups red wine

4 large or 8 small firm pears, stalks intact

Oranges in Syrup

This recipe works well with most citrus fruits – for example, try pink grapefruit or sweet, perfumed clementines, which have been peeled but left whole. Serve the oranges with 300ml/½ pint/1¼ cups whipped cream flavoured with 5ml/1 tsp ground cinnamon, or 5ml/1 tsp ground nutmeg or with Greek (US strained plain) yogurt.

SERVES SIX

6 medium oranges

200g/7oz/1 cup sugar

100ml/3¹/₂fl oz/ scant ¹/₂ cup fresh strong brewed coffee

50g/2oz/¹/₂ cup pistachio nuts, chopped (optional)

1 Finely pare, shred and reserve the rind from one orange. Peel the remaining oranges. Cut each one crossways into slices, then re-form them, with a cocktail stick (toothpick) through the centre.

2 Put the sugar in a heavy pan and add 50ml/2fl oz/¼ cup water. Heat gently until the sugar dissolves, then bring to the boil and cook until the syrup turns pale gold.

3 Remove from the heat and carefully pour 100ml/3½fl oz/ scant ½ cup freshly boiling water into the pan. Return to the heat until the syrup has dissolved in the water. Stir in the coffee.

4 Add the oranges and the rind to the coffee syrup. Simmer for 15–20 minutes, turning the oranges once during cooking. Leave to cool, then chill. Serve sprinkled with pistachio nuts, if using.

COOK'S TIP *Choose a pan in which the oranges will just fit in a single layer – use a deep frying pan if you don't have a pan that is large enough.*

Fresh Fig Compote

A vanilla and coffee syrup brings out the wonderful flavour of figs – serve Greek (US strained plain) yogurt or vanilla ice cream with the poached fruit. A good selection of different honey is available – its aroma and flavour will be subtly scented by the plants surrounding the hives. Orange blossom honey works particularly well in this recipe, although any clear variety is suitable.

SERVES FOUR TO SIX

400ml/14fl oz/ 1²/₃ cups fresh brewed coffee

115g/4oz/¹/₂ cup clear honey

1 vanilla pod (bean)

12 slightly under-ripe fresh figs

1 Choose a frying pan with a lid, large enough to hold the figs in a single layer. Pour in the coffee and add the honey.

2 Split the vanilla pod lengthways and scrape the seeds into the pan. Add the vanilla pod, then bring to a rapid boil and cook until reduced to about 175ml/6fl oz/¾ cup.

3 Wash the figs and pierce the skins several times with a sharp skewer. Cut in half and add to the syrup. Reduce the heat, cover and simmer for 5 minutes. Remove the figs from the syrup with a slotted spoon and set aside to cool.

4 Strain the syrup over the figs. Allow to stand at room temperature for 1 hour before serving.

COOK'S TIP *Figs come in three main varieties – red, white and black – and all three are suitable for cooking. They are sweet and succulent, and complement the stronger, more pervasive flavours of coffee and vanilla very well.*

Pistachio and Rose Water Oranges

This light and citrusy dessert is perfect to serve after a heavy main course, such as a hearty meat stew or a leg of roast lamb. Combining three favourite Middle Eastern ingredients, it is delightfully fragrant and refreshing. If you don't have pistachio nuts, use hazelnuts instead.

SERVES FOUR

1 Slice the top and bottom off one of the oranges to expose the flesh. Using a small serrated knife, slice down between the pith and the flesh, working round the orange, to remove all the peel and pith. Slice the orange into six rounds, reserving any juice. Repeat with the remaining oranges.

2 Arrange the orange rounds on a serving dish. Mix the reserved juice with the rose water and drizzle over the oranges. Cover the dish with clear film (plastic wrap) and chill for about 30 minutes. Sprinkle the chopped pistachio nuts over the oranges to serve.

4 large oranges

30ml/2 tbsp rose water

30ml/2 tbsp shelled pistachio nuts, roughly chopped

COOK'S TIP

Rose-scented sugar is delicious sprinkled over fresh fruit salads. Wash and thoroughly dry a handful of rose petals and place in a sealed container filled with caster (superfine) sugar for 2–3 days. Remove the petals before using the sugar.

Lychee and Elderflower Sorbet

The flavour of elderflowers is famous for bringing out the essence of gooseberries, but what is less well known is how wonderfully it complements lychees.

SERVES FOUR

175g/6oz/³/₄ cup caster sugar

400ml/14fl oz/1²/₃ cups water

500g/1¹/₄lb fresh lychees, peeled and stoned

15ml/1 tbsp elderflower cordial

dessert biscuits, to serve

1 Place the sugar and water in a saucepan and heat gently until the sugar has dissolved. Increase the heat and boil for 5 minutes, then add the lychees. Lower the heat and simmer for 7 minutes. Remove from the heat and allow to cool.

2 Purée the fruit and syrup in a blender or food processor. Place a sieve over a bowl and pour the purée into it. Press through as much of the purée as possible with a spoon.

3 Stir the elderflower cordial into the strained purée, then pour the mixture into a freezerproof container. Freeze for 2 hours, until ice crystals start to form around the edges.

4 Remove the sorbet from the freezer and process briefly in a food processor or blender to break up the crystals. Repeat this process twice more, then freeze until firm. Transfer to the fridge for 10 minutes to soften slightly before serving in scoops, with biscuits.

COOK'S TIP
Switch the freezer to the coldest setting before making the sorbet – the faster the mixture freezes, the smaller the ice crystals that form and the better the final texture will be.

Summer Fruit Brioche

Scooped-out, individual brioches make perfect containers for the fruity filling in this stylish, but simple dessert. If small brioches are not available, serve the fruit on slices cut from a large brioche. Any summer fruits can be used in this dessert – try raspberries, sliced peaches, nectarines, apricots, or pitted cherries. Serve with single (light) cream poured over.

SERVES FOUR

1 Preheat the grill (broiler). Slice the tops off the brioches and use a teaspoon to scoop out their centres, leaving a 1 cm/½in thick case. Lightly toast them, turning once and watching them carefully, as they will brown very quickly.

2 Put the strawberries in a pan with the sugar and add 60ml/4 tbsp water. Heat very gently for about 1 minute, until the strawberries are softened but still keep their shape. Remove the pan from the heat, stir in the raspberries and leave to cool.

3 Place the brioches on plates and pile the fruit mixture into them. Add plenty of juice to saturate the brioches and allow it to flood the plates. Place any extra fruit on the plates.

4 individual brioches

**300g/11oz/
2½ cups small ripe
strawberries, halved**

**30ml/2 tbsp caster
(superfine) sugar**

**115g/4oz/²/₃ cup
raspberries**

Rhubarb and Ginger Jellies

Made with bright pink, young rhubarb, these softly set jellies get the taste buds tingling. They are spiced with plenty of fresh ginger, which gives just a hint of zesty warmth. Pour the jelly into pretty glasses and serve it as it is or top it with spoonfuls of lightly whipped cream.

SERVES FIVE TO SIX

1kg/2¼lb young rhubarb

200g/7oz/1 cup caster (superfine) sugar

50g/2oz fresh root ginger, finely chopped

15ml/1 tbsp powdered gelatine

1 Cut the rhubarb into 2cm/¾in chunks and place in a pan with the sugar and ginger. Pour in 450ml/¾ pint/scant 2 cups water and bring to the boil. Reduce the heat, cover and simmer gently for 10 minutes, until the rhubarb is very soft and pulpy.

2 Meanwhile, sprinkle the gelatine over 30ml/2 tbsp cold water in a small heatproof bowl. Leave to stand, without stirring, for 5 minutes, until the gelatine has become sponge-like in texture. Set the bowl over a small pan of hot water and simmer, stirring occasionally, until the gelatine has dissolved completely into a clear liquid. Remove from the heat.

3 Strain the cooked rhubarb through a fine sieve into a bowl. Stir in the dissolved gelatine until thoroughly mixed. Leave to cool slightly before pouring into serving glasses. Chill for at least 4 hours or overnight, until set.

Papayas in Jasmine Flower Syrup

The fragrant syrup can be prepared in advance, using fresh jasmine flowers from a house plant or the garden. You can also use fresh flowers as a garnish. The syrup tastes fabulous with papayas, but it is also good with all sorts of desserts. Try it with ice cream or spooned over lychees or mangoes.

SERVES FOUR

45ml/3 tbsp palm sugar or light muscovado (brown) sugar

20–30 jasmine flowers

2 ripe papayas

juice of 1 lime

1 Place 105ml/7 tbsp water in a small pan and add the sugar. Heat gently, stirring occasionally, until the sugar has dissolved, then simmer, without stirring, over a low heat for 4 minutes.

2 Pour into a bowl, leave to cool slightly, then add the jasmine flowers. Leave to steep for at least 20 minutes.

3 Peel the papayas and slice in half lengthways. Scoop out and discard the seeds. Place the papayas on serving plates and squeeze over the lime.

4 Strain the syrup into a clean bowl, discarding the flowers. Spoon the syrup over the papayas. If you like, decorate with a few fresh jasmine flowers.

Mango and Lime Fool

Canned mangoes are used here for convenience, but this zesty, tropical fruit fool tastes even better if made with fresh ones. Choose a variety with a good flavour, such as the fragrant Alphonso mango.

SERVES FOUR

400g/14oz can sliced mango, plus extra to garnish (optional)

grated rind of 1 lime, plus juice of $^1/_2$ lime

150ml/$^1/_4$ pint/$^2/_3$ cup double (heavy) cream

90ml/6 tbsp Greek (US strained plain) yogurt

1 Drain the canned mango slices and put them in a food processor, then add the grated lime rind and lime juice. Process until the mixture forms a smooth purée.

2 Alternatively, place the mango slices in a bowl and mash with a potato masher, then press through a sieve (strainer) into a bowl with the back of a wooden spoon. Stir in the lime rind and juice.

3 Pour the cream into a bowl and add the yogurt. Whisk until the mixture is thick and then quickly whisk in the mango mixture.

4 Spoon the fool into four tall cups or glasses and chill for at least 1 hour. Just before serving, decorate each glass with fresh mango slices, if you like.

Tangy Raspberry and Lemon Tartlets

You can make the pastry cases for these little tartlets in advance and store them in an airtight container until ready to serve.

SERVES FOUR

1 Preheat the oven to 190°C/375°F/Gas 5. Roll out the pastry and use to line four 9cm/3½in tartlet tins (muffin pans). Line each tin with a circle of baking parchment and fill with baking beans or uncooked rice.

2 Bake for 15–20 minutes, or until golden and cooked through. Remove the baking beans or rice and paper and take the pastry cases out of the tins. Leave to cool completely on a wire rack.

3 Set aside 12 raspberries for decoration and fold the remaining ones into the lemon curd. Spoon the mixture into the pastry cases and top with the reserved raspberries. Serve immediately.

175g/6oz ready-made short-crust pastry, thawed if frozen

120ml/8 tbsp good quality lemon curd

115g/4oz/²⁄₃ cup fresh raspberries

3 filo pastry sheets, thawed if frozen

2 small ripe mangoes

115g/4oz/²/₃ raspberries, thawed if frozen

FROM THE STORECUPBOARD

50g/2oz/¹/₄ cup butter, melted

Crispy Mango Stacks with Raspberry Coulis

This makes a very healthy yet stunning dessert – it is low in fat and contains no added sugar. However, if the raspberries are a little sharp, you may prefer to add a pinch of sugar to the purée.

SERVES FOUR

1 Preheat the oven to 200°C/400°F/Gas 6. Lay the filo sheets on a clean work surface and cut out four 10cm/4in rounds from each. Brush each round with the melted butter and lay the rounds on two baking sheets. Bake for 5 minutes, or until crisp and golden. Place on wire racks to cool.

2 Peel the mangoes, remove the stones and cut the flesh into thin slices. Put the raspberries in a food processor with 45ml/3 tbsp water and process to a purée. Place a pastry round on each of four serving plates. Top with a quarter of the mango and drizzle with a little of the raspberry purée. Repeat until all the ingredients have been used, finishing with a layer of mango and a drizzle of raspberry purée.

Rhubarb and Ginger Trifles

Choose a good quality jar of rhubarb compote for this recipe; try to find one with large, chunky pieces of fruit.

SERVES FOUR

12 gingernut biscuits (gingersnaps)

50ml/2fl oz/¹/₄ cup rhubarb compote

450ml/³/₄ pint/scant 2 cups extra thick double (heavy) cream

1 Put the ginger biscuits in a plastic bag and seal. Bash the biscuits with a rolling pin until roughly crushed.

2 Set aside two tablespoons of crushed biscuits and divide the rest among four glasses.

3 Spoon the rhubarb compote on top of the crushed biscuits, then top with the cream. Place in the refrigerator and chill for about 30 minutes.

4 To serve, sprinkle the reserved crushed biscuits over the trifles and serve immediately.

Strawberry Cream Shortbreads

These pretty desserts are always popular. Serve them as soon as they are ready because the shortbread cookies will lose their lovely crisp texture if left to stand.

SERVES THREE

150g/5oz strawberries

450ml/³/₄ pint/scant 2 cups double (heavy) cream

6 round shortbread biscuits (cookies)

VARIATION

You can use any other berry you like for this dessert – try raspberries or blueberries. Two ripe, peeled peaches will also give great results.

1 Reserve three strawberries for decoration. Hull the remaining strawberries and cut them in half.

2 Put the halved strawberries in a bowl and gently crush using the back of a fork. (Only crush the berries lightly; they should not be reduced to a purée.)

3 Put the cream in a large, clean bowl and whip to form soft peaks. Add the crushed strawberries and gently fold in to combine. (Do not overmix.)

4 Halve the reserved strawberries, then spoon the strawberry and cream mixture on top of the shortbread cookies. Decorate each one with half a strawberry and serve immediately.

Blackberries in Port

Pour this rich fruit compote over ice cream or serve it with a spoonful of clotted cream to create an attractive, rich dessert. It's unbelievably quick and easy to make and is the perfect end to a dinner party. Blackberries can be found growing wild on hedgerows in late summer and there's nothing better than picking them yourself for this lovely dessert.

SERVES FOUR

300ml/^{1}/$_2$ pint/1^1/$_4$ cups ruby port

75g/3oz/6 tbsp caster (superfine) sugar

450g/1lb/4 cups blackberries

1 Pour the port into a pan and add the sugar and 150ml/^{1}/$_4$ pint/^{2}/$_3$ cup water. Stir over a gentle heat with a wooden spoon until the sugar has dissolved.

2 Remove the pan from the heat and stir in the blackberries. Set aside to cool, then pour into a bowl and cover with clear film (plastic wrap). Chill until ready to serve.

Baby Summer Puddings

This classic English dessert is always a favourite, and serving it in individual portions with spoonfuls of clotted cream makes it extra special. White bread that is more than a day old actually works better than fresh bread. Slices of brioche make a wonderful alternative to white bread.

SERVES FOUR

6 white bread slices, crusts removed

450g/1lb/4 cups summer fruits

75g/3oz/6 tbsp caster (superfine) sugar

COOK'S TIP *You can enjoy this lovely dessert even in the winter. Use frozen summer fruits, which are available in supermarkets all year round. Simply thaw the fruits, then cook as if using fresh fruits.*

1 Cut out four rounds from the bread slices, large enough to fit in the bottom of four 175ml/6fl oz/^{3}/$_4$ cup dariole moulds.

2 Line the moulds with clear film (plastic wrap) and place a bread round in the base of each mould. Reserve two slices of bread and cut the remaining bread into slices and use to line the sides of the moulds, pressing to fit.

3 Put the summer fruits in a pan with the sugar and heat gently until the sugar has dissolved. Bring to the boil, then simmer gently for 2–3 minutes. Remove from the heat and leave to cool slightly, then spoon into the moulds.

4 Cut four rounds out of the remaining slices of bread to fit the top of the dariole moulds. Place the bread rounds on the fruit and push down to fit. Cover each dariole mould loosely with clear film and place a small weight on top.

5 Chill the desserts overnight, then turn out on to serving plates. Remove the clear film lining and serve immediately.

Raspberry Brûlée

Cracking through the caramelized sugary top of a crème brûlée to reveal the creamy custard underneath is always so satisfying. These ones have the added bonus of a deliciously rich, fruity custard packed with crushed raspberries.

SERVES FOUR

1 Tip the raspberries into a large bowl and crush with a fork. Add the custard and gently fold in until combined.

2 Divide the mixture between four 120ml/4fl oz/^{1}/$_2$ cup ramekin dishes. Cover each one with clear film (plastic wrap) and chill in the refrigerator for 2–3 hours.

3 Preheat the grill (broiler) to high. Remove the clear film from the ramekin dishes and place them on a baking sheet. Sprinkle the sugar over the custards and grill (broil) for 3–4 minutes, or until the sugar has caramelized.

4 Remove the custards from the grill and set aside for a few minutes to allow the sugar to harden, then serve.

115g/4oz fresh raspberries

300ml/^{1}/$_2$ pint/1^1/$_4$ cups ready-made fresh custard

75g/3oz caster (superfine) sugar

COOK'S TIP *You can now buy little gas blow torches for use in the kitchen. They make quick work of caramelizing the sugar on top of the brûlées – and are also fun to use!*

Portuguese Custard Tarts

Called *pastéis de nata* in Portugal, these tarts are traditionally served with a small strong coffee as a sweet breakfast dish, but they are equally delicious served as a pastry or dessert.

MAKES TWELVE

1 Preheat the oven to 200°C/400°F/Gas 6. Roll out the pastry and cut out twelve 13cm/5in rounds. Line a 12-hole muffin tin (pan) with the pastry rounds. Line each pastry round with a circle of baking parchment and some baking beans or uncooked rice.

2 Bake the tarts for 10–15 minutes, or until the pastry is cooked through and golden. Remove the paper and baking beans or rice and set aside to cool.

3 Spoon the custard into the pastry cases and dust with the icing sugar. Place the tarts under a preheated hot grill (broiler) and cook until the sugar caramelizes. Remove from the heat and leave to cool before serving.

225g/8oz ready-made puff pastry, thawed if frozen

175ml/6fl oz/³⁄₄ cup fresh ready-made custard

30ml/2 tbsp icing (confectioners') sugar

Baked Custard with Burnt Sugar

This delicious egg custard or crème brûlée is a rich indulgent dessert that can be prepared well in advance. You can buy vanilla sugar or make your own by placing a split vanilla pod (bean) in a jar of caster (superfine) sugar – the sugar will be ready to use after a couple of days.

SERVES SIX

1 Preheat the oven to 150°C/300°F/Gas 2. Place six 120ml/4fl oz/½ cup ramekins in a roasting pan or ovenproof dish and set aside while you prepare the vanilla custard.

2 Heat the double cream in a heavy pan over a gentle heat until it is very hot, but not boiling.

3 In a bowl, whisk the egg yolks and vanilla sugar until well blended. Whisk in the hot cream and strain into a large jug (pitcher). Divide the custard equally among the ramekins.

4 Pour enough boiling water into the roasting pan to come about halfway up the sides of the ramekins. Cover the pan with foil and bake for about 30 minutes, until the custards are just set. (Push the point of a knife into the centre of one; if it comes out clean, the custards are cooked.) Remove from the pan, cool, then chill.

5 Preheat the grill (broiler). Sprinkle the sugar evenly over the surface of the custards and grill (broil) for 30–60 seconds, until the sugar melts and caramelizes, taking care not to let it burn. Place in the refrigerator to chill and set the crust.

1 litre/1³⁄₄ pints/4 cups double (heavy) cream

6 egg yolks

90g/3¹⁄₂oz/¹⁄₂ cup vanilla sugar

75g/3oz/¹⁄₃ cup soft light brown sugar

COOK'S TIP
It is best to make the custards the day before you wish to eat them and chill overnight, so that they are really cold and firm.

Passion Fruit Creams

These delicately perfumed creams are light with a fresh flavour from the passion fruit. Ripe passion fruit should look purple and wrinkled – choose fruit that are heavy for their size. When halved, the fragrant, sweet juicy flesh with small edible black seeds are revealed. These creams can be decorated with mint or geranium leaves and served with cream.

SERVES FIVE TO SIX

1 Preheat the oven to 180°C/350°F/Gas 4. Line the bases of six 120ml/4fl oz/½ cup ramekins with rounds of baking parchment and place them in a roasting pan.

2 Heat the cream to just below boiling point, then remove the pan from the heat. Sieve the flesh of four passion fruits and beat together with the sugar and eggs. Whisk in the hot cream and then ladle into the ramekins.

3 Half fill the roasting pan with boiling water. Bake the creams for 25–30 minutes, or until set, then leave to cool before chilling.

4 Run a knife around the insides of the ramekins, then invert them on to serving plates, tapping the bases firmly. Carefully peel off the baking parchment and chill in the refrigerator until ready to serve. Spoon on a little passion fruit flesh just before serving.

600ml/1 pint/2¹/₂ cups double (heavy) cream, or a mixture of single (light) and double (heavy) cream

6 passion fruits

30–45ml/2–3 tbsp vanilla sugar

5 eggs

Baked Caramel Custard

Many countries have their own version of this classic dessert. Known as *crème caramel* in France and *flan* in Spain, this chilled baked custard has a rich caramel flavour. By cooking the custard in a *bain-marie* or as here in a roasting pan with water, the mixture is cooked gently and the eggs are prevented from becoming tough or curdling. It is delicious served with fresh strawberries and thick cream.

SERVES SIX TO EIGHT

1 Put 175g/6oz/generous ¾ cup of the sugar in a small heavy pan with just enough water to moisten the sugar. Bring to the boil over a high heat, swirling the pan until the sugar has dissolved completely. Boil for about 5 minutes, without stirring, until the syrup turns a rich, dark caramel colour.

2 Working quickly, pour the caramel into a 1 litre/1¾ pint/4 cup soufflé dish. Holding the dish with oven gloves, carefully swirl it to coat the base and sides with the hot caramel mixture. Set aside to cool.

3 Preheat the oven to 160°C/325°F/Gas 3. In a bowl, whisk the eggs and egg yolks with the remaining sugar for 2–3 minutes, until smooth and creamy.

4 Heat the cream in a heavy pan until hot, but not boiling. Whisk the hot cream into the egg mixture and carefully strain the mixture into the caramel-lined dish. Cover tightly with foil.

5 Place the dish in a roasting pan and pour in just enough boiling water to come halfway up the side of the dish. Bake the custard for 40–45 minutes, until just set. To test whether the custard is set, insert a knife about 5cm/2in from the edge; if the blade comes out clean, the custard should be ready.

6 Remove the soufflé dish from the roasting pan and leave to cool for at least 30 minutes, then place in the refrigerator and chill overnight.

7 To turn out, carefully run a sharp knife around the edge of the dish to loosen the custard. Cover the dish with a serving plate and, holding them both together very tightly, invert the dish and plate, allowing the custard to drop down on to the plate.

8 Gently lift one edge of the dish, allowing the caramel to run down over the sides and on to the plate, then carefully lift off the dish. Serve immediately.

250g/9oz/1¼ cups vanilla sugar

5 large (US extra large) eggs, plus 2 extra yolks

450ml/¾ pint/scant 2 cups double (heavy) cream

VARIATION *For a special occasion, make individual baked custards in ramekin dishes. Coat six to eight ramekins with the caramel and divide the custard mixture among them. Bake, in a roasting pan of water, for 25–30 minutes or until set. Thinly slice the strawberries and marinate them in a little sugar and a liqueur or dessert wine, such as Amaretto or Muscat wine.*

Chocolate Banana Fools

This de luxe version of banana custard looks great served in glasses. It can be made a few hours in advance and chilled until ready to serve.

SERVES FOUR

1 Put the chocolate in a heatproof bowl and melt in the microwave on high power for 1–2 minutes. Stir, then set aside to cool. (Alternatively, put the chocolate in a heatproof bowl and place it over a pan of gently simmering water and leave until melted, stirring frequently.)

115g/4oz plain (semisweet) chocolate, chopped

300ml/¹/₂ pint/1¹/₄ cups fresh custard

2 bananas

2 Pour the custard into a bowl and gently fold in the melted chocolate to make a rippled effect.

3 Peel and slice the bananas and stir these into the chocolate and custard mixture. Spoon into four glasses and chill for 30 minutes–1 hour before serving.

Lemon Posset

This simple creamy dessert has distant origins, dating back to the Middle Ages. It is perfect for warm summer evenings and is particularly good served with crisp shortbread cookies.

SERVES FOUR

1 Gently heat the cream and sugar together until the sugar has dissolved, then bring to the boil, stirring constantly. Add the lemon juice and rind and stir until the mixture thickens.

2 Pour the mixture into four heatproof serving glasses and chill until just set, then serve.

600ml/1 pint/2¹/₂ cups double (heavy) cream

175g/6oz/scant 1 cup caster (superfine) sugar

grated rind and juice of 2 unwaxed lemons

COOK'S TIP *To make shortbread cookies, put 225g/8oz/1 cup chilled butter in a food processor and add 115g/4oz/²/₃ cup caster (superfine) sugar, 225g/8oz/2 cups plain (all-purpose) flour and 115g/4oz/²/₃ cup ground rice. Process to form a dough, then shape into a log 5cm/2in wide and wrap in clear film (plastic wrap). Chill for 30 minutes. Preheat the oven to 190°C/375°F/Gas 5. Cut the dough into thin slices, and bake for 15–20 minutes.*

Chilled Chocolate and Espresso Mousse

Heady, aromatic espresso coffee adds a distinctive flavour to this smooth, rich mousse. For a special occasion, serve the mousse in stylish chocolate cups decorated with sprigs of mint, with mascarpone or clotted cream on the side.

SERVES FOUR

450g/1lb plain (semisweet) chocolate

45ml/3 tbsp freshly brewed espresso

4 eggs, separated

FROM THE STORECUPBOARD

25g/1oz/2 tbsp unsalted (sweet) butter

1 For each chocolate cup, cut a double thickness 15cm/6in square of foil. Mould it around a small orange, leaving the edges and corners loose to make a cup shape. Remove the orange and press the bottom of the foil case gently on a surface to make a flat base. Repeat to make four foil cups.

2 Break half the chocolate into small pieces and place in a bowl set over a pan of very hot water. Stir occasionally until the chocolate has completely melted.

3 Spoon the chocolate into the foil cups, spreading it up the sides with the back of a spoon to give a ragged edge. Chill for 30 minutes in the refrigerator, or until set hard. Gently peel away the foil, starting at the top edge.

4 To make the chocolate mousse, put the remaining chocolate and espresso into a bowl set over a pan of hot water and melt as before, until smooth and liquid. Stir in the butter, a little at a time. Remove the pan from the heat and then stir in the egg yolks.

5 Whisk the egg whites in a bowl until stiff, but not dry, then fold them into the chocolate mixture. Pour into a bowl and chill for at least 3 hours, or until the mousse is set. Scoop the chilled mousse into the chocolate cups just before serving.

Meringue Pyramid with Chocolate Mascarpone

This impressive cake makes a perfect centrepiece for a celebration buffet. Dust the pyramid with a little sieved icing (confectioners') sugar and sprinkle with just a few rose petals for simple but stunning presentation.

SERVES ABOUT TEN

200g/7oz plain (semisweet) chocolate

4 egg whites

150g/5oz/³/₄ cup caster (superfine) sugar

115g/4oz/³/₄ cup mascarpone cheese

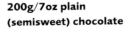
1 Preheat the oven to 150°C/300°F/Gas 2. Line two large baking sheets with baking parchment or greaseproof (waxed) paper. Grate 75g/3oz of the chocolate.

2 Whisk the egg whites in a clean, grease-free bowl until they form stiff peaks. Gradually whisk in half the sugar, then add the rest and whisk until the meringue is very stiff and glossy. Add the grated chocolate and whisk lightly to mix.

3 Draw a 20cm/8in circle on the lining paper on one of the baking sheets, turn it upside down, and spread the marked circle evenly with about half the meringue. Spoon the remaining meringue in 28–30 teaspoonfuls on both baking sheets. Bake the meringue for 1–1½ hours, or until crisp and completely dried out.

4 Make the filling. Melt the remaining chocolate in a heatproof bowl over hot water. Cool slightly, then stir in the mascarpone. Cool the mixture until firm.

5 Spoon the chocolate mixture into a large piping (pastry) bag and use to sandwich the meringues together in pairs, reserving a small amount of filling for the pyramid.

6 Arrange the filled meringues on a serving platter, piling them up in a pyramid and keeping them in position with a few well-placed dabs of the reserved filling.

Classic Chocolate Roulade

This rich, squidgy chocolate roll should be made at least eight hours before serving to allow it to soften. Expect the roulade to crack a little when you roll it up, and sprinkle with a little grated chocolate, if you like, as a final decoration. When melting chocolate, break it into even-sized pieces and place in a dry heatproof bowl over hot water. If the water is too hot the chocolate will turn grainy and scorch; if the chocolate is splashed with water it will harden and acquire a dull finish.

SERVES EIGHT

1 Preheat the oven to 180°C/350°F/Gas 4. Grease and line a 33 x 23cm/13 x 9in Swiss (jelly) roll tin (pan) with baking parchment.

2 Break the chocolate into squares and melt in a bowl over a pan of barely simmering water. Remove from the heat and leave to cool for about 5 minutes.

3 In a large bowl, whisk the sugar and egg yolks until light and fluffy. Stir in the melted chocolate.

4 Whisk the egg whites until stiff, but not dry, and then gently fold into the chocolate mixture.

5 Pour the chocolate mixture into the prepared tin, spreading it level with a palette knife (metal spatula). Bake for about 25 minutes, or until firm. Leave the cake in the tin and cover with a cooling rack, making sure that it does not touch the cake.

6 Cover the rack with a damp dishtowel, then wrap in clear film (plastic wrap). Leave in a cool place for 8 hours, preferably overnight.

7 Dust a sheet of greaseproof (waxed) paper with caster or icing sugar and turn out the roulade on to it. Peel off the lining paper.

8 To make the filling, whip the double cream until soft peaks form. Spread the cream over the roulade. Starting from one of the short ends, carefully roll it up, using the paper to help.

9 Place the roulade, seam side down, on to a serving plate and dust generously with more caster or icing sugar before serving.

200g/7oz plain (semisweet) chocolate

200g/7oz/1 cup caster (superfine) sugar, plus extra caster or icing (confectioners') sugar to dust

7 eggs, separated

300ml/¹/₂ pint/1¹/₄cups double (heavy) cream

COOK'S TIP
For a special dessert, decorate the roulade with swirls of whipped cream and chocolate coffee beans or with clusters of raspberries and mint leaves.

Cherry Chocolate Brownies

This is a modern version of the classic Black Forest gâteau. Choose really good-quality bottled fruits because this will make all the difference to the end result. Look out for bottled fruits at Christmas-time, in particular, when supermarket shelves are packed with different varieties. Other types of fruit will work equally well – try slices of orange bottled in liqueur or pears bottled in brandy.

SERVES FOUR

1 Using a sharp knife, carefully cut the brownies in half crossways to make two thin slices. Place one brownie square on each of four serving plates.

2 Pour the cream into a large bowl and whip until soft but not stiff, then divide half the whipped cream between the four brownie squares.

3 Divide half the cherries among the cream-topped brownies, then place the remaining brownie halves on top of the cherries. Press down lightly.

4 Spoon the remaining cream on top of the brownies, then top each one with more cherries and serve immediately.

4 chocolate brownies

300ml/$\frac{1}{2}$ pint/$1\frac{1}{4}$ cups double (heavy) cream

20–24 bottled cherries in Kirsch

Coffee Mascarpone Creams

For the best results, use good quality coffee beans and make the coffee as strong as possible. These little desserts are very rich so you need a really robust shot of coffee to give the desired result. They are particularly good served with a glass of liqueur or a cup of espresso.

SERVES FOUR

1 Put the mascarpone in a bowl and add the coffee. Mix well until smooth and creamy. Sift in the icing sugar and stir until thoroughly combined.

2 Spoon the mixture into little china pots or ramekin dishes and chill for 30 minutes before serving.

115g/4oz/$\frac{1}{2}$ cup mascarpone cheese

45ml/3 tbsp strong espresso coffee

45ml/3 tbsp icing (confectioners') sugar

VARIATION You can flavour mascarpone with almost anything you like to make a quick but elegant dessert. Try replacing the coffee with the same quantity of orange juice, Marsala or honey.

Ice Creams and Frozen Desserts

ICE CREAMS AND ICED DESSERTS CAN MAKE A PERFECT,

REFRESHING END TO A MEAL. HOME-MADE ICES, WHETHER

A LIGHTLY PERFUMED SORBET, A CREAMY KULFI OR A RICH

AND CREAMY ICE CREAM GÂTEAU, ARE SURPRISINGLY

EASY TO MAKE AND A WONDERFUL TREAT TO SERVE

TO GUESTS AND FAMILY ALIKE.

Lemon Sorbet

This is probably the most classic sorbet of all. Refreshingly tangy and yet deliciously smooth, it quite literally melts in the mouth. Try to buy unwaxed lemons for recipes such as this one where the lemon rind is used. The wax coating can adversely affect the flavour of the rind.

SERVES SIX

200g/7oz/1 cup caster (superfine) sugar, plus extra for coating rind to decorate

4 lemons, well scrubbed

1 egg white

1 Put the sugar in a pan and pour in 300ml/½ pint/1¼ cups water. Bring to the boil, stirring occasionally until the sugar has just dissolved.

2 Using a swivel vegetable peeler, pare the rind thinly from two of the lemons so that it falls straight into the pan.

3 Simmer for 2 minutes without stirring, then take the pan off the heat. Leave to cool, then chill.

4 Squeeze the juice from all the lemons and add it to the syrup. Strain the syrup into a shallow freezerproof container, reserving the rind. Freeze the mixture for 4 hours, until it is mushy.

5 Process the sorbet (sherbet) in a food processor until it is smooth. Lightly whisk the egg white with a fork until it is just frothy. Replace the sorbet in the container, beat in the egg white and return the mixture to the freezer for 4 hours, or until it is firm.

6 Cut the reserved lemon rind into fine shreds and cook them in boiling water for 5 minutes, or until tender. Drain, then place on a plate and sprinkle generously with caster sugar. Scoop the sorbet into bowls or glasses and decorate with the sugared lemon rind.

Strawberry and Lavender Sorbet

A hint of lavender transforms a familiar strawberry sorbet into a perfumed dinner-party dessert. When buying strawberries look for plump, shiny fruit without any signs of staining or leakage at the bottom of the punnet – this suggests that the fruit at the bottom has been squashed. To hull strawberries, prise out the leafy top with a sharp knife or a specially designed strawberry huller.

SERVES SIX

1 Place the sugar in a pan and pour in 300ml/½ pint/1¼ cups water. Bring to the boil, stirring until the sugar has dissolved.

2 Take the pan off the heat, add the lavender flowers and leave to infuse (steep) for 1 hour. If time permits, chill the syrup in the refrigerator before using.

3 Process the strawberries in a food processor or in batches in a blender, then press the purée through a large sieve into a bowl.

4 Pour the purée into a freezerproof container, strain in the syrup and freeze for 4 hours, or until mushy. Transfer to a food processor and process until smooth. Whisk the egg white until frothy, and stir into the sorbet (sherbet). Spoon the sorbet back into the container and freeze until firm.

5 Serve in scoops, piled into tall glasses, and decorate with sprigs of lavender flowers.

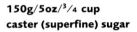

150g/5oz/³/₄ cup caster (superfine) sugar

6 fresh lavender flowers, plus extra to decorate

500g/1¹/₄lb/5 cups strawberries, hulled

1 egg white

COOK'S TIP *The size of the lavender flowers can vary; if they are very small, you may need to use eight. To double check, taste a little of the cooled lavender syrup. If you think the flavour is too mild, add two or three more flowers, reheat and cool again before using.*

Blackcurrant Sorbet

Wonderfully sharp and bursting with flavour, blackcurrants make a really fabulous sorbet. Blackcurrants are more acidic than white or redcurrants and are very rarely eaten raw. Taste the mixture after adding the syrup, and if you find it a little too tart, add a little more sugar before freezing.

500g/1¹⁄₄lb/5 cups blackcurrants, trimmed, plus extra to decorate

150g/5oz/³⁄₄ cup caster (superfine) sugar

1 egg white

SERVES SIX

1 Put the blackcurrants in a pan and add 150ml/¼ pint/²⁄₃ cup water. Cover the pan and simmer for 5 minutes, or until the fruit is soft. Cool, then process to a purée in a food processor or blender.

2 Set a large sieve over a bowl, pour the purée into the sieve, then press it through the mesh with the back of a spoon to form a smooth liquid.

3 Pour 200ml/7fl oz/scant 1 cup water into a clean pan. Add the sugar and bring to the boil, stirring until the sugar has dissolved. Pour the syrup into a bowl. Cool, then chill.

4 Mix the blackcurrant purée and sugar syrup together. Spoon into a freezerproof container and freeze until mushy. Lightly whisk the egg white until just frothy. Process the sorbet (sherbet) in a food processor until smooth, then return it to the container and stir in the egg white. Freeze for 4 hours, or until firm.

5 Transfer the sorbet to the refrigerator about 15 minutes before serving. Serve in scoops, decorated with the blackcurrant sprigs.

Damson Water Ice

Perfectly ripe damsons are sharp and full of flavour – if you can't find damsons, use another deep-red variety of plum or extra-juicy Victoria plums. To add an extra, nutty flavour to this mouthwatering ice, serve sprinkled with finely chopped toasted almonds.

SERVES SIX

> **500g/1¼ lb ripe damsons, washed**
>
> **150g/5oz/¾ cup caster (superfine) sugar**

1 Put the damsons into a pan and add 150ml/¼ pint/⅔ cup water. Cover and simmer gently for 10 minutes, or until the damsons are tender.

2 Pour 300ml/½ pint/1¼ cups water into a second pan. Add the sugar and bring to the boil, stirring until the sugar has dissolved. Pour the syrup into a bowl, leave to cool, then chill.

3 Break up the cooked damsons in the pan with a wooden spoon and scoop out any free stones (pits). Pour the fruit and juices into a large sieve set over a bowl. Press the fruit through the sieve and discard the skins and any remaining stones from the sieve.

4 Pour the damson purée into a shallow plastic container. Stir in the syrup and freeze for 6 hours, beating once or twice to break up the ice crystals.

5 Spoon into tall serving glasses or dishes and serve the water ice with wafers.

VARIATION

Apricot water ice can be made in exactly the same way. Flavour the water ice with a little lemon or orange rind or add a broken cinnamon stick to the pan when poaching the fruit. Serve garnished with sprigs of mint or nasturtium flowers.

Peach and Cardamom Yogurt Ice

Make the most of spices that are familiar in savoury cooking by discovering their potential for sweet dishes. Cardamom, often used in Indian cooking, has a warm pungent aroma and a subtle lemon flavour. Although it is made with yogurt rather than cream, this ice cream has a luxurious velvety texture and it is a healthy choice, too.

SERVES FOUR

8 cardamom pods

6 peaches, total weight about 500g/1¹/₄ lb, halved and stoned (pitted)

75g/3oz/6 tbsp caster (superfine) sugar

200ml/7fl oz/scant 1 cup natural (plain) yogurt

1 Put the cardamom pods on a board and crush them with the base of a ramekin, or place in a mortar and crush with a pestle.

2 Chop the peaches coarsely and put them in a pan. Add the crushed cardamom pods, with their black seeds, the sugar and 30ml/2 tbsp water. Cover and simmer for 10 minutes, or until the fruit is tender. Leave to cool.

3 Process the peach mixture in a food processor or blender until smooth, then press through a sieve placed over a bowl.

4 Mix the yogurt into the sieved purée and pour into a freezerproof container. Freeze for 5–6 hours, until firm, beating once or twice with a fork, electric whisk, or in a processor to break up the ice crystals.

5 Scoop the ice cream on to a large platter and serve.

Summer Berry Frozen Yogurt

Any combination of summer fruits will work for this dish, as long as they are frozen, because this helps to create a chunky texture. Whole fresh or frozen berries make an attractive decoration.

SERVES SIX

350g/12oz/3 cups frozen summer fruits

200g/7oz/scant 1 cup Greek (US strained plain) yogurt

25g/1oz icing (confectioners') sugar

VARIATION *To make a rich and creamy ice cream, use double (heavy) cream in place of the yogurt. It's a lot less healthy but the taste is irresistible.*

1 Put all the ingredients into a food processor and process until combined but still quite chunky. Spoon the mixture into six 150ml/¼ pint/⅔ cup ramekin dishes.

2 Cover each dish with clear film (plastic wrap) and place in the freezer for about 2 hours, or until firm.

3 To turn out the frozen yogurts, dip the dishes briefly in hot water and invert them on to small serving plates. Tap the base of the dishes and the yogurts should come out. Serve immediately.

Raspberry Sherbet

Traditional sherbets are made in a similar way to sorbets but with added milk. This low-fat version is made from raspberry purée blended with sugar syrup and virtually fat-free fromage frais or yogurt.

SERVES SIX

175g/6oz/scant 1 cup caster (superfine) sugar

500g/1¼lb/3½ cups raspberries, plus extra, to serve

500ml/17fl oz/2¼ cups virtually fat-free fromage frais or yogurt

COOK'S TIP *To make the sherbet by hand, pour the raspberry purée into a freezerproof container and freeze for 4 hours, beating once with a fork, electric whisk or in a food processor to break up the ice crystals. Freeze, then beat again.*

1 Put the sugar in a small pan with 150ml/¼ pint/⅔ cup water and bring to the boil, stirring until the sugar has dissolved completely. Pour into a jug (pitcher) and cool.

2 Put 350g/12oz/2½ cups of the raspberries in a food processor and blend to a purée. Press through a sieve into a large bowl and discard the seeds. Stir the sugar syrup into the raspberry purée and chill until very cold.

3 Add the fromage frais or yogurt to the chilled purée and whisk until smooth. Using an ice-cream maker, churn the mixture until it is thick but too soft to scoop. Scrape into a freezerproof container, then crush the remaining raspberries between your fingers and add to the ice cream. Mix lightly then freeze for 2–3 hours until firm. Scoop the ice cream into dishes and serve with extra raspberries.

Watermelon Ice

This simple, refreshing dessert is perfect after a hot, spicy meal. The aromatic flavour of kaffir lime leaves goes perfectly with watermelon.

SERVES FOUR TO SIX

90ml/6 tbsp caster (superfine) sugar

4 kaffir lime leaves, torn into small pieces

500g/1¼lb watermelon

1 Put the sugar and lime leaves in a pan with 105ml/7 tbsp water. Heat gently until the sugar has dissolved, then pour into a large bowl and set aside to cool.

2 Cut the watermelon into wedges with a large knife. Cut the flesh from the rind, remove the seeds and chop the flesh. Place the flesh in a food processor and process to a slush, then mix in the sugar syrup. Chill for 3–4 hours.

3 Strain the chilled mixture into a freezer container and freeze for 2 hours, then beat with a fork to break up the ice crystals. Return to the freezer and freeze for 3 hours more, beating at half-hourly intervals, then freeze until firm. Transfer the ice to the refrigerator about 30 minutes before serving.

Blackberry Ice Cream

There could scarcely be fewer ingredients in this delicious, vibrant ice cream, which is simple to make and ideal as a prepare-ahead dessert. Serve the ice cream with biscuits (cookies), such as shortbread or almond biscuits, to provide a delicious contrast in taste and texture.

SERVES FOUR TO SIX

1 Put the blackberries into a pan, add 30ml/2 tbsp water and the sugar. Cover and simmer for 5 minutes, until just soft.

2 Tip the fruit into a sieve placed over a bowl and press it through the mesh, using a wooden spoon. Leave to cool, then chill.

3 Whip the cream until it is just thick but still soft enough to fall from a spoon, then mix it with the chilled fruit purée. Pour the mixture into a freezerproof container and freeze for 2 hours, or until it is part frozen.

4 Mash the mixture with a fork or process it in a food processor to break up the ice crystals. Return it to the freezer for 4 hours more, mashing or processing the mixture again after 2 hours.

5 Scoop the ice cream into dishes and decorate with extra blackberries. Serve with crisp dessert biscuits.

COOK'S TIP

Frozen blackberries can be used instead of fresh. You will need to increase the cooking time to 10 minutes and stir occasionally.

Coffee Ice Cream

This classic ice cream is always a favourite and, despite its simplicity, has an air of sophistication and elegance about it. If you have an ice cream maker, simply pour the mixture into it and churn until firm.

SERVES EIGHT

600ml/1 pint/2¹/₂ cups fresh ready-made custard

150ml/¹/₄ pint/²/₃ cup strong black coffee

300ml/¹/₂ pint/1¹/₄ cups double (heavy) cream

1 Put the custard in a large bowl and stir in the coffee. In a separate bowl, whip the cream until soft but not stiff and fold evenly into the coffee and custard mixture.

2 Pour the mixture into a freezerproof container and cover with a tight-fitting lid or clear film (plastic wrap) and freeze for about 2 hours.

3 Remove the ice cream from the freezer and beat with a fork to break up the ice crystals.

4 Return the ice cream to the freezer, freeze for a further 2 hours, then beat again. Return it to the freezer until completely frozen, then serve.

Kulfi

This favourite Indian ice cream is traditionally made by carefully boiling milk until it has reduced to about one-third of its original quantity. Although you can save time by using condensed milk, nothing beats the luscious result achieved by using the authentic method. When they are available, rose petals are a stylish decoration in addition to the pistachio nuts.

SERVES FOUR

1.5 litres/2^1/$_2$ pints/6^1/$_4$ cups full-fat (whole) milk

3 cardamom pods

25g/1oz/2 tbsp caster (superfine) sugar

50g/2oz/^{1}/$_2$ cup pistachio nuts, skinned

1 Pour the milk into a large, heavy pan. Bring to the boil, reduce the heat and simmer gently for 1 hour, stirring occasionally.

2 Put the cardamom pods in a mortar and crush them with a pestle. Add the pods and the seeds to the milk and continue to simmer, stirring frequently, for 1–1½ hours, or until the milk has reduced to about 475ml/16fl oz/2 cups. Strain the milk into a jug (pitcher), stir in the sugar and leave to cool.

3 Grind half the pistachios in a blender or nut grinder. Cut the remaining pistachios into thin slivers and set them aside for decoration. Stir the ground nuts into the milk mixture.

4 Pour the milk and pistachio mixture into four kulfi or lolly (popsicle) moulds. Freeze the mixture overnight or until firm.

5 To unmould the kulfi, half fill a plastic container or bowl with very hot water, stand the moulds in the water and count to ten. Immediately lift out the moulds and invert them on a baking sheet. Transfer the ice creams to individual plates and sprinkle sliced pistachios over the top.

Coconut Ice

The creamy taste and texture of this ice cream comes from the natural fat content of coconut as the mixture contains neither cream nor egg and is very refreshing. The lime adds a delicious tangy flavour as well as pretty green specks to the finished ice. Decorate with toasted coconut shavings or toasted desiccated (dry unsweetened shredded) coconut (this browns very quickly, so watch it constantly).

SERVES FOUR TO SIX

115g/4oz/generous ¹/₄ cup caster (superfine) sugar

2 limes

400ml/14fl oz can coconut milk

toasted coconut shavings, to decorate (optional)

1 Pour 150ml/¼ pint/²/₃ cup water in a small pan. Tip in the caster sugar and bring to the boil, stirring constantly until the sugar has completely dissolved. Remove the pan from the heat and leave the syrup to cool, then chill well.

2 Grate the rind from the limes finely, taking care to avoid the bitter pith. Squeeze out their juice and add to the pan of syrup with the rind. Add the coconut milk.

3 Pour the mixture into a freezerproof container and freeze for 5–6 hours, or until firm. Beat twice with a fork or electric whisk, or process in a food processor to break up the crystals. Scoop into dishes and decorate with toasted coconut shavings, if you like.

COOK'S TIP *To make toasted coconut shavings, rinse the flesh from a coconut under cold water. Shave slices using a vegetable peeler, then toast under a moderate grill (broiler) until they are curled and the edges have turned golden.*

Gingered Semi-freddo

This Italian ice cream is rather like the original soft scoop ice cream. Made with a boiled sugar syrup rather than a traditional egg custard, and generously speckled with chopped stem ginger, this delicious ice cream will stay soft when frozen. For a really impressive dinner party dessert, serve the semi-freddo in plain (semisweet) chocolate cases.

SERVES SIX

1 Mix the sugar and 120ml/4fl oz/½ cup cold water in a pan and heat gently, stirring occasionally, until the sugar has dissolved.

2 Increase the heat and boil for 4–5 minutes, without stirring, until the syrup registers 119°C/238°F on a sugar thermometer. Alternatively, test by dropping a little of the syrup into a cup of cold water. Pour the water away and you should be able to mould the syrup into a small ball.

3 Put the egg yolks in a large heatproof bowl and whisk until frothy. Place the bowl over a pan of simmering water and whisk in the sugar syrup. Continue whisking until the mixture is very thick. Remove from the heat and whisk until cool.

4 Whip the cream and lightly fold it into the egg yolk mixture with the chopped stem ginger. Pour into a freezerproof container and freeze for 1 hour.

5 Stir the semi-freddo to bring any ginger that has sunk to the base of the container to the top, then return it to the freezer for 5–6 hours, until firm. Scoop into dishes or chocolate cases (see Cook's Tip). Decorate with slices of ginger and serve.

115g/4oz/generous ¹/₂ cup caster (superfine) sugar

4 egg yolks

300ml/¹/₂ pint/1¹/₄ cups double (heavy) cream

115g/4oz/²/₃ cup drained stem (preserved) ginger, finely chopped, plus extra slices, to decorate

COOK'S TIP *To make the cases, pour melted chocolate over squares of baking parchment and drape them over upturned glasses. Peel off the baking parchment when set.*

Miniature Choc-ices

These little chocolate-coated ice creams make a fun alternative to the more familiar after-dinner chocolates, especially on hot summer evenings – although they need to be eaten quickly. Serve the choc-ices in fluted paper sweet (candy) cases. If you can, buy gold cases as they will contrast very prettily with the dark chocolate coating.

MAKES ABOUT TWENTY-FIVE

750ml/1¼ pints/ 3 cups vanilla, chocolate or coffee ice cream

200g/7oz plain (semisweet) chocolate, broken into pieces

25g/1oz milk chocolate, broken into pieces

25g/1oz/¼ cup chopped hazelnuts, lightly toasted

1 Put a large baking sheet in the freezer for 10 minutes. Using a melon baller, scoop balls of ice cream and place these on the baking sheet. Freeze for at least 1 hour or until firm.

2 Line a second baking sheet with baking parchment and place in the freezer for 15 minutes. Melt the plain chocolate in a heatproof bowl set over a pan of gently simmering water. Melt the milk chocolate in a separate bowl.

3 Using a metal spatula, transfer the ice cream scoops to the parchment-lined sheet. Spoon a little plain chocolate over one scoop so that most of it is coated.

4 Sprinkle immediately with chopped nuts, before the chocolate sets. Coat half the remaining scoops in the same way, sprinkling each one with nuts before the chocolate sets. Spoon the remaining plain chocolate over all the remaining scoops.

5 Using a teaspoon, drizzle the milk chocolate over the choc-ices that are not topped with nuts. Freeze again until ready to serve.

White Chocolate Castles

With a little ingenuity, good-quality bought ice cream can masquerade as a culinary masterpiece – it's down to perfect presentation. For a professional finish, dust the castles and plates with a hint of cocoa powder or icing (confectioners') sugar.

225g/8oz white chocolate, broken into pieces

250ml/8fl oz/1 cup white chocolate ice cream

250ml/8fl oz/1 cup dark chocolate ice cream

115g/4oz/1 cup berries

SERVES SIX

1 Put the white chocolate in a heatproof bowl, set it over a pan of gently simmering water and leave until melted. Line a baking sheet with greaseproof (waxed) paper. Cut out six 30 x 13cm/12 x 5in strips of greaseproof paper, then fold each in half lengthways.

2 Stand a 7.5cm/3in pastry (cookie) cutter on the baking sheet. Roll one strip of paper into a circle and fit inside the cutter with the folded edge on the base paper. Stick the edges together with tape.

3 Remove the cutter and shape more paper collars in the same way, leaving the pastry cutter in place around the final collar.

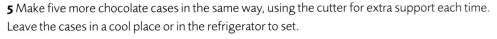
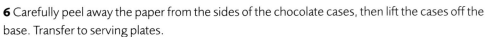

4 Spoon a little of the melted chocolate into the base of the collar supported by the cutter. Using a teaspoon, spread the chocolate over the base and up the sides of the collar, making the top edge uneven. Carefully lift away the cutter.

5 Make five more chocolate cases in the same way, using the cutter for extra support each time. Leave the cases in a cool place or in the refrigerator to set.

6 Carefully peel away the paper from the sides of the chocolate cases, then lift the cases off the base. Transfer to serving plates.

7 Using a large melon baller or teaspoon, scoop the white and dark chocolate ice creams into the cases and decorate with berries. Serve immediately.

Caramel and Pecan Terrine

Frozen or long-life cream is a useful ingredient for making impressive desserts without having a mega shopping trip. Caramel and nuts transform cream to parfait in this recipe. Take care that the syrup does not become too dark, or the ice cream will taste bitter.

SERVES SIX

**115g/4oz/generous
¹/₂ cup sugar**

**450ml/³/₄ pint/scant
2 cups double
(heavy) cream**

**30ml/2 tbsp icing
(confectioners') sugar**

**75g/3oz/³/₄ cup pecan
nuts, toasted**

COOK'S TIP

Watch the caramel syrup closely after removing it from the heat. If it starts to turn too dark, dip the base of the pan in cold water. If the syrup remains very pale, return the pan to the heat and cook it for a little longer.

1 Heat the sugar and 75ml/5 tbsp water in a small, heavy pan until the sugar dissolves. Boil rapidly until the sugar has turned pale golden. Remove the pan from the heat and leave to stand until the syrup turns a rich brown colour.

2 Pour 90ml/6 tbsp of the cream over the caramel. Heat to make a smooth sauce. Leave to cool.

3 Rinse a 450g/1lb loaf tin (pan), then line the base and sides with clear film (plastic wrap). Whip a further 150ml/¼ pint/²/₃ cup of the cream with the icing sugar until it forms soft peaks. Whip the remaining cream separately and stir in the caramel sauce and the toasted pecan nuts.

4 Spoon one-third of the caramel cream into the prepared tin and spread with half the plain whipped cream. Spread half of the remaining caramel cream over the top, then top with the last of the plain cream. Finally, add the remaining caramel cream and level the surface. Freeze for 6 hours.

5 To serve, dip the tin in very hot water for 2 seconds, invert it on to a serving plate and peel away the film. Serve sliced.

White Chocolate and Brownie Torte

This delicious dessert is easy to make and guaranteed to appeal to just about everyone. If you can't buy good quality brownies, use a moist chocolate sponge or make your own. For extra decoration, put a few fresh summer berries such as strawberries or raspberries around the edge or on the centre of the torte.

SERVES TEN

300g/11oz white chocolate, broken into pieces

600ml/1 pint/2¹/₂ cups double (heavy) cream

250g/9oz rich chocolate brownies

(unsweetened) cocoa powder, for dusting

1 Dampen the sides of a 20cm/8in springform tin (pan) and line with a strip of greaseproof (waxed) paper. Put the chocolate in a small pan. Add 150ml/¼ pint/²/₃ cup of the cream and heat very gently until the chocolate has melted. Stir until smooth, then pour into a bowl and leave to cool.

2 Break the chocolate brownies into chunky pieces and sprinkle these over the base of the tin. Pack them down lightly to make a fairly dense base.

3 Whip the remaining cream until it forms peaks, then fold in the white chocolate mixture. Spoon into the tin to cover the layer of brownies, then tap the tin gently on the work surface to level the chocolate mixture. Cover and freeze overnight.

4 Transfer the torte to the refrigerator about 45 minutes before serving to soften slightly. Decorate with a light dusting of cocoa powder just before serving.

Soft Fruit and Meringue Gâteau

This recipe takes only five minutes to prepare but looks and tastes as though a lot of preparation went into it. The trick is to use really good vanilla ice cream. For a dinner party, slice the gâteau and place on individual plates, spoon ready-made strawberry or raspberry coulis around each slice and garnish with whole strawberries or raspberries.

SERVES SIX

1 Dampen a 900g/2lb loaf tin (pan) and line it with clear film (plastic wrap). If using strawberries, chop them into small pieces. Put them in a bowl and add the raspberries or redcurrants and icing sugar. Toss until the fruit is beginning to break up, but do not let it become mushy.

2 Put the ice cream in a bowl and break it up with a fork. Crumble the meringues into the bowl and add the soft fruit mixture.

3 Fold all the ingredients together until evenly combined and lightly marbled. Pack into the prepared tin and press down gently to level. Cover and freeze overnight. To serve, invert on to a plate, peel away the clear film and cut into slices.

400g/14oz/3¹/₂ cups mixed small strawberries, raspberries and/ or redcurrants

30ml/2 tbsp icing (confectioners') sugar

750ml/1¹/₄ pints/ 3 cups vanilla ice cream

6 meringue nests or 115g/4oz meringue

Cookies and Sweet Treats

HOME-BAKED COOKIES AND SWEET SNACKS ARE THE
ULTIMATE INDULGENCE BUT ARE VIEWED BY MANY AS
TAKING TOO MUCH TIME AND EFFORT. HOWEVER, WITH
JUST A FEW BASIC INGREDIENTS, YOU CAN WHIP UP
FABULOUS CAKES, COOKIES AND CANDIES IN MOMENTS.
TRY DELICIOUS TREATS SUCH AS CHOCOLATE BROWNIES,
CHEWY FLAPJACKS OR QUICK AND EASY TEABREAD.

All Butter Cookies

Crisp, buttery cookies are perfect with strawberries and cream or any creamy dessert or fruit compote. These biscuits or cookies are known as refrigerator biscuits as the mixture is chilled until it is firm enough to cut neatly into thin biscuits. The dough can be frozen and when thawed enough to slice, can be freshly baked, but do allow a little extra cooking time.

MAKES TWENTY-EIGHT TO THIRTY

1 Put the flour in a food processor. Add the butter and process until the mixture resembles coarse breadcrumbs. Add the icing sugar and vanilla, and process until the mixture comes together to form a dough. Knead lightly and shape into a thick sausage, 30cm/12in long and 5cm/2in in diameter. Wrap and chill for at least 1 hour, until firm.

2 Preheat the oven to 200°C/400°F/Gas 6. Grease two baking sheets. Using a sharp knife, cut 5mm/¼in thick slices from the dough and space them slightly apart on the baking sheet.

3 Bake for 8–10 minutes, alternating the position of the baking sheets in the oven halfway through cooking, if necessary, until the biscuits are cooked evenly and have just turned pale golden around the edges. Leave for 5 minutes, then transfer to a wire rack to cool. Serve dusted with icing sugar.

275g/10oz/2¹/₂ cups plain (all-purpose) flour

90g/3¹/₂oz/scant 1 cup icing (confectioners') sugar, plus extra for dusting

10ml/2 tsp vanilla essence (extract)

FROM THE STORECUPBOARD

200g/7oz/scant 1 cup unsalted (sweet) butter

Almond Cookies

These short, light cookies have a melt-in-the-mouth texture. Their simplicity means they are endlessly versatile – irresistible with tea or coffee and stylish with special desserts.

MAKES ABOUT TWENTY-FOUR

115g/4oz/1 cup plain (all-purpose) flour

175g/6oz/1¹/₂ cups icing (confectioners') sugar, plus extra for dusting

50g/2oz/¹/₂ cup chopped almonds, plus halved almonds to decorate

FROM THE STORECUPBOARD

115g/4oz/¹/₂ cup unsalted (sweet) butter, softened

1 Preheat the oven to 180°C/350°F/Gas 4. Combine the flour, sugar and chopped almonds in a bowl.

2 Put the softened unsalted butter in the centre of the flour and nut mixture and use a blunt knife or your fingertips to draw the dry ingredients into the butter until a dough is formed. Shape the dough into a ball.

3 Place the dough on a lightly floured surface and roll it out to a thickness of about 3mm/¹/₈ in. Using a 7.5cm/3in cookie cutter, cut out about 24 rounds, re-rolling the dough as necessary. Place the cookie rounds on baking sheets, leaving a little space between them. Bake the cookies for about 25 minutes, until pale golden.

4 Leave the cookies on the baking sheet for 10 minutes, then transfer to wire racks to cool. Dust thickly with sifted icing sugar before serving, decorated with halved almonds.

COOK'S TIP *Use different-shaped cutters to make these cookies look even more interesting. Hearts, stars and crescents are three shapes that you might like to try.*

Chewy Flapjacks

Flapjacks are popular with adults and children alike and they are so quick and easy to make. For alternative versions of the basic recipe, stir in 50g/2oz/¼ cup finely chopped ready-to-eat dried apricots or sultanas (golden raisins). To make a really decadent treat, you can dip the cooled flapjack fingers into melted chocolate, to half cover.

MAKES TWELVE

1 Preheat the oven to 180°C/350°F/Gas 4. Line the base and sides of a 20cm/8in square cake tin (pan) with baking parchment.

2 Mix the butter, sugar and syrup in a pan and heat gently until the butter has melted. Add the oats and stir until all the ingredients are combined. Turn the mixture into the tin and level the surface.

3 Bake the flapjacks for 15–20 minutes, until just beginning to turn golden. Leave to cool slightly, then cut into fingers and remove from the tin. Store in an airtight container.

50g/2oz/¹⁄₄ cup caster (superfine) sugar

150g/5oz/scant ²⁄₃ cup golden (light corn) syrup

250g/9oz/1¹⁄₂ cups rolled oats

FROM THE STORECUPBOARD

175g/6oz/¾ cup unsalted (sweet) butter

Creamed Coconut Macaroons

Finely grated creamed coconut gives these soft-centred cookies a rich creaminess. Cooking the gooey mixture on baking parchment makes sure that the cookies are easily removed from the baking sheet. For a tangy flavour, add the grated rind of one lime to the mixture in step 2. The cooked macaroons can be stored in an airtight container for up to one week.

MAKES SIXTEEN TO EIGHTEEN

1 Preheat the oven to 180°C/350°F/Gas 4. Line a large baking sheet with baking parchment. Finely grate the creamed coconut.

2 Use an electric beater to whisk the egg whites in a large bowl until stiff. Whisk in the sugar, a little at a time, to make a stiff and glossy meringue. Fold in the grated creamed and desiccated coconut, using a large, metal spoon.

3 Place dessertspoonfuls of the mixture, spaced slightly apart, on the baking sheet. Bake for 15–20 minutes, until slightly risen and golden brown. Leave to cool on the parchment, then transfer to an airtight container.

50g/2oz creamed coconut, chilled

2 large (US extra large) egg whites

90g/3½oz/½ cup caster (superfine) sugar

75g/3oz/1 cup desiccated (dry unsweetened shredded) coconut

Orange and Pecan Scones

Serve these nutty orange scones with satiny orange or lemon curd or, for a simple, unsweetened snack, fresh and warm with unsalted (sweet) butter. Scones are best served on the day they are made, or they can be frozen. To freeze, place in an airtight container. To thaw, remove from the freezer and thaw at room temperature for an hour.

MAKES TEN

1 Preheat the oven to 220°C/425°F/Gas 7. Grease a baking sheet. Put the flour in a food processor with a pinch of salt and add the butter. Process the mixture until it resembles coarse breadcrumbs.

2 Add the orange rind. Reserve 30ml/2 tbsp of the orange juice and make the remainder up to 120ml/4fl oz/½ cup with water. Add the nuts and the juice mixture to the processor, process very briefly to a firm dough, adding a little water if the dough feels dry.

3 Turn the dough out on to a floured surface and roll out to 2cm/¾ in thick. Cut out scones using a round cutter and transfer them to the baking sheet. Re-roll the trimmings and cut more scones. Brush the scones with the reserved juice and bake for 15–20 minutes. Transfer to a wire rack to cool.

225g/8oz/2 cups self-raising (self-rising) flour

grated rind and juice of 1 orange

115g/4oz/1 cup pecan nuts, coarsely chopped

FROM THE STORECUPBOARD

50g/2oz/¼ cup unsalted (sweet) butter, chilled and diced

salt

Quick and Easy Teabread

This succulent, fruity teabread can be served just as it is, or spread with a little butter. The loaf can be stored, tightly wrapped in foil or in an airtight container, for up to five days. A great way to get children to eat some fruit, this teabread is ideal for packed lunches, picnics, or simply served with a cup of tea for afternoon tea.

SERVES EIGHT

1 Put the fruit in a bowl. Add 150ml/¼ pint/⅔ cup boiling water and leave to stand for 30 minutes.

2 Preheat the oven to 180°C/350°F/Gas 4. Grease and line the base and long sides of a 450g/1lb loaf tin (pan).

3 Beat the main quantity of sugar and the egg into the fruit. Sift the flour into the bowl and stir until combined. Turn into the prepared tin and level the surface. Sprinkle with the remaining sugar.

4 Bake the teabread for about 50 minutes, until risen and firm to the touch. When the bread is cooked, a skewer inserted into the centre will come out without any sticky mixture on it. Leave the loaf in the tin for 10 minutes before turning out on to a wire rack to cool.

350g/12oz/2 cups luxury mixed dried fruit

75g/3oz/scant ¹/₃ cup demerara (raw) sugar, plus 15ml/1 tbsp

1 large (US extra large) egg

175g/6oz/1¹/₂ cups self-raising (self-rising) flour

Cinnamon Pinwheels

These impressive sweet pastries go well with tea or coffee or as an accompaniment to ice cream and creamy desserts. If you find they turn soft during storage, re-crisp them briefly in the oven. Cinnamon is widely used in both sweet and savoury cooking: here ground cinnamon is used but it is also available as woody sticks. It has a delicious fragrant aroma and gives these simple-to-make pinwheels a warm spicy flavour.

MAKES TWENTY TO TWENTY-FOUR

50g/2oz/¹⁄₄ cup caster (superfine) sugar, plus a little extra for sprinkling

10ml/2 tsp ground cinnamon

250g/9oz puff pastry

beaten egg, to glaze

1 Preheat the oven to 220°C/425°F/Gas 7. Grease a large baking sheet. Mix the sugar with the cinnamon in a small bowl.

2 Roll out the pastry on a lightly floured surface to a 20cm/8in square and sprinkle with half the sugar mixture. Roll out the pastry to a 25cm/10in square so that the sugar is pressed into it.

3 Brush with the beaten egg and then sprinkle with the remaining sugar mixture. Loosely roll up the pastry into a log, brushing the end of the pastry with a little more egg to secure the edge in place.

4 Using a sharp knife, cut the log into thin slices and transfer them to the prepared baking sheet. Bake for 10 minutes, until golden and crisp. Sprinkle with more sugar and transfer to a wire rack to cool.

Almond Cigars

These simple, Moroccan-inspired pastries can be prepared in minutes. They are perfect served with strong black coffee or black tea, or as an after-dinner treat. They are also delicious served with traditional sweet Moroccan mint tea. To serve, the pastries look very pretty sprinkled with a little icing (confectioners') sugar as a simple finishing touch.

MAKES EIGHT TO TWELVE

250g/9oz marzipan

1 egg, lightly beaten

8–12 sheets filo pastry

FROM THE STORECUPBOARD

melted butter, for brushing

1 Knead the marzipan until soft and pliable, then put it in a mixing bowl and mix in the lightly beaten egg. Chill in the refrigerator for 1–2 hours.

2 Preheat the oven to 190°C/375°F/Gas 5. Lightly grease a baking sheet. Place a sheet of filo pastry on a piece of greaseproof (waxed) paper, keeping the remaining pastry covered with a damp cloth, and brush with the melted butter.

3 Shape 30–45ml/2–3 tbsp of the almond paste into a cylinder and place at one end of the pastry. Fold the pastry over to enclose the ends of the paste, then roll up to form a cigar shape. Place on the baking sheet and make 7–11 more cigars in the same way.

4 Bake the pastries in the preheated oven for about 15 minutes, or until golden brown in colour. Transfer to a wire rack to cool before serving.

Golden Ginger Macaroons

Macaroons are classic no-fuss biscuits – easy to whisk up in minutes from the minimum ingredients and always acceptable. A hint of ginger makes this recipe that bit different. For a darker colour and slightly richer flavour, use soft dark brown sugar instead. Bake these biscuits on non-stick baking trays or on a baking tray lined with baking parchment to prevent them from sticking.

MAKES EIGHTEEN TO TWENTY

1 Preheat the oven to 180°C/350°F/Gas 4. In a large, grease-free bowl, whisk the egg white until stiff and standing in peaks, but not dry and crumbly, then whisk in the brown sugar.

2 Sprinkle the ground almonds and ginger over the whisked egg white and gently fold them together.

3 Using two teaspoons, place spoonfuls of the mixture on baking trays, leaving plenty of space between each. Bake for about 20 minutes, until pale golden brown and just turning crisp.

4 Leave to cool slightly on the baking trays before transferring to a wire rack to cool completely.

1 egg white

75g/3oz/scant ¹/₂ cup soft light brown sugar

115g/4oz/1 cup ground almonds

5ml/1 tsp ground ginger

VARIATION *Other ground nuts, such as hazelnuts or walnuts, are good alternatives to the almonds. Ground cinnamon or mixed (apple pie) spice can be used instead of the ginger, if liked.*

Nutty Nougat

Nougat is an almost magical sweetmeat that emerges from honey-flavoured meringue made with boiled syrup. Since any other nuts or candied fruits can be used instead of almonds, as long as you have eggs, sugar and honey, you have the potential for making an impromptu gift or dinner-party treat.

MAKES ABOUT 500G/1¼ LB

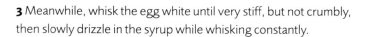

1 Line a 17.5cm/7in square cake tin (pan) with rice paper. Place the sugar, honey or syrup and 60ml/4 tbsp water in a large, heavy pan and heat gently, stirring frequently, until the sugar has completely dissolved.

2 Bring the syrup to the boil and boil gently to the soft crack stage (when the syrup dropped into cold water separates into hard but not brittle threads) or 151°C/304°F on a sugar thermometer.

3 Meanwhile, whisk the egg white until very stiff, but not crumbly, then slowly drizzle in the syrup while whisking constantly.

4 Quickly stir in the nuts and pour the mixture into the prepared tin. Leave to cool but, before the nougat becomes too hard, cut it into squares. Store in an airtight container.

225g/8oz/generous 1 cup granulated sugar

225g/8oz/1 cup clear honey or golden (light corn) syrup

1 large (US extra large) egg white

115g/4oz/1 cup flaked (sliced) almonds or chopped pistachio nuts, roasted

Rich Chocolate Brownies

These brownies are packed with both milk and plain chocolate instead of adding sugar to the mixture. Serve them in small squares as they are very rich. When buying plain chocolate, bear in mind that the higher the percentage of cocoa solids, the higher the quality of the chocolate, and the less sugar it contains. The best quality has 70 per cent cocoa solids.

MAKES SIXTEEN

1 Preheat the oven to 180°C/350°F/Gas 4. Line the base and sides of a 20cm/8in square cake tin (pan) with baking parchment.

2 Break the plain chocolate and 90g/3½oz of the milk chocolate into pieces and put in a heatproof bowl with the butter. Melt over a pan of barely simmering water, stirring frequently.

3 Chop the remaining milk chocolate into chunky pieces. Stir the flour and eggs into the melted chocolate until combined. Stir in half the chopped milk chocolate and turn the mixture into the prepared tin, spreading it into the corners. Sprinkle with the remaining chopped chocolate.

4 Bake the brownies for 30–35 minutes, until risen and just firm to the touch. Leave to cool in the tin, then cut the mixture into squares. Store the brownies in an airtight container.

300g/11oz each plain (semisweet) and milk chocolate

75g/3oz/²/₃ cup self-raising (self-rising) flour

3 large (US extra large) eggs

FROM THE STORECUPBOARD

175g/6oz/³/₄ cup unsalted (sweet) butter

Rich Chocolate Biscuit Slice

This dark chocolate refrigerator cake is packed with crisp biscuit pieces and chunks of white chocolate for colour and flavour contrast. The slice is perfect served with strong coffee, either as a teatime treat or in place of dessert. Once set, cut the cake into slices and store the slices in an airtight container in the refrigerator until ready to serve.

SERVES EIGHT TO TEN

0275g/10oz fruit and nut plain (semisweet) chocolate

90g/3½oz digestive biscuits (graham crackers)

90g/3½oz white chocolate

FROM THE STORECUPBOARD

130g/4½oz/9 tbsp unsalted (sweet) butter

1 Grease and line the base and sides of a 450g/1lb loaf tin (pan) with baking parchment. Break the fruit and nut chocolate into pieces and place in a heatproof bowl with the butter. Place the bowl over a pan of barely simmering water and stir the chocolate gently until it is melted and smooth. Remove the bowl from the pan and leave to cool for 20 minutes.

2 Break the biscuits into small pieces. Finely chop the white chocolate. Stir the biscuits and white chocolate into the melted mixture until evenly combined. Turn the mixture into the prepared tin and pack down gently. Chill for about 2 hours, or until set. Cut the mixture into slices.

Chocolate and Prune Refrigerator Bars

Wickedly self-indulgent and very easy to make, these fruity chocolate bars will keep for 2–3 days in the refrigerator – if they don't all get eaten as soon as they are ready.

MAKES TWELVE BARS

250g/9oz good quality milk chocolate

115g/4oz digestive biscuits (graham crackers)

115g/4oz/¹⁄₂ cup ready-to-eat prunes

FROM THE STORECUPBOARD

50g/2oz/¹⁄₄ cup unsalted (sweet) butter

1 Break the chocolate into small pieces and place in a heatproof bowl. Add the butter and melt in the microwave on high for 1–2 minutes. Stir to mix and set aside. (Alternatively, place the bowl over a pan of gently simmering water and leave until melted, stirring frequently.)

2 Put the biscuits in a plastic bag and seal, then bash into small pieces with a rolling pin. Roughly chop the prunes and stir into the melted chocolate with the biscuits.

3 Spoon the chocolate and prune mixture into a 20cm/8in square cake pan and chill for 1–2 hours until set. Remove the cake from the refrigerator and, using a sharp knife, cut into 12 bars.

Blueberry Cake

Cake mixes make life very easy and are available in most supermarkets. Dust with icing (confectioners') sugar and serve for a simple dessert.

SERVES SIX TO EIGHT

220g/8oz packet sponge cake mix

1 egg, if needed

115g/4oz/1 cup blueberries

1 Preheat the oven to 190°C/375°F/Gas 5. Grease a 20cm/8in cake tin (pan). Make up the sponge cake mix according to the instructions on the packet, using the egg if required. Spoon the mixture into the prepared cake tin.

2 Bake the cake according to the instructions on the packet. Ten minutes before the end of the cooking time, sprinkle the blueberries over the top of the cake. (Work quickly so that the cake is out of the oven for as short a time as possible, otherwise it may sink in the middle.)

3 Leave the cake to cool in the tin for 2–3 minutes, then carefully remove from the tin and transfer to a wire rack. Leave to cool completely before serving.

Stuffed Prunes

Prunes and plain chocolate are delectable partners, especially when the dried fruit is soaked in Armagnac. Serve these sophisticated sweetmeats dusted with cocoa powder as a dinner-party treat with coffee.

MAKES ABOUT THIRTY

1 Put the prunes in a bowl and pour the Armagnac over. Stir, then cover with clear film (plastic wrap) and set aside for 2 hours, or until the prunes have absorbed the liquid.

2 Make a slit along each prune to remove the stone (pit), making a hollow for the filling, but leaving the fruit intact.

3 Heat the cream in a pan almost to boiling point. Put 115g/4oz of the chocolate in a bowl and pour over the hot cream.

4 Stir until the chocolate has melted and the mixture is smooth. Leave to cool, until it has the consistency of softened butter.

5 Fill a piping (pastry) bag with a small plain nozzle with the chocolate mixture. Pipe into the cavities of the prunes. Chill for about 20 minutes.

6 Melt the remaining chocolate in a heatproof bowl set over a pan of barely simmering water. Using a fork, dip the prunes, one at a time, into the chocolate to coat them generously. Place on baking parchment to set.

**225g/8oz/
1 cup unpitted prunes**

**50ml/2fl oz/
¹/₄ cup Armagnac**

**150ml/¹/₂ pint/²/₃ cup
double (heavy) cream**

**350g/12oz plain
(semisweet) chocolate,
broken into squares**

COOK'S TIP *Armagnac is a type of French brandy produced in the Gascogne region in the south-west of the country. It has a pale colour and a biscuity aroma. Other types of brandy can be used in this recipe.*

Chocolate Truffles

Luxurious truffles are expensive to buy but very easy and fun to make. These rich melt-in-the-mouth treats are flavoured with coffee liqueur, but you could use whisky or brandy instead. The mixture can be rolled in cocoa powder or icing (confectioners') sugar instead of being dipped in melted chocolate. Remember to store the fresh-cream truffles in the refrigerator.

MAKES TWENTY-FOUR

1 Melt 225g/8oz of the plain chocolate in a heatproof bowl set over a pan of barely simmering water. Stir in the cream and liqueur, then chill the mixture for 4 hours, until firm.

2 Divide the mixture into 24 equal pieces and quickly roll each into a ball. Chill for about 1 hour, or until the truffles are firm again.

3 Melt the remaining plain, white or milk chocolate in separate small bowls. Using two forks, carefully dip eight of the truffles, one at a time, into the melted plain chocolate.

4 Repeat to cover the remaining 16 truffles with the melted white or milk chocolate. Place the truffles on a board or tray, covered with wax paper or foil. Leave to set before placing in individual mini paper cases or transferring to a serving dish.

350g/12oz plain (semisweet) chocolate

75ml/5 tbsp double (heavy) cream

30ml/2 tbsp coffee liqueur, such as Tia Maria, Kahlúa or Toussaint

225g/8oz good quality white or milk dessert chocolate

EXTRAS

Ring the changes by adding one of the following to the mixture:

GINGER
Stir in 40g/1½ oz/¼ cup finely chopped crystallized ginger.

CANDIED FRUIT
Stir in 50g/2oz/⅓ cup finely chopped candied fruit, such as pineapple and orange.

PISTACHIOS
Stir in 25g/1oz/¼ cup chopped skinned pistachio nuts.

HAZELNUTS
Roll each ball of chilled truffle mixture around a whole skinned hazelnut.

Chocolate Petit Four Cookies

Make these dainty cookies as stylish after-dinner snacks. If you do not have any amaretto liqueur, they will work well without it. Alternatively, you can substitute the same quantity of brandy or rum.

SERVES EIGHT

1 Preheat the oven according to the instructions on the cookie dough packet. Roll out the cookie dough on a floured surface to 1cm/½in thick. Using a 2.5cm/1in cutter, stamp out as many rounds from the dough as possible and transfer them to a lightly greased baking sheet. Bake for about 8 minutes, or until cooked through. Transfer to a wire rack to cool completely.

2 To make the filling, break the chocolate into small pieces and place in a heatproof bowl with the butter and amaretto liqueur. Sit the bowl over a pan of gently simmering water and stir occasionally, until the chocolate has melted. Remove from the heat and set aside to cool.

3 Spread a small amount of the filling on the flat bottom of one of the cookies and sandwich together with another. Repeat until all the biscuits have been used.

350g/12oz carton chocolate chip cookie dough

115g/4oz plain (semisweet) chocolate

30ml/2 tbsp Amaretto di Sarone liqueur

FROM THE STORECUPBOARD

50g/2oz/¼ cup butter

Praline Chocolate Bites

These delicate, mouthwatering little bites never fail to impress guests, but are quite simple to make. They are perfect for serving with coffee after dinner. Dust with icing sugar for a decorative finish.

SERVES FOUR

1 Put the sugar in a heavy pan with 90ml/6 tbsp water. Stir over a gentle heat until the sugar has dissolved. Bring the syrup to the boil and cook for about 5 minutes, without stirring, until the mixture is golden and caramelized.

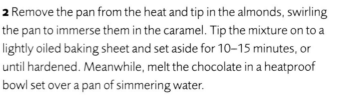

2 Remove the pan from the heat and tip in the almonds, swirling the pan to immerse them in the caramel. Tip the mixture on to a lightly oiled baking sheet and set aside for 10–15 minutes, or until hardened. Meanwhile, melt the chocolate in a heatproof bowl set over a pan of simmering water.

3 Cover the hardened caramel mixture with clear film (plastic wrap) and break up with a rolling pin then place in a food processor. Process until finely chopped, then stir into the melted chocolate. Chill until set enough to roll into balls. Roll the mixture into 16 balls and place in mini paper cases to serve.

115g/4oz/1 cup caster (superfine) sugar

115g/4oz/⅔ cup whole blanched almonds

200g/7oz plain (semisweet) chocolate

COOK'S TIP *The mixture for these bites can be made ahead and stored in the freezer for up to 2 weeks. To use, thaw the mixture at room temperature until soft enough to roll into balls.*

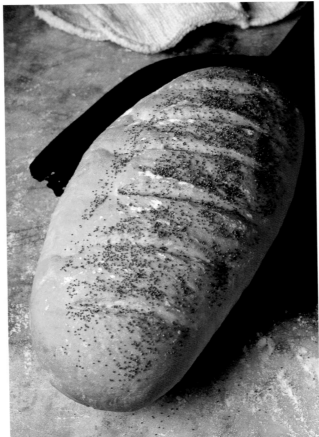

Breads

THERE ARE FEW FOODS SO DELICIOUS AND COMFORTING
AS FRESHLY BAKED BREAD. THREE BASIC INGREDIENTS —
FLOUR, SALT AND YEAST — MIXED WITH WATER ARE ALL
THAT IS NEEDED TO MAKE A BASIC LOAF, WHILE THE
ADDITION OF A FOURTH INGREDIENT SUCH AS HERBS,
SUN-DRIED TOMATOES, OLIVE OIL OR MILK CAN
CREATE WONDERFUL, ENTICING VARIATIONS.

Scottish Morning Rolls

These soft, spongy bread rolls are irresistible while still warm and aromatic. Made with milk, rather than the more usual water, they have a rich flavour. In Scotland they are a firm favourite for breakfast with fried eggs and bacon. To speed up the rising time, place the rolls in the airing cupboard or on the top of the preheated oven.

MAKES TEN ROLLS

1 Grease two baking sheets. Sift the flour and salt together into a large bowl and make a well in the centre. Mix the yeast with the milk, then mix in 150ml/¼ pint/⅔ cup lukewarm water. Add to the centre of the flour and mix together to form a soft dough.

2 Knead the dough lightly in the bowl, then cover with lightly oiled clear film (plastic wrap) and leave to rise in a warm place for 1 hour, or until doubled in bulk. Turn the dough out on to a lightly floured surface and knock back (punch down).

3 Divide the dough into ten equal pieces. Knead lightly and, using a rolling pin, shape each piece of dough into a flat oval 10 x 7.5cm/ 4 x 3in, or a flat round 9cm/3½in.

4 Transfer to the prepared baking sheets, spaced well apart, and cover the rolls with oiled clear film. Leave to rise, in a warm place, for about 30 minutes.

5 Meanwhile, preheat the oven to 200°C/400°F/Gas 6. Press each roll in the centre with the three middle fingers to equalize the air bubbles and to help prevent blistering. Brush with milk and dust with flour. Bake for 15–20 minutes, or until lightly browned. Dust with more flour and cool slightly on a wire rack. Serve warm.

450g/1lb/4 cups unbleached strong white bread flour, plus extra for dusting

20g/³/₄oz fresh yeast

150ml/¹/₄ pint/²/₃ cup lukewarm milk, plus extra for glazing

FROM THE STORECUPBOARD

10ml/2 tsp salt

Panini all'Olio

Italian-style dough enriched and flavoured with extra virgin olive oil is versatile for making decorative rolls. Children will love helping to make and shape these rolls – they can try making twists, fingers or artichoke-shapes, or just about any shape they want. The rolls are sure to disappear as soon as they are cool enough to eat.

450g/1lb/4 cups unbleached strong white bread flour

15g/¹/₂ oz fresh yeast

60ml/4 tbsp extra virgin olive oil

FROM THE STORECUPBOARD

10ml/2 tsp salt

MAKES SIXTEEN ROLLS

1 Lightly oil three baking sheets. Sift the flour and salt together in a large bowl and make a well in the centre. Measure 250ml/8fl oz/1 cup lukewarm water. Cream the yeast with half the water, then stir in the remainder. Add to the well with the oil and mix to a dough.

2 Turn the dough out on to a lightly floured surface and knead for 8–10 minutes, until smooth and elastic. Place in a lightly oiled bowl, cover with lightly oiled clear film (plastic wrap) and leave to rise in a warm place for about 1 hour, or until nearly doubled in bulk.

3 Turn the dough on to a lightly floured surface and knock back (punch down). Divide into 12 equal pieces and shape into rolls. To make twists, roll each piece of dough into a strip 30cm/12in long and 4cm/1½in wide. Twist each strip into a loose spiral and join the ends together to make a circle. Place on the baking sheets, spaced well apart. Brush lightly with olive oil, cover with lightly oiled clear film and leave to rise in a warm place for 20–30 minutes.

4 To make fingers, flatten each piece of dough into an oval and roll to about 23cm/9in long. Roll up from the wider end. Gently stretch the dough roll to 20–23cm/8–9in long. Cut in half. Place on the baking sheets, spaced well apart. Brush the dough with olive oil, cover with lightly oiled clear film and leave to rise in a warm place for 20–30 minutes.

5 To make artichoke-shapes, shape each piece of dough into a ball and space well apart on the baking sheets. Brush with oil, cover with lightly oiled clear film and leave to rise in a warm place for 20–30 minutes. Using scissors, snip 5mm/¼in deep cuts in a circle on the top of each ball, then make five larger horizontal cuts around the sides.

6 Preheat the oven to 200°C/400°F/Gas 6. Bake the rolls for 15 minutes.

French Baguette

Fine French flour is available from French delicatessens and superior supermarkets. If you cannot find any, try ordinary plain flour instead. Baguettes have a wide variety of uses: split horizontally and fill with meats, cheeses and salads; slice diagonally and toast the slices to serve with soup; or simply cut into chunks, spread with unsalted (sweet) butter and serve with French cheeses.

MAKES THREE LOAVES

500g/1¼lb/5 cups unbleached strong white bread flour

115g/4oz/1 cup fine French plain (all-purpose) flour

15g/½oz fresh yeast

FROM THE STORECUPBOARD

10ml/2 tsp salt

1 Sift the flours and salt into a bowl. Add the yeast to 550ml/18fl oz/2½ cups lukewarm water in another bowl and stir. Gradually beat in half the flour mixture to form a batter. Cover with clear film (plastic wrap) and leave for about 3 hours, or until nearly trebled in size.

2 Add the remaining flour a little at a time, beating with your hand. Turn out on to a lightly floured surface and knead for 8–10 minutes to form a moist dough. Place in a lightly oiled bowl, cover with lightly oiled clear film and leave to rise, in a warm place, for about 1 hour.

3 Knock back (punch down) the dough, turn out on to a floured surface and divide into three equal pieces. Shape each into a ball and then into a 15 x 7.5cm/6 x 3in rectangle. Fold the bottom third up lengthways and the top third down and press down. Seal the edges. Repeat two or three more times until each loaf is an oblong. Leave to rest in between folding for a few minutes.

4 Gently stretch each piece of dough into a 33–35cm/13–14in long loaf. Pleat a floured dishtowel on a baking sheet to make three moulds for the loaves. Place the loaves between the pleats, cover with lightly oiled clear film and leave to rise in a warm place for 45–60 minutes.

5 Preheat the oven to maximum, at least 230°C/450°F/Gas 8. Roll the loaves on to a baking sheet, spaced well apart. Slash the top of each loaf diagonally several times. Place at the top of the oven, spray the inside of the oven with water and bake for 20–25 minutes.

COOK'S TIP

Baguettes are difficult to reproduce at home as they require a very hot oven and steam. However, by using less yeast and a triple fermentation you can produce a bread with a superior taste and far better texture than mass-produced baguettes. It also helps if you spray the oven twice with water during the first 5 minutes of baking. These loaves are best eaten on the day of baking.

Rosemary Focaccia

If you do not need both loaves, freeze one for another time and warm it in the oven before serving. Sprinkle the loaves with finely chopped garlic, if you prefer.

MAKES TWO LOAVES

1 Put the flour and yeast in a large bowl with 5ml/1 tsp salt. Stir in 45ml/3 tbsp of the oil and 450ml/¾ pint/scant 2 cups lukewarm water. Mix with a round-bladed knife, then by hand to a soft dough, adding a little more lukewarm water if the dough feels dry.

2 Turn the dough out on to a lightly floured surface and knead for 10 minutes, until smooth and elastic. Put in a lightly oiled bowl and cover with oiled clear film (plastic wrap). Leave in a warm place for about 1 hour, until doubled in size.

3 Preheat the oven to 200°C/400°F/Gas 6. Turn out the dough on to a floured surface and cut in half. Roll out each half into a 25cm/10in round. Transfer to greased baking sheets, cover with lightly oiled clear film and leave for 20 minutes, until risen.

4 Press your fingers into the dough to make deep holes all over it about 3cm/1¼ in apart. Leave for a further 5 minutes. Sprinkle with the rosemary and plenty of sea salt. Sprinkle with water to keep the crust moist and bake for 25 minutes, until pale golden. Remove from the oven and drizzle with the remaining olive oil. Transfer to a wire rack to cool.

675g/1¹/₂lb/4 cups strong white bread flour

15ml/1 tbsp easy-blend (rapid-rise) dried yeast

45ml/3 tbsp chopped fresh rosemary

FROM THE STORECUPBOARD

75ml/5 tbsp olive oil

Granary Cob

Mixing and shaping a simple round loaf is one of the most satisfying kitchen activities and the result is incomparably excellent. This bread is made with fresh yeast – it is a similar colour and texture to putty and should crumble easily when broken. For best results, buy fresh yeast in small quantities as required: it will keep for up to one month in the refrigerator.

MAKES ONE ROUND LOAF

450g/1lb/4 cups Granary (multigrain) or malthouse flour

15g/¹/₂oz fresh yeast

wheat flakes or cracked wheat, for sprinkling

FROM THE STORECUPBOARD

12.5ml/2¹/₂ tsp salt

1 Lightly flour a baking sheet. Mix the flour and 10ml/2 tsp of the salt together in a large bowl and make a well in the centre. Place in a very low oven for 5 minutes to warm.

2 Measure 300ml/½pint/1¼ cups lukewarm water. Mix the yeast with a little of the water, then blend in the rest. Pour the yeast mixture into the centre of the flour and mix to a dough.

3 Turn out on to a lightly floured surface and knead for about 10 minutes, until smooth and elastic. Place in a lightly oiled bowl, cover with lightly oiled clear film (plastic wrap) and leave to rise in a warm place for 1¼ hours, or until doubled in bulk.

4 Turn the dough out on to a lightly floured surface and knock back (punch down). Knead for 2–3 minutes, then roll into a ball. Place in the centre of the prepared baking sheet. Cover with an inverted bowl and leave to rise in a warm place for 30–45 minutes.

5 Preheat the oven to 230°C/450°F/Gas 8 towards the end of the rising time. Mix 30ml/2 tbsp water with the remaining salt and brush evenly over the bread. Sprinkle the loaf with wheat flakes or cracked wheat.

6 Bake the bread for 15 minutes, then reduce the oven temperature to 200°C/400°F/Gas 6 and bake for a further 20 minutes, or until the loaf is firm to the touch and sounds hollow when tapped on the base. Cool on a wire rack.

Grant Loaves

This quick and easy recipe was created by a baker called Doris Grant and was published in the 1940s. It is a dream for busy cooks as the dough requires no kneading and takes only a minute to mix. Nowadays we can make the recipe even quicker by using easy-blend yeast, which is added directly to the dry ingredients.

MAKES THREE LOAVES

1 Thoroughly grease three loaf tins (pans), each 21 x 11 x 6cm/ 8½ x 4½ x 2½in and set aside in a warm place. Sift the flour and salt together in a large bowl and warm slightly to take off the chill.

2 Sprinkle the dried yeast over 150ml/¼ pint/⅔ cup lukewarm water. After a couple of minutes, stir in the muscovado sugar. Leave the mixture for 10 minutes.

3 Make a well in the centre of the flour. Pour in the yeast mixture and add a further 900ml/1½ pints/3¾ cups lukewarm water. Stir to form a slippery dough. Mix for about 1 minute, working the dry ingredients from the sides into the middle.

4 Divide among the prepared tins, cover with oiled clear film (plastic wrap) and leave to rise in a warm place for 30 minutes, or until the dough has risen by about one-third to within 1cm/ ½in of the top of the tins.

5 Meanwhile, preheat the oven to 200°C/400°F/Gas 6. Bake for 40 minutes, or until the loaves are crisp and sound hollow when tapped on the base. Turn out on to a wire rack to cool.

1.3kg/3lb/12 cups wholemeal (whole-wheat) bread flour

15ml/1 tbsp easy-blend (rapid-rise) dried yeast

15ml/1 tbsp muscovado (molasses) sugar

FROM THE STORECUPBOARD

15ml/1 tbsp salt

Cottage Loaf

Create a culinary masterpiece from a few basic ingredients and experience the satisfaction of traditional baking. Serve this classic-shaped loaf to accompany home-made soup.

MAKES ONE LARGE ROUND LOAF

675g/1½lb/6 cups unbleached strong white bread flour

20g/³/₄ oz fresh yeast

FROM THE STORECUPBOARD

10ml/2 tsp salt

1 Lightly grease two baking sheets. Sift the flour and salt together into a large bowl and make a well in the centre.

2 Mix the yeast in 150ml/¼ pint/²⁄₃ cup lukewarm water until dissolved. Pour into the centre of the flour and add a further 250ml/8fl oz/1 cup lukewarm water, then mix to a firm dough.

3 Knead the dough on a lightly floured surface for 10 minutes, until it is smooth and elastic. Place in a lightly oiled bowl, cover with lightly oiled clear film (plastic wrap) and leave to rise in a warm place for about 1 hour.

4 Turn out on to a lightly floured surface and knock back (punch down). Knead for 2–3 minutes, then divide the dough into two-thirds and one-third and shape each piece into a ball. Place the balls of dough on the prepared baking sheets. Cover with inverted bowls and leave to rise in a warm place for 30 minutes.

5 Gently flatten the top of the larger round of dough and cut a cross in the centre, about 4cm/1½ in across. Brush with a little water and place the smaller round on top. Carefully press a hole through the middle of the top ball, down into the lower part, using your thumb and first two fingers. Cover with lightly oiled clear film and leave to rest in a warm place for about 10 minutes.

6 Preheat the oven to 220°C/425°F/Gas 7 and place the bread on the lower shelf of the oven. Bake for 35–40 minutes, or until a rich golden brown colour. Cool on a wire rack before serving.

Split Tin

The deep centre split down this loaf gives it its name. The split tin loaf slices well for making thick-cut sandwiches, or for serving hearty chunks of bread to accompany robust cheese.

MAKES ONE LOAF

500g/1¹/₄lb/5 cups unbleached strong white bread flour, plus extra for dusting

15g/¹/₂oz fresh yeast

60ml/4 tbsp lukewarm milk

FROM THE STORECUPBOARD

10ml/2 tsp salt

1 Grease a 900g/2lb loaf tin (pan). Sift the flour and salt into a bowl and make a well in the centre. Mix the yeast with 150ml/¼ pint/²/₃ cup lukewarm water. Stir in another 150ml/¼ pint/²/₃ cup lukewarm water. Pour the yeast mixture into the centre of the flour and using your fingers, mix in a little flour to form a smooth batter.

2 Sprinkle a little more flour from around the edge over the batter and leave in a warm place for about 20 minutes to "sponge". Add the milk and remaining flour; mix to a firm dough.

3 Place on a lightly floured surface and knead for about 10 minutes, until smooth and elastic. Place in a lightly oiled bowl, cover with lightly oiled clear film (plastic wrap) and leave to rise in a warm place for 1–1¼ hours, or until nearly doubled in bulk.

4 Knock back (punch down) the dough and turn out on to a lightly floured surface. Shape it into a rectangle, the length of the prepared tin. Roll the dough up lengthways, tuck the ends under and place, seam side down, in the tin. Cover the loaf and leave to rise in a warm place for about 20–30 minutes.

5 Using a sharp knife, make one deep central slash. Dust the top of the loaf with a little sifted flour. Leave for 10–15 minutes. Meanwhile, preheat the oven to 230°C/450°F/Gas 8. Bake for 15 minutes, then reduce the oven temperature to 200°C/400°F/Gas 6. Bake for 20–25 minutes, until golden and it sounds hollow when tapped on the base. Cool on a wire rack.

Poppy-seeded Bloomer

This long, crusty loaf gets its fabulous flavour from poppy seeds. Cut into thick slices, the bread is perfect for mopping up the cooking juices of hearty stews, or for absorbing good dressing on summery salads. A variety of seeds can be used to add flavour, texture and colour to this loaf – try sunflower, pumpkin or sesame seeds as an alternative to the poppy seeds. Brushing the loaf with the salted water before baking helps to give it a crisp, crusty finish.

MAKES ONE LARGE LOAF

1 Lightly grease a baking sheet. Sift the flour and 10ml/2 tsp salt together into a large bowl and make a well in the centre.

2 Measure 450ml/¾ pint/scant 2 cups lukewarm water and stir about a third of it into the yeast in a bowl. Stir in the remaining water and pour into the centre of the flour. Mix, gradually incorporating the surrounding flour, to a firm dough.

3 Turn out on to a lightly floured surface and knead the dough very well, for at least 10 minutes, until smooth and elastic. Place the dough in a lightly oiled bowl, cover with lightly oiled clear film (plastic wrap) and leave to rise, at cool room temperature (about 15–18 C/60–65 F), for 5–6 hours, or until doubled in bulk.

4 Knock back (punch down) the dough, turn out on to a lightly floured surface and knead it thoroughly for about 5 minutes. Return the dough to the bowl and re-cover. Leave to rise, at cool room temperature, for a further 2 hours or slightly longer.

5 Knock back again and repeat the thorough kneading. Leave the dough to rest for 5 minutes, then roll out on a lightly floured surface into a rectangle 2.5cm/1in thick. Roll the dough up from one long side and shape it into a square-ended, thick baton shape about 33 x 13cm/13 x 5in.

6 Place the loaf, seam side up, on a lightly floured baking sheet. Cover with lightly oiled clear film and leave to rest for 15 minutes. Turn the loaf over and place on the greased baking sheet. Plump the loaf up by tucking the dough under the sides and ends. Using a sharp knife, cut six diagonal slashes on the top.

7 Leave to rest, covered, in a warm place, for 10 minutes. Meanwhile, preheat the oven to 230°C/450°F/Gas 8.

8 Mix the remaining salt with 30ml/2 tbsp water and brush this glaze over the bread. Sprinkle with poppy seeds.

9 Spray the oven with water, bake the bread immediately for 20 minutes, then reduce the oven temperature to 200°C/400°F/Gas 6. Bake for 25 minutes more, or until golden and it sounds hollow when tapped on the base. Transfer to a wire rack to cool.

675g/1½lb/6 cups unbleached strong white bread flour

15g/½oz fresh yeast

poppy seeds, for sprinkling

FROM THE STORECUPBOARD

12.5ml/2½ tsp salt

COOK'S TIP *The traditional cracked, crusty appearance of this loaf is difficult to achieve in a domestic oven. However, you can get a similar result by spraying the oven with water before baking. If the underneath of the loaf is not very crusty at the end of baking, turn it over on the baking sheet, switch off the heat and leave it in the oven for a further 5–10 minutes.*

Traditional Irish Soda Bread

Irish soda bread contains no yeast and therefore does not need to be left to rise, so it is quick and easy to make. It is best eaten on the day that it is made, preferably while still warm. You can bake a loaf in the morning, ready to take on a picnic to serve with cheese and salads.

SERVES FOUR TO SIX

450g/1lb plain wholemeal (all-purpose whole-wheat) flour

10ml/2 tsp bicarbonate of soda (baking soda)

400ml/14fl oz/1²/₃ cups buttermilk

FROM THE STORECUPBOARD

5ml/1 tsp salt

1 Preheat the oven to 200°C/400°F/Gas 6. Place the flour in a large bowl and stir in the bicarbonate of soda and salt. Make a well in the centre.

2 Gradually pour the buttermilk into the well, beating in the flour from around the edges to form a soft, not sticky, dough.

3 Turn the dough out on to a lightly floured surface and knead for 5 minutes, until smooth. Shape into a 20cm/8in round and place on a lightly greased baking sheet.

4 Using a sharp knife, cut a deep cross on the top of the dough and bake for 30–35 minutes, or until slightly risen and cooked through. Cool slightly on a wire rack before serving.

Spring Onion Flatbreads

Use these flatbreads to wrap around barbecue-cooked meat and chunky vegetable salads, or serve with tasty dips such as hummus. They're at their best as soon as they're cooked.

MAKES SIXTEEN

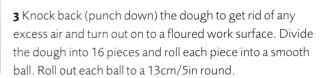

1 Place the flour in a large mixing bowl and stir in the salt, yeast and spring onions. Make a well in the centre and pour in 300ml/¹/₂ pint/1¹/₄ cups hand hot water. Mix to form a soft, but not sticky, dough.

2 Turn out the dough on to a floured work surface and knead for about 5 minutes, until smooth. Put the dough back in the bowl, cover with a damp dishtowel and leave in a warm place until doubled in size.

3 Knock back (punch down) the dough to get rid of any excess air and turn out on to a floured work surface. Divide the dough into 16 pieces and roll each piece into a smooth ball. Roll out each ball to a 13cm/5in round.

4 Heat a large frying pan until hot. Dust off any excess flour from one dough round and place in the frying pan. Cook for about 1 minute, then flip over and cook for a further 30 seconds. Repeat with the remaining dough rounds.

450g/1lb/4 cups strong white bread flour, plus extra for dusting

7g/¹/₄ oz packet easy-blend (rapid-rise) dried yeast

4 spring onions (scallions), finely chopped

FROM THE STORECUPBOARD

5ml/1 tsp salt

VARIATION

To make garlic flatbreads, use 2 finely chopped garlic cloves in place of the chopped spring onions. To add extra bite, mix in 1 finely chopped fresh red chilli as well.

Pitta Bread

Soft, slightly bubbly pitta bread is a pleasure to make. It can be eaten in a variety of ways, such as Mediterranean-style filled with salad or little chunks of meat cooked on the barbecue, or it can be torn into pieces and dipped in savoury dips such as hummus or tzatziki. Chop any leftover bread and incorporate into the Lebanese salad *fattoush* with parsley, mint, tomatoes and cucumber.

MAKES TWELVE

500g/1¼lb/5 cups strong white bread flour, or half white and half wholemeal (whole-wheat)

12.5ml/2½ tsp easy-blend (rapid-rise) dried yeast

FROM THE STORECUPBOARD

15ml/1 tbsp olive oil

15ml/1 tbsp salt

1 Combine the flour, yeast and salt. Combine the oil and 250ml/8fl oz/1 cup water, then add half of the flour mixture, stirring in the same direction, until the dough is stiff. Knead in the remaining flour. Place the dough in a clean bowl, cover with a clean dishtowel and leave in a warm place for at least 30 minutes and up to 2 hours.

2 Knead the dough for 10 minutes, or until smooth. Lightly oil the bowl, place the dough in it, cover again and leave to rise in a warm place for about 1 hour, or until doubled in size.

3 Divide the dough into 12 equal pieces. With lightly floured hands, flatten each piece, then roll out into a round measuring about 20cm/8in and about 4mm–1cm/¼–½in thick. Keep the rolled breads covered while you make the remaining pittas.

4 Heat a heavy frying pan over a medium-high heat. When hot, lay one piece of flattened dough in the pan and cook for 15–20 seconds. Turn it over and cook the second side for about 1 minute.

5 When large bubbles start to form on the bread, turn it over again. It should puff up. Using a clean dishtowel, gently press on the bread where the bubbles have formed. Cook for a total of 3 minutes, then remove the pitta from the pan. Repeat with the remaining dough. Wrap the pitta breads in a clean dishtowel, stacking them as each one is cooked. Serve the pittas hot while they are soft and moist.

VARIATION To bake the breads, preheat the oven to 220°C/425°F/Gas 7. Fill an unglazed or partially glazed dish with hot water and place in the bottom of the hot oven. Alternatively, arrange a handful of unglazed tiles in the base of the oven. Use either a non-stick baking sheet or a lightly oiled baking sheet and heat in the oven for a few minutes. Place two or three pieces of flattened dough on to the hot baking sheet and place in the hottest part of the oven. Bake for 2–3 minutes until puffed up. Repeat with the remaining dough.

Yemeni Sponge Flat Breads

These flat breads, known as *lahuhs* and made from a batter, are bubbly and soft. They are eaten with soups but are also good with salads, dips or cheese.

SERVES FOUR

1 Measure 500ml/17fl oz/generous 2 cups lukewarm water. In a bowl, dissolve the dried yeast in about 75ml/5 tbsp of the water. Leave in a warm place for about 10 minutes, or until frothy.

2 Stir the remaining water, the flour, salt and melted butter or vegetable oil into the yeast mixture and mix until it forms a smooth batter. Cover with a clean dishtowel, then leave in a warm place for about 1 hour, until doubled in size.

3 Stir the thick, frothy batter and, if it seems too thick to ladle out, add a little extra water. Cover and leave the batter to stand in a warm place for about 1 hour.

4 Cook the flat breads in a non-stick frying pan. Ladle 45–60ml/ 3–4 tbsp of batter (or less for smaller breads) into the pan and cook over a low heat until the top is bubbling and the colour has changed. (Traditionally these breads are cooked on only one side, but they can be turned over and the second side cooked for just a moment, if you like.)

5 Remove the cooked flat bread from the frying pan with a spatula and keep warm in a clean dishtowel. Continue cooking until you have used up all the remaining batter.

15ml/1 tbsp dried active yeast

350g/12oz/ 3 cups plain (all-purpose) flour

FROM THE STORECUPBOARD

50g/2oz/¹/₄ cup butter, melted, or 60ml/4 tbsp vegetable oil

5ml/1 tsp salt

COOK'S TIP *Use two or three frying pans at the same time so that the flat breads are ready together and so can be eaten piping hot.*

West Indian Flat Breads

Eclectic Caribbean food is influenced by a wide range of international cultures. It is the Anglo-Indian connection that brought the Indian flat bread called roti to Trinidad in the West Indies. Serve these simple-to-make breads straight from the pan to accompany spicy seafood chowders, curries, or any other dish that has plenty of sauce for mopping up.

MAKES EIGHT ROTIS

1 Mix the flour, baking powder and salt together in a large bowl and make a well in the centre. Gradually mix in 300ml/½ pint/ 1¼ cups water to make a firm dough.

2 Knead on a lightly floured surface until smooth. Place in a lightly oiled bowl, cover with lightly oiled clear film (plastic wrap). Leave to stand for 20 minutes.

3 Divide the dough into eight equal pieces and roll each one on a lightly floured surface into an 18cm/7in round. Brush the surface of each round with a little of the clarified butter or ghee, fold in half and half again. Cover the folded rounds with lightly oiled clear film (plastic wrap) and leave for 10 minutes.

4 Take one roti and roll out on a lightly floured surface into a round about 20–23cm/8–9in in diameter. Brush both sides with some clarified butter or ghee.

5 Heat a griddle or heavy frying pan, add the roti and cook for about 1 minute. Turn over and cook for 2 minutes, then turn over again and cook for 1 minute. Wrap in a clean dishtowel to keep warm while cooking the remaining rotis. Serve warm.

450g/1lb/4 cups atta or fine wholemeal (whole-wheat) flour

5ml/1 tsp baking powder

FROM THE STORECUPBOARD

115–150g/4–5oz/ 8–10 tbsp clarified butter or ghee, melted

5ml/1 tsp salt

Tandoori Rotis

Indian flat breads are fun to make at home: these may not be strictly authentic in terms of cooking method, but they taste fantastic. This bread would normally be baked in a tandoor, a clay oven that is heated with charcoal or wood. The oven becomes extremely hot, cooking the bread in minutes. The rotis are ready when light brown bubbles appear on the surface.

MAKES SIX ROTIS

350g/12oz/3 cups atta or fine wholemeal (whole-wheat) flour

FROM THE STORECUPBOARD

30–45ml/2–3 tbsp melted ghee or butter, for brushing

5ml/1 tsp salt

1 Sift the flour and salt into a large bowl. Add 250ml/8fl oz/1 cup water and mix to a soft dough. Knead on a lightly floured surface for 3–4 minutes, until smooth. Place the dough in a lightly oiled mixing bowl, cover with lightly oiled clear film (plastic wrap) and leave to rest for 1 hour.

2 Turn out on to a lightly floured surface. Divide the dough into six pieces and shape each piece into a ball. Press out into a larger round with the palm of your hand, cover with lightly oiled clear film (plastic wrap) and leave to rest for 10 minutes.

3 Meanwhile, preheat the oven to 230°C/450°F/Gas 8. Place three baking sheets in the oven to heat. Roll the rotis into 15cm/6in rounds, place two on each baking sheet and bake for 8–10 minutes. Brush with ghee or butter and serve warm.

Preserves, Pickles, Relishes and Sauces

SWEET AND SAVOURY PRESERVES, CONDIMENTS AND

SAUCES CAN ADD THE FINISHING TOUCH TO A SIMPLE DISH.

A SPOONFUL OF FRUIT JAM OR JELLY CAN TRANSFORM A

PLAIN SCONE INTO TEATIME TREAT, WHILE PIQUANT

PICKLES AND RELISHES CAN ENLIVEN BREAD AND CHEESE,

AND A FLAVOURSOME SAUCE CAN TURN SIMPLY COOKED

FISH INTO A REALLY SPECIAL MEAL.

Bramble Jelly

The tart, fruity flavour of wild blackberries makes this jelly one of the best, especially for serving with hot buttered toast or English muffins. When picking the fruit, include a small proportion of red unripe berries for a good set. Redcurrant jelly is made in the same way, but with less sugar. Reduce the quantity to 350g/12oz/1½ cups of sugar for every 600ml/ 1 pint/2½ cups of fruit juice.

900g/2lb/ 8 cups blackberries

juice of 1 lemon

about 900g/2lb/ 4 cups caster (superfine) sugar

MAKES 900G/2LB

1 Put the blackberries and lemon juice into a large pan (use a preserving pan with two handles if possible). Add 300ml/½ pint/1¼ cups water. Cover the pan and cook for 15–30 minutes, or until the blackberries are very soft.

2 Ladle into a jelly bag or a large sieve lined with muslin (cheesecloth) and set over a large mixing bowl. Leave the fruit to drip overnight to obtain the maximum amount of juice. Do not disturb or squeeze the bag or the jelly will be cloudy.

3 Discard the fruit pulp. Measure the juice and allow 450g/1lb/2 cups sugar to every 600ml/ 1 pint/2½ cups juice. Place the juice and sugar in a large, heavy pan and bring to the boil, stirring constantly until the sugar has dissolved.

4 Boil the mixture rapidly until the jelly registers 105°C/220°F on a sugar thermometer, or test for setting by spooning a small amount on to a chilled saucer (keep a saucer in the freezer for this purpose). Chill for 3 minutes, then push the mixture with your finger: if wrinkles form on the surface of the jelly, it is ready.

5 Skim off any scum and immediately pour the jelly into warm sterilized jars. Cover and seal immediately, then label when the jars are cold.

Strawberry Jam

This is the classic fragrant preserve for English afternoon tea, served with freshly baked scones and clotted cream. It is also extremely good stirred into plain yogurt for breakfast. When choosing strawberries for making jam, pick undamaged, slightly under-ripe fruit if possible – the pectin content will be high and ensure a good set.

1kg/2¼lb/8 cups
small strawberries

900g/2lb/4 cups
granulated sugar

juice of 2 lemons

MAKES ABOUT 1.3KG/3LB

1 Layer the strawberries and sugar in a large bowl. Cover and leave overnight.

2 The next day, scrape the strawberries and their juice into a large, heavy pan. Add the lemon juice. Gradually bring to the boil over a low heat, stirring until the sugar has dissolved.

3 Boil steadily for 10–15 minutes, or until the jam registers 105°C/220°F on a sugar thermometer. Alternatively, test for setting by spooning a small amount on to a chilled saucer. Chill for 3 minutes, then push the jam with your finger: if wrinkles form on the surface, it is ready. Cool for 10 minutes.

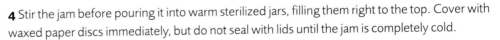

4 Stir the jam before pouring it into warm sterilized jars, filling them right to the top. Cover with waxed paper discs immediately, but do not seal with lids until the jam is completely cold.

COOK'S TIP *For best results when making jam, don't wash the strawberries unless absolutely necessary. Instead, brush off any dirt, or wipe the strawberries with a damp cloth. If you have to wash any, pat them dry and then spread them out on a clean dishtowel to dry.*

Spiced Poached Kumquats

Warm cinnamon and star anise make a heady combination with the full citrus flavour of kumquats. Star anise is an attractive spice: it is an eight-pointed star that contains tiny aniseed-flavoured, amber coloured seeds. The kumquats go well with rich meats, such as roast pork or baked ham, or with punchy goat's milk cheese. They are also good with desserts and ice creams.

SERVES SIX

1 Cut the kumquats in half and discard the pips (seeds). Place the kumquats in a pan with the caster sugar, 150ml/¼ pint/⅔ cup water and the cinnamon stick and star anise. Cook over a gentle heat, stirring until the sugar has dissolved.

2 Increase the heat, cover the pan and boil the mixture for about 8–10 minutes, until the kumquats are tender. To bottle the kumquats, spoon them into warm, sterilized jars, seal and label.

3 If you want to serve the spiced kumquats soon after making them, let the mixture cool, then chill it.

> **450g/1lb/ 4 cups kumquats**
>
> **115g/4oz/ ¹/₂ cup caster (superfine) sugar**
>
> **1 small cinnamon stick**
>
> **1 star anise**

Three-fruit Marmalade

Bitter marmalade oranges have a powerful flavour and plenty of setting power to make an excellent preserve. Known as Seville oranges, they are usually only available for a short time in January – but sweet oranges can be used in this recipe if necessary.

MAKES 2.25KG/5LB

1 Wash the fruit, halve, and squeeze their juice. Pour into a large heavy pan or preserving pan. Tip the pips (seeds) and pulp into a square of muslin (cheesecloth), gather the sides into a bag and tie the neck. Tie the bag to the pan handle so that it dangles in the juice.

2 Remove and discard the membranes and pith from the citrus skins and cut the rinds into slivers. Add to the pan with 1.75 litres/3 pints/7½ cups water. Heat until simmering and then cook gently for 2 hours. Test the rinds for softness by pressing a cooled piece with a finger.

3 Lift out the muslin bag, squeezing out the juice into the pan. Discard the bag. Stir the sugar into the pan and heat very gently, stirring occasionally, until the sugar has dissolved.

4 Bring the mixture to the boil and boil for 10–15 minutes, or until the marmalade registers 105°C/220°F on a sugar thermometer. Alternatively, test the marmalade for setting by pouring a small amount on to a chilled saucer. Chill for 3 minutes, then push the marmalade with your finger: if wrinkles form on the surface, it is ready. Cool for 15 minutes.

5 Stir the marmalade and pour it into warm, sterilized jars. Cover with waxed paper discs. Seal and label when completely cold. Store in a cool dark cupboard.

> **2 Seville (Temple) oranges**
>
> **2 lemons**
>
> **1 grapefruit**
>
> **1.5kg/3lb 6oz/ 6³/₄ cups granulated sugar**

COOK'S TIP *Allow the marmalade to cool slightly before potting so that it is thick enough to stop the fruit from sinking in the jars.*

Preserved Lemons

These are widely used in Middle Eastern cooking, for which only the peel is used and not the pulp. In this recipe the lemons are cut into wedges instead of being preserved whole, in traditional style. The wedges are more practical for potting and they are also easy to prepare before use.

MAKES TWO JARS

1 Wash the lemons well and cut each into six to eight wedges. Press a generous amount of sea salt into the cut surfaces, pushing it into every crevice.

2 Pack the salted lemon wedges into two 1.2 litre/2 pint/5 cup sterilized jars. To each jar, add 30–45ml/2–3 tbsp salt and 90ml/6 tbsp lemon juice, then top up with boiling water to cover the lemons. (If using larger jars, use more lemon juice and less water.)

3 Cover the jars and leave to stand for 2–4 weeks before serving.

4 To serve, rinse the preserved lemons well to remove some of the salty flavour, then pull off and discard the flesh. Cut the lemon peel into strips or leave in chunks and use as you like.

10 unwaxed lemons

**about 200ml/
7fl oz/scant 1 cup
fresh lemon juice or a
combination of fresh
and preserved**

FROM THE
STORECUPBOARD

sea salt

Middle Eastern Pickle

Beetroot brings attractive colour and its inimitable sweet, slightly earthy flavour to this Middle Eastern speciality. The pickle is delicious with falafel or cold roast beef. When buying beetroot, choose firm, unblemished, small- to medium-sized specimens. If you buy beetroot with green tops, reserve them and cook like spinach for a tasty vegetable accompaniment.

MAKES FOUR JARS

**1kg/2¼lb
young turnips**

**3–4 raw
beetroot (beets)**

juice of 1 lemon

FROM THE
STORECUPBOARD

**about 45ml/3 tbsp
kosher salt or
coarse sea salt**

1 Wash, but do not peel the turnips and beetroot. Then cut them into slices about 5mm/¼in thick. Put the salt in a bowl with about 1.5 litres/2½ pints/6¼ cups water, stir and leave on one side until the salt has completely dissolved.

2 Sprinkle the beetroot with lemon juice and divide among four 1.2 litre/2 pint/5 cup sterilized jars. Top with the sliced turnips, packing them in very tightly. Pour over the brine, making sure that the vegetables are completely covered.

3 Seal the jars and leave in a cool place for seven days for the flavours to develop before serving.

Horseradish and Beetroot Sauce

This is a traditional Jewish speciality. Known as *chrain*, it is often eaten at Pesah, the Passover meal, for which horseradish is one of the traditional bitter flavours. However, it complements a variety of foods and dishes of many different cooking styles, including roast meats and grilled fish.

SERVES ABOUT EIGHT

1 Put the horseradish and beetroot in a bowl and mix together, then season with sugar, vinegar and salt to taste.

2 Spoon the sauce into a sterilized jar, packing it down firmly, and seal. Store in the refrigerator, where it will keep for up to 2 weeks.

150g/5oz grated fresh horseradish

2 cooked beetroot (beets), grated

15ml/1 tbsp sugar

15–30ml/1–2 tbsp red wine vinegar

FROM THE STORECUPBOARD

salt

COOK'S TIP *Fresh horseradish is very potent and should be handled with care as it can make the skin burn as well as the eyes run. Wear fine rubber gloves to protect your hands.*

Yellow Pepper and Coriander Relish

Relishes are quick and easy to make and they are delicious with cold meats and cheese or as a sandwich filler. Here the ingredients are lightly cooked, then processed to a chunky consistency. Red or orange (bell) peppers will work just as well as yellow as they all have a sweet flavour. Don't use green peppers though, because they are not sweet.

SERVES FOUR TO SIX

1 Seed and coarsely chop the peppers. Heat the oil in a frying pan and gently cook the peppers, stirring frequently, for 8–10 minutes, until lightly coloured.

2 Meanwhile, seed the chilli and slice it as thinly as possible. Transfer the peppers and cooking juices to a food processor and process lightly until chopped. Transfer half the peppers to a bowl. Using a sharp knife, chop the fresh coriander, then add to the food processor and process briefly.

3 Tip the contents of the food processor into the bowl with the rest of the peppers and add the chilli and salt. Mix well, cover and chill until ready to serve.

3 large yellow (bell) peppers

1 large mild fresh red chilli

small handful of fresh coriander (cilantro)

FROM THE STORECUPBOARD

45ml/3 tbsp sesame oil

salt

COOK'S TIP *Other flavoured oils, such as lemon- or garlic-infused oil, can be used in place of the sesame oil.*

Hot Mango Salsa

For sweet, tangy results, select a really juicy, ripe mango for this salsa – it is not worth making the salsa with a firm, unripe mango as it will not taste as good as it should. Keep an unripe mango in the fruit bowl for a few days until it has ripened. This fruity salsa is a delicious accompaniment to chargrilled or barbecued chicken or fish.

SERVES FOUR TO SIX

1 To prepare the mango, cut the flesh off on either side of the flat stone (pit). Peel and finely dice the mango halves and cut off and chop the flesh that still clings to the stone.

2 Finely grate the lime rind and squeeze the juice. Seed and finely shred the fresh red chilli.

3 Finely chop the onion and mix it in a bowl with the mango, lime rind, 15ml/1 tbsp lime juice, the chilli and a little salt. Cover and chill until ready to serve.

1 medium ripe mango

1 lime

1 large mild fresh red chilli

$^1/_2$ small red onion

FROM THE STORECUPBOARD

salt

Harissa

This simplified version of harissa – the classic spicy North African sauce – is extremely quick to make. It can be served as a dip with wedges of Middle Eastern flat bread, as a condiment with couscous and other North African dishes, or as a flavouring to spice up meat and vegetable stews. This basic spice blend goes very well with other aromatic herbs and spices so you can vary the flavour by adding chopped fresh coriander (cilantro) or a pinch of caraway seeds along with the lemon juice, if you like.

SERVES FOUR TO SIX

1 Put the paprika, cayenne pepper, ground cumin and 250ml/8fl oz/ 1 cup water in a large, heavy pan.

2 Bring the spice mixture to the boil, then immediately remove the pan from the heat.

3 Stir in the lemon juice to taste and allow to cool completely before serving or using.

45ml/3 tbsp paprika

2.5–5ml/^{1}/$_2$–1 tsp cayenne pepper

1.5ml/^{1}/$_4$ tsp ground cumin

juice of ^{1}/$_4$–^{1}/$_2$ lemon

Aioli

This classic, creamy garlic mayonnaise from France is simple to make and absolutely delicious. Serve it with salads or as a dip with crudités, with potato wedges, or as a quick sauce for pan-fried salmon. Try to use extra virgin olive oil for this mayonnaise if you can – it has a rich and delicious flavour that really makes this sauce special.

SERVES FOUR TO SIX

1 Put the garlic cloves in a mortar, add a pinch of salt and pound to a smooth paste with a pestle.

2 Transfer the garlic paste to a bowl. Add the egg yolks and whisk for about 30 seconds, until creamy. Whisk in the olive oil, drop by drop, until the mixture begins to thicken, then add the oil in a slow drizzle until the mixture is thick and creamy.

3 Beat in the lemon juice and seasoning to taste. Serve immediately or cover with clear film (plastic wrap) and chill in the refrigerator until ready to use. Allow the aioli to return to room temperature before serving.

4 large garlic cloves, peeled

2 egg yolks

250ml/8fl oz/1 cup extra virgin olive oil

15–30ml/1–2 tbsp lemon juice

FROM THE STORECUPBOARD

salt

Roasted Garlic Sauce

A roasted garlic sauce has plenty of robust flavour without the harshness of some uncooked garlic sauces and dressings. This one keeps well in the refrigerator for several days. Serve it as an accompaniment to barbecued burgers or sausages, grilled steaks, lamb chops or pork steaks – the possibilities are endless.

SERVES SIX TO EIGHT

6 large heads of garlic

2 slices white bread, about 90g/3¹/₂oz

30–45ml/2–3 tbsp lemon juice

FROM THE STORECUPBOARD

120ml/4fl oz/¹/₂ cup olive oil

salt

1 Preheat the oven to 200°C/400°F/Gas 6. Slice the tops off the garlic and place the bulbs on a sheet of foil. Spoon over 30ml/2 tbsp of the oil and sprinkle with salt. Wrap the foil over the garlic and bake for 1 hour, until soft. Open out the foil and leave the garlic to cool.

2 Discard the crusts from the bread. Soak the bread in water for 1 minute, then squeeze dry and place in a food processor. Squeeze the garlic flesh into the processor. Process to a smooth paste.

3 Add 30ml/2 tbsp lemon juice with a little salt and pepper. With the machine running, gradually add the remaining oil in a thin stream to make a smooth paste. Check the seasoning, adding more lemon juice if needed. Turn into a bowl, cover and chill until required.

Watercress Sauce

This pretty green sauce is refreshingly tart and peppery. It is delicious served as an accompaniment to poached fish, or as a dip for simply grilled prawns (shrimp). Do not prepare the sauce more than a few hours ahead of serving, as the watercress will discolour the sauce. This peppery green sauce can also be made with rocket (arugula) leaves instead of the watercress.

SERVES SIX TO EIGHT

1 Remove the tough stems from the watercress leaves and finely chop the leaves by hand or in a food processor. Add the mayonnaise and the freshly squeezed lemon juice and process to mix.

2 Melt the unsalted butter, then add to the watercress mixture, a little at a time, processing or whisking in a bowl until the butter has been fully incorporated and the sauce is thick and smooth. Season to taste with salt and pepper, then cover and chill in the refrigerator for at least an hour before serving.

200g/7oz watercress leaves

300g/11oz/1¼ cups mayonnaise

15–30ml/1–2 tbsp freshly squeezed lemon juice

FROM THE STORECUPBOARD

200g/7oz/scant 1 cup unsalted (sweet) butter

salt and ground black pepper

EXTRAS *Garlic makes a delicious addition to this sauce. Peel and finely chop 1–2 garlic cloves and combine with the chopped watercress leaves, mayonnaise and lemon juice, before adding the melted butter in step 2.*

Shallots in Balsamic Vinegar

These whole shallots cooked in balsamic vinegar and herbs are a modern variation on pickled onions, but they have a much more gentle, smooth flavour. They are delicious served with cold pies, meats and cheese. A combination of bay leaves and thyme are used here but rosemary, oregano or marjoram sprigs would work just as well.

SERVES SIX

1 Put the unpeeled shallots in a bowl, cover with boiling water and leave for 2 minutes for the skins to loosen. Drain and peel the shallots, leaving them whole.

2 Put the sugar, bay leaves or thyme and vinegar in a heavy pan and bring to the boil. Add the shallots, cover and simmer gently for about 40 minutes, until the shallots are just tender.

3 Transfer the mixture to a sterilized jar, seal and label, then store in a cool, dark place. Alternatively, drain and transfer to a serving dish. Leave to cool, then chill until ready to serve.

500g/1¼ lb shallots

30ml/2 tbsp muscovado (molasses) sugar

several bay leaves or fresh thyme sprigs

300ml/½ pint/ 1¼ cups balsamic vinegar

Barbecue Sauce

A wide selection of ready-made barbecue sauces are available in the supermarkets, but they really don't compare with the home-made variety. This 10-minute version can be used to transform baked or grilled chicken, sausages or fish into an interesting meal that needs no more than a mixed salad and baked potatoes as accompaniments.

SERVES FOUR TO SIX

1 Tip the cans of chopped tomatoes with herbs or garlic into a medium, heavy pan and add the finely chopped onion, black treacle and Worcestershire sauce.

2 Bring to the boil and cook, uncovered, until the mixture is thickened and pulpy, stirring frequently with a wooden spoon to stop the sauce catching on the base of the pan. Season lightly with salt and plenty of freshly ground black pepper and transfer to a serving dish or jug (pitcher). Serve the sauce warm or cold.

2 x 400g/14 oz cans chopped tomatoes with herbs or garlic

1 onion, finely chopped

15ml/1 tbsp black treacle (molasses)

45ml/3 tbsp Worcestershire sauce

FROM THE STORECUPBOARD

salt and ground black pepper

Mixed Herb and Peppercorn Sauce

This lovely, refreshing sauce relies on absolutely fresh herbs (any combination will do) and good-quality olive oil for its fabulous flavour. Make it a day in advance, to allow the flavours to mingle. Serve the sauce with simply cooked fish such as salmon or with grilled beef or lamb steaks.

SERVES FOUR TO SIX

1 Crush the cumin seeds using a mortar and pestle. Alternatively, put the seeds in a small bowl and pound them with the end of a rolling pin. Add the pink or green peppercorns and pound a little to break them up slightly.

2 Remove any tough stalks from the herbs. Put the herbs in a food processor with the cumin seeds, peppercorns, oil and salt and process until the herbs are finely chopped, scraping the sauce down from the sides of the bowl if necessary.

3 Turn the sauce into a small serving dish, cover with clear film (plastic wrap) and chill until ready to serve.

10ml/2 tsp cumin seeds

15ml/1 tbsp pink or green peppercorns in brine, drained and rinsed

25g/1oz/1 cup fresh mixed herbs, such as parsley, mint, chives and coriander (cilantro)

FROM THE STORECUPBOARD

45ml/3 tbsp lemon-infused olive oil

salt

Healthy Juices and Smoothies

THERE IS SOMETHING REALLY ENTICING ABOUT FRESHLY

MADE BLENDED DRINKS AND HEALTHY JUICES. THEY CAN BE

CLEANSING, FRESH OR ZESTY, SMOOTH AND CREAMY OR

RICH AND DECADENT – BUT WHAT THEY ALL HAVE IN

COMMON IS A WONDERFULLY MOREISH QUALITY THAT

MAKES YOU FEEL THAT EVERY GLASSFUL IS A TREAT.

Leafy Apple Lift-off

This delicious blend of fruit and fresh green leaves is refreshing and healthy. The leaves are robustly flavoured and have a peppery, pungent taste. To prepare the leaves, discard any damaged and discoloured ones and rinse thoroughly in cold water to remove any grit. To prevent the juice from being watery, dry the leaves in a salad spinner or on kitchen paper before juicing.

SERVES ONE

1 Quarter the apple. Using a juice extractor, juice the fruit and watercress, rocket or spinach.

2 Add the lime juice to the apple, grape and leaf mixture and stir thoroughly to blend all the ingredients together. Pour the juice into a tall glass and serve immediately.

1 **eating apple**

150g/5oz **white grapes**

25g/1oz **watercress, rocket (arugula) or spinach**

15ml/1 tbsp **lime juice**

Fennel Fusion

The hearty combination of raw vegetables and apples makes a surprisingly delicious juice that is packed with natural goodness and is a truly wonderful pick-me-up. Use the remaining cabbage and fennel to make a really crunchy salad – slice and dress with French dressing or simply with olive oil, herb vinegar and plenty of freshly ground black pepper and sea salt to taste.

SERVES ONE

1 Coarsely slice the red cabbage and the fennel bulb and quarter the eating apples. Using a juice extractor, juice the vegetables and fruit.

2 Add the lemon juice to the red cabbage, fennel and apple mixture and stir thoroughly to blend all the ingredients together. Pour into a glass and serve immediately.

½ **small red cabbage**

½ **fennel bulb**

2 **eating apples**

15ml/1 tbsp **lemon juice**

Tropical Calm

This deliciously scented juice is packed with goodness to cleanse and calm the system. Orange fruits such as cantaloupe melons and papayas are rich in the phytochemical betacarotene, which is a valuable anti-oxidant and is thought to have many health-promoting properties.

SERVES ONE

1 papaya

½ cantaloupe melon

90g/3½ oz seedless white grapes

1 Halve the papaya, remove the seeds and skin, then cut the flesh into coarse slices. Halve the melon, remove the seeds, cut into quarters, slice the flesh away from the skin and cut into chunks.

2 Using a juicer, juice the prepared fruit. Alternatively, blend the fruit in a food processor or blender for a thicker juice. Serve immediately.

Strawberry Soother

Relax with this comforting blend of just two fruits – it is rich in vitamin C and fabulous flavour. It's a perfect drink for summer when sweet strawberries, peaches and necatarines are in season.

SERVES ONE

225g/8oz/2 cups strawberries

1 peach or nectarine

1 Hull the strawberries. Using a sharp knife, quarter the peach or nectarine and pull out the stone (pit). Cut the flesh into coarse slices or chunks.

2 Using a juice extractor, juice the fruit. Alternatively, place the fruit in a food processor or blender and process until smooth. Serve immediately.

Carrot Revitalizer

This vibrant combination of vegetables and fruit makes a lively, health-giving drink. Carrots yield generous quantities of sweet juice, which goes perfectly with the sharp flavour of pear and the zesty taste of orange. This powerful drink will nourish and stimulate the system.

SERVES ONE

1 Scrub and trim the carrots and quarter the apples. Peel the orange and cut into rough segments.

2 Using a juice extractor, juice the carrots and fruit, pour into a glass and serve immediately.

3carrots

2 apples

1 orange

Purple Pep

Jewel-coloured beetroot juice is well known for its detoxifying properties so this juice makes the perfect choice when you've been over-doing it. It offers an excellent supply of valuable nutrients that are essential for good health.

SERVES ONE

carrots

115g/4oz beetroot (beet)

25g/1oz baby spinach, washed and dried

2 celery sticks

1 Scrub and trim the carrots and beetroot. Using a sharp knife, cut the beetroot into large chunks.

2 Using a juice extractor, juice the carrots, beetroot, spinach and celery, then pour into a glass and serve immediately.

Tomato and Cucumber Juice with Basil

Some herbs don't juice well, losing their aromatic flavour and turning muddy and dull. Basil, on the other hand, is an excellent juicer, keeping its distinctive fresh fragrance. It makes the perfect partner for mild, refreshing cucumber and the ripest, juiciest tomatoes you can find. Try using cherry tomatoes for an extra sweet flavour.

MAKES TWO SMALL GLASSES

¹/₂ cucumber, peeled

a handful of fresh basil

350g/12oz tomatoes

1 Quarter the cucumber lengthways. There's no need to remove the seeds. Push it through a juicer with the basil, then do the same with the tomatoes.

2 Pour the tomato, basil and cucumber juice over ice cubes in one tall or two short glasses and echo the herb flavour by adding a few basil sprigs for decoration.

Beetroot, Ginger and Orange Juice

Despite its firmness, beetroot can be juiced raw and its intense flavour goes perfectly with tangy citrus fruits and fresh root ginger. It has the highest sugar content of any vegetable and makes a delicious juice with a vibrant colour and rich but refreshing taste.

MAKES ONE LARGE GLASS

200g/7oz raw beetroot (beets)

1cm/¹/₂in piece fresh root ginger, peeled

1 large orange

1 Scrub the beetroot, then trim them and cut into quarters. Push half the beetroot through a vegetable juicer, followed by the ginger and the remaining beetroot and pour the juice into a jug (pitcher).

2 Squeeze the juice from the orange, using a citrus juicer or by hand, and pour into the beetroot juice. Stir to combine.

3 Pour the juice over ice cubes in a glass or clear glass cup and serve immediately to enjoy the full benefit of all the nutrients. (Do not let the ice cubes melt into the juice or they will dilute its flavour.)

Melon Pick-me-up

Spicy fresh root ginger is delicious with melon and pear in this reviving and invigorating concoction. Charentais or Galia melon can be used instead of the cantaloupe melon in this recipe. To enjoy fresh root ginger at its best, buy it in small quantities and keep in a cool, dry place for up to a week. As it ages, the root will dry out and become hard.

SERVES ONE

1 Quarter the cantaloupe melon, remove the seeds using a teaspoon or a sharp knife, and carefully slice the flesh away from the skin, reserving any juice. Quarter the pears and reserve any juice.

2 Using a juice extractor, juice the melon flesh and juice, quartered pears and juice and the fresh root ginger. Pour juice into a tall glass and serve immediately.

½ **cantaloupe melon**

2 **pears**

2.5cm/1in **piece of fresh root ginger**

Apple Shiner

This refreshing fusion of sweet apple, honeydew melon, red grapes and lemon provides a reviving burst of energy and a feel-good sensation. Serve as a drink or use to pour over muesli (granola) for a quick and healthy breakfast.

SERVES ONE

1 **eating apple**

½ **honeydew melon**

90g/3½oz **red grapes**

15ml/1 tbsp **lemon juice**

1 Quarter the apple and remove the core. Cut the melon into quarters, remove the seeds and slice the flesh away from the skin.

2 Using a juice extractor, juice the apple, melon and grapes. Alternatively, process the fruit in a food processor or blender for 2–3 minutes, until smooth. Pour the juice into a long, tall glass, stir in the lemon juice and serve immediately.

Citrus Sparkle

Zesty citrus fruits are packed with vitamin C, which is necessary for a healthy immune system. Pink grapefruit have a sweeter flavour than the yellow varieties – in fact, the pinker they are, the sweeter they are likely to be. For a lighter drink to serve two, divide the juice between two glasses and top up with sparkling mineral water or soda water (club soda) and ice cubes.

SERVES ONE

1 Cut the pink grapefruit and orange in half and squeeze out the juice using a citrus fruit squeezer.

2 Pour the juice into a glass, stir in 15ml/1 tbsp lemon juice, add the remaining lemon juice if required and serve immediately.

1 pink grapefruit

1 orange

30ml/2 tbsp freshly squeezed lemon juice

Hum-zinger

Aromatic tropical fruits make a drink that is bursting with flavour and energy. Enjoy a glass first thing in the morning to kick-start your day.

SERVES ONE

½ pineapple, peeled

1 small mango, peeled and stoned (pitted)

½ small papaya, seeded and peeled

1 Remove any "eyes" left in the pineapple, then cut all the fruit into fairly coarse chunks.

2 Using a juice extractor, juice the fruit. Alternatively, use a food processor or blender and process for about 2–3 minutes until smooth. Pour into a glass and serve immediately.

Grapefruit and Pear Juice

This deliciously refreshing rose-tinged blend will keep you bright-eyed and bushy-tailed. Its sharp yet sweet flavour is perfect for breakfast or as a pick-me-up when energy levels are flagging. If the grapefruit are particularly tart, serve the juice with a little bowl of brown sugar, or even brown sugar stirrers.

MAKES TWO TALL GLASSES

1 Take a thin slice from one grapefruit half and halve it. Cut a few thin slices of pear. Squeeze the juice from the grapefruit halves, then the pears using a juicer.

2 Combine the fruit juices and pour into two glasses. Add a few ice cubes to each glass and decorate with the grapefruit and pear slices. Serve immediately.

2 pink grapefruit, halved

2 ripe pears

Strawberry Apple Slush

Sweet, juicy strawberries make a delicately fragrant juice, with a consistency that's not too thick and not too thin. The addition of apple juice and just a hint of vanilla creates a tantalizing treat that's perfect for sipping on a lazy summer's afternoon.

MAKES TWO TALL GLASSES

300g/11oz/2³/₄ cups ripe strawberries

2 small, crisp eating apples

10ml/2 tsp vanilla syrup

1 Reserve a couple of strawberries and hull the remaining ones. Roughly chop the apples and push all the fruits through a juicer. Stir in the vanilla syrup.

2 Half-fill two tall glasses with crushed ice. Pour over the juice, decorate with the reserved strawberries (slicing them if you like) and serve immediately.

Honey and Watermelon Tonic

This refreshing juice will help to cool the body, calm the digestion and cleanse the system, and may even have aphrodisiac qualities. On hot days add ice cubes to keep the juice cool. The distinctive pinkish-red flesh of the watermelon gives this tonic a beautiful hue – decorate with a few fresh mint leaves to provide a stunning colour contrast.

SERVES FOUR

1 Cut the watermelon flesh into chunks, cutting away the skin and discarding the black seeds. Place in a large bowl, pour the chilled water over and leave to stand for 10 minutes.

2 Tip the mixture into a large sieve set over a bowl. Using a wooden spoon, press gently on the fruit to extract all the liquid.

3 Stir in the lime juice and sweeten to taste with honey. Pour into a jug (pitcher) or glasses and serve.

1 watermelon

1 litre/1¾ pints/ 4 cups chilled still mineral water

juice of 2 limes

clear honey, to taste

Cranberry, Ginger and Cinnamon Spritzer

Partially freezing fruit juice gives it a refreshingly slushy texture. The combination of cranberry and apple juice is tart and clean. Add a few fresh or frozen cranberries to decorate each glass, if you like.

600ml/1 pint/2¹/₂ cups chilled cranberry juice

150ml/¹/₄ pint/²/₃ cup clear apple juice

4 cinnamon sticks

about 400ml/14fl oz/ 1²/₃ cups chilled ginger ale

SERVES FOUR

1 Pour the cranberry juice into a shallow freezerproof container and freeze for about 2 hours, or until a thick layer of ice crystals has formed around the edges.

2 Mash the semi-frozen juice with a fork to break up the ice, then return the mixture to the freezer for a further 2–3 hours or until it is almost solid.

3 Pour the apple juice into a small pan, add two cinnamon sticks and bring to just below boiling point. Pour into a jug (pitcher) and leave to cool, then remove the cinnamon sticks and set them aside. Cool, then chill the juice.

4 Spoon the cranberry ice into a food processor or blender. Add the cinnamon-flavoured apple juice and process briefly until slushy. Pile the mixture into cocktail glasses, top up with chilled ginger ale, decorate with cinnamon sticks and serve immediately.

Lavender Orange Lush

This fragrant, lavender-scented juice is guaranteed to perk up a jaded palate in no time at all. It has a heavenly aroma and distinct yet subtle taste. Make plenty and keep it in the refrigerator. Use extra lavender sprigs as fun stirrers or a pretty garnish.

SERVES FOUR TO SIX

10–12 lavender flowers

45ml/3 tbsp caster (superfine) sugar

8 large oranges

1 Pull the lavender flowers from their stalks and put them into a bowl with the sugar and 120ml/4fl oz/$^1/_2$ cup boiling water. Stir briskly until the sugar has dissolved, then leave the lavender to steep for 10 minutes.

2 Squeeze the oranges using a citrus juicer and pour the juice into a jug (pitcher). Strain the lavender syrup into the juice and chill. Serve poured over ice.

Ice Cool Currant

Intensely flavoured blackcurrants, whizzed in a blender with crushed ice, make a drink so thick and slushy that you might want to serve it with long spoons. If you have a glut of blackcurrants, make a double quantity of the juice and store it in the refrigerator for up to a week, ready to blend with ice.

SERVES TWO

125g/4¹/₄oz/generous 1 cup blackcurrants

60ml/4 tbsp light muscovado (brown) sugar

good pinch of mixed (apple pie) spice (optional)

VARIATION
Redcurrants or a mixture of redcurrants and blackcurrants could also be used instead of blackcurrants if you like. The juice will have a lighter taste.

1 Put the blackcurrants and sugar in a pan. (There is no need to string the blackcurrants first.) Add the mixed spice, if using, and pour in 100ml/3¹/₂fl oz/scant ¹/₂ cup water. Bring the mixture to the boil and cook for 2–3 minutes, or until the blackcurrants are completely soft.

2 Press the mixture through a sieve into a bowl, pressing the pulp with the back of a dessertspoon to extract as much juice as possible. Set aside to cool completely.

3 Put 225g/8oz crushed ice in a food processor or blender with the cooled juice and process for about 1 minute until slushy and thoroughly mixed. Scrape the drink into tall glasses and serve immediately.

Lemon Float

Traditional lemonade made with freshly squeezed lemons and served with scoops of ice cream and soda water makes the ultimate refresher. The lemonade can be stored in the refrigerator for up to two weeks, so make a double batch when the weather is hot.

SERVES FOUR

1 Finely grate the rind from the lemons, then squeeze out the juice using a citrus juicer. Put the rind in a bowl with the sugar and pour over 600ml/1 pint/2$\frac{1}{2}$ cups boiling water. Stir until the sugar dissolves, then leave to cool.

2 Stir the lemon juice into the cooled syrup. Strain and chill for several hours. To serve, put a scoop of ice cream in each glass, then half-fill with the lemonade and add plenty of lemon slices. Top up with soda water (club soda) and add another scoop of ice cream to each glass and serve immediately.

6 lemons

200g/7oz/1 cup caster (superfine) sugar

8 scoops vanilla ice cream

Blue Lagoon

Blueberries are not only an excellent source of betacarotene and vitamin C, but they are also rich in flavonoids, which help to cleanse the system. Mixed with other dark red fruits, such as blackberries and grapes, they make a highly nutritious and extremely delicious blend that can be stored in the refrigerator and enjoyed throughout the day.

SERVES ONE

90g/3¹/₂oz/scant 1 cup blackcurrants or blackberries

150g/5oz red grapes

130g/4¹/₂oz/generous 1 cup blueberries

1 If using blackcurrants, gently pull the stalks through the tines of a fork to remove the fruit, then remove the stalks from the grapes.

2 Push all the fruits through a juicer, saving a few for decoration. Place some ice in a medium glass and pour over the juice. Decorate with the reserved fruit and serve.

Strawberry and Banana Smoothie

The blend of perfectly ripe bananas and strawberries creates a drink that is both fruity and creamy, with a luscious texture. Papaya, mango or pineapple can be used instead of strawberries for a tropical drink. Popular with adults and children alike, this is a great way to get children to enjoy fruit – much healthier than commercial milkshakes, too.

SERVES FOUR

1 Hull the strawberries. Peel the bananas and chop them into fairly large chunks.

2 Put the fruit in a food processor or blender. Process to a thick, coarse purée, scraping down the sides of the goblet as necessary.

3 Add the skimmed milk and ice cubes, crushing the ice first unless you have a heavy-duty processor. Process until smooth and thick. Pour into tall glasses and top each with strawberry slices to decorate. Serve immediately.

200g/7oz/1³/₄ cups
strawberries, plus
extra, sliced,
to decorate

2 ripe bananas

300ml/¹/₂ pint/1¹/₄
cups skimmed milk

10 ice cubes

EXTRAS *For a rich and velvety drink, add 120ml/ 4fl oz/¹/₂ cup coconut milk and process as above. Reduce the volume of milk to 175ml/6fl oz/³/₄ cup.*

Raspberry and Orange Smoothie

Sharp-sweet raspberries and zesty oranges taste fabulous combined with the light creaminess of yogurt. This smoothie takes just minutes to prepare, making it perfect for breakfast – or any other time of the day. If you like a really tangy drink add freshly squeezed lemon or lime juice to taste.

SERVES TWO TO THREE

1 Place the raspberries and yogurt in a food processor or blender and process for about 1 minute, until smooth and creamy.

2 Add the orange juice to the raspberry and yogurt mixture and process for about 30 seconds, or until thoroughly combined. Pour into tall glasses and serve immediately.

COOK'S TIP *For a super-chilled version, use frozen raspberries or a combination of frozen summer berries such as strawberries, redcurrants and blueberries instead of fresh. You may need to blend the raspberries and yogurt slightly longer for a really smooth result.*

250g/9oz/1¹/₂ cups
fresh raspberries,
chilled

200ml/7fl oz/scant
1 cup natural (plain)
yogurt, chilled

300ml/¹/₂pint/1¹/₄
cups freshly squeezed
orange juice, chilled

New York Egg Cream

No one knows precisely why this legendary drink is called egg cream, but some say it was a witty way of describing richness at a time when no one could afford to put both expensive eggs and cream together in a drink. Use full-fat (whole) milk for a really creamy taste. Dust a little cocoa powder over the top of the egg cream before serving, if you like.

SERVES ONE

> 45–60ml/3–4 tbsp good quality
> **chocolate syrup**
>
> 120ml/4fl oz/¹/₂ cup chilled **milk**
>
> 175ml/6fl oz/³/₄ cup chilled
> **sparkling mineral water**

1 Carefully pour the chocolate syrup into the bottom of a tall glass avoiding dripping any on the inside of the glass.

2 Pour the chilled milk into the glass on to the chocolate syrup.

3 Gradually pour the chilled sparkling mineral water into the glass, sip up any foam that rises to the top of the glass and carefully continue to add the remaining chilled sparkling mineral water. Stir well before drinking.

COOK'S TIP *An authentic egg cream is made with an old-fashioned seltzer dispenser that you press and spritz. In any case, you can use soda water (club soda) rather than mineral water, if you like.*

Banana and Maple Flip

This satisfying drink is packed with so much goodness that it makes a complete breakfast in a glass – great for when you're in a hurry. Be sure to use a really fresh free-range egg. The glass can be decorated with a slice of orange or lime to serve.

SERVES ONE

1 small banana, peeled and halved

50ml/2fl oz/¼ cup thick Greek (US strained plain) yogurt

1 egg

30ml/2 tbsp maple syrup

1 Put the peeled and halved banana, thick Greek yogurt, egg and maple syrup in a food processor or blender. Add 30ml/2 tbsp chilled water.

2 Process the ingredients constantly for about 2 minutes, or until the mixture turns a really pale, creamy colour and has a nice frothy texture.

3 Pour the banana and maple flip into a tall, chilled glass and serve immediately. Decorate the glasses with an orange or lime slice, if you like.

COOK'S TIPS

To chill the drinking glass quickly, place it in the freezer while you are preparing the drink.

For a hint of sharpness, add 5ml/1 tsp lemon or lime juice or use a slightly tangy yogurt.

Chocolate Brownie Milkshake

This truly indulgent drink is so simple, yet utterly rich and luxurious, so take a quiet moment to yourself and just sit back, relax and enjoy. For an even more indulgent treat, spoon over whipped cream and sprinkle with grated chocolate to serve.

SERVES ONE

40g/1¹/₂oz chocolate brownies

200ml/7fl oz/scant 1 cup full cream (whole) milk

2 scoops vanilla ice cream

1 Crumble the chocolate brownies into a food processor or blender and add the milk. Blend until the mixture is smooth.

2 Add the ice cream to the chocolate milk mixture and blend until the shake is really smooth and frothy. Pour into a tall glass and serve immediately.

Peppermint Candy Crush

The next time you see peppermint candy canes that are on sale at Christmas time, buy a few sticks and make this fun kid's drink . All you need to do is whizz up the candy with some milk and freeze until slushy, so it's ready and waiting for thirsty youngsters.

SERVES FOUR

90g/3¹/₂oz pink peppermint candy canes, plus four extra to serve

750ml/1¹/₄ pints/3 cups milk

a few drops of pink food colouring (optional)

1 While the candy canes are still in their wrappers, break into small bits using a rolling pin. (If it is unwrapped, put the candy in a polythene bag before you crush it.) Tip the pieces into a food processor or blender.

2 Pour the milk over the candy and add a few drops of pink food colouring, if using. Process until the cane is broken up into tiny pieces, then pour the mixture into a shallow freezer container and freeze for 2 hours, or until frozen around the edges.

3 Beat the mixture with a fork, breaking up the semi-frozen areas and stirring them into the centre. Re-freeze and repeat the process once or twice more until the mixture is slushy. Spoon into tall glasses and serve with candy cane stirrers.

Drinks

FROM CHILLED COCKTAILS AND ICY SHAKES TO WINTER
WARMERS, THERE ARE MANY UNUSUAL DRINKS YOU
CAN MAKE WITH JUST THREE OR FOUR INGREDIENTS.
YOU'LL NEED A SPECIAL ELECTRIC JUICER TO MAKE
SOME OF THE JUICES BUT ALL THE OTHER DRINKS CAN
BE WHIPPED UP IN AN INSTANT USING ORDINARY
KITCHEN EQUIPMENT. WARM YOURSELF UP WITH A CUP
OF CARDAMOM HOT CHOCOLATE OR A RUM AND STAR
ANISE HOT TODDY OR TRY A REFRESHING SEA BREEZE
OR MARGARITA COCKTAIL.

Rum and Star Anise Hot Toddy

Hot toddies are normally made with whisky but rum works really well too and produces a deliciously warming drink that's perfect for a cold winter evening – or even a winter afternoon after a hearty walk out in the freezing cold countryside. You can also flavour this toddy with different spices such as a vanilla pod (bean) or cinnamon stick.

SERVES FOUR

300ml/¹/₂ pint/1¹/₄ cups dark rum

45ml/3 tbsp caster (superfine) sugar

1 star anise

1 Pour the rum into a heatproof jug (pitcher) and add the sugar and star anise. Pour in 450ml/³/₄ pint/scant 2 cups boiling water and stir thoroughly until the sugar has dissolved.

2 Carefully pour the hot toddy into heatproof glasses or mugs and serve immediately.

Cardamom Hot Chocolate

Hot chocolate is a wonderful treat at any time of day – for breakfast with a warm croissant, as a teatime treat on a cold winter afternoon or before bed to help you sleep. Adding spicy cardamom gives this hot chocolate an extra rich, fragrant aroma.

SERVES FOUR

900ml/1¹/₂ pints/3³/₄ cups milk

2 cardamom pods, bruised

200g/7oz plain (semisweet) chocolate, broken into pieces

1 Put the milk in a pan with the cardamom pods and bring to the boil. Add the chocolate and whisk until melted.

2 Using a slotted spoon, remove the cardamom pods and discard. Pour the hot chocolate into heatproof glasses, mugs or cups and serve with whipped cream.

Atole

This drink, rather like a thick milkshake in consistency, is made from Mexican cornflour (masa harina) and flavoured with piloncillo (Mexican unrefined brown sugar). Ground cinnamon and/or fresh fruit purées are often added before serving, and some recipes introduce ground almonds.

SERVES SIX

1 Combine the milk with 600ml/ 1 pint/2¹/₂ cups cold water. Put the masa harina in a heavy pan and gradually beat in the milk and water mixture to make a smooth paste.

2 Place the pan over a moderate heat, add the vanilla pod and bring the mixture to the boil, stirring constantly until it thickens. Beat in the sugar and stir until the sugar has dissolved. Remove from the heat, discard the vanilla and serve.

200g/7oz/1³/₄ cups white masa harina

600ml/1 pint/ 2¹/₂ cups milk

1 vanilla pod (bean)

50g/2oz/¹/₄ cup piloncillo or soft dark brown sugar

EXTRAS *Process 115g/4oz/ 1 cup strawberries, chopped pineapple or orange segments in a food processor or blender until smooth, then press the purée through a sieve. Stir the purée into the corn mixture and return the pan to the heat until warmed through. Remove the vanilla pod and serve.*

Café de Olla

This spiced black coffee is one of the most popular drinks in Mexico. The name means out of the pot, which refers to the heavy earthenware cooking pot, or *olla*, in which the coffee is made. Piloncillo is the local unrefined brown sugar, but any soft dark brown sugar can be used. French or Viennese roast coffees work particularly well in this hot drink.

SERVES FOUR

115g/4oz/¹/₂ cup piloncillo or soft dark brown sugar

4 cinnamon sticks, each about 15cm/ 6in long

50g/2oz/²/₃ cup freshly ground coffee, from dark-roast coffee beans

1 Pour 1 litre/1¾ pints/4 cups water into a pan. Add the sugar and cinnamon sticks. Heat gently, stirring occasionally to make sure that the sugar dissolves, then bring to the boil. Boil rapidly for about 20 minutes, until the syrup has reduced by one-quarter.

2 Add the ground coffee to the syrup and stir well, then bring the liquid back to the boil. Remove from the heat, cover the pan and leave to stand for about 5 minutes.

3 Strain the coffee through a fine sieve (strainer), and pour into cups.

Vanilla Caffè Latte

This luxurious vanilla and chocolate version of the classic coffee drink can be served at any time of the day topped with whipped cream, with cinnamon sticks to stir and flavour the drink. Caffè latte is a popular breakfast drink in Italy and France, and is now widely available elsewhere.

SERVES TWO

1 Pour the milk into a small pan and bring to the boil, then remove from the heat. Mix the espresso or very strong coffee with 500ml/16fl oz/ 2 cups of the boiled milk in a large heatproof jug (pitcher). Sweeten with vanilla sugar to taste.

2 Return the remaining boiled milk in the pan to the heat and add the 45ml/3 tbsp vanilla sugar. Stir constantly until dissolved. Bring to the boil, then reduce the heat. Add the dark chocolate and continue to heat, stirring constantly until all the chocolate has melted and the mixture is smooth and glossy.

3 Pour the chocolate milk into the jug of coffee and whisk thoroughly. Serve in tall mugs or glasses topped with whipped cream and with cinnamon sticks to stir.

700ml/24fl oz/scant 3 cups milk

250ml/8fl oz/1 cup espresso or very strong coffee

45ml/3 tbsp vanilla sugar, plus extra to taste

115g/4oz dark (bittersweet) chocolate, grated

Frothy Hot Chocolate

Real hot chocolate doesn't come as a powder in a packet – it is made with the best chocolate you can afford, whisked in hot milk until really frothy. This recipe uses dark (bittersweet) chocolate, but for a special treat you could use Mexican chocolate, which is flavoured with almonds, cinnamon and vanilla, and sweetened with sugar. All the ingredients are crushed together in a special mortar, and heated over coals. The powdered mixture is then shaped into discs, which can be bought in specialist stores.

SERVES FOUR

1 Pour the milk into a pan. Split the vanilla pod lengthways using a sharp knife to reveal the seeds, and add it to the milk; the vanilla seeds and the pod will flavour the milk.

2 Add the chocolate. The amount to use depends on personal taste – start with a smaller amount if you are unsure of the flavour and taste at the beginning of step 3, adding more if necessary.

3 Heat the chocolate milk gently, stirring until all the chocolate has melted and the mixture is smooth, then whisk with a wire whisk until the mixture boils. Remove the vanilla pod from the pan and divide the drink among four mugs or heatproof glasses. Serve the hot chocolate immediately.

1 litre/1³/₄pints/ 4 cups milk

50–115g/2–4oz dark (bittersweet) chocolate, grated

1 vanilla pod (bean)

Cuba Libre

Rum and coke takes on a much livelier, citrus flavour in this vibrant Caribbean cocktail that's sure to put you in the mood to party. The refreshing flavour and aroma of freshly squeezed limes is the dominant taste in this blend, and the dark rum really packs a punch when combined with the sweet, syrupy cola drink.

SERVES EIGHT

9 limes

250ml/8fl oz/1 cup dark rum

800ml/1¹⁄₃ pints/3¹⁄₂ cups cola drink

1 Thinly slice one lime then, using a citrus juicer, squeeze the juice from the rest of the limes.

2 Put plenty of ice cubes into a large glass jug (pitcher), tucking the lime slices around them, then pour in the lime juice.

3 Pour the rum into the jug and stir well with a long-handled spoon. Top up with cola drink and serve immediately in tall glasses with stirrers.

Tropical Fruit Royale

Based on the Kir Royale, a blend of champagne and crème de cassis, this elegant cocktail is made with tropical fruits and sparkling wine. Remember to blend the fruits ahead of time to give the mango ice cubes time to freeze.

SERVES SIX

1 Peel the mangoes, cut the flesh off the stone (pit), then put the flesh in a food processor or blender. Process until smooth, scraping the mixture down from the sides of the bowl.

2 Fill an ice cube tray with a good half of the mango purée and freeze for 2 hours until solid.

3 Cut six wedges from one or two of the passion fruits and scoop the pulp from the rest into the remaining mango purée. Process until well blended.

4 Spoon the mixture into six stemmed glasses. Divide the mango ice cubes among the glasses, top up with sparkling wine and add the passion fruit wedges. Serve with stirrers.

2 large mangoes

6 passion fruit

sparkling wine

Lemon Vodka

Very similar to the deliciously moreish Italian liqueur, Limoncello, this lemon vodka should be drunk in small quantities due to its hefty alcoholic punch. Blend the sugar, lemons and vodka and keep in a bottle in the refrigerator, ready for pouring over crushed ice, or topping up with soda or sparkling water.

SERVES TWELVE TO FIFTEEN

10 large lemons

275g/10oz/generous 1¹/₄ cups caster (superfine) sugar

250ml/8fl oz/1 cup vodka

1 Squeeze the lemons using a citrus juicer. Pour the juice into a jug (pitcher), add the sugar and whisk well until all the sugar has dissolved.

2 Strain the sweetened lemon juice into a clean bottle or narrow-necked jar and add the vodka. Shake the mixture well to combine and chill for up to 2 weeks.

3 To serve, fill small glasses with ice and pour over the lemon vodka or pour into larger, ice-filled glasses and top up with chilled soda water (club soda).

Quick Bloody Mary

Using vodka flavoured with chilli gives this drink the perfect spicy kick. You can make your own chilli vodka, simply by slipping a fresh red chilli into a bottle of vodka and leaving the flavours to infuse.

SERVES FOUR

250ml/8fl oz/1 cup chilli vodka

1.2 litres/2 pints/5 cups tomato juice

5ml/1 tsp celery salt

FROM THE STORECUPBOARD

2.5ml/¹/₂ tsp ground black pepper

1 Quarter-fill four tall glasses with a handful of ice cubes and pour over the chilli vodka. (If there's a chilli in the bottle, be careful not to pour it out!)

2 Pour the tomato juice into a jug (pitcher) and add the celery salt and pepper. Stir well to combine.

3 Pour the flavoured tomato juice over the vodka, mix well using a long-handled spoon or stirrer, and serve with a stick of celery in each glass.

Gin Fizz

The combination of sourness and fizziness in this 19th-century recipe is what makes it so refreshing.

SERVES ONE

1 Shake the gin, lemon juice and sugar with ice until the sugar is properly dissolved. Pour out into a frosted, tall, narrow glass half-filled with ice, and top up with soda.

2 Add two straws. There should be a little less soda than the other combined ingredients.

2 measures/3 tbsp gin

juice of half a large lemon

5ml/1 tsp caster (superfine) sugar

soda water

Sea Breeze

One of today's most requested cocktails, Sea Breeze was one of the first popular cocktails to use cranberry juice. Ocean Spray is one of the most famous brands, but the supermarkets nearly all have a proprietary version.

SERVES ONE

2 measures/3 tbsp vodka

2 measures/3 tbsp grapefruit juice

3 measures/4$^1/_2$ tbsp cranberry juice

1 Shake all the ingredients well with plenty of ice, and pour everything into a chilled highball glass.

2 Add a wedge of lime and a few cranberries.

Perfect Manhattan

When making Manhattans it's a matter of preference whether you use sweet vermouth, dry vermouth or a mixture of the two. Both of the former require a dash of Angostura bitters. The last, given here, is such a harmoniously balanced mixture that it doesn't need it.

SERVES ONE

2 measures/3 tbsp rye whiskey

¼ measure/1 tsp dry vermouth

¼ measure/1 tsp sweet red vermouth

1 Pour the whiskey and vermouths into a bar glass half-full of ice. Stir well for 30 seconds to mix and chill.

2 Strain on the rocks or straight up into a chilled cocktail glass.

3 Pare away a small strip of lemon rind. Tie it into a knot to help release the oils from the rind, and drop it into the cocktail.

4 Add a maraschino cherry with its stalk left intact. As any Manhattan drinker wil tell you, the cherry is essential.

Margarita

With the Tequila Sunrise, Margarita, created in Tijuana in the late 1940s, is probably the best-known tequila cocktail of them all. Its saltiness and sourness make it a great aperitif. Some recipes use lemon juice instead of lime, but lime juice sharpens its bite.

SERVES ONE

1¹⁄₂ **measures/6 tsp silver tequila**

¹⁄₂ **measure/2 tsp Cointreau**

juice of a lime

FROM THE STORECUPBOARD

salt

1 Rub the rim of a cocktail glass with a wedge of fresh lime, and then dip it in fine salt.

2 Shake the tequila, Cointreau and lime juice with ice, and strain into the prepared glass. Garnish with a twist of cucumber rind or a half-slice of lime.

Brandy Alexander

One of the greatest cocktails of them all, Alexander can be served at the end of a grand dinner with coffee as a creamy digestif, or as the first drink of the evening at a cocktail party, since the cream in it helps to line the stomach. It was possibly originally made with gin rather than brandy, and the cream was sweetened, but the formula below is undoubtedly the best of all possible worlds.

SERVES ONE

1 measure/1¹/₂ tbsp cognac

1 measure/1¹/₂ tbsp brown crème de cacao

1 measure/1¹/₂ tbsp double (heavy) cream

1 Shake the ingredients thoroughly with ice, and strain into a cocktail glass.

2 Scatter ground nutmeg, or grate a little whole nutmeg, on top. Alternatively, sprinkle with grated dark chocolate.

Spritzer

The most famous white wine cocktail is this simple fizzy creation. Everyone who drinks spritzers seems to have his or her own preferred proportions, but this recipe should be reliable. The point is that the drink is lower in alcohol than a standard glass of wine.

SERVES ONE

3 measures/4^1/$_2$ tbsp dry white wine

4 measures/6 tbsp soda water

1 Half-fill a highball glass with cracked ice, and add the wine and soda.

2 Garnish with mixed summer berries if you like, but the drink doesn't really need them.

Nutritional Information

The nutritional analysis below is **per portion**, unless otherwise stated.

p62 Zingy Papaya, Lime and Ginger Salad
Energy 58Kcal/245kJ; Protein 1g; Carbohydrate 14g, of which sugars 14g; Fat 0g, of which saturates 0g; Cholesterol 0mg; Calcium 33mg; Fibre 3.1g; Sodium 900mg.

p63 Cantaloupe Melon with Grilled Strawberries
Energy 36Kcal/150kJ; Protein 1g; Carbohydrate 8g, of which sugars 8g; Fat 0g, of which saturates 0g; Cholesterol 0mg; Calcium 18mg; Fibre 1g; Sodium 100mg.

p64 Crunchy Oat Cereal
Energy 438Kcal/1823kJ; Protein 7g; Carbohydrate 36g, of which sugars 10g; Fat 31g, of which saturates 8g; Cholesterol 27mg; Calcium 46mg; Fibre 3.4g; Sodium 100mg.

p65 Cranachan Energy 284Kcal/1182kJ; Protein 12g; Carbohydrate 14g, of which sugars 8g; Fat 22g, of which saturates 10g; Cholesterol 6mg; Calcium 251mg; Fibre 2.3g; Sodium 100mg.

p66 Porridge
Energy 115Kcal/488kJ; Protein 3.6g; Carbohydrate 20.9g, of which sugars 0g; Fat 2.5g, of which saturates 0g; Cholesterol 0mg; Calcium 16mg; Fibre 2g; Sodium 300mg.

p67 Eggy Bread Panettone
Energy 465Kcal/1934kJ; Protein 7g; Carbohydrate 37g, of which sugars 26g; Fat 33g, of which saturates 11g; Cholesterol 210mg; Calcium 58mg; Fibre 0.5g; Sodium 300mg.

p68 Chocolate Brioche Sandwiches Energy 365Kcal/1530kJ; Protein 7g;

Carbohydrate 40g, of which sugars 19g; Fat 18g, of which saturates 0g; Cholesterol 1mg; Calcium 81mg; Fibre 1.3g; Sodium 300mg.

p68 Roast Bananas with Greek Yogurt and Honey
Energy 222Kcal/926kJ; Protein 9g; Carbohydrate 18g, of which sugars 17g; Fat 14g, of which saturates 7g; Cholesterol 0mg; Calcium 194mg; Fibre 0.7g; Sodium 100mg.

p70 Apricot Turnovers
Energy 291Kcal/1225kJ; Protein 3g; Carbohydrate 43g, of which sugars 22g; Fat 14g, of which saturates 0g; Cholesterol 0mg; Calcium 35mg; Fibre 0g; Sodium 200mg.

p71 Warm Pancakes with Caramelized Pears Energy 858Kcal/3590kJ; Protein 14g; Carbohydrate 103g, of which sugars 62g; Fat 46g, of which saturates 22g; Cholesterol 177mg; Calcium 285mg; Fibre 5.3g; Sodium 200mg.

p72 Smoked Salmon and Chive Omelette
Energy 234Kcal/974kJ; Protein 22g; Carbohydrate 0g, of which sugars 0g; Fat 16g, of which saturates 5g; Cholesterol 478mg; Calcium 79mg; Fibre 0g; Sodium 900mg.

p73 Quick Kedgeree
Energy 396Kcal/1654kJ; Protein 19g; Carbohydrate 32g, of which sugars 6g; Fat 21g, of which saturates 2g; Cholesterol 248mg; Calcium 69mg; Fibre 0.8g; Sodium 700mg.

p74 Jugged Kippers Energy 202Kcal/845kJ; Protein 11.9g; Carbohydrate 13.1g, of which sugars 2g; Fat 11.8g, of which saturates 4.8g; Cholesterol 87mg; Calcium 59mg; Fibre 1.5g; Sodium 650mg.

p75 Scotch Pancakes with Bacon and Maple Syrup
Per pancake: Energy 302Kcal/1265kJ; Protein 13g; Carbohydrate 32g, of which sugars 18g; Fat 15g, of which saturates 4g; Cholesterol 43mg; Calcium 60mg; Fibre 0.9g; Sodium 1.0g.

p76 Croque-monsieur
Energy 417Kcal/1750kJ; Protein 27g; Carbohydrate 36g, of which sugars 2g; Fat 19g, of which saturates 11g;

Cholesterol 73mg; Calcium 498mg; Fibre 1.1g; Sodium 1.1g.

p76 Eggs Benedict
Energy 279Kcal/1158kJ; Protein 16g; Carbohydrate 0g, of which sugars 0g; Fat 24g, of which saturates 12g; Cholesterol 369mg; Calcium 52mg; Fibre 0g; Sodium 700mg.

p80 Hummus
Energy 125Kcal/523kJ; Protein 6g; Carbohydrate 9g, of which sugars 0g; Fat 7g, of which saturates 1g; Cholesterol 0mg; Calcium 92mg; Fibre 3.1g; Sodium 100mg.

p81 Baba Ghanoush
Energy 395Kcal/1635kJ; Protein 13g; Carbohydrate 5g, of which sugars 4g; Fat 3g, of which saturates 5g; Cholesterol 0mg; Calcium 92mg; Fibre 8.1g; Sodium 100mg.

p82 Cannellini Bean Pâté
Energy 252Kcal/1635kJ; Protein 13g; Carbohydrate 21g, of which sugars 2g; Fat 13g, of which saturates 4g; Cholesterol 12mg; Calcium 120mg; Fibre 7.6g; Sodium 900mg.

p83 Chicken Liver and Brandy Pâté
Energy 263Kcal/1091kJ; Protein 16g; Carbohydrate 0g, of which sugars 0g; Fat 20g, of which saturates 12g; Cholesterol 170mg; Calcium 91mg; Fibre 0g; Sodium 400mg.

p84 Peperonata
Energy 140Kcal/583kJ; Protein 2g; Carbohydrate 8g, of which sugars 8g; Fat 11g, of which saturates 2g; Cholesterol 0mg; Calcium 19mg; Fibre 2.0g; Sodium 100mg.

p84 Artichoke and Cumin Dip Energy 37Kcal/155kJ; Protein 2g; Carbohydrate 2g, of which sugars 1g; Fat 3g, of which saturates 0g; Cholesterol 0mg; Calcium 29mg; Fibre 0.1g; Sodium 100mg.

p86 Sweet and Salty Vegetable Crisps
Energy 64Kcal/265kJ; Protein 1g; Carbohydrate 3g, of which sugars 3g; Fat 0g, of which saturates 1g; Cholesterol 0mg; Calcium 8mg; Fibre 0.7g; Sodium 100mg.

p87 Sizzling Prawns
Energy 109Kcal/450kJ; Protein 2g; Carbohydrate 1g, of which sugars 0g; Fat 11g, of which

saturates 2g; Cholesterol 17mg; Calcium 8mg; Fibre 0.1g; Sodium 100mg.

p88 Potted shrimps
Energy 326Kcal/1389kJ; Protein 11g; Carbohydrate 0g, of which sugars 0g; Fat 31g, of which saturates 26g; Cholesterol 170mg; Calcium 91mg; Fibre 0g; Sodium 400mg.

p88 Marinated Feta with Lemon and Oregano
Energy 803Kcal/3308kJ; Protein 8g; Carbohydrate 1g, of which sugars 1g; Fat 85g, of which saturates 18g; Cholesterol 35mg; Calcium 199mg; Fibre 0g; Sodium 700mg.

p90 Mushroom Caviar
Energy 101Kcal/417kJ; Protein 3g; Carbohydrate 23g, of which sugars 92g; Fat 9g, of which saturates 1g; Cholesterol 0mg; Calcium 14mg; Fibre 1.7g; Sodium 100mg.

p91 Brandade of Salt Cod
Energy 627Kcal/2583kJ; Protein 10g; Carbohydrate 1g, of which sugars 1g; Fat 64g, of which saturates 20g; Cholesterol 57mg; Calcium 96mg; Fibre 0.1g; Sodium 100mg.

p92 Chopped Egg and Onions Energy 245Kcal/1017kJ; Protein 12g; Carbohydrate 3g, of which sugars 2g; Fat 20g, of which saturates 5g; Cholesterol 389mg; Calcium 70mg; Fibre 0.5g; Sodium 200mg.

p92 Israeli Cheese with Green Olives
Energy 252Kcal/1040kJ; Protein 4g; Carbohydrate 0g, of which sugars 0g; Fat 26g, of which saturates 16g; Cholesterol 53mg; Calcium 116mg; Fibre 0.5g; Sodium 800mg.

p94 Bacon-rolled Enokitake Mushrooms
Energy 116Kcal/483kJ; Protein 9g; Carbohydrate 1g, of which sugars 0g; Fat 9g, of which saturates 3g; Cholesterol 27mg; Calcium 10mg; Fibre 1.2g; Sodium 500mg.

p95 Walnut and Goat's Cheese Bruschetta
Energy 520Kcal/2159kJ; Protein 16g; Carbohydrate 26g, of which sugars 7g; Fat 42g, of which saturates 13g; Cholesterol 47mg; Calcium 113mg; Fibre 0.6g; Sodium 500mg.

p98 Spanish Salted Almonds
Energy 206Kcal/853kJ; Protein 8g; Carbohydrate 2g, of which sugars 1g; Fat 19g, of which saturates 1g; Cholesterol 0mg; Calcium 80mg; Fibre 2.5g; Sodium 300mg.

p99 Golden Gruyère and Basil Tortillas
Energy 430Kcal/1795kJ; Protein 20g; Carbohydrate 33g, of which sugars 1g; Fat 25g, of which saturates 13g; Cholesterol 58mg; Calcium 613mg; Fibre 1.3g; Sodium 700mg.

p100 Polenta Chips
Per chip: Energy 35Kcal/144kJ; Protein 1g; Carbohydrate 3g, of which sugars 0g; Fat 2g, of which saturates 1g; Cholesterol 4mg; Calcium 20mg; Fibre 0.1g; Sodium 100mg.

p101 Parmesan Tuiles
Energy 48Kcal/199kJ; Protein 4g; Carbohydrate 0g, of which sugars 0g; Fat 3g, of which saturates 2g; Cholesterol 11mg; Calcium 118mg; Fibre 0g; Sodium 100mg.

p102 Yogurt Cheese in Olive Oil Energy 1927kcal/7943kJ; Protein 32g; Carbohydrate 10g,of which sugars 10g; Fat

201g, of which saturates 47g; Cholesterol 0mg; Calcium 758mg; Fibre 0.0g; Sodium 400mg.

p103 Eggs Mimosa
Energy 77Kcal/318kJ; Protein 4g; Carbohydrate 0g, of which sugars 0g; Fat 7g, of which saturates 2g; Cholesterol 116mg; Calcium 18mg; Fibre 0.5g; Sodium 100mg.

p104 Marinated Smoked Salmon with Lime and Coriander Energy 65Kcal/271kJ; Protein 9g; Carbohydrate 0g, of which sugars 0g; Fat 3g, of which saturates 1g; Cholesterol 12mg; Calcium 9mg; Fibre 0g; Sodium 600mg.

p104 Blinis with Caviar and Crème Fraîche
Energy 96Kcal/398kJ; Protein 2g; Carbohydrate 5g, of which sugars 3g; Fat 8g, of which saturates 5g; Cholesterol 39mg; Calcium 19mg; Fibre 0.2g; Sodium 200mg.

p106 Marinated Anchovies
Energy 112Kcal/469kJ; Protein 14g; Carbohydrate 1g, of which sugars 1g; Fat 6g, of which saturates 1g; Cholesterol 35mg; Calcium 172mg; Fibre 0.1g; Sodium 500mg.

p107 Chilli Prawn Skewers
Energy 51Kcal/215kJ; Protein 7g; Carbohydrate 5g, of which sugars 4g; Fat 0g, of which saturates 0g; Cholesterol 78mg; Calcium 37mg; Fibre 0.3g; Sodium 700mg.

p108 Salt Cod and Potato Fritters
Energy 718Kcal/2980kJ; Protein 21.1g; Carbohydrate 33.1g, of which sugars 1.9g; Fat 56.5g, of which saturates 8.3g; Cholesterol 165mg; Calcium 67mg; Fibre 1.6g; Sodium 196mg.

p109 Asian-style Crab Cakes Energy 70Kcal/209kJ; Protein 6g; Carbohydrate 2g, of which sugars 0g; Fat 4g, of which saturates 1g; Cholesterol 20mg; Calcium 4mg; Fibre 0.1g; Sodium 100mg.

p110 Crab and Water-chestnut Wontons Energy 41Kcal/175kJ; Protein 6g; Carbohydrate 4g, of which sugars 1g; Fat 0g, of which saturates 0g; Cholesterol 21mg; Calcium 36mg; Fibre 0.1g; Sodium 300mg.

p110 Chilli-spiced Chicken Wings Energy 428Kcal/1781kJ; Protein 30g; Carbohydrate 12g, of which sugars 4g; Fat 29g, of which saturates 6g; Cholesterol 129mg; Calcium 60mg; Fibre 0.3g; Sodium 200mg.

p112 Vietnamese Spring Rolls with Pork
Energy 218Kcal/910kJ; Protein 20g; Carbohydrate 3g, of which sugars 0g; Fat 14g, of which saturates 1g; Cholesterol 0mg; Calcium 2mg; Fibre 0g; Sodium 400mg.

p113 Curried Lamb Samosas
Energy 57Kcal/238kJ; Protein 4g; Carbohydrate 1g, of which sugars 0g; Fat 4g, of which saturates 2g; Cholesterol 18mg; Calcium 8mg; Fibre 0g; Sodium 100mg.

p116 Avocado Soup Energy 301Kcal/1240kJ; Protein 4g; Carbohydrate 5g, of which sugars 3g; Fat 30g, of which saturates 12g; Cholesterol 45mg; Calcium 86mg; Fibre 2.5g; Sodium 600mg.

p117 Vichyssoise
Energy 186kcal/781kJ; Protein 5g; Carbohydrate 16g, of which sugars 4g; Fat 4g, of which saturates 2g; Cholesterol 17mg; Calcium 8mg; Fibre 0.1g; Sodium 100mg.

p118 Avgolemono
Energy 117Kcal/495kJ; Protein 7g; Carbohydrate 15g, of which sugars 1g; Fat 4g, of which saturates 1g; Cholesterol 116mg; Calcium 26mg; Fibre 0.6g; Sodium 400mg.

p119 Simple Cream of Onion Soup Energy 499kcal/2073kJ; Protein 4g; Carbohydrate 21g, of which sugars 15g; Fat 45g, of which saturates 28g; Cholesterol 118mg; Calcium 89mg; Fibre 3.5g; Sodium 600mg.

p120 Capelletti in Broth
Energy 130Kcal/551kJ; Protein 6g; Carbohydrate 22g, of which sugars 1g; Fat 3g, of which saturates 1g; Cholesterol 5mg; Calcium 68mg; Fibre 1g; Sodium 600mg.

p120 Tiny Pasta in Broth
Energy 86Kcal/366kJ; Protein 4g; Carbohydrate 15g, of which sugars 1g; Fat 2g, of which saturates 1g; Cholesterol 2mg; Calcium 33mg; Fibre 0.8g; Sodium 500mg.

p122 Potato and Roasted Garlic Broth
Energy 122Kcal/515 kJ; Protein 5g; Carbohydrate 25g, of which sugars 1g; Fat 1g, of which saturates 0g; Cholesterol 0mg; Calcium 12mg; Fibre 2.2g; Sodium 900mg.

p123 Winter Squash Soup with Tomato Salsa
Energy 255Kcal/1059kJ; Protein 3g; Carbohydrate 18g, of which sugars 12g; Fat 19g; of which saturates 3g; Cholesterol 0mg; Calcium 86mg; Fibre 3.1g; Sodium 100mg.

p124 Butter Bean, Sun-dried Tomato and Pesto Soup
Energy 305Kcal/1276kJ; Protein 14g; Carbohydrate 23g, of which sugars 3g; Fat 18g, of which saturates 4g; Cholesterol 8mg; Calcium 136mg; Fibre 7.5g; Sodium 1.5g.

p125 Stilton and Watercress Soup Energy 162Kcal/671kJ; Protein 8g; Carbohydrate 1g, of which sugars 1g; Fat 14g, of which saturates 9g; Cholesterol 38mg; Calcium 169mg; Fibre 0.6g; Sodium 400mg.

p126 Curried Cauliflower Soup Energy 137Kcal/579kJ; Protein 11g; Carbohydrate 14g, of which sugars 12g; Fat 5g, of which saturates 2g; Cholesterol 11mg; Calcium 268mg; Fibre 2.3g; Sodium 200mg.

p127 Tuscan Bean Soup
Energy 209Kcal/877kJ; Protein 8g; Carbohydrate 19g, of which sugars 9g; Fat 12g, of which saturates 2g; Cholesterol 0mg; Calcium 79mg; Fibre 6.6g; Sodium 500mg.

p128 Pea Soup with Garlic
Energy 208Kcal/874kJ; Protein 14g; Carbohydrate 22g, of which sugars 6g; Fat 8g, of which saturates 4g; Cholesterol 13mg; Calcium 81mg; Fibre

11.7g; Sodium 700mg.

p129 Star-gazer Vegetable Soup Energy 102Kcal/425kJ; Protein 4g; Carbohydrate 19g, of which sugars 9g; Fat 1g, of which saturates 0g; Cholesterol 0mg; Calcium 44mg; Fibre 3.0g; Sodium 700mg.

p132 Baked Eggs with Creamy Leeks Energy 219Kcal/905kJ; Protein 9g; Carbohydrate 2g, of which sugars 2g; Fat 19g, of which saturates 10g; Cholesterol 261mg; Calcium 61mg; Fibre 1.2g; Sodium 100mg.

p133 Red Onion and Olive Pissaladière Energy 436Kcal/1815kJ; Protein 6g; Carbohydrate 37g, of which sugars 6g; Fat 31g, of which saturates 2g; Cholesterol 0mg; Calcium 77mg; Fibre 1.5g; Sodium 500mg.

p134 Figs with Prosciutto and Roquefort Energy 192Kcal/808kJ; Protein 10g; Carbohydrate 19g, of which sugars 19g; Fat 9g, of which saturates 5g; Cholesterol 17mg; Calcium 142mg; Fibre 1.7g; Sodium 700mg.

p135 Pea and Mint Omelette Energy 216Kcal/898kJ; Protein 17g; Carbohydrate 2g, of which sugars 1g; Fat 15g, of which saturates 5g; Cholesterol 469mg; Calcium 87mg; Fibre 1.3g; Sodium 400mg.

p136 Warm Penne with Fresh Tomatoes and Basil Energy 556Kcal/2356kJ; Protein 16g; Carbohydrate 99g, of which sugars 7g; Fat 14g, of which saturates 2g; Cholesterol 0mg; Calcium 46mg; Fibre 5.1g; Sodium 100mg.

p137 Broccoli and Chilli Spaghetti Energy 675Kcal/ 2835kJ; Protein 16g; Carbohydrate 67g, of which sugars 5g; Fat 40g, of which saturates 6g; Cholesterol 0mg; Calcium 86mg; Fibre 5.5g; Sodium 100mg.

p138 Grilled Aubergine, Mint and Couscous Salad Energy 264Kcal/1101kJ; Protein 5g; Carbohydrate 35g, of which sugars 5g; Fat 12g, of which saturates 2g; Cholesterol 0mg; Calcium 39mg; Fibre 4.5g; Sodium 200mg.

p139 Marinated Courgette and Flageolet Bean Salad Energy 155Kcal/647kJ; Protein 8g; Carbohydrate 11g, of which sugars 2g; Fat 9g, of which saturates 1g; Cholesterol 0mg; Calcium 57mg; Fibre 4.7g; Sodium 300mg.

p140 Roasted Pepper and Hummus Wrap Energy 370Kcal/1533kJ; Protein 11g; Carbohydrate 53g, of which sugars 14g; Fat 14g, of which saturates 1g; Cholesterol 0mg; Calcium 101mg; Fibre 6g; Sodium 800mg.

p140 Focaccia with Sardines and Roast Tomatoes Energy 507Kcal/2134kJ; Protein 29g; Carbohydrate 54g, of which sugars 5g; Fat 21g, of which saturates 4g; Cholesterol 20mg; Calcium 205mg; Fibre 3.1g; Sodium 800mg.

p142 Jansson's Temptation Energy 688kcal/2859kJ; Protein 15g; Carbohydrate 51g, of which sugars 1g; Fat 49g, of which saturates 29g; Cholesterol 134mg; Calcium 182mg; Fibre 4.6g; Sodium 1g.

p143 Crisp Fried Whitebait Energy 591Kcal/2446kJ; Protein 22g; Carbohydrate 6g, of which sugars 0g; Fat 53g, of which saturates 0g; Cholesterol 0mg; Calcium 968mg; Fibre 0.2g; Sodium 300mg.

p144 Seared Tuna Niçoise Energy 325Kcal/1358kJ; Protein 39g; Carbohydrate 0g, of which sugars 0g; Fat 18g, of which saturates 4g; Cholesterol 158mg; Calcium 42mg; Fibre 0g; Sodium 200mg.

p144 Creamy Parmesan-Baked Eggs Energy 194Kcal/803kJ; Protein 11g; Carbohydrate 0g, of which sugars 0g; Fat 17g, of which saturates 8g; Cholesterol 280mg; Calcium 98mg; Fibre 0g; Sodium 200mg.

p146 Toasted Sourdough with Goat's Cheese Energy 414Kcal/1722kJ; Protein 13g; Carbohydrate 20g, of which sugars 2g; Fat 32g, of which saturates 11g; Cholesterol 44mg; Calcium 127mg; Fibre 0.7g; Sodium 600mg.

p147 Steak and Blue Cheese Sandwiches Energy 816Kcal/ 3418kJ; Protein 64g; Carbohydrate 52g, of which sugars 3g; Fat 41g, of which saturates 19g; Cholesterol 174mg; Calcium 434mg; Fibre 2.3g; Sodium 1.8g.

p148 Spicy Chorizo Sausage and Spring Onion Hash Energy 442Kcal/1843kJ; Protein 23g; Carbohydrate 23g, of which sugars 6g; Fat 29g, of which saturates 11g; Cholesterol 0mg; Calcium 41mg; Fibre 1.8g; Sodium 800mg.

p149 Baked Sweet Potatoes with Leeks and Gorgonzola Energy 352Kcal/1474kJ; Protein 10g; Carbohydrate 45g, of which sugars 24g; Fat 16g, of which saturates 7g; Cholesterol 26mg; Calcium 223mg; Fibre 7.2g; Sodium 700mg.

p152 Mussels in White Wine Energy 300Kcal/1252kJ; Protein 17g; Carbohydrate 5g, of which sugars 1g; Fat 13g, of which saturates 7g; Cholesterol 87mg; Calcium 83mg; Fibre 0.4g; Sodium 600mg.

p153 Crab and Cucumber Wraps Energy 310Kcal/1312kJ; Protein 15g; Carbohydrate 59g, of which sugars 2g; Fat 3g, of which saturates 0g; Cholesterol 25mg; Calcium 117mg; Fibre 2.4g; Sodium 2.8g.

p154 Scallops with Fennel and Bacon Energy 452Kcal/1870kJ; Protein 20g; Carbohydrate 4g, of which sugars 3g; Fat 40g, of which saturates 22g; Cholesterol 108mg; Calcium 114mg; Fibre 3.6g; Sodium 800mg.

p155 Prawn and New Potato Stew Energy 271Kcal/1147kJ; Protein 22g; Carbohydrate 35g, of which sugars 6g; Fat 6g, of which saturates 2g; Cholesterol 219mg; Calcium 113mg; Fibre 2.9g; Sodium 1.5g.

p156 Haddock with Fennel Butter Energy 220Kcal/921kJ; Protein 29g; Carbohydrate 1g, of which sugars 1g; Fat 11g, of which saturates 7g; Cholesterol 81mg; Calcium 123mg; Fibre 0.3g; Sodium 200mg.

p157 Baked Salmon with Caraway Seeds Energy 665Kcal/2758kJ; Protein 51g; Carbohydrate 0g, of which sugars 0g; Fat 34g, of which saturates 20g; Cholesterol 186mg; Calcium 61mg; Fibre 0g; Sodium 300mg.

p158 Sea Bass in a Salt Crust Energy 200Kcal/842kJ; Protein 39g; Carbohydrate 0g, of which sugars 0g; Fat 5g, of which saturates 1g; Cholesterol 160mg; Calcium 261mg; Fibre 0g; Sodium 2.2g.

p159 Roast Cod wrapped in Prosciutto Energy 342Kcal/1427kJ; Protein 38g; Carbohydrate 3g, of which sugars 3g; Fat 20g, of which saturates 4g; Cholesterol 98mg; Calcium 25mg; Fibre 1g; Sodium 400mg.

p160 Grilled Hake with Lemon and Chilli Energy 206Kcal/862kJ; Protein 27g; Carbohydrate 0g, of which sugars 0g; Fat 11g, of which saturates 2g; Cholesterol 35mg; Calcium 26mg; Fibre 0g; Sodium 300mg.

p161 Trout with grilled Serrano Ham Energy 236Kcal/980kJ; Protein 19g; Carbohydrate 0g, of which sugars 0g; Fat 18g, of which saturates 9g; Cholesterol 43mg; Calcium 7mg; Fibre 0g; Sodium 1.2g.

p162 Tonno con Piselli Energy 329kcal/1379kJ; Protein 30g; Carbohydrate 23g, of which sugars 8g; Fat 14g, of which saturates 4g; Cholesterol 40mg; Calcium 83mg; Fibre 6.8g; Sodium 600mg.

p163 Filo-wrapped Fish Energy 509Kcal/2135kJ; Protein 36.2g; Carbohydrate 37.2g, of which sugars 10.4g; Fat 25.1g, of which saturates 4.2g; Cholesterol 75mg; Calcium 137mg; Fibre 5g; Sodium 192mg.

p164 Poached Fish in Spicy Tomato Sauce Energy 217Kcal/915kJ; Protein 36g; Carbohydrate 7g, of which sugars 3g; Fat 5g, of which saturates 2g; Cholesterol 94mg; Calcium 33mg; Fibre 1.1g; Sodium 400mg.

p165 Fish with Tomato and Pine Nuts Energy 308Kcal/1294kJ; Protein 42g;

Carbohydrate 6g, of which sugars 3g; Fat 13g, of which saturates 2g; Cholesterol 80mg; Calcium 94mg; Fibre 1.0g; Sodium 400mg.

p167 Baked Salmon with Green Sauce Energy 1044Kcal/4323kJ; Protein 51.6g; Carbohydrate 1.4g, of which sugars 1.2g; Fat 92.4g, of which saturates 28.5g; Cholesterol 231mg; Calcium 135mg; Fibre 0.7g; Sodium 558mg.

p168 Teriyaki Salmon Energy 618Kcal/2558kJ; Protein 31g; Carbohydrate 2g, of which sugars 2g; Fat 54g, of which saturates 7g; Cholesterol 75mg; Calcium 36mg; Fibre 0g; Sodium 1.4g.

p169 Roast Mackerel in Spicy Chermoula Paste Energy 591Kcal/2449kJ; Protein 39g; Carbohydrate 6g, of which sugars 4g; Fat 46g, of which saturates 9g; Cholesterol 108mg; Calcium 66mg; Fibre 1.1g; Sodium 100mg.

p170 Pan-fried Skate Wings Energy 160Kcal/671kJ; Protein 23g; Carbohydrate 0g, of which sugars 0g; Fat 7g, of which saturates 4g; Cholesterol 18mg; Calcium 64mg; Fibre 0.1g; Sodium 300mg.

p171 Sea Bass with Parsley and Lime Butter Energy 213Kcal/890kJ; Protein 29g; Carbohydrate 0g, of which sugars 0g; Fat 11g, of which saturates 5g; Cholesterol 138mg; Calcium 199mg; Fibre 0.1g; Sodium 200mg.

p174 Beef Patties with Onions and Peppers Energy 339Kcal/1416 kJ; Protein 30g; Carbohydrate 15g, of which sugars 11g; Fat 18g, of which saturates 6g; Cholesterol 70mg; Calcium 60mg; Fibre 4.0g; Sodium 100mg.

p175 Steak with Warm Tomato Salsa Energy 175Kcal/736kJ; Protein 25g; Carbohydrate 3g, of which sugars 7g; Fat 3g, of which

saturates 69g; Cholesterol 69mg; Calcium 18mg; Fibre 0.9g; Sodium 100mg.

p176 Meatballs in Tomato Sauce Energy 309Kcal/1290kJ; Protein 22g; Carbohydrate 12g, of which sugars 7g; Fat 20g, of which saturates 8g; Cholesterol 70mg; Calcium 89mg; Fibre 2.0g; Sodium 800mg.

p177 Beef Cooked in Red Wine Energy 244Kcal/1021kJ; Protein 24g; Carbohydrate 1g, of which sugars 0g; Fat 7g, of which saturates 3g; Cholesterol 69mg; Calcium 14mg; Fibre 0.1g; Sodium 100mg.

p178 Pan-fried Gaelic steaks Energy 738Kcal/3062kJ; Protein 54.1g; Carbohydrate 1.3g, of which sugars 1.3g; Fat 54.2g, of which saturates 31.6g; Cholesterol 226mg; Calcium 49mg; Fibre 0g; Sodium 200mg.

p179 Thai-style Rare Beef and Mango Salad Energy 316Kcal/1330kJ; Protein 28g; Carbohydrate 22g, of which sugars 22g; Fat 14g, of which saturates 4g; Cholesterol 57mg; Calcium 26mg; Fibre 3.9g; Sodium 900mg.

p180 North African Lamb Energy 412Kcal/1716 kJ; Protein 34g; Carbohydrate 16g, of which sugars 14g; Fat 24g, of which saturates 11g; Cholesterol 127mg; Calcium 36mg; Fibre 2.7g; Sodium 200mg.

p181 Lamb Steaks with Redcurrant Glaze Energy 301Kcal/1258kJ; Protein 24g; Carbohydrate 12g, of which sugars 12g; Fat 17g, of which saturates 8g; Cholesterol 94mg; Calcium 10mg; Fibre 0.0g; Sodium 100mg.

p182 Lamb Chops with a Mint Jelly Crust Energy 201Kcal/845kJ; Protein 22g; Carbohydrate 11g, of which sugars 2g; Fat 8g, of which saturates 3g; Cholesterol 67mg; Calcium 41mg; Fibre 0.3g; Sodium 300mg.

p183 Marinated Lamb with Oregano and Basil Energy 251Kcal/1042kJ; Protein 21g; Carbohydrate 0g, of which sugars 0g; Fat 19g, of which saturates 5g; Cholesterol 67mg; Calcium 29mg; Fibre 0g; Sodium 1.2g.

p184 Roast Shoulder of Lamb with Whole Garlic Cloves Energy 296Kcal/1244kJ; Protein 28g; Carbohydrate 19g, of which sugars 2g; Fat 13g, of which saturates 6g; Cholesterol

90mg; Calcium 16mg; Fibre 1.4g; Sodium 100mg.

p185 Roast Leg of Lamb with Rosemary and Garlic Energy 223Kcal/931kJ; Protein 28g; Carbohydrate 0g, of which sugars 0g; Fat 12g, of which saturates 4g; Cholesterol 99mg; Calcium 9mg; Fibre 0g; Sodium 100mg.

p186 Sweet-and-sour Lamb Energy 237Kcal/988kJ; Protein 20g; Carbohydrate 8g, of which sugars 8g; Fat 13g, of which saturates 4g; Cholesterol 74mg; Calcium 13mg; Fibre 0g; Sodium 200mg.

p187 Roast Lamb with Figs Energy 446Kcal/1859kJ; Protein 33g; Carbohydrate 11g, of which sugars 11g; Fat 27g, of which saturates 11g; Cholesterol 125mg; Calcium 39mg; Fibre 1.2g; Sodium 200mg.

p188 Paprika Pork Energy 249Kcal/1049kJ; Protein 31g; Carbohydrate 15g, of which sugars 8g; Fat 8g, of which saturates 2g; Cholesterol 88mg; Calcium 44mg; Fibre 3.0g; Sodium 300mg.

p189 Pork Kebabs Energy 218Kcal/916kJ; Protein 28g; Carbohydrate 8g, of which sugars 8g; Fat 8g, of which saturates 3g; Cholesterol 79mg; Calcium 22mg; Fibre 0.5g; Sodium 400mg.

p190 Fragrant Lemon Grass and Ginger Pork Patties Energy 187Kcal/782kJ; Protein 24g; Carbohydrate 0g, of which sugars 0g; Fat 10g, of which saturates 2g; Cholesterol 71mg; Calcium 8mg; Fibre 0g; Sodium 200mg.

p191 Pan-fried Gammon with Cider Energy 448Kcal/1860kJ; Protein 40g; Carbohydrate 1g, of which sugars 1g; Fat 30g, of which saturates 11g; Cholesterol 72mg; Calcium 26mg; Fibre 0g; Sodium 2.1g.

p192 Caramelized Onion and Sausage Tarte Tatin Energy 569Kcal/2368kJ; Protein 16g; Carbohydrate 37g, of which sugars 6g; Fat 41g, of which saturates 7g; Cholesterol 42mg; Calcium 143mg; Fibre 1.6g; Sodium 1.2g.

p193 Roast Pork with Juniper Berries and Bay Energy 238Kcal/1003kJ; Protein 42g; Carbohydrate 0g, of which sugars 0g; Fat 8g, of which saturates 2g; Cholesterol

126mg; Calcium 11mg; Fibre 0g; Sodium 200mg.

p194 Sticky Glazed Pork Ribs Energy 622Kcal/2605kJ; Protein 64g; Carbohydrate 16g, of which sugars 14g; Fat 34g, of which saturates 12g; Cholesterol 218mg; Calcium 78mg; Fibre 0g; Sodium 200mg.

p194 Chinese Spiced Pork Chops Energy 231Kcal/961kJ; Protein 27g; Carbohydrate 1g, of which sugars 0g; Fat 13g, of which saturates 4g; Cholesterol 76mg; Calcium 31mg; Fibre 0g; Sodium 500mg.

p198 Pot-roasted Chicken with Preserved Lemons Energy 280Kcal/1180kJ; Protein 36g; Carbohydrate 19g, of which sugars 1g; Fat 7g, of which saturates 1g; Cholesterol 135mg; Calcium 15mg; Fibre 1.5g; Sodium 200mg.

p199 Honey Mustard Chicken Energy 244Kcal/1028kJ; Protein 27g; Carbohydrate 12g, of which sugars 12g; Fat 10g, of which saturates 2g; Cholesterol 130mg; Calcium 33mg; Fibre 0.7g; Sodium 400mg.

p200 Drunken Chicken Energy 343Kcal/1437kJ; Protein 39g; Carbohydrate 1g, of which sugars 1g; Fat 11g, of which saturates 3g; Cholesterol 158mg; Calcium 38mg; Fibre 0.1g; Sodium 100mg.

p201 Soy-marinated Chicken Energy 67Kcal/703kJ; Protein 34g; Carbohydrate 4g, of which sugars 3g; Fat 2g, of which saturates 0g; Cholesterol 88mg; Calcium 36mg; Fibre 1.7g; Sodium 500mg.

p202 Stir-fried Chicken with Thai Basil Energy 209Kcal/878kJ; Protein 31g; Carbohydrate 5g, of which sugars 5g; Fat 7g, of which saturates 1g; Cholesterol 88mg; Calcium 22mg; Fibre 1.3g; Sodium 200mg.

p203 Crème Fraîche and Coriander Chicken

Energy 164Kcal/682kJ; Protein 16g; Carbohydrate 0g, of which sugars 0g; Fat 11g, of which saturates 5g; Cholesterol 96mg; Calcium 18mg; Fibre 0g; Sodium 200mg.

p204 Chicken Escalopes with Lemon and Serrano Ham Energy 253Kcal/1058kJ; Protein 36g; Carbohydrate 0g, of which sugars 0g; Fat 12g, of which saturates 6g; Cholesterol 109mg; Calcium 9mg; Fibre 0g; Sodium 500mg.

p205 Roast Chicken with Herb Cheese, Chilli and Lime Stuffing Energy 220Kcal/921kJ; Protein 29g; Carbohydrate 0g, of which sugars 0g; Fat 12g, of which saturates 6g; Cholesterol 131mg; Calcium 27mg; Fibre 0g; Sodium 200mg.

p206 Tandoori Chicken Energy 592Kcal/2479kJ; Protein 44g; Carbohydrate 77.5g, of which sugars 4.5g; Fat 11.4g, of which saturates 1.1g; Cholesterol 105mg; Calcium 54mg; Fibre 0.4g; Sodium 826mg.

p207 Roast Chicken with Black Pudding and Sage Energy 297Kcal/1246kJ; Protein 36g; Carbohydrate 5g, of which sugars 0g; Fat 15g, of which saturates 7g; Cholesterol 161mg; Calcium 87mg; Fibre 0g; Sodium 500mg.

p208 Spatchcock Poussins with Herb Butter Energy 810Kcal/3364kJ; Protein 51g; Carbohydrate 1g, of which sugars 0g; Fat 67g, of which saturates 29g; Cholesterol 341mg; Calcium 38mg; Fibre 0.3g; Sodium 400mg.

p209 Chilli-spiced Poussin Energy 337Kcal/1403kJ; Protein 25g; Carbohydrate 0g, of which sugars 0g; Fat 27g, of which saturates 6g; Cholesterol 131mg; Calcium 28mg; Fibre 0g; Sodium 200mg.

p210 Turkey Patties Energy 155Kcal/651kJ; Protein 26g; Carbohydrate 1g, of which

sugars 1g; Fat 5g, of which saturates 1g; Cholesterol 79mg; Calcium 11mg; Fibre 0.1g; Sodium 100mg.

p211 Guinea Fowl with Whisky Sauce Energy 449Kcal/1866kJ; Protein 34g; Carbohydrate 1g, of which sugars 1g; Fat 29g, of which saturates 13g; Cholesterol 51mg; Calcium 56mg; Fibre 0g; Sodium 200mg.

p212 Pheasant Cooked in Port with Mushrooms Energy 457Kcal/1902kJ; Protein 31g; Carbohydrate 9g, of which sugars 9g; Fat 24g, of which saturates 11g; Cholesterol 263mg; Calcium 46mg; Fibre 0.8g; Sodium 200mg.

p213 Roast Pheasant with Sherry and Mustard Sauce Energy 393Kcal/1632kJ; Protein 30g; Carbohydrate 3g, of which sugars 3g; Fat 23g, of which saturates 11g; Cholesterol 263mg; Calcium 39mg; Fibre 0g; Sodium 400mg.

p214 Marmalade and Soy Roast Duck Energy 273Kcal/1144kJ; Protein 32g; Carbohydrate 8g, of which sugars 7g; Fat 13g, of which saturates 4g; Cholesterol 144mg; Calcium 20mg; Fibre 0g; Sodium 700mg.

p215 Duck with Plum Sauce Energy 334Kcal/1405kJ; Protein 33g; Carbohydrate 22g, of which sugars 21g; Fat 13g, of which saturates 4g; Cholesterol 144mg; Calcium 48mg; Fibre 2.8g; Sodium 100mg.

p218 Minty Courgette Linguine Energy 580Kcal/2442kJ; Protein 15g; Carbohydrate 87g, of which sugars 4g; Fat 21g, of which saturates 3g; Cholesterol 0mg; Calcium 61mg; Fibre 4.4g; Sodium 100mg.

p219 Pasta with Roast Tomatoes and Goat's Cheese Energy 749Kcal/3156kJ; Protein 28g; Carbohydrate 95g, of which sugars 12g; Fat 31g, of which saturates 13g; Cholesterol 49mg; Calcium 419mg; Fibre 6.5g; Sodium 500mg.

p220 Linguine with Anchovies and Capers Energy 527Kcal/2228kJ; Protein 15g; Carbohydrate 85g, of which sugars 3g; Fat 16g, of which saturates 2g; Cholesterol 4mg; Calcium 48mg; Fibre 3.5g; Sodium 300mg.

p220 Home-made Potato Gnocchi Energy 683Kcal/2892kJ; Protein 24g; Carbohydrate 136g, of which sugars 4g; Fat 8g, of which saturates 2g; Cholesterol 232mg; Calcium 164mg; Fibre 8.2g; Sodium 2.1g.

p222 Spaghettini with Roasted Garlic Energy 637Kcal/2670kJ; Protein 14g; Carbohydrate 77g, of which sugars 4g; Fat 33g, of which saturates 5g; Cholesterol 2mg; Calcium 53mg; Fibre 3.1g; Sodium 100mg.

p223 Spaghetti with Lemon Energy 450Kcal/1895kJ; Protein 11g; Carbohydrate 65g, of which sugars 3g; Fat 18g, of which saturates 3g; Cholesterol 0mg; Calcium 23mg; Fibre 2.6g; Sodium 100mg.

p224 Linguine with Rocket Energy 652Kcal/2729kJ; Protein 18g; Carbohydrate 66g, of which sugars 4g; Fat 37g, of which saturates 8g; Cholesterol 17mg; Calcium 225mg; Fibre 2.9g; Sodium 100mg.

p225 Tagliatelle with Vegetable Ribbons Energy 308Kcal/1292kJ; Protein 9g; Carbohydrate 42g, of which sugars 7g; Fat 13g, of which saturates 2g; Cholesterol 0mg; Calcium 76mg; Fibre 2.4g; Sodium 360mg.

p226 Spaghetti with Raw Tomato and Ricotta Sauce Energy 530Kcal/2230kJ; Protein 14g; Carbohydrate 69g, of which sugars 7g; Fat 24g, of which saturates 5g; Cholesterol 14mg; Calcium 100mg; Fibre 3.8g; Sodium 100mg.

p227 Farfalle with Tuna Energy 572Kcal/2433kJ; Protein 27g; Carbohydrate 89g, of which sugars 8g; Fat 15g, of which saturates 4g; Cholesterol 37mg; Calcium 63mg; Fibre 5.4g; Sodium 800mg.

p228 Fettuccine all'Alfredo Energy 697Kcal/2917kJ; Protein 16g; Carbohydrate 67g, of which sugars 3g; Fat 42g, of which saturates 26g; Cholesterol 107mg; Calcium 172mg; Fibre 2.7g; Sodium 200mg.

p229 Pansotti with Walnut Sauce Energy 550Kcal/2282kJ; Protein 11g; Carbohydrate 24g, of which sugars 2g; Fat 47g, of which saturates 13g; Cholesterol 41mg; Calcium 136mg; Fibre 1.9g; Sodium 200mg.

p230 Fettuccine with Butter and Parmesan Energy 560Kcal/2362kJ; Protein 22g; Carbohydrate 76g, of which sugars 3g; Fat 21g, of which saturates 12g; Cholesterol 53mg; Calcium 322mg; Fibre 3.1g; Sodium 300mg.

p231 Penne with Cream and Smoked Salmon Energy 475Kcal/2005kJ; Protein 18g; Carbohydrate 67g, of which sugars 3g; Fat 17g, of which saturates 9g; Cholesterol 48mg; Calcium 64mg; Fibre 2.7g; Sodium 200mg.

p232 Oven-baked Porcini Risotto Energy 288Kcal/1218kJ; Protein 6g; Carbohydrate 52g, of which sugars 2g; Fat 8g, of which saturates 1g; Cholesterol 0mg; Calcium 43mg; Fibre 1.6g; Sodium 100mg.

p233 Persian Baked Rice Energy 573Kcal/2389kJ; Protein 11g; Carbohydrate 91g, of which sugars 1g; Fat 18g, of which saturates 7g; Cholesterol 27mg; Calcium 54mg; Fibre 0.9g; Sodium 200mg.

p234 Rosemary Risotto with Borlotti Beans Energy 362Kcal/1517 kJ; Protein 11g; Carbohydrate 38g, of which sugars 4g; Fat 20g, of which saturates 8g; Cholesterol 19mg; Calcium 80mg; Fibre 65g; Sodium 900mg.

p235 Pancetta and Broad Bean Risotto Energy 526Kcal/2211kJ; Protein 18g; Carbohydrate 72g, of which sugars 4g; Fat 21g, of which saturates 6g; Cholesterol 29mg; Calcium 81mg; Fibre 3.4g; Sodium 2.4g.

p236 Mussel Risotto Energy 348Kcal/459kJ; Protein 15g; Carbohydrate 31g, of which sugars 4g; Fat 19g, of which saturates 7g; Cholesterol 351mg; Calcium 83mg; Fibre 6.5g; Sodium 700mg.

p237 Crab Risotto

Energy 345Kcal/1458kJ; Protein 20g; Carbohydrate 54g, of which sugars 0g; Fat 7g, of which saturates 1g; Cholesterol 54mg; Calcium 35mg; Fibre 0.3g; Sodium 900mg.

p238 Coconut Rice
Energy 472Kcal/2009kJ; Protein 8g; Carbohydrate 114g, of which sugars 16g; Fat 1g, of which saturates 0g; Cholesterol 0mg; Calcium 40mg; Fibre 0.6g; Sodium 400mg.

p239 Savoury Ground Rice
Energy 333Kcal/1392kJ; Protein 7g; Carbohydrate 59g, of which sugars 4g; Fat 7g, of which saturates 4g; Cholesterol 18mg; Calcium 111mg; Fibre 1.5g; Sodium 100mg.

p242 Aubergines with Cheese Sauce Energy 509Kcal/2111kJ; Protein 22g; Carbohydrate 13g, of which sugars 7g; Fat 41g, of which saturates 19g; Cholesterol 80mg; Calcium 640mg; Fibre 2.2g; Sodium 900mg.

p243 Mushroom Stroganoff Energy 318Kcal/1316kJ; Protein 10g; Carbohydrate 13g, of which sugars 7g; Fat 26g, of which saturates 13g; Cholesterol 56mg; Calcium 194mg; Fibre 2.7g; Sodium 400mg.

p244 Red Onion and Goat's Cheese Pastries
Energy 554Kcal/2308kJ; Protein 13g; Carbohydrate 48g, of which sugars 8g; Fat 36g, of which saturates 6g; Cholesterol 27mg; Calcium 128mg; Fibre 1.6g; Sodium 500mg.

p245 Baked Leek and Potato Gratin Energy 574Kcal/2394kJ; Protein 20g; Carbohydrate 43g, of which sugars 5g; Fat 37g, of which saturates 23g; Cholesterol 108mg; Calcium 257mg; Fibre 4.6g; Sodium 300mg.

p246 Mushroom Polenta
Energy 518Kcal/2155kJ; Protein 19g; Carbohydrate 46g, of which sugars 0g; Fat 26g, of which saturates 16g; Cholesterol 69mg;

Calcium 333mg; Fibre 2.5g; Sodium 400mg.

p247 Tomato and Tapenade Tarts Energy 603Kcal/2512kJ; Protein 9g; Carbohydrate 50g, of which sugars 5g; Fat 43g, of which saturates 7g; Cholesterol 21mg; Calcium 117mg; Fibre 1.7g; Sodium 800mg.

p248 Stuffed Baby Squash
Energy 469Kcal/1951kJ; Protein 14g; Carbohydrate 48g, of which sugars 1g; Fat 24g, of which saturates 10g; Cholesterol 36mg; Calcium 316mg; Fibre 2g; Sodium 300mg.

p249 Roasted Peppers with Halloumi and Pine Nuts
Energy 361Kcal/1504kJ; Protein 18g; Carbohydrate 16g, of which sugars 16g; Fat 26g, of which saturates 12g; Cholesterol 58mg; Calcium 105mg; Fibre 4.3g; Sodium 400mg.

p250 Spicy Chickpea Samosas Energy 580Kcal/2437kJ; Protein 20g; Carbohydrate 72g, of which sugars 12g; Fat 24g, of which saturates 6g; Cholesterol 17mg; Calcium 91mg; Fibre 8.3g; Sodium 500mg.

p251 Tofu and Pepper Kebabs Energy 177Kcal/738kJ; Protein 10g; Carbohydrate 13g, of which sugars 12g; Fat 10g, of which saturates 2g; Cholesterol 0mg; Calcium 342mg; Fibre 3.6g; Sodium 800mg.

p252 Mixed Bean and Tomato Chilli
Energy 216Kcal/911kJ; Protein 12g; Carbohydrate 30g, of which sugars 6g; Fat 6g, of which saturates 2g; Cholesterol 10mg; Calcium 47mg; Fibre 8.9g; Sodium 1g.

p253 Cheese and Tomato Soufflés Energy 317Kcal/1319kJ; Protein 19g; Carbohydrate 6g, of which sugars 3g; Fat 25g, of which saturates 10g; Cholesterol 203mg; Calcium 395mg; Fibre 0.1g; Sodium 600mg.

p254 Classic Margherita Pizza Energy 552Kcal/2317kJ; Protein 22g; Carbohydrate 59g, of which sugars 4g; Fat 27g, of which saturates 12g; Cholesterol 46mg; Calcium 362mg; Fibre 2.4g; Sodium 800mg.

p255 Cheesy Leek and Couscous Cake Energy 474Kcal/1973kJ; Protein 19g; Carbohydrate 41g, of which

sugars 2g; Fat 27g, of which saturates 12g; Cholesterol 49mg; Calcium 408mg; Fibre 2.2g; Sodium 500mg.

p256 Potato and Onion Tortilla Energy 512Kcal/2132kJ; Protein 15g; Carbohydrate 40g, of which sugars 5g; Fat 34g, of which saturates 6g; Cholesterol 285mg; Calcium 73mg; Fibre 3.7g; Sodium 100mg.

p257 Spiced Lentils
Energy 326Kcal/1372kJ; Protein 24g; Carbohydrate 34g, of which sugars 4g; Fat 11g, of which saturates 7g; Cholesterol 35mg; Calcium 235mg; Fibre 6.2g; Sodium 800mg.

p258 Roast Acorn Squash with Spinach and Gorgonzola Energy 317Kcal/1312kJ; Protein 12g; Carbohydrate 10g, of which sugars 2g; Fat 25g, of which saturates 12g; Cholesterol 45mg; Calcium 404mg; Fibre 3.6g; Sodium 1g.

p259 Creamy Red Lentil Dhal Energy 156Kcal/658kJ; Protein 9g; Carbohydrate 21g, of which sugars 1g; Fat 4g, of which saturates 0g; Cholesterol 0mg; Calcium 27mg; Fibre 1.8g; Sodium 200mg.

p260 Wild Mushroom and Fontina Tart
Energy 508Kcal/2110kJ; Protein 14g; Carbohydrate 25g, of which sugars 1g; Fat 40g, of which saturates 15g; Cholesterol 63mg; Calcium 309mg; Fibre 2.0g; Sodium 500mg.

p261 Parmigiana di Melanzane Energy 218Kcal/904kJ; Protein 7g; Carbohydrate 5g, of which sugars 4g; Fat 19g, of which saturates 5g; Cholesterol 13mg; Calcium 168mg; Fibre 2.8g; Sodium 200mg.

p264 Japanese-style Spinach with Toasted Sesame Seeds
Energy 51Kcal/210kJ; Protein 4g; Carbohydrate 2g, of which sugars 2g; Fat 3g, of which saturates 0g; Cholesterol 0mg; Calcium 213mg; Fibre 2.6g; Sodium 600mg.

p265 Braised Lettuce and Peas with Spring Onions
Energy 206Kcal/851kJ; Protein 8g; Carbohydrate 17g, of which sugars 8g; Fat 12g, of which saturates 7g; Cholesterol 27mg; Calcium 109mg; Fibre 6.5g; Sodium 100mg.

p266 Asparagus with Lemon

Sauce Energy 84Kcal/349kJ; Protein 6g; Carbohydrate 7g, of which sugars 4g; Fat 3g, of which saturates 1g; Cholesterol 90mg; Calcium 58mg; Fibre 2.9g; Sodium 100mg.

p267 Caramelized Shallots
Energy 109Kcal/450kJ; Protein 1g; Carbohydrate 10g, of which sugars 8g; Fat 7g, of which saturates 4g; Cholesterol 18mg; Calcium 23mg; Fibre 1.2g; Sodium 100mg.

p268 Green Beans with Almond Butter and Lemon
Energy 192Kcal/790kJ; Protein 4g; Carbohydrate 4g, of which sugars 3g; Fat 18g, of which saturates 7g; Cholesterol 27mg; Calcium 65mg; Fibre 2.9g; Sodium 200mg.

p268 Garlicky Green Salad with Raspberry Dressing
Energy 83Kcal/344kJ; Protein 1g; Carbohydrate 1g, of which sugars 1g; Fat 9g, of which saturates 1g; Cholesterol 0mg; Calcium 14mg; Fibre 0.5g; Sodium 100mg.

p270 Cauliflower with Garlic Crumbs Energy 289Kcal/1201kJ; Protein 8g; Carbohydrate 18g, of which sugars 4g; Fat 21g, of which saturates 3g; Cholesterol 0mg; Calcium 61mg; Fibre 4.0g; Sodium 200mg.

p271 Summer Squash and Baby New Potatoes in Warm Dill Sour Cream
Energy 261Kcal/1093kJ; Protein 5g; Carbohydrate 27g, of which sugars 9g; Fat 15g, of which saturates 9g; Cholesterol 45mg; Calcium 129mg; Fibre 2.7g; Sodium 100mg.

p272 Minty Broad Beans with Lemon Energy 118Kcal/493kJ; Protein 7g; Carbohydrate 9g, of which sugars 2g; Fat 7g, of which saturates 1g; Cholesterol 0mg; Calcium 35mg; Fibre 69g; Sodium 100mg.

p272 Gingered Carrot Salad
Energy 82Kcal/339kJ; Protein 1g; Carbohydrate 7g, of which

sugars 7g; Fat 7g, of which saturates 1g; Cholesterol 0mg; Calcium 70mg; Fibre 2.1g; Sodium 100mg.

p274 Baked Winter Squash with Tomatoes

Energy 139Kcal/583kJ; Protein 4g; Carbohydrate 12g, of which sugars 10g; Fat 9g, of which saturates 1g; Cholesterol 0mg; Calcium 98mg; Fibre 3.9g; Sodium 100mg.

p275 Stewed Okra with Tomatoes and Coriander

Energy 79Kcal/332 kJ; Protein 7g; Carbohydrate 9g, of which sugars 8g; Fat 2g, of which saturates 1g; Cholesterol 0mg; Calcium 355mg; Fibre 8.7g; Sodium 100mg.

p276 Roast Asparagus with Crispy Prosciutto

Energy 141Kcal/582kJ; Protein 7g; Carbohydrate 2g, of which sugars 2g; Fat 11g, of which saturates 3g; Cholesterol 18mg; Calcium 38mg; Fibre 1.5g; Sodium 400mg.

p277 Garlicky Roasties

Energy 324Kcal/1356kJ; Protein 6g; Carbohydrate 45g, of which sugars 2g; Fat 14g, of which saturates 2g; Cholesterol 0mg; Calcium 15mg; Fibre 3.9g; Sodium 100mg.

p278 Leek Fritters

Energy 331Kcal/1380kJ; Protein 11g; Carbohydrate 34g, of which sugars 6g; Fat 17g, of which saturates 3g; Cholesterol 116mg; Calcium 84mg; Fibre 5.5g; Sodium 100mg.

p279 Deep-fried Artichokes

Energy 111Kcal/459kJ; Protein 2g; Carbohydrate 2g, of which sugars 1g; Fat 11g, of which saturates 2g; Cholesterol 0mg; Calcium 24mg; Fibre 0g; Sodium 100mg.

p280 Stir-fried Broccoli with Soy Sauce and Sesame Seeds

Energy 130Kcal/538kJ; Protein 6g; Carbohydrate 4g, of which sugars 2g; Fat 10g, of which saturates 2g; Cholesterol 0mg; Calcium 267mg; Fibre

4.4g; Sodium 600mg.

p281 Stir-fried Brussel Sprouts with Bacon and Caraway Seeds

Energy 130Kcal/542kJ; Protein 7g; Carbohydrate 5g, of which sugars 3g; Fat 10g, of which saturates 2g; Cholesterol 9mg; Calcium 40mg; Fibre 4.6g; Sodium 300mg.

p282 Bocconcini with Fennel and Basil

Energy 243Kcal/1008kJ; Protein 14g; Carbohydrate 0g, of which sugars 0g; Fat 21g, of which saturates 11g; Cholesterol 44mg; Calcium 282mg; Fibre 0g; Sodium 400mg.

p283 Noodles with Sesame-roasted Spring Onions

Energy 268Kcal/1121kJ; Protein 3g; Carbohydrate 50g, of which sugars 3g; Fat 3g, of which saturates 1g; Cholesterol 0mg; Calcium 51mg; Fibre 0.5g; Sodium 400mg.

p284 Spicy Potato Wedges

Energy 205Kcal/860kJ; Protein 4g; Carbohydrate 30g, of which sugars 1g; Fat 9g, of which saturates 1g; Cholesterol 0mg; Calcium 16mg; Fibre 2.2g; Sodium 100mg.

p284 Crisp and Golden Roast Potatoes with Goose Fat and Garlic

Energy 202Kcal/848kJ; Protein 4g; Carbohydrate 30g, of which sugars 1g; Fat 1g, of which saturates 0.8g; Cholesterol 7mg; Calcium 10mg; Fibre 2.6g; Sodium 100mg.

p286 Tomato and Aubergine Gratin

Energy 229Kcal/952kJ; Protein 6g; Carbohydrate 6g, of which sugars 6g; Fat 20g, of which saturates 5g; Cholesterol 9mg; Calcium 125mg; Fibre 40g; Sodium 100mg.

p287 Bubble and Squeak

Energy 205Kcal/854kJ; Protein 3g; Carbohydrate 23g, of which sugars 4g; Fat 12g, of which saturates 1g; Cholesterol 0mg; Calcium 30mg; Fibre 2.8g; Sodium 100mg.

p288 Cheesy Creamy Leeks

Energy 333Kcal/1376kJ; Protein 9g; Carbohydrate 6g, of which sugars 5g; Fat 30g, of which saturates 17g; Cholesterol 70mg; Calcium 205mg; Fibre 4.4g; Sodium 200mg.

p289 Creamy Polenta with Dolcelatte

Energy 271Kcal/1130kJ; Protein 11g; Carbohydrate 21g, of which sugars 7g; Fat 16g, of which

saturates 6g; Cholesterol 23mg; Calcium 274mg; Fibre 0.4g; Sodium 400mg.

p290 Fennel, Potato and Garlic Mash

Energy 374Kcal/1560kJ; Protein 7g; Carbohydrate 38g, of which sugars 4g; Fat 23g, of which saturates 6g; Cholesterol 17mg; Calcium 73mg; Fibre 6.2g; Sodium 100mg.

p291 Champ

Energy 445Kcal/1858kJ; Protein 8g; Carbohydrate 49g, of which sugars 7g; Fat 25g, of which saturates 16g; Cholesterol 66mg; Calcium 143mg; Fibre 3.7g; Sodium 200mg.

p294 Sour Cucumber with Fresh Dill

Energy 18Kcal/75kJ; Protein 1g; Carbohydrate 2g, of which sugars 2g; Fat 0g, of which saturates 0g; Cholesterol 0mg; Calcium 50mg; Fibre 0.9g; Sodium 100mg.

p295 Beetroot with Fresh Mint

Energy 75Kcal/314kJ; Protein 2g; Carbohydrate 10g, of which sugars 9g; Fat 3g, of which saturates 0g; Cholesterol 0mg; Calcium 41mg; Fibre 2.4g; Sodium 100mg.

p296 Globe Artichokes with Green Beans and Garlic Dressing

Energy 371kcal/1528kJ; Protein 4g; Carbohydrate 5g, of which sugars 3g; Fat 38g, of which saturates 6g; Cholesterol 0mg; Calcium 60mg; Fibre 1.2g; Sodium 100mg.

p297 Halloumi and Grape Salad

Energy 274Kcal/1139kJ; Protein 10g; Carbohydrate 9g, of which sugars 9g; Fat 22g, of which saturates 10g; Cholesterol 14mg; Calcium 241mg; Fibre 0.6g; Sodium 1g.

p298 Watermelon and Feta Salad

Energy 211Kcal/884kJ; Protein 8g; Carbohydrate 16g, of which sugars 15g; Fat 13g, of which saturates 5g; Cholesterol 23mg; Calcium 145mg; Fibre 1.1g; Sodium 700mg.

p299 Tomato, Bean and Fried Basil Salad

Energy 201Kcal/837kJ; Protein 6g; Carbohydrate 13g, of which sugars 3g; Fat 14g, of which saturates 2g; Cholesterol 0mg; Calcium 30mg; Fibre 4.5g; Sodium 400mg.

p300 Moroccan Date, Orange and Carrot Salad

Energy 147Kcal/619kJ; Protein 4g; Carbohydrate 26g, of which

sugars 25g; Fat 4g, of which saturates 0g; Cholesterol 0mg; Calcium 98mg; Fibre 4.9g; Sodium 100mg.

p301 Pink Grapefruit and Avocado Salad

Energy 216Kcal/892kJ; Protein 2g; Carbohydrate 8g, of which sugars 7g; Fat 20g, of which saturates 3g; Cholesterol 6mg; Calcium 34mg; Fibre 3.8g; Sodium 100mg.

p302 Turnip Salad

Energy 107Kcal/443kJ; Protein 2g; Carbohydrate 8g, of which sugars 7g; Fat 8g, of which saturates 5g; Cholesterol 23mg; Calcium 82mg; Fibre 2.4g; Sodium 100mg.

p302 Moroccan Carrot Salad

Energy 85Kcal/350kJ; Protein 0g; Carbohydrate 4g, of which sugars 4g; Fat 8g, of which saturates 1g; Cholesterol 0mg; Calcium 18mg; Fibre 1.3g; Sodium 100mg.

p304 Warm Chorizo and Spinach Salad

Energy 273Kcal/1127kJ; Protein 8g; Carbohydrate 2g, of which sugars 2g; Fat 26g, of which saturates 6g; Cholesterol 0mg; Calcium 96mg; Fibre 1.2g; Sodium 300mg.

p305 Potato and Olive Salad

Energy 296Kcal/1246kJ; Protein 5g; Carbohydrate 48g, of which sugars 4g; Fat 11g, of which saturates 2g; Cholesterol 0mg; Calcium 40mg; Fibre 3.3g; Sodium 300mg.

p306 Asparagus, Bacon and Leaf Salad

Energy 239Kcal/989kJ; Protein 13g; Carbohydrate 5g, of which sugars 5g; Fat 19g, of which saturates 4g; Cholesterol 19mg; Calcium 54mg; Fibre 2.7g; Sodium 800mg.

p307 Anchovy and Roasted Pepper Salad

Energy 86Kcal/366kJ; Protein 6g; Carbohydrate 12g, of which sugars 11g; Fat 2g, of which saturates 0g; Cholesterol 8mg; Calcium 57mg; Fibre 4.0g;

Sodium 500mg.

p310 Merguez Sausages with Iced Oysters Energy 353Kcal/1469kJ; Protein 25g; Carbohydrate 5g, of which sugars 3g; Fat 26g, of which saturates 11g; Cholesterol 23mg; Calcium 56mg; Fibre 0g; Sodium 800mg.

p311 Grilled Corn on the Cob Energy 445Kcal/1846kJ; Protein 5g; Carbohydrate 24g, of which sugars 3g; Fat 37g, of which saturates 22g; Cholesterol 89mg; Calcium 16mg; Fibre 2.7g; Sodium 300mg.

p312 Butter Bean, Tomato and Red Onion Salad Energy 227Kcal/955kJ; Protein 11g; Carbohydrate 27g, of which sugars 7g; Fat 9g, of which saturates 1g; Cholesterol 0mg; Calcium 40mg; Fibre 8.9g; Sodium 100mg.

p312 Potato, Caraway Seed and Parsley Salad Energy 129Kcal/541kJ; Protein 2g; Carbohydrate 18g, of which sugars 1g; Fat 6g, of which saturates 1g; Cholesterol 0mg; Calcium 19mg; Fibre 1.2g; Sodium 100mg.

p314 Warm Halloumi and Fennel Salad Energy 209Kcal/863kJ; Protein 8g; Carbohydrate 2g, of which sugars 2g; Fat 19g, of which saturates 8g; Cholesterol 35mg; Calcium 200mg; Fibre 1.8g; Sodium 800mg.

p315 Pear and Blue Cheese Salad Energy 197Kcal/822kJ; Protein 6g; Carbohydrate 16g, of which sugars 16g; Fat 12g, of which saturates 6g; Cholesterol 26mg; Calcium 170mg; Fibre 3.5g; Sodium 600mg.

p316 Fresh Crab Sandwiches Energy 392Kcal/1636kJ; Protein 27g; Carbohydrate 28g, of which sugars 2g; Fat 20g, of which saturates 9g; Cholesterol 107mg; Calcium 74mg; Fibre 3.3g; Sodium 900mg.

p317 Warm Pasta with Crushed Tomatoes and Basil Energy 481Kcal/2038kJ; Protein 14g; Carbohydrate 88g, of which sugars 5g; Fat 11g, of which saturates 2g; Cholesterol 0mg; Calcium 40mg; Fibre 4.3g; Sodium 100mg.

p318 Roast Shallot Tart with Thyme Energy 441Kcal/1851kJ; Protein 7g; Carbohydrate 45g, of which sugars 8g; Fat 29g, of which saturates 3g; Cholesterol 13mg; Calcium 131mg; Fibre 1.6g; Sodium 400mg.

p319 Roasted Aubergines with Feta and Coriander Energy 248Kcal/1028kJ; Protein 11g; Carbohydrate 3g, of which sugars 3g; Fat 21g, of which saturates 10g; Cholesterol 47mg; Calcium 252mg; Fibre 2.0g; Sodium 1g.

p320 Barbecued Sardines with Orange and Parsley Energy 324Kcal/1353kJ; Protein 31g; Carbohydrate 2g, of which sugars 2g; Fat 21g, of which saturates 5g; Cholesterol 0mg; Calcium 144mg; Fibre 0.6g; Sodium 200mg.

p321 Soy Sauce and Star Anise Chicken Energy 210Kcal/880kJ; Protein 30g; Carbohydrate 1g, of which sugars 1g; Fat 10g, of which saturates 2g; Cholesterol 88mg; Calcium 11mg; Fibre 0.0g; Sodium 600mg.

p322 Harissa-spiced Koftas Energy 180Kcal/750kJ; Protein 23g; Carbohydrate 2g, of which sugars 1g; Fat 9g, of which saturates 4g; Cholesterol 83mg; Calcium 18mg; Fibre 0.2g; Sodium 300mg.

p323 Cumin- and Coriander-Rubbed Lamb Energy 264Kcal/1098kJ; Protein 29g; Carbohydrate 0g, of which sugars 0g; Fat 17g, of which saturates 6g; Cholesterol 104mg; Calcium 33mg; Fibre 0g; Sodium 200mg.

p326 Plum and Almond Tart Energy 491Kcal/2061kJ; Protein 7g; Carbohydrate 61g, of which sugars 28g; Fat 27g, of which saturates 0g; Cholesterol 0mg; Calcium 84mg; Fibre 1.9g; Sodium 300mg.

p327 Baked Apples with Marsala Energy 215Kcal/901kJ; Protein 1g; Carbohydrate 22g, of which sugars 22g; Fat 11g, of which saturates 7g; Cholesterol 27mg; Calcium 40mg; Fibre 3.3g; Sodium 100mg.

p328 Grilled Peaches with Meringues Energy 123Kcal/526kJ; Protein 2g; Carbohydrate 31g, of which sugars 31g; Fat 0g, of which saturates 0g; Cholesterol 0mg; Calcium 24mg; Fibre 2.3g; Sodium 100mg.

p329 Summer Berries in Sabayon Glaze Energy 217Kcal/914kJ; Protein 4g; Carbohydrate 29g, of which sugars 29g; Fat 6g, of which saturates 2g; Cholesterol 202mg; Calcium 72mg; Fibre 3.4g; Sodium 100mg.

p330 Baked Ricotta Cakes with Red Sauce Energy 176Kcal/741kJ; Protein 8g; Carbohydrate 21g, of which sugars 21g; Fat 7g, of which saturates 4g; Cholesterol 31mg; Calcium 173mg; Fibre 1.4g; Sodium 100mg.

p331 Apricot and Ginger Gratin Energy 414Kcal/1731kJ; Protein 4g; Carbohydrate 44g, of which sugars 35g; Fat 26g, of which saturates 16g; Cholesterol 48mg; Calcium 94mg; Fibre 2.4g; Sodium 200mg.

p332 Deep-fried Cherries Energy 146Kcal/612kJ; Protein 4g; Carbohydrate 18g, of which sugars 10g; Fat 7g, of which saturates 2g; Cholesterol 61mg; Calcium 65mg; Fibre 1.0g; Sodium 100mg.

p333 Hot Blackberry and Apple Soufflé Energy 128Kcal/543kJ; Protein 2g; Carbohydrate 31g, of which sugars 31g; Fat 0g, of which saturates 0g; Cholesterol 0mg; Calcium 28mg; Fibre 2.2g; Sodium 100mg.

p334 Peach Pie Energy 321Kcal/1347kJ; Protein 4g; Carbohydrate 39g, of which sugars 19g; Fat 18g, of which saturates 3g; Cholesterol 11mg; Calcium 42mg; Fibre 1.7g; Sodium 200mg.

p335 Treacle Tart Energy 416Kcal/1749kJ; Protein 4g; Carbohydrate 66g, of which sugars 35g; Fat 17g, of which saturates 0g; Cholesterol 0mg; Calcium 46mg; Fibre 1.3g; Sodium 300mg.

p336 Caramelized Upside-down Pear Pie Energy 322Kcal/1347kJ; Protein 1g; Carbohydrate 37g, of which sugars 25g; Fat 20g, of which saturates 7g; Cholesterol 31mg; Calcium 18mg; Fibre 0.8g; Sodium 100mg.

p338 Blueberry and Almond Tart Energy 316Kcal/1324kJ; Protein 6g; Carbohydrate 41g, of which sugars 23g; Fat 16g, of which saturates 0g; Cholesterol 0mg; Calcium 41mg; Fibre 1.5g; Sodium 100mg.

p339 Baked Bananas with Ice Cream and Toffee Sauce Energy 368Kcal/1545kJ; Protein 4g; Carbohydrate 55g, of which sugars 52g; Fat 16g, of which saturates 10g; Cholesterol 40mg; Calcium 81mg; Fibre 1.1g; Sodium 400mg.

p340 Roast Peaches with Amaretto Energy 111Kcal/472kJ; Protein 2g; Carbohydrate 24g, of which sugars 24g; Fat 0g, of which saturates 0g; Cholesterol 0mg; Calcium 11mg; Fibre 2.3g; Sodium 100mg.

p341 Passion Fruit Soufflés Energy 57Kcal/243kJ; Protein 4g; Carbohydrate 9g, of which sugars 6g; Fat 1g, of which saturates 1g; Cholesterol 4mg; Calcium 72mg; Fibre 0.4g; Sodium 100mg.

p342 Zabaglione Energy 131Kcal/548kJ; Protein 3g; Carbohydrate 14g, of which sugars 14g; Fat 5g, of which saturates 2g; Cholesterol 202mg; Calcium 26mg; Fibre 0.0g; Sodium 100mg.

p343 Grilled Pineapple and Rum Cream Energy 454Kcal/1869kJ; Protein 1g; Carbohydrate 4g, of which sugars 4g; Fat 45g, of which saturates 28g; Cholesterol 116mg; Calcium 43mg; Fibre 0.3g; Sodium 100mg.

p344 Warm Chocolate Zabaglione Energy 228Kcal/959kJ; Protein 4g; Carbohydrate 29g, of which sugars 29g; Fat 7g, of which saturates 3g; Cholesterol 202mg; Calcium 38mg; Fibre 0.8g; Sodium 100mg.

p345 Hot Chocolate Rum Soufflés Energy 91Kcal/382kJ; Protein 4g; Carbohydrate 12g,

of which sugars 11g; Fat 2g, of which saturates 1g; Cholesterol 0mg; Calcium 14mg; Fibre 1.0g; Sodium 100mg.

p348 Tropical Scented Fruit Salad Energy 97Kcal/410kJ; Protein 2g; Carbohydrate 19g, of which sugars 19g; Fat 0g, of which saturates 0g; Cholesterol 0mg; Calcium 89mg; Fibre 3.6g; Sodium 100mg.

p349 Juniper-scented Pears in Red Wine Energy 251Kcal/1057kJ; Protein 1g; Carbohydrate 38g, of which sugars 38g; Fat 0g, of which saturates 0g; Cholesterol 0mg; Calcium 39mg; Fibre 5.5g; Sodium 100mg.

p350 Oranges in Syrup Energy 236Kcal/1001kJ; Protein 3g; Carbohydrate 48g, of which sugars 48g; Fat 5g, of which saturates 1g; Cholesterol 0mg; Calcium 82mg; Fibre 3.0g; Sodium 100mg.

p350 Fresh Fig Compote Energy 156Kcal/667kJ; Protein 2g; Carbohydrate 38g, of which sugars 38g; Fat 0g, of which saturates 0g; Cholesterol 0mg; Calcium 67mg; Fibre 2.5g; Sodium 100mg.

p352 Pistachio and Rose Water Oranges Energy 94Kcal/400kJ; Protein 3g; Carbohydrate 18g, of which sugars 18g; Fat 2g, of which saturates 0g; Cholesterol 0mg; Calcium 102mg; Fibre 3.7g; Sodium 100mg.

p353 Lychee and Elderflower Sorbet Energy 249Kcal/1063kJ; Protein 1g; Carbohydrate 65g, of which sugars 65g; Fat 0g, of which saturates 0g; Cholesterol 0mg; Calcium 12mg; Fibre 0.9g; Sodium 100mg.

p354 Summer Fruit Brioche Energy 206Kcal/868kJ; Protein 4g; Carbohydrate 37g, of which sugars 20g; Fat 6g, of which saturates 2g; Cholesterol 5mg; Calcium 59mg; Fibre 1.5g; Sodium 200mg.

p355 Rhubarb and Ginger Jellies Energy 179Kcal/765kJ; Protein 2g; Carbohydrate 45g, of which sugars 44g; Fat 0g, of which saturates 0g; Cholesterol 0mg; Calcium 193mg; Fibre 2.8g; Sodium 100mg.

p356 Papayas in Jasmine Flower Syrup Energy 251Kcal/1057kJ; Protein 1g; Carbohydrate 38g, of which sugars 38g; Fat 0g, of which saturates 0g; Cholesterol 0mg; Calcium 39mg; Fibre 5.5g; Sodium 100mg.

p357 Mango and Lime Fool Energy 289Kcal/1204kJ; Protein 2g; Carbohydrate 21g, of which sugars 21g; Fat 22g, of which saturates 14g; Cholesterol 51mg; Calcium 62mg; Fibre 0.7g; Sodium 0mg.

p358 Tangy Raspberry and Lemon Tartlets Energy 206Kcal/868kJ; Protein 4g; Carbohydrate 37g, of which sugars 20g; Fat 6g, of which saturates 2g; Cholesterol 5mg; Calcium 59mg; Fibre 1.5g; Sodium 200mg.

p359 Crispy Mango Stacks with Raspberry Coulis Energy 189Kcal/791kJ; Protein 3g; Carbohydrate 21g, of which sugars 13g; Fat 11g, of which saturates 7g; Cholesterol 27mg; Calcium 18mg; Fibre 3.0g; Sodium 100mg.

p360 Rhubarb and Ginger Trifles Energy 690Kcal/2852kJ; Protein 4g; Carbohydrate 26g, of which sugars 13g; Fat 34g, of which saturates 39g; Cholesterol 154mg; Calcium 99mg; Fibre 0.6g; Sodium 100mg.

p361 Strawberry Cream Shortbreads Energy 890Kcal/3673kJ; Protein 4g; Carbohydrate 22g, of which sugars 10g; Fat 88g, of which saturates 55g; Cholesterol 225mg; Calcium 105mg; Fibre 1.0g; Sodium 100mg.

p362 Blackberries in Port Energy 220Kcal/923kJ; Protein 1g; Carbohydrate 34g, of which sugars 34g; Fat 0g, of which saturates 0g; Cholesterol 0mg; Calcium 51mg; Fibre 3.5g; Sodium 100mg.

p362 Baby Summer Puddings Energy 212Kcal/904kJ; Protein 5g; Carbohydrate 48g, of which sugars 23g; Fat 1g, of which saturates 0g; Cholesterol 0mg; Calcium 72mg; Fibre 1.9g; Sodium 300mg.

p364 Raspberry Brûlée Energy 152Kcal/649kJ; Protein 3g; Carbohydrate 34g, of which sugars 30g; Fat 2g, of which saturates 1g; Cholesterol 6mg; Calcium 114mg; Fibre 0.7g; Sodium 100mg.

p365 Portuguese Custard Tarts Energy 90Kcal/379kJ; Protein 2g; Carbohydrate 11g, of which sugars 4g; Fat 5g, of which saturates 0g; Cholesterol 1mg; Calcium 31mg; Fibre 0.0g; Sodium 100mg.

p366 Baked Custard with Burnt Sugar Energy 992Kcal/4099kJ; Protein 6g; Carbohydrate 31g, of which sugars 31g; Fat 95g, of which saturates 57g; Cholesterol 430mg; Calcium 114mg; Fibre 0g; Sodium 100mg.

p367 Passion Fruit Creams Energy 602Kcal/2487kJ; Protein 8g; Carbohydrate 10g, of which sugars 10g; Fat 59g, of which saturates 35g; Cholesterol 330mg; Calcium 81mg; Fibre 0.5g; Sodium 100mg.

p368 Baked Caramel Custard Energy 481Kcal/1999kJ; Protein 7g; Carbohydrate 34g, of which sugars 34g; Fat 36g, of which saturates 21g; Cholesterol 292mg; Calcium 62mg; Fibre 0g; Sodium 100mg.

p370 Chocolate Banana Fools Energy 265Kcal/1180kJ; Protein 5g; Carbohydrate 42g, of which sugars 37g; Fat 10g, of which saturates 6g; Cholesterol 8mg; Calcium 117mg; Fibre 1.3g; Sodium 100mg.

p370 Lemon Posset Energy 917Kcal/3801kJ; Protein 2g; Carbohydrate 49g, of which sugars 49g; Fat 81g, of which saturates 50g; Cholesterol 206mg; Calcium 79mg; Fibre 0g; Sodium 100mg.

p372 Chilled Chocolate and Espresso Mousse Energy 710Kcal/2974kJ; Protein 13g; Carbohydrate 71g, of which sugars 70g; Fat 43g, of which saturates 24g; Cholesterol 253mg; Calcium 74mg; Fibre 2.8g; Sodium 100mg.

p373 Meringue Pyramid with Chocolate Mascarpone Energy 216Kcal/907kJ; Protein 3g; Carbohydrate 28g, of which sugars 28g; Fat 11g, of which saturates 7g; Cholesterol 12mg; Calcium 20mg; Fibre 0.5g; Sodium 100mg.

p375 Classic Chocolate Roulade Energy 434Kcal/1815kJ; Protein 9g; Carbohydrate 43g, of which sugars 43g; Fat 26g, of which saturates 15g; Cholesterol 208mg; Calcium 72mg; Fibre 0.7g; Sodium 100mg.

p376 Cherry Chocolate Brownies Energy 522Kcal/2159kJ; Protein 3g; Carbohydrate 23g, of which sugars 12g; Fat 47g, of which saturates 27g; Cholesterol 128mg; Calcium 62mg; Fibre 0.5g; Sodium 100mg.

p376 Coffee Mascarpone Creams Energy 146Kcal/604kJ; Protein 1g; Carbohydrate 5g, of which sugars 5g; Fat 14g, of which saturates 9g; Cholesterol 27mg; Calcium 29mg; Fibre 0g; Sodium 100mg.

p380 Lemon Sorbet Energy 135Kcal/577kJ; Protein 1g; Carbohydrate 35g, of which sugars 35g; Fat 0g, of which saturates 0g; Cholesterol 0mg; Calcium 6mg; Fibre 0g; Sodium 100mg.

p381 Strawberry and Lavender Sorbet Energy 123Kcal/522kJ; Protein 1g; Carbohydrate 31g, of which sugars 31g; Fat 0g, of which saturates 0g; Cholesterol 0mg; Calcium 16mg; Fibre 0.9g; Sodium 100mg.

p382 Blackcurrant Sorbet Energy 124Kcal/529kJ; Protein 1g; Carbohydrate 32g, of which sugars 32g; Fat 0g, of which saturates 0g; Cholesterol 0mg; Calcium 53mg; Fibre 3g; Sodium 100mg.

p383 Damson Water Ice Energy 130Kcal/555kJ; Protein 0g; Carbohydrate 34g, of which sugars 34g; Fat 0g, of which saturates 0g; Cholesterol 0mg; Calcium 23mg; Fibre 1.5g; Sodium 100mg.

p384 Peach and Cardamom Yogurt Ice Energy 155Kcal/659kJ; Protein 4g; Carbohydrate 33g, of which sugars 33g; Fat 2g, of which saturates 0g; Cholesterol 1mg; Calcium 126mg; Fibre 1.9g; Sodium 100mg.

p385 Summer Berry Frozen Yogurt Energy 74Kcal/311kJ; Protein 3g; Carbohydrate 10g, of which sugars 10g; Fat 3g, of which saturates 2g; Cholesterol 0mg; Calcium 61mg; Fibre 0.7g; Sodium 100mg.

p386 Raspberry Sherbet
Energy 179Kcal/763kJ; Protein 8g; Carbohydrate 39g, of which sugars 39g; Fat 0g, of which saturates 0g; Cholesterol 1mg; Calcium 132mg; Fibre 2.3g; Sodium 100mg.

p387 Watermelon Ice
Energy 85Kcal/363kJ; Protein 0g; Carbohydrate 22g, of which sugars 22g; Fat 0g, of which saturates 0g; Cholesterol 0mg; Calcium 7mg; Fibre 0.1g; Sodium 100mg.

p388 Blackberry Ice Cream
Energy 391Kcal/1621kJ; Protein 3g; Carbohydrate 28g, of which sugars 28g; Fat 30g, of which saturates 19g; Cholesterol 79mg; Calcium 97mg; Fibre 3.9g; Sodium 100mg.

p389 Coffee Ice Cream
Energy 164Kcal/686kJ; Protein 3g; Carbohydrate 13g, of which sugars 9g; Fat 11g, of which saturates 7g; Cholesterol 32mg; Calcium 115mg; Fibre 0g; Sodium 100mg.

p390 Kulfi
Energy 334Kcal/1389kJ; Protein 14g; Carbohydrate 24g, of which sugars 24g; Fat 20g, of which saturates 10g; Cholesterol 53mg; Calcium 455mg; Fibre 0.6g; Sodium 200mg.

p391 Coconut Ice
Energy 137Kcal/583kJ; Protein 0g; Carbohydrate 35g, of which sugars 35g; Fat 0g, of which saturates 0g; Cholesterol 0mg; Calcium 33mg; Fibre 0g; Sodium 100mg.

p392 Gingered Semi-freddo
Energy 397Kcal/1694kJ; Protein 3g; Carbohydrate 29g, of which sugars 28g; Fat 31g, of which saturates 18g; Cholesterol 203mg; Calcium 45mg; Fibre 0g; Sodium 100mg.

p393 Miniature Choc-ices
Energy 106Kcal/442kJ; Protein 2g; Carbohydrate 12g, of which sugars 11g; Fat 6g, of which saturates 3g; Cholesterol 8mg; Calcium 36mg; Fibre 0.3g; Sodium 100mg.

p394 White Chocolate Castles Energy 352Kcal/1476kJ; Protein 6g; Carbohydrate 43g, of which sugars 42g; Fat 18g, of which saturates 11g; Cholesterol 22mg; Calcium 198mg; Fibre 0.5g; Sodium 100mg.

p395 Caramel and Pecan Terrine Energy 553Kcal/2292kJ; Protein 2g; Carbohydrate 27g, of which sugars 27g; Fat 49g, of which saturates 26g; Cholesterol 103mg; Calcium 46mg; Fibre 0.6g; Sodium 100mg.

p396 White Chocolate and Brownie Torte Energy 572Kcal/2374kJ; Protein 5g; Carbohydrate 35g, of which sugars 25g; Fat 47g, of which saturates 27g; Cholesterol 103mg; Calcium 130mg; Fibre 0.4g; Sodium 100mg.

p397 Soft Fruit and Meringue Gâteau Energy 331Kcal/1392kJ; Protein 6g; Carbohydrate 52g, of which sugars 50g; Fat 12g, of which saturates 8g; Cholesterol 30mg; Calcium 143mg; Fibre 1.4g; Sodium 100mg.

p400 All Butter Cookies Energy 99Kcal/419kJ; Protein 1g; Carbohydrate 11g, of which sugars 3g; Fat 6g, of which saturates 4g; Cholesterol 16mg; Calcium 15mg; Fibre 0.3g; Sodium 100mg.

p401 Almond Cookies Energy 94Kcal/394kJ; Protein 1g; Carbohydrate 12g, of which sugars 8g; Fat 5g, of which saturates 3g; Cholesterol 11mg; Calcium 13mg; Fibre 0.3g; Sodium 100mg.

p402 Chewy Flapjacks Energy 276Kcal/1038kJ; Protein 3g; Carbohydrate 29g, of which sugars 14g; Fat 14g, of which saturates 8g; Cholesterol 34mg; Calcium 16mg; Fibre 1.4g; Sodium 100mg.

p403 Creamed Coconut Macaroons Energy 83Kcal/344kJ; Protein 1g; Carbohydrate 6g, of which sugars 6g; Fat 10g, of which saturates 5g; Cholesterol 29mg; Calcium 7mg; Fibre 0.6g; Sodium 100mg.

p404 Orange and Pecan Scones Energy 192Kcal/806kJ; Protein 3g; Carbohydrate 18g, of which sugars 1g; Fat 12g, of which saturates 3g; Cholesterol 12mg; Calcium 87mg; Fibre 1.2g; Sodium 100mg.

p405 Quick and Easy Teabread Energy 239Kcal/1017kJ; Protein 4g; Carbohydrate 56g, of which sugars 40g; Fat 1g, of which saturates 0g; Cholesterol 32mg; Calcium 116mg; Fibre 1.6g; Sodium 600mg.

p406 Cinnamon Pinwheels Energy 45Kcal/189kJ; Protein 1g; Carbohydrate 6g, of which sugars 2g; Fat 2g, of which saturates 0g; Cholesterol 5mg; Calcium 9mg; Fibre 0.0g; Sodium 100mg.

p407 Almond Cigars Energy 171Kcal/721kJ; Protein 4g; Carbohydrate 28g, of which sugars 22g; Fat 5g, of which saturates 1g; Cholesterol 29mg; Calcium 25mg; Fibre 0.8g; Sodium 100mg.

p408 Golden Ginger Macaroons Energy 59kKcal/248kJ; Protein 2g; Carbohydrate 5g, of which sugars 5g; Fat 4g, of which saturates 0g; Cholesterol 13mg; Calcium 20mg; Fibre 0.5g; Sodium 100mg.

p408 Nutty Nougat Energy 2251Kcal/9514kJ; Protein 28g; Carbohydrate 416g, of which sugars 413g; Fat 64g, of which saturates 5g; Cholesterol 312mg; Calcium 25mg; Fibre 0.8g; Sodium 100mg.

p410 Rich Chocolate Brownies Energy 213Kcal/892kJ; Protein 4g; Carbohydrate 14g, of which sugars 11g; Fat 16g, of which saturates 10g; Cholesterol 77mg; Calcium 67mg; Fibre 0.3g; Sodium 100mg.

p411 Rich Chocolate Biscuit Slice Energy 408Kcal/1711kJ; Protein 3g; Carbohydrate 36g, of which sugars 30g; Fat 29g, of which saturates 18g; Cholesterol 44mg; Calcium 55mg; Fibre 1.1g; Sodium 100mg.

p412 Chocolate and Prune Refrigerator Bars Energy 198Kcal/829kJ; Protein 2g; Carbohydrate 22g, of which sugars 16g; Fat 12g, of which saturates 7g; Cholesterol 18mg; Calcium 59mg; Fibre 0.9g; Sodium 100mg.

p413 Blueberry Cake Energy 240Kcal/1005kJ; Protein 3g; Carbohydrate 28g, of which sugars 17g; Fat 14g, of which saturates 3g; Cholesterol 56mg; Calcium 36mg; Fibre 0.6g; Sodium 200mg.

p414 Stuffed Prunes Energy 98Kcal/411kJ; Protein 1g; Carbohydrate 10g, of which sugars 10g; Fat 6g, of which saturates 4g; Cholesterol 8mg; Calcium 9mg; Fibre 0.7g; Sodium 100mg.

p415 Chocolate Truffles Energy 143Kcal/596kJ; Protein 2g; Carbohydrate 15g, of which sugars 15g; Fat 9g, of which saturates 5g; Cholesterol 5mg; Calcium 32mg; Fibre 0.4g; Sodium 100mg.

p416 Chocolate Petit Four Cookies Energy 366Kcal/1533kJ; Protein 4g; Carbohydrate 43g, of which sugars 26g; Fat 21g, of which saturates 11g; Cholesterol 15mg; Calcium 47mg; Fibre 1.4g; Sodium 200mg.

p416 Praline Chocolate Bites Energy 544Kcal/2280kJ; Protein 9g; Carbohydrate 64g, of which sugars 63g; Fat 30g, of which saturates 10g; Cholesterol 3mg; Calcium 88mg; Fibre 3.4g; Sodium 100mg.

p420 Scottish Morning Rolls Energy 165Kcal/701kJ; Protein 6g; Carbohydrate 35g, of which sugars 1g; Fat 1g, of which saturates 0g; Cholesterol 2mg; Calcium 2mg; Fibre 1.4g; Sodium 200mg.

p421 Panini all'Olio Energy 121Kcal/510kJ; Protein 3g; Carbohydrate 21g, of which sugars 0g; Fat 3g, of which saturates 0g; Cholesterol 0mg; Calcium 40mg; Fibre 0.9g; Sodium 200mg.

p422 French Baguette Energy 702Kcal/3285kJ; Protein 23g; Carbohydrate 155g, of which sugars 3g; Fat 3g, of which saturates 0g; Cholesterol 0mg; Calcium 289mg; Fibre 6.4g; Sodium 1.3g.

p423 Rosemary Focaccia Energy 1504Kcal/6349kJ; Protein 42g; Carbohydrate 255g, of which sugars 5g; Fat 42g, of which saturates 6g; Cholesterol 0mg; Calcium 490mg; Fibre 10.5g; Sodium 100mg.

p424 Granary Cob
Per loaf: Energy 1403Kcal/ 5965kJ; Protein 59g; Carbohydrate 288g, of which sugars 9g; Fat 10g, of which saturates 1g; Cholesterol 0mg; Calcium 176mg; Fibre 40.5g; Sodium 4.9g.

p425 Grant Loaves Per loaf: Energy 1371Kcal/5831kJ; Protein 57g; Carbohydrate 282g, of which sugars 14g; Fat 10g, of which saturates 1g; Cholesterol 0mg; Calcium 17.1mg; Fibre 39g; Sodium 2.

p426 Cottage Loaf
Per loaf: Energy 2312Kcal/ 9839kJ; Protein 80g; Carbohydrate 508g, of which sugars 9g; Fat 10g, of which saturates 1g; Cholesterol 0mg; Calcium 951mg; Fibre 20.9g; Sodium 4g.

p427 Split Tin
Per loaf: Energy 1770kcal/7527kJ; Protein 65g; Carbohydrate 380g, of which sugars 10g; Fat 10g, of which saturates 3g; Cholesterol 8mg; Calcium 784mg; Fibre 15.5g; Sodium 4g.

p429 Poppy-seeded Bloomer Per loaf: Energy 2310Kcal/9828kJ; Protein 82g; Carbohydrate 508g, of which sugars 9g; Fat 15g, of which saturates 2g; Cholesterol 0mg; Calcium 1140mg; Fibre 20.9g; Sodium 4.9g.

p430 Traditional Irish Soda Bread Energy 257Kcal/1093kJ; Protein 12g; Carbohydrate 5g, of which sugars 2g; Fat 0g, of which saturates 0g; Cholesterol 11mg; Calcium 109mg; Fibre 6.8g; Sodium 800mg.

p430 Spring Onion Flatbreads Energy 97Kcal/414kJ; Protein 3g; Carbohydrate 21g, of which sugars 0g; Fat 0g, of which saturates 0g; Cholesterol 0mg; Calcium 41mg; Fibre 0.9g; Sodium 100mg.

p432 Pitta Bread
Energy 151Kcal/641kJ; Protein 5g; Carbohydrate 31g, of which sugars 1g; Fat 2g, of which saturates 0g; Cholesterol 0mg; Calcium 59mg; Fibre 1.3g; Sodium 500mg.

p433 Yemeni Sponge Flat Breads Energy 393Kcal/1660kJ; Protein 9g; Carbohydrate 68g, of which sugars 1g; Fat 11g, of which saturates 7g; Cholesterol 27mg; Calcium 126mg; Fibre 2.7g; Sodium 600mg.

p434 West Indian Flat Breads Energy 316Kcal/1322kJ; Protein 7g; Carbohydrate 36g, of which sugars 1g; Fat 17g, of which saturates 10g; Cholesterol 44mg; Calcium 27mg; Fibre 5.1g; Sodium 300mg.

p435 Tandoori Rotis
Energy 218Kcal/922kJ; Protein 7g; Carbohydrate 37g, of which sugars 1g; Fat 5g, of which saturates 3g; Cholesterol 11mg; Calcium 23mg; Fibre 5.3g; Sodium 400mg.

p438 Bramble Jelly
Per 15ml/1 tbsp: Energy 63Kcal/268kJ; Protein 0g; Carbohydrate 17g, of which sugars 17g; Fat 0g, of which saturates 0g; Cholesterol 0mg; Calcium 8mg; Fibre 0g; Sodium 0mg.

p439 Strawberry Jam
Per 15ml/1 tbsp: Energy 42Kcal/161kJ: Protein 0g; Carbohydrate 11g, of which sugars 11g; Fat 0g, of which saturates 0g; Cholesterol 0mg; Calcium 3mg; Fibre 0.1g; Sodium 0mg.

p440 Spiced Poached Kumquats
Energy 108Kcal/459kJ; Protein 1g; Carbohydrate 27g, of which sugars 0g; Fat 0g, of which saturates 0g; Cholesterol 0mg; Calcium 21mg; Fibre 2.9g; Sodium 100mg.

p440 Three-fruit Marmalade
Per jar: Energy 1225Kcal/ 5223kJ; Protein 1324g; Carbohydrate 324g, of which sugars 324g; Fat 0g, of which saturates 0g; Cholesterol 0mg; Calcium 71mg; Fibre 0.1g; Sodium 2.2g.

p442 Preserved Lemons
Per jar: Energy 41Kcal/174kJ; Protein 2g; Carbohydrate 7g, of which sugars 7g; Fat 1g, of which saturates 0g; Cholesterol 0mg; Calcium 71mg; Fibre 0.1g; Sodium 2.2g.

p443 Middle Eastern Pickles
Per jar: Energy 86Kcal/365kJ; Protein 4g; Carbohydrate 18g, of which sugars 17g; Fat 1g, of which saturates 0g; Cholesterol 0mg; Calcium 137mg; Fibre 7.4g; Sodium 4.5g.

p444 Horseradish and Beetroot Sauce Energy 28Kcal/121kJ; Protein 1g; Carbohydrate 6g, of which sugars 5g; Fat 0g, of which saturates 0g; Cholesterol 0mg; Calcium 28mg; Fibre 1.5g; Sodium 100mg.

p445 Yellow Pepper and Coriander Relish
Energy 77Kcal/324kJ; Protein 1g; Carbohydrate 6g, of which sugars 5g; Fat 6g, of which saturates 1g; Cholesterol 0mg; Calcium 12mg; Fibre 1.7g; Sodium 100mg.

p446 Hot Mango Salsa
Energy 18Kcal/76kJ; Protein 0g; Carbohydrate 4g, of which sugars 4g; Fat 0g, of which saturates 0g; Cholesterol 0mg; Calcium 6mg; Fibre 0.7g; Sodium 100mg.

p447 Harissa
Energy 35Kcal/148kJ; Protein 2g; Carbohydrate 4g, of which sugars 0g; Fat 2g, of which saturates 0g; Cholesterol 0mg; Calcium 23mg; Fibre 0.0g; Sodium 100mg.

p448 Aioli
Energy 400Kcal/1646kJ; Protein 1g; Carbohydrate 0g, of which sugars 0g; Fat 7g, of which saturates 75g; Cholesterol 10mg; Calcium 10mg; Fibre 0.1g; Sodium 100mg.

p449 Roasted Garlic Sauce
Energy 184Kcal/761kJ; Protein 3g; Carbohydrate 9g, of which sugars 1g; Fat 15g, of which saturates 2g; Cholesterol 0mg; Calcium 17mg; Fibre 1.1g; Sodium 100mg.

p450 Watercress Sauce
Energy 451Kcal/1856kJ; Protein 1g; Carbohydrate 1g, of which sugars 1g; Fat 49g, of which saturates 16g; Cholesterol 98mg; Calcium 50mg; Fibre 0.4g; Sodium 300mg.

p451 Shallots in Balsamic Vinegar Energy 59Kcal/247kJ; Protein 1g; Carbohydrate 12g, of which sugars 10g; Fat 0g, of which saturates 0g; Cholesterol 0mg; Calcium 25mg; Fibre 1.2g; Sodium 100mg.

p452 Barbecue Sauce
Energy 31Kcal/132kJ; Protein 1g; Carbohydrate 7g, of which sugars 6g; Fat 0g, of which saturates 0g; Cholesterol 0mg; Calcium 42mg; Fibre 0.8g; Sodium 100mg.

p453 Mixed Herb and Peppercorn Sauce
Energy 50Kcal/207kJ; Protein 0g; Carbohydrate 0g, of which sugars 0g; Fat 6g, of which saturates 1g; Cholesterol 0mg; Calcium 15mg; Fibre 0g; Sodium 100mg.

p456 Leafy Apple Lift-off
Energy 169Kcal/719kJ; Protein 2g; Carbohydrate 41g, of which sugars 41g; Fat 1g, of which saturates 0g; Cholesterol 0mg; Calcium 69mg; Fibre 4.2g; Sodium 100mg.

p456 Fennel Fusion
Energy 127Kcal/539kJ; Protein 3g; Carbohydrate 29g, of which sugars 29g; Fat 1g, of which saturates 0g; Cholesterol 0mg; Calcium 96mg; Fibre 7.9g; Sodium 100mg.

p458 Tropical Calm
Energy 149Kcal/633kJ; Protein 3g; Carbohydrate 34g, of which sugars 26g; Fat 1g, of which saturates 0g; Cholesterol 0mg; Calcium 118mg; Fibre 5.7g; Sodium 100mg.

p458 Strawberry Soother
Energy 111Kcal/471kJ; Protein 3g; Carbohydrate 26g, of which sugars 26g; Fat 0g, of which saturates 0g; Cholesterol 0mg; Calcium 50mg; Fibre 4.4g; Sodium 100mg.

p459 Carrot Revitalizer
Energy 232Kcal/981kJ; Protein 4g; Carbohydrate 55g, of which sugars 54g; Fat 1g, of which saturates 0g; Cholesterol 0mg; Calcium 137mg; Fibre 11.9g; Sodium 100mg.

p459 Purple Pep
Energy 136Kcal/571kJ; Protein 4g; Carbohydrate 29g, of which sugars 27g; Fat 1g, of which saturates 0g; Cholesterol 0mg; Calcium 150mg; Fibre 9.1g; Sodium 200mg.

p460 Tomato and Cucumber Juice with Basil
Energy 41Kcal/175kJ; Protein 2g; Carbohydrate 7g, of which sugars 6g; Fat 1g, of which saturates 0g; Cholesterol 0mg;

Calcium 51mg; Fibre 2.2g; Sodium 100mg.

p461 Beetroot, Ginger and Orange Juice
Energy 155Kcal/666kJ; Protein 6g; Carbohydrate 34g, of which sugars 31g; Fat 1g, of which saturates 0g; Cholesterol 0mg; Calcium 134mg; Fibre 7.1g; Sodium 100mg.

p462 Melon Pick-me-up
Energy 189Kcal/799kJ; Protein 3g; Carbohydrate 45g, of which sugars 45g; Fat 1g, of which saturates 0g; Cholesterol 0mg; Calcium 95mg; Fibre 10.2g; Sodium 100mg.

p462 Apple Shiner
Energy 228Kcal/970kJ; Protein 4g; Carbohydrate 56g, of which sugars 56g; Fat 1g, of which saturates 0g; Cholesterol 0mg; Calcium 57mg; Fibre 5.1g; Sodium 100mg.

p463 Citrus Sparkle
Energy 167Kcal/705kJ; Protein 5g; Carbohydrate 38g, of which sugars 38g; Fat 0g, of which saturates 0g; Cholesterol 0mg; Calcium 167mg; Fibre 7.4g; Sodium 100mg.

p463 Hum-zinger
Energy 227Kcal/975kJ; Protein 3g; Carbohydrate 55g, of which sugars 51g; Fat 1g, of which saturates 0g; Cholesterol 0mg; Calcium 95mg; Fibre 8.6g; Sodium 100mg.

p464 Grapefruit and Pear Juice
Energy 140Kcal/597kJ; Protein 2g; Carbohydrate 33g, of which sugars 33g; Fat 1g, of which saturates 0g; Cholesterol 0mg; Calcium 78mg; Fibre 6.9g; Sodium 100mg.

p465 Strawberry Apple Slush
Energy 95Kcal/400kJ; Protein 2g; Carbohydrate 23g, of which sugars 23g; Fat 0g, of which saturates 0g; Cholesterol 0mg; Calcium 28mg; Fibre 3.5g; Sodium 100mg.

p466 Honey and Watermelon Tonic
Energy 96Kcal/399kJ; Protein 1g; Carbohydrate 22g, of which

sugars 22g; Fat 10g, of which saturates 0g; Cholesterol 0mg; Calcium 19mg; Fibre 0.3g; Sodium 100mg.

p467 Cranberry, Ginger and Cinnamon Spritzer
Energy 121Kcal/512kJ; Protein 8g; Carbohydrate 29g, of which sugars 8g; Fat 0g, of which saturates 0g; Cholesterol 0mg; Calcium 3mg; Fibre 0g; Sodium 100mg.

p468 Lavender Orange Lush
Energy 133Kcal/568kJ; Protein 3g; Carbohydrate 32g, of which sugars 32g; Fat 0g, of which saturates 0g; Cholesterol 0mg; Calcium 132mg; Fibre 4.8g; Sodium 100mg.

p469 Ice Cool Currant
Energy 126Kcal/539kJ; Protein 1g; Carbohydrate 35g, of which sugars 35g; Fat 0g, of which saturates 0g; Cholesterol 0mg; Calcium 54mg; Fibre 2.3g; Sodium 100mg.

p470 Lemon Float
Energy 345Kcal/1461kJ; Protein 3g; Carbohydrate 70g, of which sugars 69g; Fat 8g, of which saturates 5g; Cholesterol 19mg; Calcium 91mg; Fibre 0.1g; Sodium 100mg.

p471 Blue Lagoon
Energy 148Kcal/630kJ; Protein 3g; Carbohydrate 36g, of which sugars 36g; Fat 0g, of which saturates 0g; Cholesterol 0mg; Calcium 127mg; Fibre 8.3g; Sodium 100mg.

p472 Strawberry and Banana Smoothie
Energy 85Kcal/360kJ; Protein 4g; Carbohydrate 18g, of which sugars 17g; Fat 0g, of which saturates 0g; Cholesterol 2mg; Calcium 103mg; Fibre 1.1g; Sodium 100mg.

p472 Raspberry and Orange Smoothie
Energy 110Kcal/466kJ; Protein 5g; Carbohydrate 18g, of which sugars 18g; Fat 2g, of which saturates 1g; Cholesterol 7mg; Calcium 164mg; Fibre 2.2g; Sodium 100mg.

p474 New York Egg Cream
Energy 271Kcal/1132kJ; Protein 6g; Carbohydrate 20g, of which sugars 19g; Fat 19g, of which saturates 1g; Cholesterol 7mg; Calcium 207mg; Fibre 0g; Sodium 100mg.

p475 Banana and Maple Flip
Energy 376Kcal/1573kJ; Protein 12g; Carbohydrate 58g, of which sugars 52g; Fat 12g, of which saturates 5g; Cholesterol 240mg; Calcium 141mg; Fibre 0.9g; Sodium 100mg.

p476 Chocolate Brownie Milkshake
Energy 454Kcal/1899kJ; Protein 12g; Carbohydrate 50g, of which sugars 36g; Fat 24g, of which saturates 14g; Cholesterol 47mg; Calcium 344mg; Fibre 0.8g; Sodium 300mg.

p477 Peppermint Candy Crush
Energy 175Kcal/743kJ; Protein 6g; Carbohydrate 32g, of which sugars 32g; Fat 3g, of which saturates 2g; Cholesterol 11mg; Calcium 227mg; Fibre 0g; Sodium 100mg.

p480 Rum and Star Anise Hot Toddy
Energy 200Kcal/833kJ; Protein 0g; Carbohydrate 12g, of which sugars 12g; Fat 0g, of which saturates 0g; Cholesterol 0mg; Calcium 1mg; Fibre 0g; Sodium 100mg.

p481 Cardamom Hot Chocolate
Energy 359Kcal/1567kJ; Protein 10g; Carbohydrate 42g, of which sugars 42g; Fat 18g, of which saturates 11g; Cholesterol 6mg; Calcium 127mg; Fibre 0g; Sodium 100mg.

p482 Atole
Energy 197Kcal/838kJ; Protein 4g; Carbohydrate 44g, of which sugars 13g; Fat 2g, of which saturates 1g; Cholesterol 6mg; Calcium 127mg; Fibre 0g; Sodium 100mg.

p482 Café de Olla
Energy 149Kcal/634kJ; Protein 1g; Carbohydrate 34g, of which sugars 30g; Fat 2g, of which saturates 0g; Cholesterol 0mg; Calcium 25mg; Fibre 0g; Sodium 100mg.

p484 Vanilla Caffè Latte
Energy 545Kcal/2299kJ; Protein 15g; Carbohydrate 77g, of which sugars 76g; Fat 22g, of which saturates 13g; Cholesterol 24mg; Calcium 445mg; Fibre 1.4g; Sodium 200mg.

p485 Frothy Hot Chocolate
Energy 223Kcal/942kJ; Protein 10g; Carbohydrate 25g, of which sugars 25g; Fat 10g, of which saturates 6g; Cholesterol 16mg; Calcium 307mg; Fibre 0.5g; Sodium 100mg.

p486 Cuba Libre
Energy 109Kcal/454kJ; Protein 0g; Carbohydrate 11g, of which sugars 11g; Fat 0g, of which saturates 0g; Cholesterol 0mg; Calcium 9mg; Fibre 0g; Sodium 100mg.

p487 Tropical Fruit Royale
Energy 94Kcal/396kJ; Protein 1g; Carbohydrate 13g, of which sugars 13g; Fat 0g, of which saturates 0g; Cholesterol 0mg; Calcium 15mg; Fibre 2.0g;

Sodium 100mg.

p488 Lemon Vodka
Energy 111Kcal/470kJ; Protein 0g; Carbohydrate 20g, of which sugars 20g; Fat 0g, of which saturates 0g; Cholesterol 0mg; Calcium 10mg; Fibre 0g; Sodium 100mg.

p489 Quick Bloody Mary
Energy 171Kcal/722kJ; Protein 2g; Carbohydrate 9g, of which sugars 9g; Fat 0g, of which saturates 0g; Cholesterol 0mg; Calcium 30mg; Fibre 1.8g; Sodium 1.2g.

p490 Gin Fizz
Energy 200Kcal/840kJ; Protein 0g; Carbohydrate 28g, of which sugars 7g; Fat 0g, of which saturates 0g; Cholesterol 0mg; Calcium 11mg; Fibre 0g; Sodium 100mg.

p491 Sea Breeze
Energy 135Kcal/566kJ; Protein 0g; Carbohydrate 10g, of which sugars 4g; Fat 0g, of which saturates 0g; Cholesterol 0mg; Calcium 6mg; Fibre 0g; Sodium 100mg.

p492 Perfect Manhattan
Energy 106Kcal/440kJ; Protein 0g; Carbohydrate 1g, of which sugars 1g; Fat 0g, of which saturates 0g; Cholesterol 0mg; Calcium 1mg; Fibre 0g; Sodium 100mg.

p493 Margarita
Energy 90Kcal/376kJ; Protein 0g; Carbohydrate 4g, of which sugars 4g; Fat 0g, of which saturates 0g; Cholesterol 0mg; Calcium 3mg; Fibre 0g; Sodium 100mg.

p494 Brandy Alexander
Energy 218Kcal/894kJ; Protein 0g; Carbohydrate 8g, of which sugars 8g; Fat 12g, of which saturates 8g; Cholesterol 31mg; Calcium 11mg; Fibre 0g; Sodium 100mg.

p495 Spritzer
Energy 30Kcal/124kJ; Protein 0g; Carbohydrate 0g, of which sugars 0g; Fat 0g, of which saturates 0g; Cholesterol 0mg; Calcium 9mg; Fibre 0.1g; Sodium 100mg.

Index